Designing for Virtual Communities in the Service of Learning

While many of us are concerned with the loss of communal spaces and ties that broaden one's sense of self beyond the "me" or "I" and into the "we" and "us," less clear are the educational advantages of a community approach in terms of learning curricular content. We know even less about whether something resembling community can be designed and about how to measure whether it has emerged. The authors of the chapters in this volume explore the theoretical, design, learning, and methodological questions with respect to designing for and researching Web-based communities to support learning. Coming from diverse academic backgrounds (computer science, information science, instructional systems technology, educational psychology, sociology, and anthropology), they are frank in examining what we do and do not know about the processes and practices of designing communities to support learning. Taken as a collection, these writings point to the challenges and complex tensions that emerge when designing for a Web-supported community, especially when the focal practice of the community is learning.

Dr. Sasha A. Barab is Associate Professor of Education and Cognitive Science at Indiana University, where he is the Associate Director of the Center for Research on Learning and Technology.

Dr. Rob Kling was Professor of Information Science and Information Systems at Indiana University, where he directed the Center for Social Informatics.

Dr. James H. Gray is a developmental psychologist, media designer, and educational researcher interested in the design and study of tools to foster deeper understanding of the social world among children and youth. He works currently as a researcher at SRI International.

LEARNING IN DOING: Social, Cognitive, and
Computational Perspectives

Series Editor Emeritus
John Seely Brown   *Xerox Palo Alto Research Center*
General Editors
Roy Pea   *Professor of Education and the Learning Sciences and Director,
Stanford Center for Innovations in Learning, Stanford University*
Christian Heath   *The Management Centre, King's College, London*
Lucy A. Suchman   *Centre for Science Studies and Department of Sociology,
Lancaster University, UK*

Continued on page following index

Designing for Virtual Communities in the Service of Learning

Edited by

SASHA A. BARAB

Indiana University

ROB KLING

Indiana University

JAMES H. GRAY

SRI International

PUBLISHED BY THE PRESS SYNDICATE OF THE UNIVERSITY OF CAMBRIDGE
The Pitt Building, Trumpington Street, Cambridge, United Kingdom

CAMBRIDGE UNIVERSITY PRESS
The Edinburgh Building, Cambridge CB2 2RU, UK
40 West 20th Street, New York, NY 10011-4211, USA
477 Williamstown Road, Port Melbourne, VIC 3207, Australia
Ruiz de Alarcón 13, 28014 Madrid, Spain
Dock House, The Waterfront, Cape Town 8001, South Africa

http://www.cambridge.org

First published 2004

Printed in the United States of America

Typeface Palatino 10/12 pt.   *System* LATEX 2_ε [TB]

A catalog record for this book is available from the British Library.

Library of Congress Cataloging in Publication data

Designing virtual communities in the service of learning / edited by Sasha A. Barab,
Rob Kling, James H. Gray.
    p.   cm. – (Learning in doing)
Includes bibliographical references (p.) and index.
ISBN 0-521-81755-2 – ISBN 0-521-52081-9 (pb.)
1. Distance education – Computer-assisted instruction.   2. Internet in education.
3. Virtual reality in education.   4. Cognition and culture.   I. Barab, Sasha A.   II. Kling, Rob.
III. Gray, James H.   IV. Series.
LC5803.C65D47   2003
371.3'58–dc21   2003051524

ISBN 0 521 81755 2 hardback
ISBN 0 521 52081 9 paperback

Contents

Contributors

Sasha A. Barab, Indiana University

Amy Bruckman, Georgia Institute of Technology

Blaise Cronin, Indiana University

Christina Courtright, Indiana University

Sharon J. Derry, University of Wisconsin-Madison

Judith Fusco, SRI International

James H. Gray, SRI International

Noriko Hara, Indiana University

Christian Heath, King's College

Susan C. Herring, Indiana University

Jim Hewitt, University of Toronto

Kirk Job-Sluder, Indiana University

Rob Kling, Indiana University

Emmanuel F. Koku, University of Toronto

Julia Lee, University of Wisconsin-Madison

James G. MaKinster, Hobart and William Smith Colleges

Roy Pea, Stanford University

Linda Polin, Pepperdine University

K. Ann Renninger, Swarthmore College

Margaret Riel, University of California-Irvine

Rebecca Scheckler, Virginia Polytechnic Institute and State University

Mark S. Schlager, SRI International

Thomas M. Schwen, Indiana University

Jennifer Seymour, University of Wisconsin-Madison

Wesley Shumar, Drexel University

Marcelle A. Siegel, University of Wisconsin-Madison

Constance Steinkuehler, University of Wisconsin-Madison

Lucy A. Suchman, Lancaster University

Deborah Tatar, SRI International

Barry Wellman, University of Toronto

Series Foreword

This series for Cambridge University Press is becoming widely known as an international forum for studies of situated learning and cognition.

Innovative contributions are being made by anthropology; by cognitive, developmental, and cultural psychology; by computer science; by education; and by social theory. These contributions are providing the basis for new ways of understanding the social, historical, and contextual nature of learning, thinking, and practice that emerges from human activity. The empirical settings of these research inquiries range from the classroom to the workplace, to the high-technology office, and to learning in the streets and in other communities of practice.

The situated nature of learning and remembering through activity is a central fact. It may appear obvious that human minds develop in social situations and extend their spheres of activity and communicative competencies. But cognitive theories of knowledge representation and learning alone have not provided sufficient insight into these relationships.

This series was born of the conviction that new and exciting interdisciplinary syntheses are underway as scholars and practitioners from diverse fields seek to develop theory and empirical investigations adequate for characterizing the complex relations of social and mental life and for understanding successful learning wherever it occurs. The series invites contributions that advance our understanding of these seminal issues.

Roy Pea
Christian Heath
Lucy A. Suchman

Foreword

These are early days in the exploration of how *the concept of community* – challenging enough in its own right for inquiries in social science, politics, and education – is to be understood in the emerging hybrid worlds in which people live. These worlds are not simply governed through face-to-face communication. Conversations and relationships are, for a growing number of people, mediated through new tools enabled by computing and telecommunications. These are exciting times, akin to the first decades of the written word and the discourse that might have ensued around what it meant to have the new "virtual talk" that texts created. An examination of Socrates' dialogues in Plato's *Phaedrus* may provide some insight into what such discourse might have been like as Socrates questions the wisdom of writing and books. In these dialogues, Socrates outlines the myth of how the ancient god Theuth gave writing to Thamus, the king of Egypt, and although Theuth advocates that his discovery of writing "provides a recipe for memory and wisdom" that ought to be imparted to other Egyptians, Thamus challenges the gift:

If men learn this, it will implant forgetfulness in their souls; they will cease to exercise memory because they rely on that which is written, calling things to remembrance no longer from within themselves, but by means of external marks. What you have discovered is a recipe not for memory, but for reminder. And it is no true wisdom that you offer your disciples, but only its semblance, for by telling them of many things without teaching them you will make them seem to know much, while for the most part they know nothing, and as men filled, not with wisdom, but with the conceit of wisdom, they will be a burden to their fellows (Plato, *Phaedrus*, 274c–75b, trans. Hackforth).

The editors have assembled a number of the most active researchers in the field of "virtual communities" for learning, and, to varying degrees, the authors take on the voice of Theuth, Thamus, or the dialectic between them as they challenge us to consider what the designs and implementations of virtual learning communities are accomplishing and how we might learn to more successfully contribute to learning with our design features and processes for online communities. To this end, many of the authors ask: What is a community? What makes a community? And once we move online in our activities: What is a virtual community? What does it mean to "design" a community, whether real or virtual? What is special about designing virtual communities in the service of learning rather than for other purposes? How do virtual learning communities relate to place-based "communities of learning"? And how can systematic methods of investigation of online community participation contribute not only to scientific understanding of human behaviors in such systems but to new design cycles that improve the fit between community member needs and system properties?

Many, but not all, of the chapters investigate issues affiliated with K–12 education–related communities of learning that are conducted to a significant degree online. We learn about several different environments developed to support online community engagement among pre-service and in-service mathematics and science teachers, about a campus of virtual places used by teaching professionals throughout the K–12 continuum and those who support their learning, about a community forum for mathematics educators at all levels, and about several online communities established to foster learning for schoolchildren. In the realm beyond K–12, there are accounts also of several scholarly learning networks, in technology and in linguistics, and of workplace communities. There are rich profiles of developing methods for studying virtual learning communities, including social network analysis and computer-mediated discourse analysis. Throughout the book, we learn about the struggles, dilemmas, cautions, and dualities that surface in designing for virtual communities. Although often optimistic in tone, these works do not promote online community as a panacea for learning. They deepen our appreciation for the subtle and intricate nature of motives, trust, and identity displayed in social engagements.

I would caution the reader not to be too swept up in a quest to find "the right" definition for learning community, virtual community, or community more generally. I am fond of telling my students that definitions, like maps, are developed for a purpose, and that they become useful to the extent that they enable wayfinding for those who are using them. The philosopher Ludwig Wittgenstein pushed us far in thinking about definitions when he argued that the meaning of the concept "game" is not one governed so simply as by an Aristotelian definition of necessary and sufficient conditions for category membership. He makes the case that concepts are organized in mental and social life by prototypic exemplars, a view rediscovered and developed in cognitive science during the 1970s as Eleanor Rosch and colleagues at Berkeley demonstrated prototype effects in experimental studies of categorization, including "typicality," a finding that people reliably judge certain exemplars as more representative of a concept than others.

My sense from reading the contributions to this volume is that there is an emerging vision here of prototypic exemplars of virtual communities designed in the service of learning. This book chronicles an initial cartography for the terrain in which investigations of virtual learning community are taking place, and it launches a wayfinding process for those seeking to identify the key issues for learning in online communities as they exist or as they are being designed. The fascinating exercise for readers will be to find their own ways through the territory the authors have begun to map and to bring their own discoveries back to the quest for understanding and exploring the future of learning served by virtual community tools and systems.

Finally, I wish to acknowledge my grief and sadness at the loss of such a valuable colleague and friend as co-editor Rob Kling, whose clarion voice representing the importance of constant consideration of values of social justice, fairness, and community in the face of technology-centered design has inspired so many of us.

Roy Pea
Stanford University
June 16, 2003

Preface and Acknowledgments

This volume brings together a series of chapters focused on the theoretical, design, learning, and methodological questions with respect to designing for and researching virtual communities to support learning. We are at an interesting time in education and technology, with terms such as *communities of learners, discourse communities, learning communities, knowledge-building communities, school communities,* and *communities of practice* being the zeitgeists of education and the Internet serving as a much touted medium to support their emergence. More generally, any time a new technology is introduced, it suggests the promise of the revolution of education. Thomas Edison was convinced that film would transform education and make the teacher obsolete. Although the Internet offers much promise and the potential to support new environments for learning, we are just beginning to understand the educational potential of community models for learning and whether community can be designed online or face-to-face. In fact, we know very little about whether something such as community can be designed and, if so, whether this can be done online. We are witnessing instructional designers employing *usability* strategies effective for understanding human-computer interactions, but we have little appreciation of how to design to facilitate sociability – that is, supporting human–human interactions as mediated by technology.

The authors of this edited volume came together to advance a critical and in-depth look at what we *do* and *do not* know about the process and practices of designing for virtual communities in the service of learning. Some of the core questions taken up by the authors include: What constitutes community? How do these electronic environments relate to more familiar place-based pedagogical ones? How well do the techniques and constructs that are used to understand the processes of learning and enculturation in traditional face-to-face community settings suffice for these new settings? What is the educational value of a community approach to learning? How do we capture and what are the relations among individual, group, and community trajectories?

Our collaborative pursuit of these questions began with the planning and coordination of two symposia for the annual meeting of the American Educational Research Association, at which eleven of the authors presented. To expand the dialogue and broaden our understanding, we asked the participation of other authors from multiple disciplines who are interested also in community and design questions. With support from an NSF CAREER grant and the NSF-funded Center for Innovative Learning Technologies (CILT), we organized two face-to-face author meetings and hosted a Web site with the goals of enhancing communication among authors and producing a more conceptually cohesive book than would otherwise have been possible. As a result, chapter authors read and commented on each other's work, and the group as a whole grappled with a range of common concerns, such as the meaning of "virtual," "designing community" versus "designing *for* community," and the goal of designing "in the service of learning."

Throughout this process we strived for much cross-fertilization of ideas, as authors from diverse backgrounds read and reviewed drafts of each other's papers, incorporating their responses into subsequent drafts of their own papers. It was our commitment to develop a volume that had a distinctive intertextuality, thereby distinguishing it from the (relatively) disconnected contributions of many edited volumes. We view this intertextuality as a strength of the book, allowing for a more cohesive yet multilayered look at the diverse theoretical perspectives and empirical cases presented. The book also was not to be simply more theoretical arguments touting the virtues of community or glossing over the complexities of building for them online. Instead, in their own work, all the authors were committed to clarifying their theoretical assumptions at the same time as they exposed the challenges and inherent dualities involved in designing for and researching virtual communities.

Taken as a whole, this volume offers a much needed critical examination and reflection of what is being learned about the educational potential and challenges of designing for virtual communities. The authors are neither evangelical nor pessimistic about this process, and, at the same time, they have worked to avoid hyperbole and unsubstantiated claims. They are academic and rigorous in their research and in the claims they advance, offering a critical gaze about the challenges and potential of virtual communities to support learning. Each author presents his or her struggles and lessons learned in a manner that provides insight into local struggles while also serving as a resource for others doing similar work in other contexts. It is our hope that by sharing our experiences we as participants in a design field can better understand how to develop contexts for learning that will best meet the needs of those who will be learning through them.

ACKNOWLEDGMENTS

We are grateful for the encouragement and guidance of Philip Laughlin, our editor at Cambridge University Press, for his support as this volume moved from inception to the printed book you have before you. We thank Melanie Misanchuk for her careful reading and editing of each of the articles in this volume. We thank the Center for Research on Learning and Technology for developing and hosting the Web site and collaboration tools that supported the virtual collaborations among the authors. We thank all the willing participants who signed the informed consent forms and participated in the various spaces so that we could conduct our research. Finally, we recognize the National Science Foundation (CAREER Grant # 0092831) and the Center for Innovative Learning Technologies (NSF Grant # 9720384) for their support. Any opinions, findings, and conclusions or recommendations expressed in this volume, however, are those of the author(s) and do not necessarily reflect the views of the National Science Foundation.

In Memoriam

From AI (Artificial Intelligence) to SI (Social Informatics): Rob Kling's Intellectual Odyssey

In 1971 Rob Kling presented a paper on reasoning by analogy at an international conference on artificial intelligence held in London. He had been a doctoral student with Edward Feigenbaum at Stanford and his early output reflected his formal research training and also suggested a certain kind of career trajectory within computer science. But a mere couple of years later Rob was delivering a paper at the ACM national conference in Georgia titled, "Towards a person-centered computer technology." And again, in 1973, he published "Notes on the social impacts of AI." The scene was set.

I don't know exactly when Rob's Paul of Tarsus moment occurred, but it is safe to say that his interest in the social dimensions of computing, a set of concerns he was to corral years later with the rubric *social informatics*, dates from the early 1970s. Even a cursory look at the titles of some of the publications included in his curriculum vitae conveys a sense of his evolving intellectual concerns: "Computing as social action," "Computers and social power," "Computer based social movements," "The social design of worklife with computers and networks," "Computing for our future in a social world." For thirty years, until his untimely death, Rob Kling had been doing what some of us were only beginning to think about doing decades later. In fairness, a discerning group of colleagues and scholars recognized the significance of his work early on; others, a growing band of fellow travelers, only came to appreciate his manifold contributions relatively late in his life. But I am already getting ahead of myself.

This appreciation of Rob Kling is being written at very short notice and under the Damoclean sword of a publisher's deadline. That said, I am most grateful to Sasha Barab for the invitation to append a few words to the present volume. After all, Rob was/is his co-editor: it is nothing less than fitting. My only regret is that I shall necessarily fail to capture the many rich (a favorite Klingian epithet) and highly nuanced insights the Great Man generated in the course of his remarkably productive life. More to the point, I am not especially well qualified to write on the significance of Rob Kling's empirical and theoretical contributions to the nascent domain of social informatics. There are many others who knew him and his work much better than I; collaborators and friends, who could do him justice in print. Ken Kramer and Mark Poster of the University of California-Irvine spring to mind, as do other former members of the "Irvine school" such as John King, now at the University of Michigan, and Suzanne Iacono, currently a program director at the National Science Foundation. My short reflection does not really conform to any established genre of academic writing. It is certainly not a detailed critical assessment of his life's work – that is for another day and another hand – better still, a platoon of knowing hands. It is part an *in memoriam*, part a personal reminiscence. The *Festschriften* will follow in good time.

I first met Rob Kling in 1995, shortly before he uprooted from the West Coast to come, to many people's surprise, not least my own, to the cornfields of Indiana. But let me here quote verbatim the comments I made immediately after his death. They are still fresh and reflect accurately my enduring sense of, and personal feelings for, the man.

Recruiting Rob Kling was like reeling in a prize marlin: a wrenching struggle, but also a massively gratifying experience. Not that he was rapacious; Rob actually took a salary drop coming to IU from UC Irvine. That spoke volumes. Our negotiations were protracted, but we got to know one another well as draft letters of offer winged their way westward and back. He played according to the Queensbury rules. Rob Kling's accomplishments are legion, and well documented. They don't require retelling here.

He was quite simply the brightest bloke with whom I have had the pleasure of working. Infectiously curious, playfully serious, razor sharp, generous of spirit, and wonderfully open-minded. Which isn't to say that we always saw eye-to-eye; over the years we had a couple of serious spats; on both occasions he ate humble pie in a way that only a special kind of colleague could have. He probably didn't need to, but he did. That, too, spoke volumes. We regularly read and commented on one another's drafts. And we chatted a lot, to the point that we could complete one another's sentences. He'd laugh, the upper body juddering, a cross between sometime UK Prime Minister Edward Heath and a pneumatic drill. I can see him vividly as I write; eyes sparkling, mischief never a million miles away.

Rob cared about the academy, and was passionately committed to maintaining scholastic standards and collegiality. He juggled a workload that made the rest of us blanch. Yet, as soon as a new problem, challenge, or opportunity presented itself, he was off. Another ball was tossed up into the already seriously congested air. I'd routinely tease him that he had more bees in his bonnet than an apiarist, but the man was not for turning. Such was Rob, and we would not have had it otherwise. He added so much to the life of our school and IU in a relatively short time. He enthused and inspired us all, young and old, seasoned and wet behind the ears. I cannot bear to think that the Big Man's face will never again peer around my door.

Those of us who have had the pleasure of working with Rob Kling know just how fortunate we are.

These comments were posted along with many others on the School of Library and Information Science's Web site. I revisited these touching tributes and was struck by the profound effect Rob had on the lives of so many people in so many vectors of academic life. I thought I had a good sense of the man after seven years as his colleague, but in the days and weeks following his death I discovered so much more about him simply by listening to, and reading, what others had to say. Rob was indefatigable and extraordinarily generous in terms of his willingness to engage with, advise, and mentor all and sundry. He would as happily debate or work with a graduate student as a distinguished coeval peer. That says a lot. He didn't just understand the social aspects of computing, but recognized the social aspects of thinking and writing about the social dimensions of computing. In fact, Rob exemplified classic Mertonian norms, such as communism and disinterestedness, to say nothing of organized skepticism. He was an exemplary scholar, for whom the values of the academy (collegiality, faculty governance, peer review) mattered greatly. And, as he confessed to me not so long before he passed away, he still got nervous before teaching his class, a sure sign of an individual who took his pedagogic responsibilities seriously. Rob's intellectual vibrancy was matched by his passion for disciplined enquiry. He was the perfect "trusted assessor," a colleague who always managed to ask a penetrating question, reframe an argument, or critique a draft manuscript in a way that simply didn't occur to most of us.

He did not accept things at face value (such as the presumed benefits or limitations of online learning), was wary of punditry (he would challenge utopian and dystopian IT futures with equal relish), and was deeply suspicious of one-size-fits-all solutions (the electronic publishing regimes that work for high-energy physicists won't work for everyone else, he stressed often in his later publications). Kling understood that choices relating to the adoption and use of ICTs (information and communication technologies) were not apolitical; he understood the role of power in organizations and work groups. Through fieldwork and empirical studies he deftly explored the soft underbelly (or "underside," to use his term) of ICTs in organizations of all kinds, trying to understand the interaction (a key construct in his *oeuvre*) of human behaviors and information technology. The compendious (961 pages to be exact) second edition of his edited volume, *Computerization and Controversy: Value Conflicts and Social Choices* (Academic Press, 1996), particularly the introductory and linking sessions written by him, give a good idea of what motivated Rob Kling. We need to move beyond analysis of technology "effects" and "impacts" to an understanding of the mutual shaping of technology and human behavior. He was not the only one to think thusly, but he was certainly one of the most vocal cheerleaders in the sociotechnical systems camp. But let me here defer to his words: "I believe that understanding the social repercussions of any technological system requires that we be able to see it from the perspectives of the people who are likely to use it and live with it, or even, in part, live within it. It takes some empathy to appreciate their perceptions; it takes courage to unflinchingly acknowledge the pains as well as the pleasures that new technologies bring to people's lives" (p. 9). Rob Kling was no saint, but he was a humane man with a well-developed social conscience and a sterling sense of professional propriety.

In an elegantly written and well-informed obituary in the *Los Angeles Times* (May 26, 2003, B11), Myrna Oliver, a staff writer, remarked that Kling often used automotive analogies to explain social informatics: "Technological debates could be likened to discussing the latest sports car model . . . while informatics addresses how the automobile has affected society, including construction of highways and developments of suburbs." Not altogether surprising, then, that he should have co-edited with Spencer Olin and Mark Poster the award-winning *Postsuburban California: The Transformation of Postwar Orange County* (University of California Press, 1991). This was just another example of his fecundity and breadth of scholarly interests. In his research, publications, and presentations Rob would frequently use telling metaphors and analogies to vivify abstractions (think "web of computing"). It was the same on the administrative plane. Invariably, he would illuminate the dullest of procedural discussions with an eye-opening or dissension-resolving observation.

When Rob came to Indiana University it was on the understanding that he would establish the Center for Social Informatics (CSI) and also act as editor-in-chief of *The Information Society*, a journal he improved greatly during his time at the helm. The CSI's mission statement (http://www.slis.indiana.edu/CSI/mission.html) notes that the Center is dedicated to supporting research into IT and social change. In his words, "[s]ocial Informatics (SI) refers to the body of research and study that examines the social aspects of computerization – including the roles of information technology in social and organizational change, the uses of information technology in social contexts, and ways that the social organization of information technologies is influenced by social forces and social practices." Rob's Center acted as a campus agora for debate on the social aspects of computing. Fellows of the Center were drawn from a range of academic units, including business, instructional systems technology, political science, informatics, library and information science, telecommunications, and journalism. It was a testimony to Rob's sapient leadership that he could seed interest so broadly.

Social informatics is a rather protean notion, one that has still not achieved universal acceptance, although the term "informatics" has recently migrated from Europe to the New World: witness the number of embryonic schools of informatics dotting the academic landscape. Rob may indeed be "the founding father of social informatics," as the *LA Times* stated. Kling's ideas will surely continue to have an impact across fields and disciplines. His scholarly spoors are to be found in many different literatures, for he talked to and influenced quite a few academic tribes in the course of his career. Rob's research has been demonstrably influential in the fields of management, computer science, public administration, and sociology, to name but a few. In short, he wore seven-league boots.

Rob Kling had unquenchable intellectual curiosity and a trencherman's appetite for life. His brain fizzed and his personality sparkled. He was a singularly vivid presence in our lives, and he will live on in his many stimulating and original writings.

Blaise Cronin
Indiana University

PART I

COMING TO TERMS WITH COMMUNITY

1

Introduction

Designing for Virtual Communities in the Service of Learning

Sasha A. Barab, Rob Kling, and James H. Gray

Currently, numerous educators and policy makers are advocating a move away from teacher-centered models of instruction and toward more learner-centered and community-based models. However, at present the word "community" is at risk of losing its meaning. We have little appreciation and few criteria for distinguishing between a *community* of learners and a *group* of students learning collaboratively (Barab & Duffy, 2000; Grossman, Wineburg, & Woolworth, 2000; Wineburg & Grossman, 1998). Given the proliferation of terms such as communities of learners, discourse communities, learning communities, knowledge-building communities, school communities, and communities of practice, it is clear that

> *community* has become an obligatory appendage to every educational innovation. Yet aside from linguistic kinship, it is not clear what features, if any, are shared across terms. This confusion is most pronounced in the ubiquitous "virtual community," where, by paying a fee or typing a password, anyone who visits a web site automatically becomes a "member" of the community . . . Groups of people become community, or so it would seem, by the flourish of a researcher's pen. (Grossman, Wineburg, & Woolworth, 2000, p. 2, italics in original)

Too little of the education literature provides clear criteria for what does and does not constitute community; the term is too often employed as a slogan rather than as an analytical category. We also know little about the educational value of employing a community model for supporting learning.

While many of us are concerned with the loss of communal spaces and ties that broaden one's sense of self beyond the "me" or "I" into the "we" and "us" (Putnam, 2001), less clear are the educational advantages of a community approach in terms of learning curricular content. We know even less about whether something resembling community can be designed, and how to measure whether it has emerged. This is glaringly apparent in terms of virtual communities where designers are employing

3

usability strategies to develop innovative designs but have not adequately taken into account issues of *sociability* – that is, how does the design make links to and support people's social interactions, focusing on issues of trust, time, value, collaboration, and gatekeeping (Preece, 2000)? Regardless, there is a rapid growth in the efforts to create web-based learning environments to supplement or replace traditional modes and even institutions of learning.

Developing an online forum is not very difficult. Almost any "off the shelf" listserv or web-based conferencing system can provide an adequate underlying technology. However, attracting a group of people to the forum who will form a community is a considerable accomplishment. It is common for many people to visit and leave without posting messages and for many others to stay and only read public messages (lurking). Further, when online discussions are unmoderated, some debates can be transformed into hostile *flame wars* that all too easily spiral out of control (Sproull & Kiesler, 1986, 1991;[1] Herring, Sluder, Scheckler, & Barab, 2002). Nonetheless, there are many examples of sustained civil online groups, some of which have important communal dimensions.

According to Barab and Duffy (2000) a community has a significant history, a shared cosmology, a common cultural and historical heritage, social interdependence, and a reproduction cycle. With respect to fostering learning, many current educators are interested in creating new intentional online communities that support learning. The intentionality is often linked to the start of a new course or professional development effort. In these cases, identifying potential participants is usually easy. However, we know relatively little about how to develop such online (or online and offline) intentional communities (see Kim, 2000; Wenger, McDermott, & Snyder, 2002 for useful exceptions). Many such efforts end with fragile and even fractured groups communicating intermittently. It is yet another leap to have such communities support substantial learning (rather than other pursuits, such as conviviality). *Building online communities in the service of learning is a major accomplishment about which we have much to learn.*

As more and more of these online communities are being designed, we must ask whether they are succeeding and what exactly they are accomplishing. The chapters in this volume are frank in examining what we *do* and *do not* know about the processes and practices of designing communities to support learning. Some of the central questions addressed herein include: What constitutes community? How do these electronic environments relate to more familiar place-based pedagogical ones? How well do the techniques and constructs that are used to understand the processes of learning and enculturation in traditional face-to-face community settings suffice for these new settings? What is the educational value of a

---

[1] Flaming was identified in the mid-1980s.

community approach to learning? How do we capture and what are the relations among individual, group, and community trajectories?

Specifically, the chapters in this volume explore the theoretical, design, learning, and methodological questions with respect to designing for and researching online communities to support learning. We highlight what we mean by *community*, which is a core issue for each of the chapters in this volume and addressed with special emphasis in Part I. In fact, each of the words in this title can be thought of as a problematic issue for investigation. Moving beyond community and taking the term "virtual" as another example, the term implies something that is different from the "real." However, given the fluency with which people are transacting with the technical world, one wonders how to distinguish between the virtual and the real. As a case in point, consider the telephone. At one time communicating on the telephone must have seemed like a "virtual" discussion. Today, most people who use telephones do not consider these types of conversations as virtual or "unreal," yet these same people probably consider an online synchronous text-based discussion to be a virtual conversation.

So what is it that constitutes something as virtual? Is it an extension in time and space from that which we directly experience with our senses? It is a significant question when one considers the design of an intimate space in which, as pointed out by many of the authors of this volume, trust is fundamental to participation. Another problematic term is *design*, a topic that is central to Part II. In fact, the problematic nature of designing something such as a community led us to change the title of this volume from "Designing Virtual Communities . . ." to "Designing *For* Virtual Communities. . . ." While a seemingly trivial change, it captures the overriding assumption of each of the authors that someone external cannot simply impose a predesigned community onto a group, but rather community is something that must evolve from within a group around their particular needs and for purposes that they value as meaningful. In fact, a core struggle emerges when one designs something for someone else to use, especially when the desired outcome of community participation is to support the learning (or even reform) of another group.

Following the sections on community and designing for community, the next set of authors focus on fostering community/member participation. They explore questions of volunteer versus mandated participation, and ways of supporting participation and collaboration without stealing ownership and intrinsic buy-in. The final set of chapters, in Part IV, focuses on research in online communities. These authors each present methodological approaches and begin the process of applying these methods to a particular case so as to illustrate the value of the approach being advocated. Taken as a collection, these chapters, whose authors come from diverse academic backgrounds (computer science, information science, instructional systems technology, educational psychology, sociology, and anthropology), point to the challenges and complex tensions that emerge when designing for an online community, especially when the focal practice of the community is learning.

PART I: COMING TO TERMS WITH COMMUNITY

There is a long social-theoretical history of the concept of community. Different social scientists have characterized communities in different ways in order to understand different social phenomena and also based on different underlying social philosophies. Anthropologists traditionally studied pre-industrial societies, which involved village-scale communities where kinship was a basic organizing element. In the early twentieth century, sociologists who studied urbanization were especially interested in the contrasts between tightly woven village life and the more multicultural and possibly alienating cities. In the last few decades, sociologists have examined communities that are not place-based – art worlds whose participants form strong ties across national boundaries and professions whose communities often constitute standards of good practice nationally, rather than only locally (Becker, 1984;[2] Wellman & Gulia, 1999). Political scientists have been interested in political groupings – from local to national scale – including those "imagined communities" that could fuel nationalistic political movements. Progressive urban planners have been interested in place-based communities to identify those who should have a voice in planning or to create "urban villages" where neighborly relationships provide important kinds of sociality as well as safer neighborhoods.

A conception of community that helps to advance one of these research or action agendas may not be as helpful for understanding communities that can support learning. For example, anthropologist Sharon Traweek (1988) defined a community as a "group of people who have a shared past, hope to have a shared future, have some means of acquiring new members, and have some means of recognizing and maintaining differences between themselves and other communities" (p. 6). This conception worked well for her study of experimental particle physics collaborations; it is less helpful in understanding, for example, the core issues and challenges involved in supporting a group of students in a ten-week online course (i.e., little shared past, perhaps no shared future, no need for recruitment or even differentiation from other courses). However, it may be more relevant to understanding relationships among teachers in an ongoing open-ended professional development group. Building on the definition advanced by Barab, MaKinster, and Scheckler (this volume), we view an online community as *"a persistent, sustained [socio-technical] network of individuals who share and develop an overlapping knowledge base, set of beliefs, values, history*

---

[2] Wellman builds on Becker, H. (1984). *Art Worlds*. Berkeley: University of California Press.

and experiences focused on a common practice and/or mutual enterprise" (p. 23, italics in original).

Political sociologist Robert Bellah and his colleagues conceived of a community as "a group of people who are socially interdependent, who participate together in discussion and decision making, and who share certain practices that both define the community and are nurtured by it" (1985, p. 333). This conception may be helpful for identifying key issues for learning in both the ten-week course and for the ongoing professional development group. Lave and Wenger (1991) advanced the term *communities of practice* to capture the importance of activity in fusing individuals to communities, and of communities in legitimizing individual practices. Lave and Wenger define a community of practice state thusly:

[Community does not] imply necessarily co-presence, a well-defined identifiable group, or socially visible boundaries. It does imply participation in an activity system about which participants share understandings concerning what they are doing and what that means in their lives and for their communities. (1991, p. 98)

Predicated on work in anthropology (Geertz, 1983; Jackson, 1996; Lave & Wenger, 1991; Rogoff, 1990; Traweek, 1988; Wenger, 1998), sociology (Shaffer & Anundsen, 1993; Wellman, 1999), and education (Bradsher & Hogan, 1995; Brown & Duguid, 1991; Lipman, 1988; Quartz, 1995; Roth, 1998; Scardamalia & Bereiter, 1993; Sergiovanni, 1994; Tanner, 1997), Barab and Duffy (2000) identified four features that are consistently present and, they argued, requisite of communities. First, they conceptualize a community as having a significant history, a common cultural and historical heritage. Second, they describe communities as having a shared cosmology, especially related to shared goals, practices, belief systems, and collective stories that capture canonical practices (Brown & Campione, 1990). Third, the notion of community suggests something larger than any one member; as a part of something larger, the various members form a collective whole as they work toward the joint goals of the community and its members (Lemke, 1997; Rogoff, 1990). Fourth, a community is constantly reproducing itself such that new members contribute, support, and eventually lead the community into the future; new members move from peripheral participant to core member through a process of enculturation (Lave, 1988, 1993; Wenger, 1998).

Barab, MaKinster, and Scheckler (this volume) introduce additional characteristics: a common practice and/or mutual enterprise; opportunities for interactions and participation; meaningful relationships; and respect for diverse perspectives and minority views. Still others have different lists (see, for example, Wenger, McDermott, & Snyder, 2002). The important point is not the specifics of the list but developing an appreciation for the complexity of community, a complexity that is only exacerbated when one wishes to intentionally design for its emergence.

A central focus of this volume is to better understand what constitutes community in ways that are especially relevant for learning and to investigate the difficulties of designing for the emergence of one online. Following this introduction, Riel and Polin (this volume) further take up the delicate task of defining community, especially those communities designed to support learning. More specifically, they distinguish among three types of learning communities (task-based, practice-based, and knowledge-based), providing rich descriptions of each type and advancing a typology for categorizing different types of learning communities.

While Riel and Polin readily acknowledge the difficulty in categorizing different forms of community, at the same time they provide a useful distinction for others interested in understanding and characterizing communities explicitly designed to support learning. Moving beyond theoretical arguments, they draw on a wealth of examples, especially technology-rich innovations, to clarify and illuminate the distinctions being advocated. Last, they provide a more synergistic vision of a learning organization that aggregates these different forms of communities into a comprehensive structure to support learning. Offering this vision as the ultimate goal, they then describe how graduate education provides a fertile setting for the task-based, practice-based, and knowledge-based learning communities to co-exist. All chapters return to this issue of what constitutes community.

PART II: DESIGNING FOR WEB-SUPPORTED COMMUNITY

Introducing Part II, Barab, MaKinster, and Scheckler discuss the challenges of supporting the development of the Inquiry Learning Forum, an online community of practice for grade 5–12 mathematics and science teachers. Their project involves the design and evaluation of an electronic knowledge network through which in-service and pre-service mathematics and science teachers can create, reflect, share, and improve their inquiry-based pedagogical practices. Their research examines the interplay among a variety of variables that characterize the dynamics of building a social network and in understanding the challenges associated with fostering, sustaining, and scaling a web-supported community in which the value of sharing one's practice and engaging in the dialogue outweighs the "costs" associated with participation. Toward this end, they adopt and expand Wenger's (1998) notion of dualities to characterize the emergent design and use struggles. Their research suggests that designing for virtual communities involves balancing and leveraging complex dualities (Participation/Reification; Designed/Emergent; Local/Global; Identification/Negotiation; Online/Face-to-Face; Coherence/Diversity) from the "inside" rather than applying some set of design principles from the "outside." This chapter provides an illuminating case study from which others can more readily identify patterns occurring in their own interventions and navigate the challenges they face more intelligently.

Kling and Courtright, also researching the Inquiry Learning Forum, critique the oversimplification of some authors' use of the word community, distinguishing between empirical observations of groups in practice and theoretical aspirations or assumptions. Their analysis further suggests that rather than thinking about "instructional technology-led group development," designers would be more usefully served by thinking about "instructional technology-supported group development." They also show how developing a group into a community is a major accomplishment that requires special processes and practices to develop trust among the participants, and the experience is often both frustrating and satisfying for many of the participants. This argument is consistent with the arguments being advanced by Schlager and Fusco (this volume) and Schwen and Hara (this volume) as well.

Over the past several years, Schlager and Fusco have been developing and refining the socio-technical infrastructure of a virtual environment called Tapped In (*www.tappedin.org*), intended to support the online activities of a large and diverse community of education professionals. While they have succeeded in growing and supporting a thriving community of thousands of education professionals, in this chapter they question whether the users of the Tapped In environment collectively constitute a *community of practice* and whether their participation in the Tapped In environment fundamentally changes their teaching practices outside of Tapped In. Consistent with Kling's argument, they similarly propose that an effective model of design would not begin with the virtual environment but with locating existing functioning groups and determining how to best use technological infrastructures to support their continued growth. This model is also consistent with the findings of Barab et al., whose data suggest that the Inquiry Learning Forum was most successful in supporting existing groups of inquiry rather than growing new ones.

Along similar lines, Schwen and Hara further challenge the overly simplistic assumption that communities can just be built, online or face-to-face. Their chapter summarizes and then compares and contrasts four cases that describe rich patterns of online and face-to-face workplace community. Based on their interpretations from these cases, they challenge some of the theoretical optimism around building online community by presenting five "cautionary notes" to designers attempting to build communities of practice regardless of whether they employ technical supports.

PART III: FOSTERING COMMUNITY/MEMBER PARTICIPATION

Renninger and Shumar begin the next part of this volume by describing their research examining The Math Forum, a highly successful, inquiry-informed digital library, or virtual resources center, for mathematics education. More specifically, they problematize notions of culture and community, arguing how the collaborative Math Forum site culture facilitates the ongoing development of community. They demonstrate how site interactivity and substantial mathematics content engages learners. Because the design of the site includes many paths and opportunities, it is responsive to the needs and interests of a diverse set of participants. In their chapter, they argue that the internet provides an expanded possibility for different forms of community. Central to building community are myriad services, yet while members appreciate the site complexity they simultaneously have a simplistic path through which to use the site. Members frequently begin by using just a few resources on the site, then expanding their work as they become aware of other resources and services with an established culture that encourages taking on responsibility for the evolution of community.

Hewitt, illustrating Riel and Polin's theoretical discussion of knowledge-building communities, takes up the empirical challenge of examining a knowledge-based community in action. His chapter begins with a discussion of knowledge-based community and how this relates to the more general notion of community. From there, he carries out an activity systems analysis of a grade 5–6 classroom implementing the Knowledge Forum, a networked educational software program that supports learners' dialogue through publishing multimedia "notes" in a collaborative technical space. Hewitt's analysis is based on three years of data collection and includes both face-to-face and online interactions. These interactions are examined at both an individual (subject) and social (community) level, using activity theory to examine the relations among subjects, tools, objects, rules, community, and division of labor. His analysis illuminates the power of networked technologies to support a knowledge-building community through which members develop more sophisticated understandings about the processes and products of learning. Further, his chapter reveals how the particular learning community he investigated emerged out of the multiple, interrelated ways in which knowledge advancement was facilitated by the sociocultural context of the classroom in combination with the online environment. This chapter suggests that the goal of knowledge construction was interwoven into both the cultural fabric of the classroom community and the participant structures of the online environment, resulting in a knowledge-based learning community.

Bruckman describes the design of an online learning community for children in her chapter. A core challenge facing this project has been to determine how to encourage participation and learning, yet maintain the self-motivating, constructivist context that underlies the development of the project. The environment is primarily a self-motivated context, with a decentralized process in which anyone can create virtual spaces in a simple programming language and anyone can read the code underlying their creations. Participants can easily create spaces and add objects and interactive elements to their spaces with which other participants can interact. The online environment is unique in that it has attracted a large following of girls and that everyone is considered a participant/creator. However, participation in the space is mostly voluntary and has resulted in highly uneven participation as well as participant programming achievements. Central to the challenges of designing for community, Bruckman's work directly addresses the tension between facilitating self-motivation and structuring (even requiring) participation.

In the next chapter, Derry, Seymour, Steinkuehler, Lee, and Siegel also examine a knowledge-building community. They share their research and development of a socio-technical system, the Secondary Teacher Education Project, a problem-based learning web environment, designed to facilitate the continual evolution of a knowledge-based community to support pre-service teacher education. Focusing on their own conceptual and technical development, they share insights on both the challenges of supporting shared collaborative work and how this might be scaffolded using a web-based environment. To help the reader understand the complexity of the task involved in designing a web-based community that has practice as its core – knowledge building through a problem-based learning framework – they begin with an overview of their initial vision and how this process occurs in a face-to-face context. It is because of an appreciation of the challenges involved in face-to-face social contexts that they began to examine social processes within the newly developing program, trying to gain a better understanding of what kinds of interactions their socio-technical design must mediate. Their discussion includes a contextual analysis of their existing teacher education program as well as an interaction analysis of a representative, face-to-face discourse from a group learning activity that occurred in that program. From there, and consistent with many of the other chapters in this edited volume, they then discuss how a deeper appreciation of the complexity of this task led to a modified goal from developing an "online community" to structuring and supporting group learning through which something like "community" might develop.

PART IV: RESEARCHING ONLINE COMMUNITY

In this section, we present four methodological approaches to the study of virtual community, learning, and related issues of design. Each chapter addresses, from its own perspective, the complexity of these topics. Collectively they call for the use and further development of multiple methods to grasp the myriad aspects of community that span the boundaries between online and offline activities.

First, Koku and Wellman employ social network analysis as an approach to understanding the structure of relations underlying a community of practice. The authors present methods for describing the kind of loose ties and distributed interaction networks that increasingly characterize collaborative work relations in present-day society. By describing the complex patterns of social networks such as density, tie strength, clustering, and multiplexity, the authors are able to examine the specific social contexts of the interpersonal relationships that comprise the larger community. Rather than seeing virtual communities as separate from face-to-face ones, the authors suggest that designers of online educational communities need to look at the broader social networks of community members – both on- and offline – and how their internal structure and media use affect peer-to-peer learning.

Next, Herring presents a detailed examination of computer-mediated discourse analysis (CMDA) as a kind of methodological toolkit adapted from language-oriented disciplines and applied to one or more domains of language: structure, meaning, interaction, social behavior, or participation patterns. Through adherence to five conceptual skills of scientific methodology (e.g., crafting empirically answerable research questions, defining and operationalizing key concepts), CMDA can bring a "fine-grain empirical rigor" to social-psychological questions like the existence of community. However, despite the potential analytic power of CMDA, Herring is careful to acknowledge its limits. Drawing inferences about participants' inner states or experience of something as abstract as community is best approached by combining CMDA with other methods such as surveys, interviews, and ethnographic observation.

Building on Herring's work, Job-Sluder and Barab then provide a methodological process that can be used to identify and characterize shared group identity. More specifically, they provide a coding scheme for identifying and comparing shared group identity of an online environment. Describing two types of discursive strategies, linking and contrasting identity, they advance a methodology for evaluating the sociability of learning environments. Specifically, they describe three stages of computer-mediated discourse analysis: beginning with procedures for carrying out contextual analysis, then describing the process of conducting content analysis, and last, building a qualitative case characterization. Their approach, while still in its infancy, provides a much needed mixed methodology for evaluating shared group identity and, thereby, building an argument for the occurrence of something like community.

Finally, Gray and Tatar present a four-part sociocultural approach to the study of learning and development online. They analyze the complex interplay of individual, interpersonal, community, and technological aspects of activity (cf. Rogoff, 1990) through a case study of "Robert," a highly active participant in the Tapped In environment. Key to Robert's professional development is the connection he maintains between his online and offline professional worlds. Based on their findings and related literature, Gray and Tatar offer several design suggestions. For example, they recommend a multidimensional needs analysis to understand target community members in terms of personal identity and life trajectory, existing patterns of interpersonal interactions, and community affiliations as they relate to the goals of a new online environment. This sort of analysis might lead, for instance, to the design of private "whisper" functions and personal office space that motivate new teachers to discuss professional challenges they face during their first year of teaching.

SUMMARY

We are currently in an exciting time in which pedagogical theory and technological advances have created an opportunity to design innovative and powerful environments to support learning. We also have this enthusiasm and have had the luxury of researching and designing a number of interventions based on a community approach to support learning. However, as researchers in the learning sciences community, we need to be careful not to get caught up in the whirlwind of theoretical aspirations and the current zeitgeist. We need to be visionary while at the same time examining empirical data. As educators and research scientists, we need to be critical about our claims. Nonevidenced-based claims can lead to over-simplistic interpretations and, to the extent that these claims result in designs that impact real people, damaging consequences for those we are trying to help.

In this edited volume, the authors have worked to balance their claims, remaining optimistic and visionary while at the same time avoiding hyperbole and unsubstantiated assumptions. Just as design work is filled with tensions, so is advancing new theory. We hope that readers will develop useful insights into their own work, sharpening their critical gaze while at the same time advancing their thinking about what can be done. Innovation is not a simplistic practice; it involves taking risks and making mistakes. However, good research involves examining these risks and what is being learned. Each of the authors has worked to present his or her struggles and lessons learned in a manner that not only captures the local struggles but provides them in a manner that could be useful to readers in their own work. To the extent that this book can support the field in designing for new communities and facilitating new groups of learners, we have accomplished our goals. We look forward to hearing reactions and learning from you, the reader, as you engage in your design struggles and successes as well.

References

Barab, S. A., & Duffy, T. (2000). From practice fields to communities of practice. In D. Jonassen & S. M. Land (Eds.), *Theoretical Foundations of Learning Environments* (pp. 25–56). Mahwah, NJ: Erlbaum.

Becker, H. (1984). *Art Worlds*. Berkeley: University of California Press.

Bellah, R. N., Madson, N., Sullivan, W. M., Swidler, A., & Tipton, S. M. (1985). *Habits of the Heart: Individualism and Commitment in American Life.* Berkeley: University of California Press.

Bradsher, M., & Hogan, L. (1995). The Kids Network: Student scientists pool resources. *Educational Leadership, 53* (Oct.), 38–43.

Brown, A., Ash, D., Rutherford, M., Nakagawa, K., Gordon, A. & Campione, J. (1994). Distributed expertise in the classroom. In M. D. Cohen & L. S. Sproull (Eds.), *Organizational Learning* (pp. 188–228). London: SAGE Publications.

Brown, A. L., & Campione, J. C. (1990). Communities of learning and thinking, or a context by any other name. *Contributions to Human Development, 21,* 108–126.

Brown, J. S., & Duguid, P. (1991). Organizational learning and communities of practice: Toward a unifying view of working, learning, and innovation. In M. D. Cohen & L. S. Sproull (Eds.), *Organizational Learning* (pp. 59–82). London: SAGE Publications.

Geertz, C. (1983). From the native's point of view: On the nature of anthropological understanding. In C. Geertz (Ed.), *Local Knowledge* (pp. 55–70). New York: Basic Books.

Grossman, P., Wineburg, S., and Woolworth, S. (May, 2000). In pursuit of teacher community. Paper presented at the American Educational Research Association, New Orleans.

Herring, S., Sluder, K., Scheckler, R., and Barab, S. (2002). Searching for safety online: Managing "trolling" on a feminist bulletin board. *The Information Society 18* (5) 371–384.

Jackson, M. (Ed.). (1996). *Things as They Are: New Directions in Phenomenological Anthropology.* Bloomington: Indiana University Press.

Kim, A. J. (2000). *Community Building: Secret Strategies for Successful Online Communities on the Web.* Berkeley, CA: Peachpit Press.

Lave, J. (1988). *Cognition in Practice: Mind, Mathematics, and Culture in Everyday Life.* Cambridge: Cambridge University Press.

Lave, J. (1993). Situating learning in communities of practice. In L. B. Resnick, J. M. Levine, & S. D. Teasley (Eds.), *Perspectives on Socially Shared Cognition* (pp. 17–36). Washington, DC: American Psychological Association.

Lave J., & Wenger, E. (1991). *Situated Learning: Legitimate Peripheral Participation.* New York: Cambridge University Press.

Lemke, J. (1997). Cognition, context, and learning: A social semiotic perspective. In D. Kirshner & J. A. Whitson (Eds.), *Situated Cognition: Social, Semiotic, and Psychological Perspectives* (pp. 37–56). Mahwah, NJ: Erlbaum.

Lipman, M. (1988). *Philosophy Goes to School.* Philadelphia: Temple University Press.

Preece, J. (2000). *Online communities: Designing usability, supporting sociability.* Chichester, UK: John Wiley & Sons.

Putnam, R. (2001). *Bowling Alone: The Collapse and Revival of American Community.* New York: Touchstone Books.

Quartz, K. H. (1995). Sustaining new educational communities: Toward a new culture of school reform. In J. Oakes & K. H. Quartz (Eds.), *Creating New Educational Communities* (ninety-fourth yearbook of the National Society for the Study of Education, Part 1, pp. 240–254). Chicago: University of Chicago Press.

Rogoff, B. (1990). *Apprenticeship in Thinking: Cognitive Development in Social Context.* New York: Oxford University Press.

Roth, W.-M. (1998). *Designing Communities*. Dordrecht: Kluwer Academic Publishers.

Scardamalia, M., & Bereiter, C. (1993). Technologies for knowledge-building discourse. *Communications of the ACM, 36*, 37–41.

Sergiovanni, T. J. (1994). *Building Community in Schools*. San Francisco: Jossey-Bass.

Shaffer, C. R., & Anundsen, K. (1993). *Creating Community Anywhere: Finding Support and Connection in a Fragmented World*. Los Angeles: Tarcher/Perigee.

Sproull, L. & Kiesler, S. (1986). Reducing social context cues: electronic mail in organizational communication. *Management Science, 32* (11): 1492–1512.

Sproull, L., & Kiesler, S. (1991). *Connections*. Cambridge, MA: MIT Press.

Tanner, L. N. (1997). *Dewey's Laboratory School: Lessons for Today*. New York: Teachers College Press.

Traweek, S. (1988). *Beamtimes and Lifetimes: The World of High Energy Physicists*. Cambridge, MA: Harvard University Press.

Wellman, B. (1999). *Networks in the Global Village: Life in Contemporary Communities*. Boulder, CO: Westview Press.

Wellman, B., & Gulia, M. (1999). Net surfers don't ride alone. In B. Wellman (Ed.), *Networks in the Global Village* (pp. 331–366). Boulder, CO: Westview Press.

Wenger, E. (1998). *Communities of Practice: Learning, Meaning, and Identity*. Cambridge: Cambridge University Press.

Wenger, E., McDermott, R., & Snyder, W. M. (2002). *Cultivating Communities of Practice: A Guide to Managing Knowledge*. Boston: Harvard Business School Press.

Wineburg, S., & Grossman, P. (1998). Creating a community of learners among high school teachers. *Phi Delta Kappan, 79*, 350–353.

2

Online Learning Communities

*Common Ground and Critical Differences
in Designing Technical Environments*

Margaret Riel and Linda Polin

The psychological model we hold for the mind influences the way we think and act in designing and participating in intentional learning settings. Social and cognitive scientists have been expanding educational models of learning with their examinations of the distinctions between individual cognition and social cognition, promoting a conception of shared mind. Using terms such as *collective sense-making, distributed intelligence, dialogue, group mind, systems thinking,* or *activity theory,* they suggest a view of learning in which there is a shift in power relationships, a respect for practitioner knowledge, and an emphasis on group learning through intentional activity, collective reflection, and participatory decision-making. This view gives rise to a range of popular phrases in the field of education, including: *learning communities, communities of learners, Learning Circles, learning organizations, knowledge communities, communities of practice, professional community,* and *learning organizations.* These terms are attempts to characterize new forms of social/cultural learning. They are often used interchangeably, despite the fact that each evolves out of a different research tradition, thus highlighting different aspects of collaborative work and group structure.

Our objective in this chapter is to provide common language for understanding the different forms of social organization, goals, and outcomes of learning in communities. We suggest three distinct but overlapping forms of learning within communities (task-based, practice-based, and knowledge-based learning) and discuss practical design implications of these distinctions. In doing so, we keep a focus on how networked technologies support these variations in perspectives on collaborative work. Finally, we offer the concept of a *learning organization* to describe organizational efforts that aggregate different forms of learning communities into a larger structure. In the overlap of different types of communities engaged in learning, we find a common cultural core of continuous reflection and change.

LEARNING AS SOCIAL CONSTRUCTION

Over the past three decades, learning theory has evolved from a cognitive theory of acquisition of knowledge to a social theory of increased participation in activity (Bruner, 1973; Cole, 1988; Lave, 1988; Mehan, 1983; Norman, 1980; Rogoff, 1994; Wertsch, 1997). A social view of learning adopts a systems or network view of interaction and activity. Intellectual development becomes a process of negotiation of meaning in everyday practice with others (Dewey, 1916; Vygotsky, 1978). Learning occurs through engagement in authentic experiences involving the active manipulation and experimentation with ideas and artifacts – rather than through an accumulation of static knowledge (Bruner, 1973; Cole, 1988; Dewey, 1916).

While it may appear that some learning is an individual accomplishment, in fact, even when "alone" the individual relies upon and is influenced by socio-cultural tools, signs, and symbols to make sense and produce work. Studies of craft workers, for example, reveal that, though they may appear to stand alone beside their work, their work identity and production is very much influenced by and exerting influence upon a surrounding network of colleagues, friends, and family (Mishler, 1999; John-Steiner, 2000). People co-construct knowledge by building on the ideas and practices of group members. Social scientists from cognitive anthropology (Chaiklin & Lave, 1993; Rogoff, 1998), sociolinguistics (Smagorinksy, 2000), sociology (Cicourel, 1973, LaTour, 1987; Mehan, 1983), anthropology (Hutchins, 1996; Lave & Wenger, 1991), and cross-cultural psychology (Cole & Scribner 1974) have studied ways in which the actions of the individual both acquire and contribute to meaning within a larger context of the group as shared understandings, "group mind," distributed cognition, or cultural practice (Brown & Duguid, 2000; Newman, Griffin, & Cole, 1989; Pea, 1993). The incubation of most great ideas has taken place in groups (LaTour, 1987). Competing ideas and creative inventions are often the outcomes of cohesive work groups, through the natural evolution of practice that comes from the infusion of new members and from the critical, dialectical tension that arises from the social and economic conditions in which the community lives (Lave & Wenger, 1991; Cole & Engeström, 1993; Pea & Gomez, 1994; Wenger, 1998).

LEARNING EMBEDDED IN COMMUNITY

The term *community* has rapidly become a clichéd bit of jargon used to refer to a social group in which learning is an intentional, explicit goal. To understand the functional meaning of learning communities, communities of practice, and knowledge-building learning communities, we must first anchor our definition of the term community.

A *community* is a multigenerational group of people, at work or play, whose identities are defined in large part by the roles they play and relationships they share in that group activity. The community derives its cohesion from the joint construction of a culture of daily life built upon behavioral norms, routines, and rules, and from a sense of shared purpose. Community activity also precipitates shared artifacts and ideas that support group activity and individual sense-making. A community can be multigenerational; that is, it can exist over time in the comings and goings of individuals. In short, a community differs from a mere collection of people by the strength and depth of the culture it is able to establish and which in turn supports group activity and cohesion.

Communities are not always healthy contexts of close interpersonal relationships. A community may be dysfunctional or troubled, stemming from a failure to accommodate change or variation. Sometimes a community is scattered and isolated. Unable to interact with each other or sequestered from community cultural resources, members may find it difficult to develop common practices or shared values. Sometimes a community becomes insular by demanding unquestioned conformity or because the enduring purpose of the group becomes unclear or contested. If a community fails to attract new members, it will not be able to ensure its continuation and development. Where the community is dormant, or where membership is static, there may be no development or evolution of the system, the activity, and the roles that support it. In these cases, learning is more problematic and limited. In short, simply labeling a group of people as a community neither ensures that it functions as one, nor that it is a beneficial, cohesive unit in which learning will take place readily.

Successful communities are able to sustain themselves over multiple generations of members and yet do so without becoming brittle. They grow their collective knowledge-in-use, or "practice," by incorporating variations or responding to contradictions that arise from the diversity of their dynamic membership and their collective interaction with the larger communities, such as political systems or institutions in which their community exists and with which it interacts (Engeström, 1987). As communities continue to exist over time, embracing new members, switching roles and functions among members, altering practices, tweaking tools, and expanding activity, they are, in a very real sense, learning from their collective experience. Over time, the residue of these experiences remains available to newcomers in the tools, tales, talk, and traditions of the group. In this way, the newcomers find a rich environment for learning. They can have access to current practitioners at various degrees of experience, and to the past development of the activity.

Identity is socially constructed in part by the function the individual fills in the group. But how do individuals acquire different roles and responsibilities as they continue to participate in a community?

Communities are social organizations, and over time they precipitate a culture, with all the features and mechanisms associated with cultural systems (Durkheim, 1915). Members occupy roles only with the implicit or explicit support of the community. Where the community is small and its time together quite bounded, there may be little opportunity for individuals to do or be other than they were at the outset. Where the community is newly formed, with little history to guide activity, there may be much ambiguity about roles and activities.

LEARNING COMMUNITIES

Variations in explanatory models of community-based learning mirror variations of focus within the notion of community. At a micro level, a small group of people toils on a task, and over time accomplishes it together. In the process, individuals learn from their interactions with others, with objects of the effort, and from their own participation. At a most macro level, a widely dispersed organization accomplishes its work, evolving, developing, and improving, through the collective contribution of generations of individuals and subgroups over time. From the largest to the smallest unit, these groups are often referred to as communities, because of their cohesiveness and purposefulness. Both macro and micro views consider the same issues in their analyses, but focus them on different *units* of analysis. For instance, in the micro view, researchers examine participation structures to understand how the group is organized to support interaction among participants. The same analysis at a macro level might consider the division of labor and power in an activity system, and how that organizes participation opportunities.

Two theories in particular, Communities of Practice (Lave & Wenger, 1991; Wenger, 1998) and Activity Theory (Cole & Engeström, 1993), suggest that the individual's changing role in the community or activity system enables his or her developing knowledge. That is, they suggest that learning is a process of identity transformation – a socially constructed and socially managed experience.

In this chapter, we discuss three distinct but overlapping types of learning communities: task-based, practice-based, and knowledge-based learning communities. When we refer to learning communities, we are specifically referring to communities intentionally designed to support learning. To examine these different forms of learning communities, we consider their similarities and differences along four dimensions of community: membership, task features and learning goals, participation structures, and mechanisms for further growth and reproduction.

MEMBERSHIP. An important element of community is membership. Who joins? How do they find their way to the group? What is the life cycle of their participation in the group? What sort of differentiation, if any, exists among members?

TASK FEATURES / LEARNING GOALS. Groups come together for a purpose. In some instances, the group may be explicitly tasked with a product to develop or an activity to complete. For others, the group is simply engaged in joint activity as part of some larger enterprise.

PARTICIPATION STRUCTURES. A critical distinction among groups arises from the formal or informal means of group members with access to the full range of community activity, for example, tools, events, history, and other members. Furthermore, groups differ in the opportunities they afford members to participate in a variety of ways. Some communities are very open to and supportive of shifts in members' roles and identities in the group.

REPRODUCTION AND GROWTH MECHANISMS. These are the means by which the community grows and the mechanisms by which the community continues to exist independent of members who might join or leave the community.

The structure of this chapter is provided by our examination of three different types of learning communities and the technical environments that support them. After a summary of the differences, we examine programs or systems of activities where there is an intentional effort to use the parallel structure of different layers and types of learning communities to help facilitate the growth and development of each of the communities. *Learning organizations* create a system of interchange between different communities with a goal of supporting the development across communities. We end the chapter with some observations about designs for the future.

Technical Designs for Learning Communities

In designing technical environments for learning communities, it is important to understand that there is variation within their structure and goals. We describe three distinct but overlapping types of learning communities.

Task-based learning communities are groups of people organized around a task who work intently together for a specified period of time to produce a product. While the specific group may not, in the strictest sense, share all of the properties of a community, the people who participate in them often experience a strong sense of identification with their partners, the task, and the organization that supports them. The use of community as a context that modifies learning signals a form of learning that is very different from simple collaboration (Schrage, 1995).

Practice-based learning communities are larger groups with shared goals that offer their members richly contextualized and supported arenas for learning. Indeed, some corporate organizational groups are evolving their approach to workplace learning to leverage the learning power of community. The term *community of practice* (Lave & Wenger, 1991) was created to provide a way of talking about the institutional and interpersonal activities that unite groups of people who are engaged in the same occupation or career.

Knowledge-based learning communities often share many of the features of a community of practice but focus on the deliberate and formal production of external knowledge about the practice. Where a community of practice might rely on ongoing participation of members to transmit embodied knowledge, knowledge-building learning communities have made the overt commitment to record and share knowledge outside of its immediate use or active context.

TASK-BASED LEARNING COMMUNITIES

The explicit goal of task-based *learning communities* is to assemble a set of people with a maximum diversity of perspectives that can be focused on a common issue or problem, and then, through the processes of group formation, discourse, and common work, create a common systemic understanding (See Table 2.1). Their shared goal is the communal use of diversity to achieve a deeper understanding of issues, to find a solution to problems, or to complete a task in a way that is beyond the capabilities of any single person. Close interpersonal relationships and work patterns often arise in the process of creating the product or completing the task together.

The group product or outcome reflects the learning process and stands as a completed static object. While the product may be used by others, it is not likely to be revisited or revised by others. For example, a task-based learning team might be formed to study the pollution in local rivers. Each member has a better understanding and leaves what she or he has learned. A report might be written and sent to other people in the neighborhood or to local officials, but it exists as a finished document. This stands in contrast to a "living" document or database that continues to develop in knowledge-based learning communities.

Learning communities in the formal school setting are most often task-based and emphasize group learning as a way to scaffold individual learning. We begin our discussion of task-based learning communities with an exploration of the distinctions between community models of learning in schools and more traditional forms of classroom learning.

Studies of children in the home neighborhood offer evidence of how deeply learning is embedded in social activity (Greenfield, 1999; Cole, 1996; Heath, 1983; Scribner, 1990; Rogoff, 1995). Children in school are certainly located in a social context, with roles, traditions, language, and have cultural tools at their disposal. However, the goals of their group efforts are often unclear. Is their task to do well on standardized tests? To pass

TABLE 2.1. *Task-Based Learning Communities*

Community Dimensions	Product-Based Learning Communities
Membership	Membership is assigned or grouped.
	Members know one another.
	Group identity is temporary.
	Leadership is assigned or evolves through interaction.
Task Features and/or Group Goals	Topic, project, or group goal is well specified.
	Learning goals are defined as a part of the project.
	Timeline used, often with phases and a specified deadline.
	Value of the product assessed by others.
Participation Structures	Participation is often defined with specific roles and responsibilities.
	Small-group interaction, which may be shaped by explicit division of labor.
Reproduction and Growth Mechanisms	Specific Learning Community ends with the production of the product that reflects the learning.
	Transfer of practices and procedures from one community to the next through products, procedures, and guidelines.
	Community practices carried between discontinuous groups by organizational leaders or programs.

to the next grade level? To get "high marks" from the teacher? To acquire specific pieces of information such as times tables? To avoid punishment? To become a good citizen? To prepare to enter the workforce?

Traditional classrooms, weighed down by the burden of a prescribed curriculum, constrained by the limitations of age and ability grouping, and with compulsory attendance, lack the defining characteristics of a cohesive community. Collaborative learning might be employed for a specific lesson, as an instructional strategy. However, for most of the time, the traditional classroom is a thinly contextualized, unfocused collection of tasks that does not support community-based learning.

There are, however, striking contrasts to this model where individual classrooms are involved in projects like Knowledge Forum (Hewitt, this volume), Kids as Global Scientists (Songer, 1993), The Jason Project

(Eklund, 1993), The Globe Project (Means, 1998), the iEARN Projects (Rennebohm-Franz, 1996), and Learning Circles (Riel, 1998). In some cases, whole schools (Brown, Ellery, & Campione, 1998; Goldman & The Cognition and Technology Group at Vanderbilt, 1997; Coalition for Essential Schools, 2000) are transformed into communities of learners that extend across grade levels and involve interactions with experts beyond the classroom. In these examples, there is an effort to modify classroom norms and student identities to create workspaces in which students collaborate with teams of students and experts, building knowledge together. In our discussion of task-based learning communities, we offer a description of how the community-learning model operates in these connected classrooms, in what we call task-based learning communities.

Task-based learning communities in the classroom may be the beginning of a more extensive school structure for learning or they may be temporary communities with the specific purpose of helping students learn how to work in communities. They are in some ways micro-communities because they do not share all of the characteristics of full-blown communities. The timeline on task-based learning is relatively short, making it more difficult to develop community mechanisms such as shared discourse and shared sets of practices, values, and tools. Also, a task-based learning experience begins with the same set of people and ends with the production of a product. The regeneration is with a new cohort and any knowledge across "generations" of groups may be carried by people in the larger community identified for this purpose or through program materials left for the new group. And perhaps most important, they are not voluntary groupings. A student cannot decide to physically leave the classroom communities (although students can refuse to participate). For these reasons, some of the authors of this volume questioned the use of the term community within the classroom context.

Recognizing these differences, we nevertheless use community to index a fundamental shift in classroom social organization that moves closer to patterns of community interaction and a social-cultural framework for learning. Often these task-based learning communities do continue but with new groups of students, and these bounded groups do in small ways contribute to the knowledge of the larger community – the school or project organization.

DESIGNING TECHNICAL ENVIRONMENTS TO SUPPORT TASK-BASED LEARNING COMMUNITIES

Communication technology makes it much easier to find and work with people who share a common learning goal. These people can come from different regions and be part of different organizations and different experiences and interests. Spontaneous support groups and interest groups can arise and develop into virtual communities (Rheingold, 1993), and a great deal of learning might occur in these virtual communities. However, a task-based learning community requires an intentional focus on advancing the knowledge of the collective. The transformation to a learning community requires the development of group goals focused intentionally on a learning outcome. This structuring is often accomplished from within a project, program, community, or organization.

Teachers often become members of online task-based learning communities, perhaps with the goal of creating a lesson facilitated by collaborative tools such as those found on Harvard's Education with New Technologies Web site,[1] Indiana University's Inquiry Learning Forum (Barab, MaKinster, & Scheckler, this volume), or in SRI International's Tapped In (Schlager & Fusco, this volume). Organizations such as ThinkQuest encourage students and teachers to join task-based learning communities outside of the school with a goal of fostering learning both in and out of schools. Many learning communities that meet in face-to-face settings also use technology to support their collaborative work.

A comparison of two task-based learning communities, one sponsored by an organization and one by an international teacher community, illustrates the dimensions of supporting a task-based learning community online. The International Education and Resources Network (iEARN) supports Learning Circles,[2] highly interactive, project-based partnerships among eight to ten schools located throughout the world. The Learning Circle participants design and complete a series of projects that are summarized in a group publication. Network Learning Services, a company, sponsors the ThinkQuest Challenge,[3] a contest in which teams of students and adults, often from three different countries, work over the Internet to design an educational Web site. The development work generally takes place out of school but often involves teachers as team members.

iEARN uses discussion forums and email notices to announce the start of a Learning Circle session to teachers from diverse regional, social, linguistic, cultural, and national diversity. ThinkQuest sets a date for team formation and students use the ThinkQuest Web site to advertise for teams members with specific skills. With a competitive advantage for team diversity (gender, ethnicity, and socio-economic status), students use a variety of strategies to locate team members from distant locations. In both cases, the smaller task-based learning communities are dependent on a larger community structure for their formation, organization, and support. Once a ThinkQuest team or Learning Circle is formed, the members are set.

---

[1] Harvard's Education with New Technologies Web site: http://learnweb.harvard.edu/ent/home/index.cfm
[2] Learning Circle Web site: http://www.iearn.org/circles
[3] ThinkQuest Web site: http//www.thinkquest.org

Participants in both of these learning communities begin by learning more about their partners and discussing their shared task. They share a goal of designing a project or set of projects, collecting group ideas, data, and writing, and finally publishing their collected materials.

Collaboration over the Internet makes it possible for each class participating in a Learning Circle, or member of a ThinkQuest team, to be an active part of the management team. School-based Learning Circles and extracurricular ThinkQuest teams have a similar structure to Quality Circles in the business community (Deming, 1993), where the hierarchical boundaries between workers and managers are reduced through a cooperative approach to decision-making and product development.

Learning Circle and ThinkQuest interaction is organized into phases, each with goals and tasks facilitating cooperative planning among the participants. Timelines published on the Web and email announcements at the beginning of each phase help organize the group exchange. In Learning Circles, each school sponsors one of the Circle projects and in doing so, takes on the role of expert in that area. All schools have the opportunity to sponsor a project and the responsibility to respond to the projects of the other classroom teams. In ThinkQuest, each student takes on responsibility for part of the shared task. Students assume roles like researcher, writer, and programmer, and often find coaches who can help with content and structure and design.

Completing the Circle, for Learning Circles, or submitting the Web site for ThinkQuest teams, marks the completion of a round of the learning community. All of the interaction in these activities is mediated by technology, both as the tool of communication and as productivity tools for creating the shared artifact. This technical product is the reflection of group process. If schools continue to participate in Learning Circles, they join a new Circle in the next cycle. Students who continue in ThinkQuest form new teams. The teacher and coaches, as well as the social-technical design of the Learning Circle and ThinkQuest programs, carry the continuity from one session to the next. Student products, either a Web site or digital or print publication, reflect what they accomplished as a team and can serve to guide future teams as an example. The product might be displayed in a class or school library or posted in online libraries. These reports and Web sites serve primarily to document the group learning processes.

In these task-based learning communities, the learning takes place both online, facilitated by many different forms of distant communication, and through interaction that takes place locally *as a direct result* of either sending or receiving the messages. The technology is used to create both technical and social environments (Kling & Courtright, this volume) where members depend on one another and are asked to incorporate different worldviews into their frame of perception.

Technology structures for task-based learning communities may also have as an implicit goal the introduction of students to professional communities and the learning that takes place in these settings. For example, The Jason Project, Passport to Knowledge projects, and a number of other electronic field trips use combinations of live video, feeds of data collection, and Web and communication tools to give students a sense of being part of a team of researchers and support staff engaged in doing real science. Participation structures provide students with opportunities to handle the tools of authentic science inquiry, to converse using specialized language, and to observe more sophisticated members of the community going about their work. For instance, when Passport to Knowledge presented "Live from the Hubble Telescope," American students were allocated time on the Hubble telescope. They could use this powerful tool and focus it into space and receive their data for analysis. They could not do this alone, but with planet "advocates" who were able to scaffold student thinking with questions, observations, and anecdotes to engage in an online discussion of which planet to examine and why. Once the decisions were made, students were able to watch via live televised broadcasts as their data were received. The scientists then responded, and engaged the students with questions intended to help the students to interpret "their data." In this task-based learning community, they are also able to participate somewhat like "tourists" in a community of practicing astronomers, but they are not really members of a community of practice of scientists.

PRACTICE-BASED LEARNING COMMUNITIES

A practice-based learning community arises around a profession, discipline, or field of endeavor (see Table 2.2). It may be as broad as a group of Linux programmers around the world developing and sharing their work in journals, conferences, and online forums. It can be as narrow as a team of teachers at a single school who are working together to improve the practice of reading instruction on site by meeting, discussing, and sharing around their practicing with new methods and materials. It differs from a task-based learning community in significant ways, most of which are captured by the *voluntary participation* in field or "practice."

There is a strong emphasis on the notion of a community as a shared activity and goals, though there may be differences in expertise and experience. Members of a community of practice have identities that are defined in part by the nature and extent of their participation in the practice. Additionally, members share a social responsibility to learn from and learn for the community.

When the emphasis is on practice, the concept of community indexes a view of learning as increased participation and responsibility in activity, and a view of knowledge as knowledge-in-use. These terms characterize

TABLE 2.2. *Practice-Based Learning Communities*

Community Dimensions	Practice-Based Learning Community
Membership	Members join and are frequently acknowledged formally by the community through dues, licenses, or certification.
	Community identity is defined in terms of evolving expertise and by the division of labor in the practice of the community.
	Leadership identified through roles in the community.
Task Features and/or Group Goals	Reproduction and preservation of the practices that have been found most effective in the past.
	Design and experimentation with new practices to solve evolving community challenges.
	Development of tasks, tools, or roles in the practice arising in response to internal and external changes.
Participation Structures	Access to peers, near-peers, and experts engaged in practices.
	Opportunity to participate in authentic tasks of the practice, and to become more fully involved. Access to the rituals, tools (including language), and history of the practice as support for learning.
Reproduction and Growth Mechanisms	Tension between new and old experts and expertise within the practice resulting in modification and development.
	Development of the practice and community through development of discourse, tools, and artifacts of work, action routines, anecdotes about practice, and other cultural mechanisms.
	Exchanges with adjacent practice communities, e.g., across companies in an industry, across departments in a company, or across schools in a district.

the reproduction and distribution of knowledge throughout a group of people who constitute a working community on the basis of their shared goals and interests in productive activity of some sort, such as work. These *practice-based learning communities* focus on the evolution, preservation, and reproduction of the common or shared understandings of the group beyond the current social grouping.

In a community of practice, the knowledge is embedded in the performance and the organizational culture in which it occurs (Lave & Wenger, 1991). Each of the participants helps to shape the knowledge but mostly as a consequence of modifying practice, not explicitly to build knowledge. Indeed, a community of practice often relies on tacit understandings that are shared among members and passed along through mentoring and apprentice experiences.

Practice-based learning communities locate knowledge in two symbiotic activities: reification and participation (Barab, MaKinster, & Scheckler, this volume; Wenger, 1998). Reified knowledge is codified and captured. It resides in policies, documents, talk, and even in tools themselves. This provides the community with a stable but brittle knowledge base, made more flexible by the complementary notion of participation. Participative knowledge, or experiential or lived knowledge, is the wisdom that is actualized through people, their practices, and their stories. This is dynamic knowledge that develops and changes over time and across practitioners. If only tacit, experiential knowledge exists, the community is vulnerable to the loss of key individuals. Both sources of knowledge are critical to the health of the community.

A characteristic of healthy communities of practice is their permeability by "brokers" – members of multiple, related communities who move between them, functioning as conduits between the communities. Communities avoid isolation and support their own development by interacting with groups engaged in tangentially related practices. In this way, a community of practice that is quite focused on its own activity can avoid becoming an isolated cult of practice.

We define a practice-based learning community as a culture that has grown up around an activity system and in which there is a focus on continually improving one's practices so as to support the effective functioning of the activity system. As a cultural system, it relies on cultural tools to hold the community together and ensure continuity across generations: language, artifacts, rituals, routines, and stories. In the everyday and work worlds, outside of formal public education, practice communities abound. But, unlike task-based learning communities or knowledge-based communities, their cultural work is frequently tacit. They are not consciously building dynamic knowledge systems for future generations of practice; they are instead going about their work refining procedures or developing new tools. Further, not all practices develop strong community structures; many are dysfunctional, locking their members out of opportunities to grow and develop further, and limiting the evolution and development of the practice. Such communities still have a strong cultural dimension, but the tools of cultural work are used to limit and control. In their seminal work on communities of practice, Lave and Wenger (1991) offer the tale of the meat cutters, a community that has stunted its own growth by the isolation of new workers from "old-timers." Though Lave and Wenger do not discuss school in terms of a community of practice, it is not a far reach to see teachers as equally isolated and sequestered from each other, and from greater expertise in their field.

Practice-based learning communities share the same vulnerabilities as cultures. Much of their knowledge is knowledge-in-action that comes from tacit understanding and familiarity with tools, signs, and symbols of practice. When we try to capture the tacit knowledge of communities, we end up with a snapshot of current practice, current knowledge, and current cultural routines. This reified knowledge is useful, but brittle and fragile, for it has only captured a moment in time, a version of activity. However, both the ongoing participation of diverse members, and the access that makes that participation possible, provide a balance to the rigidity and limitations of frozen, reified knowledge. Participation and reification are complementary characteristic activities of practice-based learning communities.

Practice-based learning communities need nurturing and protection. Wenger (2000) uses the metaphor of a garden to describe the nature of support that works for something as delicate as a community of practice. You cannot, he says, make the flowers grow by pulling on their leaves. You can, however, keep the flower beds free of weeds and pests, ensure there is water and sunlight, and you can even apply some plant food. But the flowers must do their own growing. What does that sort of support for the flowerbed look like in an isolated and troubled profession such as teaching?

The Japanese method of lesson research or study (Lewis & Tsuchida, 1998) provides a model of how the educational profession might be different if teachers were engaged in a practice-based learning community. Teachers in Japan and increasingly in the United States[4] form small groups to design, review, and modify lesson plans. They observe one another teaching the group lesson and analyze the differences, trying to better understand the relationship between the teaching and the learning. The goal of this shared work is to find ways to improve their practice. Teachers see lesson study as a part of teaching. "If we didn't do lesson research," one Japanese teacher commented, "we wouldn't be teachers." Their identity as teachers includes a commitment to analyze their practice as a method of continuous improvement. Teaching is learning to teach.

The Problem of School as a Practice Community

A practice-based learning community best describes a particular way of organizing associations of people in a field of endeavor, a profession, an avocation, or other activity system. In most cases, when the term *community of practice* is invoked in the classroom setting, it is associated with

---

4 For more information and video segments, see www.schoolrenewal.edu/renewal/feature/ lesson_study

efforts to liberate students from the confines of the classroom and connect them, immerse them, in an active formal community in which knowledge is instrumental and in practical use by knowledgeable professionals. However, this almost always results in an experience that is more like an extended site visit with people engaged in professional practice, rather than joining as members of the practice. Students get limited access and have limited participation opportunities in otherwise genuine work efforts that are underway in the real world. Projects like Globe, Co-Vis, Jason, and Passport to Knowledge use networking technology to connect students with peer and adult experts engaged in specific fields of endeavor that lend authenticity to the school's inert curricular knowledge.

Brown, Ellery, and Campione (1998) assert that a school can be constituted as a community of practice where the practice is school learning. Their work with a school in Oakland shifts the focus from fragmented knowledge acquisition to an intense program of learning how to be learners. The grade school students are viewed as novice learners working with more expert learners (teachers and researchers) and more experienced learners (other students including graduate-level students) to develop the practice of learning. The students select major and minor subjects of study and are made responsible for both learning and teaching in these areas of expertise. There is multi-age and multi-ability student grouping to help facilitate the informal mentoring and apprentice learning that is a part of community life. The research team helped the school employ a number of participant structures that are very different from conventional classrooms, such as reciprocal teaching meta-cognitive strategies, jigsaw patterns of collaborative research, guided writing, benchmark lessons, and cross talk (Brown, Ellery, & Campione, 1997). All of these procedures have become community mechanisms that help define roles and responsibilities and provide a strong sense of group identity.

While these examples seem to suggest that classrooms can approximate communities of practice, the temporary time period and the students' lack of choice to participate make it difficult to characterize them as members of a community of practice. Furthermore, the classroom routines do not evolve out of the practice of the teachers and researchers as "expert" learners themselves, nor do students see their community experts at work. And finally, the larger socio-cultural, political contexts of public schooling (e.g., standardized testing) and researcher intervention (i.e., temporary and specially funded) cloud the authenticity of the enterprise.

DESIGNING TECHNICAL ENVIRONMENTS TO SUPPORT PRACTICE-BASED LEARNING COMMUNITIES

The dawn of computer networking across geographic boundaries was also the beginning of much experimentation with network-based support for otherwise isolated practice-based learning communities outside the business world, such as classroom teachers or university researchers (Harasim, Hiltz, Teles, & Turoff, 1994). Efforts to use technology tools to develop and facilitate online communities of practice continue to grow.

TERC used email and online conferencing to foster a community of teachers of project-based science in LabNet (Ruopp, Gal, Drayton, & Pfister, 1993). While this community is no longer active, it was one of the first to develop a community of practice online with tele-mentoring. The connections help many teachers take a more reflective stance toward their practice and to experiment with shifts to new forms of teaching in a supportive environment. This was one of the early projects to demonstrate how an online community of practice could form an alternative to traditional methods of diffusion of knowledge with a community.

The Math Forum[5] brings together teachers, students, and researchers working with schools (Shumar & Renninger, this volume). The resulting math community relies on a range of web communication tools, including the virtual environment developed by SRI International, Tapped In.[6] These tools help support diverse participation structures in the community. For example, pre-service teachers are employed in a process of analysis of students' work and enlisted to provide online feedback to students who submit their reasoning on the "problem of the week."

Other online communities include Education with New Technology (ENT) at Harvard[7] and the Inquiry Learning Forum[8] at Indiana University (Barab, MaKinster, & Scheckler, this volume), both of which provide extensive online contexts for reflection on practice by a community of practicing teachers. Teachers of art can find others who share this identity through the Getty ArtsEd Network.[9]

Teachers who see service learning and global citizenship as an important function of schooling have connected with one another in the International Education and Resource Network (iEARN).[10] The levels of participation have resulted in a structure of management that uses the United Nations as a model. Each country has a regional community that grows as volunteers in the community take on leadership roles. Once they have developed a structure, they can participate on the management council that manages the international community. The international secretariat moves from country to country. Their annual meetings in face-to-face settings move from one continent to the next. The rest of the work is facilitated by work in online conferences.

---

5 Math Forum's Web site: www.mathforums.org
6 Tapped In Web site: tappedin.org
7 Education with New Technology Web site: learnweb.harvard.edu/ent/home/
8 The Inquiry Learning Forum Web site: http://ilf.crlt.indiana.edu
9 The Getty Arts Ed. Web site: www.getty.edu/artsednet/
10 iEARN Web site: www.iearn.org

The Virtual High School[11] and the Global Educator Network[12] are online communities for educators who teach online in high schools and universities. In both cases, there are efforts to use the online tools to provide community support, to develop roles, and to evolve a structure of continued participation and with it an identity.

These examples highlight the roles that technology plays in fostering online communities of practice. The participants may not know everyone in the community and there will be many different levels of participation from highly active members who play critical roles in the continuity of the community to those who have registered and yet remain on the fringe.

Designing online communities of practice presents new challenges because the participation structures are new. New members engaged in learning their practice must also learn new conventions and skills for engaging one another. Communities require channels for communicating among members and for accumulating and archiving the history of their group interactions. When communities are spread across time and space, networking tools support those actions. But virtual networks must also be able to support subtle cultural mechanisms that shape interaction, identity, and access, such as rituals and traditions that distinguish newcomers from old-timers in communities that rely on face-to-face encounters.

KNOWLEDGE-BASED LEARNING COMMUNITIES

Knowledge-based learning communities construct, use, reconstruct, and reuse knowledge in deliberate, continuous cycles (Scardamalia & Bereiter, 1994; Bereiter, 2001; Hewitt, this volume; also see Table 2.3). A knowledge-based learning community seeks to advance the collective knowledge in a subject or field of inquiry, and to do so in a way that supports the growth of each of the individuals in the community, that is, the intentional development of experts within the community. The group is engaged in a process of thinking about knowledge as knowledge. Knowledge-based learning community members continue to adapt the knowledge product to new and emerging conditions, to better understand processes that are dynamic in nature. The clearest example of a knowledge-based community is a set of researchers who work toward understanding a phenomenon, concept, or relationship, for example, earthquakes, black holes, or the effect of divorce on children. Like most learning communities, these groupings exist within programs, organizations, and professional societies. They function to make program, organizational, or community knowledge an object externalized from the tacit understandings, unbundled from practice, and available for iterative evolution.

---

[11] The Virtual High School Web site: www.concord.org/vhs
[12] The Global Educator Network Web site: http://vu.cs.sfu.ca/GEN/

TABLE 2.3. *Knowledge-Based Learning Communities*

Community Dimensions	Knowledge-Based Communities
Membership	Membership is defined by credentials as knowledge-builders.
	Members may or may not know each other personally.
	Strong identity with the knowledge-building endeavor.
	Leadership evolves from the efforts of knowledge-building.
Task Features and/or Group Goals	Evolution of the knowledge base through current use and for future users.
	Focus on validation knowledge, e.g., through peer review of cycles of generation of knowledge products.
	Focus on learning how to learn, or learning how to strengthen or counter ideas or arguments.
	Shared interest in development of the community.
Participation Structures	Long-term commitment to construct and reconstruct knowledge base.
	Organized and defined by the tasks of production of intellectual work.
Reproduction and Growth Mechanisms	Construction of a shared language for characterizing group work.
	Development and evolution of a set of procedures for evidence and interpretation that are passed from one group to the next.
	Interchanges with similar knowledge-building learning communities.

What makes a knowledge-building community distinct from a task-based learning community is a central focus on the design of an external representation of the community thought. While a task-based learning community is also engaged in the process of making knowledge, it is generally making it as a reflection of what members have learned. Task-based learning community members create a collection, an anthology, a lesson plan, a set of procedures, or a publication that is finished. It can be read or used by others but does not invite republishing, amendments, or modifications. The task-based learning community often disbands after the product is designed. They may not look at the product again other than to suggest others use it. In this regard, the knowledge-building learning community shares some characteristics with the task-based learning community. However, here the task is much broader, and the group commitment much deeper.

Unlike a task community, a knowledge-building learning community does not complete a product, publication, or gallery as an end point of effort. Instead, members work on living documents or databases of ideas, which form a living, changing record of their shared mind. Their contribution moves in a larger discourse where each contribution is examined, reviewed, and analyzed for clues on how to take the next turn in the community discourse. It is an intellectual conversation, which leaves a trace that can be revisited and rewritten to fit new notions of the ongoing activities. A knowledge-based community views its work as one move in a process of continual change to a common, external, codified knowledge base around the practice.

An important distinction between a knowledge-based learning community and a practice-based learning community is a consequence of this intentionality. In the latter, the development of practice relies on the natural evolution of practice over time and individuals. That is, it relies upon the natural variation that emerges as novices advance in the practice and add their own modifications, and the reciprocal shaping of tool and practice. In practice-based learning communities, these mechanisms create tension in the community that further pushes the evolution of practice and practical knowledge. However, in the knowledge-based community, the intentionality is explicit, not tacit. Members actively seek to evolve the practice of knowledge building as well as the content.

DESIGNING TECHNICAL ENVIRONMENTS TO SUPPORT KNOWLEDGE-BASED COMMUNITIES

An educational example of a knowledge-building learning community can be found in the social infrastructure that is created around groups of school-age students using the networking software, Knowledge Forum,[TM] as the tool for externalizing their understandings (Hewitt, this volume). In the schools Hewitt describes, the goal was to transform the whole social organization of the classrooms to a knowledge-building learning community. Students engaged in a number of different knowledge-building activities, some of which involved the use of Knowledge Forum[TM] as the tool for externalizing their understandings. In knowledge-building learning communities, tools evolve that make it possible for groups to store and reuse knowledge, but the group use of a tool does not necessarily index a knowledge-building learning community.

For example, Bugscope,[13] is a Web-accessible electron microscope available for student and teacher use from the classrooms. Students send their collected bug samples through postal mail and Bugscope technicians mount them for viewing with the electron microscope. Using a Web interface, the students can examine and save images of the eyes, skin, hair, mouth, parts, and legs of even the tiniest creatures. The pictures taken by one class are added to a database so that everyone can view them. In this way they are collectively creating a visual database of what a group of students chooses to examine on bugs, spiders, worms, and flies. While these students are collectively building a database of information, they are doing so as individuals with no ties to a larger community. The pictures are not individually labeled, which makes it difficult to view images of other schools. To be participants in a knowledge-building learning community, they would need to work together to understand the knowledge that can be derived from the data collection. As yet, there has been no real community development around this online tool, but it is an example of a technical tool that could provide the online technology support for a knowledge-building learning community of educators and students who are interested in the study of small organisms.

An example of the role of technology in a knowledge-building learning community can be seen in the partnerships that the city parks and recreation department of Apple Valley, Minnesota, forms with the local high school program of environmental studies. Students in this interdisciplinary program use a range of technical tools to make careful measurements of the quality of water, types of organisms present, and characteristics of the water environment in a city pond (NCREL, 1998). They do so at the request of the city parks and recreation services, and they work in teams and share their data with the community in multimedia products. Because each new class begins the activity when they enter the science course and they do not use or build on the work of prior students, their collaborative work in this system of classification would be an example of a task-based learning community. The city parks and recreation department, by organizing these data measurements in a flexible system for repeated use over time, would be characterized as a knowledge-building learning community. It might make sense to think of the high school students as visiting "interns" in this knowledge-building learning community.

In a similar project organized by a primary teacher, Kristi Rennebohm-Franz, very young students are active participants in building the knowledge about a pond of water in their community.[14] The students and teacher

---

[13] Bugscope Web site: bugscope.beckman.uiuc.edu/
[14] Water Habitat Project Web site: www.psd267.wednet.edu/%7Ekfranz/Science/
WaterHabitat/waterhabitat.htm

are using Web-based technologies to record what they are learning and to save it so that each successive class of students can build on the previous class's work. The knowledge building is evident in the students' Web pages in both written and visual forms. While mindful of the reasons that we discussed earlier challenging the use of communities to describe student groups, this group of primary students comes as close to a knowledge-building learning community as one is likely to find in a school setting.

The Knowledge Loom[15] is a knowledge-building learning community organized around best practices in teaching and learning. The Knowledge Loom is a Web-based resource developed by the Northeast & Islands Regional Educational Laboratory at Brown University (LAB) with the support of the U.S. Department of Education. It features a database of best-practice resources for elementary, middle, and high school teachers. The website provides a meeting place as well as the technical structure for members to continually "add their own threads of wisdom and experience to the content." They can do this by sharing their teaching knowledge in the form of "success stories," responding to one of the posted success stories, or participating in panel discussions. Community experts are available to respond to questions posed by members, and leaders in the field are available for online panel discussions on different topics.

Membership in the community is through a process of registration, and communication with the community is achieved through a biweekly electronic newsletter. Members can move from passive observer to active contributor through their actions and the reactions of the community. All members can contribute their ideas while other more central community members serve as peer reviewers to assure quality of content. The site helps to generate a language and a structure for the sharing of teaching practices. A practice is defined and then illustrated by stories and supported by research. The loom is a technical-social infrastructure for the building of knowledge as an ongoing task of the community.

In the workplace, outside of formal educational settings, the notion of intentional knowledge building has emerged from a perceived crisis of competition. As companies strive to improve production and capture market share, they have turned to the deliberate capture and reuse of workplace knowledge as a critical strategy (Davenport & Prusak, 1998). This notion of knowledge includes worker knowledge and expertise as well as the development of "knowledge" out of raw information mined from clients. Obligingly, technology companies in the 1990s generated a variety of "knowledge management" software systems, designed to allow for worker contributions in many forms (documents, email, images, sounds, and so on) and offering an array of actions that could be performed on archived data, such as linking and context-sensitive searching. A second

---

[15] Knowledge Loom Web site: knowledgeloom.org

major class of software development, also a database of sorts, is the customer relations management package (CRM and e-CRM). Customers, especially e-customers, are now viewed as niche communities from which valuable development information can be gathered (Hagel & Armstrong, 1997). In the late 1990s companies began to develop "information policies" and hire high-level executives for positions like Chief Learning Officer or Chief Knowledge Officer to direct these activities. Because the production of knowledge is still generally not perceived as the main goal of these companies and organizations, companies must establish an organizational culture in which this activity is highly valued (Dixon, 2000).

Knowledge-based communities share many of the characteristics of practice-based learning communities, but add the intentional, focused activity of building, managing, and using information over time. Technical environments for knowledge-building learning communities must support the development of communities of practice, but have at least two additional requirements. First, the technical environment must support a fairly sophisticated knowledge handling system, that is, a means for identifying, adding, annotating, modifying, or extending, for making connections, for searching, retrieving, and unpacking contributions. Further, this system must be able to handle contributions in a variety of formats. Second, there must be a mechanism for warranting knowledge, that is, a means for validating its worth according to community values.

SUMMARY OF TOPOLOGY OF LEARNING COMMUNITIES

We have characterized three types of learning communities. As a summary of the preceding discussion, Table 2.4 provides a comparison of task-based, practice-based, and knowledge-based learning communities, as we have discussed them.

We recognize that there are social entities that contain all three of these types of learning communities, and membership in these different communities varies in ways that are not always clear. This echoes the discussion at the beginning of this chapter about macro or micro perspective on communities. It complicates the issue of how to characterize the collection of learning communities. However, for the final section of the chapter we will propose a group system that emerges from the intersection of the three discussed communities: the learning organization.

TECHNICAL DESIGNS FOR LEARNING ORGANIZATIONS

Learning communities are often subdivisions of larger organizations or activity systems. Although they may be brief in duration or longer lasting, they support the work of ongoing groups to further their understanding and to develop their ability to work creatively. In this section, we focus

TABLE 2.4. *Comparison of Task-Based, Practice-Based, and Knowledge-Based Learning Communities*

Dimensions	Task-Based	Practice-Based	Knowledge-Based
Membership	Members assigned or grouped on the basis of task features	Members seek participation to become more experienced practitioners	Members participate by virtue of relevant expertise and common interest
	Members know one another	Members may or may not all know each other	Members may or may not know each other
	Temporary group identity with task	Strong identity with role in ongoing practice/profession	Strong identity with knowledge/expertise
	Informal or emergent division of labor	Formal division of labor based on roles and identities	Formal division of labor based on roles and identities
	Formal or informal leadership, linked to completion of task	Leadership emerges from acknowledged experience and expertise, a source of ongoing tension in the community	Leadership evolves from knowledge-building successes and reputation in the knowledge field
Task Features and/or Group Learning Goals	Well-defined topic, project, or problem, with clear start and finish	Productive, collective activity comprised of many tasks	Evolution of the knowledge base through current use and for future users to improve practice
	Learning goals as a part of the project	Learning as the tacit or explicit consequence of ongoing practice; continual redesign and experimentation to solve challenges, accommodate variation, and integrate development of tools	Learning as knowledge; focus on knowledge production, validation, and dissemination

Participation Structures	Small-group interaction with informal division of labor	Open access to practice, practitioners, culture, and tools of practice; changes in members' roles reflect changes in their knowledge; roles related to division of labor	Written dialogue and documents used to externalize, construct, and reconstruct the knowledge base
	Ends with the completion of the product that reflects the learning	Engaged in continual production of practical work, in the course of which learning opportunities arise	Organized and defined by the production of intellectual work and theoretical constructs
Reproduction and Growth Mechanisms	Explicit transfer of practices and procedures across groups through products, procedures, and guidelines	Evolution of the practice through discourse, tools, and artifacts of work, action routines, anecdotes about practice, and other cultural mechanisms, both tacit and explicit	Develops and evolves a set of procedures for evidence and interpretation that are passed from one group to the next
	Shared vocabulary and agreed-upon practice for the duration of the task	Shared values and language; reproduction and evolution of valued practices, i.e., an evolving culture	Shared values and language; reproduction and evolution of valued practices, i.e., an evolving culture
	Community practices carried between discontinuous groups by organizational leaders or programs	Exchanges with adjacent, relevant practice communities, e.g., across companies in an industry, or across departments in a company or school, often through intentional brokering	Interaction with similar knowledge-building learning communities, often through intentional brokering

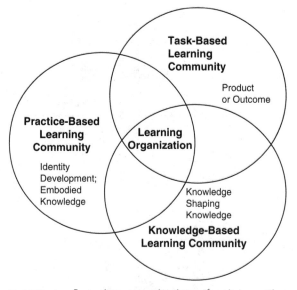

FIGURE 2.1. Learning organization: the intersection of task-, practice-, and knowledge-based communities

on the overlapping or shared features of the three kinds of communities we have discussed. Figure 2.1 illustrates the three types of learning communities that we have described in a system of overlapping circles. In the common core, where all three overlap, lies the fertile ground of organizational learning (Senge, 1990).

These different communities are strengthened by the activities and interaction with other communities in a larger structure of a learning organization. Creating systems of interchange between different communities with a goal of supporting the development across communities promotes a culture of community learning within learning organizations (Argyris, 1977; Senge, 1990).

Each of these three community types shares common characteristics. For instance, all have a working culture that members can rely upon to help them make sense of the work underway. However, time and other constraints in a learning community may keep that culture from developing into a more enduring, rich resource for future work. Also, while each community type is goal-directed, differences in goal or intent or the organized social activity mean differences in the nature of activity. A community of practice is focused on the accomplishment of the practice, not the protection of knowledge about the practice gained as a by-product. On the other hand, the knowledge-building learning community can be viewed as a practice-based learning community that has taken as its practice the deliberate construction of an ongoing, dynamic, knowledge base about some productive field of endeavor, such as second language acquisition or ABS braking systems.

We believe each type of community has a particular emphasis or focus that best defines it. The practice-based learning community is largely about learning as the transformation of identity within the practice, for example, novices becoming more expert. And, because it is focused on a "real-world" practice, the practice-based learning community situates knowledge in the context of its use in practice. The task-based learning community is a work group, focused on a time-limited task or effort. The knowledge-building learning community is oriented toward the intentional development of reusable knowledge, and more importantly to its continued growth and development.

The practice-based learning community and the knowledge-building learning community are able to rely upon cultural mechanisms to aid members in their participation. Both are most functional when they provide for access and participation among members of varying degrees of experience and expertise. The practice-based learning community and the task-based learning community may share far fewer characteristics, but both rely on the mechanism of interpersonal interaction to move the activity forward. The learning community and knowledge-building learning community share the common element of deliberate, explicit efforts to accomplish learning.

All three kinds of community activity exist within one larger sociocultural organization such as a business, school, or an institution. We use the term *organizational learning* to describe a collective unit under which these groups are nested.

The notion of the *learning organization* is a relatively new description of workplace culture as the source of tacit and explicit learning that supports and develops the organizational enterprise. This idea emerged in the field of business management and leadership from seminal work by Argyris (1977) and extended by Senge (1990).

Kofman and Senge (1995) describe a learning organization as a "culture of systems" in which innovations evolve through generative conversations and concerted actions in contrast to fragmentary competitive organizations, which are driven by reactions to problems without a sense of the whole. A learning organization is a system in which knowledge sharing is overtly valued and supported within the culture of the workplace. The refinement and extension of networking and database technologies and the crush of competition in the economy are two influences that have pressed on the practice of business and begun to evolve the practice of knowledge creation, use, and sharing in the organization (Barksdale, 1998; Davenport & Prusak, 1998; Dixon, 2000; Nonaka & Takeuchi, 1995).

Some corporate workplaces deliberately design and implement cultural and technical mechanisms to harvest and share workplace knowledge

(Dixon, 2000; Davenport, 1997; Davenport & Prusak, 1998; Koulopouls, Spinello, & Toms, 1997.) Since the 1990s, paralleling the increasing sophistication of networked applications, we have seen the rise of high-level corporate positions tasked with establishing and supporting this process. Job titles have evolved, from "Chief Information Officer" to "Chief Learning Officer" or "Chief Knowledge Officer." This represents a deep conviction about the knowledge value of community culture and a serious effort to make tacit knowledge or knowledge-in-use explicit and capture it for reuse by others. This effort is made possible by advances in networking and software, and has spawned a niche business in enterprise portals and knowledge management networks.

The Learning Organization: An Example

Graduate education is one setting in which task-based, practice-based, and knowledge-based communities co-exist, potentially. If the institution deliberately takes on this role, it can function to connect individual practitioners with the larger community of professional practice, which contextualizes their work and generates formal knowledge for the field. We believe this is a powerful role for higher education in the future and one that is well supported by network applications even today. When positioned in this way, the professional graduate school becomes a learning organization, deliberately self-aware and constantly evolving both its practice as an organization and the knowledge base upon which it relies. To illustrate this, we use as an example the online Masters in Educational Technology Program at Pepperdine University. The Graduate School of Education and Psychology (GSEP) designed this program with the explicit goal of helping students develop a deeper understanding of community through their reflections on task-based learning experiences in the program and, more importantly, through transforming their identities in their local communities of practice. Throughout the process, a reflective metacognitive stance is accomplished by making changes in their thinking observable through explicit knowledge construction.

TASK-BASED LEARNING COMMUNITY. While students bring with them their membership in a local practice (e.g., teachers in a K–12 classroom, designers working in industry, etc.), their participation in the graduate program also places them in a task-based learning community, the goal of which is explicitly to carry out work and learn something in the process. When admitted into the program, students are grouped into cadres and take all of their courses together. Their first week of the program is a series of face-to-face activities often with a range of technology tools structured by the cadre that has just completed their degrees. They pass on the learning culture in a "camp" experience. After the first week, they continue to interact through a series of task-based learning communities organized online as part of their coursework. Their work together in different learning communities provides access to variations in practice, and thus to discussions and work groups aimed at improving practice.

PRACTICE-BASED LEARNING COMMUNITY. Students come to the program from primary and secondary education communities, from universities and the corporate sector. They represent regions as distant as Japan or as different as Alaska. Thus each student brings a personal, local version of technology in education as practiced in his or her workplace. The program is designed to embrace this, rather than ignore, reject, or deny it. The work experiences students share in the ongoing discourse of the program's year-long action research project and companion courses offer a view of the variations and the commonalities in problems, issues, objects, histories, and goals. The elementary school computer lab teacher and the aerospace information technology worker share common frustrations at the consequences of working on the peripheries of their organizations. The high school English teacher and the university media specialist share their common concerns about information literacy and acceptable use policies for student Internet use. For each of these students, their roles in communities of practice are the basic unit of design of each learning experience. The overarching goal of the program is for each student to understand his or her role in a primary community of practice and then develop new strategies for how to serve this community in effective ways.

KNOWLEDGE-BASED LEARNING COMMUNITY. Students and faculty also have experiences as members of knowledge-building learning communities. For example, in learning about mentoring and team leadership, the students inherit the Pepperdine Mentor Center, an online repository of what past cadres have learned about mentoring. They also inherit the responsibility to improve the database of cases. The medium of the Web with multi-user access to information stored in databases makes it possible for students to leave their work for future generations of students and, at the same time, maintain access for their own use. This property of the technology to provide students intellectual ownership of their property and, simultaneously, permit them to share it with future students changes the way teachers and students can work in classrooms. It allows for the multi-generational form of knowledge building.

Faculty and students are also jointly engaged in a knowledge-building learning community as they collectively reshape the program in an iterative fashion. In contrast to face-to-face teaching, most of the dialogue of each online course is stored and made available online for visits by other faculty or students. This provides a framework for how the course was taught in the past. Faculty and sometimes students share ideas for assignments, activities, and projects in the online teaching area, and so effective strategies diffuse rapidly through the program. New faculty can visit courses from the past to see how they were taught. In this way each year faculty are learning from one another. Students, faculty, and alumni of the program also participate in an annual program debrief, conducted during the final face-to-face meeting, as a greatly modified version of the Future Search (Weisbord & Janoff, 1995).

TECHNICAL SUPPORT FOR THE LEARNING ORGANIZATION

Over the past five years, the impact of social, community-based models of learning and the rise of the Internet and Intranet webs have combined to give birth to software designed to support online teaching and learning as well as knowledge capture and sharing in organizations.

Rather then work within the limitations of packaged software, faculty model for students different ways of constructing the learning context. They set this example as they expect that students will also learn to use the technology to create similar models that can be used in their communities of practice. Asynchronous, threaded discussions (newsgroups) are a foundational part of online learning. In addition, the synchronous, multi-user, chat environment Tapped In (see Schlager & Fusco, this volume) provides students, faculty, and guests with a landscaped, real-time space for interaction. Where newsgroups support longer reflective pieces, Tapped In supports fast-paced, short conversational turns.

In newsgroups, students have the time and space to reference their workplace, in anecdotes or as examples to illustrate course ideas. This sharing is probably most useful as students use their own community contexts to make sense of theoretical and empirical content of the courses. This opportunity is heightened by the responses of peers and the opportunity to see peer versions of the workplace. Students move flexibly from the narrow confines of the specifics of their school or organization, or from ideas presented in a book, to a more expansive view of how many schools and organizations deal with a problem or implement ideas. Students also have access to server space and build their online portfolio as a central location to keep information about their learning process.

In the learning organization, there is a deliberate, self-conscious attempt to support all three kinds of community systems by harvesting experience and supporting its shared use among members. To support the continuity and evolution of the culture that students in the graduate programs are creating, the tacit and explicit knowledge embedded in the many community activities must find a repository that is accessible to members of the organization. There are many varieties of specific knowledge management (KM) software packages, but most share these characteristics: backbone of a searchable database of Web objects (text, images, graphs, spreadsheets, and so on), ability to link objects together for personal use, support

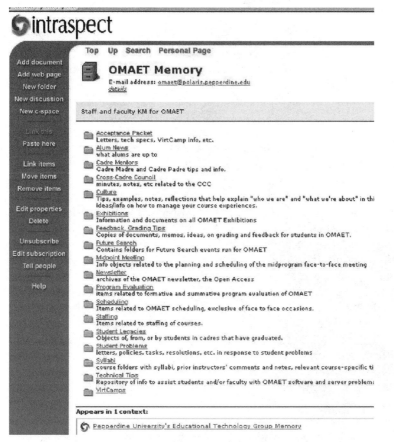

FIGURE 2.2. Pepperdine's Group Memory database

of collaborative or shared workspace, and ability to push information to others (through publishing or email or other broadcast methods). Four interesting KM packages include: Intraspect,[16] Simplify,[17] BSCW,[18] and Lotus.[19]

Pepperdine has been using Intraspect for three years. Figure 2.2 shows the listing of folders in the OMAET Group Memory database. As the titles suggest, the database holds artifacts that capture tacit dimensions of program culture and tradition.

[16] http://www.intraspect.com
[17] http://www.tomoye.com
[18] http://bscw.gmd.de/
[19] http://www.lotus.com

LEARNING DESIGNS FOR THE FUTURE

This example suggests a shift not only at the classroom level, but at the institutional level as well. A learning organization requires a redefinition of learning as a social activity – one that is inherently tied to group membership and identity. We have suggested that this culture will include a range of different forms of community learning, focused on the development of products, practice, and knowledge. While schools at present are divided into autonomous "class" units, to create the culture of learning necessary for learning organization means engaging learners in a system that supports collaborative designs and the preservation and sharing of knowledge. Networking technology can support the aggregation of these communities across distance and time into a learning landscape that looks very different than the schools of the past century. This offers a dramatically different role for technology integration in schooling than we have seen over the past three decades, during which time technology was largely viewed as a conduit for delivering curriculum to individuals.

In this chapter, we have discussed learning as a function of situated activity, whether that activity be situated in a task-based, practice-based, or knowledge-based community. In fields other than education, the activity is focused on something other than learning and knowledge is the by-product of other productive work. It is much less threatening and much less difficult to support intentional knowledge-building enterprises in organizations that do not have learning as their chief product and process (Wenger, 2000). Yet, teaching is a professional practice, with an evolving body of knowledge and a diverse and divided workforce. Networking technology offers the teaching profession an opportunity to organize as a distributed learning organization, to integrate historically divided groups, particularly researchers and teachers, and to more effectively evolve practice through collaborative reconceptualization of learning practices.

References

Argyris, C. (1977). Double Loop Learning in organizations. *Harvard Business Review* (September–October), 115–125.

Barab, S. & Duffy, T. (2000). From practice fields to communities of practice. Chapter 2 in Jonassen & Land (Eds.), *Theoretical Foundations of Learning Environments*. Hillsdale, NJ: Lawrence Erlbaum Associates.

Barksdale, J. (1998). Communications technology in dynamic organizational communities. Chapter 9 in Hesselbein, Goldsmith, Beckhard, & Schubert (Eds.), *The Community of the Future*. San Francisco: Jossey-Bass.

Bereiter, C. (2001). *Education and the Mind in the Knowledge Age*. Hillsdale, NJ: Lawrence Erlbaum Associates.

Brown, A. L. & Campione, J. C. (1994). Guided discovery in a community of learners. In K. McGilly (Eds.), *Classroom Lessons: Integrating Cognitive Theory and Classroom Practice* (pp. 229–270). Cambridge, MA: MIT Press/Bradford Books.

Brown, A., Ellery, S., & Campione, J. (1998). Creating zones of proximal development electronically. In James Greeno & Shelly Goldman (Eds.), *Thinking Practices in Mathematics and Science Learning*. Hillsdale, NJ: Lawrence Erlbaum Associates.

Brown, J. S. & Duguid, P. (2000). *The Social Life of Information*. Boston: Harvard Business School Press.

Bruckman, A. & Resnick, M. (1993). Virtual Professional Community: Results from the MediaMOO Project. In Third International Conference on Cyberspace, (3Cybercon) Austin, Texas, May.

Bruner, J. S. (1973). *Beyond the Information Given*. New York: Norton.

Chaiklin, S. & Lave, J. (Eds.) (1993). *Understanding Practice: Perspectives on Activity and Context*. New York: Cambridge University Press.

Cicourel, A. (1973) *Cognitive Sociology: Language and Meaning in Social Interaction*. London: Penguin.

Coalition for Essential Schools. (2000). Reinventing high schools: Six case studies of change. Jobs for the Future. Available online at www.essentialschools.org.

Cole, M. (1988). Cross-cultural research in the sociohistorical tradition. *Human Development*, 31, 137–157.

Cole, M. (1996). *Cultural Psychology: The Once and Future Discipline*. New York: Cambridge University Press.

Cole, M. & Engeström, Y. (1993). A cultural-historical approach to distributed cognition. In G. Salomon (Ed.), *Distributed Cognitions: Psychological and Educational Considerations*. New York: Cambridge University Press.

Cole, M. & Scribner, S. (1974). *Culture and Thought: A Psychological Introduction*. New York: John Wiley.

Davenport, T. H. (1997). *Information Ecology: Why Technology Is Not Enough for Success in the Information Age*. New York: Oxford University Press.

Davenport, T. H. & Prusak, L. (1998). *Working Knowledge: How Organizations Manage What They Know*. Cambridge, MA: Harvard Business School Press.

Deming, W. E. (1993). *The New Economics for Industry, Government, Education*. Boston: MIT Press.

Dewey, J. (1916). *Democracy and Education*. New York: The Free Press.

Dixon, N. (2000). *Common Knowledge: How Companies Thrive by Sharing What They Know*. Cambridge, MA: Harvard Business School Press.

Durkheim, E. (1915, reprinted 1995). *Elementary Forms of Religious Life*. Glencoe, IL: The Free Press.

Eklund, J. (1993). Interview with Robert Ballard. Division of Computers, Information, & Society, National Museum of American History, Smithsonian Institution. Available online at http://americanhistory.si.edu/csr/comphist/ballard.html.

Engeström, Y. (1987). *Learning by Expanding: An Activity-Theoretical Approach to Developmental Research*. Helsinki: Orienta-Konsultit.

Engeström, Y. (1999). Activity theory and individual and social transformation. Chapter 1 in Engestrom, Miettinen, & Punamaki (Eds.), *Perspectives on Activity Theory*. New York: Cambridge University Press.

Gergen, K. (1995). Social construction and the educational process. Chapter 2 in Steffe & Gale, (Eds.), *Constructivism in Education*. Hillsdale, NJ: Lawrence Erlbaum Associates.

Goldman, S. & The Cognition and Technology Group at Vanderbilt (1997). Supporting Student Learning in Schools for Thought Environments. Paper presented at the August 1997 biannual meeting of the European Association for Research on Learning and Instruction. Athens, Greece. Available online at http://peabody.vanderbilt.edu/projects/funded/sft/formoreinfo/srg/srgearli97.html.

Greenfield, P. M. (1999). Historical change and cognitive change: A two-decade follow-up Study in Zinacantan, a Maya Community in Chiapas, Mexico. *Mind, Culture, and Activity*, 6, 92–98.

Hagel, J. & Armstrong, A. (1997). *Net.gain: Expanding Markets through Virtual Communities*. Cambridge, MA: Harvard Business School Press.

Harasim, L., Hiltz, S., Teles, L., & Turoff, M. (1994). *Learning Networks: A Field Guide*. Cambridge, MA: MIT Press.

Heath, S. B. (1983). *Ways with Words: Language, Life, and Work in Communities and Classrooms*. Cambridge: Cambridge University Press.

Hewitt, J. (this volume).

Kofman, F. & Senge, P. (1995). Communities of Committment: The heart of learning organizations. In S. Chawla & J. Renesch (Eds.), *Learning Organizations: Developing Cultures for Tomorrow's Workplace* (pp. 15–44). Portland: Productivity Press.

Khoulopoulos, T., Spinello, R., & Toms, W. (1997). *Corporate instinct: Building a Knowing Enterprise for the 21st Century*. New York: John Wilay & Sons.

Hutchins, E. (1996). *Cognition in the Wild*. Cambridge, MA: MIT Press.

John-Steiner, V. (2000). *Creative Collaboration*. New York: Oxford University Press.

LaTour, B. (1987). *Science in Action*. Cambridge, MA: Harvard University Press.

Lave, J. (1988). *Cognition in Practice*. New York: Cambridge University Press.

Lave, J. (1993). The practice of learning. Chapter 1 in Lave & Chaiklin (Eds.), *Understanding Practice: Perspectives on Activity and Context*. New York: Cambridge University Press.

Lave, J. & Wenger, E. (1991). *Situated Learning: Legitimate Peripheral Participation*. New York: Cambridge University Press.

Lewis, C. C. & Tsuchida, I. (1998). A lesson is like a swiftly flowing river: How lesson research improves Japanese education. *American Educator* (Winter, 14–17 & 50–52). Also available online at http://lessonresearch.net/lesson.pdf).

Means, B. (1998). Melding authentic science, technology, and inquiry-based teaching: Experiences of the GLOBE Program. *Journal of Science Education and Technology*, 7, 1, 97–105.

Mehan, H. (1979). *Learning Lessons: Social Organization in the Classroom*. Cambridge, MA: Harvard University Press.

Mehan, H. (1983). Social constructivism in psychology and sociology. *Sociologie et Societes. XIV* (2), 77–96.

Mishler, E. (1999). *Storylines: Craft Artists' Narratives of Identity*. Cambridge, MA: Harvard University Press.

Newman, D., Griffin, P., and Cole, M. (1989). *The Construction Zone: Working for Cognitive Change in Schools*. Cambridge: Cambridge University Press.

Nonaka, I. & Takeuchi, H. (1995). The *Knowledge-Creating Company*. New York: Oxford University Press.

Norman, D. (1980). Twelve Issues for Cognitive Science, *Cognitive Science*, 4, 1–32.

North Central Regional Educational Laboratory (NCREL) (1998). "The Pond." Learning with Technology Captured Wisdom Library #2, NCREL.

Pea, R. (1993). Practices of distributed intelligence and designs for education. In G. Salomon (Ed.), *Distributed Cognitions: Psychological and Educational Considerations* (pp. 47–87). Cambridge: Cambridge University Press.

Pea, R. D. & Gomez, L. M. (1994). Distributed multimedia learning environments: Why and how? *Interactive Learning Environments*, 2(2), 73–109.

Rennebohm-Franz, K. (1996). Toward a critical social consciousness in children: multicultural peace education in a first grade classroom. *Theory into Practice* (Autumn 1996), 264–270.

Rheingold, H. (1993). *The Virtual Communities*. New York: Addison-Wesley.

Riel, M. (1998). Learning communities through computer networking. In James Greeno & Shelly Goldman (Eds.), *Thinking Practices in Mathematics and Science Learning*. Hillsdale, NJ: Lawrence Erlbaum Associates.

Riel, M. & Fulton, K. (2001). The role of technology in supporting learning communities. *Kappan*, 82:518–523.

Rogoff, B. (1994). Developing understanding of the idea of communities of learners. *Mind, Culture, and Activity*, 4, 209–229.

Rogoff, B. (1995). Observing sociocultural activity on three planes: participatory appropriation, guided participation, and apprenticeship. In Wertsch, Del Rio, & Alvarez (Eds.), *Sociocultural Studies of Mind*. New York: Cambridge University Press.

Rogoff, B. (1998). Cognition as a collaborative process. In W. Damon (Ed.), *Handbook of Child Psychology*. (5th ed.). New York: John Wiley & Sons.

Rogoff, B. & Lave, J. (Eds.) (1984). *Everyday Cognition: Its Development in Social Context*. Cambridge, MA: Harvard University Press.

Ruopp, R., Gal, S., Drayton, B., & Pfister, M. (1993). *LabNet: Toward a Community of Practice*. Hillsdale, NJ: Lawrence & Erlbaum Associates.

Scardamalia, M. & Bereiter, C. (1994). Computer support for knowledge-building learning communities. *The Journal of the Learning Sciences*, 3(3), 265–283.

Schlager, M. & Fusco J. (this volume).

Schrage, M. (1995). *No More Teams!: Mastering the Dynamics of Creative Collaboration*. New York: Doubleday.

Scribner, S. (1990). A sociocultural approach to the study of mind. In Greenberg & Tobach (Eds.), *Theories of the Evolution of Knowing*. Hillsdale, NJ: Lawrence Erlbaum Associates.

Senge, P. (1990). *The Fifth Discipline*. London: Doubleday.

Singleton, J. C. (1998). *Learning in Likely Places: Varieties of Apprenticeship in Japan*. New York: Cambridge University Press.

Sizer, T. (1992). *Horace's School: Redesigning the American High School*. New York: Houghton Mifflin.

Smagorinksy, P. (2000). If meaning is constructed, what is it made from? *Invited address, Annual Meeting of the American Educational Research Association*, New Orleans, April 24–28, 2000.

Songer, N. (1993). Learning science with a child-focused resource: A case study of kids as global scientists. *Proceedings of the Fifteenth Annual Meeting of the Cognitive Science Society* (pp. 935–940). Hillsdale, NJ: Lawrence Erlbaum Associates.

Turkle, S. (1984). *The Second Self: Computers and the Human Spirit.* New York: Simon and Schuster.

Vygotsky, L. S. (1978). In M. Cole., B. John-Steiner, S. Scribner, & E. Souberman, Eds. and Trans., *Mind in Society: The Development of Higher Psychological Processes.* Cambridge, MA: Harvard University Press.

Weisbord, M. & Janoff, S. (1995). Future Search: *An Action Guide to Finding Common Ground in Organizations and Communities.* San Francisco: Berrett-Koehler Publishers.

Wenger, E. (1998). *Communities of Practice: Learning, Meaning, and Identity.* New York: Cambridge University Press.

Wenger, E. (2000). Building communities of practice. Invited speaker, Call to Leadership, Pepperdine University. Culver City, CA, September.

Wertsch, J. (1997) *Mind As Action.* London: Oxford University Press.

PART II

DESIGNING FOR WEB-SUPPORTED COMMUNITY

3

Designing System Dualities

Characterizing an Online Professional Development Community

Sasha A. Barab, James G. MaKinster,
and Rebecca Scheckler

> The advent of cyberspace is apt to be seen in two ways, each of which can
> be regretted or welcomed, either as a new stage in the etherealization of
> the world we live in, the real world of people and things and places, or,
> conversely, as a new stage in the concretization of the world we dream and
> think in, the world of abstractions, memory and knowledge.
>
> – Benedikt, 1991, p. 124

The idea of "virtual communities" has captured popular, as well as scholarly, attention. Numerous websites and dot.com companies advertise their
"online communities." In hundreds of books and articles, virtual communities are championed by educators, cognitive scientists, sociologists,
anthropologists, computer scientists, and even CEOs. This outpouring of
interest takes place in an America that is increasingly concerned about the
loss of face-to-face community (Putnam, 2001). Advocates of online communities hope that by leveraging technology, they can recreate a "we" that
has steadily eroded into many isolated "I's." There is confusion, though,
about the definition of a virtual community, which includes anything from
a tight-knit group of people who share important parts of their lives on
a day-to-day basis to an amorphous chat group that can be joined (and
left) by anyone with a valid password. Many educators are participating
in this movement as well, exploring the educational value of employing
a "community" model for supporting learning. The idea is that through
participating in a community, novices can learn through collaboration with
others and by working alongside more experienced members. Much like in
an apprenticeship, newcomers work with old-timers, and then gradually
begin to adopt the practices of the community. This social view of learning
involves whole persons, and treats learning as a process of constructing

This material is based on work supported by the National Science Foundation under Grant
9980081.

practice, meaning, and identity all in relation to a community of practice (Lave & Wenger, 1991; Wenger, 1998).

Lave and Wenger (1991) advanced the term *community of practice* (CoP) to capture the importance of activity in fusing individuals to communities, and of communities in legitimizing individual practices. Within the context of CoPs, learning is conceived as a trajectory in which learners move from legitimate peripheral participants to core participants of a community of practice. Barab and Duffy (2000) discussed a CoP as a collection of individuals sharing mutually defined practices, beliefs, and understandings over an extended time frame in the pursuit of a shared enterprise. They discussed a CoP as having the following characteristics: (1) shared knowledge, values, and beliefs; (2) overlapping histories among members; (3) mutual interdependence; and (4) mechanisms for reproduction. We argue for the additional characteristics, suggesting that CoPs also include: (5) a common practice and/or mutual enterprise; (6) opportunities for interactions and participation; (7) meaningful relationships; and (8) respect for diverse perspectives and minority views. Many of these ideas are based on the work of Wenger (1998); however, despite his intense focus on understanding CoPs and the theoretical commitments behind this lens, he does not provide an operational definition for a CoP within this book.

One example of an educational community of practice is a Community of Teachers, a professional development program at Indiana University for pre-service teachers working toward teacher certification (Barab & Duffy, 2000; Barab, Barnett, & Squire, 2002). It is highly field-based with each participant being expected to commit to one school where she will do all her fieldwork. Pre-service teachers are not assigned to a teacher, but rather, spend time visiting the classes of and talking with teachers who are a part of the program. An apprenticeship relation is formed with one of the teachers based on a social negotiation and a mutual determination that the relationship will be beneficial. Hence, each student is paired with an "old-timer" in the first year in the program and continues to work with him or her for the duration. Similarly, each student negotiates membership in a community of students who are studying to be teachers. Students join an ongoing community and remain a part of that community for the duration of their study. Students in the community attend seminars together and, as with any community, there are wizened old-timers (seniors/students with teaching experience), newcomers (sophomores), and levels in between, mixed together in a common endeavor.

In the Community of Teachers program, students are continually negotiating goals and meanings of the community as well as the profession (Barab, Barnett, & Squire, 2002). Further, there is a growing collection of personal narratives that come to embody the canonical practices of the community, and students have developed a shared language to describe particular group practices. The community has a tradition and heritage at

Indiana University that captures much of the community's understandings. This heritage is continually developed and inherited by members as they become a part of the community program. The community also has a trajectory that extends across multiple classrooms and multiple occasions. Individuals view themselves as becoming a part of the community as well as the communities (those formed by in-service teachers) for which the project is nested. Lastly, the community continually reproduces itself as "rolling cohorts" cycle from newcomers to grizzled veterans.

More generally, based on a review of the literature and our previous work, we define a CoP as *a persistent, sustained social network of individuals who share and develop an overlapping knowledge base, set of beliefs, values, history, and experiences focused on a common practice and/or mutual enterprise.* CoPs have histories, cultural identities, interdependence among members, and mechanisms for reproduction (Lave & Wenger, 1991). The important point is not whether another researcher can add or delete indicators from the above list, or produce a different definition, but the acknowledgment that CoPs are more than a temporary coming together of individuals around a particular goal, for a workshop, or for a course (see Riel and Polin's discussion of this issue in this volume). Much like a living organism, they are self-organizing, and cannot be designed prima facie. They grow, evolve, and change dynamically, transcending any particular member and outliving any particular task.

A central conviction underlying the CoP conception is that learning is a social process that involves building connections: connections between what is being learned and what is important to the learner, connections between what is being learned and those situations in which it is applied, and connections between the learner and other learners with similar goals (Barab, 1999; Barab, Cherkes-Julkowski, Swenson, Garret, Shaw, & Young, 1999; Lave, 1997; Lemke, 1997). The CoP model supports learners in collaboratively working with others who have similar goals of building a community context that best supports their needs and stimulates them in their learning trajectory (Rogoff, 1990; Roth, 1998; Scardamalia & Bereiter, 1993). While CoPs do not necessarily result in positive outcomes for members (see Schwen & Hara, this volume), Westheimer (1998) suggests that the anticipated effects of CoP membership for individuals include "a sense of identity and belonging, affirmation, commitment to the group, strong bonds, and the development of both common purposes and collective responsibility" (p. 12). The community-based approach to learning has enormous theoretical and practical potential but it is imperative that these environments be studied empirically.

Recently, several books have been published about online communities. Some of the topics covered are designing and building online communities (Kim, 2000; Preece, 2000), researching online communities (Hakken, 1999; Jones, 1999; Smith & Kollock, 1999), supporting online communities

(Collison, Elbaum, Haavind, & Tinker, 2000), and the impact of online communities on other institutions (Werry & Mowbray, 2001). These books cover a wide array of topics that are important to those dealing with online communities in their entire developmental cycles. From this proliferation of books we can correctly assume an urgent interest in online communities. Some of the recurring topics in these texts are the differences between online and copresent communities. Building and maintaining online communities involves the design and manipulation of technologies in ways that foster human connection (Barab, MaKinster, Moore, Cunningham, & The ILF Design Team, 2001; Kim, 2000; Preece, 2000; Schlager, Fusco, & Schank, 2002). Indeed, online communities face all the challenges of copresent communities with the extra challenges added by the technologies and by the physical distancing these technologies both permit and cause.

In this chapter we focus on the challenges we have encountered in attempting to support the development of a web-supported community of practice for grade 5–12 mathematics and science teachers. Specifically, this project involves the design and evaluation of an electronic knowledge network, the Inquiry Learning Forum (ILF), a web-based professional development system designed to support a CoP of in-service and pre-service mathematics and science teachers who are creating, reflecting upon, sharing, and improving inquiry-based pedagogical practices (see http://ilf.crlt.indiana.edu). A central research goal of our work has been to understand the design principles for fostering, sustaining, and scaling a CoP in which the value of sharing one's practice and engaging in the dialogue outweighs the "costs" of participation. While the effective use of technology in supporting a CoP provides one focus, it is clear that technological structures are only one component of an overall strategy (Preece, 2000; Roupp et al., 1993). Thus, our research examines the interplay among a variety of variables that characterize the dynamics of building a social network through which participating teachers will seek to share and improve their pedagogical practices.

Our analytical lens for understanding design decisions and emergent happenings consists of initially identifying system *tensions* (Engeström, 1987), or what Wenger (1998) referred to as *dualities*. Tensions, or dualities, refer to overlapping yet conflicting activities and needs that drive the dynamics of the system (Engeström, 1987). Engeström (1999) viewed tensions as characterizing system activity and driving system innovation, and Wenger (1998) similarly discussed the importance of understanding the design of community in terms of the interplay among four sets of system dualities. Within this chapter, we will interpret our data and experiences in terms of the core dualities that were identified by Wenger (1998) as characterizing community dynamics and design, as well as the additional two dualities of face-to-face versus online participation and encouraging community cohesion versus supporting diversity. By characterizing community life in terms of dualities, we hope to provide other educators/ designers with an illuminative case study from which they can build what Stake (1983, 1995) referred to as *petite generalizations*; that is, use this discussion to more readily identify patterns occurring in their own interventions and navigate the challenges they face more intelligently (Barab, Barnett, & Squire, 2002).

ANALYTICAL TOOLS FOR CHARACTERIZING COMMUNITY

Traditionally, at least in anthropological circles, ethnography is the common methodological technique for understanding community life (Marcus, 1998). Building an ethnography involves extended engagement with the community being researched, collecting field notes, locating and interviewing informants, examining artifacts, and interviewing community members, frequently as a participant observer (Emerson, Fretz, & Shaw, 1995). Our role as co-designers in this project complicates our roles as researchers, in that at the same time as we are building a thick description of community life, we are also positioned in a role where we have a clear and invested agenda to provide service to that community.[1] Once the data are collected, the researcher sifts through the data, frequently creating descriptive codes and building larger interpretive categories from which themes and patterns are identified. Using this process, the ethnographer can then give a "grounded" and "thick" description of community life (Geertz, 1983; Marcus, 1998). However, there is also an advantage to qualitative research that makes a commitment to an analytical framework that then both guides observations and provides a useful lens through which the data can be interpreted. When there is a well-documented literature base, having a pre-existing analytical lens is especially useful for researchers who are also designers of the work. For researcher-designers, such a lens can serve an evaluative function while at the same time guiding design.

We approach our design and research as a series of design experiments (Brown, 1992). This process involves carrying out design work, conducting research on its implementation, cycling what we are learning into future design iterations, and then again examining how these innovations impact the learning process. In addition, over the course of our design/research work we have come to adopt two theoretical frameworks that are central to our work and that structure the reporting of the data in this chapter. First is the notion of socio-technical interaction networks (STINs) (Kling

---

[1] We are more than participant observers in that we have an agenda as a change agent with a goal of bringing about transformation (Eden & Huxham, 1996; Grills, 1998; McNiff, 1995; Stringer, 1996; Wells, 1999). We view our roles as having a mix of what Adler and Adler (1997) called *peripheral membership* (referring to our position outside the CoP) and *active membership* (referring to our position as change agent on the CoP).

2000), and second is the conception of communities as being characterized by tensions or dualities.

The STIN model, developed by Kling (2000), focuses on the interactions between social and technical, with technology-in-use and the social world viewed as co-constitutive. The concept of STIN highlights the interaction of people and technologies, but encompasses the actors, artifacts, interactions, resources, technologies, and relationships among participants both inside and outside the community. Interactions and activities in any one part of the STIN, and even outside the STIN, may affect interactions elsewhere. When analyzing the evolution of a STIN, one looks at resource dependencies (between actors, between actors and artifacts, and between artifacts) and account-taking (other actors or STINs that participants seek to emulate or not emulate in their behavior). Instead of focusing on the most obvious pieces of the online community (the website or, in our case, what we call the electronic-ILF), we gain a powerful insight into the complexity of online communities by examining interactions among all of the features within the STIN framework. It was the adoption of the STIN framework that shifted our thinking as designers from a focus on usability issues to sociability issues (Preece, 2000), and as researchers we began to conceptualize the ILF as more than the electronic-ILF (e-ILF) (Barab et al., 2001).

The second framework we adopted had to do with an acknowledgment of understanding design/use practices in terms of core dualities (Barab & Schatz, 2001; Engeström, 1987; Wenger, 1998). These dualities refer to core struggles that are endemic to system activity and that characterize the design struggles of such a system within these dualities. Engeström (1999), whose work is grounded in Activity Theory,[2] described tensions as characterizing system activity and driving system innovation. In our own work examining learning environments and copresent communities, we have found tensions to be a useful analytical principle to characterize participant behavior (Barab, Barnett, Yamagata-Lynch, Squire, & Keating, 2002; Barab, Barnett, & Squire, 2002). Wenger (1998) similarly discussed the utility of understanding community in terms of the interplay of system dualities. He views a duality as a "single conceptual unit that is formed by two inseparable and mutually constitutive elements whose inherent tensions and complementarity give the concept richness and dynamism" (p. 66). Although both sides of a duality are considered separate units, the

---

[2] Activity Theory is a psychological theory with a naturalistic emphasis that offers a framework for describing activity and provides a set of perspectives on practice that interlink individual and social levels (see Engeström, 1987, 1993; Leont'ev, 1974, 1981, 1989; Nardi, 1996; Vygotsky, 1978). When discussing activity, activity theorists are not simply concerned with "doing" as a disembodied action, but are referring to "doing in order to transform something," with the focus on the contextualized activity of the system as a whole (Barab, in press; Kuttii, 1996; Engeström, 1987, 1993).

effective functioning of one pole (e.g., participation) of a duality necessitates and is dependent on the existence of the other (e.g., reification) (Shaw et al., 1992). As such, while the term *duality* implies two separate units, in terms of their usefulness for design, the term also acknowledges their simultaneous bond. That is, while the analytical lens of dualities provides a useful framework for characterizing community dynamics, their usefulness in terms of a design/research framework lies in uncovering the system dynamics and understanding how the interplay between both sides of the duality (as well as among dualities) contributes to community life. Wenger (1998) describes four dualities as being central to understanding community life: Participation/Reification; Designed/Emergent; Local/Global; and Identification/Negotiation. Given that our community exists, in part, online, we have added the additional tensions of Online/Face-to-Face, and given our commitment to empowerment of all teachers we have added the Coherence/Diversity tension as well. It is these six dualities that guided our data collection, data interpretations, and the body of this chapter.

The Inquiry Learning Forum

This ILF is designed to support a virtual community of in-service and pre-service mathematics and science teachers sharing, improving, and creating inquiry-based, pedagogical practices (register or take a tour at: http://ilf.crlt.indiana.edu/). Founded in our previous research and consistent with our pedagogical commitment (Barab & Duffy, 2000; Chaney-Cullen & Duffy, 1998), we have designed the ILF with the belief that teachers need to be full participants in and owners of *their* virtual space. Specifically, four design principles guided our design.

1. *Foster Ownership and Participation.* We believe that a truly effective professional development environment must include a community of professional practitioners with varied experiences and skills who accept responsibility for building and maintaining *their* environment.
2. *Focus on Inquiry.* Our goal is to foster inquiry, both in terms of inquiry pedagogy in the classroom and teacher inquiry into his or her own practices.
3. *Visit the Classroom.* A central strategy in the design and implementation of our knowledge network is the use of video streaming and web-based technologies to situate participants in the social context of other community members' teaching practice.
4. *Support Communities of Purpose.* We hope to bring together and support groups of teachers organized around some collective experience and/or curricular interest.

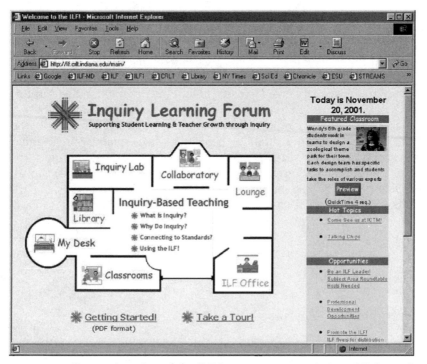

FIGURE 3.1. Current iteration of the ILF home screen, consisting of links to the *Classrooms, ILF Office, Collaboratory, Lounge, Library,* and *My Desk*

The hallmark of this environment is that teachers with a broad range of experiences and expertise come together in a virtual space to observe, discuss, and reflect upon pedagogical theory and practice anchored to video-based teaching vignettes.

The ILF consists of a variety of participant structures, all related to encouraging online dialogue and collaboration. One of the primary areas of interest is the ILF *Classrooms* that enable ILF members to virtually visit the classrooms of other teachers. The home screen of the ILF is shown in Figure 3.1, in which the classrooms are available through the Classrooms space. When ILF members select a specific classroom lesson, they can watch seven or eight video segments of the implemented lesson. Additionally, they can view an overview of the lesson, reflective commentary from the teachers, descriptions of teaching activity, lesson plans, student examples, and connections to both state and national standards (see Figure 3.2).

The other primary area of interest in the ILF is the *Collaboratory*. The ILF Collaboratory is a space in which groups of teachers can come together in an online space around some collective experience and/or curricular interest. Each group within the Collaboratory is referred to as an Inquiry

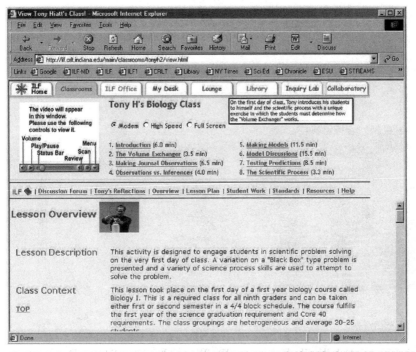

FIGURE 3.2. Current iteration of a specific *Classroom*, including links to an overview of the lesson, reflective commentary, descriptions of teaching activity, lesson plans, student examples, and connections to both state and national standards

Circle (Figure 3.3) and the contents of the Inquiry Circle are visible only to its members. An Inquiry Circle can be a group of members who are part of a class, workshop, or share a similar curricular interest. Currently there are thirty-nine Inquiry Circles in the ILF Collaboratory that range in focus from elementary science methods classes from four different universities, a group of middle and high school science teachers who participated in a summer workshop on teaching science through inquiry, and teachers who use water ecology and water quality as a focus in their classroom. The important point is that there is a common purpose of the group, whether it be a class focus, a workshop focus, or a topic focus. Each Inquiry Circle space enables teachers to: (a) organize the ILF classrooms and resources, and create discussion forums that are of interest to this group; (b) share announcements, ideas, weblinks, and electronic documents; (c) collaboratively create and edit documents; and (d) organize the efforts and interests of this group as they use this space as a way to keep in touch. The Inquiry Circles allow for smaller subgroups to collaborate (membership is determined by the facilitator) and give members control of adding documents, discussion threads, web resources, and other ILF resources without having to contact an ILF staff member.

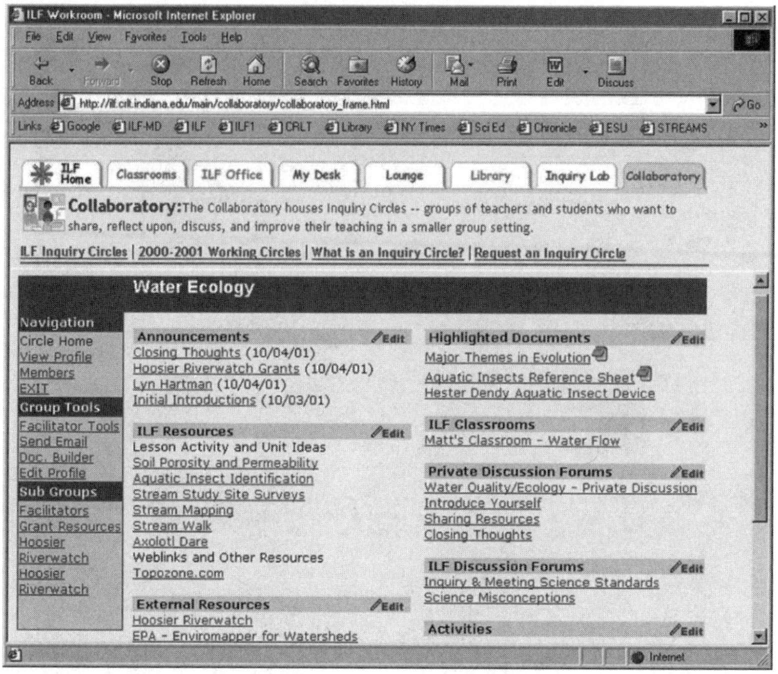

FIGURE 3.3. Current iteration of an ILF Inquiry Circle (Water Ecology). The sections within an Inquiry Circle include *Announcements, Highlighted Documents, External Resources, ILF Resources, ILF Classrooms, ILF Discussion Forums, Private Discussion Forums*, and *Activities*

In addition to the Classroom and Collaboratory spaces, there are also four other virtual spaces designed to support the professional development needs of ILF teachers. The *ILF Office* is the place where new participants can secure a password (the site is password-protected), get help with technology, or make suggestions. The *Lounge* contains general asynchronous discussion forums that are not tied to a particular classroom. The *Inquiry Lab* entails a series of professional development activities that members can use to address their current professional development needs. ILF Labs are based on the Concerns-Based Adoption Model, commonly referred to as "CBAM" (Hall, 1979). This model of teacher change suggests that teachers go through various stages of change characterized by different concerns they have regarding a particular change or innovation. Our Professional Development Labs are organized around these stages and the types of concerns teachers have at each stage. Teachers can go to the *Library* to access resources and reference materials, including teaching resource materials (software, other classroom artifacts like the graphing calculator, manipulatives, sensory probes), state and national standards, grants, applied research and theory, relevant state initiatives, and other materials the ILF teachers identify as relevant. Finally, *My Desk* is the teacher's "office" (since entry into ILF is password-protected, the office is that of the person who logged in) in which she can store bookmarks to resources and classrooms that are of personal relevance and return to those at a later visit. The owner can also maintain a journal which she can later email to any ILF member, a feature that has been especially useful in pre-service classes.

CORE DUALITIES

Designed/Emergent

A core challenge in fostering a CoP is to manage the interplay between the designed and the emergent (Wenger, 1998). At one level, Wenger's (1998) argument is that community cannot be designed; however, at another level he attempts to provide educators with a conceptual and architectural framework for facilitating the development and perpetuation of CoPs. In addition, as has been known in the systems design literature, there is an inherent uncertainty between design and its realization in practice. In terms of designing a CoP, as opposed to a simple computer program, the challenges of bridging design and use are further complicated because "no community can fully design the learning of another . . . [however] no community can fully design its own learning" (Wenger, 1998, p. 234). Communities, in a very real sense, are self-organizing, emerging in response to local conditions and the needs of their users (Barab, Cherkes-Julkowski, et al., 1999). The challenge for designers is to not over-design but instead work to accomplish what Wenger (1998) referred to as a minimalist design. The idea behind a minimalist design is to create a tentative platform and then facilitate the community in growing and evolving its own space, a process that involves walking the tightrope between designing the community and allowing it to emerge from the needs and agendas of its members. While working toward a minimalist design, one of the first challenges is to determine what constitutes minimalist design. We wanted the space to evolve based on teacher participation and individual negotiation while at the same time retaining some sense of an identity. As in the development of any website or piece of software, we began with a needs analysis in which we talked with teachers about what they wanted (MaKinster, Barab, & Keating, 2001). The design then began in earnest with the university team mocking up a website based on a school metaphor. Despite our best intentions (including usability tests), this first iteration of the ILF took a production path that was likely to cause problems of over-design. The design team was proud of their production and, consistent with notions of participatory design, we even worked with our users in developing the site, but unfortunately this early conception of the e-ILF was heavily critiqued by the Teacher Advisory Board. An interview with one of the designers revealed the state of the project at that time.

> There's always a tension between over designing something, rather than doing some minimal stuff and seeing what happens. I think in the first iteration of this we tried to do too much. We tried to anticipate what teachers would think. What the teachers told us was "that's confusing, we don't need all that. First thing you should be able to do is go right to those classrooms." That's where the heart of it is. It became more user-centered. We got our design slapped. In a project where there's a lot of talented designers there's always this need to design. Sometimes you worry about over designing vs. letting the participants in the community decide what the site ought to be. (Cunningham, interview, 2/15/00)

The teachers unanimously expressed that the current virtual hallway look of the system was too complicated, and they wanted something very simple. They wanted an interface that would allow them to obtain the information they wanted in a single click.

It was at this time that the design team became more aware of the clear divide between the design team and the contributing teachers (whose classrooms were being videotaped and digitized so there would be some initial classrooms to visit on the ILF). At one meeting, the project teacher liaison expressed, with discomfort: "I feel like a funnel, with all comments coming through me. I am the go-between, talking to teachers and telling you all and then talking to you all and telling the teachers" (Haas, field note, 2/23/00). With this rocky start, we began to work more closely with a subset of teachers from our Teacher Advisory Board. The feeling was that if we simply included more members from our target population we could design the "correct" framework. Over the next couple of months the design team developed a site that was usable by teachers, but did not necessarily support social interactions.

It was at this point, six months into the project, that one of the Co-Principal Investigators shared his paper regarding Socio-Technical Interaction Networks (Kling et al., 2001). At design and research meetings, earnest discussions began about better understanding the social issues as opposed to simply technical issues of participation. A distinction occurred between the larger ILF community and the website, which was now referred to as the electronic-ILF (e-ILF). One design team member commented, "I was gone for a couple of weeks and when I came back, everyone was talking about the e-ILF and I wasn't sure if this was something new, or a new label, or what" (Moore, interview, 4/25/00). Additionally, another team member returned from an academic conference where he had heard the distinction between usability and sociability (Preece, 2000). A greater acknowledgment of the social component of online community brought a shift in the thinking of the design team. This shift changed the focus from supporting human-computer interactions to supporting human-human interactions as mediated by computer interactions (Barab, in press; Nardi, 1996). There was also a growing appreciation within the design team that sociability could not necessarily be designed, only supported.

Elsewhere we discuss the resultant changes (Barab, MaKinster, et al., 2001), some of which were in the e-ILF and some of which had to do with interactions fostered outside the e-ILF. The important point is that this project is a design experiment and, as such, we have continually supported the emergence of the ILF based on a cycle of design, research, and re-design. This responsive type design, while allowing for community member input, has in some sense kept primary ownership in the university team's hands. An interesting phenomenon occurred when a classroom teacher suggested he would like to start and moderate a new discussion topic in the ILF Lounge. During that semester, that forum (Useless Math) became the most active and potentially interesting of the lounge discussions; all the others had been initiated by the university designers. This suggests that emergent topics introduced by teachers may prove more meaningful to community members than those pre-designed or formatted by the developers.

As stated earlier, while we cannot expect to fully design the learning space for the teachers successfully, they cannot be expected to fully design their own space either. The challenges of being university designers with a reform agenda has meant that the identity of the site, with its need for prolonged engagement of the user, has in some ways been at odds with the needs of teachers who frequently simply want a place to acquire lesson ideas that can be used the following day (this issue is discussed more fully below in the other dualities). The design challenge is to understand the interplay among these multiple agendas and to support a space that meets both needs and agendas. We initially chose to build a space and then work with teachers to modify it so that it would better meet their needs. It is our current realization that this may have resulted in over-design in that we developed a large and complex space that may often appear daunting to the user. Due to the lack of exit costs and perceived gains, it is much easier to simply log off of the ILF than to grapple with its complexity, with the expectation of some long-term payoff.

Given the challenges of fostering sustained participation and the importance of local support, we believe that a more bottom-up approach in which we developed trust and community support first might be a more effective design trajectory when attempting to foster an online CoP where the practices being fostered (i.e., critical dialogue among teachers, inquiry-based teaching, ongoing interactions online) are somewhat inconsistent with the current culture. Toward this end, we have been working to develop bounded "communities of purpose" (Schagler & Fusco, 2001). These bounded groups have a shared agenda and interest in terms of a particular project or curricular unit (e.g., create a water quality curriculum). We are providing these groups with a semi-private online space that is customized to address their local needs.

Consistent with Barab, Squire, and Dueber's (2000) co-evolutionary model, we view the design process as self-organizing, beginning with a minimalist design and then working collaboratively with members as they are using the designed space to evolve participant structures that meet their own needs. This process does not result in a designed end state but is a continual process of remaking based on users' changing localized needs in conjunction with the designers' more global reform agenda.

Participation and Reification

The term Community of Practice highlights the centrality of *practice*[3] in defining the community and of communities in legitimizing and supporting individual practices. This is because it is through participating in community-recognized practices that members become part of the larger community. It is in this way that participation reflects both *action* and *connection* and that participation is both *personal* and *social*. Wenger (1998) writes that participation "involves our whole person, including our bodies, minds, emotions, and social relations . . . [and that] . . . a defining characteristic of participation is the possibility of developing an 'identity of participation,' that is, an identity constituted through relations of participation" (p. 56). In this way, the concept of participation captures the social character of our experience of life, as well as the notion that through participation we create meanings and identities; that is, individuals are fundamentally constituted through their relations with the world (Barab & Duffy, 2000; Lave, 1993; Lemke, 1997). It is this realization that led Lave (1993) to conclude that "developing an identity as a member of a community and becoming knowledgeably skillful are part of the same process, with the former motivating, shaping, and giving meaning to the latter, which it subsumes" (p. 65).

Frequently, participation results in some outcome, whether it is an idea, a tool, drawing, an online post, or simply becoming more knowledgeably skillful with respect to the practice. This process of transforming experience and the outcome of experience into a thing is known as *reification*. According to Wenger (1998), the process of reification allows CoPs to capture and share meanings as they turn their local experience into something that is portable and potentially has global significance. However, the power of

---

[3] When we use the term practice, we are not evoking some behaviorist notion of activity. Rather, and akin to Schön (1987), we view practice as "chunks of activity, divisible into more or less familiar types, each of which is seen as calling for the exercise of a certain kind of knowledge" (pp. 32–33).

reification – its conciseness, portability, potential physical form, focusing effect – is also its danger, in that the reification itself can come to replace a deeper understanding of and commitment to that for which the reification stands. Wenger writes:

Reification as a constituent of meaning is always incomplete, ongoing, potentially enriching, and potentially misleading. The notion of assigning the status of object to something that really is not an object conveys a sense of mistaken solidarity, of projected concreteness. It conveys a sense of useful illusion. The use of the term reification stands both as a tribute to the generative power of the process and as a gentle reminder of its delusory perils. (1998, p. 62)

Reification is an abridged and concise representation of a typically messy, convoluted practice, making practice easier to share, while at the same time offering an incomplete account of that same practice. It is in this way that reification provides a double-edged sword, at the same time it allows experience to be captured and shared it undermines the very experiences that give the reification value and use.

Wenger (1998) argued that participation and reification form a duality that is fundamental to the negotiation of meaning and that design for practice must be distributed between participation and reification with its realization being dependent on how these two sides fit together. In this section, we will begin with a discussion of ILF participation, followed by discussion of the challenges of avoiding reification in a community of practice that primarily exists online.

In the design of the ILF we have created a number of participant structures that allow members to virtually visit the classrooms of other teachers, participate in online discussions, and develop a sense of belonging to the ILF community. Similar to other online environments, participation in the ILF can take on a variety of forms. *Team Members* refers to those individuals at the university level who are involved in either the research or development aspects of this project. *Observers* are those registered members who visit various places in the site, view other members' comments and videos, but do not post their own. *Active Members* are those who participate in viewing other members' comments and videos and engage in online discussion with other ILF members. *Contributing Members* are those who share their classroom with the community. This involves videotaping a lesson or unit, organizing the accompanying materials, and posing questions within their associated discussion forum. *Bounded Group Members* are those individuals who join and participate in the ILF as part of some collective experience and/or curricular interest, either a teacher education class, a workshop, or a group of teachers sharing resources and ideas around a particular curricular topic. Their participation is usually centered in an Inquiry Circle. ILF members can move through these levels of membership as their situation and interests allow. In addition, we have begun to identify some of the other roles that ILF members can choose to adopt such as discussion moderators, critical friends, and project facilitators.

In any project that requires production of tools, there is the tension of reification versus participation of function and knowledge in the designed tools. Software is by nature a reification of design and implementation decisions. To date, it has been primarily through our design and member participation that the ILF reified its beliefs, culture, and mission. Much of this is embodied in the ILF classrooms. As discussed below in the Identification/ Negotiation section, the process by which these teachers were solicited, their reputations, the video review process, and the structure of the ILF classrooms themselves create an e-ILF identity that frames the socially acceptable types of negotiation and participation. Reifications of practice both support and limit the types of emergent meanings (and identities).

One place we have really struggled with the interplay between supporting participation versus the reification of our beliefs and commitments is in terms of our individual and collective understandings of *inquiry-based teaching and learning*. Inquiry is the central focus of the ILF community and a term that has come to mean a number of different things to science teachers and researchers. At its core is the idea of affording students some level of ownership over their science investigation in terms of their research questions and/or methods. Fortunately, the science education community has put forth several documents that attempt to describe a current understanding of inquiry and what it looks like in the classroom (Dewey, 1938/1986; National Research Council, 2000).

Since its conception, the ILF has chosen not to put forth an explicit description of what inquiry entails or looks like in the science classroom. Our hope was to support ILF community members in coming to their own conclusions regarding the nature of inquiry through participation and negotiation. For example, one of the main Lounge discussions has been *Inquiry-Based Learning: So what is inquiry-based learning anyhow?* Within the forum there are several lines of discussion that include: the importance of background knowledge, inquiry and the standards, methods of promoting inquiry, and two discussion threads that begin to discuss what *inquiry* is in the first place. In one discussion, we see a member struggling with inquiry:

ALEX: My current notion of "inquiry" involves the investigation of a driving question. The question out of which inquiry is born can be either broad or specific, but must be structured such that it provides ample opportunity for investigation. Often, the best questions to investigate are those which provide a discrepancy or ill-structured problem to the inquirer. The method of inquiry need not adhere to scripts or be specific, but should allow for many different paths to arrive at a conclusion. The "scientific method" that is often taught is just one model for investigation of a question, and I emphasize to my students that it is not a prescriptive set of rules by which inquiry must be conducted. One thing I always tell them is that "I am more interested in the questions you ask rather than the answers you give." This emphasizes my belief that inquiry should open more doors than it closes – successful inquiry leads to many new driving questions, and therefore new inquiries. Truths are relative. The day we have all of the "answers" is the day we stop learning.

TIA: I liked your description of the inquiry-based classroom. I particularly like the comparison of it to opening more doors than closing them. I get really excited when in the process of investigating one question, my students come up with more that they want to investigate. I feel you are right in being more interested in the questions than the answers.

Despite the thoughtfulness of these comments, these posts do not embody a collective understanding of inquiry-based teaching and learning. Consequently, one of the complaints of users is that it is unclear what the ILF is about, and what is meant by inquiry.

The ILF research and development teams recently have developed their own understandings of different levels of inquiry (structured, guided, and open) (MaKinster & Barab, in preparation). One debate has been whether or not to "publish" these descriptions within the ILF site as a means of reifying our understanding of inquiry. The fear has been that putting forth such a document will limit conversations regarding the nature of inquiry in the classroom as members simply defer to the "ILF's reification" of inquiry teaching and learning. The result is a distinct tension of how do we define inquiry in a way that supports ILF members in continuing to negotiate what it is and through participation develop their own identity in terms of inquiry in their classroom. Recently, in response to this tension, we added a tentative definition of inquiry to the front screen with the stated caveat that inquiry is a dynamic process and will look somewhat different for each member depending on his or her particular context.

An additional challenge faced by the ILF arises out of the way that, as mentioned above, identity is fundamentally constituted through participation. This is most important in relation to the ILF's *Contributing Members*. As individuals participating in and contributing to the ILF, their beliefs, values, and understandings are reified within their videos, reflections, and discussion forum settings. These teachers have chosen to participate in the community by sharing their classrooms and in turn have established their identity through this participation. Within an online CoP, an individual's identity is reified within any permanent artifact created during participation. A significant problem arises when one considers that the ILF is designed to foster critical dialogue among participating teachers. When one's classroom practice is the object of critical discussion, it is impossible to avoid the fact that we are critiquing the identity of that person as well as his or her practice. This notion is exacerbated in the context of teaching versus other practices. For example, the culture of science accepts, to a certain point, that critical dialogue within a scientific investigation is a natural part of the scientific enterprise (Latour, 1987), whereas within the culture of teaching, a teacher's classroom practice is much more closely tied to her identity as a person (Cochran-Smith & Lytle, 1999). This may explain some of the ILF members' reluctance to critique the practice of other teachers. Additionally, posts, like any other reification, run the risk of being later interpreted out of context and, thereby, the reader may misjudge the intended meaning. Although we have begun to implement steps to communicate the importance and desire for critical feedback (e.g., contributing members now ask explicit questions of visitors to their classroom), we see in our research a large divide between face-to-face discussions of ILF classrooms and what gets posted online.

Local/Global

The third duality Wenger (1998) described is that between the local and the global. While talking about the challenges of sharing one's local practice with others, Wenger argued that, "due to the inherently limited scope of our engagement, now practice is itself global" (p. 234). As we get more specific so as to highlight the contextualized nuances of practice, we enter into a series of trade-offs in terms of its global significance. In some sense, the more local the unit of analysis (e.g., sharing videos of the interactions in a particular classroom), the less significance this experience may have for other individuals in other locations. For example, suppose a classroom teacher achieves a series of successes with her children. How can she then share her local experience and insights in a manner that will have global relevance to others who have a different context with different constraints and goals? In addition to challenges in terms of local practice having global meaning, there is the notion of local practices being so determined by immediate constraints that teacher practice often remains unaffected by more global reform agendas.

One of the primary challenges that the ILF has faced since its inception is that its global reform agenda does not meet the immediate needs of teachers. Teachers have a persistent need to identify readily available curricular resources in order to meet the day-to-day demands of their teaching. This fundamental need to address what a teacher will teach "tomorrow" led Gomez, Fishman, and Pea (1998) to declare that "the currency of the classroom is curriculum and activities!" The ILF, on the other hand, is designed to support a community of in-service and pre-service mathematics and science teachers creating, sharing, and improving inquiry-based pedagogical practices through virtually visiting the classrooms of other teachers. This sharing and critiquing is seen as a means to building relations among teachers who share similar beliefs and classroom practices. The problem is that visiting the classroom of another teacher within this framework of "improving inquiry-based practices" is not relevant to the immediate needs of teachers. Teachers are most concerned about what they will use as a lesson or unit tomorrow or how they will deal with a particular student problem. However, what we have conceived as meaningful participation in the ILF is something that may take an extended period of time and require multiple visits and interactions before a teacher even begins to reap any tangible benefits. This tension hinges on the local, immediate needs of the classroom teachers versus the global reform agenda of the university designers. The focus of the ILF is on improving inquiry teaching across the state. We have worked to locate and videotape reform-minded teachers; that is, teachers who have decided to employ inquiry-based pedagogical practices. A central question is how to capture and share these local success stories in a manner that will be useful and motivating to other teachers throughout the state, while at the same time meeting their immediate professional development and curricular needs.

A second challenge in terms of the local/global duality is grounded in the use of the "visiting the classroom" metaphor as a core focus of the ILF. ILF classrooms are very local, intimate portrayals of teachers whose practice is supposed to have relevance to the global reform agenda of the ILF. Because an ILF classroom as a reification of a teacher's practice is so local, it is likely that relatively few teachers can identify with all of the contextual factors in a manner that allows them to meaningfully make connections to their particular classroom. Capturing a lesson or unit through video, text, and graphics leaves out much of what happened in the classroom and most of the contextual factors of the classroom and school. ILF members do not have access to the political climate of the school, the recent activities within the classroom, personalities of the students, and a variety of other elements that would provide a more complete representation of that lesson or unit – even if they did, the climate of one classroom may be very different than that of another classroom. Consequently, both pre-service and in-service teachers have argued that it is very difficult to engage in critical discussions without having such an understanding.

One reason that ILF classrooms are often perceived as so local is that there are important aspects to face-to-face conversations and live classroom visitations that are not captured in an online environment, resulting in a limited representation of that visit. For example, an ILF contributing teacher, Kyle, visited a pre-service secondary science methods classroom that had been using the ILF to talk with the students about his experience. Kyle shared his ILF classroom with the students, describing his school, the classroom setting, his goals, and the struggles that he had during this lesson. Together they watched two different video clips from his ILF lesson and talked about what happened in each. As the discussion was winding down, Kyle asked the class what they thought of the ILF, did they think it was useful, and would they feel comfortable posting feedback to ILF teachers. Several of the students responded that they would now feel very comfortable giving Kyle feedback on his teaching since they had a chance to talk with him and better understand the context of his classroom and lesson. During the next two weeks, the students in this class visited Kyle's ILF classroom and posted their thoughts and responses.

Many of the students from this pre-service class were able to post thoughtful and detailed responses that even contained elements of personal connections such as using Kyle's first name in the greeting and statements of encouragement or appreciation at the end of the message. For example, here Kyle is asking a question in reference to his ILF classroom.

KYLE: Having gone through so many steps to determine the age of the universe, have the students lost sight of the goal? Should the lesson have been broken up into smaller bits?

STEVE: Kyle, after looking at the clip again and your response, I agree more with how you were going around to the specific groups. I at first thought that the reason you should address a problem with the entire class was because everyone had the same questions. If they do, I believe that you should maybe first address the question in class and then go from group to group if it is needed. But, if the students don't have the same question throughout the groups, no reason to address the question to the entire class. I agree with how you're doing things, I just thought maybe you should give an answer to the entire class and then work with groups individually if they're still not grasping the concept.

However, even after this in-class interaction, one or two of the students still found it difficult to provide Kyle with feedback.

KYLE: Did I give them too much information and suggestions about classifying their galaxies? Is this part of the instruction too scripted?

RACHEL: Is this a first year physics class? I wish that I could see more of your class to get a real feel for what you are doing and so I could understand the topic better. It may have an effect on what I write here . . . I think that you did a good job with the section. You obviously have an idea where you want the students to go and you lead the students there – mostly through questions so they have to think about it.

Rachel was still struggling with trying to understand the context of Kyle's classroom and was frustrated with the limited perspective afforded by what was presented within the ILF. This situation becomes compounded when members visit ILF classrooms with lessons or units that are outside of their content area (biology, chemistry, physics, etc.). Not only do these ILF members have to wrestle with understanding the contextual elements of the classroom, they have to make generalizations from a different subject and make interpretations about how it applies to their own area of expertise. Finally, even if a teacher can connect with another teacher, and if they have a common subject and context, teachers seldom have the time to spend determining if this is the case and then responding.

From this standpoint, design decisions create relations not simply between the global and the local but, rather, "among their localities in their constitution of the global" (Wenger, 1998, p. 234). The challenge is to find means of sharing these local particulars in ways that can have global significance. Conversely, an additional challenge is to communicate a global reform agenda in a manner that will have local relevance and value. We have attempted to identify local particulars through user-centered design and through discussions with teachers in which they share the aspects of the e-ILF that are most useful. We have developed video "trailers" for each classroom so that teachers can gain an overview about the local specifics before investing large amounts of time in the classroom. We have also developed member activities, such as Contrasting Cases, that ILF users can attempt in order to develop particular skills or understandings. For example, in the Contrasting Cases activity, members are able to examine two classrooms in terms of their level of inquiry, having access to other teachers' comments and being expected to relate this contrast to their own teaching. In presenting these challenges, we define the task and communicate the local value of completing the challenge. Lastly, we have become more explicit in communicating to teachers our global reform agenda, why the ILF is important, and how ILF participation can be useful for developing useful pedagogical skills. The success of these efforts still remains to be determined.

Identification/Negotiability

Wenger (1998) refers to identification as that which provides experiences through which individuals can build their identities via "relations of association and differentiation." New members of a community are able to assess the extent to which they can identify with the mutual enterprise, culture, and history of a community. The extent to which new members identify with a community, in part, determines the nature of their membership and participation. For example, as a visitor to a church, an individual will assess the extent to which he or she can relate to its members, beliefs, and mission, which will in turn dictate how this person chooses to participate within this church community. It is through this dynamic and generative process that individuals become identified as something (a certain type of individual), and also identify with something or someone in the community (Wenger, 1998).

Negotiability refers to "the degree to which we have control over the meanings in which we are invested" (Wenger, 1998, p. 235). This includes how an individual perceives his or her ability, facility, and legitimacy to contribute to and take responsibility for the direction of a CoP. In turn, opportunities for negotiability determine the extent to which we develop ownership over the community's mutual enterprise and practice. Community members assume different levels of participation (Lave & Wenger, 1991; Wenger, 1998) or roles (Kim, 2000). Members at the center of the community typically have been able to identify with the community to a greater extent and thus are willing to play a more integrated role in the future success and direction of the community. Throughout the design and implementation of the ILF, it has become increasingly clear that identification and negotiability can foster participation as well as nonparticipation.

The ILF was originally designed to support teachers in visiting the classrooms of other teachers, something that teachers at all levels feel is one of the best ways to improve their teaching (MaKinster, Barab, & Keating, 2001). Despite this recognition, most ILF members seem very reluctant to engage in dialogue with the ILF contributing teachers. One potential explanation for this is that the stakes for negotiation within the ILF are high. Unlike many other online communities, the ILF only has limited potential for anonymity. In fact, the ILF encourages its members to create and edit their member profiles so other ILF members can learn more about one another. This enables ILF members to control how they are perceived by others within the community, and ideally, these profiles help ILF members to decide with whom they want to communicate and how they might interpret statements or attitudes of others (Kim, 2000). However, at the same time, the ILF is limiting its ability to get teachers to critique the practice of other teachers perhaps because critical dialogue online may be limited in the absence of anonymity.

> BEN: I put my video up, now I know it has only been there for a couple weeks, but there's, you know the only person that has posted any responses to my discussion things is someone on the ILF team. And that's great, and I write back to her, but I email her a couple times a week, so I am not getting that aspect. That larger community criticism. . . . I guess probably one of the challenges is to, you know . . . to keep wanting to do it for some reason, when I am not getting a lot of feedback right now. I mean I am still interested in taping another lesson and putting it up there . . . you know, I think it's kind of admirable that I want to do that when I haven't had any feedback on the one that's already up there. I mean why would I want to do this? I guess

that the selfish reason is that it forces me to really in-depth analyze my teaching. The whole video process and reflecting on my teaching is very beneficial.

An additional risk of designing an environment such as the e-ILF is that it creates fragmentation among the different groups involved (Design Team Members, Contributing Teachers, ILF Members). An increasing focus on design by the ILF team results in new members having fewer opportunities for negotiation because the identity of the community appears already established. This struggle arises out of the fact that teachers do not have the time to create this type of electronic environment on their own and at the same time, we as designers are limited by both our time and resources in terms of enabling all teachers to be full participants in the design process. We have chosen to involve ILF members in our design decisions by conducting usability tests and interviews with a variety of teachers, as well as having participant advisory board meetings during which several ILF teachers spend 2–3 days giving us feedback in a variety of settings (large group discussions, focus groups, workshops, etc.). Given the sometimes limited nature of our participatory design model, all ILF members are not afforded opportunities for negotiation in terms of the electronic structure of the ILF. Implicit, and sometimes explicit, within this electronic structure is a specific agenda for participation developed and embraced by the ILF development and research teams. Therefore, participation in the ILF involves the process of exploring, identifying, and potentially embracing the practices and collective identity of both the e-ILF and the ILF community prior to legitimate participation and being able to contribute to the ILF in a way that will affect its future trajectory.

The ILF classrooms embody a significant portion of what new ILF members used to identify with the ILF community. The ILF has been seeded with a number of contributing teachers who have agreed to share their classroom and experiences with the ILF during its initial stages. The goal was to create a critical mass of teachers and experiences with which new ILF members could identify. In the process, the ideas, philosophies, and commitments of the ILF were embodied within these teachers due to how they were selected (most were recommended by university faculty), how their classrooms were presented (all content was reviewed and edited by ILF Development Team members), and electronic structures through which participation takes place. Consequently, there are limited opportunities for negotiation. New members first have the Herculean task of trying to identify what the ILF is about, where and how they can find information that is relevant to their own teaching, and then deciding to what extent they can identify with the mission and commitments of the ILF community.

Our primary solution to the problem of identification in the ILF was to expand and develop the ILF Collaboratory as a space in which groups of teachers can come together in an online space around some collective experience and/or curricular interest. As mentioned above, an Inquiry Circle can be a group of teachers who are part of a class, workshop, or who simply share a similar curricular interest. Again we are concerned that supporting the development of such groups may create fragmentation within the ILF community. We may see very little interaction between the different groups of teachers that use an Inquiry Circle as their primary focus and entry point. Many ILF participants may spend the majority, if not all, of their time only using their Inquiry Circle space and contribute very little to the e-ILF outside of this space. This highlights the importance of structuring an Inquiry Circle space as a way of both communicating and sharing things privately, but also organizing the e-ILF elements and discussions that are of interest to this group. This effort would facilitate focused interactions among this group and other ILF members.

We do believe that the ILF Inquiry Circles offer a powerful way for members to quickly identify themselves with other teachers in the ILF. An ILF member can enter the ILF as part of an existing group of in-service or pre-service teachers or can identify teachers who share similar curricular or pedagogical interests. It is our hope that we can support these *Communities of Purpose* as they attempt to address their professional development needs. This is not unlike the constellation of communities of purpose in Tapped-In (Schlager, Fusco, & Schank, 2002); however, unlike Tapped-In, the ILF is focused on working together to share, improve, reflect, and create learner-centered classrooms through better understanding learning and teaching through inquiry and inquiring into our own practices.

Online/Face-to-Face

ILF presents an additional tension, one that is largely unexamined in Wenger's book: the tension between online and face-to-face. It is a tension that is knotted with the previously mentioned tensions of local/global, participation/reification, and designed/emergent and may indeed be a part of all the other tensions. For instance, when we talk about designed and emergent, we have to acknowledge that an online CoP requires a great deal more design up front than a face-to-face CoP. The technology de-termines the epistemology. By this we mean that the programming that creates the designed technological interface is composed of decisions that incorporate certain ideologies. At the least, they limit some types of ex-change and encourage others. In the e-ILF, a member cannot start a new discussion forum. This has to be done through administrative channels that are friendly but still serve as filters to participant initiative and enforces a very definite power hierarchy between designers and participants of the ILF. There are literally thousands of design decisions that go into an online project as complex as ILF and each of these decisions could be regarded as a limit – or a boon – to an emergent community.

There are so many components to this online/face-to-face tension that many believe it is a binary dualism rather than a duality, as evident in the initial chapter quote by Benedikt. The question of whether being online is fundamentally different from face-to-face communications is a difficult one. While few people dispute that there is a functional difference, characterization of this as essential and ontological raises questions. Both viewpoints have their vocal adherents. If the online is fundamentally different from the real or face-to-face, this leads to a radical reconstruction of selfhood, identity, and communication. However, treating the virtual as a continuity of the real allows for the application of tools and theories that have been in use for decades to understand community. The virtual as an extension, but not fundamentally different from the real, is consistent with the view held by anthropologist David Hakken (1999), who argues against a concept of a computer revolution or essential break between how we think about the online and the copresent. By extrapolation, we can assume that John Dewey, a unifier of Cartesian dualisms, would have found reason to see a functional, but not essential, difference between online and copresent participation. We will take the position that there is a continuity and connection between online and copresent communities, a position that allows us to view online spaces with the knowledge and skills garnered from the study of copresent communities. The functions that help a community of practice cohere are social functions since communities are overwhelmingly social spaces (Barab & Duffy, 2000; Preece, 2000). The goals of the ILF, to encourage the critiquing of and reflection on teaching practices and to help foster knowledge and use of inquiry pedagogy, cannot occur without communicative functions. This type of critical reflection and public criticism is both personal and social. The work of Jenny Preece (2000) on sociability emphasizes the holistic needs of online communities where the social and the technological interact to form community. This points to the maintenance of sociability as one of the biggest tasks of a successful online community of practice. It is within these social functions that we see the tensions that arise from the online/face-to-face duality.

We see two different issues illustrating this duality. The first is difficulty with the use of ILF online tools. The e-ILF poses difficulties to some users. The digital tools become a hindrance to participation if they block communication. Some teachers talked to us about getting lost in the electronic space. They had trouble navigating to the parts of the website they were interested in visiting. We supplied help on our website through an email link to our project director. However, dealing with the technical issues of navigation, firewalls in K–12 schools, and having appropriate software, hardware, and Internet connectivity are all challenges that need to be bridged for online participation to occur.

A busy teacher has many demands on her time. When a teacher is having difficulty with the forum software, other matters might easily distract her from following up on her difficulties. This is particularly true if the problem is intricate and might take a fair amount of time to type. ILF is vying for her attention and loses when the cost of logging off is less than the time and energy costs of continuing the ILF. Like Lankshear and Knobel (2000), we have found that time is a limiting commodity in our world. A messy problem, such as a technical impediment, is more easily mentioned in a copresent situation where words can be modified until other participants exhibit understanding. Another possible deterrent to asking for help online is the matter of trust. Typing messages online can seem for all practical purposes as if the words are being sent to some unknown place. Without trust of the motives of the recipient, a user might fear inappropriate circulation of their communication, especially in the context of a research project. Asking help from someone who is copresent provides the opportunity to read facial expression and other body language.

The second issue, alluded to above, is trust. Teachers are expected to do some inherently risky things, to put examples of their teaching online in the form of videos, to critically reflect on these videos, and to critique other teachers' videos and beliefs. Whenever a member types a message online there are the issues of: where will this message be dispersed? How widely will it travel? Who will see it? If it is archived, will it hinder future growth and credibility if one moves away from the currently held (and printed) opinion? This may be a particularly difficult issue for teachers who are accustomed to closing their classroom doors and acting autonomously (Grossman, Wineburg, & Woolworth, 2000). Opening oneself to criticism almost always evokes a sense of insecurity. This sense may be magnified in the minds of people like teachers who devote themselves to other people's children, often for low salaries and with varying support from administration and parents, out of a sense of duty to humanity (Hansen, 1995).

In what could be interpreted as a desire to foster a more trusting environment, ILF members commented on the need for copresent contact before engaging in communications online. One participant advisory board member said, "I've never felt like that [e-ILF] has been as useful as our physical community's use of that electronic community." Another participant advisory board member remarked, "I have not spent a lot of time in anybody's video. Okay? But now that I've met these people, I'll go home and do it. What's missing is I don't want to look at home movies if I don't know the people." Both these statements indicate the need for familiarity with the people in the community before online communications can be substantive or even sometimes initiated.

Online spaces, while having their challenges, also have some advantages over copresent spaces, for example, when teachers' needs for support cannot be met in their usual copresent situations. One of our driving commitments is that leveraging the Internet allows for enlarging the matrix of colleagues and thereby increasing the chance that an individual's innovation will find a niche with someone else. This seemed to be true in regard to support for inquiry pedagogy. As one teacher said, "it's [e-ILF] exposed me to at least a community of people out there that I know are intelligent and carry on interesting conversations." Several of the teachers most involved in ILF work are in rural schools where they feel like they are quite isolated from their peers doing innovative activities. Even those teachers not physically isolated often experience animosity from other teachers in their school who were characterized as "not understanding what we're doing." There were many comments from the participant advisory board that indicated the support and affirmation they got from ILF made a difference in their practice and their perceptions of their practice. In this way, we see the e-ILF's usefulness was enhanced precisely because it is an online space that allows access where copresent communications do not suffice. The separations that online communications potentially bridge include those constructed by time, space, and interest.

Diversity/Coherence

When those who have the power to name and to socially construct reality choose not to see you or hear you, whether you are dark-skinned, old, disabled, female, or speak with a different accent or dialect than theirs, when someone with the authority of a teacher, say, describes the world and you are not in it, there is a moment of psychic disequilibrium, as if you looked into a mirror and saw nothing. (Rich, 1986, p. 199)

During the characterization of our design decisions we recognized a sixth tension that we view as essential in terms of characterizing our work. The duality of having a system that allows diversity, while at the same time maintaining a certain level of coherence in communities, has been noticed and discussed by Joel Westheimer (1998). Gardner (1991, p. 32) explains that "the common good is first of all preservation of a system in which all kinds of people can – within the law – pursue their various visions." This suggests that attempts to support the community development must ensure there are multiple voices and perspectives, even in the face of advancing a particular agenda or framework. This trade-off of diversity for coherence is such a basic tension within communities that it may often be accepted as a standard cost for building and maintaining communal relations. However, we argue that ignoring this tension endangers the formation, let alone the sustainability and value, of community. Individual needs and opportunities for participation require as much attention as group needs and community agendas.

Communities benefit from diversity in a number of ways. Dewey stressed the need for difference among community members in order to provide multiple perspectives and viewpoints (1909/1965). By having a diverse population, ideas and perspectives are continually challenged, revised, and often result in new collective agendas or beliefs. Lave and Wenger (1991) argue that change over time is a fundamental property of communities of practice and that the knowledge and perspectives of a community are mutually constitutive. Therefore, as the level of diversity within a community increases, so does the opportunity for collective and individual development. It is the diversity of skills, abilities, and perspectives that drives the growth of the community. As designers, we need to ensure that we are creating a system that is inviting and receptive to individuals with a variety of ideas, needs, and agendas (Barab, Barnett, & Squire, 2002).

By using convenience sampling to find teacher participants in our initial efforts and by strictly advancing a professional development model that embraces personal reflection and critical dialogue with other teachers, the ILF has failed to adequately address the need for a certain level of diversity. This may have resulted in the ILF participating teachers being an outlier group, those interested in inquiring into their own teaching and those interested in implementing inquiry-based teacher practices regardless of issues of meeting – what Songer, Lee, Hartman, and McDonald (2001) referred to as *maverick* teachers. Additionally, the commitment of the site to math and science inquiry may be excluding other teacher voices that would offer important perspectives and experiences around best practices. Another area in which lack of diversity is apparent is in the gender ratio of the ILF Contributing Teachers.

At the end of our first year, based on convenience sampling, we realized that there were no ILF classrooms of female science teachers. This is a serious omission, especially since women comprise the majority of ILF members (both pre-service and in-service). Since the ILF classrooms are seriously imbalanced in terms of gender diversity, we are not surprised to find that there is a distinct lack of participation by female teachers in the discussions around the ILF classrooms of male teachers and conversely the lack of male participants in the discussion around the videos of female math teachers (Herring, Martinson, & Scheckler, 2001). In addition, Herring et al. also found that questions asked by women are less likely to be answered by men than by women.

The other area in which the ILF has struggled in terms of diversity versus coherence is in regard to supporting the articulation of multiple and varied voices within the ILF discussion forums. Thus far there has been very little critical dialogue within the ILF. Most of the discussion posts are either complimentary or are simply people stating their ideas and opinions. It is very seldom that an ILF member challenges the opinions of another person, or gives critical feedback to one of the ILF Contributing Teachers. We argue that, in part, this has to do with American culture in general and the culture of teaching specifically. "[T]he anthropologist Paul Bohannan notes that Americans have two categories of behavior: polite and rude. The British, he says, add a third: civil, meaning that you pull no punches when you criticize, but that you do so without jeering. As he puts it, an American has to be your close friend before giving you anything but praise" (Nader, 2001, p. 15). American culture is not one where critical feedback is offered and received openly. In addition, as stated previously, providing one another with critical feedback is not something teachers do on a day-to-day basis. The culture of teaching is primarily one of isolation, where teachers are most concerned with and motivated by improving student learning, rather than improving their own teaching practice (Dunn & Shriner, 1999). Fortunately, the culture of most pre-service programs encourages these future students to provide one another with feedback on a regular basis – this was consistent with the level of critical dialogue that we observed in the areas of the e-ILF devoted to pre-service teachers. However, this practice is usually pushed aside once pre-service teachers enter the teaching profession.

These conditions create significant design challenges for the ILF in terms of fostering critical dialogue and supporting multiple and diverse voices. We need to provide our members with a variety of opportunities in which teachers at all levels feel like their ideas and opinions will be valued and respected. Most important, we need to provide models and mentors that new ILF members can relate to and interact with in ways that will help them to perceive themselves as valued and legitimate participants. To this end, we are currently making a concerted effort to get several ILF classrooms of female science teachers online as well as initiate new discussion forums that have female science teachers as moderators. Our hope is that the central presence of these women as core members in the ILF will result in more balanced levels of female participation overall.

The other design decision that may have a significant impact on the diversity of ILF members is to support "bounded groups" of teachers that share some common curricular, professional development, or pedagogical interest. For example, we are currently working to support a number of Indiana science teachers who conduct water quality investigations in their classrooms. The new ILF Collaboratory provides these teachers with a virtual space in which they can share resources, identify ILF resources and discussions that are of interest to them, and keep in touch with a growing group of teachers who have similar interests and needs. Ironically, it is our belief, and consistent with our initial observations, that by creating groups with a common focus we will actually increase the opportunity for diverse voices. Our assumption is that these settings allow for more attention to be focused on the needs of individuals and on the nuances of supporting inquiry within the context of a common ground.

At the same time, the semiprivate nature of these groups will allow for the development of trust and camaraderie. Establishing a certain level of trust with a particular group of teachers will most likely result in a greater willingness of these teachers to serve as "critical friends" (Costa & Kallick, 1993) of one another. Critical friends are willing to challenge the thoughts or ideas of one another in a manner that is supportive, yet honestly critical. Our hope is that these types of dialogue and interactions will encourage a greater level of diversity in terms of ILF membership and in the thoughts and ideas expressed both face-to-face and online. As more and more bounded groups arise, we run the risk of fragmenting the ILF into a constellation of subcommunities, rather than supporting the emergence of a single, coherent, legitimate community of practice. As we initiate our support of these bounded groups, the diversity/coherence duality is central to our thinking.

CONCLUSIONS AND IMPLICATIONS

The notion of tensions, or dualities, provides a useful lens for better understanding the life-cycle of community systems more generally (Barab, Barnett, & Squire, 2002; Engeström, 1987, 1999; Wenger, 1998). Wenger discussed these tensions as dualities, with the challenge not being to eliminate tensions or treat the pieces as polarities along a continuum, but to understand their interplay, harnessing it in a manner that invigorates system dynamics and learning. Using Wenger's (1998) dualities as a means for understanding how to support a community of practice can serve as a powerful framework that informs both design and research. We have attempted to provide other educators/designers with an illuminative case from which they can build their own generalizations as they confront and potentially overcome the challenges that they face when "designing for community."

Although we often discussed each of the dualities as if they exist independently from the others, clearly they are overlapping. Not only does each duality serve as an interacting dimension, but the six dualities knot together in ways that make them almost inseparable. This means that when designing online communities it is difficult not to consider at least two or three dualities at a time. Consideration of these dualities and their overlapping nature is both a challenge and at the same time has been instrumental in informing the directions of our design work, helping us to develop the ILF in innovative and meaningful ways. In this chapter we attempted to show how the interplay of the dimensions that constitute these dualities, as well as the dynamic interactions among dualities, have been manifest in the ILF.

We view these dynamics as driving system innovations, as well as change, and understanding these dynamics is essential to the future success of the ILF. If we weigh too heavily on one dimension to the exclusion of another, we will undermine the system as a whole. To be clear, we view the potential success or failure of the ILF to be dependent on our (including designers and community members') ability to foster and maintain a healthy dynamic within and among the above discussed dualities/tensions.

Examining our work in light of dualities has resulted in a number of design decisions that have implications for others designing online communities and especially online communities of practice. First, it is clear that online communities are not simply technical spaces, but instead are networks (STINs) constituted by social and technical relations (Kling et al., 2001). As mentioned previously, it was necessary at one point during the project to distinguish between the ILF as a socio-technical network and the ILF website or e-ILF. The e-ILF refers only to the website, which includes the web pages, videos, online conversations, and the electronic database that serves as the backbone of the ILF. One of the primary implications is that designers of online communities need to explicitly acknowledge the sociability issues they face (Preece, 2000). Given the challenges of supporting community development online, we have been attempting to create more copresent opportunities that can then be supported and integrated with online participation. The important point is not to spend time debating whether differences between online and copresent CoPs are ontological or simply functional, but rather to focus on understanding how, in a community context, we can best support social relations so that communication and learning trajectories can flow freely.

Many of the aforementioned ideas have helped us to see that the term *online community* does not really capture the nature of the ILF and most other educationally focused electronically networked communities. Therefore, we have chosen to advance the label of *web-supported communities*. There are many organizations or social entities that exist almost exclusively online and can legitimately be referred to as online communities. Online gaming communities such as those within Everquest® and Asheron's Call® are the most populated examples of viable social networks of individuals that interact and collaborate almost exclusively through electronic networking technologies (Kim, 2000). In addition, there is a long history of social MUDs and MOOs that involve thousands of individuals that interact with one another solely through networked technologies. However, educational researchers and designers are quickly coming to realize that face-to-face and other socially mediated interactions are essential supplements to online interactions in educational settings. We have experienced our greatest success when online interactions in the ILF have served as extensions of face-to-face workshops, meetings, and classes, or when we bring together individuals that had previously interacted only in online settings and allow them to develop relationships outside of the e-ILF.

Another significant issue that arose within this project was the divide between the immediate needs and desires of ILF teachers (for lesson plans, resources, etc.) versus the global reform agenda of the university educators, while we made efforts to collapse this tension between the global reform agenda of the ILF community and the immediate local needs of the teachers. Although the goal was not to eliminate this tension, we are university educators who, consistent with the research community to which we are most centrally located, believe that more science and math teachers need to be using inquiry-based teaching techniques in the classroom. This call is consistent with national reform movements and with the focus of the grant. However, teachers are confronted with multiple constraints, including 45-minute class periods, minimal lesson preparation time, 1 teacher to 20–30 students, content-based accountability on standardized tests, and student and parent focus on grades as opposed to meaningful engagement as the measure of success influences the practices of teachers. In the course of the school day and school year, teachers' plates are so full they rarely have the luxury or inclination to consider and learn new pedagogies, reflect on their current practice, decide to change their approach, then revise their curriculum to support new pedagogies. So, a systemic tension between teachers' immediate needs and long-term reform efforts that require learning, reflection, reworking curriculum, and collegial critique exists within the project. The challenge is to balance the local needs of the teachers with the global reform agenda of the university educators. By supporting the interplay of these goals, we support reform that is grounded in practice, not simply in the minds and articles of university educators – what we call *grounded reform*. We have come to realize that some systemic reform work that reduces the constraints in teachers' time and makes "anytime, anywhere" professional development more appealing is necessary before the ILF will have widespread adoption in an in-service teacher context. Finally, we have clearly been convinced that community cannot be designed a priori or by someone other than the community members. As such, our current commitments in this project are even more focused on a minimalist design through which we collaboratively develop participant structures that will initiate dialogue and then evaluate how our efforts support local adaptation and continued development. This bottom-up approach is consistent with Kim's (2000) discussion of the goal for designers interested in supporting online community being to support a timeline in which staff starts out as very active but drops off relative to the community members in terms of evolving the online space and defining what it means to be a community member. Based on Barab, Squire, and Dueber's (2000) work, we call this approach *co-evolutionary design*, a process that is similar to participatory design but with an evolutionary component involving extended time scales and with the focus being to work with community members over time to co-develop and evolve participant structures as well as the norms and rules of participation.

We view co-evolutionary design as particularly appropriate, and possibly necessary, when designers are trying to "build" online communities to support learning; this is because within our definition of communities, they are self-organizing systems whose continual health and functioning is dependent upon local ownership and member identification (Barab, Cherkes-Julkowski et al., 1999). This bottom-up, or self-organizing, approach does not result in a static, fixed, "designed" space to which new members can assimilate. Instead, we are arguing for an ongoing collaboration among designers, educators, and users. In this way, designers are supporting the evolution of a community identity, while at the same time creating a space for continued negotiability by individual members. In recommending this approach for design we must still locate and encourage participation from the absent voices. There is a conundrum of wanting both diversity and emergent design. Those participating in the developing design of an online community are those who are comfortable with the hegemony of that space. We feel that our latest design focus on the ILF Collaboratory reflects many of the aforementioned commitments and ideas. As described above, the Collaboratory is a space within the e-ILF in which groups of teachers can come together around some collective experience and/or curricular interest. As such, the Collaboratory is simply a space to organize resources, documents, and ILF areas of interest. Therefore, it is the community or Inquiry Circle members that decide what things are of relevance in each electronic space including what private discussions take place or ILF Lounge discussions are of greatest interest. As a result, each Inquiry Circle member is able to customize his or her space to meet his or her local needs and interests. This allows the identity and interests of each group to emerge out of the community members and facilitators, rather than being imposed by designers or project leaders. While this situation also allows for the development of Inquiry Circles that are not at all tied to the global reform agenda of the ILF, we feel that the other, more heavily designed areas of the ILF contextualize the Inquiry Circle activities so they are less likely to discuss noninquiry activities than it might be in other electronically networked settings. Currently there are 39 Inquiry Circles ranging from pre-service classrooms at six different universities, to in-service teacher workshops, to curricular focused groups centered around topics such as evolution, water ecology, and elementary teaching with salamanders. The development of the ILF Collaboratory (August 2001) and using the ILF within math and science pre-service classrooms (Fall 2001) has resulted in a significant increase in activity in ILF private and public discussion forums as members of these Inquiry Circles post inside and outside their circles (see Figure 3.4).

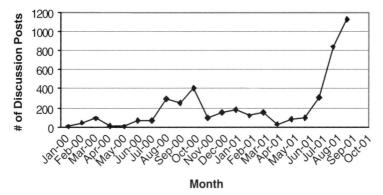

Month

FIGURE 3.4. ILF discussion postings per month since the beginning of the project

SUMMARY

In this chapter, we have used six dualities as an analytical lens to characterize the ILF and to illuminate the design struggles that arose in the design of an online CoP in the service of learning. It is through understanding and balancing the interplay within and among these dualities that designers can inform and evolve their design efforts. We have argued that dualities are made up of reciprocal components whose interplay can drive system innovation and are useful for characterizing system dynamics. By examining community life in terms of these dualities, we have been able to better understand the ILF dynamics, and have tried to share these insights in a manner that will provide other designers with an illuminative case study. More generally, we hope that this discussion will allow designers to readily identify patterns occurring in their own community interventions and intelligently navigate the challenges they face when designing for community.

References

Adler, P. A., & Adler, P. (1997). *Membership Roles in Field Research*. Thousand Oaks, CA: Sage.

Barab, S. A. (1999). Ecologizing instruction through integrated units. *Middle School Journal, 30,* 21–28.

Barab, S. A. (2002). Commentary: Human-field interaction as mediated by mobile computers. In T. Koschmann, R. Hall, & N. Miyake (Eds.), *Computer Supported Collaborative Learning*. Mahwah, NJ: Erlbaum.

Barab, S. A., Barnett, M., Yamagata-Lynch, L., Squire, K., & Keating, T. (2002). Using activity theory to understand the contradictions characterizing a technology-rich introductory astronomy course. *Mind, Culture, and Activity, 9*(2), 76–107.

Barab, S. A., Barnett, M. G., & Squire, K. (2002). Building a community of teachers: Navigating the essential tensions in practice. *The Journal of The Learning Sciences, 11*(4), 489–542.

Barab, S. A., Cherkes-Julkowski, M., Swenson, R., Garrett. S., Shaw, R. E., & Young, M. (1999). Principles of self-organization: Ecologizing the learner-facilitator system. *The Journal of The Learning Sciences, 8*(3&4), 349–390.

Barab, S. A., & Duffy, T. (2000). From practice fields to communities of practice. In D. Jonassen, & S. M. Land (Eds.), *Theoretical Foundations of Learning Environments* (pp. 25–56). Mahwah, NJ: Erlbaum.

Barab, S. A., MaKinster, J. G., Moore, J., Cunningham, D., & the ILF Design Team. (2001). Designing and building an online community: The struggle to support sociability in the Inquiry Learning Forum. *Educational Technology Research and Development, 49*(4), 71–96.

Barab, S. A., & Schatz, S. (2001, April). *Using Activity Theory to Conceptualize Online Community and Using Online Community to Conceptualize Activity Theory.* Presented at the annual meeting of the American Educational Research Association, Seattle, WA.

Barab, S. A., Squire, K., & Dueber, B. (2000). Supporting authenticity through participatory learning. *Educational Technology Research and Development, 48*(2), 37–62.

Benedikt, M. (1991). "Cyberspace" Some proposals. In M. Benedikt (Ed.), *Cyberspace: First steps* (pp. 119–224). Cambridge, MA: MIT Press.

Brown, A. L. (1992). Design experiments: Theoretical and methodological challenges in creating complex interventions in classroom settings. *The Journal of The Learning Sciences, 2*(2), 141–178.

Chaney-Cullen, T., & Duffy, T. (1998). Strategic Teaching Frameworks: Multimedia to support teacher change. *The Journal of The Learning Sciences, 8*, 1–40.

Cochran-Smith, M. & Lytle, S. L. (1999). Relationships of knowledge and practice: Teacher learning in communities. In A. Iran-Nejad, & Pearson, P. D. (Eds.). *Review of Research in Education* (pp. 249–305). Washington D.C.: American Educational Research Association.

Collison, G., Elbaum, B., Haavind, S., & Tinker, R. (2000). *Facilitating Online Learning: Effective Strategies for Moderators.* Madison, WI: Atwood Publishing.

Costa, A. L., & Kallick, B. (1993). Through the lens of a critical friend. *Educational Leadership, 51*(2), 49–52.

Dewey, J. (1903–1906/1977). *Collected Articles, Book Reviews, and Miscellany* (Vol. 3). Carbondale: Southern Illinois University Press.

Dewey, J. (1909/1965). *The Influence of Darwin on Philosophy and Other Essays in Contemporary Thought.* Bloomington: Indiana University Press.

Dewey, J. (1938/1986). Logic: The theory of inquiry. In J. A. Boydston (Ed.), *John Dewey: The Later Works 1925–1953* (Vol. 12, pp. 1–506). Carbondale: Southern Illinois University Press.

Dunn, T. G., & Shriner, C. (1999). Deliberate practice in teaching: What teachers do for self-improvement. *Teaching & Teacher Education, 15*(6), 631–651.

Eden, C., & Huxham, C. (1996). Action research for the study of organizations. In S. Clegg., C. Hardy, & W. Nord (Eds.), *Handbook of Organizational Studies*. Thousand Oaks, CA: Sage.

Emerson, R. E., Fretz, R. L., & Shaw, L. L. (1995). *Writing Ethnographic Fieldnotes.* Chicago: University of Chicago Press.

Engeström, Y. (1987). *Learning by Expanding.* Helsinki: Orienta-konsultit.

Engeström, Y. (1993). Developmental studies of work as a testbench of activity theory: The case of primary care medical practice. In S. Chaiklin & J. Lave (Eds.),

Understanding Practice: Perspectives on Activity and Context (pp. 64–103). Cambridge, MA: Cambridge University Press.

Engeström, Y. (1999). Activity theory and individual and social transformation. In Y. Engeström, R. Miettinen, & R. Punamaki (Eds.), *Perspectives on Activity Theory* (pp. 19–38). Cambridge, MA: Cambridge University Press.

Fowler, R. B. (1991). *The Dance with Community: The Contemporary Debate in American Political Thought.* Lawrence: University Press of Kansas.

Gardner, John. (1991). *Building Community.* Washington, D.C.: Independent Sector.

Geertz, C. (1983). From the native's point of view: On the nature of anthropological understanding. In C. Geertz (Ed.), *Local Knowledge* (pp. 55–70). New York: Basic Books.

Gomez, L., Fishman, B., & Pea, R. (1998). The CoVis Project: Building a large scale science education testbed. *Interactive Learning Environments, 6*(1–2), 59–92.

Grills, S. (1998). *Doing ethnographic research: Field settings.* Thousand Oaks, CA: Sage.

Grossman, P., Wineburg, S., & Woolworth, S. (2000). *In Pursuit of Teacher Community.* Paper presented at the American Educational Research Association, New Orleans.

Hakken, D. (1999). *Cyborgs@cyberspace: An Ethnographer Looks to the Future.* New York: Routledge.

Hall, Gene E. (1979). The concerns-based approach to facilitating change. *Educational-Horizons, 57*(4), 202–208.

Hansen, D. T. (1995). *The Call to Teach.* New York: Teacher's College Press.

Herring, S., Martinson, A., and Scheckler, R. (2001). A Multimodal Web-based Community for Math and Science Educators: A Feminist Critique. National Women's Studies Association Minneapolis, MN, June 13–17, 2001.

Hickman, L. A. (1992). *John Dewey's Pragmatic Technology.* Bloomington: Indiana University Press.

Hickman, L. A. (2000, April 10–13). *Johndewey.com: What Dewey Would Have Liked – and Disliked – about the Internet.* Paper presented at the Philosophy and Education for Democracy International Conference, the Inaugural Conference of the European John Dewey Society, Unical, Aula Magna, Italy.

Jackson, M. (Ed.). (1996). *Things as They Are: New Directions in Phenomenological Anthropology.* Bloomington: Indiana University Press.

Jones, S. (Ed.). (1999). *Doing Internet Research.* Thousand Oak, CA: Sage.

Kaufman-Osborn, T. V. (1997). *Creatures of Prometheus: Gender and the Politics of Technology.* New York: Rowman and Littlefield.

Kim, A. J. (2000). *Community Building: Secret Strategies for Successful Online Communities on the Web.* Berkeley, CA: Peachpit Press.

Kling, R. (2000). Learning about information technologies and social change: The contribution of social informatics. *The Information Society, 16*(3), 217–232.

Kuttii, K. (1996). Activity theory as a potential framework for human-computer interaction research. In B. Nardi (Ed.), *Context and Consciousness: Activity Theory and Human-Computer Interaction.* Cambridge, MA: MIT Press.

Lankshear, C., & Knobel, M. (2000). Why 'digital epistemologies'? *Re-open, 1*(1).

Latour, B. (1987). *Science in Action: How to Follow Scientists and Engineers through Society.* Milton Keynes, UK: Open University Press.

Lave, J. (1993). Situating learning in communities of practice. In L. B. Resnick, J. M. Levine, & S. D. Teasley (Eds.), *Perspectives on Socially Shared Cognition* (pp. 17–36). Washington, DC: American Psychological Association.

Lave, J. (1997). The culture of acquisition and the practice of understanding. In D. Kirshner & J. A. Whitson (Eds.), *Situated Cognition: Social, Semiotic, and Psychological Perspectives* (pp. 63–82). Mahwah, NJ: Erlbaum.

Lave, J., & Wenger, E. (1991). *Situated Learning: Legitimate Peripheral Participation.* New York: Cambridge University Press.

Lemke, J. (1997). Cognition, context, and learning: A social semiotic perspective. In D. Kirshner & J. A. Whitson (Eds.), *Situated Cognition: Social, Semiotic, and Psychological Perspectives* (pp. 37–56). Mahwah, NJ: Erlbaum.

Leont'ev, A. (1974). The problem of activity in psychology. *Soviet Psychology, 13*(2), 4–33.

Leont'ev, A. (1981). *Problems of the Development of Mind.* Moscow: Progress.

Leont'ev, A. (1989). The problem of activity in the history of Soviet psychology. *Soviet Psychology, 27*(1), 22–39.

Lipman, M. (1988). *Philosophy Goes to School.* Philadelphia: Temple University Press.

MaKinster, J. G., Barab, S. A., & Keating, T. M. (2001). Design and implementation of an online professional development community: A project-based learning approach. *Electronic Journal of Science Education, 5*(3). Available at: http://unr.edu/homepage/crowther/ejse/ejsev5n3.html.

Marcus, G. E. (1998). *Ethnography through Thick and Thin.* Princeton, NJ: Princeton University Press.

McNiff, J. (1995). *Action Research Principles and Practice.* New York: Routledge.

Nader, L. (2001). Harmony coerced is freedom denied. *The Chronicle of Higher Education, 47*, July 13, B13–B16.

Nardi, B. (Ed.). (1996). *Context and Consciousness: Activity Theory and Human-Computer Interaction.* Cambridge, MA: MIT Press.

National Research Council. (2000). *National Science Education Standards.* Washington, DC: National Academy Press.

Preece, J. (2000). *Online Communities: Designing Usability, Supporting Sociability.* Chichester, UK: John Wiley & Sons.

Putnam, R. (2001). *Bowling Alone: The Collapse and Revival of American Community.* New York: Touchstone Books.

Quartz, K. H. (1995). Sustaining new educational communities: Toward a new culture of school reform. In J. Oakes & K. H. Quartz (Eds.), *Creating New Educational Communities* (ninety-fourth yearbook of the National Society for the Study of Education, Part 1, pp. 240–254). Chicago: University of Chicago Press.

Rich, A. (1986). Invisibility in academe (1984). In A. Rich (Ed.), *Blood, Bread, and Poetry: Selected Prose, 1979–1985* (pp. 198–201). New York: Norton.

Rogoff, B. (1990). *Apprenticeship in Thinking: Cognitive Development in Social Context.* New York: Oxford University Press.

Roth, W.-M. (1998). *Designing Communities.* Dordrecht: Kluwer Academic Publishers.

Ruopp, R., Gal, S., Drayton, B., & Pfister, M. (1993). *LabNet: Toward a Community of Practice.* Hillsdale, NJ: Lawrence Erlbaum Associates.

Scardamalia, M., & Bereiter, C. (1993). Technologies for knowledge-building discourse. *Communications of the ACM, 36*, 37–41.

Scheckler, R. (2000). *Weaving Feminism, Pragmatism, and Distance Education*. Unpublished Dissertation, Virginia Polytechnic Institute and State University, Blacksburg, VA.

Schlager, M. S., Fusco, J., & Schank, P. (2002). Evolution of an on-line education community of practice. In K. A. Renniger & W. Shumar, (Eds.), *Building Virtual Communities: Learning and Change in Cyberspace* (pp. 129–158). New York: Cambridge University Press.

Schön, D. A. (1987). *Educating the Reflective Practitioner*. San Francisco: Jossey-Bass.

Sergiovanni, T. J. (1994). *Building Community in Schools*. San Francisco, CA: Jossey-Bass.

Shaffer, C. R., & Anundsen, K. (1993). *Creating Community Anywhere: Finding Support and Connection in a Fragmented World*. Los Angeles: Tarcher/Perigee.

Shaw, R. E., Kadar, E., Sim, M., & Repperger, D. W. (1992). The intentional spring: A strategy for modeling systems that learn to perform intentional acts. *Journal of Motor Behavior*, 24(1), 3–28.

Smith, M. and Kollock, P. (Eds.) (1999). *Communities in Cyberspace*. London: Routledge.

Songer, N. B., Lee, H. S., Hartman, M., & McDonald, S. (2001, April). Towards a repertoire of exemplars of classroom science inquiry. Paper presented at the American Educational Research Association, Seattle, WA.

Stake, R. E. (1983). Program evaluation, particularly responsive evaluation. In G. F. Madaus, M. S. Scriven., and D. L. Stufflebeam (Eds.), *Evaluation Models: Viewpoints on Educational and Human Services Evaluation* (pp. 287–310). Boston: Kluwer-Nijhoff Publishing.

Stake, R. E. (1995). *The Art of Case Study Research*. Thousand Oaks, CA: Sage.

Stringer, E. T. (1996). *Action Research : A Handbook for Practitioners*. Thousand Oaks, CA: Sage.

Vygotsky, L. (1978). *Mind in Society: The Development of Higher Psychological Processes*. Cambridge, MA: Harvard University Press.

Watson, N. (1997). Why we argue about virtual community: A case study of the phish.net fan community. In S. G. Jones (Ed.), *Virtual Culture: Identity and Communication in Cybersociety* (pp. 102–132). London: Sage.

Wellman, B. (1999). *Networks in the Global Village: Life in Contemporary Communities*. Boulder, CO: Westview Press.

Wells, G. (1999). *Dialogic Inquiry: Towards a Sociocultural Practice and Theory of Education*. Cambridge, MA: Cambridge University Press.

Wenger, E. (1998). *Communities of Practice: Leaning, Meaning, and Identity*. Cambridge, UK: Cambridge University Press.

Wenger, E., McDermott, R., & Synder, W. M. (2002). *Cultivating Communities of Practice: A Guide to Managing Knowledge*. Boston, MA: Harvard Business School Press.

Werry, C., & Mowbray, M. (2001). *Online Communities: Commerce, Community Action, and the virtual university*. Upper Saddle River, NJ: Prentice Hall.

Westheimer, J. (1998). *Among school teachers: Community, autonomy, and ideology in Teachers' Work*. New York: Teachers College Press.

Wineburg, S., & Grossman, P. (1998). Creating a community of learners among high school teachers. *Phi Delta Kappan*, 79, 350–353.

4

Group Behavior and Learning in Electronic Forums

A Socio-Technical Approach

Rob Kling and Christina Courtright

The term *community* is widely and often uncritically used to characterize two kinds of groups that are central to this book. First, there are groups that come together to learn, in classes, workshops, and professional associations. Most professionals would refer to these as classes, workshops, and associations. Some educators like to refer to all of these kinds of groups as learning communities. The second kind of group is one that participates in an electronic forum (e-forum), such as an Internet Relay Chatroom, a professional listserv, a distance education course, or an online auction. It has become equally commonplace to refer to such groups as communities – virtual communities. This book examines issues for the developers and participants of electronic forums that could facilitate learning.

We believe that the casual use of the term community to characterize groups that are engaged in learning, or groups that participate in e-forums, is seriously misguided. As we shall see, developing a group into a community is a major accomplishment that requires special processes and practices, and the experience is often both frustrating and satisfying for many of the participants. The extent to which a group develops certain desirable community-like characteristics should be based on empirical observation rather than on assumptions or aspirations.

Since 1999, we have been involved in the development and study of an e-forum designed to support science and math teachers who want to improve their abilities to teach with inquiry approaches. The Inquiry Learning Forum (ILF) is a large project that has directly involved eight faculty members and eight graduate students, with a research advisory board of

This research was supported in part by National Science Foundation Grants, REC-9980081 and 9872961. We have also benefited from discussions about professional development with Cathy Brown and Mitzi Lewison. Blaise Cronin, Andrew Feenberg, Rebecca Scheckler, and Murali Venkatesh also provided helpful comments.

nine faculty and a participant advisory board of eight teachers. The ILF's e-forums were opened for teachers' access in the Spring of 2000, and by mid-2001, several hundred teachers had registered and visited them.

Groups of this scale and diversity rarely have a consensus about the processes and practices that will support teachers in improving their teaching. We have participated in numerous meetings and informal discussions of the nature of participants' behavior in the ILF's e-forum (which we call the e-ILF). We have heard the term community used in a wide variety of ways, and have seen important evidence that the "assumption of community" on the e-ILF has undermined our ability to effectively support reflective discussions by the participating teachers.

This chapter examines how group behavior in e-forums could be supported to meet the kinds of aspirations of trust and reciprocity that people who use the term community desire. We will start with a discussion of the structure of the Internet, to address some of the prevailing misconceptions regarding its nature as a medium for human interaction and community development. We will then discuss a variety of social forms, from teams and groups to communities. We will also examine some of the available research concerning how the crucial element of trust is developed in groups, both face-to-face and those that meet or work online. Finally, we will discuss some of the relevant experiences of the ILF, and provide suggestions for structural changes that could enhance its community-oriented features.

CONTRASTING CONCEPTIONS OF THE INTERNET

Standard Model of the Internet

The growth of the Internet as both a tool and an environment for human interaction has generated a concomitant growth of popular and academic literature seeking to describe, interpret, and explain the nature and forms of such interaction. Underlying much of this literature is a conception of the Internet as a "level playing field" whose architecture allows people to engage in many of the activities that they have traditionally performed off-line, including conversation, work, commerce, hobbies, meetings, worship, reading, and learning, yet without the usual constraints of space and time. This "level" or "standard" model of the Internet is conceptualized most fundamentally as a network of computer networks connected by virtue of the TCP/IP protocol, which allows unlimited sending and receiving of electronic files (Cerf, 2001; Zakon, 2001). What derives from this essentially technological characterization is a portrait of human online activity that mimics the fluid, boundless nature of file transfer: people can communicate with anyone, at any time, in groups or one-on-one; anything can be located, read, or purchased; work can be conducted from anywhere; and so on.[1] Even the complaint that "there is a lot of unreliable information on the Internet" rests on this standard model.

Socio-Technical Model of the Internet

An alternative model conceptualizes how the Internet is structured technically, socially, and socio-technically. The term *socio-technical* refers to an ensemble, a practice, or even an analysis of any of these that integrates social and technical elements in a way that reveals their interactions and interpenetration. In conventional approaches, an ensemble could be seen as wholly social, such as an organization, a high school for example. More accurately, an analysis of the high school could be wholly social, and focus on such behaviors as the formations of informal student cliques. Or the ensemble could be seen as wholly technical. The high school could be the subject of a technical analysis of its structures: the likelihood that it would collapse in an earthquake. A socio-technical analysis of behavior in the high school would focus on a mix of social and technical elements. For example, if the classroom chairs are bolted to the floor in some rooms and not in others, one may examine different kinds of class organization and communication in these rooms with different physical capabilities. The structuring of spaces, such as rooms that are assigned to student clubs, may influence the ways that cliques form and how they manage their social boundaries with technologies (i.e., closed doors). High schools are neither completely social entities nor completely technological entities, even though social psychologists and structural engineers may analyze them as if they were. Socio-technical analysts see social behavior and the organization of artifacts (such as buildings or websites) in a much more integrative manner.

Consider websites as varied as newspapers (such as the *New York Times* online edition), travel sites (such as *expedia.com*), financial services (such as *schwab.com*), and e-magazines (such as *salon.com*). The conventions for these sites vary considerably. They allow their readers few places to post, if any. Some e-zines, such as *salon.com*, have areas that anyone can read, along with premium areas that require a paid subscription. In contrast, the *New York Times* online edition requires a potential reader to register in order to read stories that are less than seven days old, and to pay a fee for accessing older stories from the *Times'* archives. Financial services such as *schwab.com* provide scant financial information for people who have not established a brokerage account with the firm. Schwab's account holders,

---

[1] For example: "File transfers allow Internet users to access remote machines and retrieve programs or text. Many Internet computers – some two thousand of them, so far – allow any person to access them anonymously, and to simply copy their public files, free of charge" (Sterling, 1993).

however, can enter the site and find extensive reports, charts, and other means for evaluating potential investments. Some of these sites rely upon passwords for protection; others use IP addresses. In short, rather than the level and undifferentiated view of the Internet that emphasizes highways from a user to every site, this socio-technical view emphasizes carefully structured electronic forums where people experience walls, hallways, and doors with electronic locks.

A different class of websites is structured to support more open communication among participants, and sometimes high degrees of sociality. Clubs on *Yahoo.com* and *America Online* require simple subscriptions. But some of them screen applicants and limit membership to certain classes of people, such as adults, or teenagers, or women. *ArXiv.org*, a repository of scientific working papers, allows authors to post their own works. Anyone can visit the site and read articles without registering. However, those who wish to post articles must register and demonstrate their legitimacy (by having accounts with .edu or .gov domains). Even though scientists may post articles on *arXiv.org*, there are no spaces to discuss articles that have been posted.

Online games support a different kind of sociality. Popular games, such as *Ultima Online* and *Everquest*, each have several hundred thousand players paying monthly subscription fees. In order to advance in these games, the players join groups, called guilds. Not only are the spaces structured to help players form guilds, but some game designers also create incentives for players to recruit and assist new guild members by awarding them additional credits and other resources for their efforts. Sanctioned behavior varies among games, from healthy competition to group murder (Ahuna, 2001; Kolbert, 2001). Thus, sites like these are structured socio-technically, in that they are co-configured not only by the constraints and affordances of the technologies involved, but also – and primarily – by social, economic, and institutional factors. The sites also differ in their rules and norms about:

- who can participate (and who is excluded)
- the genres of acceptable communication
- participants' activities (speak/post, read, role-play, buy, sell)
- acceptable conventions (are newbies in a game welcomed or killed? do you criticize others or flame them?)
- their social control agents and their practices (established and enforced by e-forum organizers? by participants?).

In our view, e-forums can be designed socio-technically (Kling, 2000). Designers may try technical means (such as IP-address checking or personally reviewed registration) to limit participation to some kinds of people or groups. An e-forum's charter may describe the kinds of acceptable communications, but without human review, it may be difficult to enforce. The e-forum may enable some specific kinds of activities, while providing no explicit support for others. The e-forum may be designed so that any participants may easily form their own (private) group, or they may require the assistance of an e-forum administrator, or it may be effectively impossible.

These socio-technical design elements may tend to support some kinds of social relationships between participants, but they do not effectively control the array of possible and even likely behavior. In fact, participants in e-forums can – and do – subvert designed structures for their own purposes, just as members of a club or association can push the group to act in a manner not foreseen by its founders. For example, the BioNet newsgroups (http://www.bio.net/) were established to enable research biologists to discuss specific topics; lists were created in the early 1990s for specialized topics such as automated DNA sequencing, microbial biofilms, and the science and profession of biophysics. By 2001, the unmoderated BioNet newsgroups had become loaded with spam (i.e., advertisements for "easy credit," "find out anything about anyone"), and some seem to have died as scientific e-forums. A related example: the members of one Usenet newsgroup, alt.tasteless, once decided to "raid" another unmoderated newsgroup, rec.pets.cats, and filled it with posts that the cat lovers found deeply offensive (Quittner, 1994).

Sometimes participants will subvert the e-forum structures in an effort to be constructive. One of the authors (Kling) was invited to give a guest lecture for a two-week period on social informatics in a doctoral course that was organized through a set of e-forums. One of his social informatics articles was posted as a lecture, and about twenty doctoral students were required to post one or two questions in response. The e-forum was structured with a special area (list) for Questions, and a separate area (list) for Answers. After reading some of the posted questions, it seemed that an online discussion would be more useful than simply posting static answers. Kling thus posted replies, comments, and questions of his own in the Questions area exclusively, and encouraged the doctoral students to respond there as well. He succeeded in developing a discussion that engaged over forty doctoral students during the two weeks; this would probably not have occurred if questions and answers had been kept to separate realms.

In this socio-technical view, then, the Internet is a "chunky" environment populated by many different kinds of spaces, each structured both socially and technically. Of particular interest to this chapter are the e-forums that support high levels of communication among participants. *Groups form around e-forums*, rather than simply "on the Internet." Among such e-forums, no one mode of social interaction predominates. Nor can they be easily aggregated into an umbrella Internet community. Instead, just as in face-to-face life, there are forums that resemble fan clubs, for example, while others resemble flea markets, and yet others look like task forces working closely on a project. And some may form communities. Each e-forum has its own norms, purpose, accessibility, and expectations, although many bear family resemblances to a cluster of similar e-forums and their participants. This forum-centered socio-technical approach will frame our examination of the e-ILF, following a more detailed discussion of forms of social organization.

SOCIAL ORGANIZATION: FROM TEAMS AND GROUPS TO COMMUNITIES

Empirical research in the social sciences has generated a plethora of categories to describe forms of social organization, ranging from teams and task forces to groups and communities. One convenient way to organize these types of social organization is to divide them according to their relationship to paid employment. Work-oriented forms of social organization include, for example, task forces and work teams, trade unions and guilds, professional associations and study groups, classrooms and skills centers. Each has notably different attributes, but what they share in general is their members' recognition that participation is either compulsory or highly beneficial for work-related advancement.

Non-work groups can be further divided into voluntary associations, which are generally task-oriented even if sociability plays a large role (Sills, 1968), and "hangouts," or non–task-oriented social formations (Oldenburg, 1999). Among the former can be found, for instance, clubs and nonprofessional associations, fan clubs, mutual self-help groups, congregations, resource centers, interest groups, and even gangs. Purely social hangouts include, for example, cafés, taverns, bookstores, farmers' markets, parks, beaches, malls, downtown, water coolers, and hair salons.

Sociological and anthropological studies have carefully examined these formations, and it is not difficult to identify and illustrate "typical" attributes and roles found in each. Communities, however, constitute a much more elusive analytical category, yet the term is used with increasing frequency in both lay and academic literature, particularly with regard to online social formations (cf. Hagel & Armstrong, 1997; Kim, 2000; Preece, 2000; Werry & Mowbray, 2001). We will examine both lay and academic uses of the term in the next section.

Sociological Communities?

Community is a strange and particularly resonant term in North American public life. Like many key concepts in the social sciences – including culture, learning, politics, and power – it has specific and restricted meanings for scholars, and broader connotations when it is used in lay language. As a lay term, community usually connotes a group that shares warm, caring, and reciprocal social relationships among its members. It is invoked routinely by politicians and real estate developers to set aspirations for places and their residents. As an analytical term, sociologists, anthropologists, and others have examined alternative definitions and the complex, multivalent social relationships between people who participate in various communities, including spatially concentrated villages and geographically dispersed professional associations (reviewed in Brint, 2001; Hillery, 1955; Morris, 1996). A major analytical effort by F. Tönnies (1887/1955) that gave a new empirical anchoring to German sociology in the late nineteenth century distinguished between two broadly conceived ideal types: village-style *Gemeinschaft* (community), associated with close ties and shared values, and city-style *Gesellschaft* (society), characterized by dispersed ties and dissimilar views.

In practice, Tönnies' categories are essentially mid-level social constructs used to characterize an intermediate level of social organization between individuals (or households) and the totality of a society, whose value is more practical than analytical. In particular, the term community has achieved this practical meaning in everyday life. For example, a call for "community management" of a federal program implies involvement by a potential range of nongovernmental actors including nonprofits, churches, or coalitions that are local to those who receive services. In this case, community is implicitly contrasted with a larger entity, the state, in terms of its style of management. Analytically, however, the term community must be more carefully examined. In a review of empirical studies, sociologist Stephen Brint (2001) has identified six dimensions of community that are well supported by the sociological research literature: (1) dense and demanding social ties; (2) social attachments to and involvements with institutions; (3) ritual occasions; (4) small group size; (5) perceptions of similarity with the physical characteristics, expressive style, way of life, or historical experience of others; and (6) common beliefs in an idea, a moral order, an institution, or a group. Brint notes that few groups share all of these characteristics simultaneously. In addition, research has associated each of these six dimensions with other social outcomes and characteristics. For example, dense social ties can be associated with conformity to the dominant morality in the group.

Brint also notes that careful empirical studies of communities do not reinforce their popular image in lay usage. For example, cooperation is not a defining characteristic of communities. In the 1930s and 1940s American sociologists were discovering hidden patterns of privilege, power, and inequality in communities that at first glance seemed cohesive. Sociologists also learned that what seemed like the spontaneous development of group consensus could often be a by-product of the self-interest of dominant status groups. Nevertheless, not only in lay and professional literatures, but also in scholarly literature, communities are most often represented as a highly desirable form of social relations, characterized by warmth, cooperation, and mutual support. This characterization is particularly prevalent in popular and professional literatures addressing education, business, and online sociability.

When a term is used to depict an ideal or desired state of affairs rather than to analyze an existing reality, it can be considered aspirational. One of the best-known examples is the stirring affirmation in the U.S. Declaration of Independence that "all men are created equal," despite the widespread practice of slavery in the colonies at the time, even among some of the declaration's authors. Of course, stating aspirations is important (as in the case of Martin Luther King's "I Have a Dream" speech), and sets a sense of direction for a common enterprise. Nevertheless, aspirational definitions are, by intent, empirically inaccurate. Their purpose is not to analyze existing realities, but rather to envision desirable future situations and thereby motivate change from the current conditions. We find that many uses of the term community are, in fact, aspirational rather than empirically grounded. Unfortunately, too many authors do not communicate the scope of the challenge involved in moving from what exists to what is desired. As a result, community-building tends to involve unforeseen levels of hard work, conflict, and renewed efforts at group mobilization to achieve.

Virtual Communities?

Another example of the aspirational use of the term community can be found in the vast literature describing online social interaction. Howard Rheingold (1993), who is frequently cited on the subject, defines virtual communities as "social aggregations that emerge from the Net when enough people carry on [. . .] public discussions long enough, with sufficient human feeling, to form webs of personal relations in cyberspace" (p. 5).

Our criticism of this definition is that it does not distinguish among the kinds of organizations that are basically groups, hangouts, associations, fan clubs, and, of course, communities (Kling, 1996). His descriptions of the activities that transpire inside online communities correspond to a rich range of human interaction found in any group situation, from commerce to flirting, but the focus on a conversational forum as the essence of community essentially flattens the concept and strips it of its social complexity.

Rheingold's definition of virtual communities has been highly influential in subsequent literature, and most published descriptions of online groups quite casually characterize the forum in question as a community, almost by virtue of the fact that its members interact online. Sometimes the use of the term is almost apologetic, in recognition of its market dominance. For example, according to Preece (2000), community is, in the final analysis, the best term to use for online social interaction, given that its "[w]idespread use by e-commerce entrepreneurs has in fact made the term a buzzword" (p. 9), and that it "has also become a blanket term to describe any collection of people who communicate online" (p. 17).

What writers most praise about virtual communities appears to be a sense of mutual engagement and openness among members, a "feeling" of community that is not analytical (cf. Bays & Mowbray, 2001; Bird, 1999; Kim, 2000; Rheingold, 1996). There seems to be an underlying equation of the term with solidarity, reciprocity, and support, even when criticism and conflict are acknowledged (Komito, 1998). These traits are very important, but they are equally characteristic of many kinds of groups, clubs, and other social forms that do not call themselves communities. In lay language, "sense of community" is often an idiomatic shorthand for these kinds of feelings, and particularly widespread in the North American cultural context. In short, community has a strong *symbolic* value that does not necessarily characterize real-life group interaction (Cohen, 1985; Miller, 1999). This implicit understanding of community issues a normative expectation regarding how participants in online forums ought to interact, but provides no clue as to how such interaction can be structured and motivated.

An extreme example of the misconceptions generated by the casual use of the term virtual community can be found in a recently published description of a website, *Through Our Parents' Eyes: Tucson's Diverse Community* (Glogoff, 2001).[2] The project, an online multimedia resource that brings together a wealth of heretofore unavailable information on the cultural heritage of Tucson residents, has inspired e-mail comments to the site's author from readers who express their appreciation, and who often share further details about their heritage and how the site has contributed to their self-awareness and pride. These social interactions, in the form of letters written directly to the site's owner and not published on the site for further discussion, form the basis for what Glogoff calls a *virtual community*, when in fact they are semi-private, bilateral communications. The site offers no support for visitors to identify and communicate with other interested visitors. It is a strange form of community where the participants do not and cannot easily recognize and interact with each other! We are in no sense critical of Glogoff's Tucson project, but rather of the sloppy, romantic way in which he has characterized the kind of social formation that has developed around it:

William J. Mitchell, in his important forward-looking book *City of Bits: Space, Place, and the Infobahn* (1995), predicted that "being online may soon become a more important mark of community membership than being in residence." This certainly has been the case with many of the Web exhibits in *Through Our Parents' Eyes.* They

<hr>

[2] http://www.library.arizona.edu/parents/

have attracted, for several years, people who self-identify with its content and seek out some degree of membership. Such behavior is consistent with the view that an essential element of building a climate of trust involves "feeling secure in revealing vulnerable parts of ourselves to others."

It could be argued that a kind of "imagined community" of Tucson is being developed through the website, analogous to Anderson's (1991) discussion of nations as "both inherently limited and sovereign," in which "the members of even the smallest nation will never know most of their fellow-members, meet them, or even hear of them, yet in the minds of each lives the image of their communion" (p. 6).

Glogoff's uncritical characterizations of social formations as communities do not promote understanding of the different types of social relationships that actually develop in electronic forums. Nor do they help devise ways to support e-forums through design, based on the characteristics of the target population and the theme of the venue. Using the term community to describe as diverse a range of groups as auction bidders, students in a distance education course, investors, and cancer patients (cf. Hagel & Armstrong, 1997; Werry & Mowbray, 2001), is unhelpful to scholars, designers, and even prospective participants. The use of the term is aspirational, and may be largely based on the need for recruitment of members, rather than on a description of empirical reality.

In contrast, Haythornthwaite, Kazmer, Robins, and Shoemaker (2000) found that the extent to which the students in an online degree program can be characterized as a community is a question to be resolved empirically, rather than by assumption. Analysis of the interpersonal ties that students developed in a distance education course that began with a face-to-face "boot camp" revealed many traits that are consistent with accepted definitions of community: recognition of members and nonmembers, a shared history, a common meeting place, commitment to a common purpose, adoption of normative standards of behavior, and emergence of hierarchy and roles. These data, although not identical to Brint's (2001) findings, would also support a community conception based on his six criteria. Interestingly enough, the study also documents how students eventually "disengaged" from the community as they finished the program.

Learning Communities?

According to Liana Nan Graves (1992), the term *learning communities* became popular among educators in the 1990s. Educators seem to take two major approaches in conceptualizing learning communities. One approach characterizes them in terms of *curricular organization*, such as "linked courses, which link cohorts of students taking two courses in common with one course typically content-based and the other application-based"

(Kellogg, 1999). Kellogg discusses five different models that emphasize the curricular structure for learning communities in higher education. This approach, centered around resource-sharing and structural arrangements, is similar to many existing e-forums, where the arrangement and accessibility of resources through socio-technical design can be central.

Other educators emphasize the *social relationships among participants* as most critical in conceptualizing learning communities. In particular, they stress certain kinds of human sociality that they believe are desirable, such as high levels of cooperation and collaboration between students, as well as between students and teachers (Graves, 1992). In this sense of the term, Graves uses the term community to signify "an inherently cooperative, cohesive, and self-reflective group entity whose members work on a regular, face-to-face basis toward common goals while respecting a variety of perspectives, values, and life styles." She itemizes several additional characteristics of learning communities: (1) "where everyone feels they belong and are respected"; (2) "where interaction is on-going, face-to-face, regular, and focused around common goals"; and (3) "a cohesive yet self-reflective group."

Developing and supporting cooperative learning groups is a major challenge, since the participants are asked to engage in more personal risk-taking behavior than in typical courses. Instructors are encouraged to step down from their stages (pedestals), and to act as coaches and co-participants who can display ignorance as well as knowledge. Social relationships may be multivalent, as when students are supposed to collaborate, but are also graded individually, and thus competitively. Graves (1992) discusses some approaches to developing learning communities, which rely on carefully planned stages of activity for encouraging trust and strengthening ties among members. Although a significant amount of work is required by teachers or facilitators, the concept of building a scaffolding for learning communities may be very useful for developing other kinds of communities as well.

Riel and Fulton (2001) discuss the ways that e-forums may support the development of geographically distributed learning communities. They write, however, as if face-to-face learning communities are an easily accomplished practice. Their example of a geographically dispersed learning community of teachers emphasizes the technological complexities (and anxieties) that teachers face and the ways that the participating teachers can require significant time to find ways to effectively use electronic media in their own teaching. In contrast with Graves, Riel and Fulton do not discuss how participating in a normative community can be difficult in terms of negotiating identities, learning to trust other participants, and taking professional risks (such as frankly acknowledging difficulties and failures).

In our own experience, observation, and reading of empirically reliable research, creating online groups of any form tacitly requires finding ways to support the social processes that would be typical of face-to-face groups, in addition to dealing with the complications of communication in a specific e-forum. When authors such as Riel and Fulton ignore the fragility of the social processes for developing effective learning communities of any kind, they set up unrealistic expectations about the issues that must be engaged in fostering distributed learning communities via e-forums.

A COMMON THEME: BUILDING TRUST

While many people portray groups as caring arrangements in which to share experiences and thoughts and learn new ideas and practices, group participation can involve risks – and thus require trust between participants. Students who share good information risk earning a lower grade than if they did not share when they are graded in a competitive environment. Students who ask for help may be seen as incapable (although that may also be a mark of pride in some schools for some topics). In professional development groups, teachers who share experiences of troubled teaching, and even of failure, risk being viewed as incompetent by their peers. Those who propose a novel idea risk the possibility of being seen as strange and perhaps even ostracized. We say that people are more willing to take risks in groups that develop a high level of trust.

There are several ways to characterize trust, and one of these is as a measure of risk. For example, Mayer, Davis, and Schoorman (1995) define trust as "the willingness of a party to be vulnerable to the actions of another party based on the expectation that the other will perform a particular action, irrespective of the ability to monitor or control that other party" (cited in Grabowski & Roberts, 1998). We can interpret each of the activities in the previous paragraph through the lens of this definition. Trust can develop over time, as people reciprocate in sharing information, demonstrate respect for one another, are careful in maintaining certain information as confidential, and so on. Each of these steps involves a certain measure of risk, and when that risk is rewarded, trust is more likely to develop.

While trusting relationships can facilitate learning in groups, they also facilitate the practical work of a wide variety of organizations. Thus, "trust at work" has been the subject of notable research in the field of organization studies (Kramer & Tyler, 1996). Of course, not all workplaces exemplify high levels of trust. For example, it is common for telephone operators and the staff of "800 number" service call centers to risk having any telephone call monitored, and may have their productivity measured daily. In contrast, the participants of engineering design teams must collaborate for months or even years before they have a "product" that can be assessed.

Working online complicates the formation of sustainable trust between people. In a face-to-face setting, people can see each other's appearance and gauge some emotional reactions during a conversation. Appearances can be deceiving or simply lead to stereotyping. But we are sufficiently accustomed to living with appearances that we all develop ways to interpret them for developing trust. In online communication, the participants have to work hard (through writing) to communicate something about themselves, and about each of their reactions. Grabowski and Roberts (1998) note that "[d]eveloping trust in VO's [virtual organizations] requires constant, continual communication among members to build relationships that provide the foundation for trust."

Jarvenpaa and Leidner (1998) studied the behavior of approximately seventy virtual teams composed of students in different countries enrolled in master's degree programs. They noted that e-forums offer the possibility for teams of people to work in different countries and collaborate. But they noted that "a dark side to the new form also exists: such dysfunctions as low individual commitment, role overload, role ambiguity, absenteeism, and social loafing may be exaggerated." They collected systematic data about these teams, and selected twelve for detailed investigation. In particular, they were interested in teams that started with low trust and those that started with high trust, and that also ended with either low trust or high trust. They examined trust trajectories over the lives of the teams. They found that some behaviors facilitated trust early in a group's life (i.e., communication of enthusiasm, coping with technical uncertainty). Other behaviors helped to maintain or enhance trust during a team's activities (i.e., predictable communication, substantial and timely responses).

Jarvenpaa and Leidner's study is important reading for anyone who is trying to develop learning communities online. Their specific findings may or may not translate literally to other settings. But some key ideas stand out: the importance of trust in teamwork; that groups may begin with varying levels of trust; and that the groups that increase their levels of trust or maintain high levels of trust work hard to do so in ways that are describable. In short, group solidarity online in the service of anything – work or play – is a fragile accomplishment rather than a gift that just "comes with the territory." Some educators have found that it is easier to develop the bases for trust in online groups through face-to-face means, and then to continue group work online. An interesting example, mentioned earlier, is Haythornthwaite et al.'s (2000) account of an online master's degree program at the University of Illinois. Each new cohort of students is required to visit the Urbana-Champaign campus to study together for a week in a "boot camp" at the beginning of each academic year. The students learn how to use various relevant technologies at boot camp. But they also work in varied groups, and the workload is such that high levels of cooperation are required. At boot camp, these students come to know and trust others in the class. Haythornthwaite et al.'s interviews with students during their work in the program indicate that these ties are exceptionally helpful after the students disperse and continue their study online. We realize that a practice that may be workable for an elite graduate program may not be feasible or even meaningful for other online courses and study groups. But it anchors the point that trust does not automatically develop for many groups online; it may require significant intervention for e-forum organizers to foster trust, either online or face-to-face, or both.

PARTICIPATING IN THE E-ILF

Initial Conceptions and Aspirations for the e-ILF

The Inquiry Learning Forum (ILF) was created in 1999 by researchers at the Indiana University School of Education as an online forum to support inquiry-based teaching and learning practices among Indiana science and math teachers at the secondary school level (see http://ilf.crlt. indiana.edu). The underlying conception was to provide a set of interesting teaching materials and online forums, the e-ILF, where teachers could discuss them and reflect on their own teaching practices, and function as a "community of practice" (Barab, MaKinster, Moore, et al., 2001).

"Communities of practice are informal networks that support professional practitioners to develop a shared meaning and engage in knowledge building among the members" (Hara, 2000, p. 11). This definition is based on Wenger's elements of communities of practice (CoPs): negotiating meaning among participants; preserving and creating knowledge; and supporting the development of identities (Wenger, 1998). Some recent studies of how people learn technical, craft, and professional skills found that new entrants to an occupation learn informally through discussions and observations with others who do similar work. These studies include a wide range of occupations, including flute-makers, office equipment technicians, and lawyers in public defenders' offices (Hara, 2000).

The ILF research team was concerned that in-service teachers have limited opportunities to discuss and observe teaching practices with other teachers because they are often all in their own classrooms at the same time. In contrast, for example, Hara (2000) found that the public defenders in a county court would attend each others' major trials to observe how their co-workers interacted with juries, judges, and witnesses. Being a good public defender is not simply based on knowing the law, or in developing the basis for a case. A public defender has to work with witnesses and evidence, in front of a judge, to convince a jury of a particular position. In a similar way, being a great math teacher is not based simply on knowing a great deal of mathematics. Great teachers develop strategies and a language for communicating mathematical concepts to their students and stimulating their interests in mathematics. However, teachers have little opportunity to visit each others' classrooms to observe and to discuss their teaching in action.

In 1999, the School of Education faculty who were associated with the ILF interviewed a number of science and mathematics teachers about their professional development experiences (see MaKinster, Barab, & Keating, 2001; Barab, MaKinster, Moore, et al., 2001). They found that many of their in-service teacher informants expressed an interest in seeing other teachers teach. These faculty translated these interests into a conception in which an e-ILF would provide facilities that illustrated some of the key elements of a classroom visit, such as videos of class segments, the relevant lesson plans, and reflections by the teacher about his or her class. In addition, each virtual classroom would support a local discussion list in which teachers could reflect on the class materials and on their own teaching. The Education faculty expected communities of practice that focused on inquiry learning in math and in science to develop through these online discussions. Other features of the e-ILF include a lounge, for more general threaded online conversation, and thus further support for the development of CoPs, as well as spaces for closed working groups and a resource center. (See Barab, MaKinster, & Scheckler, this volume, for a more detailed discussion of the e-ILF's design.)

The ILF researchers took a strong stance that fostering inquiry-oriented teaching by enhancing teachers' understanding of their own classroom practice was a primary focus of the site. The research team knew that certain services, such as providing a large library of "canned lesson plans" that teachers could download and apply immediately, would almost certainly attract many more teachers. But they did not see such a lesson plan service as enhancing teachers' capabilities in the long run. They saw it as more akin to enabling students to download term papers, rather than developing the skills to write their own. Thus, the lesson plans on the e-ILF were part of a larger portfolio of materials in a specific classroom that illustrated teaching a specific topic (such as the concept of temperature or Pythagorus's theorem).

In 2000, the ILF staff identified fourteen Indiana teachers who were willing to have parts of their classroom activities videotaped and posted in an online classroom about their teaching on the e-ILF. In addition, these teachers provided their lesson plans and notes about teaching this lesson, which were also posted in their e-ILF virtual classrooms. We estimate that each teacher spent about thirty hours working with the ILF staff to develop a virtual classroom that was organized around one lesson.

The ILF research team expected teachers to develop reflective online discussion groups on their own. In fact, one major research question was, "How do the ILF members structure themselves into communities and how do we promote boundary crossing?" Barab and Duffy (2002) characterized communities of practice in these terms: "Much like a living organism, they are self-organizing, and cannot be designed *prima facie*. They grow, evolve, and change dynamically, transcending any particular member and outliving any particular task."

Some structures, such as the sample classrooms and a lounge, were created by the ILF staff, who worked with specific teachers to develop materials for each online classroom. But the ILF staff were not expected to moderate any of the resulting discussions. There were also few cues and clues for participants about how they should behave in the e-ILF, or what specific expectations they could have about others' participation (i.e., frequency of posting). This model of autonomous group organization has been very successful for such professional e-forums as scientific Usenet Newsgroups, Bionet, and nonrecreational services such as the message boards on ParentsPlace.com. The registered e-ILF members include in-service and pre-service teachers, along with ILF researchers and developers. Those who wish to participate in the e-ILF are screened by ILF staff to ensure that they are appropriate teachers, student teachers, or associates of the project. Potential participants such as parents and journalists are not accorded access to the e-ILF, by request of the teachers who helped to create its virtual classrooms.[3] The participants on the e-ILF are identified by pseudonyms they choose themselves (often compressed versions of real names), although ILF researchers and highly active teachers include their real names in their postings and profiles. ILF staff have access to the identities and profiles of all members, who in turn can control the level of personal and professional information revealed to other members on the site.

e-ILF Activity from Spring 2000 to Mid-2001

By late 2001, there were twenty-one videotaped "classrooms" on the ILF website. Over 300 in-service teachers out of approximately 26,000 secondary math and science teachers in Indiana had registered for the ILF, along with some 430 pre-service teachers at Indiana University. However, participation in the e-ILF has not reflected the breadth of this membership: statistics collected in February 2001 show that only 14 percent of in-service teachers had visited the site five or more times, and 9 percent had visited ten or more times. Online discussion by in-service teachers has been limited to a relatively small group, whose numbers have increased rather slowly: 58 of the site's 320 registered in-service teachers (18%) had posted a total of five or more messages by October 2001, up from 35 of 202 (17%)

---

[3] Originally, school administrators were denied access to the site at the request of teachers, but this restriction was removed in early 2001.

by February. Only 6 percent had posted a total of ten or more times by October. Pre-service teachers have recently begun posting more actively on the site, principally because e-ILF participation is often part of their learning requirements: 147 of 432 pre-service teachers (34%) had posted five or more times by October 2001, up sharply from 51 of 183 (28%) before February.

The number of posted messages connected to each classroom varies widely, but a typical set of fifteen posts is threaded into 6–7 topics with anywhere from 0–3 responses each. The "lounge" section of the website contains general topics for discussion, with a typical topic taking up 15–30 posts over a one-year period.

These levels of participation are not unusual, particularly for such a new forum. Empirical research on other e-forums also shows evidence of highly concentrated levels of participation. For example, Nonnecke and Preece (2000) found that over 70 percent of subscribers to health-related discussion groups posted three or fewer times in a twelve-week period; lurking levels for software-related discussion groups exceeded 90 percent. Selwyn (2000), in his analysis of two years of postings to an electronic discussion group for teachers in Great Britain, found that one-third of all posted messages came from only 26 of its 900 members.

But ILF research team members have expressed concern that the on-line exchanges among teachers do not display the levels of engagement and critical reflection that were initially expected from what was to be a community of learners. An example of a typical supportive post:

Just watched your video. It's good to see someone brave enough to go on film. You seem to enjoy what you are doing and your class seems to show you much respect. I think it is great to see a teacher laugh with her students and they laugh back. Great job!

The videotaped classrooms nevertheless represent a touchstone for discussion and learning. Many teachers' posts are requests for further information that could help them link their own methods to the practices observed on the video clips:

I think you had a good idea of using 2 people in a group and having two questions (one for each to do) and one to do together. What do you do if you have a student who doesn't want to participate at all?

In the lounge section of the e-ILF, teachers discuss substantive issues that arise in math and science teaching, and present many different views on inquiry-based teaching and learning. In this area, the teachers' posts consist of opinions or questions without reference to the videotaped classrooms, and they often mention useful outside resources. Although there is little evidence of direct critical engagement with other opinions, and many postings go unanswered, the tone of the postings is self-reflective, helpful, and engaging. For example:

Many of my students lack this background knowledge and I am at a loss on how to teach the standards that are expected, encourage inquiry and supply sufficient background knowledge.
    . . . I think the important thing to do is to find out what your students know and go from there. If your students are struggling with open or guided inquiry, go back and try something more concrete.
    . . . What does everyone feel about that? Have you experienced problems with open inquiry in advanced or basic classes?

In response to the perceived lack of critical engagement, some ILF staff have posted messages to stimulate more engagement, by asking questions in response to comments, making critical observations, and referring to specific aspects of the videos. For example:

Can you be more specific. What subject? What techniques?
    . . . I would have liked to see your lecture extended and given as a separate lesson. You were covering so much relevant and necessary information. I felt like you were trying to hurry through information and especially at first you were simply feeding the information, *instead of trying to elicit it from the students.*

According to Selwyn (2000), one indicator of community is an explicit sense of group identity that some participants mention in their discussions. In his study of teachers' use of an electronic discussion list, Selwyn found little if any evidence of such a "sense of community," of engagement among members in a common mission. Likewise, in the e-ILF, the messages posted in both the classroom and the lounge forums lack any mention of the group. The postings tend to be about general and specific aspects of the forum's common idea, inquiry teaching and learning, but do not express a bond among its members as Indiana teachers engaged in a common mission or as e-ILF participants. More importantly, Selwyn also found that participants carefully maintained a professional and formal air as teachers, taking care not to risk exposure as incompetent. This appears to be replicated in the e-ILF. As in Selwyn's group, there is no "staff-room talk" on the e-ILF that could build trust and help forge closer personal relationships among members, thereby adding another dimension of community.

The e-ILF might be contrasted, for example, to an online financial site visited over a one-year period by one of the authors. The site was organized into dozens of individual discussion groups. In a few of these, participants gradually revealed additional information regarding their identities if they felt confidence in the group's usefulness and in the reliability of other members; conversely, new members were often asked to reveal personal information or "bona fides" in order to obtain a thoughtful response to a question. Moreover, in those groups in which mutual confidence was rewarded, there were numerous references to group identity and a common mission, and members often engaged in other forms of social interaction, such as migrating together to new groups, meeting offline, or interspersing philosophical and personal discussions. Some participants criticized others harshly, although the more cohesive groups tended to exercise peer pressure to maintain norms of civility and encourage open, trusting exchanges.

Thus, with the exception of commitment to the common idea of inquiry-based teaching, the e-ILF does not correspond to the sociological criteria for community identified by Brint (see above). Nor does it satisfy Graves' aspirational criteria for learning communities. Nevertheless, some teachers are using the e-ILF to learn and share new ideas among peers, and their numbers are steadily growing. In this sense, the site is a valuable peer-to-peer resource center for in-service and pre-service teachers to view teaching examples, obtain ideas for their own practice, and share opinions on the subject of inquiry-based teaching and learning. As such, the continuation of the e-ILF along present lines suggests an online social formation equivalent to a useful drop-in center for teachers' professional development in the area of inquiry-based teaching. The ILF could provide important benefits to its members and their students, but the activity is still in a very early stage, and it is too soon to assess productively.

Even in face-to-face situations, promoting both collegiality and critical engagement among teachers has long been perceived as a problem. In fact, the nature of the ILF interactions described above are consistent with empirical research on teachers' interactions in general, which are characterized by a lack of direct advice or criticism (Ellis, 1993; Little, 1985, 1990). Overcoming this "etiquette" (Little, 1985) and promoting greater critical engagement and a sense of group identity might require mechanisms – both online and offline – conducive to forging greater trust among ILF members for open, frank discussions and engagement. If the e-ILF aspires to move beyond its present resemblance to a professional development site in order to build stronger mutual ties among members that more resemble a community, certain structural changes might be necessary to stimulate such engagement, trust, and group identity.

Building Support for Community Activity in the e-ILF

In her discussion of learning communities, Graves (1992) notes:

In the early stages of building a community – whether classroom, school, faculty group, or administrative team – people are concerned with finding a place for themselves within the group. This involves:
- becoming acquainted with other group members on a friendly basis: Who are you?
- presenting oneself to the group and being accepted as a valuable member: Who am I? . . .

... classrooms, schools, and educator support groups are not natural communities – that is, there is usually no built-in reason such as kinship or generational village ties to bring these people together. . . . We need to encourage strong standards of equality and honoring of diversity . . . We can do this in two ways. The first is by offering opportunities to get to know one another under circumstances that maximize enjoyable interaction while creating opportunities for information exchange and problem solving.

Graves goes on to discuss a wide variety of group-building activities that may help people come to know each other and work together under differing levels of risk-taking and accomplishment. Many of these observations are applicable to the challenges facing the e-ILF. Here, building community among its members will probably require structural changes to provide both spaces and mechanisms in which trust, familiarity, and group identity can be forged among members. In keeping with our conceptual understanding of online spaces as both socially and technically structured, *we believe that such changes cannot only be instituted through technological redesign, but must include offline measures as well.*

The expectation that teachers would self-organize CoPs in the e-ILF's virtual classrooms has not yet been realized. In light of Graves' observations, we suspect that the development of CoPs could require a much more interventionist strategy in which moderators try to encourage participants to get to know each other (for example, by posting some personal as well as professional information in their online bios) and help to focus and deepen the online discussions. These kinds of interventionist activities are difficult because they make more demands on participants for self-revelation, and for reading and posting in specific time frames, while the ILF strategy has been to attract participants by making no demands upon them after they register.

Bounded Groups

During the first year of the e-ILF's operation, there were several requests to support the discussions of groups that wanted private spaces. One such group, which is developing a curricular framework for mathematics (Collaboration to Enhance Mathematics Instruction, CEMI), is led by a key faculty member of the ILF research team. The workspaces for the bounded groups include private discussion lists, as well as spaces to post documents, link to external resources, and so on.

This request for a space on the e-ILF was accepted, although the research team was initially reluctant to encourage more bounded groups. Subsequently, several additional groups requested bounded spaces for their own discussions. These included a group of high school physics teachers and a physics professor who are developing a collaborative experimental project, a group of biology teachers who are developing curricular plans to study watersheds, and another group of biology teachers who use salamanders in their classes. After continuing deliberations, the ILF team decided to support such groups and encourage others.

As of early 2002, over two dozen bounded groups have been formed on the e-ILF. These groups constitute naturally forming teams and potential communities of practice, in which relations of trust among members might be expected to develop more easily than in the open forums, for reasons we have explained above. The hard work of team or community development – including trust-building, and of recruiting participants – is done by others who are usually based outside of the ILF. The e-ILF has the relatively easy task of providing some of the communications infrastructure to enable these groups of teachers to carry out their work, although it is likely that the ILF will also have to play a role in encouraging their formation and stimulating both online and offline activities. It remains to be seen whether the growth of interactions within bounded groups will also eventually lead to interactions across them, a development that could strengthen the ILF in a way that is consistent with its designers' goals.

Ironically, the importance of bounding groups to facilitate trust in electronic forums has been known before the development of the ILF project. Feenberg (1986) identified its importance for electronic conferences, and Bakardjieva and Feenberg (2002) note that it is an important feature to support democratic relationships in electronic forums. DiMauro and Gal (1994) recommended that online forums have space for bounded groups to support trust between teachers. Somehow, these ideas did not travel rapidly enough to Bloomington!

THE E-ILF IN COMPARATIVE PERSPECTIVE

Reflective Dialogue and Trusting Group Behavior Online

We began this chapter with a provocative stance, by claiming that "the casual use of community to characterize groups that are engaged in learning, or groups that participate in e-forums, is seriously misguided." The ILF project has a set of ambitious goals that rest on the possibility of *developing online forums that enable teachers to improve their abilities to teach in an inquiry style through participating in communities of practice.* This approach rests on several complex assumptions: (a) that a critical mass of teachers would be willing to participate actively in some kind of online forums about inquiry-learning; (b) that open-ended discussions of sample teaching episodes would be valuable to participating teachers; (c) that teachers would self-initiate reflective dialogue about the online classroom materials and their own teaching; (d) that teachers who were participating in the e-ILF would develop a sense of group identity and forge mutual trust via online interactions; and (e) that their group identities would be transformed over time into lively communities of practice.

Translating each of these assumptions into a practice on the e-ILF is a significant accomplishment. As Graves noted, developing a community *is* an accomplishment. Unfortunately, in the early stages of the ILF Project, the tendency to characterize the e-ILF as a community space distracted attention from the vexing issues about what would be required to transform it from an electronic forum with facilities that could support conversations into a space in which communities of practice were actually forming. Our examination of interactions on e-ILF shows that although it has value as an online resource for teachers, it does not at this time resemble a community. It is easier to provide communication infrastructure for pre-existing groups than it is to use an e-forum to develop high-performing groups and CoPs directly. Thus, the e-ILF may benefit from the addition of bounded groups, which involve greater engagement, stimulate trust, and are complemented by offline activities, thereby enabling the ILF to support a wider variety of inquiry projects. At the same time, the ILF could play a less demanding social role of having to support all stages of development of the community of practice it envisions. Unfortunately, the difficulties of supporting reflective dialogue and community building in online forums seem to be under-appreciated within the educational communities. The best research that we have found about trust building for online groups has been conducted by Information Systems faculty who study teamwork online (see earlier discussion). In contrast, Sherry (2000) is all too typical in unreflectively reporting claims that: "One advantage of text-based communication is that written communication tends to be more reflective than spoken interaction. The very act of assembling one's thoughts and articulating them in writing for a conference audience appears to involve deeper cognitive processing'" (Berge, 1997, p. 10).

Claims framed in this way make it appear that the use of text-based electronic communication will almost certainly lead to reflective dialogues where assumptions are evaluated, alternatives discussed, and contexts carefully explored. Yet, according to research on typical teaching practices in the United States, teachers rarely engage in this kind of discussion when they are meeting face-to-face (Little, 1982, 1985, 1990). Perhaps we should not be surprised to find that such reflective discussion does not spontaneously arise in the e-ILF.

Our observations of the e-ILF discussions are consistent with mid-1990s research findings from the LabNet project, an e-forum to support the professional development of science teachers. DiMauro and Gal (1994) examined the online discussions of a group of science teacher leaders who were acting as liaisons to the staff of an online professional development project. A network infrastructure was designed to enable these teachers to "exchange to reflect upon their involvement with peer leadership and teacher-teacher support." They characterized messages as informative, responsive (to a query), or reflective (one in which a participant "thinks out loud" about some teaching practice and different ways of approaching it). DiMauro and Gal note that reflective postings were very infrequent. Most seriously, they observe, "Reflective responses are difficult to formulate and risky to post because of the personal nature of the content." They speculate about the conditions that support reflective postings, and suggest that they include "protected workspace for reflection, retrieved text base, collaborative research, access and response to messages, structure dialogue, linking action with reflection, forming reflective practice inquiry, and participatory motivation." Some of these conditions are found on the e-ILF (i.e., retrieved text base). However, only the bounded groups have a protected workspace for reflection. In contrast, postings in the virtual classrooms may be read by any student teacher or in-service teacher who joins the e-ILF in the future and, as a result of recent changes to the site, by school administrators.

In a related study that is also based on observations of LabNet dialogues, Spitzer, Wedding, and DiMauro (1995) published a significant set of suggestions for promoting more reflective discussions on LabNet. Apparently, the LabNet discussion groups were usually moderated. Like Graves, they recommended that the forum moderators explicitly find ways to build trust among participants, such as "get to know each other by talking about your situation, interests, etc." They tried to promote group development with suggestions such as, "Invite people to join via e-mail and e-mail lists"; "Move a private e-mail dialogue to a public forum"; and "Ask thought-provoking questions that ask for another's idea or point of view, and make your intentions explicit." Their strategies, which encourage the moderators to engage members in thinking and doing, are extremely labor-intensive. Unfortunately, they provide no data about how well various Lab-Net moderators adopted these strategies (or other interventions), and with what effects. Nonetheless, Spitzer et al. suggest that supporting reflective dialogues online and developing community require significant and committed communicative and social work.

In the end, community development is likely to be a complex accomplishment that is difficult to initiate without purposive interventions from some kind of leaders or stewards. It will rarely happen online alone through self-organizing.

How do Lively Online Places Happen?

This discussion leaves open the question about how some professional e-forums such as scientific Usenet Newsgroups, Bionet, and nonrecreational services such as the message boards on ParentsPlace.com, become lively places. In our view, they demand less from their participants than does the e-ILF. Most of the sites like these that we know are organized as professional or personal help groups. For example, the postings that we have read on BioNet are often focused on questions raised by a stymied researcher who has trouble getting some specific piece of equipment to work.

For example, a posting in a forum for discussing ACEDB (A C.Elegans database) in June 2001, was framed as follows:

Hello, I am trying to set up saceserver on my machine, following the "User Guide To Sockets-based Client/Server"; I experience some troubles.

I am using acedb 4.9a. saceserver (and saceclient) are doing just fine when launched in the foreground. But when launched through inetd (actually, it is xinetd on my machine), I get a FATAL ERROR – (fc on grun.marseille.inserm.fr) reported by program saceclient (ACEDB 4.9a), in file acesocketlib.c, at line 284: connect error system error 111 – Connection refused

/etc/services :
acedb 20113/tcp

/etc/xinetd.conf:
acedb stream tcp wait acedb /usr/local/bin/saceserver saceserver
/database/acedb 200:200:0

acedb is a valid user on my machine

saceserver is -rwxr-xr-x

Any help will be appreciated!

A response one week later resulted in a technical dialogue that lasted another two weeks. The question and answer form of dialogue is also common for teachers (Lewison, 2001). It is similar to the informative postings identified by DiMauro and Gal (1994) on LabNet, and by Selwyn (2000) on a teachers' discussion list. We have seen a significant amount of highly focused technical Q&As on the BioNet groups, and no significant discussions that sound like scientific reflections. Some of the lists on BioNet support researchers who participate in a tightly knit research community and who have numerous complex interactions offline as colleagues, in conferences, as editors and reviewers, and so on. (In this sense, in fact, BioNet resembles some aspects of the e-ILF's bounded groups.)

In another realm, ParentsPlace.com offers its participants an opportunity to raise questions about parenting and affords them a good chance of hearing comments from other parents. The primary dialogic format is also question and answer. Further, most participants are pseudonymous. One recent paragraph-long post about toddlers began:

Hi everybody, I don't usually post here but . . . desperate times call for desperate measures! I babysit for four kids, and the boy who's 3.5 has had some aaawful tantrums lately and I have no idea what to do about it.

The writer received a pseudonymous reply asking some questions and offering some advice within a day. Most of the dialogues on

ParentsPlace.com seem to be Q&A; few comments are reflective. Most seriously, the pseudonymous writer is able to express extreme despera-tion based on her inability to manage her relationship with the 3-1/2-year-old boy. Yet based on the experience of the teachers' online forum studied by Selwyn (2000), it would be implausible for an e-ILF partic-ipant to express this level of interpersonal incapability (and thus pro-fessional vulnerability) in discussing dilemmas of teaching. In terms of willingness to risk looking incompetent, there appears to be a significant difference between the situation of entirely pseudonymous parents and caregivers, on the one hand, and that of teachers – whose anonymity is not fully ensured by the e-ILF, for example – on the other. Yet in order to build the type of community of practice sought by the ILF, teachers must become willing to engage in professionally risky conversations in order to build trust and group identity. The overall level of support work re-quired by its moderators and organizers, therefore, will be concomitantly greater.

CONCLUSIONS

The ILF has ambitious goals in encouraging both reflective discussions of teaching via inquiry and also supporting the development of com-munities of practice in support of inquiry teaching. To fulfill these goals, the ILF must be capable of supporting a high level of trust-building and other social practices that cannot be readily "wired into" the design of an e-forum, but instead require a significant investment of time and human resources, and perhaps even offline work as well. It is possible that some arrangements that offload the community-building to others, such as the bounded groups, may enable the e-ILF to provide a different kind of useful role in supporting professional development activities of geographically dispersed teachers.

We have illustrated two approaches to building online groups that differ sharply. The original ILF strategy of bringing teachers together via discus-sions of classrooms illustrates "IT-led group development." In contrast, the bounded groups illustrate "IT-supported group development." The IT-led strategies are much more difficult to make workable. Some of the best examples that we know of, such as ParentsPlace.com, do not place a strong emphasis upon group formation, but instead function essentially as peer-run resource and mutual help centers. Other examples, such as online group game sites, offer their players a form of entertainment by participat-ing in game-playing "guilds." Yet the expectation of using IT to play the leading role in forming close, trusting groups is not likely to be fulfilled. In contrast, effective IT-*supported* groups are very common, since they do not require that the various and complex processes of group formation and group development rely principally on an electronic forum. Instead, the role of the e-forum is to enhance, extend, and support wider group processes and goals. We believe that this approach will be more fruitful, not only for the ILF, but also for a wide range of professional, group, and learning endeavors.

References

Ahuna, C. (2001). *Online game communities are social in nature.* Retrieved July 15, 2001, from the World Wide Web: http://switch.sjsu.edu/v7n1/articles/cindy02.html.

Anderson, B. R. (1991). *Imagined communities: Reflections on the origin and spread of nationalism* (rev. and extended ed.). London: Verso.

Bakardjieva, M., & A. Feenberg. (2002). Community technology and democratic rationalization. *The Information Society, 18*(3), 181–192.

Barab, S. A., & Duffy, T. M. (2000). From practice fields to communities of practice. In D. Jonassen & S. M. Land (Eds.), *Theoretical foundations of learning environments* (pp. 25–56). Mahwah, NJ: Lawrence Erlbaum Associates.

Barab, S. A., MaKinster, J., Moore, J., Cunningham, D., & the ILF Design Team. (2001). The Inquiry Learning Forum: A new model for online professional development. *Educational Technology Research and Development, 49*(4), 71–96.

Barab, S. A., MaKinster, J., & Scheckler, R. (in press). Designing system dualities: Building online community. (this volume).

Bays, H., & Mowbray, M. (2001). Cookies, gift-giving, and online communities. In C. Werry & M. Mowbray (Eds.), *Online communities: Commerce, community action, and the virtual university* (pp. 47–70). Upper Saddle River, NJ: Prentice Hall.

Berge, Z. (1997). Computer conferencing and the on-line classroom. *International Journal of Educational Telecommunications, 3*(1), 3–21.

Bird, S. E. (1999). Chatting on Cynthia's porch: Creating community in an e-mail fan group. *Southern Communication Journal, 65*(1), 49–65.

Brint, S. (2001). *Gemeinschaft* revisited: A critique and reconstruction of the community concept. *Sociological Theory, 19*(1), 1–23.

Cerf, V. (2001, May 15). *A brief history of the Internet and related networks.* Internet Society. Retrieved June 22, 2001, from the World Wide Web: http://www.isoc.org/internet-history/.

Cohen, A. P. (1985). *The symbolic construction of community.* London: Tavistock Publications.

DiMauro, V., & Gal, S. (1994). The use of telecommunications for reflective discourse of science teacher leaders. *Journal of Science Education and Technology, 3*(2). Retrieved October 2, 2001, from the World Wide Web: http://www.terc.edu/papers/labnet/Articles/Reflective/reflective.html.

Ellis, N. E. (1993). Collegiality from the teacher's perspective: Social contexts for professional development. *Action in Teacher Education, 15*(1), 42–48.

Feenberg, A. (1986). Network design: An operating manual for computer conferencing. *IEEE Transactions on Professional Communications, PC29*(1), 2–7.

Glogoff, S. (2001). Virtual connections: Community bonding on the net. *First Monday, 6*(3). Retrieved March 7, 2001, from the World Wide Web: http://firstmonday. org/issues/issue6_3/glogoff/.

Grabowski, M., & Roberts, K. H. (1998). Risk mitigation in virtual organizations. *Journal of Computer-Mediated Communication, 3*(4). Retrieved July 18, 2001, from the World Wide Web: http://www.ascusc.org/jcmc/vol3/issue4/ grabowski.html.

Graves, L. N. (1992). Cooperative learning communities: Context for a new vision of education and society. *Journal of Education, 174*(2), 57–79.

Hagel, J., & Armstrong, A. G. (1997). *Net gain: Expanding markets through virtual communities.* Boston, MA: Harvard Business School Press.

Hara, N. (2000). *Social construction of knowledge in professional communities of practice: Tales in courtrooms.* Unpublished doctoral dissertation, Indiana University, Bloomington.

Haythornthwaite, C., Kazmer, M. M., Robins, J., & Shoemaker, S. (2000). Community development among distance learners: Temporal and technological dimensions. *Journal of Computer-Mediated Communication, 6*(1). Retrieved Oct 2, 2000, from the World Wide Web: http://www.ascusc.org/jcmc/vol6/issue1/ haythornthwaite.html.

Hillery, G. A. (1955). Definitions of community: Areas of agreement. *Rural Sociology, 20,* 111–123.

Jarvenpaa, S. L., & Leidner, D. E. (1998). Communication and trust in global virtual teams. *Journal of Computer-Mediated Communication, 3*(4). Retrieved July 11, 2001, from the World Wide Web: http://www.ascusc.org/jcmc/vol3/ issue4/jarvenpaa.html.

Kellogg, K. (1999). *Learning communities* (EDO-HE-1999–1). Washington, DC: ERIC Digest.

Kim, A. J. (2000). *Community building on the Web: Secret strategies for successful online communities.* Berkeley, CA: Peachpit Press.

Kling, R. (1996). Social relationships in electronic forums: Hangouts, Salons, workplaces and communities. In R. Kling (Ed.), *Computerization and controversy: Value conflicts and social choice* (2d ed.) (pp. 112–139). San Diego: Academic Press.

Kling, R. (2000). Learning about information technologies and social change: The contribution of social informatics. *The Information Society, 16*(3), 217–232.

Kolbert, E. (2001, May 28). Pimps and dragons. *The New Yorker,* 88–98.

Komito, L. (1998). The Net as a foraging society: Flexible communities. *The Information Society, 14,* 97–106.

Kramer, R. M., & Tyler, T. R. (Eds.). (1996). *Trust in organizations.* Thousand Oaks, CA: Sage.

Lewison, M. (2001). Personal communication.

Little, J. W. (1982). Norms of collegiality and experimentation: Workplace conditions of school success. *American Educational Research Journal, 19,* 325–340.

Little, J. W. (1985, November). Teachers as teacher advisors: The delicacy of collegial leadership. *Educational Leadership,* 34–36.

Little, J. W. (1990). The persistence of privacy: Autonomy and initiative in teachers' professional relations. *Teachers College Record, 91*(4), 509–536.

MaKinster, J. G., Barab, S. A., & Keating, T. M. (2001). Design and implementation of an on-line professional development community: A project-based learning approach in a graduate seminar. *Electronic Journal of Science Education, 5*(3). Retrieved October 2, 2001, from the World Wide Web: http://unr.edu/homepage/crowther/ejse/ejsev5n3.html.

Mayer, R. C., Davis, J. H., & Schoorman, F. D. (1995). An integrative model of organizational trust. *Academy of Management Review, 20,* 709–734.

Miller, L. J. (1999). Shopping for community: The transformation of the bookstore into a vital community institution. *Media Culture and Society, 21*(3), 385–407.

Morris, E. W. (1996). Community in theory and practice: A framework for intellectual renewal. *Journal of Planning Literature, 11*(1), 127–150.

Nonnecke, B., & Preece, J. (2000, April). *Lurker demographics: Counting the silent.* Paper presented at the CHI 2000 Conference on Human Factors in Computing Systems, The Hague, Netherlands.

Oldenburg, R. (1999). *The great good place: Cafés, coffee shops, bookstores, bars, hair salons, and other hangouts at the heart of a community* (2d ed.). New York: Marlowe.

Preece, J. (2000). *Online communities: Designing usability and supporting sociability.* New York: John Wiley & Sons.

Quittner, J. (1994, May). The war between alt.tasteless and rec.pets.cats. *Wired, 2.05.* Retrieved July 11, 2001, from the World Wide Web: http://www.wired.com/wired/archive/2.05/alt.tasteless pr.html.

Rheingold, H. (1993). *The virtual community: Homesteading on the electronic frontier.* Reading, MA: Addison-Wesley.

Rheingold, H. (1996). A slice of my life in my virtual community. In P. Ludlow (Ed.), *High noon on the electronic frontier: Conceptual issues in cyberspace* (pp. 413–436). Cambridge, MA: MIT Press.

Riel, M., & Fulton, K. (2001, March). The role of technology in supporting learning communities. *Phi Delta Kappan, 82,* 518–523.

Selwyn, N. (2000). Creating a 'connected' community? Teachers' use of an electronic discussion group. *Teachers College Record, 102*(4), 750–778.

Sherry, L. (2000). The nature and purpose of online conversations: A brief synthesis of current research. *International Journal of Educational Telecommunications, 6*(1), 19–52.

Sills, D. L. (1968). Voluntary associations: Sociological aspects. In D. L. Sills (Ed.), *International encyclopedia of the social sciences* (vol. 16, pp. 362–379). New York: Macmillan.

Spitzer, W., Wedding, K., & DiMauro, V. (1995). Fostering Reflective Dialogues for Teacher Professional Development. TERC. Retrieved October 2, 2001, from the World Wide Web: http://www.terc.edu/papers/labnet/Guide/Fostering Refl Dialogues.html.

Sterling, B. (1993). Short history of the Internet. Retrieved July 19, 2001, from the World Wide Web: http://w3.aces.uiuc.edu/AIM/scale/nethistory.html.

Tönnies, F. (1887/1955). *Community and association.* London: Routledge & Kegan Paul.

Weber, M. (1949). *The methodology of the social sciences.* Glencoe, IL: Free Press.

Wenger, E. (1998). *Communities of practice: Learning, meaning, and identity.* Cambridge: Cambridge University Press.

Werry, C., & Mowbray, M. (Eds.). (2001). *Online communities: Commerce, community action, and the virtual university.* Upper Saddle River, NJ: Prentice Hall.

Zakon, R. H. (2001, April 15). *Hobbes' Internet Timeline v5.3.* Retrieved June 22, 2001, from the World Wide Web: http://www.zakon.org/robert/internet/timeline/.

5

Teacher Professional Development, Technology, and Communities of Practice

Are We Putting the Cart before the Horse?

Mark S. Schlager and Judith Fusco

> Practice, then, both shapes and supports learning. We wouldn't need to labor this point so heavily were it not that unenlightened teaching and training often pulls in the opposite direction.
>
> Brown & Duguid (2000, p. 129)

In their book *The Social Life of Information*, Brown and Duguid (2000) analyze examples of learning in the context of professional practice and the ways in which information technology supports or fails to support professional learning. Failure is related to neglect of ways in which people learn, their resourcefulness in solving problems, and the communities of practice in which they participate. As the opening quotation suggests, training (and technology that supports a training model of learning) tends to pull professionals away from their practice, focusing on information about a practice rather than on how to put that knowledge into practice. Only by engaging in work and talking about it from inside the practice can one learn to be a competent practitioner. They conclude that "practice is an effective teacher and the community of practice an ideal learning environment" (p. 127).

Over the past several years, we have been developing and refining the sociotechnical infrastructure of a virtual environment called Tapped In® (www.tappedin.org) that is intended to support the online activities of a large and diverse community of education professionals. We have described the design principles that underlie our efforts and documented

The work presented in this chapter was supported in part by National Science Foundation Grant REC-9725528. We are grateful to the editors of this volume and the other authors for their support and commentary on drafts of the chapter. We are indebted to the other members of our own community of practice, the Tapped In project team at SRI: Patti Schank, Melissa Koch, Deb Tatar, Richard Godard, Kari Holsinger, and B. J. Berquist. Finally, we thank the many Tapped In community leaders, from whom we have learned much about the culture of K–12 education professionals. We dedicate this chapter to Natalie and Adi.

how educators have used the environment for their own purposes and in the context of formal professional development (Schlager & Schank, 1997; Schank, Fenton, Schlager, & Fusco, 1999). We have also tracked the growth and evolution of what we have called an *online education community of practice* (Schlager, Fusco, & Schank, 1998; Fusco, Gehlbach, & Schlager, 2000; Schlager, Fusco, & Schank, 2002).

Along the way, we have struggled with the choice of label. We have succeeded in growing and supporting a thriving community of thousands of education professionals, but the question of whether the users of the Tapped In environment collectively constitute a community *of practice* remains unresolved. Although we have tried ardently to cultivate a social entity that reflects all the major characteristics of communities of practice described in the literature, and in many ways have been very successful, we have struggled to define *the practice*. The members of Tapped In appear to participate in many, sometimes overlapping, communities of practice in and outside of the Tapped In environment (Schlager et al., 2002; Tatar, Gray, & Fusco, 2002; Gray & Tatar, this volume), suggesting that Tapped In may be better described as a *network of practice* (Brown & Duguid, 2000), a *constellation of practices* (Wenger, 1998), or a *crossroads*[1] of multiple educator communities.

Although such a distinction may appear inconsequential on the surface, we believe that it can have important consequences for online infrastructure design (Schank et al., 1999). As an online crossroads, Tapped In has been quite successful in achieving its original goal of bringing together and forging new relationships among education practitioners, providers, and researchers from around the world on a daily basis. Thousands of different people log in each month to engage in activities that include course and workshop sessions, group meetings, and public discussions spanning a wide range of K–12 topics. Many of our members are drawn to Tapped In because they seek ideas and colleagues outside of their local practice. Others introduce their local colleagues (or, in the case of university faculty, their students) to Tapped In to demonstrate the affordances of online communities. In this way, the community grows and evolves.

In optimizing our design to cultivate and support an *online* community, we have almost certainly ignored or rejected design alternatives that would have supported more effectively the professional activities in which our members participate in their local context of practice (i.e., their own schools or districts). We do not regret the choices we have made, but we are concerned that, as in many professional development projects (online and face-to-face), teachers' experiences in Tapped In will remain only tangentially related to the predominant practices of professional development in their own school districts. In our eyes, that would constitute failure of

---

[1] This term came from Linda Polin, Pepperdine University.

our mission – helping teachers to break out of their isolation only to grow apart from their local practice professionally is not our intent.

In the conclusion to our most recent paper (Schlager et al., 2002), we began to "think aloud" about how our online community concepts and design principles might play a more integral role in local- and state-level teacher professional development. We envisioned the development of *systemic* (i.e., district- or statewide) online education communities of practice that serve the professional development needs of teachers and support the missions of professional development providers across a district, state, or region. We argued that, as a shared sociotechnical infrastructure, a systemic online education community of practice could not only provide more equitable access to professional development opportunities but also help build the capacity of, and provide incentives for, teachers to participate in formal and self-organized professional learning activities. Such an online infrastructure could also help build the capacity of professional development providers to offer the kinds of experiences that reflect research-derived principles and strategies.

This chapter takes up that line of thought, beginning a new stage in our research. We step back from a focus on *online* communities as designed and built by researchers and professional development providers to serve a particular purpose and examine communities of practice *as they exist* in local education systems. We seek to understand the nature of local education communities of practice, their reciprocal relationship with teacher professional development and instructional improvement interventions, and the sociotechnical infrastructure through which the community supports the professional growth of its teachers.

THEORETICAL UNDERPINNINGS OF OUR WORK

As in our prior work, we draw from the community of practice literature. The characteristics of workplace communities of practice and how members work and grow professionally within them have been documented extensively in sociological and anthropological research (Lave & Wenger, 1991; Orr, 1996; Wenger, 1998; Cothrel & Williams, 1999; Brown & Duguid, 1991, 2000) outside of public education. Communities of practice are viewed as emergent, self-reproducing, and evolving entities that are distinct from, and frequently extend beyond, formal organizational structures, with their own organizing structures, norms of behavior, communication channels, and history (Brown & Duguid, 1991; Lave & Wenger, 1991; Barab & Duffy, 2000; Schlager et al., 2002). Members often come from a larger professional network spanning multiple organizations, drawn to one another for both social and professional reasons. Newcomers gain access to the community's professional knowledge tools and social norms through peripheral participation in authentic activities with other members. New practices and technologies are brought into the community by leaders, newcomers, and outsiders, and are adopted by the community through the discourse of its members and the evolution of practice over time. Thus, from a community of practice perspective, one's work and one's professional development are inextricably entwined with those with whom one works.

This characterization of communities of practice has been documented in many craft and professional workplaces, but it appears to be the exception rather than the rule in the workplaces that we call schools. Thus, we begin our exploration with a focused summary of research on the characteristics of effective professional development and the complex web of challenges to implementing programs that exhibit those characteristics within the traditional professional development paradigm.[2] We then ask: *Why do education researchers, policy-makers, district leaders, and technologists need to understand, nurture, and support communities of practice in K–12 education?* To understand the roles that communities of practice play in K–12 education and the relationship between education communities of practice and teacher professional development, we appeal to the richly descriptive literature on the teaching profession, teacher communities, and teacher professional development. Finally, we ask: *What can education technologists do to help nurture and support communities of practice in K–12 education?* By understanding the characteristics of communities of practice and the forms they take in the education profession, we hope to find more effective ways to apply what we have learned about online community processes and structures to foster more effective, scalable, and sustainable professional development in local education systems. We enumerate eight characteristics of education communities of practice and their implications for the design of online capabilities to support the roles that such communities can play in the professional development of K–12 education professionals.

TEACHER PROFESSIONAL DEVELOPMENT: THE VISION AND THE REALITY

To design online technology and services that support effective professional development, education technologists must understand the participants, processes, and structures that comprise effective professional development, the extent to which existing professional development projects reflect those components, and the local professional norms and practices that support or inhibit effective professional development. Researchers (Putnam & Borko, 2000; Smylie, Allensworth, Greenberg, Harris, &

---

[2] For a more in-depth overview, we encourage the reader to refer to Loucks-Horsley, Hewson, Love, and Stiles (1998) and to Darling-Hammond and Sykes (1999).

Luppescu, 2001; Darling-Hammond & Ball, 1997; Loucks-Horsley et al., 1998; Little, 1993), practitioners (Wilson & Berne, 1999; AACTE, 2000), and policy-makers (Rényi, 1996; PCAST, 1997; National Commission on Mathematics and Science Teaching for the 21st Century, 2000) are converging on a shared vision of the characteristics of effective teacher professional development. Professional development is viewed as a career-long, context-specific, continuous endeavor that is guided by standards, grounded in the teacher's own work, focused on student learning, and tailored to the teacher's stage of career development. Its objective is to develop, implement, and share practices, knowledge, and values that address the needs of all students. It is a collaborative effort, in which teachers receive support from peer networks, local administration, teacher educators, and outside experts. Formal school-based and external professional development programs are aligned with one another and balanced with informal professional development activities.

We recognize that this brief description does not capture the complexities and nuances inherent in the vision, but we hope it conveys that teacher professional development is more than a series of training workshops, institutes, meetings, and in-service days. It is a process of learning how to put knowledge into practice through engagement *in* practice within a community of practitioners. The description also suggests that professional development can be treated as a socio-organizational *system* that requires communication and close cooperation among several stakeholder groups to assure access to professional development opportunities for all teachers, continuity and cohesion of professional development pedagogy across providers, capacity to support sustained adoption and practice, sharing of knowledge and professional norms of practice, and formation of coherent policies. We conjecture that fulfilling these requirements is where a local community of practice, and the sociotechnical infrastructure that supports it, can play a crucial role in achieving effective professional development district-wide.

This vision, and the system it implies, have been difficult to put into practice. Studies of school-based professional development, programs developed and implemented by outside providers, and informal teacher networks at both the local (McLaughlin & Mitra, 2001; Smylie et al., 2001) and national levels (Corcoran, Shields, & Zucker, 1998; Garet, Porter, Desimone, Birman, & Yoon, 2001) have consistently found that professional development programs are disconnected from practice, fragmented, and misaligned. Many programs lack key pedagogical, content, and structural characteristics of effective professional development that are needed by the teachers they serve. Few professional development providers have the resources to address all stages of career development or the capacity to provide support on an ongoing basis. There is little coordination among providers or continuity across stages of the career development ladder, creating gaps and redundancies that hamper teachers' abilities to assess and satisfy their ongoing professional development needs.

Obstacles to professional development have also been documented within schools themselves. Local values and norms of practice have proved formidable barriers to effective professional development. For example, a common challenge is the reluctance of teachers to engage in inquiry or dialogue that critiques the practice of their peers (Grossman, Wineburg, & Woolworth, 2000; Barab, MaKinster, & Scheckler, this volume). Research has cited the importance and difficulty of building trusting and respectful relationships across school departments (Grossman et al., 2000) and career development levels. Teachers also find it difficult to reflect on their own practice, perhaps because teachers' classroom practice is closely tied to their identity as a person, because teachers lack certain professional dispositions (Ball & Cohen, 1999), or because teaching has largely developed a culture of privacy (Little, 1990).

Clearly, the challenges to achieving the kinds of work-embedded professional development processes envisioned here are formidable and multifaceted. Because the problems extend beyond the traditional foci of professional development research (e.g., content, pedagogy, and assessment) into the realm of social and organizational issues, they have been extremely resistant to efforts by professional development programs and systemic reform projects to address them (Stein, Silver, & Smith, 1998; Corcoran et al., 1998; Smylie et al., 2001; Gallego, Hollingsworth, & Whitenack, 2001; Blumenfeld, Fishman, Krajcik, & Marx, 2000). The state of research in this area is aptly summarized by Wilson and Berne (1999): "across this incoherent and cobbled-together nonsystem, structured and unstructured, formal and informal, we have little sense . . . of what exactly it is that teachers learn and by what mechanisms that learning takes place" (p. 174).

This chapter is not intended to offer a conceptual or technological "silver-bullet" solution to those challenges, but we do describe a conceptual thread that we have observed weaving through recent teacher research, policy studies, and evaluations of systemic reform programs: reference to the characteristics and benefits of communities of practice. We take up that thread in an attempt to derive lessons that will guide research into the development of sociotechnical infrastructures that can help practitioners and policy-makers overcome some of the challenges to achieving the vision above.

TEACHER PROFESSIONAL DEVELOPMENT AND COMMUNITIES OF PRACTICE

Researchers and reform advocates consistently cite participation in communities of practice as an integral factor in achieving effective, sustainable professional development systems. For example, a recent study of professional development in Chicago (Smylie et al., 2001) indicates that a teacher's community of practice can play both catalytic and direct roles in the teacher's professional development.

A professional community characterized by a focus on student learning, peer collaboration, and reflective dialog provides social and normative support for teacher participation in professional development. (pp. 57–58)

In schools with strong norms for innovation and strong professional communities, teachers find motivation, direction, and accountability for continuous learning and development. They find among their colleagues sources of new ideas, intellectual stimulation, and feedback essential to deepen learning and promote instructional change. They also find encouragement and safety in challenging taken-for-granted assumptions, risk-taking, and experimenting with new ideas. (p. 50)

The first quotation suggests that a teaching professional's community of practice is a preexisting social entity (in relation to a particular professional development intervention) that can (at least under some circumstances) serve an enabling or catalytic function, establishing and spreading professional norms of practice, encouraging collaboration among community members, and instilling dispositions (Ball & Cohen, 1999) needed for effective professional development. The second quotation also suggests that a teacher's community can have a direct impact on development through various forms of informal collegial interaction. In a national survey of teachers, Riel and Becker (2000) found significant differences in the classroom practices of professionally engaged teachers and those who engaged in "private" practice, isolated in their classrooms. Teachers who played important roles in a larger educational community were more likely to use constructivist and collaborative instructional strategies in their classrooms, while teachers who became less involved in collaborative activities with other colleagues were more likely to use direct instruction and individualized learning tasks.

The recognition that communities of practice can play important direct and catalytic roles in teacher learning has spurred great interest in how to harness the power of communities of practice in the context of systemic school reform and professional development projects. For example, Blumenfeld and her colleagues (2000) argue that "instructional reform requires a school culture that supports professionalism and provides opportunities for sharing, risk taking, and reflection among teachers about pedagogy and student learning. It is also more likely to take root when there are norms of open communication and cooperation among administrators and teachers" (p. 151). McLaughlin and Mitra (2001) argue that sustaining large-scale theory-based reform efforts "requires a community of practice to provide support, deflect challenges from the broader environment, and furnish the feedback and encouragement essential to going deeper" (p. 10). In their study of one such effort, they found that a local community of practice was the primary vehicle for learning, for sustaining project norms and values, and for inducting new teachers into the reform-based culture.

But the questions of what assemblage of people constitutes a community of practice in education and how, and under what conditions, a community of practice catalyzes positive learning outcomes remain largely unresolved (for more discussion, see Riel & Polin, this volume). If communities of practice can be so powerful and useful to professional development, why do so few school districts reflect the conditions described in the Smylie et al. (2001) passages just cited or exhibit the characteristics of effective professional development described in the vision above? What is it about communities of practice that supports the effective professional development of their members? Is there a relationship between a community of practice and each individual professional development intervention, such that if we can find ways to enhance the functioning of the former, the latter will also improve?

Although on the surface the questions we raise appear to have more to do with policy and professional development strategy than technology, we argue that the answers to these questions are also central to the design of technical infrastructure that supports the professional development of our nation's teachers. The large scale and distributed nature of many reform projects, along with an imperative to sustain and scale-up change, have led many research and development projects to explore the role of the Internet in delivering teacher training and creating online communities that can help sustain the learning after formal professional development (Ruopp, Gal, Drayton, & Pfister, 1993; Schlager & Schank, 1997; Palloff & Pratt, 1999; Marx, Blumenfeld, Krajcik, & Soloway, 1998; Barab et al., this volume).

Today, it would be rare to find a professional development project of any magnitude and duration that does not use at least some generic Internet technologies to foster dialogue and/or information sharing. Yet, simply having the ability to interact more frequently and for longer durations on-line than face-to-face does not translate directly into high-quality learning experiences or sustainable communities (Hawkins, 1996; Feldman, Konold, & Coulter, 2000). Few professional development projects have resulted in online communities that are sustainable enough to support teachers as they engage in the extended process of classroom reform (Donnelly, Dove, Tiffany, Adelman, & Zucker, 2000) or scalable enough to support all teachers as they enter the profession and grow professionally toward mastery (Corcoran et al., 1998).

Perhaps in applying Internet technology to deliver teacher training and create online teacher networks, we have placed the cart before the horse by ignoring the Internet's even greater potential to help support the local communities of practice within which teacher training and networking already take place. We are convinced that more traction might be gained by understanding and, as appropriate, using Internet technology to help strengthen,

grow, sustain, and/or change an extant education community's membership, culture, structures, and processes. We next explore this supposition
and its implications for the role and design of online technology in support
of local education communities of practice.

EDUCATION COMMUNITIES OF PRACTICE IN THE WILD

The nature of education communities of practice and the ways they come
to play a supportive role in teacher professional development are not well
understood. In education research, the term *community* has been invoked
as a classroom strategy (Bransford, Brown, & Cocking, 1999), a professional development strategy (Ruopp et al., 1993; Wilson & Berne, 1999), an
alternative to formal professional development (Schlager & Schank, 1997),
a small group of educators engaged in some activity (Scribner, Cockrell,
Cockrell, & Valentine, 1999; Grossman et al., 2000), and a label to instill a
sense of trust and interdependence among the members of a group (Palloff
& Pratt, 1999; Loucks-Horsley et al., 1998).[3] A first step in understanding the
leverage that technologists can bring to supporting communities of practice and their role in promoting effective professional development is to
detect them (Brown & Duguid, 1991). In our effort to understand the scope,
boundaries, and characteristics of education communities of practice, we
turned to a rich body of literature on teacher learning and professional
practice.[4]

BREAKING DOWN ARTIFICIAL WALLS. Professional development research and implementation projects often treat a community of practice
as an artifact to be built in the context of some form of intervention, suggesting that infrastructure for supporting interventions and communities
of practice are synonymous, and that both are divorced from practices and
practitioners that are not part of the intervention. We conjecture that this
artificial distinction between community inside and outside the intervention may be one reason why many professional development and reform
projects remain islands of exemplary practice in a sea of system-wide dysfunctional practice. Studies describing professional development interventions that have been sustainable and scalable over time have found a quite
different relationship, in which an *extant* education community of practice
coalesces around, interacts with, and influences formal teacher professional
development and reform programs (Elmore, 1996).

---

[3] In their chapter in this volume, Riel and Polin provide an excellent analysis of the distinctions among different types of education communities.

[4] Wilson and Berne (1999) and Cochran-Smith and Lytle (1999) provide illuminating
overviews of the field. Lortie (1975) and, more recently, McLaughlin and Talbert (2001)
provide excellent overviews of the characteristics of teaching practitioner communities,
particularly in relation to school and district administration.

Much of what a teacher needs to know (and know how to do) is learned in the context of practice. Little (2001) suggests that resources for the improvement of teaching are created through interaction among teachers and others in what she calls *traditional communities* (as opposed to those that are organized specifically around a particular intervention) as they work with teaching and learning artifacts in the context of daily practice. She suggests that "it is in the ordinary, mundane exchanges among teachers . . . that professional community is forged and opportunities to learn are created or foreclosed" (p. 8). To help nurture, sustain, and spread instructional improvement throughout an entire education system and reverse the decontextualization, misalignment, and fragmentation of professional development, we must understand communities of practice as integral components of education systems apart from professional development interventions. We must recognize the reciprocal and sometimes dialectical relationship between the norms and practices of the extant community and those of a particular intervention. Only then can we design infrastructure to support the processes of system-wide improvement.

EXTENDING THE BOUNDARIES. Most studies of education communities of practice focus on the activities of small groups of educators in individual schools, suggesting that our analytical lens, and thus our infrastructure designs, should focus on small, relatively homogeneous groups (Grossman et al., 2000). Recently, however, reports have begun to suggest that teachers need to form communities with colleagues and experts outside their own schools or districts (Hawkins, 1996; Darling-Hammond & Ball, 1997; PCAST, 1997; Web-based Education Commission, 2000; National Commission on Mathematics and Science Teaching for the 21st Century, 2000). This research raises the question of what the boundaries of education communities of practice should be. Do small-scale studies capture the structures and processes of communities of practice or only the characteristics of particular factions within them?

McLaughlin and Talbert (2001) point to the importance of the relationship between district and school staff in supporting teacher communities. They describe both the negative effects on professional development of an antagonistic relationship and the positive effects where the district office and the local teacher community work together. In one exemplary district, they describe how professional development is "planned by teachers and implemented by the district" (p. 111). District staff also serve communication and brokering roles on behalf of teachers. McLaughlin and Talbert conclude that in strong district communities, "shared norms, values, and expectations that support teacher innovation are communicated throughout the district." In contrast, weak district communities are "fractured by disputes, disrespect, and inconsistent leadership" (p. 114). Similarly, Elmore (1996) describes how in New York City's District 2 "professional development activities are specifically designed to connect teachers, principals, professional developers, and district administrators with each other and with outside experts around specific problems of practice" (p. 28).

These studies suggest to us that all education professionals – those who work in the schools, district leadership, and outside professional development partners – play a part in establishing values and perpetuating norms of instructional improvement; fostering communication and cooperation; building human capacity for coaching, mentoring, and peer support; sharing tools and artifacts; and building the social networks and infrastructure needed to generate and diffuse new knowledge. When these stakeholder groups work together as a community – communicating, cooperating, building trusting reciprocal relationships, and sharing norms, values, tools, and accountability for instructional improvement – improvement can occur (Elmore, 2000). How these sociocultural preconditions for improvement come into being district-wide and what sociotechnical structures enable them to work are questions that require empirical research aimed at understanding the sociocultural processes of district communities of practice.

ALIGNING COMMUNITY STRUCTURES WITH PROFESSIONAL
DEVELOPMENT ACTIVITY STRUCTURES

To help us understand the sociotechnical structures needed to support, nurture, and harness the power of education communities of practice, we need a framework for representing the structural relationships among a community of practice, individual practices, and professional development projects. The Activity Theory framework (Engeström, 1987, 1999; Mwanza, 2001; Cole & Engeström, 1993; Blanton, Mooremn, & Trathen, 1998) provides a good first step, enabling us to zoom in on individual groups and their activities and then zoom out to view those activities in the context of the larger community of practice.

Briefly, the core of the Activity Theory framework focuses on the activities in which individuals and groups (called *subjects*) engage. As depicted in Figure 5.1, *subjects* engage in *actions* (e.g., dialogue, construction, search) to accomplish the *object* (also called *objective*) of the activity, which leads to some *outcome(s)*. Activities are mediated by the *tools* (technical and conceptual) and other artifacts that are available to the subjects. Activities take place in the context of, and are influenced by, a surrounding *community*. The community exerts influence on the activity through the mediation of established *rules* (e.g., values, norms of behavior, dispositions toward inquiry, trust, and commitment), *tools* that have been institutionalized in the community, and *division of labor* (the allocation of roles and responsibilities). We find the framework useful in understanding the relationship between the community engaged in a professional development project and the community (or communities) of practice from which the teachers involved in

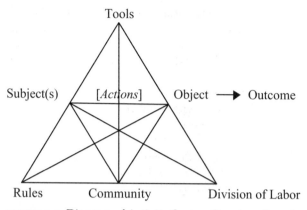

FIGURE 5.1. Diagram of Activity System Structure (based on Engeström, 1987)

the project have come. Both can be represented by similar activity system diagrams. The key to understanding the relationship between the two, and thus the roles that a community of practice can play in professional development activities, is the degree of alignment in tools, rules, and division of labor.

Professional development programs typically involve a selected group of teachers engaged in a prescribed, highly structured set of interventions to accomplish specific learning objectives. We have found it useful to describe this type of assemblage as a *community of purpose*.[5] From the professional development provider's perspective, the social context is the program and the participants and staff are the community. The norms of engagement and tools to be employed are designed to support a particular pedagogy for a specified duration. Barab et al. (this volume) and Grossman et al. (2000) offer descriptive accounts of how professional development activities of teachers are influenced by the tools, rules, and division of labor established by leaders of a professional development project and the tensions created when forging a new community of purpose.

The framework highlights the fundamental relationship between the activity structures of professional development projects (and other professional activities, such as examining student work, lesson study, etc.) and the existing structures at each teacher's place of practice – the school. Imagine, for example, that fifty teachers are invited by a university to participate in a professional development project. The project (the *activity*) is designed to train the teachers (the *subjects*) to use a particular set of inquiry methods and technologies (*tools*) that have not been part of the teachers' prior repertoire or their schools' infrastructure (the *object*). The teachers are asked to

---

[5] We first heard this term from Vicki Suter. Riel and Polin (this volume) use the term *task-based learning community*.

take on new collaborative roles (*division of labor*) based on values and social *norms* that are internal to the project. The participants are also encouraged to develop trust in and form a lasting *community* with one another in the hope that they will support one another (*outcome 1*) in applying what they have learned (*outcome 2*) and disseminate the knowledge they gained to other teachers in their schools (*outcome 3*).

MISALIGNMENT. The professional development project may overlap to a greater or lesser extent with the universe of prior activities, tools, values, and norms of practice that the fifty teachers bring to the activity from their practice. It would not be difficult to imagine that at least some of the teachers come from schools where outdated conceptual tools, inadequate technological tools, an entrenched culture of privacy, and top-down allocation of roles and responsibilities are the norm. The activity diagram also brings into focus some of the challenges faced by staff and teachers in many professional development projects. For example, the participants (and, in many cases, the staff) have no prior history with one another or the tools they are expected to use to achieve the object. They must learn to use new tools and negotiate new roles and rules of engagement, resulting in a great deal of "overhead" activity before they can focus on the object of the activity (Schlager et al., 2002).

The diagram also encourages us to ask what happens to the knowledge and skills developed in the professional development project and whether the intended outcomes are realized in practice (e.g., sustained improvements in teaching and learning outcomes; dissemination of new knowledge, tools, and practices). We might imagine problems arising when the teachers return to their classes with their new palette of activities, rules, tools, and roles and must concurrently apply them in their own practice and introduce them to their colleagues. Many find that the sense of community that they established with one another takes a back seat to the demands of their daily responsibilities. They are too busy to support one another as they try to apply their new knowledge and skills in their own teaching and try to "disseminate" their new knowledge and skills. Nor can the returning teachers count on support from their local communities of practice. Other local professional development providers and accomplished teachers within the local communities of practice (neither of whom were part of the summer institute) can offer little support because the tools and strategies employed by the "outsiders" are unfamiliar to them. In some cases, the returning teachers find that they are no longer in tune with, and therefore are marginalized by, their colleagues.

ALIGNMENT. In contrast to the scenario just described, imagine the same professional development project taking place within the kinds of community of practice on which Smylie et al. (2001), Stein et al. (1998), McLaughlin and Talbert (2001), and others base their descriptions of the catalytic properties of a community of practice. When professional development is embedded in a strong community of practice focused on instructional improvement, the community of practice owns a stake in the outcome of the activity. As a result, the success of the activity (*object*) and the *outcomes* of the activity become a community-wide responsibility (*division of labor*). For example, Stein et al. (1998) describe how a mathematics professional development project was implemented in the context of ongoing reform in a middle school. They describe an array of activities that they viewed as different from the support that teachers attempting innovation typically receive.

> Although some of the assistance activities can be seen as pedagogically struc-
> tured, event-specific occasions for teacher assistance (e.g., MME workshops, elec-
> tive coursework, monthly staff development meetings, retreats), others were more
> informal and ongoing (e.g., teachers mentoring teachers, ongoing classroom vis-
> its by consulting teachers, tagging up). Still others represented opportunities to
> actually do the work of the project. (pp. 26–27)

The extant community forms a social support structure that can help a new professional development project introduce its teachers to new knowledge and skills in the context of conceptual *tools, rules*, and *allocation of roles* that are already well established in the community and therefore familiar to the participants. After a professional development project ends, the community reabsorbs the participating teachers into its ranks, providing support structures that can help sustain the teachers' nascent collaborative efforts and collegial relationships. At the same time, the community benefits from the infusion and spread of knowledge gained by the teachers in the project, thus helping teachers who have not participated in formal projects take charge of their own professional development (Koppich, Asher, & Kerchner, 2002; Rényi, 1996). Individual professional development projects also become a source of new community members with new skills, which enables the community of practice to grow, spread innovation, and reproduce itself (Barab & Duffy, 2000).

COMMUNITY AS CATALYST. The activity framework suggests that the catalytic effects of an education community of practice on professional development stem from the alignment of the community's existing *rules* and *tools*, as well as a *division of labor* that draws members of the community of practice into a particular activity for ongoing support and expertise. When the tools, rules, and division of labor experienced in a particular professional development activity are aligned with those of the established culture at the teacher's school (as well as with other professional development activities), the community itself also benefits. Figure 5.2 illustrates the community processes that can support capacity-building, knowledge-building, and the spread of innovative ideas. The arrows in the diagram illustrate how the community serves as a memory and diffusion mechanism for new ideas, tools, and outcomes of the project. The curved arrow

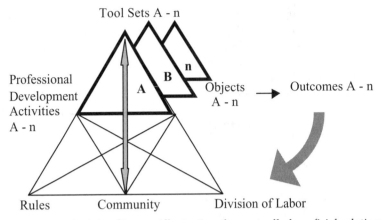

FIGURE 5.2. Activity diagram illustrating the mutually beneficial relationship between professional development activities and a local education community of practice

indicates that knowledge and capacity generated in individual activities make their way back into the community in three forms: (1) the new values, skills, and expertise of the members of the group return to the community as those members participate in new activities with other members of the community; (2) the group may create new artifacts (e.g., rubrics, lessons) that become part of the community's knowledge base; and (3) the tools used by the group (e.g., video cases, e-portfolios, modeling and simulation tools) and knowledge of how to use them make their way into community discourse and other activities (Hoadley & Pea, 2002). The vertical double-headed arrow indicates that the project both uses tools that exist within the community and introduces new tools to the community.

Research describing successful district-wide professional development systems that are integrated with the district's community of practice in this way (i.e., most or all teachers in the district are involved) to achieve collective improvement is rare, but exemplary instances do exist (e.g., Koppich et al., 2002; Honey, Carrigg, & Hawkins, 1998; Elmore & Burney, 1999). One such effort is the 8-year-old Union City Online project in Union City, New Jersey, a district of 11 schools serving 10,000 inner-city students in grades K–12. All professional development programs in Union City are designed to respond to the evolving needs of the educator community. Each follows a five-stage process that involves formal and informal, large- and small-group activities (Honey et al., 1998): Awareness, Practice, Sharing, Peer Coaching, and Mentoring. District leaders and researchers cite reforms in cultural norms as key preconditions for establishing curricular reforms, helping "to establish both a climate and an infrastructure that support and embrace innovation" (p. 136). These changes in norms include collaborative decision-making among school staff, district administrators, researchers, and unions and ownership of curricular changes by the teaching community.

Another example of effective integration of practice and professional development in a district-wide system is New York City's District 2, a district of 48 schools serving 22,000 students in grades K–8. Elmore and Burney (1999) describe how over more than ten years the district has evolved a strategy for the use of professional development to improve teaching and learning that "consists of a set of organizing principles about the process of systemic change and the role of professional development in that process," along with specific models of staff development that focus on "system-wide improvement of instruction" (p. 266). These models include a Professional Development Laboratory staffed by an expert "teacher in residence," peer visitation, an advising network, and outside consultants who work directly with teachers at their schools to solve concrete problems or develop new instructional interventions.

To be clear, we are not claiming that a strong community of practice was the root or primary cause of successful reform in these two districts. The two districts' policies, leadership, and reform strategies (along with an acute sense of urgency) were the primary drivers of improvement. Those drivers sparked cultural changes within the community of practice that enabled the community to enact, sustain, and spread new norms and activities. In both these cases, the local education community of practice now helps build the capacity of, and provides social incentives for, teachers to participate in formal and self-organized activities for professional growth. In both cases, the community helps build the capacity of professional development providers to offer high-quality activities that are aligned with the needs and professional norms of the community members. In both, we see communication channels, shared norms of practice and cooperation among stakeholder groups, continuity and cohesion across providers, and the capacity to support sustained adoption within the community of practice.

COMMUNITY INFRASTRUCTURE AS ACCELERANT. Whether and how these catalytic functions can be improved and accelerated by improving the community's sociotechnical infrastructure remains a question. Research is needed to understand where weaknesses, gaps, and lack of capacity persist and to develop ways in which the appropriate use of online technology might overcome them. The Activity Theory framework focuses our investigation on the intersection of tools, rules, and division of labor between the professional development activities and the community. One example coming out of research on theory-based reform is the need to more effectively convey to teachers the "first principles" on which the reform practices are based (McLaughlin & Mitra, 2001). If we think of these first principles as conceptual *tools*, without which the community cannot build sustainable reform, we begin to see that teachers must become comfortable with those tools before they can learn to construct new practices that are robust (the *object*). Using traditional professional development approaches, such a process can take several years per cadre of teachers. Perhaps a different division of labor, supported by a more effective communication infrastructure, could help new conceptual tools become part of the community culture more quickly and in a more sustainable manner.

Another issue that has been a growing concern of many districts is their capacity for mentoring, coaching, and peer support. Many states are enacting policies that mandate those forms of informal professional development for teachers at all stages of the career development continuum (National Commission on Teaching and America's Future, 1996). However, few local networks or programs have the expert capacity to provide the frequency and duration of contact with mentors and coaches needed to address the challenges of teacher retention and renewal. Accomplished practitioners who would serve as coaches and mentors are in shortest supply where they are needed most, in schools with high rates of under-qualified teachers (Shields, Esch, Young, & Humphrey, 2000) and under-performing students. This capacity issue suggests that we look closely at the models for allocating expertise (division of labor) in the programs (typically, a hub-and-spoke model) and the opportunities for developing new models that make better use of the expertise that resides in the larger community of practice (a network or matrix model). Online environments could help enact and support those new organizational models, thereby increasing access to the right expertise at the right time.

CORRECTING DYSFUNCTIONAL COMMUNITIES OF PRACTICE

The literature clearly suggests that a strong community of practice can play an integral role in the professional development of a district's teaching workforce, and the Activity Theory framework points to social structures through which a community of practice comes to be a positive force. However, the mere existence of a community of practice does not imply that the community is a well-functioning social entity or a positive catalyst for effective professional development; it can also be dysfunctional in a number of ways that (along with other factors) can militate against improvement (McLaughlin & Talbert, 2001; Wenger, 1998; Schwen & Hara, this volume). We need to detect when, how, and why a community is exhibiting dysfunctional symptoms in order to understand how to correct them.

Like other large social entities, an education community of practice is a complex beast. A strong community can wield the power to enact policies or subvert them, foster change or resist it, spread innovation or impede it. A community of practice is also subject to influence from formal policies and hierarchies. It can be subordinated, undermined, or disrupted, either deliberately or inadvertently, through acts (reorganization, changes in leadership, or new policies) and omissions (e.g., not providing opportunities, tools, and support for communication and collaboration) of the formal organizational leadership (department chairs, principals, superintendents, school boards, and unions) (Scribner et al., 1999). The community itself can exhibit strong or weak leadership, foster or inhibit member diversity, and support dense webs of social relationships or sparse, disconnected threads of communication. Nor is a community of practice inherently a unifying, cooperative entity. Members can form competing factions or simply not interact with one another. A community can be so weak and fractious as to appear to be multiple communities.

Incompatibilities in culture, leadership, tools, and cooperation both within and between stakeholder groups in a local education community of practice can hinder development of an effective system of professional development. Many schools have a history of separation among teachers across disciplinary lines and career stages, of communication channels that inhibit rather than support professional networking, of discouraging informal leadership, and of erecting barriers between *inside* and *outside* expertise (Loucks-Horsley et al., 1998). All of these factors can promote a culture of privacy and autonomy that can reinforce ineffective professional development strategies and discourage collaboration and sharing of expertise and resources (Little, 1990; Elmore, 2000).

We also know that, under some circumstances, dysfunctional district communities of practice can change for the better. The Union City and District 2 examples demonstrate that dysfunctional communities of practice can, over several years, grow a strong, cohesive culture that supports fundamental system-wide improvement. Elmore (2000) gives an eloquent account of how policies and leadership focused on instructional improvement can foster such change. What remains unclear is the role that community of practice infrastructure can play in supporting, and perhaps accelerating, the evolution from a dysfunctional to a strong, well-functioning community of practice. Can the efforts of education technologists help promote changes in *sociotechnical* infrastructure that can improve the health of the community? Can they help a strong but entrenched educator community embrace change? Can they help unify a fractious community?

There is evidence that online sociotechnical support structures and pedagogically sound online professional development activities can foster "healthy" cultural norms, membership diversity and growth, distributed leadership, public and private dialogue, and professional networking on a large scale (Constant, Sproull, & Kiesler, 1996; Derry, Gance, Gance, & Schlager, 2000; Dunlap, Neale, & Carroll, 2000; Evertson, Smithey, & Hough, 2000; Fusco et al., 2000; Ruopp et al., 1993; PCAST, 1997; Schlager et al., 1998, 2002; Web-based Education Commission, 2000; National Commission on Mathematics and Science Teaching for the 21st Century, 2000).

To our knowledge, however, such strategies have not been applied systematically to the challenge of diagnosing and helping to correct dysfunctional aspects of education communities of practice. If we can bring online community strategies to bear on the ills of education communities of practice, we may be able to shorten the time it takes to establish the norms, values, and relationships needed to support system-wide improvement, increase the likelihood that healthy norms and practices will take root, and thereby decrease the risk that instructional reform efforts will falter or fail.

GUIDEPOSTS FOR TECHNOLOGY DESIGN THAT SUPPORTS SYSTEM-WIDE IMPROVEMENT

Throughout this chapter, we have discussed several highly interwoven characteristics of communities of practice that we believe are particularly salient to understanding how communities of practice differ from other groupings of education professionals, how they exhibit symptoms of dysfunction, and how to harness their power in support of teacher professional development and instructional improvement. In this section, we attempt to untangle the characteristics we have discussed and suggest ways in which online sociotechnical infrastructure might be used to nurture and support local education communities of practice. We do not intend the following descriptions to be complete definitions, but rather a set of guideposts that together form a conceptual framework for research. Nor do we claim that the design implications we draw are the only implications that can be drawn; they are intended as examples that we hope will spur the reader to think of and research new designs for online infrastructure to support education communities of practice.

GUIDEPOST 1. LEARNING PROCESSES. The growing interest in community of practice concepts in teacher professional development stems largely from the rich and compelling descriptions of how newcomers enter and learn the ropes of workplace communities. Learning is viewed as a social activity that occurs primarily in the context of work (as opposed to training) as new and less-skilled members participate peripherally in activities with more-experienced colleagues and as journeymen take on new roles on a path toward expertise. Informal learning opportunities occur regularly in the context of daily practice, typically in the form of focused episodes dealing with real problems. Support from peers and more-accomplished colleagues is common; access to and interaction with the *master* practitioner is relatively infrequent. New ideas are often learned through peer networks that transcend organizational boundaries. Formal training supplements informal learning to build competencies that contribute to the collective enterprise.

Countless online learning initiatives and many *e-learning* systems justify their designs and approaches on the basis of this characterization of learning relationships and processes. Unfortunately, in most cases, the designs of online tools and pedagogies do not support the social structures that promote community learning processes. For example, course management technologies used in most e-learning applications (e.g., WebCT and Blackboard) are designed to support highly structured, university-style learning situations and therefore may not be the most appropriate for informal, highly contextualized learning in an education community of practice. Only people who are officially part of the course are part of the "community"; when the course is over, so is the community. Such technologies may actually hinder informal learning processes more than they help by reinforcing the type of training model that Brown and Duguid (2000) and others argue against. Although we see a place for highly structured e-learning environments, we also see a need for teachers to have a set of online learning and collaboration capabilities that they can *own* and tailor to meet their own needs and the needs of the community. Sophisticated knowledge management and collaboration capabilities are commonly found in online environments intended for business (Cothrel & Williams, 1999), scientific (Finholt, Lewis, & Mott; 1995), and even elementary classroom (Hewitt, this volume; Gomez, Fishman, & Pea, 1998) learning communities, but they are not common in environments intended to support communities of education practitioners.

GUIDEPOST 2. HISTORY AND CULTURE. A community of practice develops – and continually reproduces – its own dominant cultural artifacts, norms, and values over time. Members of a community of practice inherit norms and practices that have been previously negotiated and agreed on through the experiences of those who have come before them (Barab & Duffy, 2000). Online technology can enable new members of a community of practice to learn established norms, values, and practices of the culture through participation in the community's online activities. New members also inherit the community's memory, embodied in historical artifacts that the community reuses and modifies over time. Policy-makers and change agents could also benefit from analyzing the records of online discourse and digital artifacts that are modified by the community through use over time.

As we have seen, however, cultural norms and values can become very resistant to change in communities with a long and rich history, requiring drastic measures on the part of school reform leaders to implement and sustain reform efforts. Online technology could help encourage members of a community of practice to unlearn old norms and learn new norms, values, and practices through participation in new forms of activity (e.g., from hierarchical to collegial interaction patterns, structured to conversational discourse, passive to active participation).

Thus, education communities of practice could benefit from online capabilities that make it possible to create, manage, reuse, and modify workplace artifacts (e.g., lesson plans, assessments, action research, student and teacher portfolios) and records of community discourse. Developers of online environments must also be aware of the match between historically evolved norms and values and those that their technology promotes. The two need not, and in some cases should not, match, but if the designers are not aware of the mismatch, they may not build appropriate scaffolds to help users bridge the mismatch.

GUIDEPOST 3. MEMBERSHIP IDENTITY AND MULTIPLICITY. Education communities of practice differ from other groupings of educators (e.g., study groups, work teams, or occupational societies) in the heterogeneity and diversity of their membership. By this we mean that community membership spans a continuum of types of expertise and levels of competency rather than being defined by domain or rank. Groups within communities form and disband; participants, objectives, tools, and division of labor change over time. Community members take on multiple roles – such as broker, moderator, mentor, and learner – in different contexts. The transition between roles is not scripted, designated, or assigned as in formal training or organizational hierarchies. Membership tends to cross formal organizational and social boundaries rather than being defined by them.

Thus, online infrastructure needs to be designed to help members of a community of practice build and manage their professional identity, find and collaborate with one another, and function in multiple roles. Such capabilities are not needed by homogeneous communities of purpose in which roles are relatively static (e.g., projects, courses, formal organizations). Community of practice infrastructure must support the process of forming a group for a specific activity, based on the expertise and prior experiences of the members of the community; it must also support the transfer of knowledge from groups back into the larger community. For example, Barab et al. (this volume) describe a design process in which they moved away from designing spaces through which all members of a large community could interact to supporting spaces in which smaller, bounded groups could form and interact around a particular practice, topic, or issue. In contrast, *groupware* systems are typically designed to support defined groups, not the larger social entity from which groups are formed. They may support sharing and awareness within a group but not across groups, thereby inhibiting peripheral participation by novices and outside experts and constraining knowledge diffusion throughout the community.

GUIDEPOST 4. COMMUNITY REPRODUCTION AND EVOLUTION. A major objective of many professional development interventions is the transformation of a community of purpose into a community of practice, which rarely occurs; the time, cost, commitment, and effort required are simply too great for most projects. Instead, the literature suggests that projects leverage the ongoing growth and reproductive processes of extant communities from which the participants come. One hallmark of a community of practice that distinguishes it from other forms of community is the ability to grow, evolve, and reproduce its membership. A community of practice grows and reproduces itself as new members join and embark on paths toward mastery and leadership and as existing members join other communities (Lave & Wenger, 1991; Schlager et al., 1998, 2002; Barab & Duffy, 2000). A major premise of this chapter is that professional development efforts need to leverage this existing capacity for sustainability more effectively.

Online technology could be used to support a division of labor in which accomplished members of a local community of practice participate peripherally in formal professional development interventions in which their less-accomplished colleagues are participating. This arrangement would help new teachers form relationships with more senior members of their new community (not just with other new teachers and professional development providers). Bringing members of the community into formal teacher education and professional development interventions could also help the community reproduce itself by helping to decrease the epidemic rates of teacher attrition in many underserved areas.

Online technology can also support community evolution and reproduction by enabling the community to build its capacity for resource-intensive *informal* professional development activities such as mentoring and coaching. Harnessing the diverse expertise available among community of practice members to engage in mentoring and coaching on a district-wide scale requires a different type of support infrastructure than is commonly implemented today. Most mentoring programs assume that expertise is a very limited resource (mentors must be "officially designated"); therefore, most programs employ a hub-and-spoke model in which a single mentor is assigned to some number of mentees. This model works well in small projects, in which a sufficient number of mentors can be recruited and trained, and the technology needed to support such a model is fairly straightforward (e.g., the participants need to be able to communicate and share artifacts). However, the hub-and-spoke model is inherently unscalable, especially in school districts with high turnover rates. In districts with the most need, there simply are not enough *designated* mentor teachers to go around.

A networked model, which makes use of technology to create a web or network of expertise from across the district, would make better, more efficient use of the district's human capacity, but it also requires more sophisticated technology than the hub-and-spoke model to implement. Matching seekers to providers, load balancing, reputation and reward management, and quality control are some of the challenges that must be addressed for a networked model to work.

GUIDEPOST 5. SOCIAL NETWORKS. Professionals in a community of practice develop, manage, and participate in multiple overlapping social networks within and across community of practice boundaries (Wenger, 1998;

Cothrel & Williams, 1999). We believe that online technologies can influence the formation, structure, and evolution of social networks within education communities of practice in either positive or negative ways. For example, built-in administrative control structures in some intranet systems may tend to encourage top-down, hierarchical communication and dissemination of information. Such structures may not allow ad hoc groups to set up their own private (or public) channels of communication and information sharing. Moreover, intranet systems can exclude outsiders from participating in discourse through gate-keeping policies and security mechanisms. Finally, intranets can inhibit communication among members of a community by blocking access from outside the school or district server, forcing teachers to seek other means of communication after school hours (such as Tapped In for many of its users). List server, chat, and discussion board technologies may also facilitate or constrain social networks within communities of practice in ways that are not fully understood, suggesting the need for both new strategies and technologies to track and analyze technology-mediated social networks.

Analyzing the online activities among members of a community of practice and across communities can help to uncover patterns of interaction, group and individual relationships, and roles played by different members – the social structures through which knowledge is generated and spread through the community (Koku & Wellman, this volume; Wellman, 1997; Wellman & Gulia, 1999; Bozeman, Dietz, & Gaughan, 1998). Thus, the size, strength, density, and structure of social networks may serve as indicators of community health and growth.

Assessing social roles or positions in the network can provide information about a group and the place of group members in the overall community. Members with similar patterns of relationships may share a particular role or social position. An individual who has close ties to those at the center of a network may be in a better position to acquire new knowledge, whereas an individual who has direct ties to other members in the periphery may be in a better position to disseminate information (Granovetter, 1973, 1982). Understanding the substructures in a network can also be important to understanding how the network is likely to behave. For example, a clique is a subgroup in a network in which everyone has connections to everyone else. A network with overlapping cliques may experience less conflict and enable innovations to spread more readily than a network with non-overlapping cliques because members are part of multiple cliques. Moreover, it is possible that members who belong to multiple cliques may have more opportunities for learning.

We are beginning to explore what social network analysis tools and techniques, in conjunction with other methodologies, can tell us about education communities of practice (Tatar et al., 2002). For example, social network analysis tools might help identify community members who play central roles, who are members of several groupings, or who are in the periphery and, therefore, in need of support. If we look at a social network over time, we expect to see members' centrality in the network change; peripheral members may move toward the center, and central members may move to the periphery or leave. New members may join a group, or members from one group may join another group, and all of this movement could change information flow in a network. In addition, we might find similar network patterns among "successful" groups and then be able to use social network analysis as a tool to analyze groups as they are developing and intervene if a group does not show structures that promote success. Groups, their purposes, and their members will need to be categorized, and metrics of what constitutes a successful group need to be created.

GUIDEPOST 6. LEADERS AND CONTRIBUTORS. Leadership is a central aspect of membership identity (Guidepost 3) that promotes social networking (Guidepost 5) and community reproduction (Guidepost 4). We have chosen to discuss it separately to highlight the differences between community leadership and the more traditional concepts of organizational (e.g., department heads, principals, district staff) and academic (instructor-student, mentor-mentee) leadership. More importantly, we want to raise the issue of whether and how online technology can support, and help districts build capacity for, community leadership.

Community leadership may intersect with, but is not synonymous with, an organization's formal management structure. Community leaders perform organizing, governance, networking, brokering, and other social support services (Lieberman, 1996; Spillane, Halverson, & Diamond, 1999; Schlager et al., 1998, 2002) for the community. For example, leaders model and reinforce community rules and norms of practice; they encourage and support the growth of others toward leadership. Leadership can also be conveyed by someone through contributions to the community (e.g., volunteering expertise, materials, or even emotional support). Consequently, community leaders can be difficult for others (especially outsiders) to spot, both because they may have no formally recognized position or title and because their contributions may only have been experienced by certain other members of the community.

Most e-learning technologies are designed to support traditional instructional leadership, in which roles and associated capabilities are well defined, usually in advance. For example, course instructors are given administrative capabilities and controls that students do not have; professional development staff members typically have the power to create discussion forums, while participants do not. Similarly, most intranet systems have levels of permissions that reflect the organization's formal leadership hierarchy. There are no designated and immutable roles and hierarchies in communities of practice; technology should not force people into them.

Leadership might take the form of setting up and moderating one's own study group, developing and publishing materials, or offering one's services to other community members in a particular area of expertise. Environments that support communities of practice should enable any member of the community to have the technical capabilities and social support required to take on leadership roles in a given context.

GUIDEPOST 7. TOOLS, ARTIFACTS, AND PLACES. When we think of how technology can support communities of practice, what typically comes to mind is the design of tools and artifacts (e.g., curriculum, assessments, rubrics, and teaching and learning samples) that the members of the community might use to help them learn. We believe that equally important is consideration of how and when new tools and artifacts are introduced to, and assimilated into the practice of, members of a community. Technological tools and learning artifacts are frequently introduced to groups of teachers with little or no advance planning for how those tools and artifacts will be introduced into, and become an integral part of, the overarching culture of a community. As a result, different groups within and across schools in a district champion their own favorite tools and artifacts to accomplish the same functions and the community as a whole suffers from the fragmentation and isolation among factions. From a community of practice perspective, we should be concerned with these issues. Communication, productivity, coordination, and knowledge generation depend on the broad use of a common palette of tools and the generation, reuse, and refinement of community artifacts, not only within projects but also across projects over time. Thus, professional development providers should think hard about whether and when to introduce new tools and artifacts instead of making use of those that are already part of the culture. When new tools and artifacts are warranted, designers need to think about compatibility, interoperability, and overlap with existing infrastructure, as well as how the tools could be used in contexts other than the current project.

Public and private meeting places (physical and virtual) are components of the permanent infrastructure of a community of practice (Schlager & Schank, 1997; Schlager et al., 1998) that are not well represented in online design. Online education technologies tend to focus on representing "the classroom." In the physical world, classrooms and teachers' lounges tend not to be the preferred venues for professional collaboration; consequently, they may not be the best metaphors for online meeting places. Instead, communities of practice may require virtual *third* places (Oldenburg, 1997) and the social structures that those places afford. Lieberman's (1996; Lieberman & Grolnick, 1999) research on teacher networks suggests that meeting in community gathering places *outside* the workplace can help build professional relationships and socialize new members into the fold, thereby solidifying teachers' commitment to the community. Similarly, Orr's (1996) copier repair technicians were able to share "war stories" because they were able to gather in the lunchroom. The Tapped In and Inquiry Learning Forum (Barab et al., this volume) projects represent two anchor points in the design and use of different types of online third places for education professionals. More research is needed to understand how online technology can be used to support the range of professional activities that take place in education communities of practice.

GUIDEPOST 8. THE PRACTICE. A community of practice can be distinguished from other groupings of professionals that we call communities of purpose or occupational communities (Van Maanen & Barley, 1984) by a mutual engagement in a collective enterprise (Wenger, 1998). We might say that the practice of a school is *educating children*, and the education professionals in a school are members of that practice.[6] Or one might argue that *school administration* is a practice separate from classroom teaching. Beyond the school, the lines become even more blurred. Is the enterprise of *managing a district* a practice separate from the enterprise of educating children within each school? Are all members of a state science teacher association mutually engaged in a single practice? Are district staff developers, professional development consultants, university faculty who conduct summer institutes, and other professionals practitioners of yet another practice – that of *training teachers*? We raise these questions not simply to encourage philosophical debate, but rather to better understand the boundaries and scope of the collective enterprise that community of practice infrastructure is intended to support.

When researchers observe schools that violate community of practice characteristics – where teachers, administrators, and librarians rarely interact informally; where professional development is taken outside the workplace and placed in the hands of outside providers – we are tempted to conclude that those who teach children, those who run schools, and those who train teachers *should not* be considered one community of practice. If they are practitioners of the same practice, we would expect educators of children, administrators, and teacher trainers to share the community characteristics listed here. If, however, those practitioners are engaged in separate practices, we would expect to find fundamental differences between the communities in norms of practice, values, tools of the trade, professional relationships, and leaders. Clearly, research has most frequently found the latter to be the case.

These findings pose a dilemma for school reform researchers and technologists alike. Should we generalize from the observation of how things are today to conclude that school districts are made up of multiple, only loosely connected practices? Our understanding of the literature suggests

---

[6] We distinguish our use of the term *practice* from the individual practices, or activities, that members of the practice engage in as part of their work.

that doing so would be a mistake (perhaps one that has been made in large-scale professional development and reform efforts). The practice – the *collective enterprise* – of educating children demands that members of multiple occupational communities and levels of management hierarchy work together in ways that transcend occupational or managerial structures. That they do not, in many cases, appear to be engaged in a joint practice may be a failing of the formal system, not a desired state of affairs (see Elmore, 2000). Thus, we believe that resolving the question of *what is the practice that our technologies are being designed to support* is not simply an academic exercise but rather a necessary design inquiry. Fundamental differences between *practices* should lead technologists to make different design choices tailored to the characteristics of each practice. One need only look at the differences between online course management systems used for teacher education and professional development and the much more advanced visualization, modeling, and knowledge-building systems developed for inquiry-based K–12 science classrooms to see how differently designers think about the two aspects of a teacher's practice: they are treated as separate and unrelated. We know that this sort of fractionation is not desirable if we seek overall improvement in our education systems.

In rejecting the premise that district management and professional development are separate from the practice of educating children, we are forced to think anew how, and for whom, we design sociotechnical infrastructure. It no longer makes sense to build separate systems to support school principals, beginning teachers, math teachers, professional development courses, and classroom practice. In developing technology to support community-based teacher professional development, we must support the mutual engagement of all stakeholders in the practice of educating children, not merely the individual parts of the practice in isolation from one another. At least for the purposes of analysis and design, we must treat all stakeholder groups as a single community of practice.

TOWARD A NEW EDUCATION COMMUNITY CROSSROADS

In his article on school leadership, Elmore (2000) characterizes large-scale improvement as a *property of organizations*, capturing several of the characteristics of communities of practice enumerated previously in a single paragraph:

Organizations that improve do so because they create and nurture agreement on what is worth achieving, and they set in motion the internal processes by which people progressively learn how to do what they need to do in order to achieve what is worthwhile.... Improvement occurs through organized social learning, not through the idiosyncratic experimentation and discovery of variously talented individuals. Experimentation and discovery can be harnessed to social learning by connecting people with new ideas to each other in an environment in which the ideas are subjected to scrutiny, measured against the collective purposes of the organization, and tested by the history of what has already been learned and is known. (p. 25)

Elmore clearly puts the cart of experimentation and discovery (what we have been calling innovation or intervention) behind the horse of established social learning processes and structures within a district. Formal professional development programs represent a form of experimentation leading to discovery of how to improve instruction. But if that and other forms of experimentation and innovation remain disconnected from the larger learning context – the norms and practices of the collective community – then the system will not improve.

This chapter represents the start of a journey to find ways in which we might leverage online technology, activities, and services to help districts realize cohesive, well-aligned, career-long professional development and system-wide improvement. We have used the community of practice framework to expand the focus of analysis beyond individual schools, professional development programs, or online communities. We have argued that *community of practice* is not just another term used to convey a sense of professional kinship or shared interest; it is an integral, evolving entity that spans stakeholder groups within a school system. It may promote improvement or militate against instructional improvement in a number of ways. Even dysfunctional communities of practice can, with leadership toward a common improvement goal, grow over time to be effective contexts for learning and strong catalysts for district-wide improvement. We also conjecture that specific aspects of communities (e.g., tools, rules, and division of labor) can help diagnose the health of an education community of practice (how well it is functioning), signaling whether a professional development intervention or other innovation is likely to be accepted, take root, and spread.

As a starting point for our journey, we have enumerated eight characteristics of an education community of practice that represent guideposts for designing infrastructure to support communities of practice. We have taken the strong position that the eight characteristics are *not* a menu from which technologists can choose which ones to address in developing tools and environments intended to support an education community of practice. We believe that community of practice infrastructure must address all of the characteristics. In the sociotechnical design of Tapped In, we have worked on all of these dimensions, and we have been more successful in some areas than in others. Tapped In lacks certain communication, database, and search tools that we believe are necessary components of a community of practice infrastructure. For example, Tapped In needs stronger tools for content-specific authoring and reflective inquiry to support a local practice more effectively. We have focused on leadership and culture in relation to the online community, but not in relation to one's local community.

Moving forward, we must develop new ways that online technology and social structures can be used to help (1) identify, diagnose, and mend dysfunctional structural aspects of an education community of practice and (2) support the community in its role as a context and catalyst for improved instruction and professional development. We recognize, however, that understanding and addressing the characteristic *structures* of education communities of practice is only half the battle. The greater challenge is to understand the *processes* through which a district-wide community of practice works, evolves, and interacts with policies, programs, and informal activities to help teachers become accomplished educators and adult learners.

Education technology researchers know well that even technology-mediated interventions that are well designed to support the *envisioned* structures and activities of a school community often are not taken up by the community because of what Orlikowski (1992) calls the *duality of technology* – the influence of the technology on the organization and the influence of the organization on the technology. "The ongoing interaction of technology with organizations must be understood dialectically, as involving reciprocal causation, where the specific institutional context and the actions of knowledgeable, reflexive humans always mediate the relationship" (p. 423). To meet this challenge, we must step outside the *online* world to study the sociocultural processes of communities of practice in both well-functioning and dysfunctional districts. By understanding the structures *and* the processes of education communities of practice, we hope to construct analytical tools to diagnose community health, formulate strategies to help strengthen the community, and develop social models and technological tools that support the community's role in the professional development of its members. Our goal is to build a new *crossroads* that brings together, and helps forge stronger relationships among, education practitioners, providers, and researchers within a local community of practice to engage in the work of instructional improvement.

References

American Association of Colleges for Teacher Education (AACTE). (2000). *Log on or lose out*. Washington, DC: AACTE Publications.

Ball, D. L., & Cohen, D. K. (1999). Developing practice, developing practitioners: Toward a practice-based theory of professional education. In L. Darling-Hammond & G. Sykes (Eds.), *Teaching as the learning profession: Handbook of policy and practice* (pp. 3–32). San Francisco, CA: Jossey-Bass.

Barab, S. A., & Duffy, T. M. (2000). From practice fields to communities of practice. In D. Jonassen & S. Land (Eds.), *Theoretical foundations of learning environments* (pp. 25–56). Mahwah, NJ: Erlbaum.

Barab, S., MaKinster, J., & Scheckler, R. (this volume). Designing system dualities: Characterizing an online professional development community.

Blanton, W. E., Mooreman, G., & Trathen, W. (1998). Telecommunications and teacher education: A social constructivist review. In P. D. Pearson & A. Iran-Nejad (Eds.), *Review of research in education, 23* (pp. 235–275). Washington, DC: AERA.

Blumenfeld, P. C., Fishman, B. J., Krajcik, J. S., &. Marx, R. W. (2000). Creating usable innovations in systemic reform: Scaling up technology-embedded project-based science in urban schools. *Educational Psychologist, 35*(3), 149–164.

Bozeman, B., Dietz, J. S., & Gaughan, M. (1998, August). Scientific and technical human capital: An alternative model for research evaluation. Draft for presentation at the American Political Science Association, September 5, Atlanta, GA.

Bransford, J., Brown, A., & Cocking, R. (Eds.). (1999). *How people learn: Brain, mind, experience, and school*. Washington, DC: National Academy Press.

Brown, J. S., & Duguid, P. (1991). Organizational learning and communities-of-practice: Toward a unified view of working, learning and innovation. *Organization Science, 2*(1) 40–57.

Brown, J. S., & Duguid, P. (2000). *The social life of information*. Cambridge, MA: Harvard Business School Press.

Cochran-Smith, M., & Lytle, S. L. (1999). Relationships of knowledge and practice: Teacher learning in communities. In A. Iran-Nejad & P. D. Pearson (Eds.), *Review of research in education 24* (pp. 249–305). Washington, DC: AERA.

Cole, M., & Engeström, Y. (1993). A cultural-historical approach to distributed cognition. In G. Solomon (Ed.), *Distributed cognitions: Psychological and educational consideration* (pp. 1–46). Cambridge: Cambridge University Press.

Constant, D., Sproull, L., & Kiesler, S. (1996). The kindness of strangers: The usefulness of electronic weak ties for technical advice. *Organization Science, 7*(2), 119–135.

Corcoran, T. B., Shields, P. M., & Zucker, A. A. (1998, March). *The SSIs and professional development for teachers*. Menlo Park, CA: SRI International.

Cothrel, J., & Williams, R. (1999). Online communities: Helping them form and grow. *Journal of Knowledge Management, 3*(1), 54–60.

Darling-Hammond, L., & Ball, D. L. (1997, June). *Teaching for high standards: What policymakers need to know and be able to do*. Available online at http://www.negp. gov/reports/highstds.htm.

Darling-Hammond, L., & Sykes, G. (Eds.) (1999). *Teaching as the learning profession: Handbook of policy and practice*. San Francisco, CA: Jossey-Bass.

Derry, S. J., Gance, S., Gance, L. L., & Schlager, M. S. (2000). Toward assessment of knowledge building practices in technology-mediated work group interactions. In S. Lajoie (Ed.), *Computers as cognitive tools II* (pp. 29–68). Mahwah, NJ: Erlbaum.

Donnelly, M. B., Dove, T., Tiffany, J., Adelman, N., & Zucker, A. (2000, January). *Evaluation of key factors impacting the effective use of technology in schools. Subtask 5: Professional development study literature review*. Draft report. Menlo Park, CA: SRI International.

Dunlap, D. R., Neale, D. C., & Carroll, J. M. (2000). Teacher collaboration in a networked community. *Educational Technology and Society 3*(3) (pp. 442–454), Special Issue on On-Line Collaborative Learning Environments.

Elmore, R. F. (1996). Getting to scale with good educational practice. *Harvard Educational Review, 66*(1), 1–26.

Elmore, R. F. (2000). *Building a new structure for school leadership.* Washington, DC: Albert Shanker Institute.

Elmore, R. F., & Burney, D. (1999). Investing in teacher learning: Staff development and instructional improvement. In L. Darling-Hammond & G. Sykes (Eds.), *Teaching as the learning profession: Handbook of policy and practice* (pp. 265–291). San Francisco, CA: Jossey-Bass.

Evertson, C. M., Smithey, M. W., & Hough, B. W. (2000). Exploring the use of Web-based conferences for new teacher professional development. Final Report, NPEAT Project 2.4.3. National Partnership for Excellence and Accountability in Teaching (NPEAT). Washington, DC: U.S. Department of Education.

Engeström, Y. (1987). *Learning by expanding: An activity-theoretical approach to developmental research.* Helsinki: Orienta-Konsultit.

Engeström, Y. (1999). Expansive visibilization of work: An activity-theoretical perspective. *Computer Supported Cooperative Work (CSCW), 8*(1–2), 63–93.

Feldman, A., Konold, C., & Coulter, B. (2000). *Network science a decade later: The Internet and classroom learning.* Mahwah, NJ: Erlbaum.

Finholt, T. A., Lewis, S. A., & Mott, W. H. (1995). *Distance learning in the Upper Atmospheric Research Collaboratory.* Unpublished manuscript. Collaboratory for Research on Electronic Work. University of Michigan, Ann Arbor.

Fusco, J., Gehlbach, H., & Schlager, M. (2000). Assessing the impact of a large-scale online teacher professional development community. In *Proceedings of the 11th International Conference for the Society for Information Technology and Teacher Education* (pp. 2178–2183).

Gallego, M. A., Hollingsworth, S., & Whitenack, D. A. (2001). Relational knowing in the reform of educational cultures. *Teachers College Record, 103*(2), 240–266.

Garet, M. S., Porter, A. C., Desimone, L., Birman, B. F., & Yoon, K. S. (2001, Winter). What makes professional development effective? Results from a national sample of teachers. *American Educational Research Journal, 38*(4), 915–945.

Gomez, L., Fishman, B., & Pea, R. (1998). The CoV is project: Building a large-scale science education testbed. *Interactive Learning Environments, 6*(1–2), 59–92.

Granovetter, M. (1973). The strength of weak ties. *American Journal of Sociology, 78,* 1360–1380.

Granovetter, M. (1982). The strength of weak ties: A network theory revisited. In P. M. N. Lin (Ed.), *Social structure and network analysis* (pp. 105–130). Beverly Hills, CA: Sage.

Gray, J., & Tatar, D. (this volume). Sociocultural analysis of online professional development: A case study of personal, interpersonal, community, and technical aspects.

Grossman, P., Wineburg, S., & Woolworth, S. (2000, April). *In pursuit of teacher community.* Paper presented at the Annual Meeting of the American Educational Research Association, New Orleans.

Hawkins, J. (1996). Dilemmas. In C. Fisher, D. C. Dwyer, & K. Yocam (Eds.), *Education and technology* (pp. 33–50). San Francisco, CA: Jossey-Bass.

Hewitt, J. (this volume). An exploration of community in a Knowledge Forum classroom: An activity system analysis.

Hoadley, C. M., & Pea, R. D. (2002). Finding the ties that bind: Tools in support of a knowledge-building community. In K. A. Renninger & W. Shumar (Eds.), *Building virtual communities: Learning and change in cyberspace* (pp. 321–354). New York: Cambridge University Press.

Honey, M., Carrigg, F., & Hawkins, J. (1998). Union City Online: An architecture for networking and reform. In C. Dede (Ed.), *The 1998 ASCD yearbook: Learning with technology* (pp. 121–139). Alexandria, VA: ASCD.

Koku, E. F., & Wellman, B. (this volume). Scholarly networks as learning communities: The case of TechNet.

Koppich, J., Asher, C., & Kerchner, C. (2002). Developing careers, building a profession: The Rochester Career in Teaching plan. New York: National Commission on Teaching & America's Future.

Lave, J., & Wenger, E. (1991). *Situated learning: Legitimate peripheral participation.* Cambridge: Cambridge University Press.

Lieberman, A. (1996). Creating intentional learning communities. *Educational Leadership, 54*(3), 51–55.

Lieberman, A., & Grolnick, M. (1999). Networks and reform in American education. In L. Darling-Hammond & G. Sykes (Eds.), *Teaching as the learning profession: Handbook of policy and practice* (pp. 292–312). San Francisco, CA: Jossey-Bass.

Little, J. W. (1990). The persistence of privacy: Autonomy and initiative in teachers' professional relations. *Teachers College Record, 91*(4), 509–536.

Little, J. (1993). Teachers' professional development in a climate of educational reform. *Educational Evaluation and Policy Analysis, 15*(2), 129–151.

Little, J. W. (2001, September). *Inside teacher community: Representations of classroom practice.* Paper presented at the conference of International Study Association on Teachers and Teaching, Faro, Portugal.

Lortie, D. C. (1975). *Schoolteacher: A sociological study.* Chicago: University of Chicago Press.

Loucks-Horsley, S., Hewson, P. W., Love, N., & Stiles, K. E. (1998). *Designing professional development for teachers of science and mathematics.* Thousand Oaks, CA: Corwin.

Marx, R. W., Blumenfeld, P. C., Krajcik, J. S., & Soloway, E. (1998). New technologies of teacher professional development. *Teaching and Teacher Education, 14,* 33–52.

McLaughlin, M. W., & Mitra, D. (2001). Theory-based change and change-based theory: Going deeper, going broader. *Journal of Educational Change, 1*(2), 1–24.

McLaughlin, M. W., & Talbert, J. E. (2001). *Professional communities and the work of high school teaching.* Chicago: University of Chicago Press.

Mwanza, D. (2001). Where theory meets practice: A case for an Activity Theory based methodology to guide computer system design. In M. Hirose (Ed.), *Proceedings of INTERACT'2001: Eighth IFIP TC 13 International Conference on Human-Computer Interaction.* Oxford, UK: IOS Press.

National Commission on Mathematics and Science Teaching for the 21st Century. (2000). *Before it's too late.* U.S. Department of Education. Available online at www.ed.gov/americacounts/glenn.

National Commission on Teaching and America's Future (NCTAF). (1996). *What matters most: Teaching for America's future.* New York: Author.

Oldenburg, R. (1997). *The great good place.* New York: Marlowe.

Orlikowski, W. J. (1992). The duality of technology: Rethinking the concept of technology in organizations. *Organization Science, 3*(3), 398–427.

Orr, J. (1996). *Talking about machines: An ethnography of a modern job.* Ithaca, NY: IRL Press.

Palloff, R. M., & Pratt, K. (1999). *Building learning communities in cyberspace.* San Francisco, CA: Jossey-Bass.

President's Committee of Advisors on Science and Technology (PCAST), Panel on Educational Technology. (1997, March). *Report to the President on the use of technology to strengthen K–12 education in the United States.* Available online at http://www.ostp.gov/PCAST/k-12ed.html.

Putnam, R. T., & Borko, H. (2000). What do new views of knowledge and thinking have to say about research on teacher learning? *Educational Researcher, 29*(1), 4–15.

Rényi, J. (1996). *Teachers take charge of their learning: Transforming professional development for student success.* NEA Foundation for the Improvement of Education. Available online at http://nfie.org/publications/takecharge.htm.

Riel, M., & Becker, H. (2000, April). *The beliefs, practices, and computer use of teacher leaders.* AERA presentation, New Orleans. Available online at http://www.crito.uci.edu/tlc/findings/aera.

Riel, M., & Polin, L. (this volume). Online learning communities: Common ground and critical differences in designing technical environments.

Ruopp, R., Gal, S., Drayton, B., & Pfister, M. (1993). *LabNet: Toward a community of practice.* Hillsdale, NJ: Erlbaum.

Schank, P., Fenton, J., Schlager, M., & Fusco, J. (1999). From MOO to MEOW: Domesticating technology for online communities. In C. Hoadley (Ed.), *Computer Support for Collaborative Learning (CSCL) 1999* (pp. 518–526). Hillsdale, NJ: Erlbaum.

Schlager, M. S., Fusco, J., & Schank, P. (1998). Cornerstones for an online community of education professionals. *IEEE Technology and Society, 17*, 15–21, 40.

Schlager, M., Fusco, J., & Schank, P. (2002). Evolution of an online education community of practice. In K. A. Renninger & W. Shumar (Eds.), *Building virtual communities: Learning and change in cyberspace* (pp. 129–158). New York: Cambridge University Press.

Schlager, M. S., & Schank, P. K. (1997). TAPPED IN: A new online teacher community concept for the next generation of Internet technology. In *Proceedings of CSCL 97, The Second International Conference on Computer Support for Collaborative Learning* (pp. 230–241). Hillsdale, NJ: Erlbaum.

Schwen, T. M., & Hara, N. (this volume). Communities of practice: A metaphor for online design?

Scribner, J. P., Cockrell, K. S., Cockrell, D. H., & Valentine, J. W. (1999). Creating professional communities in schools through organizational learning. *Educational Administration Quarterly, 35*(1), 130–161.

Shields, P. M., Esch, C., Young, V. M., & Humphrey, D. C. (2000). *White paper on teacher induction*. Menlo Park, CA: SRI International.

Smylie, M. A., Allensworth, E., Greenberg, R. C., Harris, R., & Luppescu, S. (2001). *Teacher professional development in Chicago: Supporting effective practice*. Chicago, IL: Consortium on Chicago School Research.

Spillane, J. P., Halverson, R., & Diamond, J. B. (1999). *Toward a theory of leadership practice: A distributed perspective*. Evanston, IL: Northwestern University.

Stein, M. K., Silver, E. A., & Smith, M. S. (1998). Mathematics reform and teacher development: A community of practice perspective. In J. G. Greeno & S. V. Goldman (Eds.), *Thinking practices in mathematics and science learning* (pp. 17–52). Mahwah, NJ: Erlbaum.

Tatar, D. G., Gray, J., & Fusco, J. (2002). Rich social interaction in a synchronous online community for learning. In G. Stahl (Ed.), *Proceedings of the Conference on Computer Support for Collaborative Learning* (pp. 633–634). Hillsdale, NJ: Erlbaum.

Van Maanen, J., & Barley, S. R. (1984). Occupational communities: Culture and control in organizations. *Research in Organizational Behavior, 6*, 287–365.

Web-based Education Commission. (2000). *The power of the Internet for learning: Moving from promise to practice*. Washington, DC: Author.

Wellman, B. (1997). An electronic group is virtually a social network. In S. Kiesler (Ed.), *Culture of the Internet* (pp. 179–205). Mahwah, NJ: Erlbaum.

Wellman, B., & Gulia, M. (1999). Net surfers don't ride alone: Virtual communities as communities. In M. Smith & P. Kollock (Eds.), *Communities in cyberspace* (pp. 169–194). London: Routledge.

Wenger, E. (1998). *Communities of practice: Learning, meaning, and identity*. New York: Cambridge University Press.

Wilson, S. M., & Berne, J. (1999). Teacher learning and the acquisition of professional knowledge: An examination of research on contemporary professional development. In A. Iran-Nejad & P. D. Pearson (Eds.), *Review of research in education, 24* (pp. 173–209). Washington, DC: AERA.

6

Community of Practice

A Metaphor for Online Design?

Thomas M. Schwen and Noriko Hara

The field of Instructional Technology has a long tradition of design to support learning, using both soft technology (e.g., coaching or mentoring) and hard technology (e.g., computer-assisted instruction). A new commercial communications technology is released in the marketplace, and then within a few years the scholarly journals develop a series of claims, and some preliminary data, about the potential for teaching and learning. Current enthusiasm that a community of practice (CoP) would be a compelling tool to support learning in organizations is well beyond empirical evidence and is inconsistent with related theory for nurturing CoPs. The major assumption of this chapter is that there is a historic tautology in the field of educational technology that is extremely seductive and persistent. The major thesis is: the enthusiasm for online communities seems premature in the sense that the technology is the natural vehicle for CoPs.

The readers of this volume are certainly well acquainted with Lave and Wenger's (1991) and Wenger's (1998) seminal work on communities of practice. One can reasonably credit the authors with dramatically influencing both research and development efforts in an extremely wide variety of contexts. Legitimate peripheral participation in a community of practice is a compelling and relatively fresh theoretical approach to the complicated pattern of workplace learning and related identity formation. Caught up in this enthusiasm, several of the first author's students have conducted case studies examining professional business consultants, engineers, and defense lawyers. The data from these studies both confirm and extend the work of Lave and Wenger (1991) as they describe rich patterns of workplace community nurturing of professional identity formation and learning. We have become convinced that these constructs are extremely useful descriptions of the situated learning patterns prevalent in many work settings.

We thank Sasha Barab and Rob Kling for their helpful comments.

We began to be concerned about the potential misapplication of the constructs as we became swept up in what appeared to be the next logical step, online communities. This chapter was written in response to these concerns. We begin by reviewing four cases and offering a brief comparison and contrast. From there, we challenge some of the theoretical optimism, instead highlighting five challenges facing the design of CoPs. Acknowledging these challenges, we finally offer an alternative design approach and a design allegory to illustrate these concepts more concretely.

CASE DESCRIPTIONS

Case 1: CoPs and IT

Hara (2000) completed an ethnographic study that followed two communities of defense lawyers. She was particularly interested in the use of communication technology among the professionals, whether it contributed to, was independent of, or detracted from productive CoP behavior. In the first group she observed seven practicing defense lawyers, who were employees of a modest-sized county in a large Midwestern state. These lawyers practiced in a collaborative fashion, actively sharing their knowledge of the law with one another and other private defense lawyers in their county. They regarded themselves as "underdogs" in the judicial system, underfinanced, underpaid, and not particularly appreciated by the public at large. They expressed both satisfaction and commitment to the values in the law, which provide for equal protection of all citizens. Some had left more lucrative private practices to follow a career of service, mainly to the indigent. Contrary to general norms in this type of professional practice, they were relatively stable in their employment. The youngest person in service had been with the office for six years, and some of the others' service exceeded ten years. They would spontaneously rally around a colleague with serious felony cases, offering moral support, sharing stories of similar cases, and listening to and critiquing alternate theories of defense. They would informally develop specialties in the law to provide updates to the rest of the practice on new or changing interpretations in the law. There were few physical boundaries in their offices, as they often moved from workspace to workspace dialoging with one another in an animated fashion. They were proud of their history and the respect they had gained in the for-profit legal community. While more than 70 percent of their clients were found guilty, they were especially satisfied with the minority of cases where innocent clients were vindicated. While continually dealing with the hostile environment of public perception, better-funded opponents, and often hostile clients they managed to find an identity in their underdog image that was sustaining and constructive. Regarding technology, they were not well enough funded to have elaborate connectivity to legal services such as Lexis-Nexis. There was one terminal in the office connected to those services. They did have a listserv provided by the state government on which they could share stories, pursue legal issues, or ask for assistance. They were very modest users of all the electronic services. They seemed to resist the services from the state, reasoning that the advice was less effective and predictable than they would receive in their own practice. Although they would use the standard Lexis-Nexis services when needed, they often assigned the research to legal assistants or interns.

A second practice of defense lawyers was much larger. There were sixty-five lawyers and thirty legal assistants in the office. This practice was divided into four categories ranging from least to most serious offenses. Their specialties corresponded to the structure of a court system in a much larger community than the one in the previously described county. The pay and public perception was similar to the smaller community. The compensation was actually somewhat higher. However, the turnover for professional lawyers was about 50 percent annually. These lawyers would often be recruited or find other more lucrative employment in the community as they developed their expertise. In addition, the specialization offered significantly fewer opportunities for practicing and developing a wide range of defense skills. The lawyers in the misdemeanor court could represent as many as 120 clients in a single day, merely going through pro forma protocols without much knowledge of the individuals or their circumstances. To further complicate the opportunity to form productive community relationships, the lawyers in the latter group were physically separated from the rest of the practice. Despite best efforts from leadership, there was very little community sharing between the separated units (they were in government offices about a city block apart). Some of the lawyers in the major felony and capital case portion of the practice were better supported. However, they did not achieve the level of mutual supportive behavior that was observed in the small county practice. This group of professionals was better funded, and each professional had full access to the electronic service mentioned above. The youngest and least advantaged group serving the least important misdemeanor and class D felony clients frequently used the services for community support. In an interesting turn of events, they did not interact with members of their own practice, but occasionally took advantage of the state listserv service. They would sporadically share case scenarios and ask for advice from (and offer advice to) other defense lawyers in the state. They seemed to, at some level, use this extended community to replace what was lacking in their primary practice. However, the use of the listserv was episodic and did not seem to sustain this practice as well as the small county practice described above. Hara did not find much support for the beneficial effects of technology. The least sophisticated, perhaps most needy group used standard collaborative software almost as an escape from a reasonably unrewarding practice. The most successful CoP, in terms of mutual support and productive learning behaviors, actively eschewed the use of collaborative technology.

Case 2: Expensive CoP

Yi (2000) was a participant observer in a Fortune 50 company's attempt to design a CoP. This high-technology company is well known for its sophisticated educational enterprises. The company routinely invests a significant proportion of its income in a variety of strategic efforts to improve learning and performance. The company leaders were well aware of Wenger's work and decided that they could increase the effectiveness and efficiency of learning by forming a CoP on the basis of a new and necessary change in engineering design practice. There was strong agreement in the leadership of design engineers that the changes in practice were important individually and collectively. The firm had a strong history of competitiveness by adopting new technology at a very rapid rate. Lead engineers were often rewarded for their responsiveness to industry challenges. To test this new concept of learning at work, the leadership of the firm assembled an impressive array of resources for the CoP experiment.

CoP designers, technical support personnel, world-class experts in the new design technology, world-class consultants, evaluation experts, and leaders of the engineering community from across the firm were assembled and given whatever reasonable requests for communication technology they needed. A multi-month plan was put in place to transfer the knowledge of the new design technology to those portions of the firm that would most likely take advantage of the new design tools and processes. A curriculum plan was put in place where one of the best-known experts in the new design process would be made available to teach a few formal sessions, but more importantly to coach the leading engineers as they attempted to apply the new knowledge to extant problems. The curriculum plan involved some initial formal presentations and quickly evolved to a work group activity with regular electronic meetings using NetMeeting™ and related technologies. The presenters would vary as they attempted to apply the new design technology. The expert quickly adopted a coaching role, assisting where necessary, and encouraging others to accept leadership. After some difficulties with the technology, the group settled into a rhythm of work exploring the tools and concepts. Whereas the engineers with the most pressing relevant problems made a great deal of progress, the engineers with less relevant work problems at the time participated in a more peripheral manner.

As the work group continued, their participation began to wane as the immediate problem of acquiring the tools and concepts had been accomplished. What was interesting and unexpected by corporate leadership was that established CoP structures began to be the primary mediators of the new design process. These established CoP structures seemed to co-alesce around functional specialties in the firm, although the "designed CoP" continued to support boundary activities of the kind that Wenger describes. Engineers of long standing in the firm would often share their information on the basis of known associations resulting from workplace rotation or previous common projects in the firm. The designed CoP was eventually abandoned as a project. The firm declared success concerning the objective or rapid dissemination of new design knowledge. However, the significant cost of designing such an enterprise was considered too severe when compared with the gain and the lack of permanency of the constructed social structure.

Case 3: Extensive Legitimate Peripheral Participation (LPP)

Chao (2001) observed and interviewed fast-rising managers in one of the nation's larger consulting firms. She was concerned with the nature of their learning processes as they were initiated into the practice of busi-ness consulting. As an employee of the firm in its educational arm, she identified those new employees who had received initial high ratings in their regular personnel reviews. These ratings were sufficient to identify the most promising recruits of the previous two years. Her intention was to examine the dynamics of these recruits' learning processes. The firm had an established pattern of coaching and mentoring, formal training, prompt personnel reviews of new employee performance, and reasonably effective rotation of work assignments to provide both breadth and depth in assign-ments. The success of the recruits seemed to be a function of assignments that were challenging but not overwhelming, the opportunity to provide service while being coached but not tightly managed, the determination and drive to learn new skills rapidly, and thoughtful mentoring including constructive personnel reviews. Nearly all the informants in this study at-tributed a substantial portion of their early success to "luck," especially luck in work assignments that were a stretch but not devastating, and luck in mentors who were supportive but not oppressive in their style of su-pervision. Formal training was important in some cases but uniformly a minor portion of the reported causes of success.

Chao (2001) found extensive legitimate peripheral participation as de-scribed by Lave and Wenger (1991), but little mature CoP behavior on the part of the individuals or the work groups in which they participated. This finding is consistent with Wenger's (1998) discussion of trajectories. It was as if the tacit policy of the firm was to extend the apprenticeship for at least three years while the hardiest of the new recruits survived the Darwinian environment. What was interesting to this discussion was that the new recruits had access to an extensive electronic environment for sharing consulting information. The environment was designed to support collaboration, reports about consulting success and failure, employee profiles, proprietary business practices, and so forth. The virtual environment was endowed with massive sums of money to support the infrastructure, the consultants, and more. Despite these "advantages," this infrastructure was hardly used by the new recruits or their mentors to communicate with the recruits. This modest use of the virtual environment occurred despite special incentives and other forms of encouragement and threats by management.

Case 4: Online CoP

Haney (2003) observed work groups in one of the most technologically sophisticated firms in the world where she was a participant observer for a little more than a year. Her commission was to observe the knowledge-sharing behavior of a group of professionals in the firm. She was expected to critique the group's use of collaboration and performance support technology in a manner that would enhance the group's performance. She was also allowed to pursue dissertation research to examine one of the most extensive support environments in the world.

The firm can support individual and collective work with an array of virtual tools that is quite unique. A work group can define itself by its own authority, construct databases of relevant documents, schedule virtual or face-to-face meetings, share individual databases, search and retrieve relevant databases from the firm's public archives, seek help from information specialists and technical experts within the firm, and construct personal time management support tools. Additionally, they can post special tools for group decision-making, schedule online learning events, locate similar work groups, and find and reference the firm's vision, strategic planning documents, and leadership communications relevant to their task. Multiple millions of dollars have been spent on developing and promoting the virtual environment.

The firm is generally successful and the work group observed in this study is well regarded for its productivity and its contribution to the overall success of the firm. The work culture is highly competitive and rewards for exceptional performance are usually given to individuals rather than groups. The firm recruits top graduates of a variety of business and technical specialties that support the work of the practice. Ultimate success in the firm is achieved by reaching a level of management where financial rewards are determined by the overall success of the firm as well as individual productivity. Less than a third of those entering the firm stay with it after four years. By that point, the new recruits usually know whether they are likely to achieve management status. Many leave voluntarily when their future with the firm becomes well understood. This work environment still requires collaboration for success. Many business opportunities

require a team of specialists and less expensive peripheral players to produce a profit. Management recognizes this tension between its reward
system and the need for teamwork. Although it is not explicitly a part of
the culture, it appears that the extensive investment in collaboration and
productivity tools is an attempt to deal with this incongruity or tension in
the firm.

As in Chao's (2001) study, there were considerable incentives for employees to explore the array of support technologies. Further, the tools
were well grounded in the most contemporary theories of knowledge
management, social cultural learning, and ergonomic research. Despite
these advantages, Haney found the tools were not used in the patterns
that most advocates of online community would expect. There were simply no discernable patterns of online CoP behavior in this setting. The
occasional flurries of small group work that seemed to offer promise of
maturing to online CoP behavior were often informal mechanisms lightly
challenging the authority or power of management. A small group would
form around an issue or theme of work practice, a flurry of productive
antiestablishment rhetoric would punctuate the useful exchange, and the
group behavior would fade quickly as the problem or theme was resolved.
There were many attempts to meet management's expectations about the
use of tools by creating publicly observable structures that resembled formal and informal norms and standards created by trainers and consultants. Often a young manager or aspiring manager would create a forum
with accompanying databases to initiate a new project or reform within
the practice. These structures or frameworks would rarely be used in any
dynamic fashion to negotiate meaning, share stories, or seek resolution
to conflict. Especially absent were communications that reflected on the
personal and group efforts and achieving professional identity. The effect seemed quite flat and sterile when contrasted with Hara's defense
lawyers or Yi's established CoP engineers working at the boundary of the
designed CoP.

Cross-Case Discussion

These case descriptions offer interesting contrasts with regard to the difficulty of establishing or observing CoP behavior in online environments
(see Table 6.1 for an overview of the cases). Hara (2000) found that the
strongest CoP used collaborative technologies the least, and Haney (2003)
notes that, despite elaborate, sophisticated, and expensive technology, no
discernable online CoP was observed. Lave and Wenger (1991) used butchers, tailors, midwives, quartermasters, and alcoholics as their primary
data set when they first introduced legitimate peripheral participation.
What we find interesting, in retrospect, is this situated learning of longstanding practice. In Lave and Wenger (1991), the weakest example of a

TABLE 6.1. *Cross-Case Description*

Case	Description
Case 1: CoP & Technology by Hara (2000)	The strongest CoP used collaborative technologies the least.
Case 2: Expensive CoP by Yi (2000)	All efforts were focused on design of a new CoP. Existing CoPs absorbed new design. Corporation discontinued support of new CoP.
Case 3: Extensive LPP by Chao (2001)	Extensive LPP was found among younger consultants, but little mature CoP behaviors were found.
Case 4: Online CoP by Haney (2003)	Despite elaborate, sophisticated, and expensive technology, no discernable online CoP was observed.

productive CoP was the butchers. The designers of this system had made an important modification to a prior practice. The introduction of formal training and the restriction of practice on economic grounds in supermarkets made the practice far more restrictive, sterile, and mechanical. There seemed to be far less negotiated meaning around a clear sense of professional identity formation. The exchanges were less about the practice of butchers and more about the routines that created efficiency. It is not that these topics are mutually exclusive, but it is the ratio that is at issue.

In our experience, a healthy CoP is one in which the practitioners find personal and profound meaning in their work. Learning is often not a formal agenda, but it is a secondary outcome of becoming knowledgeable while working in the field. The lawyers in Hara's study and the engineers in Yi's naturally occurring CoPs also had these attributes. Their identity formation was deeply rooted and tacitly held in their practice. The explicit goal of these enterprises seemed to be supporting the work, and the equally important tacit goal seemed to be forming identity. They were continually challenged by the work practice; they found solace, support, and satisfaction in the intimate local longstanding traditions that were known to improve practice. We wonder about the impediments to community formation in an online environment of practitioners who do not know one another, do not practice in intimate proximity to one another and therefore have little incentive or opportunity to negotiate their tacit agenda, as in Haney's case (2003).

Where designers attempt to foster or create community, even in enterprises where the employer is the same for all potential members, we find resistance or benign neglect of the community infrastructure. Although the employers invest large sums of money for knowledgeable consultants and extensive software systems, we still find struggle and benign neglect or cynical participation.

CAUTIONARY NOTES

These experiences have created a "return to fundamentals" motivation in our research group. We have gone back to Orr (1990), Wenger (1990), and the early examples that are often cited in support of the construct generally and as antecedents to the notion of online CoPs specifically. On the basis of these original studies and our more recent studies, we have some cautions to suggest regarding the design of online communities.

These cautions challenge the widespread enthusiasm about the CoP construct and online communities (e.g., Barab & Duffy, 2000; Cochran-Smith & Lytle, 1999; Collison et al., 2000; Kim, 2000; Preece, 2000) and problematize the construct in what we have found to be a more realistic perspective (see Kling & Courtright, this volume). This analysis points to problems that should be considered before developing an online CoP. These five problems seem to account for much of the data we have collected and we find comparable ideas in the literature for most of these notions (see Table 6.2).

Problem 1: Prescriptive versus Description Distinction

The original CoP formulation (Lave & Wenger, 1991) is descriptive, social, middle-level theory. It is not a warrant or prescription for the

TABLE 6.2. *List of Cautionary Notes*

Cautionary Note	Description of Problem
Prescriptive vs. Description Distinction	The foundational social theory is not a warrant for designing or nurturing a CoP.
Ready-Made vs. Communities in the Making	Situated learning theory has more to offer the "formed" community. Little is known about the early life cycle of CoPs. The best opportunity for online design is with formed CoPs.
Knowledge of Possession vs. Knowing in Practice	CoPs are rarely centered around declarative knowledge acquisition. Rather CoPs support knowledge in action.
Mid-Level Social Theory vs. Micro Learning Theory	Situated learning theory is a "middle-level" social theory; mixing learning theory and related pedagogy is either an inappropriate or untested mixing of levels of theory and methodology.
Motivated Members vs. Unwilling Subjects	The intentions of the community members are often subverted in "designs of" CoP.

construction of a CoP. While Wenger acknowledges the origins of the theory and is in many ways faithful to the original formulation, there has been a recent shift to a prescriptive posture. In the different contexts of applied theory building, Dubin (1978) and Bruner (1966) argued that prescriptive and descriptive theories serve different purposes. They observed that the twin purposes of understanding and prediction in this context are not interchangeable. That is, a rich descriptive theory is not a warrant or recipe for the construction of certain phenomena and a useful prescriptive theory may not provide a full understanding of the phenomena but rather a perspective on the conditions or circumstances of its applied use. While anthropologists and related social theorists do not commonly use the prescriptive/descriptive distinction, today one may find a similar understanding in their dialogue about pragmatic applications of their discipline (Gaver, 1996; Lassiter, 2000; Wasson, 2000; Sanday, 1998).

To apply this distinction to the current issue, Wenger's (1998) book, especially the last few chapters, may be viewed as a rich theoretical description of a fully mature and constructive CoP. In effect, Wenger seems to be defining the most complete and robust CoP that he finds plausible in his review of the literature. Since the data for such a formulation are few, we find his description to be an *interpretation* of what a fully functioning CoP could achieve. The rich set of subconstruct relationships offers the designer a set of hypotheses about diagnosing established or forming CoPs. Any interventions based on this sort of analysis would be quite speculative, because there are few, if any, empirical studies of interventions applying the theory. Although this type of analysis is certainly better than no analysis at all, it simply does not inform design efforts directly. Perhaps the best analogy of this circumstance for educators would be Gagne's (1965) early work. He originally summarized eight different genres of learning prototype research (signal, s-r, chaining, verbal association, discrimination, concept, rule, problem solving) into a hierarchical, progressive, predictive theory. The rearrangement of descriptive theory into a prescriptive format required years of additional research to achieve status as a classic design tool.

Although Wenger's work is a provocative ideal to achieve and useful as a tool for dialogue between designers and client systems, it is not a recipe for construction of such phenomena. While Yi (2000) observed fully functioning CoPs, none of the attempts at design shed light on how to construct these social structures. In fact, the design efforts were weakly or negatively correlated with CoP activity. All of the fully functioning CoPs we have observed in our work and have read about in the literature were not designed. Instead, they evolved quite naturally over several years. This state of affairs does not support a traditional design posture as was seen in Yi's (2000) or Haney's (2003) studies. Indeed, Wenger (1998, 2000) is clear about the style of design that is appropriate as warranted by his theory.

Communities of Practice are about content – about learning as a living experience of negotiating meaning – not about form. In this sense they cannot be legislated into existence or defined by decree. They can be recognized, supported, encouraged and nurtured, but they are not designable reified units. Practice itself is not amenable to design. (Wenger, 1998, p. 229)

The problem therefore is not with what Wenger advocates but how his theory is interpreted.

Problem 2. Ready-Made versus Communities in the Making

Wenger offers little insight into the formation of CoPs. He offers no longitudinal studies of CoP formation. Wenger (1999), in an internal document, describes a kind of stylized evolution of CoPs. He offers no data about such an evolutionary process. This evolutionary pattern resembles social theorizing about organizations, such as Aplin and Cosier (1980), where an organization cycles from early problem identification and uncertainty to collective action and eventually disintegration. Such models are indebted to birth, development, and death metaphors. The issue for designers is that the evolutionary pattern of CoP development is poorly understood. The early stages of CoP development may not resemble later stages that are better understood. Therefore, it will be extremely difficult to differentiate between healthy and unhealthy development under design. An interesting analogy may be found in child and adolescent development in which there are all sorts of specialties in physical and psychological practice that have evolved because the adult model is not a useful description of early developmental stages.

The studies of Yi (2000), Chao (2001), and Haney (2003) are particularly relevant here. Yi's organization abandoned its designed CoP after twelve months of extensive effort. Since the theory of development of CoPs is incomplete, there exist limited means of knowing whether the decision was appropriate or premature. Chao observed a group of employees frozen in a state of legitimate peripheral participation. While Wenger (1998) posits that this pattern is possible (presumably observed in the past), it is hard to determine whether this is an exception to development or one alternate development path. If this is an alternative path, it raises the issue of other alternative paths.

Problem 3. Knowledge of Possession versus Knowing in Practice

There appears to be a fundamental confusion between the epistemology of possession and the epistemology of practice among advocates of online design of CoPs. Cook and Brown (1999), writing in the social cultural learning tradition of Xerox PARC, raise a series of important epistemological issues. A simplified version of their argument is that there is a fundamental qualitative difference between the epistemology of possession (the traditional approach to learning and *knowledge*) and the epistemology of practice (which deals with the interactive *knowing* that occurs in professional and work practice). There are parallel ideas in the educational literature. Nickerson (1993) speaks thoughtfully to the dilemma of collective knowing in the well-known book of readings on situated cognition edited by Gavriel Solomon. Sfard (1998) raised the issue of acquisition and participation metaphors coexisting in educational practice. Liberally paraphrasing these authors and Resnick (1997), leading theoreticians argue that knowledge and knowing epistemologies are distinct processes that require different designs to support optimal community learning. Further, it is our opinion that acquisition of declarative knowledge is largely incompatible with the formation of CoPs or especially online CoPs.

What these authors find in both corporate and educational designs of CoPs is a heavy emphasis on knowledge (possession or acquisition). Often we see extensive learning objectives, curriculum lists of descriptions of knowledge deficits that justify the creation of online communities (Burroughs, 2000; Yi, 2000; Schlager & Fusco, this volume). An imposed intention on community members is an arrogance of intentionality that subverts the social foundation. We argue that these justifications and corresponding designs miss the point of the CoP theory. The theory is about knowing. The theory is about the kind of thoughtful, reflective dialogues that occur between Hara's attorneys as they solve everyday problems, Yi's engineers as they consider new design tools and applications, or Yanow's (2000) flute manufacturers as they collectively create world-class flutes. Workers in a CoP are responding to their work environment by sharing stories, problematizing work-related issues, and actively constructing their knowing processes. This process is much closer to Weick's (1995) sense-making than Gagne's learning conditions. The designs for knowing should be quite different than the designs for knowledge of possession.

Our reading of Cook and Brown (1999) and especially Sfard (1998) and Resnick (1997) is that the designs of knowing should not be sacrificed for designs of knowledge. It is the ratio that is at issue and perhaps the compatibility of the forms of expressing the two epistemologies. Thus, a CoP design could certainly entertain traditional knowledge goals and designs, but the ratio of such designs would be far less. Perhaps that would resemble the practice fields described by Barab and Duffy (2000). However, our limited experience suggests, as in Yi's study and perhaps some of the data in this volume would suggest, a kind of incompatibility in mixing traditional knowledge and knowing designs. The engineers seemed to breathe an audible (virtual) sigh of relief when the style of the electronic environment moved from a classroom style to a participatory style (see also the discussion of Problem 4). We find that the two epistemologies require different social support that is difficult to coordinate appropriately.

Problem 4. Mid-Level Social Theory versus Micro Learning Theory

There is a serious dilemma in applying a middle-level social theory in combination with an individual micro learning theory. Dubin (1978) is the theoretician we find most clear on the problem of aggregating levels in theory construction and application. He argues that combining theories across levels of analysis does not necessarily produce expected results. One cannot assume individual learning aggregates in predictable fashion to become collective learning. In this situation, designers are often applying a middle-level social theory of learning with prescriptive micro level theories of learning in online CoP designs. As in Problem 3, we find many mixed designs with a tilt toward knowledge objectives. To commit an injustice to Shakespeare, "Learning by another name is not necessarily learning." There is an analogy to this type of problem among educators in the corporate world. A dominant model of evaluation of training outcomes has been addressed in Kirkpatrick's (1998) Four Level Model. He argued that perceptions of training, learning outcomes, transfer outcomes, and results in business terms should be positively and, presumably, linearly related. Only recently have analysts understood that this is a classic case of faulty aggregation across theoretical levels of analysis, and is therefore a faulty assumption on which to build an evaluation paradigm. Individual learning may not be reliably aggregated to the level of institutional outcomes.

In some CoP designs, it would appear, designers assume that learning is learning and that knowing and knowledge "fit together" in a hand-in-glove manner. The socio-cultural theorists such as Wertsch (1995), Cole (1995), Rogoff (1995), Engeström (1987), and Lave and Wenger (1991) have certainly raised our sensitivity to social mediation of learning. What isn't as clear is that these "forms" of learning can or should always be combined in the same vessel.

By reexamining Lave and Wenger's examples and the work of Yi (2000), Chao (2001), and Haney (2003), a different kind of interpretation has emerged. In the study by Yi (2000), the early attempts to teach engineers the new design concepts resembled a traditional distance education class. There were manuals, lectures, examples, and so on. While the "instruction" was successful at some level, the expert and the designers became painfully aware that the kind of CoP behavior they expected was obviously absent. There was a teacher-pupil ethos. When the engineers and designers moved quickly away from this pattern to an agenda of professional dialogue that involved shared leadership, individual "think alouds" about possibilities and problems in application, demonstrations of personal breakthroughs and failures, and so on, there were early signs of community, changes in power relationships, and even some signs of identity formation. It was as if the social expectations about traditional knowledge-building and knowing practiced in this setting were largely incompatible. Chao (2001) found that fast-rising managers in the large consulting firm struggled to see a utilitarian or functional relationship between the knowledge gained in "training" and the knowing activity that was a part of their legitimate peripheral participation. Categorically, these were held as different, almost oppositional, events even though they shared the same vocabulary. Both were necessary, but they were perceived to be different, almost incompatible in the social practice of their work. Also, as reexamined in the examples in Lave and Wenger (1991) and the largely repeated examples in Wenger (1998), we noted that the technicians, flute makers, claims processors, butchers, and others were having dialogues about their work, and learning is not distinct. They are articulating the everyday problems or dilemmas of practice. One wonders if the social dynamics typically associated with acquisition of knowledge may be incompatible with the social practice of knowing at work.

Problem 5. Motivated Members versus Unwilling Subjects

While the CoP theoretical model has changed, some important dimensions have not been evaluated. In the vast chorus of enthusiasm about CoP theory and application there have been a few thoughtful criticisms that should be of concern to designers. First is an appreciation of intentionality as possibly undermining member participation, and second is an appreciation of the potential destructive aspects of a CoP.

Regarding intentionality, Henriksson (2000), Contu and Willmont (1999, 2000), Fox (1999), and Easterby-Smith et al. (1998) express important reservations about CoP research. Contu and Willmont express it particularly well: "we encounter an (unacknowledged) shift or slippage from an earlier presentation of learning as praxis fashioned within a discourse of critiques to a formulation as technology conceived within a discourse of regulation and performance" (p. 272). Our interpretation of this criticism is that there is an interesting irony in Marxist critical theory being adapted to large corporate organizational purposes. What started as recognition of the informal, nonhierarchical, social frame for considering situated learning became a tool for implementing managerial change. We see this shift as a dilemma for designers because the original articulation of the theory is being applied to a significantly different purpose. This new emphasis leads to a different social dynamic.

Regarding destructive CoPs in Yi, Haney, and Hara, there was active resistance to the espoused concept of online community. In the Yi case, an accommodation with leadership was achieved when the agenda for the engineers was given to the participants. The loss of power and participant determination of intention that shifted to designers or agents of authority may be seen in some of the chapters in this volume. The common justification for federal funding of CoPs for teachers stems from their "inadequate preparation" or "poor performance." This asserting control over the professional intentions of teachers, while consistent with Wenger's current position (2000), is an important deviation from the original definition of CoP by Lave and Wenger (1991): "Agents' activities and the world (presumably of CoP) mutually constitute each other" (p. 33). The consequences for social system design or actualization of community seem dramatically changed by such a shift. We have no data about the resistance that could normally be expected about such a loss of power, but certainly teacher CoPs with dwindling participation or low participation should consider the hypothesis that their community membership has been disenfranchised.

The positive connotations of community have been retained while the negative or destructive aspects of community have been moved to footnotes or underrepresented by the exclusive use of positive examples. Henriksson (2000), Contu and Willmont (2000), Chao (2001), Haney (2003), and Hara (2000) gave us some insight to the issues associated with destructive community behavior. Chao observed what could reasonably be described as intentional hazing of new hires. A protracted period of intense, powerless apprenticeship seemed to be a part of the organizational design. Admittedly, no informants were quite willing to risk that assertion. A Darwinian conception of organizational survival was the modus operandi leading to a 33 percent retention rate over three years. A reasonable amount of serendipity as well as skill seemed to determine success or failure.

In the Haney case, in another consulting firm, there was such an atmosphere of competition and corresponding lack of trust that the fleeting CoP behavior seemed to be a feeble expression of collective passive aggression. The online "practice" was often a cynical expression of resistance. As previously observed in the Hara case, the weakest and most poorly supported employees in the law office turned to an outside legal listserv service to supplement the inadequate support found inside the organization. While Wenger (1998) allows for these patterns, the emphasis recently has only been on positive or productive behavior of CoPs (Contu & Willmont, 2000; Henriksson, 2000). The story is incomplete, and designers are not well served by such omissions. Designers will have both substantive issues of design as well as ethical trade-offs to consider when such destructive patterns emerge.

A DESIGN APPROACH

What then, is the alternative? What kind of design is possible when informed by such a complex social theory? What do this and related theories afford the designer? What use can be made of Wenger's notions

TABLE 6.3. *Educational Design Strategy*

Phase	Description
1. Possible design interventions	Identify an existing community and evaluate whether design interventions would be possible and useful.
2. Analysis	What are the social patterns of learning and identity formation? What are the untapped possibilities for achieving the goals of the population?
3. Design	The design process could incorporate iterative strategies such as social technical design, rapid prototyping design, or user-centered design.
4. Evaluation and revision	The issue of intention is central to goal setting and evaluation. Participatory decision-making is the only ethical stance possible in this social theory context.

of educational design? What design concepts that form other fields can be applied? This approach would be more consistent with the original Lave and Wenger (1991) perspectives, especially in the matter of co-creating the intentions and interventions of such an enterprise. The general strategy would be to describe existing patterns of community learning and then co-design appropriate interventions and evaluation cycles with those constituents. While this general strategy resembles Wenger's (1998) advice, this approach would also incorporate design strategies that can be found in other social theory applications (Cole, 1995; Rogoff, 1995; Engeström, 1987). This approach is presented in very broad strokes and would need to be developed with more precision in specific circumstances (see Table 6.3).

Phase 1: Possible Design Interventions

The first phase of socio-cultural educational design would be to understand the social fabric of the community in which a design is to be considered. Cole and Rogoff, it seems, would consider social theory analysis in the Russian tradition. Rogoff (1995) would, additionally, consider the levels of apprenticeship she has articulated. Wenger (1998) would take his design CoP theory and determine the nature of CoP activity, the constellations in which these CoPs exist. All points of view are portraying the social landscape as it naturally exists. Ethnographic or ecological description would be the tools of choice (Yanow, 2000). Further, Rogoff (1995) describes graphical analysis, which, to this reader, resembles the form and structure of social activity theory analysis. The point of this early phase of design would be to recognize those social structures that currently serve the population and engage the population in determining its social learning needs and possible intentions in a new or expanded community function. It would be a very rare circumstance in which a collective would immediately recognize and proceed to form a completely new community. More often the design would lead to a boundary intervention that facilitated communication between contemporary CoPs or facilitated the learning processes of a contemporary CoP or both. For teachers and designers the starting questions would be: What is the nature of socialization in teaching practice? What CoP activities do they engage in at the present time? Are these CoP activities connected? Do the CoP activities significantly extend beyond the geographic region of practice? If so, what are their boundary, binding, or enabling characteristics? Do the processes of the CoP(s) lead to productive professional development? Is there potential to enhance the learning processes?

It is our assertion that design in this genre does not occur without intention of the learners and designers fully participating in the process. The very nature of the social cultural theory would argue for co-design of the intention as well as the interventions. The authors believe that social theorists such as Sanday (1998), Gaver (1996), and Wasson (2000) would argue for an intention derived through full participation of the target population. The learners are co-designers mutually determining the purpose, value, and worth of the emergent design. We as designers of the conditions for a virtual CoP would not impose our intentions directly or inadvertently. While it is easy to agree in principle to co-design, we have found it much harder in practice (Schwen, Goodrum, & Dorsey, 1993). The volatile nature of a virtual CoP means that a large segment of the "community" is in transition, not having played a significant role in the negotiations of intention. There is a real risk of either renegotiating intention ad infinitum or coercing participation, thereby creating a dynamic that was not intended.

Phase 2: Analysis

The analysis phase of such a design process would have at least two central themes: (1) What are the social patterns of learning and identity formation in this population? and (2) What are the untapped possibilities for achieving the goals of the population? One would face the same dilemma that Wenger (1998) faced in creating his book. While there is strength in relying on the increasing sophistication of the descriptive social cultural theories, there is not much prescriptive theoretical or practical experience in constructing interventions, even interventions that purport to modify rather than construct social structures or dynamics. We, as a profession, are not practiced social designers. We have just barely become sophisticated enough to do harm. Various analysis tools such as social network analysis, activity theory portrayal, and process analysis would bring a deeper understanding to the field in which we may choose to intervene. Negotiation with the population about the nature of intervention seems both ethically and conceptually appropriate.

Wenger offers an especially fresh look at such analysis issues. He posits four dimensions of dualities or tensions in mature CoPs: participation/reification, designed/emergent, identification/negotiability, and local/global (see also Barab, MaKinster, & Scheckler, this volume, for application of these dualities). These are CoP system characteristics that exist in a natural tension with one another. For example, the duality of designed/emergent expresses the tension between over- and underdesign. Some elements of the CoP must emerge to fulfill the learning needs of the population. This is a natural expression of intention. On the other hand, some minimal elements or structures would be required in an online CoP to provide for the necessary baseline of communication efficacy to attract and retain community activity. This and the other tensions are dynamic in Wenger's conception and their determination would be a necessary part of the analysis study.

Wenger also argues for three infrastructures or modes for learning: architecture imagination, alignment, and engagement. These are attributes or characteristics of a mature productive CoP. Taking engagement as an example, Wenger further calls for mutuality, competence, and continuity. To continue sampling from the theory (and illustrating the complexity), mutuality has three subcharacteristics: interactional facilities, joint tasks, and legitimate boundary participation or "peripherality." Wenger's descriptive elements of a mature system become a portion of the hypothetical framework of mature construct relationships that could be considered in analyzing contemporary and developing community behavior.

Later in the same section, Wenger combines the four dimensions or tensions (participation/reification, designed/emergent, local/global, identification/negotiability) and the three infrastructures (engagement, imagination, and alignment) to create a 4 × 3 matrix for his complex description of a mature CoP. In the first author's experience of thirty years as an instructional designer, only one theory for applied intervention comes close to this level of complexity. Engeström (1987) and his colleagues' activity theory is as complex and equally challenging for designers to apprehend and apply. As noted above, while this is a very rich theory, it has not been well tested in application studies. Analysis in this kind of design is a speculative process of seeking hypotheses for causal links in the learning behavior of a collective. The richness of the descriptive theory does not speak to empirical experience with intervention, but offers a plausible insight that remains to be tested.

Phase 3: Design

The design phase of such an ambitious process would most likely have the appearance of social technical design, rapid prototyping design, or user-centered design. These design approaches often have the common characteristics of: co-design teams consisting of all affected constituents, rapid prototype development, immediate test–revise cycles, simultaneous consideration of the social as well as technological determinants of behavior, and process negotiation and renegotiation with the affected constituents leading to joint ownership of the design and consequences of the design. These design practices can be unwieldy to manage and they can be informal, inelegant, and downright messy, but they do bring the designers and affected constituents to a new state of understanding and acceptance of their common goals. Our designs in the past and the designs of those we have seen in the literature often emphasize support of work processes.

Wenger is one of the first to emphasize the tacit aspect of identity formation. As he has noted, one does not design identity formation, one hopes to arrange the conditions that would support identity formation. This theoretical relationship is neither well understood conceptually nor explored empirically. Excepting the work of Nonaka and Takeuchi (1995) and his colleagues von Krough et al. (2000) and Baumard (1999), the design of conditions for sharing or converting tacit knowledge is unexplored. Burton (2001) offers some insight into these sorts of relationships. Following Nonaka and Burton, the designer and her clients would need to carefully build environments of trust and caring with ample opportunities for sharing stories, metaphors, and mental models.

Creating the conditions for a healthy community would foster "productive" behaviors in the community. The community could not be expected to follow the blueprint of a social design. Interestingly, Wenger argues for "minimalist" design, allowing the communities to find their natural levels of identity and learning as a result of well-nurtured conditions. Presumably this form of minimalism refers to using the extremely complex theory as a descriptive lens for seeking causal links in the behavior of the population under consideration. The interventions that would result would be inserted, by consent, in the online CoP, tested and revised in rapid succession until a level of satisfaction is achieved with the patterns of learning behavior. Computer application designers have perfected such a rapid prototyping approach. Li (2001) offers a useful summary of rapid prototyping literature. A socio-technical approach that simultaneously considers and implements the social and technical aspects of the design may also be considered as a means of expediting the complex tensions of design (Schwen et al., 1993; Kling, McKim, & King, 2003).

Phase 4. Evaluation and Revision

To be consistent with the larger ethical and substantive considerations of applied social theorists (Sanday, 1998; Lassiter, 2000) and to honor the original Lave and Wenger (1991) formulation (see Problem 5), the intended and unintended consequences of design would need to be evaluated. Issues of consequences to aesthetics, loss of autonomy, and abuse of power as well as the central issues of learning patterns, identity formation, and collective accomplishment would be considered. The fundamental tools would be the same tools as used in the first four phases. In fact, the so-called phases would often be indistinct or blurred. Negative consequences of the contemporary community behavior could surface in Phase 1 problem definition. The co-design process would insure that the evaluation is completed with the constituents rather than to the constituents. Negative or destructive consequences of contemporary community behavior would become part of the agenda of the community. The skilled designer could present data in a concise and neutral fashion creating a decision-making structure that allowed the community to confront their issues and reach appropriate consequences. Chao could have found a forum for the consulting company to consider the consequences of their protracted Darwinian period of legitimate peripheral participation.

Issues of ethics, treatment of employees, and high turnover costs could be presented in such a fashion to facilitate a collective, perhaps tacit, understanding of the socialization of new employees. For example, the collective decisions of federal funding agencies and local teaching hospitals place economic issues ahead of patient welfare. Interns are often required to work 36- and 48-hour shifts during which they are primarily responsible for patient care in the early morning hours. Clearly, their judgment is impaired in such circumstances and there is no doubt that patients have been harmed in such situations. This example makes the point that a social cultural design is not complete until the social consequences of learning interventions are fully considered, whether they be native to the situation or caused by design interventions.

A DESIGN ALLEGORY

To illustrate these design concepts more concretely, the following hypothetical scenario is offered as an alternative to a conventional conclusion.

We recently completed an exciting three-year project in which we were commissioned to implement an educational design involving the professional development of K–3 teachers. Federal and state funding was available to improve the performance of K–3 teachers' reading instruction.

At the same time, the State of Nirvana had experienced a dramatic decline in its standardized reading test scores. The public outcry was quite shrill. Many different explanations were offered for the decline, including a criticism of the test, high rates of immigration into Nirvana, pedagogical confusion and conflict, under-funding, and so on. Teacher performance was widely considered to be a significant cause of the problem by all constituents except the teachers. After some discussion with teachers, teacher educators, public leaders, and minority representatives, interested parties came together to create a teacher development proposal to take advantage of public funding. The initial agreement was to fund a demonstration teacher development activity served by a community of practice website.

We were hesitant to accept the problem as given, and proceeded to Phase 1 analysis. The designers lobbied for time to more completely engage the local teachers and teaching leadership. They worked to locate formal and informal teaching networks. They especially concentrated on local networks that seemed to promote open, active dialogue. They were concerned with teacher groups that had reading performance problems and were actively engaged and mutually supportive. They found a number of different patterns of learning community and as expected found a number of different definitions of the "reading problem." Using focus group techniques among teachers and town meetings with interested community members, they attempted to co-define different versions of the reading problem. As the different views of the reading problem became more articulate, partially motivated by federal funding, they encouraged the teacher leadership to find a common structure for communicating the problem definition process. This included use of the website provided by the designers. They were sensitive to the vagaries of funding as well. A useful simplification of the number of problems occurred in time to meet funding deadlines. Throughout this process of problem definition, the designers eased themselves out of leadership roles and assumed the role of facilitators.

The teacher leaders and funding authorities initiated a round of funding analysis projects. Teacher groups in the local community could propose a funded project that would further define their analysis of the local reading problem. They could seek assistance from university, state, and regional authorities in framing the analysis. Four projects representing a reasonable cross-section of teacher opinion emerged. All the while the designers collected relevant data, provided connections to outside experts, supported internal dialogue, located regional and national projects that were comparable and supported the communication that resulted from these efforts on the web site. Regarding the local activists, they were especially concerned with teacher groups in their schools. They observed meetings, classrooms, lunchroom conversations, and parent-teacher interactions to find the salient forms of problems and related communication to relocate some of the communication where possible to the web services. As the analysis phase was completed, the teachers in combination with university and regional experts produced a number of analytic documents to address the K–3 reading performance issues. Each document included a local action plan. This process naturally moved or evolved to the web as the local activists had now come to find most relevant data they needed on the web.

In a second round of funding, the implementation grant forms and related instructions were only available on the web. By this time a reasonable amount of daily chat could be observed with lively discussions of different points of view, sharing of ideas, professional socialization, and random chatter. The designers facilitated this process in an unobtrusive fashion. The next round of proposals for implementation projects had just a few constraints: (1) the interventions dealt with teacher-teacher collaboration, teacher-student interaction, and teacher-family transactions; and (2) the standard for evaluating success had prior approval of the teacher leadership and the federal authorities. The process of intervention was open to public inspection mostly by using web tools but also by controlled visitation. The designers began to facilitate cross-project comparisons, teacher-parent interactions, and federal school interactions on the web. The designers also created a rapid response team that supported all the implementation projects, some of the instruction as well as the more extensive dialogue among teachers, parents, and peripheral participants. The rapid response team included a call center for technological support, guaranteed 24-hour modifications to instructional and communication bugs, and "rapid" analysis of important communication and instructional dilemmas from a conceptual point of view. The designers were socio-cultural analysts on demand.

There were rewards for success in performance improvement. About half of the implementation projects were refunded. New project proposals were also accepted in the second and third years of the project. In the last year of the project, grant leaders commissioned a group of educational anthropologists to evaluate the project. They found mixed results in the improvement of reading performance with lessons learned in both the successful and unsuccessful projects. They found some unintended negative consequences for some minority students involving technology access from the students and parents. They recommended solutions that were funded locally. In a footnote, they explained that the process of reform was well served by excellent democratic communication, including the local web service.

In conclusion, we have presented cautionary notes to designers who are sometimes overly enthusiastic about building online CoPs. We illustrated that descriptive theories including Lave and Wenger (1991), Orr (1996), and Wenger (1998) could provide insights to analyze established CoPs. However, we need to further examine the hypothesis of the life cycle of CoPs in order to facilitate earlier stages of CoPs.

References

Aplin, J. C., & Cosier, R. A. (1980). Managing creative and maintenance organizations. *The Business Quarterly*, Spring, 56–63.

Barab, S. A., & Duffy, T. (2000). From practice fields to communities of practice. In D. Jonassen & S. M. Land (Eds.), *Theoretical foundations of learning environments* (pp. 26–56). Mahwah, N.J.: Erlbaum.

Baumard, P. (1999). *Tacit knowledge in organizations*. London: Sage Publications.

Bruner, J. S. (1966). *Toward a theory of instruction*. Cambridge, MA: Harvard University Press.

Burroughs, R. (2000). Communities of practice and discourse communities: Negotiating boundaries in NBPTS Certification. *Teachers College Record, 102*(2) 344–375.

Burton, C. L. (2001). *Knowledge transfer in a corporate setting: A case study*. Unpublished doctoral dissertation, Indiana University, Bloomington.

Chao, C. A. (2001). *Workplace learning as legitimate peripheral participation: A case study of newcomers in a management consulting organization*. Unpublished doctoral dissertation, Indiana University, Bloomington.

Cochran-Smith, M., & Lytle, S. L. (1999). Relationships of knowledge and practice: Teacher learning in communities. In A. Iran-Nejad & P. D. Pearson (Eds.), *Review of research in education* (pp. 249–303). American Educational Research Association: Washington D.C.

Cole, M. (1995). Socio-cultural-historical psychology: some general remarks and a proposal for a new kind of cultural-genetic methodology. In J. V. Wertsch, P. del Rio, & A. Alvarez (Eds.), *Sociocultural studies of mind* (pp. 187–214). New York: Cambridge University Press.

Collison, G., Elbaum, B., Haavind, S. & Tinker, R. (2000). *Facilitating online learning: Effective strategies for moderators*. Madison, WI: Atwood Publishing.

Contu, A., & Willmont, H. (1999). Learning and practice: Focusing on Power Relationships. Paper presented at the *Society for Organizational Learning*, Cambridge, MA, October 8–9.

Contu, A., & Willmont, H. (2000). Comment on Wenger and Yanow. Knowing in practice: A 'delicate flower' in the organizational learning field. *Organization, 7*(2) 269–276.

Cook, S., & Brown, J. S. (1999). Bridging epistemologies: The generative dance between organizational knowledge and organizational knowing. *Organizational Science, 10*(4), 381–400.

Dubin, R. (1978). *Theory building*. New York: Free Press, Macmillan.

Easterby-Smith, M., Snell, R. & Gherwidi, S. (1998). Organizational learning: diverging Communities of Practice? *Management Learning, 29*(30), 258–272.

Engeström, Y. (1987). *Learning by expanding*. Helsinki: Orienta-konsultit.

Fox, S. (1999). 'Communities of Practice Foucault and Actor Network Theory,' *Proceedings of Organisational Learning Third International Conference*, Lancaster University, 397–417.

Gagne, R. (1965). *The conditions of learning*. New York: Holt Reinhart & Winston.

Gaver, W. W. (1996). Affordances for interaction: The social is material for design. *Ecological Psychology, 8*(2), 111–129.

Haney, D. (2003). *Knowledge management in a professional service firm*. Unpublished manuscript, Indiana University, Bloomington.

Hara, N. (2000). *Social construction of knowledge in professional communities of practice: Tales in the courtrooms*. Unpublished doctoral dissertation, Indiana University, Bloomington.

Henriksson, K. (2000). When communities of practice came to town: On culture and contradiction in emerging theories of organizational learning. *Institute of Economic Research Working Paper Series*, Lund University, Sweden.

Kim, A. J. (2000). *Community building: Secret strategies for successful online communities on the web*. Berkeley, CA: Peachpit Press.

Kirkpatrick, D. (1998). *Evaluating training problems: The four levels* (2nd ed.). San Francisco: Berrett-Koehler Publishers.

Kling, R., McKim, G., & King, A. (2003). A bit more to IT: Scientific Communication forums as socio-technical interaction networks. *Journal of American Society for Information Science & Technology, 54*(1), 47–67.

Lassiter, E. (2000). Engaging in localized public anthropology. *Anthropology News, 42*(2), 7–8.

Lave, J. (1997). The culture of acquisition and the practice of understanding. In D. Kirshner & J. A. Whitson (Eds.), *Situated cognition: Social semiotic, and psychological perspectives* (pp. 37–56). Mahwah, NJ: Erlbaum.

Lave, J., & Wenger, E. (1991). *Situated learning: Legitimate peripheral participation.* New York: Cambridge University Press.

Li, S. (2001). *Contingent scaffolding strategies in computer-based learning environment.* Unpublished doctoral dissertation, Indiana University, Bloomington.

Nardi, B. (Ed.) (1996). *Context and consciousness: Activity theory and human-computer interaction.* Cambridge, MA: MIT Press.

Nickerson, R. S. (1993). On the distribution of cognition: Some reflections. In G. Solomon (Ed.), *Distributed cognitions: Psychological and educational considerations* (pp. 229–261). New York: Cambridge University Press.

Nonaka, I., & Takeuchi, H. (1995). *The knowledge creating company.* New York: Oxford University Press.

Orr, J. E. (1990). Sharing knowledge, celebrating identity: community memory in a service culture. In D. S. Middleton & D. Edwards (Eds.), *Collective remembering: Memory in society* (pp. 169–189). Beverly Hills, CA: Sage.

Preece, J. (2000). *Online communities: Designing usability, supporting sociability.* Chichester, UK: John Wiley and Sons.

Reil, M. (2001, April). Models of community learning and online learning in communities. Paper presented at *American Educational Research Association*, Seattle, WA, April 10–14.

Resnick, L. B. (1987). Learning in school and out. *Educational Researcher, 16,* 13–20.

Resnick, L. B. (1997). *Discourse, tools, and reasoning: Essays on situated cognition.* New York: Springer.

Rogoff, B. (1995). Observing sociocultural activity on three planes: Participatory appropriation, guided participation, and apprenticeship. In J. V. Wertsch, P. del Rio, & A. Alvarez (Eds.), *Sociocultural studies of mind* (pp. 139–164). New York: Cambridge University Press.

Sanday, P. (1998). *Opening statement: Defining public interest anthropology.* Available online at http://www.sas.upenn.edu/~psanday/pia.99.html.

Schwen, T. M., Goodrum, D. A. & Dorsey, L. T. (1993). On the design of an Enriched Learning and Information Environment (ELIE). *Educational Technology, 33*(11), 5–9.

Sfard, A. (1998). On two metaphors for learning and the dangers of choosing just one. *Educational Researcher, 27,* 4–13.

von Krough, G., Nishiguchi, T., & Nonaka, I. (2000). *Enabling knowledge creation: How to unlock the mystery of tacit knowledge and release the power of innovation.* New York: Oxford University Press.

Wasson, C. (2000). Ethnography in the field of design. *Human Organization, 59*(4), 377–389.

Weick, K. E. (1995). *Sensemaking in organizations*. Thousand Oaks, CA: Sage Publications.

Wenger, E. (1990). *Toward a theory of cultural transparency: Elements toward a discourse on the visible and invisible*. Unpublished doctoral dissertation, University of California, Irvine.

Wenger, E. (1998). *Communities of practice: Learning, meaning, and identity*. Cambridge, MA: Cambridge University Press.

Wenger, E. (1999). *Communities of practice: Stewarding knowledge*. Internal document: P.O. Box 810, North San Juan, CA 95960. USA.

Wenger, E. (2000). Communities of practice and social learning systems. *Organization*, 7(2), 225–246.

Wertsch, J. (1995). The need for action in sociocultural research. In J. V. Wertsch, P. del Rio, & A. Alvarez (Eds.), *Sociocultural studies of mind* (pp. 56–74). New York: Cambridge University Press.

Yanow, D. (2000). Seeing organizational learning: A 'cultural' view. *Organization*, 7(2), 247–268.

Yi, J. Q. (2000). *Supporting business by facilitating organizational learning and knowledge creation in the MOT community of practice (CoP)*. Unpublished doctoral dissertation, Indiana University, Bloomington.

PART III

FOSTERING COMMUNITY/MEMBER PARTICIPATION

7

The Centrality of Culture and Community to Participant Learning at and with The Math Forum

K. Ann Renninger and Wesley Shumar[1]

In this chapter, the terms *culture* and *community* are problematized, and their centrality to participant learning at and with The Math Forum (math-forum.org) is discussed.[2] Culture, as it is used here, refers to the rituals and norms that come to be associated with a site and its functioning. Community describes recognition of connections to and identification with other participants.

The Math Forum is an interactive and inquiry-informed digital library, or virtual resource center, for mathematics education. Previous chapters have addressed the ways in which The Math Forum has leveraged the concept of community in order to become a dynamic and resource-rich educational site (Renninger & Shumar, 2002; Shumar & Renninger, 2002). In the present chapter, this analysis is taken a step further. The culture of The Math Forum is described as providing its participants with a unique set of opportunities for learning and for making the relationship between the individual and the community one in which individual and community

---

[1] Order of authorship is alphabetical.

[2] The present discussion is informed by in-depth structured interviews with teacher partici-pants over three years of work with The Math Forum (Renninger & Shumar, 2002), study of student responses to the Problems of the Week (Renninger, Farra, & Feldman-Riordan, 2000), study of participant-mentor exchanges in the Ask Dr. Math service (Renninger & Farra, 2003), study of collaboration in the context of site projects (Shumar, 2003), study of site participation using Internet questionnaires (Renninger & Shumar, in press), participant observation in workshops and projects, and focus group discussions with staff (Renninger & Shumar, 2000).

We acknowledge the many contributions that our students, colleagues, and the participants of The Math Forum have made to our thinking about the roles of culture and community in learning at and with the site. We thank Vanessa Gorman for her help in preparing this chapter for publication and Sasha Barab and Rob Kling for their comments on an earlier draft. Finally, we gratefully acknowledge support for research reported in this chapter from National Science Foundation funding (grants #9618223 and #9805289). The analysis presented in this chapter does not necessarily represent the views of the National Science Foundation.

needs can both be met. Site culture enables contributions from individuals that by definition help to build out and sustain this community.

Math Forum participants include Math Forum staff members and a mix of teachers, students, and other individuals such as parents, software developers, mathematicians, math educators, professionals, and tradespeople, many of whom also volunteer their time as mentors for the site. Participants differ not only in terms of their roles, but in their experience, level of expertise, and interest for mathematics (Renninger & Shumar, 2002). Thus, partnerships and mentoring on the site typically take the form of cross-age tutoring, in that participants with different strengths work to scaffold each other's understanding of mathematics.

Two prepositions (*at* and *with*) can be used to describe the kinds of connections that Math Forum participants make between what they know and what they learn in working with site resources. This is because The Math Forum is both (a) a content site that has extensive archives and links to information and (b) an interactive site that promotes information exchange, discussion, and community-building. The Math Forum resources are rich, deep, and interactive. It is the site's interactivity, however, that distinguishes its resources from those provided by an encyclopedia or a compendium of tables. The design of the site leads participants to try out and select different ways of working with its content. Participants are not told what they need to do or learn on the site. The learning that takes place is driven by the questions and interests of participants and is facilitated by the design of the site.

The Math Forum presently consists of over a million and a half pages. It offers a number of services: five problems of the week, or *PoWs*, which are weekly, interactive, nonroutine, challenge problems that are archived along with explanations and answers; the interactive *Ask Dr. Math* service and its archives of frequently asked questions; and *Teacher2Teacher*, a question-and-answer discussion forum that is also archived. In addition, the site includes lessons, projects, games, discussions, and a newsletter.

The learning that characterizes participant engagement at and with The Math Forum appears to have its roots in both the site's culture and community (Holland et al., 1998; Lave, 1993; Smolka, DeGoes, & Pino, 1995), as well as in the staff members' goals to facilitate the development of mathematical thinking (DeCorte, Verschaffel, & Op T'Eynde, 2000; Ginsberg, Klein, & Starkey, 1998; Schoenfeld, 1987; 1992). Prior studies of Math Forum participation (see Renninger & Farra, in press; Renninger, Farra, & Feldman-Riordan, 2000; Renninger & Shumar, 2002; Renninger, Weimar, & Klotz, 1998; Shumar, in press) suggest that it is the interactive resources that (a) enable participants to make connections to serious mathematics content; (b) lead participants to engage their own questions and persevere in finding solutions or answers to them; and (c) provide models for working with challenging problems and topics

(Pea, 1993). These studies further suggest that interactive resources can provide a basis for interested engagement if interest for mathematics (pedagogy or technology) is less-developed initially. They also indicate that interactive resources can also lead to deepened interest(s) if participants bring a well-developed interest for mathematics (pedagogy or technology) to their work with the site (Renninger & Shumar, 2003).

In exploring the new social spaces opened up by the Internet, the staff appears to be enabling Math Forum participants to engage in forms of interaction that differ from those with which they are familiar. Thus, for example, elementary children may work on answering a question with a world famous mathematician (e.g., Renninger, Weimar, & Klotz, 1998); teachers may work with programmers to more effectively gauge the type of support students need (e.g., Shumar, 2003), and mathematicians may end up in a conversation with a pipe fitter or other tradesperson. Opportunities to work with people who are not part of one's everyday world lead participants to new senses of identity and identification. These new options for working and sharing together also promote the development of renewable resources for a site like The Math Forum that has archives.

The site provides individuals and groups of individuals with opportunities and support to experience optimal levels of autonomy. Also, it provides opportunities and support to engage in interactions that cause them to stretch what they know about mathematics, math pedagogy, and/or technologies that enhance mathematics teaching and learning (e.g., Renninger & Farra, 2003; Renninger, Farra, & Feldman-Riordan, 2000; Renninger & Shumar, 2002). Importantly, staff members' decision-making about the design and refinement of Math Forum services is informed by both their goals for the service and formal and informal sources of data, including research on service usage (e.g., Renninger & Farra, in press; Renninger, Farra, & Feldman-Riordan, 2000; Renninger & Shumar, 2002; Renninger, Weimar, & Klotz, 1998), feedback to the webmaster and the staff, and Internet questionnaires distributed to all participants.

Interviews with its participants suggest that the culture of The Math Forum typically contrasts with participants' other experiences as learners because it is a community to which they are welcomed and with which they feel comfortable working, regardless of how strong or weak their skills are (see discussion in Renninger & Shumar, 2002). Participants report that in their work with the site they are led to create opportunities and support for themselves that, in turn, lead to change in their participation over time. Resources that are used at The Math Forum lead to continued work with The Math Forum, which in turn leads to the development of new resources. Moreover, the tracks of these interactions are the raw materials out of which the different archives are developed. As such, work at and with The Math Forum is dialectical.

THE MATH FORUM

The Math Forum is a situated context for learning (Barab & Duffy, 2000; Chaiklin & Lave, 1993; Cole, Engestrom, & Vasquez, 1997; Kirshner & Whitson, 1997; Lave & Wenger, 1991) in which participants can be involved whenever, wherever, and however they choose as long as they have a connection to the Internet. The combination of site interactivity and substantial content appears to enable the site to be responsive to all types of learners. Across services, the culture or norms for interacting with others include (a) assuming that participants are using the site to learn or figure something out, (b) accepting at face value what a person says about both their interest and understanding, and (c) using an inquiry approach of questioning, exploring, and modeling in order to enable the participant to understand (c.f., Bruner, 1966). Participants using the Ask Dr. Math service, for example, typically do not receive answers to questions. Rather, if a participant asks how to solve a problem, the mentor is likely to ask what the participant needs to know in order to be able to solve the given problem, or others like it, on his or her own (see discussion in Renninger & Farra, 2003).

Interactive services that enable the asking of questions, searching for answers with partial information or misspelled words, and reviewing of past questions or problems and solutions encourage participant engagement. They also provide reinforcement for participation. The process of working with services such as these positions participants to work on their own questions. They are assisted with clarifying their questions so that they can answer them by themselves and/or realize related or alternative solution paths. Because the services help participants to clarify their questions, they also make it possible for the mentors to better adjust their responses to address the questions that the participants are posing and increase the likelihood of their responses meeting the participants' interests and needs (Pea, 1993).

One reason that The Math Forum can begin to meet the needs of its participants is that it has a large corps of participants who serve as volunteer mentors. Volunteer mentors are not simply ceded the responsibility of working with others on the site, however. They are trained and supported as they assume these roles. Volunteers are considered to be in training with a particular service until each of them has demonstrated the ability to listen and provide questions or pointers to the questions as posed. Student mentors for the cross-age tutoring, which is a component of the Elementary Problem of the Week service, are also given instruction about how to write constructive responses to submissions, and the responses that are sent to other student participants are reviewed by their teachers and/or Math Forum staff members.

The design of the site also includes a set of Ask Dr. Math offices, PoW offices, and other service offices that are accessible by staff members and volunteer mentors. Math Forum staff and volunteer mentors use these offices for training and for facilitating discussions among volunteers who have already been trained and tenured. These discussions often address staff members' and volunteers' concerns about particular problems that reoccur and dilemmas that arise. They work together and with Math Forum staff to generate alternate answers to questions, check that their intuitions are correct, and so forth. Also, they can request more information about answers to questions for which they do not know the answers (Renninger & Farra, 2003).

Importantly, the interactivity of Math Forum services is complemented by mathematics content that has depth and breadth. It is unlikely that the design of services alone would support participant learning or the willingness to be a volunteer mentor without the site's content (see related discussion in Shulman, 1986). Math Forum resources include a range of formats for topics in mathematics that typically span the K–12, undergraduate, and postgraduate levels. Just as participants who come to the site typically find and work with topics in the forms that work best for them given their dispositions, abilities, and levels of math, volunteers on the site can choose which problems/questions to mentor based on the topic being addressed because of the setup of the office for each service. This enables mentors to continue to develop their own thinking about particular topics, in addition to helping others to understand or think about them.

The fact that the same protocol for working with participants on the site characterizes (a) each of the services, (b) the webmaster's responses, and (c) staff members' interactions with each other and other participants means that newer participants feel welcome and realize that they too can ask questions and offer answers. Participants' ease in identifying the interactivity of the site has also been found to lead them to explore the site and identify other services and resources with which they then typically begin to work over time (see Renninger & Shumar, 2002). The design of the site includes many paths and many opportunities through which participants can anchor their knowledge (CTGV, 1990, 1991). Participants are encouraged to ask questions and learn using formats that make sense to them. If participants do best pursuing questions in the archives, the search function is set up to help them. If they do better talking with others about their questions, services and discussion groups are available.

Participants who continue to return to the site also report that their site involvement expands over time (Renninger & Shumar, 2002). Even if they initially sought only to support their students, teacher participants typically find themselves learning, teaching, and doing math themselves as they work with the site. In the process of designing a lesson on understanding how to find the volume of three-dimensional figures, for example, a middle-school mathematics teacher might look for:

- Sample lessons to help students understand the difference between two-dimensional and three-dimensional figures (e.g., mathforum. org/alejandre/workshops/recprism.html; mathforum.org/alejandre/ workshops/net.html; mathforum.org/brap/wrap/midlesson.html);
- Questions and answers in the Dr. Math archives that provide explanations of the characteristics of two- and three-dimensional figures (e.g., mathforum.org/dr.math/faq/faq.formulas.html);
- Problems of the Week at different levels of difficulty (e.g., mathforum. org/midpow/solutions/solution.ehtml?puzzle=64; mathforum.org/ calcpow/solutions/solution.ehtml?puzzle=15; mathforum.org/ calcpow/solutions/solution.ehtml?puzzle=16); and/or
- Discussions comparing students' responses to and questions about the volume of two cylinders made from the same size paper, one turned vertically and the other horizontally, in the Bridging Research and Practice videopaper (mathforum.org/wrap/brap).[3]

Teacher participants typically describe their use of Math Forum resources in terms of discrete resource-related goals such as finding answers to questions or providing students with nonroutine challenge problems. They talk about The Math Forum as different from their everyday experience of mathematics, and they return to use the site again and again, citing the availability of resources, the way in which people respond to their students or to them, and all of the things that they still want to check out (Renninger & Shumar, 2002). In contrast to discussions that suggest that culture is invisible to its participants (e.g., Rogoff, 1998), Math Forum participants talk about their own work with The Math Forum site as distinct from experiences they have had with other sites or mathematics resources, and/or with mathematics as a discipline (Renninger & Shumar, 2002). It appears that the site adds value to their experiences (CTGV, 1996). Participants

---

[3] Similarly, students have a range of resources that involve different types of learning on the site. Elementary-aged students who are assigned to work with the Elementary Problem of the Week (ElemPoWs), for example, may use other site resources to help them explain their solution path (part of the ElemPoW task). They can search the PoW, Frequently Asked Questions (FAQs), or Dr. Math archives. Also, if they have not been able to answer their question based on their own searching, they can write to Dr. Math. While they cannot get a Dr. Math mentor to do problems for them, they can get help that will allow them to proceed in their work if they explain what their questions are, resources with which they have worked, and what they still do not understand. Through their teachers, elementary-aged students may also get involved in developing challenge problems that will later be posted for other students as ElemPoWs. Once problems they help to write are live (posted), they can work to mentor solutions that are submitted to the problems they helped develop, be led to think through the range of solution types submitted, and rethink the framing of the problems developed.

may be attuned to the culture of the site because they work with the site as an extension of individual culture. The site is not a replacement for the classroom and the school curriculum, but the culture of the site encourages individuals to extend their own interests and enrich their experience of their school curriculum. As such, the culture serves to enhance their experience with mathematics.

The site holds value for its participants, at least in part, because it has been designed and built out in collaboration with its participants (including the staff members). In fact, it could be argued that technology facilitates the tweaking, revision, and/or reorganization of norms or rituals, the culture that participants associate with the site. Moreover, as participants adjust their understanding of the site and contribute suggestions for its further development, they come to identify with the site in some way. Since the site uses participant input to refine its services, it could be said to be fine tuning its culture to its participants' strengths, needs, and interests.

Renninger and Shumar (2002), reporting on findings from in-depth structured interviews with site participants, suggest that it is possible to identify three types of Math Forum teacher participation: (a) those who find the site and are positioned to immediately make use of the resources it provides; (b) those who find the site and have a sense of what they might do to use its resources but need support to do so; and (c) those who find the site only because they have to and need a substantial amount of support both from the site and from others in their environment to persevere to make use of its resources. Importantly, over the three years of their study, those participants who were identified as needing particular levels of support when they were first interviewed were eventually positioned to help their colleagues or students to work with the site. The change typically meant that over time they needed less support from site staff members, and they were able and willing to help others. Changed participation was enabled by several forms of support: (a) the autonomy or space for participants to work with the site on their own questions whenever, however, and wherever they choose; (b) participant interaction with others and site resources to address their questions; and (c) opportunities for participants to extend or stretch what they know (Renninger & Shumar, 2002).

It seems that in their interactions with the site, Math Forum participants are led to new senses of possibility for themselves (Markus & Nurius, 1986; Renninger & Shumar, 2002), and they are positioned to explore and to shift their identities as learners (Barab & Duffy, 2000; Linehan & McCarthy, 2000). Take, for example, the case of the teacher who once thought she was neither mathematical nor able to work with technology. Forced to do something with technology because her school was becoming a model tech school, she found and decided to print out Math Forum problems of the week for her classes. Over the three years that she and her use of The Math Forum were studied, she became increasingly confident about mathematics and teaching mathematics, and descriptions of her classroom instruction suggested shifts to reform practices. By the end of the second year, she had assumed a position in a different school as a lead teacher helping others to teach mathematics and use technology (see case description and discussion in Renninger & Shumar, 2002).[4]

Even though The Math Forum differs from most other sites because its participants are heterogeneous, it seems that the differences that exist between participants actually reinforce the participants' sense of the site as a community. On The Math Forum site many participants have strong mathematics backgrounds, and many do not. Some of these participants can also be identified as having a well-developed interest for mathematics; others cannot. There are participants who may have answers to one kind of question and others who can help think about other types of questions. Furthermore, some participants have been working with the site since The Math Forum's beginnings as a listserv discussion of the Visual Geometry Project (which produced The Geometer's Sketchpad), and some began working with the site when it evolved into The Geometry Forum. Other participants became involved with the site when the National Science Foundation (NSF) first encouraged the site to broaden its base to become The Math Forum, whereas others have only just located the site.

There are always possibilities for collaborating to figure something out on The Math Forum site. There are others with whom to check in and people for whom a person may have answers. Moreover, based on Internet questionnaires, it appears that approximately a third of the site's participants can be considered sticky traffic, a core group of participants who return to the site over time who are familiar with Math Forum culture. These participants can be assumed to have worked with site services, have had site practices modeled for them, and/or have received support that pushed them to think and work with mathematics. Thus, these participants can also be expected to support newer participants as they work with the site and learn how to participate in ways that lead them to stretch

---

[4] Similarly, weak and strong students who work with The Math Forum's PoWs over time have been found to make more connections to, generate more effective strategies for, and work more independently with PoW challenge problems than before working with problems that require them to explain how they arrived at the answer that they submit (Renninger, Farra, & Feldman-Riordan, 2000). Such findings suggest that at an individual level participants are not only seeking and using resources in their work with the site, but they are being supported in ways that deepen their understanding of the culture of mathematics (Schoenfeld, 1992). Because they can approach the problems in any of a number of ways, the approach they select is theirs, and any discussions they engage in with PoW mentors in build on their questions or work. Thus, the interactions that they have involve thinking about the solutions they have posed or on which they are trying to work. The process of these interactions leads them to a more developed understanding of mathematics, and it provides the foundation for asking the kind of curiosity questions that characterize interested engagement (Renninger, 2000) and deepen their connections to the community that they call The Math Forum.

themselves. Once archived, these interactions also make a contribution to the larger community.

CULTURE AND COMMUNITY PROBLEMATIZED

In previous work, The Math Forum has been described as a community and the role of community in virtual spaces has been addressed (Renninger & Shumar, 2002; Shumar & Renninger, 2002). As Kling and Courtright (this volume) argue, the term community may be overused in online environments; every discussion list does not necessarily constitute a community. In contrast to many sites, The Math Forum staff was invested in building community long before the term community became so widespread. The staff members use community to describe themselves and other participants who work together to build out The Math Forum site. In fact, it may be because of The Math Forum's success as an online community that others have chosen to emulate it.

Community

The usefulness of the term community has been questioned especially as it applies to virtual space. Rather than being focused on problems associated with the use of the term to refer to a group with whom others come to identify, per se, these questions claim that virtual communities (a) point to a loss of community in the modern world, (b) are distinct from physical communities, and (c) describe one-dimensional groups (e.g., a discussion listserv) (Nie & Erbring, 2000; Kraut et al., 1998; Putnam, 2000).

Building on the work of Barth (1981) and Cohen (1985), Shumar and Renninger (2002) suggest that modern society has not eliminated community. Traditional communities are typically presented as homogeneous, and modern society is presented as heterogeneous and, as such, not as community. Cohen (1985) points out that all communities – modern or traditional – are based on symbolic boundaries, which may actually be more complex in small, traditional fishing villages than they are in large, contemporary cities. If symbolic boundaries define communities, then attachment and belonging can be understood as socially produced and reinforced through rituals and other symbols. From an analytic point of view, community describes the way boundaries work and the forms of attachment and connection experienced by social actors. All communities are virtual in the sense that they are the product of social imagination and must be defined symbolically (Anderson, 1991). Thus, the distinction between virtual and physical to which some people point may more accurately represent a continuum of community types instead of two specific forms of community (see also Barab, MaKinster, & Scheckler, this volume; Hewitt, this volume).

Many people have suggested that Internet communities may be less deep and involve more superficial forms of attachment and belonging than physical communities (Nie & Erbring, 2000; Kraut et al., 2000). It also can be argued, however, that the Internet has made the experience of different forms of community more of a possibility than it ever has been in the past (Shumar & Renninger, 2002). The Internet allows for greater flexibility of forms of interaction and symbolic communication, and these, in turn, have stretched the realm of possibilities about community. There is a greater "virtualism" to Internet-based communities than there is to physical communities. Many online groups have thin connections, weak attachments, and not much of a sense of identity and belonging. These groups may or may not be communities. In contrast, The Math Forum site is an example of a very complex network of groups and individuals who work together virtually and face-to-face. They are not engaged in a simple, one-dimensional discussion group that self-identifies as a community. The Math Forum includes a multi-faceted and heterogeneous group of individuals who are positioned to learn, think, and do mathematics. For groups such as The Math Forum, the term community has proven to be a very useful and appropriate concept for thinking about the potential of social spaces.

While one conception of community holds that it is a homogeneous and simply bounded entity, most contemporary thinkers reject that model (Barth, 1981; Cohen, 1985, 1994; Goody, 1994). They suggest instead that community is a complex set of overlapping boundaries. These overlapping boundaries are subtle and are often only seen by insiders to the group whereas external boundaries are those seen by outsiders. For example, the very boundary that is more important to the outsider, such as, "Oh, you are from New York," is not often considered by those who live and work together within the city boundary. For a member of a community, the boundaries that matter are those that separate neighborhoods and groups from each other. These boundaries are the symbols of belonging and attachment. These boundaries also are manipulated by social actors and are often contested, resulting in a patchwork of connections and discourses about imagined connections. Social networks can be a useful tool for understanding the relationships between individuals and arrangements of connections (Barnes, 1972; Barth, 1981; Gulliver, 1971; Koku & Wellman, this volume; Wellman, 2001; Wellman & Gulia, 1999). From this perspective, community and culture are closely related and can be said to share the same complex structure.

Online, recognition that community is a symbolic construction is useful because it addresses the roles of participants' imaginations about attachment and belonging to others. The Math Forum community is comprised of groups that have distinct projects and resources. Participant observations and interviews with participants suggest that individuals imagine

The Math Forum community differently from each other. The boundaries they describe overlap and reflect varying visions of The Math Forum. As Renninger and Shumar (2002) suggest, participant imagination builds on participants' experiences, including the nature of exchanges participants have had, as well as the design of services and availability of resources that the site makes possible. Thus, Math Forum teacher participants, looking for lesson plans, find resources that are available when they have the time and space to work with them. Textual interactions such as student submissions to the Problem of the Week, online discussions, or archives of FAQs provide teachers with different formats and levels of materials that allow them to find the match for their interests and abilities. In this way, they can build on what they know. These interactions are not formulaic; they have been adjusted to meet the strengths, needs, interests, and experiences of participants. As such, they also provide models of how teachers might work with their students, or other participants (Collins, Brown, & Newman, 1989; Renninger & Shumar, 2002).

The culture of the site is explicit. There is an assumption that everyone working with the site (including staff members) is trying to learn and can, given support, appreciate the elegance of a well-worked problem and develop the perseverance and sense of humor necessary to continue working to understand. This context is one in which both imagination and sense of creative play are freed because both the culture and the community of The Math Forum acknowledge that there are always more questions to ask and to answer. Also, The Math Forum appreciates that one needs to start with what he or she does understand in order to learn. Given the assumption that participants want to learn, learning then appears to yield participation, even for those who are initially "required" to use the site (Renninger & Shumar, 2002).

Those who do not know The Math Forum site may equate it with other math education sites, discussion lists, or virtual communities. However, interviews with Math Forum participants who have used the site over time suggest that they focus on other boundaries, such as those of the site's services, partners, or projects. These are the type of symbolic boundaries that define the outsider (Cohen, 1985). On a site as large as The Math Forum, however, there are also projects to which even the staff may refer as though the projects were homogeneous entities. Thus, participants in such projects appreciate the nuanced subgroups that exist and the differences that emerge, for example, between participants and staff, staff and staff, those who are strong in math versus those who are strong in pedagogy, and those who are strong in both. Participation in or increased knowledge of a given project shifts the perception of homogeneity that initially existed for participants.

Importantly, the culture that is experienced and associated with The Math Forum by individuals, groups, or other communities when they begin work with The Math Forum is recognizable and distinctive. The site culture facilitates participants moving from feeling like outsiders to becoming insiders in the community. Presumably, it is also this ease of participant movement that accounts for return visits to the site, continued work with and willingness to volunteer on the site, and identification of opportunities to learn.

Culture

Just as there have been questions about the applicability of the term community to virtual spaces, there have also been questions about the usefulness of the term culture. There are at least three reasons that this is the case. (a) Culture could imply homogeneity within a clearly demarcated border; (b) culture could imply an entity with boundaries that are static and nonoverlapping; and (c) culture, as entity, raises questions of whose power, voice, and vision are used to represent the social group described as a culture (Clifford, 1988; Ewing, 1990; Holland et al., 1998; Paul, 1990; Rosaldo, 1989; Stewart, 1996; Strauss & Quinn, 1997). While valid, these problems could also be argued to enhance understanding of the role of the social group in an online learning community if they were used to reconceptualize the meaning of the term.

On one level, the evolution of the concept of culture mirrors the experience of newcomers to a culture that is unfamiliar. Anthropologists, for example, began doing research as outsiders to different cultures. At first, their tendencies were to make a strength out of a weakness by arguing that outsiders could understand the contours of the culture better than insiders (Bourdieu, 1977). There is a parallel between the theories and concerns of anthropologists and the folk taxonomies of individuals. Newcomers to a culture see that it is bounded, homogeneous, and static. Over time, the newcomer gets to know the members of a community and develops a basic model on which to base an understanding of a group. With an increasingly complex understanding of the culture, the person who once was a newcomer becomes more dynamic and fluid. Thus, boundaries can be understood as overlapping, and struggles for power and the assertion of different values, knowledge, and concerns surface (Holland et al., 1998).

People may hold onto simpler visions of culture even when their understandings include more complexity because these provide them with an easy shorthand for representing a group. It may be because anthropologists traditionally study groups in which the language and ways of interacting are unfamiliar that they inadvertently saddled themselves with a simplistic model of culture. Bourdieu (1980) suggests something similar to this in his observation that the methodological objectivism of structuralism and functionalist anthropology really involves making strength out of a weakness. In fact, anthropologists have argued that it was an advantage to not know a culture intimately because an outsider can objectively define the rules of the game and the structure of the system. By taking such a position, the traditional social scientist limits him- or herself to a newcomer's understanding of rules and structure. Official rules and structure often are not an accurate reflection of the complexity of a group's actual structure and process. Identifying rules does not necessarily allow for a more intimate (Herzfeld, 1997) appreciation of the strategies that are employed by social actors.

While earlier discussions of culture identified a simple boundary and everyone within that boundary as homogeneous, more recent models have specified overlapping sets of boundaries and pointed to heterogeneity that is intertwined with homogeneity (Barth, 1981; Cohen, 1985, 1994; Goody, 1994). To borrow a botanical metaphor, if the older models identified culture as a plant bulb, more contemporary models describe culture as a rhizome (Deleuze & Guattari, 1987). A rhizome has structure and pattern. It also has diversity and a separation of parts. Within any specific community, there are many subgroups, alliances, overlapping boundaries, and differences that make up the whole. These groups have both an individual and a shared culture that informs their senses of community. The more dynamic structures may lead to a great deal of identity confusion and conflict, but they may also become very dynamic, active, and productive social groups. The question that surfaces is whether to consider these groups one culture, multiple cultures, or to drop the term culture altogether and refer to the social group in some other way. Here, the term culture is used to refer to the dynamic interplay of ideologies, values, practices, and so on that comprises rhizomatic social groups.

The classic problems of difference and identity, which characterize all cultures, are compounded by the hybrid collaborations of people and groups that are possible in virtual spaces. Poster (2001), reflecting on the possibilities of the Internet, suggests, "Culture has lost its boundary" (p. 1). He points out that debates about the determining role of technology in the development of culture miss a very significant point. The Internet constitutes a space, "which encourages practices and which, in turn, serves to construct new types of subjects" (p. 3). In a richly textured and interactive virtual space such as The Math Forum, the Internet appears to enable possibilities for learning that facilitate a changed sense of possibility for participants and for the organizations building sites on the Internet (Renninger & Shumar, 2002).

In fact, Math Forum data suggest an even more nuanced view of culture than Poster's. Interviews with participants who return to the site over time suggest that they simultaneously hold both a simplistic and a heterogeneous model of the site. They think of the site as amazing or rich. They also are aware of and appreciative of the site's complexity and that it is hard to have everything work perfectly. In the past, the layers suggested by this kind of description have led many researchers to jettison the term culture in favor of the rubric of practice. Lumping all social interaction under practice, however, does not yield clarity about the role of culture in learning.

For present purposes, it seems appropriate to use the term culture to describe both a group's social imagination about the rules, models, strategies, and understanding of conflict and success, as well as the intersection of this group understanding with individual understanding (Holland et al., 1998; Shore, 1996; Strauss & Quinn, 1997). For example, some participants who submitted questions to Ask Dr. Math were told that the staff was receiving too many questions if the answer to their question already existed in the FAQ portion of the site. Their responses to questionnaires specifically asking about being pointed back to the FAQs indicated that they understood the problem of scaling, may have found the FAQs useful, and had not changed their sense of the service, or the site, as a resource that they wanted to continue to use. By providing information about their situation, the staff members involved participants in helping them to figure out how to make the site go forward. The staff took what could have been understood as individual rebuff and provided information that involved participants whose questions were not answered in the larger group issues of how to scale services.

In keeping with site culture, the staff members are inclusive. They seek and make use of feedback from all participants. They have been able to leverage the heterogeneity of the population and side-step possible complications that could be introduced by differences of cognition, power, and representation.[5] It was similar feedback to participants submitting answers to the Problems of the Week service that led to the development of a volunteer group who could help respond to the many solutions that service receives each week.

Presumably because of the way that they are received (heard, enlisted, etc.), participants of all types identify with the site. These participants also typically characterize Math Forum staff members as problem solvers, citing the fact that they can and do work along with the participants, so learning and working with mathematics (or new or different mathematics)

---

[5] Divisions within a social group typically involve differences of power, including the subordination of one group to another. In such situations, the dominant group may speak for the subordinated group because of the privilege of its position. Feminists were among the first to call attention to the problems of voice and representation. They recognized that many traditional ethnographic accounts of cultures involved male informants talking with male anthropologists and constructed a version of male culture that may not fit the realities or imaginations of women within the social group they described. The silencing of women within the social group and within the ethnographic literature is one example of how difficult it is for the subaltern to speak (Spivak, 1988). There are also cases where the dominated group is not represented or able to speak for itself.

becomes possible. For example, when Math Forum staff members began running workshops for the Urban Systemic Initiative teachers, they neither assumed that workshops needed to be held in 90-degree classrooms with no air conditioning, nor that they should give up when assigned to these classrooms. The staff members began rounding up fans from their homes and neighbors and opening windows to make the air flow. Once conditions were tolerable, they moved on to talking about doing mathematics on the Internet. On feedback forms from the workshop, the teachers reported that they had never seen anything like The Math Forum staff in action. They said that other groups would have given up. They also said that they were glad The Math Forum had not.

Math Forum staff members respond similarly to developments on the site by involving others in helping them to describe the problem, its attributes, and its possibilities and using these data to problem solve. After The Math Forum began posting PoWs and facilitating teacher and student use of these problems, it also began receiving questions from teachers, students, and others working with mathematics. Instead of responding that it was not a question and answer service, the staff members responded to the questions, viewing them as an indicator of participant need. They resurrected a defunct question and answer service that another site had mounted, and they launched the service that is now known as Ask Dr. Math. Then, because Ask Dr. Math was quickly overwhelmed with submissions and publicity that yielded even more submissions, they decided to develop a tenuring process for volunteers who were willing to help mentor other participants. The tenuring process allowed them to enlist help from participants and maintain a focus on enabling participants to become resourceful problem solvers without needing to single-handedly do all of the support that this entails. Furthermore, by refining the way in which questions are submitted, the service also guaranteed that the mathematics with which volunteer mentor doctors worked was not routine. It also ensured that the problem was of interest and would increase the likelihood that the doctor would want to continue to mentor problems from the queue in the Dr. Math office (see related discussion in Renninger & Farra, 2003).[6]

On The Math Forum site, structural features of information technology are used to facilitate forms of interaction where participants can begin work from the position of their own strengths, and then move on to different challenges and/or types of questions about mathematics as they are ready to do so. The design of the site and the staff members' approaches to working with participants distinguish The Math Forum from the bureaucracy that

---

[6] Presently, the Dr. Math service has one full-time staff member, who answers questions and facilitates the tenuring and mentoring of volunteers, and two part-time people assisting with programming and archiving. This service alone receives over 350 questions a day and could not exist if it were not for the support of volunteer mentor doctors.

characterizes most schools and many teacher professional development programs. The culture of The Math Forum provides its participants with a context for thinking and working with mathematics that is characterized by individual autonomy and opportunities for interaction and knowledge-building. In fact, it may be the staff's democratic focus on problem solving that accounts for the positive feelings for the site held by participants who do not have an interest for mathematics and/or technology.

The culture of The Math Forum is not embodied in either its participants or in the resources or text of the site, however. The culture is dynamic, and, as such, it is in an ongoing process of being recreated as participants work with the site, their exchanges are archived, and their understanding of their own sense of possibility shifts. As successive refinements to the Ask Dr. Math service suggest, the culture is one of both creative and substantial problem solving. The staff members developed a tenuring process because of the unevenness in the responses being provided by volunteer mentors to participants posing questions. Although they had a huge need for the kind of support that a volunteer corps of mentors could provide, their vision for the service was that mentors would help participants to use their own resources to think through the question and not simply answer them. The process of tenuring was designed to help mentors "hear" the questions posed so that they can support participants to think mathematically. The process of tenuring takes as much or as little time as the mentor in training needs. All levels of mentors, including Ph.D.s, high school students, and former teachers, have to be tenured before they are permitted to respond directly to participant questions.

The staff works to help participants engage mathematics by focusing on what is understood and providing a context that enables participants to stretch their understanding. The staff members communicate an appreciation of the field of mathematics as broad and deep and a playful approach to the process of problem solving (Winnicott, 1971). At times, this means that the environment needs to be altered (e.g., volunteers need to be trained) so mathematics can be taken up. At other times, it means that, in order to address a problem, participants are encouraged to either identify the complications that they experience and revise what they are doing or work on identifying the problem to be answered (cf., Sternberg, 1985). This type of interaction about mathematics reinforces the perception of the site as distinctive, and it enables the individuals who find and become participants on the site to think of it as a place as well as a community.

MATH FORUM CULTURE AND COMMUNITY

Like a rhizome, Math Forum culture and community have emerged from and within a diverse set of forces. The Math Forum is a product of existing educational institutions, the individuals who first came together to create The Math Forum, and technology that has facilitated the collection of resources that both support and reflect inquiry-based approaches to instruction (Renninger, Weimar, & Klotz, 1998). The culture and the community are a dialectical interplay of (a) the people and institutions that are and have been a part of site and its development and (b) the technological possibilities brought into being by personal computers and the Internet.

In fact, the community that formed The Math Forum in 1992 can be likened to a foraging band in that it was (and continues to be) a highly egalitarian structure where the norms of reciprocity fuel its development. The staff was a small group. Everyone worked alongside of and knew everyone else. Its beginnings were a response to the desire of geometers working with The Geometer's Sketchpad[7] to exchange figures. Some teachers and students found The Geometry Forum, The Math Forum's predecessor, and these "lone rangers," as the staff referred to them, were welcomed to think about and discuss geometry along with the geometers and developers. The staff members thought of those people with whom they worked as collaborators and referred to themselves as a community; they did not think of the participant list as something to protect, but instead they worked to pool a range of perspectives from this diverse population.

Without realizing that they were doing so, the staff members had begun to establish a utopia, infused by the values of the early Internet and the privileges of being housed in the liberal arts college environment of Swarthmore College and funded by the NSF. Like other pioneers of Internet use, the staff members shared a problem-solving orientation toward the world and the beliefs that (a) individuals have great things to contribute and the Internet can make it possible for these contributions to be understood by others, (b) learning is essential and the Internet can be a medium for communicating about ideas, and (c) everyone can learn and the Internet can bring people together so that they can work on their understanding(s) with others. Like other Internet groups at the time, a lot of the everyday social niceties from official titles and positions down to style of dress were also considered to have little to do with real value. Consistent with these values, The Math Forum was designed and built out to model democratic education (e.g., Dewey, 1938).

The habitus (Bourdieu, 1977, 1980) of the early days of the site included various forms of privilege. It combined the excitement of the new "digerati," the technologically elite who understand and can use the new technologies, with the intellectual surety of mathematicians. Furthermore, it was nurtured in the intellectual and pedagogical milieu of a small liberal arts college. This context was powerful for fueling a group that felt it could

---

[7] The Visual Geometry Project, which produced software for visualizing geometric figures, including *The Geometer's Sketchpad*, was the first of a series of National Science Foundation-funded projects that evolved into what is currently known as The Math Forum.

use technology to make a real contribution to mathematics education – a field that concurrently was undergoing self-examination about exactly what reform practices in mathematics involved and needed to look like.

Having established itself in geometry, the staff was encouraged by the NSF to build out their offerings in mathematics topics in 1997 as The Math Forum. As a condition of this funding, however, staff members were also asked to train teachers in two large, urban school districts that were part of the NSF's Urban Systemic Initiative (USI). These were school districts in which the technology and math skills of the teaching staff were largely undeveloped. The NSF was interested in harnessing the capacity of projects such as The Math Forum to help meet the needs of students and teachers in underprivileged settings. Not all of the teachers for whom The Math Forum was to be responsible as part of this plan were mathematics teachers, however. Unlike The Math Forum's work with teachers prior to this, USI teachers had not sought to be supported by The Math Forum staff.

The Math Forum staff members worked to figure out what would be useful to USI teachers. In the course of face-to-face and, eventually, virtual work, they were able to adjust their services and begin to develop forms of social interaction that a number of these teachers found to be beneficial.[8] Teachers in these districts voted to allot their in-service funding to continued support by The Math Forum staff following its support by federal funding. The experience of working with the USI teachers helped the staff to build out the site in ways that made it more accessible to people who were uncomfortable with mathematics and technology. Work with USI teachers also led the staff to realize that they could not be all things for all people. The staff members knew that in face-to-face workshops they could support teachers in ways that made them want to work with the site. They also recognized that they needed to focus their efforts. Either they could focus on building out site services with participants who had their own questions about mathematics, technology, and the use of technology in classrooms, or they could focus on staffing workshops to encourage teachers to consider working with technology. They could not continue to do both things well. Because of the rate at which the site was growing in terms of both pages and participant numbers, it rapidly became clear to the staff that its choice had to be providing and refining site services if theirs was to be a site that others would want to learn to use.

---

[8] Because the teachers for whom The Math Forum was responsible were not all mathematics teachers, staff time on this project involved helping the teachers to learn and work with technology. Thus, they were thinking through the issues that learning to work with technology required and ways in which the site might be better developed to help those who needed this type of support to work with the site.

Even though its beginnings were rich in social and cultural capital, like all small Internet organizations, The Math Forum has been shaped by limitations on support and problems of scaling and sustainability. Ironically, rapid success with services like the PoWs and Ask Dr. Math meant that there were many people using the services and few staff members to manage the needs of participants. Furthermore, there were limited financial resources to address issues of additional staff, space, and equipment.[9] The staff recruited help, streamlined the need for participants to ask questions, and developed tools and procedures to enable mentors to more easily assess the strengths and needs of participants.

Over time, the culture of The Math Forum has become more complex and polyvocal (Turner, 1969, 1974). Following work with USI teachers and publicity in the mass media, the site has grown to include an increasingly diverse group of participants and these participants have become integral to the site's expansion and existence. Participants bring their questions and concerns to the site or work with site problems and content. They help to provide the interactivity of the site's resources. Some participants contribute web pages, answer students' questions about math, have their students submitting problems, and work with their colleagues to build site resources into their classes. Many participants retain contact with The Math Forum through workshops, professional meetings, projects, and their collaborations with others on the site – which in other parlance might have been identified as rituals of belonging.

The Math Forum as an organization has always put individuals first in the sense that it is individual strengths and needs that have informed the building out and tweaking of its services. The staff has constantly asked itself, "what do participants want and how can resources be made more useful?" To this end, for example, the staff takes feedback on the questionnaire that might to some be considered eccentric and an indication of not knowing how to use a particular set of problems, and it proceeds to develop pages to address this understanding. The presumption is that if one teacher had a misunderstanding or need, this perspective is likely to be shared by others. In this way, the staff has broadened the site's base of services, the nature of the explanations, and the resources available to participants. Importantly, although the response of the site has been to meet individuals' needs as learners, social interaction has consistently been

---

[9] This chapter does not detail the contradictions that emerge in the process of scaling and the need for sites to be sustainable, even though these issues have had and continue to have an impact on the activity of The Math Forum. Such issues are the focus of a number of other papers (Shumar & Renninger, 2000; Renninger & Shumar, 2001). Briefly, these papers suggest that scaling and sustainability could be understood as the instigators of cultural change at The Math Forum because they necessitated that the staff grow quickly albeit with modest remuneration, and that the staff as a whole found ways to sell its services to potential buyers who could provide sustainability.

perceived as central to learning. Thus, site development has also focused on enhancing the possibilities of interaction.

In addition to work with the USI teachers and other teacher groups, Math Forum staff have also been partners on a number of NSF projects, which have brought participants to The Math Forum (physically and virtually) to work together in ways that benefit participants and further expand the resources of the site (e.g., www.mathforum.org/brap/wrap/; Shumar, 2003). The Math Forum staff does not reify social interaction by creating forms, lists, and rules (Wenger, 1999). Rather it interacts and facilitates interactions. Participants in these projects, like participants in site services, are typically given a wide range of choices about what they want to know and do – whether they are a staff member, workshop participant, or participant. Reification takes place only at the point of archiving what is useful and effective in these learning interactions for others.

Although critiques of progressive approaches to education typically suggest that focusing on pedagogy undermines attention to content, The Math Forum has been and continues to be both person-centered in its attention to learners' strengths and needs and strong in its mathematics content. Participants are attracted to and willing to help this staff that models creative problem solving – whether this is an alternative solution path to a challenging problem, the ability to figure out how to deal with hot weather so that a workshop can proceed, or refining a service to better meet the strengths and needs of participants. The Math Forum is a community of practice where newcomers apprentice with more senior and skilled participants (Lave & Wenger, 1991; Renninger et al., 1998; Renninger & Shumar, 2002), and learning on the site is considered a social activity, whether the learning is modeled, learned through apprenticeship, or scaffolded through interactions with or conversations about text (Collins, Brown, & Newman, 1989). Consistent with reform pedagogy, site design focuses the process of participants' engagement on thinking mathematically with others, and the content of this engagement is rigorous mathematics.

LEARNING, A POSSIBILITY BECAUSE OF CULTURE AND COMMUNITY

A central question for a site such as The Math Forum is how it can continue to effectively facilitate learning online, given rapidly increasing usage. Moreover, how can participants who require a lot of time be supported, given the needs to continue to scale services and become sustainable? The answer to these questions seems to be that once the culture and community of a site are articulated and sustained, in the sense that the site becomes an entity for participants, the culture and the community of the site lead participants to help. Participants facilitate interactions, help others to stretch mathematical thinking, and so forth, allowing staff attention to be directed to figuring out how to scale services and address the need to be financially sustainable.

Based on in-depth structured interviews with participants, it appears that early in their work with technology, participants need to form a sense of social identity online (Renninger & Shumar, 2002). This identity provides them with a sense of with whom they are talking and working, and it allows them to feel a sense of belonging. The sense of belonging, like the ability to cross symbolic borders, is facilitated by interactive services that scaffold participants to feel welcomed, heard, and taken seriously as learners. Thus, as Renninger and Shumar (2002) point out, participants typically use one or only a few resources or services when they first find the site. Then, they expand their work with the site by exploring and finding other resources or services with which to work and learn. They also begin to assume some responsibility for aspects of those resources to which they previously had connected. Over time, participants who continue to work with the service continue to stretch and deepen their work with mathematics and become co-creators of the site. The developmental course of participation proceeds from processes involving identity formation to those associated with identification (Virilio, 1995).

Similarly, students' work with the Problems of the Week service over a ten-month period has been found to have an impact on their abilities to (a) make connections to the mathematics of the nonroutine word problems they were presented, (b) generate and revise strategies for working with these problems, and (c) become increasingly independent in their abilities to accurately work with this type of problem (Renninger, Farra, & Feldman-Riordan, 2000). Because student work in this service is highlighted in the archive, the students are at once learning and making contributions to the learning of others who will use their work as resource material.

The connection between changed participation and site functioning was further examined in the Math Forum's Bridging Research and Practice (BRAP) project[10] using microanalytic methods, including study of participant observation in workshops, videotapes of classroom practice, interviews, and email exchanges. The BRAP project was (and continues to be) a collaboration of teacher and staff participants who worked face-to-face and online over a three-year period to (a) read and think together about applications of the research on mathematics learning to their work with students and (b) write a live videopaper (mathforum.org/brap/wrap/) that describes their insights about the research they read and its application, provides detail about their study of their own students' work with the

---

[10] The Math Forum's Bridging Research and Practice (BRAP) project was The Math Forum's contribution to a Math Forum, TERC, and Michigan State University collaboration sponsored by the NSF to study the value of video in online learning.

cylinder problem, a classic challenge problem,[11] and allows them to continue this conversation among themselves and with others over the web through links in the videopaper.

The learning of those involved with this project took two complementary forms. First, participants stretched their thinking and experience with mathematics, pedagogy, and technology. Second, participants also shifted some of the assumptions with which they began the project, including concerns about their abilities to do mathematics, research and write a paper, and collaborate in thinking about the content and direction of their work together. Findings from this study suggest that staff members' efforts both to share power and to learn through their own participation in the project supported collaboration and resulted in learning for all participants. Through collaboration, the teachers and the staff members came to identify (or reaffirm) The Math Forum as a community that they are helping to build (Harasim, 2002). Their participation in the project was not simply part of a received identity.

Importantly, community for the BRAP project participants appears to be an experience or process and not a product. It included the activity and work that went into creating the videopaper; the close friendships created in this process; the learning about mathematics, pedagogy, and technology that each individual continues to realize from the group's work, and the changed imagination of participants' individual identities and that of the group. This process of identifying with, contributing to, and growing through participation is critical for identifying the BRAP group as a community distinct from a collection of resources. Moreover, as mentioned above, participants not only established a group identity through association, but they took part in an active process of building identifications with the other community members as well as the site. Interestingly, this process of identification mirrored the characteristics of the larger site culture, suggesting that on The Math Forum site, community and culture are co-dependent.

While change in participants' work with and perception of the BRAP project might have been expected over the three-year period of the project, there was no reason to expect this particular group of teachers and staff members to cohere, especially given the precarious status of The Math Forum at the time. The BRAP project was launched in the midst of rapid scaling and a need for the site to find financial sustainability for its infrastructure since the infrastructure could no longer be covered by NSF grants. Furthermore, the BRAP project was undertaken with some staff who were being trained during the project. Unlike the way the site requires its

---

[11] The cylinder problem: Form two cylinders from a rectangular piece of paper, one by joining the long sides, one by joining the short sides. Which of these cylinders will have greater volume, or will they hold the same amount?

volunteers to practice mentoring before they begin responding to others, the conditions at The Math Forum at that time necessitated that new staff leap into the project alongside experienced staff and work though the challenges of understanding site culture and its implications for collaborative process as the project evolved.

In spite of complications, participants in the BRAP project did cohere. It is likely that site culture and the community that this culture fosters account for participant learning in this project. The expectation that participants come to a site project to learn meant that the staff worked with the participants as learners. The expectation that participants should be welcomed and able to work at the level for which they are ready not only made teacher participants feel welcome but appears to have enabled them to maintain the esteem they felt for Math Forum staff coming into the project and to accept the strengths and needs of various staff members as the project unfolded. It also appears that connections made to participants' questions, or interests, in the design of the project meant that both teacher and staff participants focused on these in their discussions rather than site difficulties. This enabled all of the participants to deepen and/or develop their understanding of the BRAP project content, including discourse, mathematics, mathematical thinking, and the applications of research to practice.

There was no hidden curriculum (Jackson, 1968). The Math Forum staff did not hold a goal to reform or change participants (nor did the teachers who joined the project have a goal to change the staff, for that matter). Rather, the staff and teacher participants in the BRAP project came together to explore issues of research and practice in mathematics. In the process, they stretched what they knew not only about research and practice, but about mathematics, teachers doing research and writing, and collaboration. They also deepened their connections to each other and to the site.

Study of individual and group participation in The Math Forum's BRAP project suggests that as long as there is rich content in addition to multiple opportunities and support for engaging this content, there is no particular ratio of autonomy, interaction, or opportunity to think with others that needs to be in place for participants to be supported. Rather, like findings from studies of project-based learning (Blumenfeld et al., 1991; Brown & Campione, 1994), an open-ended project such as the BRAP project allows participants to (a) connect to content in the way that they can, (b) assume the autonomy that they need, and (c) take advantage of opportunities to think with others as they are ready. Motivation for participating in the project grew from participant and group questions and the interest that these questions held (Renninger, 2000). Staff members' support of participants' questions as the focus of the project meant that participants developed their understandings of mathematics, pedagogy, and technology at a pace and in a way that matched their strengths, needs, and interests. The process of participants addressing their own questions also led them to additional questions and the need for resources to address them. The site held some of the resources they needed, and they brought additional resources that they identified to the site. In this way, participants addressed their own questions and shared them and the resources that they found with others through the site.

It might be argued that the combination of face-to-face and online communication of the project's design was important to the cohesion that the BRAP participants developed during the project. It is possible, however, that a well-facilitated online discussion could have been as compelling for participants. This is an open question.

CONCLUSIONS

Face-to-face workshops and projects have been important to developing the participant base that constitutes The Math Forum. In fact, participation in the BRAP project replicates and extends previous descriptions of learning at and with The Math Forum (Renninger et al., 1998; Renninger et al., 2000; Renninger & Shumar, 2002). The Math Forum has leveraged the concept of community by fostering interactions and contributions that increase opportunities for individuals to work together to think, do, and learn mathematics. The focus on interaction and provision of support for the strengths, needs, and interests of individuals working with the site are central to Math Forum culture.

The Math Forum has always worked virtually and through face-to-face meetings with participants. Participants' shared goals of creating a place where thinking about mathematics is supported has been more critical than a specific site design. Design decisions have been undertaken in response to and at the suggestion of participants. As site participation has changed, the design of the services has been adjusted. Because of its increased size, The Math Forum staff has had to leverage the concept of community in order to foster interactions on the site, to encourage people to volunteer to staff services, and to help create resources for the site. These recruiting efforts have been very successful. For example, teachers, who at one time may have seen their professional community as being made up of their local colleagues, have come to view online colleagues as part of their professional community. At times teachers blur the boundaries of these communities by drawing on Math Forum staff and resources during staff meetings and/or their school-based colleagues for online discussions. This blurring of boundaries has led to a much more complex sense of professional community. Parallel findings can be reported for student participants too. For them, based on site questionnaires, it appears that the site represents an expanded sense of mathematics. They point to opportunities to ask questions without fear of ridicule, do mathematics that challenges them, and extend the learning they do in school.

The Math Forum is a community rich in resources. These resources are not simply resources compiled for others; rather, they have been built out through participants and the mining of archived learning interactions. These resources are community resources and they contribute to participants' senses of ownership and belonging.

As study of BRAP participation suggests, the site appears to have evolved to a point where the culture and the community can be considered entities (albeit complex and heterogeneous), which while continuing to be supported by staff, are also sustained by the imagination and participation of participants. The relationships between staff participants and other participants on the site continue to be reciprocal (Pea, 1993). Participants who are experienced in their work with the site are able to make use of it and help support the work of others. Participants who are new to the site continue to need additional support in order to use the site well, but over time they are able to become more independent in their efforts – in fact, as evidenced by the BRAP project, helping others appears to heighten the likelihood of independence (Shumar, 2003).

Because the Math Forum culture is increasingly complex and polyvocal, it can and does enable the learning of all types of participants – those who are strong in mathematics and those who are weak, those who have interest for mathematics and those who do not, those who have lots of previous experience and those who do not, and those who come to the site in different roles (e.g., teachers, students, mathematicians). For each of these individuals or groups of individuals the culture and the community of the site provide support to continue to think with others about mathematics. The staff builds on participants' stated or evident needs and uses these to inform refinements of site options and services. It may be that because The Math Forum provides a contrast to the other experiences of its participants, that it is a site to which they tend to return over time. It does appear that The Math Forum provides its participants with a unique set of opportunities for learning, and that the relationship between the individual and the community on the site is one in which individual needs are met while the community benefits.

References

Anderson, B. R. O. G. (1991). *Imagined communities: Reflections on the origin and spread of nationalism*. (rev. and extended ed.). New York: Verso.

Barab, S. A., & Duffy, T. M. (2000). From practice fields to communities of practice. In D. Jonassen & S. Land (Eds.), *Theoretical foundations of learning environments* (pp. 25–56). Mahwah, NJ: Erlbaum.

Barnes, J. A. (1972). *Social networks*. (Module in anthropology 26.) Reading, MA: Addison-Wesley.

Barth, F. (1981). *Process and form in social life*. Boston: Routledge & Kegan Paul.

Blumenfeld, P. C., Soloway, E., Marx, R. W., Krajcik, J. S., Guzdial, M., & Palincsar, A. (1991). Motivating project-based learning: Sustaining the doing, supporting the learning. *Educational Psychologist, 26,* 369–398.

Bourdieu, P. (1977). *Outline of a theory of practice.* Richard Nice, Trans. New York: Cambridge University Press.

Bourdieu, P. (1980). *The logic of practice.* Stanford, CA: Stanford University Press.

Brown, A. L., & Campione, J. C. (1994). Guided discovery in a community of learners. In K. McGilly (Ed.), *Classroom lessons: Integrating cognitive theory and classroom practice* (pp. 229–272). Cambridge, MA: MIT Press.

Bruner, J. S. (1966). *Toward a theory of instruction.* Cambridge, MA: Harvard University Press.

Chaiklin, S., & Lave, J. (Eds.) (1993). *Understanding practice: Perspectives on activity and context.* New York: Cambridge University Press.

Clifford, J. (1988). *The predicament of culture: Twentieth-century ethnography, literature, and art.* Cambridge, MA: Harvard University Press.

Cobb, P. (1995). Mathematical learning and small-group interaction: Four case studies. In P. Cobb & H. Bauersfeld (Eds.), *The emergence of mathematical meaning: Interaction in classroom cultures* (pp. 25–129). Hillsdale, NJ: Erlbaum.

Cochran-Smith, M., & Lytle, S. L. (1993). *Inside/outside: Teacher research and knowledge.* New York: Teachers College Press.

Cognition and Technology Group at Vanderbilt (1990). Anchored instruction and its relationship to situated cognition. *Educational Researcher, 19*(6) 2–10.

Cognition and Technology Group at Vanderbilt (1991). Technology and the design of generative learning environments. *Educational Technology, 31,* 34–40.

Cognition and Technology Group at Vanderbilt (1996). Looking at technology in context: A framework for understanding technology and education research. In D. C. Berliner & R. C. Calfee (Eds.), *Handbook of educational psychology* (pp. 807–840). New York: Macmillan.

Cohen, A. (1985). *The symbolic construction of community.* London: Tavistock Publications.

Cohen, A. (1994). *Self consciousness: An alternate anthropology of identity.* London and New York: Routledge.

Cole, M., Engestrom, Y., & Vasquez, O. (Eds.) (1997). *Mind, culture and activity: Seminal papers from the Laboratory of Comparative Human Cognition.* New York: Cambridge University Press.

Collins, A., Brown, J. S., & Newman, S. E. (1989). Cognitive apprenticeship: Teaching the crafts of reading, writing, and mathematics. In L. B. Resnick (Ed.), *Knowing, learning, and instruction: Essays in honor of Robert Glaser* (pp. 455–494). Hillsdale, NJ: Erlbaum.

De Corte, E., Verschaffel, L., & Op T'Eynde, P. (2000). Self-regulation: A characteristic and a goal of mathematics education. In M. Boekaert, P. R. Pintrich, & M. Zeidner (Eds.), *Handbook of self-regulation* (pp. 687–726). New York: Academic Press.

Deleuze, G., & Guattari, F. (1987). *A thousand plateaus: Capitalism and schizophrenia.* Brian Massumi, Trans. Minneapolis: University of Minnesota Press.

Dewey, J. (1938). *Experience and education.* New York: Collier Books.

Ewing, K. (1990). The illusion of wholeness: Culture, self and the experience of inconsistency. *Ethos, 18*(3):251–278.

Ginsberg, H. P., Klein, A., & Starkey, P. (1998). The development of children's mathematical thinking: Connecting research with practice. In I. E. Sigel & K. A. Renninger (Vol. Eds.), *Child psychology and practice* (Vol. 4), in W. Damon (Gen. Ed.), *Handbook of child psychology* (5th ed., pp. 401–476). New York: John Wiley and Sons.

Goody, J. (1994). Culture and its boundaries: A European view. In R. Borofsky (Ed.), *Assessing cultural anthropology* (pp. 250–260). New York: McGraw-Hill.

Gulliver, P. H. (1971). *Neighbours and networks: The idiom of kinship in social action among the Ndendeuli of Tanzania.* Berkeley: University of California Press.

Harasim, L. (2002). What makes online learning communities successful? In C. Vrasidas & G. Glass (Eds.), *Distance education and distributed learning* (pp. 181–200). CT: Information Age Publishing.

Herzfeld, M. (1997). *Cultural intimacy: Social poetics in the nation-state.* New York: Routledge.

Holland, D., Lachicotte, W. Jr., Skinner, D., & Cain, C. (1998). *Identity and agency in cultural worlds.* Cambridge, MA: Harvard University Press.

Jackson, P. W. (1968). *Life in classrooms.* New York: Holt, Rhinehart, & Winston.

Kirshner, D., & Whitson, J. A. (1997). *Situated cognition: Social, semiotic and psychological perspectives.* Mahwah, NJ: Erlbaum.

Krapp, A. (1999). Interest, motivation, and learning: An educational-psychological perspective. *European Journal of Psychology of Education, 14*(1), 23–40.

Krapp, A., & Fink, B. (1992). The development and function of interests during the critical transition from home to preschool. In K. A. Renninger, S. Hidi, & A. Krapp (Eds.), *The role of interest in learning and development* (pp. 397–431). Hillsdale, NJ: Erlbaum.

Kraut, R., Lundmark, V., Patterson, M., Kiesler, S., Mukopadhyay, T., & Scherlis, W. (1998). Internet paradox: A social technology that reduces social involvement and psychological well-being? *American Psychologist, 53*(9), 1017–1031.

Lave, J. (1993). The practice of learning. In S. Chaiklin & J. Lave (Eds.). *Understanding practice: Perspectives on activity and context* (pp. 3–32). New York: Cambridge University Press.

Lave, J. & Wenger, E. (1991). *Situated learning: Legitimate peripheral participation.* New York: Cambridge University Press.

Linehan, C., & McCarthy, J. (2000). Positioning in practice: Understanding participation in the social world. *Journal for the Theory of Social Behavior 30*(4).

Marcus, H., & Nurius, P. (1986). Possible selves. *American Psychologist, 4*(9), 954–969.

National Research Council (1989). *Everybody counts: A report to the nation on the future of mathematics education.* Washington, DC: National Academy Press.

Neumann, A. (April, 1999). *Passionate talk about passionate thought: The view from professors at early midcareer.* Paper presented at the annual meeting of the American Educational Research Association. Montreal, Canada.

Nie, N. H., & Erbring, L. (2000). *Internet and society: A preliminary report.* Stanford, CA: Stanford Institute for the Quantitative Study of Society.

Paul, R. (1990). What does anybody want? Desire, purpose and the acting subject in the study of culture. *Cultural Anthropology 5*, 431–451.

Pea, R. D. (1993). Learning scientific concepts through material and social activities: Conversational analysis meets conceptual change. *Educational Psychologist, 28*(3), 265–277.

Poster, M. (2001). *What's the matter with the Internet?* Minneapolis: University of Minnesota Press.

Putnam, R. D. (2000). *Bowling alone: The collapse and revival of American community.* New York: Simon & Schuster.

Renninger, K. A. (2000). Individual interest and its implications for understanding intrinsic motivation. In C. Sansone & J. M. Harackiewicz (Eds.), *Intrinsic and extrinsic motivation: The search for optimal motivation and performance* (pp. 375–404). New York: Academic.

Renninger, K. A., & Farra, L. (2003). Mentor-participant exchange in the Ask Dr. Math service: Design and implementation considerations. In M. Mardis (Ed.), *Developing digital libraries for K–12 Education.* Syracuse, NY: ERIC IT Clearinghouse.

Renninger, K. A., Farra, L., & Feldman-Riordan, C. (2000). The impact of The Math Forum's Problems of the Week on students' mathematical thinking. *Proceedings of ICLS 2000.* Mahwah, NJ: Erlbaum.

Renninger, K. A., & Shumar, W. (2000). *Report of the local evaluation team to The Math Forum and the National Science Foundation regarding NSF Grant #9618223.* Available online at mathforum.org/build/build/NSFreport/report.html; semiprivate password: forum/forumfriend.

Renninger, K. A., & Shumar, W. (April, 2001). Multidimensional aspects of on-line community building: The Math Forum. Paper presented as part of the symposium, *Understanding online learning communities: Sociocultural views.* American Educational Research Association. Seattle, WA.

Renninger, K. A., & Shumar, W. (2002). Community building with and for teachers: *The Math Forum* as a resource for teacher professional development. In K. A. Renninger & W. Shumar (Eds.), *Building virtual communities: Learning and change in cyberspace* (pp. 60–95). New York: Cambridge University Press.

Renninger, K. A., & Shumar, W. (April, 2003). The role of the social in teachers' interest development and learning with an online community. Paper presented as part of the symposium, *Sociocultural Aspects of Interest Development and Their Implications for Education* (S. Nolen, Chair). Chicago, IL.

Renninger, K. A., & Shumar, W. (in press). Participant learning and activity in an interactive digital library: *The Math Forum community.* In J. Weiss, J. Nolan, & P. Trifonas (Eds.), *International handbook of virtual learning environments.* Amsterdam: Kluwer Press.

Renninger, K. A., Weimar, S. A., & Klotz, E. A. (1998). Teachers and students investigating and communicating about geometry: The Math Forum. In R. Lehrer & D. Chazen (Eds.), *Designing learning environments for developing understanding about geometry and space* (pp. 465–487). Mahwah, NJ: Erlbaum.

Rogoff, B. (1998). Cognition as a collaborative process. In R. Siegler & D. Kuhn (Vol. Eds.), *Cognition, perception and language* (Vol. 2). In W. Damon (Gen. Ed.) *Handbook of child psychology* (pp. 679–730). New York: John Wiley & Sons.

Rosaldo, R. (1989). *Culture and truth: The remaking of social analysis.* Boston, MA: Beacon Press.

Schoenfeld, A. (1987). What's all the fuss about metacognition? In A. Schoenfeld (Ed.), *Cognitive science and mathematics education* (pp. 189–215). Hillsdale, NJ: Erlbaum.

Schoenfeld, A. (1992). Learning to think mathematically: Problem solving, metacognition, and sense making in mathematics. In D. A. Grouws (Ed.), *Handbook of research on mathematics teaching and learning: A project of the National Council of Teachers of Mathematics* (pp. 334–370). New York: Macmillan.

Shore, B. (1996). *Culture in mind: Cognition, culture, and the problem of meaning.* New York: Oxford University Press.

Shulman, L. S. (1986). Those who understand: Knowledge growth in teaching. *Educational Researcher, 15,* 4–14.

Shumar, W. (2003). The role of community and belonging in online learning. In M. Mardis (Ed.), *Developing digital libraries for K–12 education.* Syracuse, NY: ERIC IT Clearinghouse.

Shumar, W., & Renninger, K. A. (September, 2000). *Commerce and community: Walking the line between quality and sustainability at a virtual education center.* Paper presented to the meetings of the Association of Internet Researchers. Lawrence, KS.

Shumar, W., & Renninger, K. A. (2002). On conceptualizing community. In K. A. Renninger & W. Shumar (Eds.), *Building virtual communities: Learning and change in cyberspace* (pp. 1–17). New York: Cambridge University Press.

Smolka, A. B., DeGoes, M. C., & Pino, A. (1995). The constitution of the subject: A persistent question. In J. V. Wertsch (Ed.), *Sociocultural studies of mind* (pp. 165–184). New York: Cambridge University Press.

Spivak, G. C. (1988). Can the Subaltern Speak? In C. Nelson & L. Grossberg (Eds.), *Marxism and the interpretation of culture* (pp. 271–313). Chicago: University of Illinois Press.

Sternberg, R. J. (1985). *Beyond IQ.* New York: Cambridge University Press.

Stewart, K. (1996). *A space on the side of the road: Cultural poetics in an "other" America.* Princeton, NJ: Princeton University Press.

Strauss, C., & Quinn, N. (1997). *A cognitive theory of cultural meaning.* New York: Cambridge University Press.

Turner, V. (1969). *The ritual process: Structure and anti-structure.* Ithaca, NY: Cornell University Press.

Turner, V. (1974). *Dramas, fields, and metaphors: Symbolic action in human society.* Ithaca, NY: Cornell University Press.

Virilio, P. (1995). *The art of the motor.* J. Rose, Trans. Minneapolis: University of Minnesota Press.

Wellman, B. (2001). Physical place and CyberPlace: The rise of personalized networking. *International Journal of Urban and Regional Research, 25,* 227–252.

Wellman, B., & Gulia, M. (1999). Net surfers don't ride alone: Virtual communities as communities. In M. A. Smith & P. Kollack (Eds.), *Communities in cyberspace* (pp. 167–194). New York: Routledge.

Wenger, E. (1999). *Communities of practice.* New York: Cambridge University Press.

Winnicott, D. W. (1971). *Playing and reality.* London: Tavistock Publications.

8

An Exploration of Community in a Knowledge Forum Classroom

An Activity System Analysis

Jim Hewitt

The past two decades have witnessed a remarkable transformation in the theoretical landscape of educational research. Classical in-the-head conceptions of thinking and learning are now sharing the epistemic spotlight with the sociocultural and sociohistorical theories of Vygotsky, Leont'ev, and Luria (Kuutti, 1996). These new perspectives argue that learning is fundamentally a social activity, inextricably tied to participation in communal practices (Lave & Wenger, 1991; Rogoff, Baker-Sennett, Lacasa, & Goldsmith, 1995). Accordingly, there has been a growing interest in the notion of community in educational circles, and the ways in which social groupings can be designed to advance individual and collective cognitions.

Like any theory of learning, sociocultural perspectives are susceptible to misinterpretation and oversimplification. The notion that development "is a process of participation in sociocultural activities" (Rogoff et al., 1995, p. 45) offers a new way of thinking about cognition and meaning, but it can also lead to unwarranted optimism regarding the educational efficacy of community-based strategies. While sociocultural theory has been widely interpreted as a call for framing pedagogies around social engagement, it would be a mistake to assume that any form of group activity will yield desirable educational outcomes. The word *community* is popularly (and sometimes erroneously) applied to a broad range of social organizations, from informal Internet chat rooms to carefully crafted models of classroom activity (e.g., CTGV, 1992; Brown & Campione, 1990; Riel, 1992; Scardamalia, Bereiter, McLean, Swallow, & Woodruff, 1989). Clearly, some kinds of community engagement offer more educational promise than others. Thus, the research challenge is not one of drawing overarching conclusions regarding the efficacy of community models in general, but rather one of understanding how communities can be designed to effectively support individual and collective growth.

Over the past decade, the introduction and rapid expansion of Internet technologies have allowed communities to have a virtual existence in addition to, or in place of, conventional face-to-face interaction. This chapter seeks to improve our understanding of the complex relationships that can exist between the online and face-to-face worlds, and the ways in which communal practices and supports can be distributed across these modalities in pedagogically powerful ways. The focus of analysis is on a grade 5–6 classroom instantiation of an educational community model called a Knowledge Building Community (KBC) (Scardamalia & Bereiter, 1994). The core work of the class takes place "virtually" in an asynchronous electronic environment, but many aspects of online behavior are shaped by daily face-to-face interactions. No effort is made to classify this particular community as virtual or face-to-face, since such labels fail to capture the fluidity with which participants move from one medium to the other. The chapter begins by describing some of the characteristics of a Knowledge Building Community and how a KBC relates to the more general notion of *community*. This is followed by an Activity System analysis of a KBC that examines the distribution of power and responsibilities, the framing of individual and collective goals, and how online and face-to-face elements can combine to support learning.

WHAT IS A KNOWLEDGE BUILDING COMMUNITY?

A knowledge building community (KBC) is a type of community of practice (CoP). Barab, MaKinster, and Scheckler (this volume) describe a CoP as being characterized by: (1) shared knowledge, values, and beliefs; (2) overlapping histories among members; (3) mutual interdependence; (4) mechanisms for reproduction; (5) a common practice and/or mutual enterprise; (6) opportunities for interactions and participation; (7) meaningful relationships; and (8) respect for diverse perspectives and minority views. However, a KBC is a special kind of CoP, one in which the primary enterprise is knowledge creation rather than the construction of specific products or the completion of tasks (Riel & Polin, this volume). Academic research teams serve as a prototypical example. The members of a research team are expected to continually work toward the production of new knowledge, and their day-to-day responsibilities (writing papers, collecting data, presenting at conferences) are in service of that larger objective. Scardamalia and Bereiter (1994) propose that the research team model can be applied to many kinds of organizations (e.g., corporations, elementary and secondary classrooms, clubs, and even families).

As might be imagined, transforming a classroom into a KBC requires a significant shift in classroom norms and student and teacher identities. For students, the challenge is no longer one of completing teacher-designated tasks (e.g., worksheets, assignments, projects), but one of actively and collaboratively defining research problems that interest them, developing plans, identifying intellectual impasses, synthesizing ideas, and generally working with others to make sense of their area of inquiry. To support these kinds of activities, Scardamalia and Bereiter (1994) have created an online environment called Knowledge Forum (formerly known as Computer Supported Intentional Learning Environments, or CSILE). Knowledge Forum is a networked educational software program in which learners publish multimedia "notes" in a collaborative space and continually push forward the boundaries of communal knowledge (Scardamalia et al., 1989; Scardamalia et al., 1992). The teacher is seen as the expert learner in the classroom, one who supports and mentors students in their knowledge building efforts. Class investigations typically last for weeks, or even months. These investigations evolve in an iterative style, where discoveries inspire new questions that continually drive the research deeper.

To what extent is a classroom-based KBC a genuine community? At first glance, it appears to fit most conventional definitions. For example, it is consistent with Barab and Duffy's (2000) description of a CoP: "a collection of individuals sharing mutually defined practices, beliefs, and understandings over an extended time frame in the pursuit of a shared enterprise" (Wenger, 1998, p. 36). On the other hand, Barab and Duffy also point out that it is difficult for most classrooms to be genuine communities. One problem is that a class often lacks the historic context of conventional communities (Barab & Duffy, 2000). There is no heritage of shared goals, beliefs, and practices, nor is there a dynamic membership, where participants have overlapping histories and newcomers work alongside established practitioners. A second problem concerns the authenticity, or legitimacy, of student activity (Barab & Duffy, 2000). Schoolwork generally does not have meaning or purpose beyond the walls of the classroom. Students spend most of their time generating contrived products (projects, essays) as a means of learning course content, but the products themselves have little value beyond assessment. Lave (1993) refers to this as the commoditization of knowledge and learning in schools.

The implications of the aforementioned problems for classroom-based KBCs are unclear. Concerns about the authenticity of student activity may be less of an issue in KBC classrooms than in regular classrooms. Students in a KBC define problems of understanding that are personally relevant to them and then work to resolve them. There are no products to speak of – no final presentations or essays – just the preserved trace of electronic discourse. The students' goal is an intrinsically meaningful one: to deepen their personal and collective knowledge in a particular domain area. Thus, Barab and Duffy's (2000) concerns about authenticity may not be applicable to knowledge building classrooms. The knowledge constructed in such classrooms is not a commodity, but something that the participants find personally valuable and that the community as a whole legitimizes.

Concerns about a lack of historical context are more germane to knowledge building classrooms. Some split-grade classes (like the one described later in this chapter) do have a sense of continuity, since students cycle through the class over several years. However, many Knowledge Forum classrooms are reconstituted entirely each September. Naturally, they lack a sense of history. One possible way to think about these classrooms is to classify them as *new communities* or *proto-communities* – communities in the early stages of development. In the initial stages of any community, everyone is a novice and roles, protocols, practices, and tools have yet to be established. In much the same fashion, KBC classrooms are populated by newcomers who slowly develop their own rules, knowledge base, and sense of identity. As the school year progresses, pockets of expertise begin to develop, and artifacts emerge that have meaning for classroom members. However, the key distinction between a conventional community and a KBC is that the latter does not always have an opportunity to fulfill its potential. When the academic session ends, the class is disbanded, and the cycle starts anew the following year.

One argument in favor of using the word community to describe Knowledge Forum classrooms is purely pragmatic: a phrase like *knowledge building community* evokes a sense of a paradigmatic shift in teaching practice, which is important for teacher development. Traditional school culture is extremely resistant to change (Elmore, 1996), and innovative instructional approaches are constantly at risk of being routinized or subsumed into familiar, comfortable categories (e.g., "group work"). A phrase like knowledge building community is valuable precisely because it suggests a methodology that separates it from traditional teaching practice. The word community, in particular, helps convey many of the essential attributes of the KBC model. Thus, regardless of whether or not a classroom can be technically classified as a community, it may be helpful, in some circumstances, to label it as such.

This chapter examines a specific grade 5–6 classroom that adheres to many of the KBC practices described by Scardamalia and Bereiter. The teacher of this class is widely considered to be one of the more successful and effective Knowledge Forum instructors. His transition from conventional teaching to teaching with Knowledge Forum has already been documented in a previous study (Hewitt, 2002). The following analysis will examine the relationship between online and face-to-face processes in his class, and how the two come together to support community. Activity Theory is used as a framework for this investigation.

ACTIVITY THEORY

A sociocultural shift in the thinking of the educational psychology community has called into question the validity of traditional research methodologies. In particular, researchers like Lave (1988) propose that knowledge is not something that simply exists in the head, but also exists in the way that social groups communicate, make use of symbols and tools, and organize their belief systems. Learning, by extension, is a fundamentally situated activity in which expertise is gained by taking a legitimate role in the ongoing activities of a community and gradually moving to fuller participation (see also Brown, Collins, & Duguid, 1989 and Collins et al., 1989). However, if cognitions are fundamentally situated, then research that neglects the social and contextual dimensions of learning are at risk of drawing unwarranted conclusions about complex phenomena (Salomon, 1995). Such ideas call into question the epistemic assumptions of traditional experimental methodologies and argue for new forms of educational research. The alternative to conventional experimentation, and its philosophy of simplification by isolation, is to observe how individuals learn *in situ* – that is, in authentic, real-world contexts like a school classroom.

A classroom is a complicated environment in which many interacting factors influence the learning process. Discerning how and why cognitions change at a detailed level is extremely difficult and open to interpretive bias. Indeed, this complexity is one of the reasons why reductionist approaches were originally so popular. However, the apparent trade-off between ecological validity and rigor may only be problematic if the individual remains as the unit of study. Since theories of situated cognition suggest that learning involves much more than just those processes that go on in the head, it may be appropriate to consider larger units of analysis (Barab & Kirshner, 2001). Salomon (1995) suggests that it is these larger "composites" on which we should be focusing.

The meaning of the configuration, Gestalt, composite or constellation of factors is qualitatively different from that of its components. It is the composite that students and teachers experience; it is that composite which they interact with, not each of the ingredients taken one at a time; and it is that composite that we should be studying. (p. 17)

The problem, as Rogoff (1997) points out, is one of identifying units of analysis that capture the events of interest while simultaneously honoring the dynamic interdependence of individual, social, and cultural influences. Activity theory (AT) provides one useful lens for studying these interrelationships. As its name suggests, Activity Theory posits that human learning is fundamentally grounded in activity (thus blurring the traditional distinction between knowing and doing). Activity Theory is neither a methodology, nor is it a prescriptive or diagnostic tool (Jonassen & Rohrer-Murphy, 1999). Rather, it serves as a philosophical framework for studying the interweaving of human praxis at the individual and social levels. Engeström (1990) describes AT as an interdependent view of human activity involving the individual (or subject), tools, a problem space (or object), the community of people who are similarly concerned with

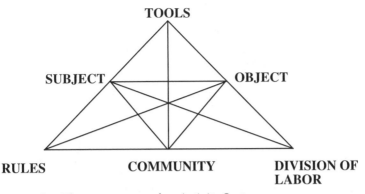

FIGURE 8.1. The components of an Activity System

the problem, the division of labor between community members, and the conventions (rules) regarding actions.

A triangular diagram (Figure 8.1) is often used to depict this relationship. Note that the activity of the individual (top three components) is not viewed in isolation, but is tied to the larger cultural context. Human activity is socially bound and is not merely the sum of individual actions (Engeström, 1987, 1990, 1993; Kuutti, 1996). Furthermore, Activity Systems are dynamic and may evolve over time. For example, changes in the design of a tool may influence a subject's orientation toward an object, which in turn may influence the cultural practices (rules) of the community. Or, changes to cultural practice may inspire the creation or reworking of a tool. Perturbations at any one point produce ripples, and occasionally, major transformations across the system. Thus, the model provides a composite view that recognizes the socially distributed nature of human activity, the activity of the individual, and the transformative nature of activity systems in general. And as Wells (1994) points out, it suggests ways of inducing cultural change:

[The Activity Theory model] also draws attention to possible points of leverage in the attempt to overcome the sequestered nature of schooling. For example, changing the nature of the rules that prescribe the sorts of actions that participants engage in and the expected outcomes, modifying the division of labor, or valuing other tools in addition to the textbook – for example, collaborative, exploratory talk – all create quite different activity systems, and ones that may encourage rather than resist student initiative and creativity. (p. 5)

Figure 8.2 serves as a rough model of the Activity System of a typical classroom. Most classroom activities involve students (subject) using pencils, erasers, calculators, and so forth (tools) to complete a task (object) that has been assigned by the teacher. This activity is constrained and guided by the rules and norms that govern classroom behavior (rules). The outcome,

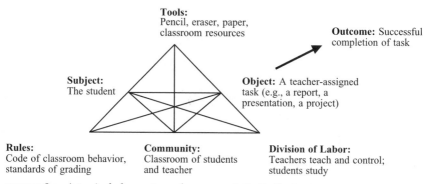

FIGURE 8.2. A typical elementary classroom Activity System

or product of this system, is student success or failure to complete the task according to the instructor's predefined criteria. Obviously, this Activity System is a rather generic one, and the components are not deeply fleshed out. However, Figure 8.2 does serve as a representation of a common – and in many ways dominant – task-based classroom Activity System, one that has endured in schools for decades.

The Activity System of a KBC takes a form that is quite different from that of Figure 8.2. Scardamalia and Bereiter (1993) describe a classroom-based KBC as follows:

1. There is a sustained study of topics in depth, sometimes over a period of months, rather than superficial coverage.
2. The focus is on problems rather than on categories of knowledge: not "the heart" but "how does the heart work?"
3. Inquiry is driven by students' questions. The teacher helps students formulate better questions and encourages them to reformulate questions at higher levels as inquiry proceeds.
4. Explaining is the major challenge. Students are encouraged to produce their own theories to account for facts and to criticize one another's theories by confronting them with facts.
5. Although teachers pay close attention to how each student is doing, the day-to-day focus is progress toward collective goals of understanding and judgment rather than on individual learning and performance.
6. There is little schoolwork of the conventional kind, where the students are working individually but all doing the same thing. More typically, students work in small groups; each group has a different task related to the central topic and plans how to distribute work among its members.
7. Discourse is taken seriously. Students are expected to respond to one another's work and are taught how to do so in helpful, supportive ways.
8. The teacher's own knowledge does not curtail what is to be learned or investigated. Teachers can contribute what they know to the discourse, but there are other sources of information.

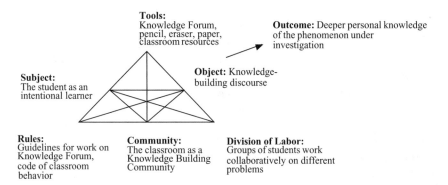

FIGURE 8.3. The Activity System of a Knowledge Building Community classroom

9. The teacher remains the leader, but the teacher's role shifts from standing outside the learning process and guiding it to participating actively in the learning process and leading by virtue of being a more expert learner. (pp. 14–15)

Using this description, the Activity System of a KBC can be represented by the framework in Figure 8.3.

Comparing the Knowledge Forum Activity System (Figure 8.3) to that of typical classrooms (Figure 8.2) reveals key differences. In a regular classroom, the product of activity is often a report, a presentation, or a project. Knowledge Forum classrooms, by comparison, often have no tangible product beyond that of written discourse (Bereiter et al., 1997). In a sense, the product and the process of inquiry are the same thing. Rather than focus on completing a teacher-designated task, students are encouraged and expected to take an intentional stance on their own learning (Bereiter & Scardamalia, 1989).

A CASE STUDY OF A KNOWLEDGE FORUM CLASSROOM

The following case study employs an Activity System framework to analyze individual and communal practices, both face-to-face and online, in a grade 5–6 Knowledge Forum classroom. The research methodology can be characterized as naturalistic inquiry supported by both quantitative and qualitative data (Guba & Lincoln, 1994). Data were gathered over a span of three years from researcher field notes, teacher interviews, student interviews, the contents of the Knowledge Forum database, and videotaped interactions between the instructor and students. The class contained between 25 and 32 students each year and typically 8 to 10 of the grade 6 students would have also been in the class during grade 5. Each student worked on Knowledge Forum for approximately 30 minutes per school day. The class studied a series of science-related topics (e.g., human biology, electricity, plants and animals) with each topic lasting approximately two months. Over the three-year span, the researcher spent approximately 150 hours in the classroom. The researcher conducted interviews, observed class activity, and provided occasional technical support for students, but did not assist or advise students with regard to their Knowledge Forum investigations. Neither the researcher nor the teacher participated extensively in the Knowledge Forum database.

In the following investigation, online and face-to-face processes are examined at both an individual (subject) and social (community) level. To carry out this analysis, the subject-community relationship is highlighted on the Activity System triangle, and this relationship is considered relative to each of the remaining Activity System components. This arrangement yields the following four subtriangle analyses: (1) subject-community-object; (2) subject-community-division of labor; (3) subject-community-rules; and (4) subject-community-tools. Considered collectively, these analyses are intended to provide a rich description of an exemplary Knowledge Forum instructor's classroom.

Subject-Community-Object: Online Discourse as an Individual and Collective Object of Analysis

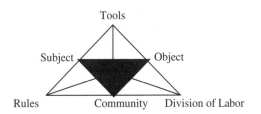

The learner discourse on Knowledge Forum (object) was the focal point of the community. It held the questions, theories, findings, and summaries of the entire class. At the beginning of a unit, students would be prompted to think about what they didn't understand about the given subject area. For example, if the topic was human biology, students might wonder where blood comes from or how the human eye works. These questions would serve as starting points in Knowledge Forum, and it would be the students' responsibility to make progress on both the questions that they contributed and those of their classmates in the shared online environment. "Progress" in this case is defined as adding notes that advance the existing discourse (e.g., providing a new theory, asking a question that no one had previously considered, or sharing information that had been obtained from resource materials). Usually, students were also required to associate an epistemological scaffold (e.g., "My Theory," "I Need To Understand") with each of their contributions, giving rise to discussions like the one in Example 8.1 involving three students (AR, JD, and AK).

Example 8.1. A Knowledge Forum discussion about nerve cells

PROBLEM (AR): How does a nerve cell work?

MY THEORY (AR): I think a nerve cell is just like any other cell except it can send messages to other parts of the body and it can feel. For example: Let's say an arm has been hurt. A nerve cell would feel that and then would send a message to the brain saying that the arm has been hurt.

MY THEORY (JD): I agree with you but where you say that the nerve cell sends messages to the ear. I think that the brain tells the ear.

MY THEORY (AK): I think that the nerve cell sends messages to the brain not the parts of the body that's been hurt. I think after the brain receives the message it reacts to them.

NEW INFORMATION (AR): Nerve cells are very long. They are longer than any other cell. Nerve cells have thin parts sticking out that send the messages. These parts are called axons.

I NEED TO UNDERSTAND (AK): How does the body react to the messages the nerve cell sends?

NEW INFORMATION (AR): Let's say the arm has been hurt. First an arm nerve cell will send a message up to the brain, through the spinal cord, saying that the arm has been hurt. Then the brain will send a message to, for instance, a hand saying that the arm has been hurt and needs help. Finally the hand will reach out and help the arm, maybe by squeezing it or rubbing it. I will try to explain this more clearly in my chart called a nerve cell.

I NEED TO UNDERSTAND (JD): What kind of parts are there in a nerve cell?

NEW INFORMATION (AR): A part in the nerve cell is the myelin. This is a very thick layer that covers the axon. Axons are another part of a nerve cell. Axons are long and skinny and can be as small as a fraction of an inch to three feet! Another part is the dendrites. They are very small and stick out from the cell. Nerve cells have a nucleus just like any other cell. Please look at my chart parts of the nerve cell.

Typically, the class worked on several dozen discussions simultaneously. Collectively, these discussions served as a reification of the evolving understanding of the entire class. The global accessibility of this corpus, combined with the teacher's emphasis on making progress, led to a reciprocal and mutually reinforcing relationship between the classroom as a whole (community) and the individual learner (subject). To make a worthwhile contribution to a Knowledge Forum discourse, a student had to first learn what the community already knew about the issue at hand (Scardamalia & Bereiter, 1996). Thus, individual learning was continually driven forward by a need to build on the community's existing knowledge base. Communal knowledge, in turn, was continually advanced by the ongoing contributions of individuals. Each time a student introduced a new question or a new theory, it upped the ante for the rest of the class who were now responsible for pushing the discourse even deeper.

Focusing on knowledge advancement and understanding was a common theme in the teacher's discussions with the class. Some students initially found it to be a difficult concept to grasp. After four or five years of conventional schooling, they were accustomed to producing specific artifacts for the teacher (e.g., a story, or a project). Few of them were initially comfortable with the notion of focusing on something as intangible as personal comprehension, and in September there was sometimes a clash between the new students' expectations and the teacher's efforts to foster knowledge building. For example, new students would be more reluctant to offer their personal theories, for fear of being wrong. However, the teacher's practice of describing the class as a research team and his use of experienced grade 6 students (i.e., those who had participated in the class during the previous year) as mentors to the grade 5 students helped quicken the pace of enculturation.

Face-to-face discourse in the classroom was unlike the discourse on Knowledge Forum. The latter was organized around epistemological scaffolds and was specifically targeted at making progress on the problems of understanding. Face-to-face discourse, on the other hand, was used for a much wider range of purposes (e.g., how to use certain features of the software, deciding what problems the group would pursue next, alerting others to database developments, and the challenge of finding resources that pertained to their particular online interests). One notable aspect of both kinds of discourse is that they frequently included phrases like "my theory" or "John's question" or "her findings." Such phrases are not usually heard in traditional classrooms. However, Knowledge Forum turns theories, questions, and findings into screen objects that can be pointed at, organized, and talked about. A theory is not an ethereal construct in a Knowledge Forum classroom, but a meaningful community artifact.

Subject-Community-Division of Labor: Roles and Responsibilities of Community Members

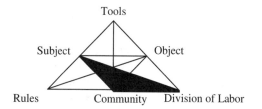

Typically, in elementary classrooms, everyone in the class is taught the same curriculum material. In the case study classroom, the entire class worked together on the same overarching topic, but different students specialized in different subdomains. For example, if the topic was human biology, one group would become experts on the respiratory system, another group would become experts on vision, and so forth. Rather than providing all students with the same broad (and shallow) biology curriculum, the labor was divided so individuals could investigate personal areas of interest in depth.

The teacher arranged the classroom schedule so that each student had 30 minutes per day on Knowledge Forum, and an additional 15 to 30 minutes for research in the library or at their desks. Virtually all of the notes in Knowledge Forum belonged to the students. The teacher monitored developments in the Knowledge Forum database, but rarely contributed notes of his own.

As the unit progressed, students were expected to submit a few of their notes to the teacher for grading. Notes that were grammatically correct, were free of spelling errors, and made a reasonable contribution to the class discourse were assigned a "published" designation in the database. The teacher adjusted the publication criterion to match the needs and abilities of each learner. He felt it was important to challenge each student, but not set standards so high that publication was impossible for some individuals. Report card grades were determined, in part, by the quantity and quality of published notes. The scientific accuracy of the student submissions was not one of the criteria for publication. Some student notes contained misconceptions.

To publish a note, a student would approach the teacher at his desk during the Knowledge Forum work period. Videotaped studies of these exchanges indicate that the teacher used these one-on-one meetings as opportunities to suggest profitable directions for future inquiry, or to raise issues that the student had not previously considered. The discourse in Example 8.2 transpired when the teacher was asked to publish a student's theory that the cerebrum was responsible for actions like walking and talking.

Example 8.2. A videotaped teacher-student exchange

[*Teacher reads the student's note while the student stands by.*]

TEACHER: Oh, that's a good idea . . . so do you think the memory is the most important . . . do you think you first have to remember something even . . . even if you are thinking about walking it has to go through the memory process and then whatever happens after that . . .

STUDENT: But you still have to remember how to do it, cause I think once you learn it, you still remember it, you still have to remember it when you want to do it . . .

TEACHER: . . . and you still have to decide you want to do it and you think that happens in the cerebrum.

[*2-second pause*]

TEACHER: Have you ever heard the expression, "Running around like a chicken with its head cut off?" It's an old expression referring to people who are confused, hyperactive, things like that . . . the expression comes from when farmers used to decide they want to kill a chicken for supper, so they'd cut its head off and the chicken would still run around. How do you explain that if the cerebrum is not even there?

STUDENT: [*Pause*] Well, maybe they . . . maybe they just . . . it was a reflex or something? . . .

TEACHER: Yeah . . . What is a reflex?

STUDENT: A thing you do automatically without really thinking about it.

TEACHER: So do you think the cerebrum is involved in reflexes?

[*Student smiles but doesn't answer*]

TEACHER: Be nice . . . well maybe in some of your readings you might have a look at that.

STUDENT: [*Nods*] Yeah, I have some books.

[*The teacher publishes the student's note and the student leaves. Ten minutes later, the student returns with a reference book and points to a section entitled "Actions and Reflexes." The teacher pages through it.*]

TEACHER: This looks like a good book. I'll also take a look through some of my books and see if I can find more information.

STUDENT: Thanks. [*Leaves*]

The teacher chose to use publication as his primary vehicle for coaching students. He rarely wrote notes to them in Knowledge Forum. Interestingly, the instructor's lack of online presence was at odds with Scardamalia and Bereiter's (1993) recommendation that teachers participate in Knowledge Forum as co-learners and mentors. When queried, the instructor's rationale for his lack of online involvement was as follows:

TEACHER: If I were to write in the database, I'd have to do all of that after the students had left, so I think that method is too similar to methods in which the teacher assigns work to be done, and the student does it, and then the teacher marks it after hours and returns it to the student. It becomes some sort of automatic process that everyone gets involved in. It's not very interactive. There are many opportunities for misunderstanding, or worse, for the student not to notice, or not to bother with, what the teacher has written.

Thus, in part, the teacher didn't feel that he had the time to work in Knowledge Forum. However, beyond issues of time constraints, he believed that the software was not interactive enough for his purposes. While Knowledge Forum served as a useful support for collaborative student inquiry, it did not, in his view, have the immediacy required for exchanges like the one in Example 8.2. Consequently, the students were wholly responsible for online knowledge building, and the teacher was responsible for observing their progress and coaching individuals privately.

In some respects, the teacher organized the division of labor in such a way that he stood outside the KBC, rather than working within it. During his first few years as a Knowledge Forum instructor, he contributed frequently to the database. Over time, he gradually reduced his online involvement in favor of greater face-to-face interaction with students. This decision involved trade-offs. Had he assisted students through Knowledge Forum, his suggestions would have been preserved and made available to the entire class. On the other hand, coaching students in person permitted more rapid conversational exchanges than would be possible in asynchronous environments, and it reduced the risk of embarrassing a student in front of his or her peers. It may have had other benefits as well. The teacher commented that "students who come to me to have their notes published are ready to talk about their research." He felt that these students were more likely to be focused on the contents of their notes and intellectually receptive to his suggestions.

The teacher felt uneasy about some aspects of his publication methods. On one hand, he wanted students to take increasing responsibility for the regulatory processes governing their own intellectual growth. On the other hand, he felt that he needed to use his publishing scheme as a task-based incentive for quantity and quality in student online productions. The problem was that a heavy focus on the latter could subvert the former. On several occasions, the teacher expressed concern about whether his marking scheme was unintentionally undermining his efforts to foster student ownership of knowledge building activity. What were the students' goals? Were they genuinely taking charge of their own investigations and trying to push forward the boundaries of classroom knowledge? Or were their actions primarily aimed at publishing as many notes as possible? This was an ongoing dilemma for the teacher, and while he tried to keep knowledge building as the primary focus, he also recognized a need to establish standards that would bear on report card grades.

To summarize, online and offline processes served different but interrelated functions that were tied to classroom roles and responsibilities. Students were expected to work in Knowledge Forum toward becoming experts in areas of their own choosing. The teacher did not participate directly in online discourse, but used a publication mechanism as a means of coaching students, face-to-face. This allowed him to evaluate performance and tailor standards of achievement to the needs and abilities of individual students. Thus, students became classroom experts in various subdomains and interacted with each other in the online environment, and felt a sense of ownership over that environment, while the teacher mentored them privately and in-person.

Subject-Community-Rules: Guidelines for Knowledge Building Activities

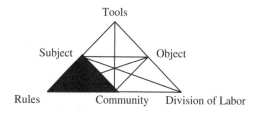

In addition to traditional classroom codes of behavior, the instructor also introduced guidelines for student work in Knowledge Forum (see also Hewitt, 2002). The guidelines included:

- Students should associate an epistemological scaffold (e.g., "My Theory," "I Need To Understand," "New Information") with each Knowledge Forum note. One of the effects of this rule was to change the language of the class, as these words became increasingly used in face-to-face settings as well as in Knowledge Forum.
- All Knowledge Forum investigations should begin with a problem statement. The students were told that certain kinds of problems were more educationally productive than others. For example, the problem, "How many bones are in the human hand?" doesn't lead to a very deep investigation. However, questions of the form "How does x work?" or "Why . . . ?" lead to deeper analysis.
- Students were asked to not bring reference books with them to the computer. The teacher was concerned that students might copy passages or phrases from the reference book into Knowledge Forum without fully understanding the content. Instead, students were encouraged to take brief notes at their desk, and make an effort to understand what they were reading. They would then take their handwritten notes to the computer during their Knowledge Forum session.
- To encourage students to construct explanations, students were expected to use "My Theory" in response to "Problem" and "I Need To Understand" entries in all online discussions. The teacher introduced this guideline to encourage conjecture-building. Students were discouraged from consulting classroom resources until after they had shared their theories about the question at hand.

- Students were given instructions regarding constructive criticism, including strategies for responding to each other's work in a positive fashion. The teacher explained that most "My Theory" notes would be incorrect and it was important to not criticize people for early explanations, which tend to be inaccurate.

Perhaps the most distinctive rule in this community was the emphasis on student theories and the tolerance of partial understandings or misconceptions. The teacher wanted the students to feel safe proposing explanations and sharing them with their classmates. Students were allowed to disagree with one another, but only in ways that respected each other's work. The teacher modeled this behavior in his own face-to-face interactions with students. For instance, in the discussion in Example 8.3, the teacher is uncritical of a student's (incorrect) hypothesis that pain occurs when blood fails to provide cells with an adequate supply of oxygen.

Example 8.3. A videotaped teacher-student exchange

[*Teacher reads student note while student stands by*]
TEACHER: So you think pain is caused by a lack of oxygen.
STUDENT: Yep.
TEACHER: What makes you think that?
STUDENT: Well when you get cut – the blood, the blood usually comes out. The blood comes out which momentarily stops the flow of blood. Because you keep bleeding.
TEACHER: Yeah? Stops the flow of blood?
STUDENT: Yes, because –
TEACHER: To where?
STUDENT: To wherever it was going.
TEACHER: Oh I see! So, you're saying, those cells . . .
STUDENT: The blood carries oxygen . . .
TEACHER: . . . don't have their oxygen any more?
STUDENT: Yeah.
TEACHER: They start to hurt.
STUDENT: Yeah.
TEACHER: Oh that's interesting!
[*They both start to look at the screen together as the teacher scrolls through the note.*]
STUDENT: Maybe oxygen keeps the blood from hurting.
TEACHER: Well first, yes, if this is going on . . . I'd like to know, if it's ok with you, why the loss of oxygen causes pain. We're not sure if it does yet. You should maybe put . . .
STUDENT: [*suggests a phrase to insert into his note*] "If it does?"
TEACHER: [*repeats*] "I would like to know why, if it does, why loss of oxygen causes pain."

TEACHER: [*Pointing to a spelling error*] This I think we need to revise a bit
more. Did you run it through? [*the spell-checker*]
STUDENT: I did in spots.
TEACHER: Did you? Well just run it through and bring it back and we'll
take a look at it. That's an interesting idea.

In the dialogue in Example 8.3, the student hypothesized that some cells
failed to receive an adequate amount of oxygen when blood escaped from
the body through a cut. This absence of oxygen causes pain. It is not clear
if the student believed his explanation was scientifically accurate. However, he had produced a promising hypothesis because it combined some
of his knowledge about blood (it carries oxygen) with his observation that
cuts are painful. What is notable in this example is the teacher's willingness to allow (at least temporarily) a student to entertain a misconception,
as long as the explanation was rational given the student's knowledge of
the world. Episodes like this one suggest that the teacher placed higher
value on reasoning, risk-taking, and the invention of explanations than on
making sure that the students were aware of the scientifically accepted
accounts.

TEACHER: . . . we have never allowed students before to express [their
theories]. In fact, the name of the game in school is to keep
them hidden, not to bring them out in the open, not to ask a
question in case it's a stupid one, not to write something down
in case it's the wrong answer. Instead now with this format
we are encouraging students to be unafraid of saying what
they actually believe and then work towards seeing whether
or not they are correct.

One should not interpret the teacher's support of student theories as
acceptance for all kinds of student-invented conjectures. The teacher often
walked a delicate line between allowing students to express and explore
their theories, and keeping them from floundering down intellectual blind
alleys. He wanted to provide students with the freedom to define and
pursue their theories, and to feel safe in doing so. However, he also felt
a need to nudge students toward more promising lines of inquiry should
their theories prove to be unproductive.

Much of the teacher-student discourse appears to be consistent with
Fosnot's (1989) four-step mentoring strategy:

1. The mentor learns the protégé's point of view through careful listening and probing.
2. The mentor teaches by inquiring at the "leading edge" of the
   protégé's thinking and by attempting to facilitate disequilibrium.

3. The mentor constructs a line of inquiry meaningful to the protégé and the protégé constructs a line of reasoning meaningful to the mentor.
4. The mentor acknowledges that the protégé has the intellectual freedom to adopt and modify the pedagogical orientation of his or her choice (Fosnot, 1989, p. 97).

The effort to provoke disequilibrium is clearly visible in the Example 8.2 "chicken with its head cut off" dialogue. During that discussion, the teacher invented a scenario that challenged the student's theory – a challenge that ultimately led the student to a more productive line of research. The dialogue in Example 8.3 illustrates the teacher's willingness to support student explanations that may be scientifically inaccurate, but are coherent and sensible given the learner's world view.

In an attempt to better grasp the community's emphasis on theory building, a series of student interviews was conducted at the end of the third year. The sample of grade 5 and 6 students who took part in this exercise contained a disproportionate number of high achievers, so their responses may not be entirely representative. However, there were some interesting trends and these are presented with the caveat that a more rigorous investigation is required. The responses from three questions are examined:

Interview Question 1: *What is the most important thing to do when you are trying to learn something?*

An examination of the responses reveals two re-occurring themes. The first is the importance of identifying what you need to understand. For example:

RACHEL: I think the most important thing is you should understand your problem first and you know what you are trying to learn. And then go to different resources, look at different books, to see if there is different information in them. Because a lot of books have . . . if you compare two books, sometimes they have different information.

JULIE: I think it is to understand the problem and then to think about what you could learn if you researched it in a certain way. Supposing you had a topic on static electricity, you could think of all the different aspects of electricity, and see which one you wanted to learn about.

TODD: Well first you have to understand what you are trying to learn. And if you don't do that you might not get the right information, because if you don't quite understand the problem, you might . . . I am not sure.

A second theme running through many of the responses was the notion of making understanding a key part of the process:

BILL: I think that you should understand what you are trying to learn first, and not, like . . . when you read something and you know what it says and you know what it means . . . well, you don't know what it means, but you know what it says and you say, I read it. That is not . . . like, learning, you have to understand how it works and how it fits together with your problem.

MARGE: I think that the most important thing when you are trying to learn something is to understand what you are trying to learn, and not just memorize it, just try and understand what it is.

Both themes were effectively combined in one student's response:

NANCY: I think the most important thing to do is understand the problem and understand the new information. Because if you understand the problem, then you are able to make sure that your answers are direct and that they answer the question as well as possible. And if you get new information, if you make sure you know exactly what all the new information means, then you are able to make it make more sense to the people reading and make more sense to yourself. It will make more sense to yourself if you understand the new information in the problem.

Interview Question 2: *How can you tell when you have learned something?*

Again, several types of responses were identified. Some students reported that they could tell they had learned something if they could respond to other people's questions.

JIM: Because I know it, like if somebody were to ask me about it I could just tell them right off. I just know it.

ANNE: I can, if somebody asks me a question about it, if I am able to answer it to [*inaudible*] what the person asked.

For other students, knowing that you've learned something is more of an internal process. The following student related it to an increased ability to create new explanations that "fit together" and "make sense":

NANCY: I think I can tell if I have learned something when I am able to form substantial theories that seem to fit in with the information that I have already got. So it isn't necessarily that I have everything, that I have all the information, but I am able to piece things in that make sense, and to form theories on the questions that would get all fit together.

Echoes of this idea were also evident in the following response, but to a lesser extent.

TODD: Well, when I have learned something I will know because I will be able to form my own theories and also be able to explain it better to someone else.

Interview Question 3: *What happens if there are wrong things in the database?*

All students who were asked this question expressed a tolerance for notes that contained misconceptions. Most students seemed to view "wrong theories" as just an expected initial step in the process of trying to learn something.

NANCY: Wrong theories . . . I don't think there really is such a thing as a wrong theory, because I consider it that theories are just what somebody thinks. Theories . . . if there was wrong information you could correct it. But with theories I think that there isn't a wrong answer with theories because it is just what somebody thinks, and if it is wrong, then that is fine, because it is just a theory, it is just what somebody thought, and they are able to correct themselves by new information and things like that. So I don't really think that there could be a wrong theory.

MARGE: I think that wrong theories are okay because they are just what people think and they can be corrected. But if you put a right theory down, then you can just think to yourself, well maybe I am getting better at this because it is a right theory. But wrong theory, you think, okay, well that is fine, I have learned from it that it doesn't work this way, it works this way.

RUTH: Then you learn. Most theories aren't right. It is very rare that someone will get an exact theory. So if you get one that is wrong you just think, oh, well, gee! This is the way it works. And then you learn and you just revise your theory.

BILL: That is fine, because the theory isn't the information that they think. It isn't carved in stone or anything. You can always change what you think of a certain problem.

Common to most student responses was an implicit or explicit recognition that learning was an active process of improving one's understanding. Of course, it is difficult to know to what extent students had genuinely adopted that philosophy or whether they were simply saying what they thought the interviewer wanted to hear. However, there is a high level of consistency between the student interview responses, the way that students interacted with the teacher, and student actions in Knowledge Forum. Even if some students privately harbored doubts about the classroom emphasis on progressive, collaborative sense-making, they at least seemed to have a rudimentary understanding of what it entailed.

Clearly, student attitudes about learning and their day-to-day practices in Knowledge Forum were largely a product of a knowledge building culture that the teacher fostered in his classroom. Knowledge Forum technology offered a medium through which learners could engage in knowledge building operations, but the students' sense of mutual trust, their priorities, and their tolerance for each other's ideas were largely forged through face-to-face processes.

Subject-Community-Tools: Design Supports for Knowledge Building

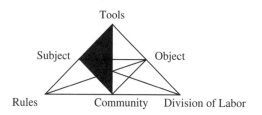

Knowledge Forum software was designed to support individuals and groups in their efforts to collaboratively advance knowledge. The principal tool for student interaction in this class was an experimental facility known as the "Discussion Note" or "Discussion Window" (Figure 8.4). The Discussion Window contained two parts: a small problem area at the top and a scrollable discourse area below. This arrangement allowed students to engage in lengthy discussions without losing sight of the core problem (Hewitt & Scardamalia, 1998).

The discussion facility was designed to focus students on the collective efforts of a group of people. Many computer conferencing environments (especially web-based environments) display the contents of each participant's note in its own individual window. In the discussion facility, the contents of the notes are displayed together in the same scrollable region. In fact, it is difficult (although not impossible) for students to view their contributions in isolation and out of context. Thus, this aspect of the software highlights the mission of the group rather than the performance of the individual. From an Activity System perspective, Knowledge Forum not only mediates the Subject's work with the Object, but it also amplifies communal goals and the Subject's perception of his or her role in the Community.

Knowledge Forum software also contains supports that relate directly to the teacher's instructions and the classroom protocols that he developed. To add a note to a Knowledge Forum discussion, learners click on the "Add" button at the bottom of the Discussion Window. Doing so produces a

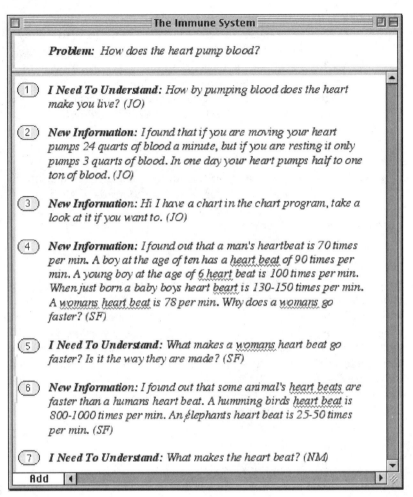

The Immune System

Problem: *How does the heart pump blood?*

(1) *I Need To Understand: How by pumping blood does the heart make you live? (JO)*

(2) *New Information: I found that if you are moving your heart pumps 24 quarts of blood a minute, but if you are resting it only pumps 3 quarts of blood. In one day your heart pumps half to one ton of blood. (JO)*

(3) *New Information: Hi I have a chart in the chart program, take a look at it if you want to. (JO)*

(4) *New Information: I found out that a man's heartbeat is 70 times per min. A boy at the age of ten has a heart beat of 90 times per min. A young boy at the age of 6 heart beat is 100 times per min. When just born a baby boys heart beart is 130-150 times per min. A womans heart beat is 78 per min. Why does a womans go faster? (SF)*

(5) *I Need To Understand: What makes a womans heart beat go faster? Is it the way they are made? (SF)*

(6) *New Information: I found out that some animal's heart beats are faster than a humans heart beat. A humming birds heart beat is 800-1000 times per min. An elephants heart beat is 25-50 times per min. (SF)*

(7) *I Need To Understand: What makes the heart beat? (NM)*

Add

FIGURE 8.4. A Discussion Note window

pop-up list of scaffolds: My Theory, I Need To Understand, Comment, New Information, and What We Have Learned. Students must decide which scaffold best describes the contribution that they are planning to make. When the student's work is finally saved, the selected scaffold is displayed in boldface in front of the text.

The design of the Discussion Window emerged, in part, out of concerns about cognitive load. When Knowledge Forum is used without the discussion facility, each note is displayed in its own separate window, connected to another note by threads. To read an entire discussion, students must open a note, read its contents, identify the next note in the chain, open that note, read its contents, and so forth. While single-note threaded discussion interfaces are common in distance education circles, it was felt that they could be problematic for elementary students. The need to constantly open, arrange, and close windows can interfere with learner efforts to follow a line of thought that spans many notes. Accordingly, the discussion facility was invented to minimize the effort required to review a discussion and keep students focused on a central problem statement. A comparative study of the single-note interface and the discussion interface revealed significant advantages in favor of the latter. Individuals using the discussion format responded to other people's notes more frequently, engaged in lengthier discussions, and were more likely to focus their work on the problems that they had set out. Students spent less time on window management, and more time focusing on the content of the investigation. In general, the discussion interface better matched the needs of a classroom community that valued progressive, collaborative knowledge advancement around specific problems of understanding.

DISCUSSION

The preceding analysis describes how the strength of this particular learning community emerged out of the multiple interrelated ways in which knowledge advancement was supported by the full sociocultural context of the classroom and the online environment. Learning was both an individual and a collective goal, and it was supported in numerous ways by the rules governing classroom behavior, the allocation of roles and responsibilities, and the design of the Knowledge Forum interface. Specifically, an examination of the Subject-Community relationship from four different perspectives yielded the following findings:

Subject-Community-Object

The goals and intentions of the Knowledge Forum classroom were unlike those of conventional classrooms. The teacher worked to foster a culture of collaborative knowledge building, one in which advancement of communal knowledge was the central objective. Knowledge Forum discussions (Object) made this process tangible (and achievable) by serving as an ongoing record of the community's investigations. By preserving discourse electronically, the work of the community became an object that could be studied and progressively improved upon. Thus, the Subject-Community relationship was conceptualized as one of mutually reinforcing growth: individuals learned from the online knowledge base of the collective, while simultaneously working to increase that knowledge base.

Subject-Community-Division of Labor

The Subject-Community relationship was also defined by the way in which responsibilities were divided in class. Within a particular unit (e.g., human biology), different groups of students had different areas of expertise and each group contributed something new and meaningful to the collective. The teacher didn't directly participate in the online discourse. However, through his publication assessment technique he counseled students on their Knowledge Forum productions, encouraging them to work at the leading edge of their thinking and facilitating disequilibrium when the opportunity arose.

Subject-Community-Rules

A key element of any community involves the accepted protocols for interaction. A shared language is one part of that protocol (Lewis, 1997). For example, phrases like "My Theory," "New Information," and "I Need To Understand" were made a part of the classroom culture. Another part of the protocol involves how people are expected to interact with one another. During class meetings and in one-on-one situations, the teacher emphasized that each class member is expected to be tolerant of other people's conjectures and ideas. This outlook was reinforced by the teacher's own assessment scheme. For example, he frequently published student theories that contained incomplete or incorrect explanations. Interview data suggest that students accepted the notion that their initial theories were tentative and that they should work to improve them. Thus, the Subject-Community relationship was focused on building and sharing conjectures, identifying what is not understood, conducting research, respecting other people's beliefs, and working to continually improve upon what is known. The teacher forged this culture of mutual trust and respect in his day-to-day classroom interactions with students.

Subject-Community-Tools

The user interface of Discussion Notes was designed to emphasize communal discourse over individual productions. It was also designed to keep difficult problems in view, and to support, through scaffolds, the discourse of the classroom (e.g., "My Theory," "New Information," "I Need to Understand"). Thus, Knowledge Forum not only mediated the Subject's work on the Object, but it also reinforced the communal nature of the students' research endeavor and the established language protocols of the classroom. More specifically, the online environment contributed to a sense of community in the following ways:

- Access: The online environment transformed the intellectual resources of the community into tangible objects of inquiry.
- Amplification of Individual's Role in Community: The online environment amplified a sense of community by presenting individual work

within a communal context. Knowledge Forum emphasizes community artifacts over individual productions.
- Problem Focus: The online environment kept the pressing problems of
  the community in view.
- Language Support: The software scaffolds (e.g., My Theory) fostered the
  development of a specialized language – one used by the community
  both on and off Knowledge Forum.
- Mentoring Support: The teacher, in his meetings with individual students, used the online environment as an aid for mentoring students
  and better focusing them on communal artifacts.

What is striking from the preceding analysis is the intricate way in which
the goal of knowledge construction was interwoven into both the online environment and the cultural fabric of the classroom community. It is unlikely
that Knowledge Forum would have operated as effectively in a context that
was less supportive of the students' expression of personal theories or of an
inquiry-based approach. In the past, Knowledge Forum has occasionally
been introduced into classrooms where the dominant cultural practices
were inconsistent with the KBC model. The results were rarely positive.
Sometimes Knowledge Forum was abandoned altogether. In other cases,
the technology was used in unconventional ways to serve different goals.
Such outcomes are consistent with findings that teachers often use educational software to sustain existing pedagogical practices rather than alter
the way that they teach (Cuban, Kirkpatrick, & Peck, 2002). Knowledge
Forum software, by itself, is unlikely to bring about significant change in
the classroom. However, for teachers who are working to transform their
practice, the technology makes possible new models of classroom learning
that would otherwise be difficult or impossible to implement.

CONCLUSIONS

Sociocultural theory suggests that learning should be viewed as a process
of increasing one's participation in communal practices (Lave & Wenger,
1991). This perspective provides researchers with a powerful theoretical
lens for thinking about educational processes. However, for the purposes of
educational reform, sociocultural theory is frustratingly vague. While communal participation may be a necessary condition for individual growth,
it is not a sufficient one. The pressing questions for educators are "What
kind of community?" and "What kind of participation?" These questions
become even more urgent when viewed in light of recent advances in electronic communication. Networked technologies now allow communities
to be connected in entirely new ways.

As researchers explore the possibilities that new technologies offer, it
is important to remember that community building is a difficult process,

and there are some aspects of community that technology simply does not support very well. For example, trust is a key part of teamwork, yet trust is difficult to establish through electronic communication (Kling & Courtright, this volume; Vaillancourt, 2002). In the grade 5–6 Knowledge Forum classroom, students were willing to publicly post their (often erroneous) theories because the teacher had fostered an atmosphere of mutual trust and tolerance for tentative understandings. It is highly unlikely that this level of trust could have developed through online interaction alone.

In some respects, an expression like *virtual community* may not be particularly useful for educational research. Fundamentally, it is a technocentric phrase that says nothing about educational rationale or purpose.[1] Instead, it conjures up images of a community in which relationships and interactions are completely circumscribed by an electronic medium. As already discussed, such a community may be difficult to develop. Some of the more compelling computer-assisted communities include ones in which subsets of community members occasionally meet face-to-face (e.g., Barab et al., this volume; Derry, Seymour, Steinkuehler, Lee, & Siegel, this volume; Schlager & Fusco, this volume). Nor is it unusual for users of online environments to be colleagues from the same institution, or students from the same class (e.g., Bruckman, this volume). The problem with the word "virtual" is that it de-emphasizes and devalues any face-to-face communication that might be taking place behind the scenes – even though these conversations may be contributing to the development of community.

Arguably, if one's overarching research goal is to design educationally effective communities, then the expression virtual community is unnecessarily constraining. Most real-world communities do not confine their constituents to a single mode of communication. Instead, people benefit from the ability to interact with one another in a rich variety of ways (e.g., face-to-face discussion, paper, telephone, fax, email, computer conferencing). In the same fashion, educational communities should ideally be designed to exploit synergies across different communication modalities.

This chapter's Activity System analysis of a classroom-based KBC describes an innovative way in which computer-based and classroom-based processes can be combined to forge a new kind of learning community. Within this classroom model, students purposefully carry out investigations of their own design. This chapter described how different elements of the community – objectives, rules, language – were distributed across face-to-face and online contexts, reinforcing one another. The result is a culture that is quite unlike that of traditional classrooms. In a regular class, questions, theories, ideas, and discussions are personal, ethereal constructs. In a KBC classroom, they are public artifacts that have a permanent

---

[1] The phrase *virtual community* stands in stark contrast to phrases that describe principled educational models, such as *community of learners* or *Knowledge Building Community*.

presence in the classroom database. As such, they can be analyzed, pointed at, talked about, and progressively refined over time. Knowledge Forum technology supports a new approach to classroom learning, one that focuses learners directly on the process of knowledge production. This ability to support previously undreamed of community models may be one of the more important educational dividends of networked technologies.

References

Barab, S. A., & Duffy, T. (2000). From practice fields to communities of practice. In D. Jonassen & S. M. Land (Eds.). *Theoretical Foundations of Learning Environments* (pp. 25–56). Mahwah, NJ: Lawrence Erlbaum Associates.

Barab, S. A., & Kirshner, D. (2001). Methodologies for capturing learner practices occurring as part of dynamic learning environments. *The Journal of The Learning Sciences*, 10(1&2), 5–15.

Barab, S., MaKinster, J., & Scheckler, R. (this volume). Characterizing an online professional development community.

Bereiter, C., & Scardamalia, M. (1989). Intentional learning as a goal of instruction. In L. B. Resnick (Ed.). *Knowing, Learning and Instruction: Essays in Honor of Robert Glaser* (pp. 361–392). Hillsdale, NJ: Lawrence Erlbaum Associates.

Bereiter, C., Scardamalia, M., Cassells, C., & Hewitt, J. (1997). Postmodernism, knowledge building, and elementary science. *The Elementary School Journal*, 97(4), 329–340.

Brown, A. L., & Campione, J. C. (1990). Communities of learning and thinking, or a context by any other name. *Human Development*, 21, 108–125.

Brown, J. S., Collins, A., & Duguid, P. (1989). Situated cognition and the culture of learning. *Educational Researcher*, 18, 32–42.

Bruckman, A. (this volume). Co-evolution of technological design and pedagogy in an online learning community.

Cognition and Technology Group at Vanderbilt (1992). Technology and the design of generative learning environments. In T. Duffy and D. Jonassen (eds.). *Constructivism and the Technology of Instruction: A Conversation* (pp. 77–89). Hillsdale, NJ: Lawrence Erlbaum Associates.

Collins, A., Brown, J. S., & Newman, S. E. (1989). Cognitive Apprenticeship: Teaching the crafts of reading, writing, and mathematics. In L. B. Resnick (Ed.). *Knowing, Learning and Instruction: Essays in Honor of Robert Glaser* (pp. 453–494). Hillsdale, NJ: Lawrence Erlbaum Associates.

Cuban, L., Kirkpatrick, H., & Peck, C. (2002). High access and low use of technologies in high school classrooms: Explaining an apparent paradox. *American Educational Research Journal*, 38(4), 813–836.

Derry, S., Seymour, J., Steinkuehler, C., & Lee, J., & Siegel, M. (this volume). From ambitious vision to partially satisfying reality: An evolving sociotechnical design supporting community and collaborative learning in teacher education.

Elmore, R. (1996). Getting to scale with good educational practice. *Harvard Educational Review*, 66(1), 1–26.

Engeström, Y. (1987). *Learning by expanding*. Helsinki: Orienta-konsultit.

Engeström, Y. (1990). *Learning, working and imagining: Twelve studies in activity theory.* Helsinki: Orienta-Konsultit Oy.

Engeström, Y. (1993). Developmental studies of work as a testbench of activity theory: The case of primary care medical practice. In S. Chaiklin & J. Lave (Eds.). *Understanding Practice: Perspectives on Activity and Context* (pp. 64–103). Cambridge, MA: Cambridge University Press.

Fosnot, C. T. (1989). *Enquiring Teachers Enquiring Learners. A Constructivist Approach to Teaching.* New York: Teacher's College Press.

Guba, E. G., & Lincoln, Y. S. (1994). Competing paradigms in qualitative research. In N. Denzin & Y. Lincoln (Eds.). *Handbook of Qualitative Research* (pp. 105–117). Thousand Oaks, CA: Sage Publications.

Hewitt, J. (2002). From a focus on tasks to a focus on understanding: The cultural transformation of a Toronto classroom. In T. D. Koschmann and N. Myake (Eds.). *Computer Supported Cooperative Learning Volume 2: Carrying forward the conversation* (pp. 11–41). Mahwah, NJ: Lawrence Erlbaum Associates.

Hewitt, J., & Scardamalia, M. (1998). Design principles for distributed knowledge building processes. *Educational Psychology Review, 10*(1), 75–96.

Jonassen, D. H., & Rohrer-Murphy, L. (1999). Activity theory as a framework for designing constructivist learning environments. *Educational Technology: Research and Development, 47*(1), 61–79.

Kling, R., & Courtright, C. (this volume). Group behavior and learning in electronic forums: A socio-technical approach.

Kuutti, K. (1996). Activity theory as a potential framework for human-computer research. In B. A. Nardi (Ed.). *Context and Consciousness: Activity Theory and Human-Computer Interaction* (pp. 17–44). Cambridge, MA: MIT Press.

Lave, J. (1988). *Cognition in Practice: Mind, Mathematics and Culture in Everyday Life.* Cambridge: Cambridge University Press.

Lave, J. (1993). Situating learning in communities of practice. In L. B. Resnick, J. M. Levine, & S. D. Teasley (Eds.). *Perspectives on Socially Shared Cognition* (pp. 17–36). Washington, DC: American Psychological Association.

Lave, J., & Wenger, E. (1991). *Situated Learning: Legitimate Peripheral Participation.* New York: Cambridge University Press.

Lewis, R. (1997). An Activity Theory framework to explore distributed communities. *Journal of Computer Assisted Learning, 13*, 210–218.

Riel, M. (1992). A functional analysis of educational telecomputing: A case study of learning circles. *Interactive Learning Environments, 2*(1), 15–29.

Riel, M., & Polin, L. (this volume). Online learning communities.

Rogoff, B. (1997). Observing sociocultural activity on three planes: participatory appropriation, guided participation, and apprenticeship. In J. Wertsch, P. del Rio, & A. Alvarez (Eds.). *Sociocultural Studies of the Mind* (pp. 139–164). New York: Cambridge University Press.

Rogoff, B., Baker-Sennett, J., Lacasa, P., & Goldsmith, D. (1995). Development through participation in sociocultural activity. *New Directions for Child Development, 67*, 45–65.

Salomon, G. (1995). *Real Individuals in Complex Environments: A New Conception of Educational Psychology.* Draft Document.

Scardamalia, M., & Bereiter, C. (1993). *Computer Support for Knowledge-Building Communities.* Draft Document.

Scardamalia, M., & Bereiter, C. (1994). Computer support for knowledge-building communities. *Journal of the Learning Sciences, 3*(3), 265–283.

Scardamalia, M., & Bereiter, C. (1996). Adaptation and understanding: A case for new cultures of schooling. In S. Vosniadou, E. DeCorte, R. Glaser, and H. Mandl (Eds.). *International Perspectives on the Design of Technology-Supported Learning Environments* (pp. 149–163). Mahwah, NJ: Lawrence Erlbaum Associates.

Scardamalia, M., Bereiter, C., Brett, C., Burtis, P. J., Calhoun, C., & Smith Lea, N. (1992). Educational applications of a networked communal database. *Interactive Learning Environments, 2*(1), 45–71.

Scardamalia, M., Bereiter, C., McLean, R., Swallow, J., & Woodruff, E. (1989). Computer-supported intentional learning environments. *Journal of Educational Computing Research, 5*(1), 51–68.

Schlager, M., & Fusco, J. (this volume). Teacher professional development, technology, and communities of practice.

Vaillancourt, D. (2002). *Exploration of an online networking innovation with women entrepreneurs: A case study.* Unpublished doctoral thesis. Ontario Institute for Studies in Education, University of Toronto.

Wells, G. (1994, April). *Discourse as a tool in the activity of learning and teaching.* Paper presented at the meeting of the American Educational Research Association, New Orleans, LA.

Wenger, E. (1998). *Communites of Practice: Learning, Meaning, and Identity.* Cambridge: Cambridge University Press.

9

Co-Evolution of Technological Design and Pedagogy in an Online Learning Community

Amy Bruckman

The design of any piece of technology intended for human use – whether for entertainment, work, or education – is ideally iterative and user-centered. Designers cannot anticipate all the needs of users, but most begin with a prototype and revise it based on user feedback. This is even more true of online learning communities, where designers must understand the needs not just of individual users, but of groups of users and their complex inter-relationships as facilitated by the technology. Designers begin with theory, create a prototype, test, and then revise. However, it is not just the technology that can be revised, but also the underlying theory. Technological design and pedagogy have the potential to co-evolve in this new medium.

In this chapter, I will describe in detail one example of this co-evolution: a new perspective on motivation in constructionist learning environments, which evolved through quantitative and qualitative observations of an online learning community[1] called MOOSE Crossing. These observations

[1] I use the word community here in the loosest possible sense: a group of people interacting in some fashion over an extended period of time. I concur with Kling et al. (this volume) that the value of "online community" is often over-hyped. One solution to this problem is, as Kling proposes, to be vigilant to only apply the word community to groups that meet appropriate criteria. A second solution is to choose to use the word community in a looser, non–value-laden way, separating the issue of value from the issue of word choice. I prefer this second solution.

Parts of this chapter were originally presented at ICLS 2000, with additional co-authors Elizabeth Edwards (who contributed to portfolio scoring and creation of charts and graphs), Jason Elliott (scoring), and Carlos Jensen (scoring and statistical analysis). The author thanks current and past contributors to the MOOSE Crossing project, especially Mitchel Resnick, Alisa Bandlow, Austina DeBonte, Elizabeth Edwards, Tysen Perszyk, Will Scott, Steve Shapiro, Adam Skwersky, Trevor Stricker, Steve Tamm, and Adam Tegen. Special thanks to the kids of MOOSE Crossing and their parents. We also thank the teachers who have tried it in their classrooms, especially B. J. Conn. Research in the Electronic Learning Communities group at Georgia Tech is supported by grants from IBM, Intel, Microsoft, Neometron, Ricoh, and The National Science Foundation. For more information, see http://www.cc.gatech.edu/elc.

led to a significant design change to the environment (the addition of a system of "merit badges"), and this in turn led to further reflections on pedagogy.

BACKGROUND: CONSTRUCTIONISM IN A COMMUNITY CONTEXT

In *Mindstorms*, Seymour Papert has a vision of a "technological samba school." At samba schools in Brazil, a community of people of all ages gather together to prepare a presentation for Carnival. "Members of the school range in age from children to grandparents and in ability from novice to professional. But they dance together and as they dance everyone is learning and teaching as well as dancing. Even the stars are there to learn their difficult parts" (Papert, 1980, p. 178). People go to samba schools not just to work on their presentations, but also to socialize and be with one another. Learning is spontaneous, self-motivated, and richly connected to popular culture. Papert imagines a kind of technological samba school where people of all ages gather together to work on creative projects using computers.

Papert calls his approach to learning *constructionism*, and views it as an extension of Jean Piaget's constructivism:

> We understand "constructionism" as including, but going beyond, what Piaget would call "constructivism." The word with the v expresses the theory that knowledge is built by the learner, not supplied by the teacher. The word with the n expresses the further idea that this happens especially felicitously when the learner is engaged in the construction of something external or at least shareable . . . a sand castle, a machine, a computer program, a book. This leads us to a model of using a cycle of internalization of what is outside, then externalization of what is inside. (Papert, 1991, p. 1)

Much research on constructionist learning has an individualistic implementation, focusing on providing the individual with "tools to think with" and the freedom to pursue self-selected goals (Kafai & Resnick, 1996). Papert's samba school metaphor goes beyond that individualistic focus, highlighting the social nature of learning (Newman, Griffin, & Cole, 1989) and the role that a community context can play in scaffolding learning (Rogoff, 1994).

MOOSE Crossing is a text-based virtual reality environment (or MUD) whose design was inspired by the idea of a virtual samba school. In this online world, children create magical places and creatures that have behaviors. In the process, they practice creative writing and learn object-oriented programming. Past research on MOOSE Crossing has focused on the power of the Internet to create a supportive community context for constructionist learning (Bruckman, 1997, 1998). In many experiments in constructionist learning done to date, exciting learning results are observed during trials; however, those gains are not sustained after the researchers go home. The researchers provide important support for both learners and teachers. Online communities have the potential to provide ongoing support for innovative pedagogy under realistic settings. Past research on MOOSE Crossing has found that the community provides:

1. Role models
2. Situated, ubiquitous project models
3. Emotional support to overcome technophobia
4. Technical support, and
5. An appreciative audience for completed work. (Bruckman, 1998)

"Situated, ubiquitous project models" require special explanation. A good example of such models is HTML coding on the World Wide Web. On the Web, you can often view the HTML source for a document. When you want to know how to do something yourself, you can remember something you saw that uses that technique and look at the HTML source code. As you are going about your daily business using the Web, you are developing an ever richer vocabulary of models to which you can refer back. Most software products come with detailed instruction manuals and sometimes libraries of examples; however, it is well-known that users tend not to take the time to read them. Most people cannot learn from an example they have not seen. On the Web, a user's knowledge of available examples increases continually in the course of normal activity.

Similar to the Web, every object on MOOSE Crossing is an example from which the user can learn. A learner in a virtual place can look at every object present – objects, other characters, the room itself – and use those as models from which to learn. Since the set of examples to learn from is the set of all things everyone in the community has ever made, those examples reflect the interests of the community. That set of examples is not static; it grows and evolves as the community grows. A single centralized author of a set of examples could never reflect the community's interests and needs as well as the decentralized process of using everyone's creations as examples to learn from – it could be argued that this is a core advantage of online communities for learning.

Note in particular that examples on MOOSE Crossing are created by specific people. A child using another's work as a model typically has the opportunity to meet the more experienced programmer and ask questions. As a result, role models, project models, technical support, and emotional support for learning are all linked and become mutually reinforcing sources of support. Internet technology has unique affordances to help make a constructionist approach to learning viable in realistic settings.

Children and adults began using MOOSE Crossing in October 1995. It continues to be an active site at the time of this writing, with participants connecting from home, school, and after-school programs. An after-school program was held at the MIT Media Lab from that date until February 1997 for the purpose of helping us to better understand the environment in use and the learning that takes place there. Children participating in the program were observed closely and interviewed regularly. In addition to those local users, the environment was made freely available on the Internet to anyone interested. Many new participants simply heard about the project online or from friends and participated from home. A few teachers have brought their classes online. Teachers hear about MOOSE Crossing by word of mouth and through presentations about the environment at conferences like the National Educational Computing Conference (NECC). Participation from home or after-school programs is almost always voluntary, while from schools it may or may not be. In some classes, MOOSE Crossing is offered as just one of many options during unstructured computer lab time; in others, students are assigned to participate. Where participation is mandatory, teachers assess student work in some cases but not in others. To further complicate the picture, many students who participate from school also have access from home, and a significant number of students whose in-school participation is required choose to participate voluntarily from home as well. However, taking all these factors into account, required participation in MOOSE Crossing is unusual and forms only a small fraction of total activity.

Every command typed on MOOSE Crossing is recorded, with written informed consent from parents and assent from kids. The log files used for this analysis comprise 3.1 GB data, and provide an opportunity for quantitative analysis to complement the ongoing process of qualitative observation and interviewing.

Like many educational online communities, participation in MOOSE Crossing is primarily voluntary. A few kids participate from classes, but most do so from home or from after-school programs. Even those who participate in school are often given total or near total freedom in deciding what to do while online. Voluntary participation has advantages but also raises significant challenges for learning.

CHALLENGES TO VOLUNTARY PARTICIPATION AND LEARNING

The 1989 movie *Field of Dreams* popularized the phrase "If you build it, they will come." In the early 1990s, this was an apt description for developing online communities. For example, in 1992, a few email messages were all that was necessary to attract over a thousand members and create a thriving community on MediaMOO, a MUD designed to be a professional community for media researchers (Bruckman & Resnick, 1995). By the mid-1990s, the situation had changed: an exponentially increasing number of sites competed for users' time and attention. Participation in most sites is voluntary, and a wide variety of sites compete for users' limited time.

Voluntary participation is the norm for entertainment forums but is a little more unusual in the field of education. After all, school work is typically required. Progressive pedagogy, however, suggests that students should learn better when they do so in the context of self-selected, self-motivated activities. At the radical extreme, Joel Spring argues that school:

> makes alien the very ability of the individual to act or create. In school the ability to act is no longer an individual matter but is turned over to the experts who grade, rank, and prescribe. Activity itself no longer belongs to the individual but to the institution and its experts. (Spring, 1972, pp. 153–154)

Taking this radical rethinking of school and power relations seriously, generations of educational researchers have experimented with new ways to foster learning on a purely voluntary, self-motivated basis. However, moving from an extreme authoritarian to extreme anti-authoritarian view does not eliminate all problems – it simply introduces different ones. Given the freedom to direct their own learning, what if some students choose to learn little? What if they learn a great deal in some areas but neglect others? For example, Friskolen 70 is an elementary through middle school in Denmark with absolutely no requirements for students. In this open environment, children tend to excel at topics related to history, literature, and culture, but often fail to learn much mathematics. Students typically have difficulty moving to a traditional high school because of gaps in their mathematical background (Falbel, 1989).

As early as the 1930s, John Dewey was aware of this tension and struggled to find a resolution:

> What is the place and meaning of subject-matter and of organization *within* experience? How does subject-matter function? Is there anything inherent in experience which tends towards progressive organization of its contents? What results follow when the materials of experience are not progressively organized? A philosophy which proceeds on the basis of rejection, of sheer opposition, will neglect these questions. It will tend to suppose that because the old education was based on ready-made organization, therefore it suffices to reject the principle of organization *in toto*, instead of striving to discover what it means and how it is to be attained on the basis of experience. We might go through all the points of difference between the new and the old education and reach similar conclusions. When external control is rejected, the problem becomes that of finding the factors of control that are inherent within experience. When external authority is rejected, it does not follow that all authority should be rejected, but rather that there is need to search for a more effective source of authority. Because the older education imposed the knowledge, methods, and the rules of conduct of the mature person upon the young, it does not follow, except on the basis of the extreme *Either-Or* philosophy, that the knowledge and skill of the mature person has no directive value for the experience of the immature. On the contrary, basing education upon personal experience may mean multiplied and more intimate contacts between the mature and the immature than ever existed in the traditional school, and consequently more, rather

than less, guidance by others. The problem, then is: how these contacts can be established without violating the principle of learning through personal experience. The solution of this problem requires a well thought-out philosophy of the social factors that operate in the constitution of individual experience. (Dewey, 1938, pp. 20–21)

Many online learning communities are organized around the principle of voluntary participation either in whole or part. Consequently, they face the challenge of finding a middle ground between the "extreme either-or philosophies" Dewey describes. Designers of online learning communities face the challenge first of eliciting any form of participation and second of creating a high likelihood that participation leads to learning gains.

PORTFOLIO SCORING

How effective is voluntary participation on MOOSE Crossing in fostering learning? Based on our first four years of observation and analysis of MOOSE Crossing from 1995 to 1999, the system designers and administrators developed an impression that achievement in the environment is quite uneven. In fall 1999, we set out to explore variations in achievement systematically.

To begin our analysis, we decided to use portfolio scoring (Baron & Wolf, 1996; Chi, 1997) to examine achievement levels systematically. We randomly selected 50 children from the 803 total MOOSE Crossing users (as of November 1999). All chosen child participants were under the age of 18 during their time of participation and all had logged into the system at least once. Of the 50 kids selected, we had 23 girls and 27 boys. Further information about the children and their level of involvement can be found in Table 9.1. Degree of participation is a key factor to track and in most research is typically measured by time on task. On MOOSE Crossing, as in many online environments, time on task is not equivalent to total connection time. Many users may be multitasking or just leave themselves logged in and inactive for long periods of time. Therefore, in order to get a more accurate measure of time on task, we chose to count the number of commands issued by each child.

We performed a portfolio-based assessment of each participant's scripting ability. While children do significant creative writing as well as programming in this environment, the writing data are harder to interpret since children can learn to improve their writing through a variety of activities and sources of support. For this reason, we are focusing this analysis on their programming ability. Each child's portfolio contains all the scripts the child has written on MOOSE Crossing. Two independent judges reviewed and scored the portfolios. In cases where they did not

TABLE 9.1. *Levels of Participation and Programming Achievement in MOOSE Crossing*

	Minimum	Maximum	Median	Mean *(std. dev.)*
Age	7	17	12	12 *(2.3)*
Period of Participation	7 minutes	4 years, 1 month	3 months, 25 days	9 months, 12 days *(1 year, 1 month)*
Commands Typed	6	51,850	788	6,638 (11,958)
Scripts Written	0	234	2	19.5 *(43.3)*
Portfolio Score	0	4	1	1.36 *(1.47)*

agree, a third judge scored the student's work, and then compared the three scores and assigned a final score. The children were scored on their highest level of achievement using the following scale and criteria:

0: Wrote no scripts
1: Demonstrated understanding of basic input/output
2: Used variables and properties
3: Performed list manipulation and flow control
4: Demonstrated mastery of all aspects of the system

RESULTS

The children we examined exhibit uneven levels of both participation and programming achievement in MOOSE Crossing (Table 9.1). It is clear that while some of the users have attained a high level of programming mastery, a larger subset have not written any MOOSE scripts at all (Figure 9.1).

This supports our informal observation that a small subset of MOOSE users are deeply involved and learn significant programming skills, but a large portion of the community learns only the most basic programming concepts. While over a quarter of the students (categories 3 and 4) are achieving a level of programming knowledge comparable to that taught in a high school class, over 40% do not appear to be learning anything. Despite a reasonable sample size (50 of 405, 12% of children participating), the standard deviations on all mean values are high. The difference between the mean and median scores shows that a small group of kids are greatly offsetting the average. The mean time on task of 6,638 commands typed and the median of 788 shows that a few enthusiastic users are spending enormous amounts of time on MOOSE Crossing, while the majority are much less active. The median number of scripts written is only two, as

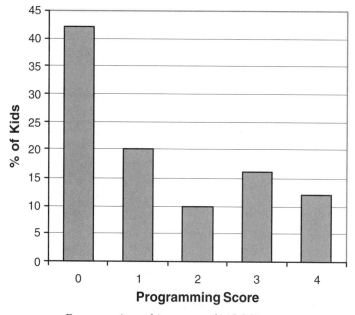

FIGURE 9.1. Programming achievement of MOOSE users

opposed to the mean of 19.5. Again, a very active part of the community is skewing the average score, whereas the median presents a more realistic measure of participation.

In order to address this uneven level of achievement, we have considered several influences on children's programming performance in MOOSE Crossing. We recognize that users with previous exposure to some form of programming are likely to do better. In addition, we must consider the obvious relation between the users' time on task and their achievement. Finally, we pose some interesting questions about the relevance of gender and home versus school use with respect to children's participation and programming scores.

Prior programming experience is an influential factor on achievement. For the purposes of this study, we considered use of any programming or markup language (such as HTML) as prior programming experience. Of the 50 kids, 16 had some form of previous programming experience (4 girls and 12 boys). As expected, the kids with previous exposure achieved significantly higher scores than those without ($p < 0.05$ [Mann-Whitney Test]). There was no significant difference regarding the time on task between the two groups ($p > 0.05$ [nonpooled t test]). The children with previous experience had a mean score of 2.4 and a median of 3; those with no previous experience achieved only a mean score of 0.9 and a median of 0 (Figure 9.2).

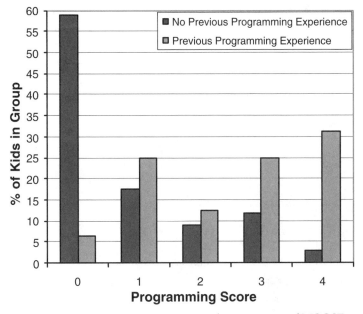

FIGURE 9.2. Programming experience and mean scores of MOOSE users

It is interesting to note that the group with prior experience consisted mostly of boys. Only 17% of the girls had previous experience, compared with 44% of the boys.

We are not surprised that our data support the established concept that time on task is directly related to achievement. However, we are encouraged by the logarithmic trend in the children's programming scores based on the number of commands typed. The users who made it past the initial threshold usually went on to create more complex projects. This illustrates that the amount of participation required to gain understanding of more complex programming concepts in MOOSE Crossing is low. It does not appear that gender affects this trend, as shown by the nearly identical curves for both boys and girls (Figure 9.3). It should be noted, however, that children generally self-select their time on task. We cannot say for sure whether the children who chose not to continue would learn more if they were encouraged or required to persist. From these data, we cannot separate the element of self-selection from time on task.

Noting the heavy gender bias with previous programming experience, we examined whether programming achievement on MOOSE Crossing is directly related to gender (Table 9.2). While the boys had a higher mean programming score (1.63 boys, 1.04 girls) and a higher median score (1 boys, 0 girls), the curves for both boys and girls have the same approximate

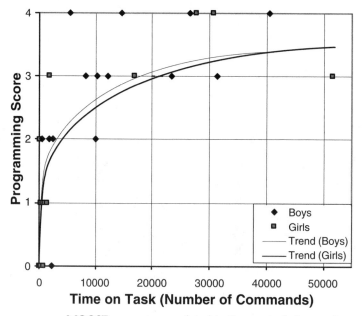

FIGURE 9.3. MOOSE users scores related to time on task, by gender

shape as the composite (Figure 9.4). The slightly higher performance of the boys may be explained by their prior programming experience and slightly higher time on task, but these differences are not significant. Our data indicate that gender does not affect the kids' level of achievement or involvement ($p > 0.05$ [Mann-Whitney Test for programming scores and nonpooled t test for involvement]).

MOOSE Crossing is used in-class (42% of participants), in after-school programs (8%), and as a free-time activity (50%) in school. We found no significant differences in time on task or programming achievement (Figure 9.5) among these groups ($p > 0.05$ [Nonpooled t test for time-on-task and Mann-Whitney Test for achievement]). (Note that some school users also have access at home. These students were classified as school users. This complicates the interpretation of these data.)

COMBATING UNEVENNESS: A CHANGE TO BOTH THEORY AND DESIGN

We do not believe this unevenness to be a problem unique to MOOSE Crossing, but rather a fundamental issue that arises in the design of many learning environments, especially self-motivated ones. In a self-motivated learning environment, students are given the freedom to choose whether to get involved in the hopes that they will embrace the opportunity with genuine enthusiasm. However, inevitably some will decline what is offered.

TABLE 9.2. *Programming Experience and Achievement, by Gender*

	Minimum		Maximum		Median		Mean (*std. dev.*)	
	Boys	**Girls**	**Boys**	**Girls**	**Boys**	**Girls**	**Boys**	**Girls**
Age	7	7	17	16	12	11	12 (2.23)	12 (2.36)
Period of Participation	7 min	13 min	4 yrs, 1 mo	3 yrs, 5 mo	4 mo, 28 days	3 mo, 1 day	10 mo, 23 days (*1 year, 1 mo*)	7 mo, 24 days (*11 mo, 21 days*)
Commands Typed	6	41	40,436	51,850	1,632	241	7,267 (*10,974*)	5,900 (*13,233*)
Scripts Written	0	0	234	124	8	0	26.6 (*52.8*)	11.3 (*27.2*)
Portfolio Score	0	0	4	4	1	0	1.63 (*1.50*)	1.04 (*1.40*)

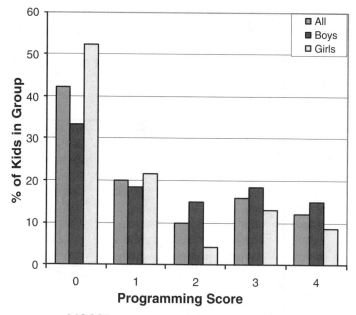

FIGURE 9.4. MOOSE users programming scores, by gender

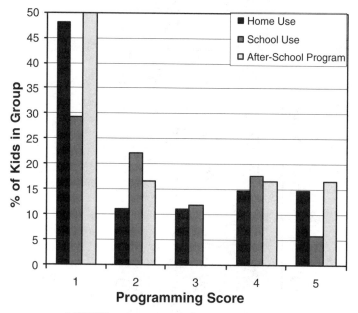

FIGURE 9.5. MOOSE users scores and activity location

This unevenness of achievement is undesirable, particularly for an in-school activity. A free-time activity can not be expected to appeal to all children, and unevenness in both interest and achievement is acceptable. However, for an in-school activity, we have a greater expectation that a large percentage of children will benefit at least to some degree, or the activity should be removed from the curriculum.

This led us to a question: how can we begin to remedy this problem without spoiling the open-ended, self-motivated nature of the learning environment? Children who use MOOSE Crossing in school are generally given a great deal of freedom in how they spend their time online. We do not want to require that specific programming tasks be accomplished but to encourage the students to choose to learn more.

In winter 2000, this led to the design of a system of "merit badges." Children are able to earn badges for a variety of programming and writing tasks. Special badges are awarded for community service. To earn a badge, a child first finds a sponsor. A sponsor is someone who already has earned that badge (or one of a group of community leaders designated to give badges to the first applicants). With help from the sponsor, the applicant prepares a project portfolio demonstrating understanding of the designated concept (for example, using a conditional statement, using a property reference, writing something funny, writing something beautiful, etc. A list of currently offered badges appears in Figure 9.6). When the student and sponsor feel the portfolio is ready, it is submitted for anonymous review. If the reviewer approves the application, the student is awarded the badge. The sponsor is also rewarded for this achievement: sponsoring

---

Programming Badges:

Rooms

Properties

Conditionals

List 1

Input

Operators

Writing Badges:

General

Descriptive

Funny

FIGURE 9.6. MOOSE Crossing merit badges

one other person changes your badge in that area to silver, sponsoring five others changes it to gold. When you have a gold badge, you are eligible to be an anonymous reviewer for that badge.

Thus, the new merit badge system combines elements of portfolio assessment and peer tutoring (Johnson & Johnson, 1987). Our design goal is to raise the level of achievement without spoiling the self-motivated nature of the learning environment (a fundamental tension discussed by others in this volume, e.g., Barab, MaKinster, & Scheckler, this volume; Derry, Lee, Seymour, Steinkuehler, & Siegel this volume). This is a delicate balance. Twenty-three members have earned badges as of November 2002. Sarah[2] (girl, age 13) is the most enthusiastic of the initial badge earners. She has been participating in MOOSE Crossing regularly since she was nine years old. Since the introduction of the badge system, she has earned six badges and at the time of this writing is working on two more. (A total of eleven badges are currently offered.) She has also sponsored three other members for badges, including her father, Jim. Jim is the technology coordinator for a suburban school district and takes a special interest in educational technology. Neither Sarah nor Jim are "typical" of either the population at large or the MOOSE population; they both have unusual interest in and knowledge of educational technology. However, Sarah's involvement with the badge system puts her in a good position to offer insights into both the strengths and weaknesses of the system.

In a telephone interview in July 2001, Sarah captured the complexity of the change that the badge system represents:

AMY: Do you think the merit badge system has changed the mood of the place at all?

SARAH: Slightly. Kind of. Well, I don't know why, but it's just like . . . it seems to a little bit.

AMY: In what way?

SARAH: It's like, more . . . I mean, I like the merit badge system, but it's more of a . . . well, I don't know. There's nothing that says you **have** to do merit badges, but everyone's like "merit badge! merit badge!" Like, the talk of the town. It's more, like, learning? That sounds kinda weird. But um, it's like, the mood is like more directed towards learning new things.

AMY: As opposed to what was it before?

SARAH: Slackers? [*giggles*]

AMY: [*laughs*]

SARAH: No, it's . . . before it was too, but it's just more, like, you have to, like . . . teaching to the test. We're learning what we need to know on the requirements.

---

[2] All real names and online pseudonyms of subjects have been changed.

Jim said in an interview that he feels that the badge system has had a positive impact on Sarah. He and Sarah often participate in MOOSE together. Before the introduction of the badge system, they had just finished working on a project together. After finishing the project, he noticed that Sarah lost interest to some extent. However, the badge system revived her enthusiasm. Like his daughter, he has mixed feelings about the badge system, but is on the whole positive:

> JIM: I see MOOSE Crossing as really having two purposes. One is, it's a playground – an after-school club, a place where you can go and develop an online community. And it's free-form. You have your own ideas about what you want to do and you do them. So having this thing that you have to do that has requirements seems very antithetical to that. [...]
>
> But I think that the badge system is very motivating, and if one of your goals is to get students to become more proficient in the programming, then this is certainly a way to do that. Because you set not a very high bar toward attaining these things and some of them I think are quite challenging – you know, doing the ones for lists, and the if-thens, and all that. If you haven't had exposure to that, well that's a good motivation to learn it. So, I think it goes back and forth. The fact that MOOSE Crossing is so open-ended means that you could choose to do or not to do the badges. And the fact that they're there is fine.

We hope that the merit badge system will help teachers to structure the use of MOOSE Crossing in their classrooms. In informal conversations, teachers using MOOSE Crossing have expressed great enthusiasm for this addition to the learning environment. One teacher commented that she would like to use the badge system as a form of assessment for her students: they will be assigned to earn a certain number of badges during the course of the school year. Unfortunately, using the badge system as an assessment detracts from the self-motivated nature of the learning environment. It is possible that this change will negatively impact the atmosphere of the online community.

We are attempting to achieve a delicate balance between a radical constructionist perspective (which eschews assessment and insists that the project should be its own reward) and a more traditional perspective (which sees assessment as an essential component of any learning environment that can meet the demands of functioning in real classrooms). At the time of this writing, the badge system is undergoing iterative design. We are conducting interviews, observing interactions online, and trying to refine the model to support learning both through earning a badge and being a sponsor. In future work, we plan to perform a detailed study of changes in both students' perceptions of the learning environment and in

their level of achievement. Our ultimate goal is not just to create a successful learning environment, but more importantly to test our evolving ideas
about motivation and arrive at a more generally applicable advance to the
underlying theory of learning.

CONCLUSION: CO-EVOLUTION OF THEORY
AND TECHNOLOGICAL DESIGN

The MOOSE Crossing project began in 1992 as an exploration of the application of constructionist learning theory to the design of an online learning
community. Online communities have the potential to provide social support for learning and teaching, making this approach to learning more
scalable and sustainable in real-world settings. Initially, the project began
with a commitment to self-motivated learning. In the first few years of using the software with kids from our first working version in 1995 through
1999, we informally observed that achievement in the environment was
uneven. Portfolio scoring techniques confirmed this observation.

Taking the time to confirm informal observations is of great importance
to progress in the theory and design of online learning communities. Researchers are prone to make mistakes in informal observations. Perception
is guided by expectations, and all researchers are vulnerable to seeing what
they hope to see. Administrators of online communities are particularly
vulnerable to being overly influenced by community regulars. Regulars
form the heart of any "third place" (neither work nor home) community
(Oldenburg, 1989). Most of an administrator's daily interactions are with
these regulars; however, they are often not representative of the population
at large. For example, in informal observations of MOOSE Crossing users,
we developed a suspicion that girls' achievement exceeded that of boys.
In reality, gender does not predict programming achievement (Bruckman,
Jensen, & DeBonte, 2002). The highest achieving regular members are dis-
proportionately female, but this does not extend to the broader population.
While systematic analysis refuted our informal ideas about gender and programming achievement, this analysis confirmed our informal observations
about unevenness of student achievement.

These findings have guided our ongoing work on improving both the
system's technological design and our understanding of underlying learning phenomena. These findings support the conjecture that fully self-
motivated learning environments can be successful for free-time use, but
are problematic for in-school use. To address this issue, we are experimenting with a form of compromise between traditional and radical constructionist approaches to student motivation. Over the next year, we
will continue to improve the design of the merit badge system through
continual formative evaluation and iterative design. After this lengthy
process is completed, we will be in a position to once again undertake

more systematic data collection to test our hypothesis that our hybrid approach to motivation can be an effective compromise. Improvements in both technological design and pedagogy for online learning communities can best be achieved through a combination of quantitative and qualitative methods over an extended timeframe.

References

Baron, J. B., & Wolf, D. P. (Eds.). (1996). *Performance-Based Student Assessment: Challenges and Possibilities*. Chicago: University of Chicago Press.

Bruckman, A. (1997). *MOOSE Crossing: Construction, Community, and Learning in a Networked Virtual World for Kids*. Unpublished doctoral dissertation, MIT.

Bruckman, A. (1998). Community Support for Constructionist Learning. *Computer Supported Cooperative Work, 7*, 47–86.

Bruckman, A., Jensen, C., & DeBonte, A. (2002). *Gender and Programming Achievement in a CSCL Environment*. Paper presented at the CSCL, Boulder, CO, January 1, 2002.

Bruckman, A., & Resnick, M. (1995). The MediaMOO Project: Constructionism and Professional Community. *Convergence, 1*(1), 94–109.

Chi, M. T. (1997). Quantifying Qualitative Analyses of Verbal Data: A Practical Guide. *Journal of the Learning Sciences, 6*(3), 271–315.

Dewey, J. (1938). *Experience and Education*. New York: Macmillan.

Falbel, A. (1989). *Friskolen 70: An Ethnographically Informed Inquiry Into the Social Context of Learning*. Unpublished doctoral dissertation, MIT.

Johnson, D. W., & Johnson, R. T. (1987). *Learning Together & Alone*. Englewood Cliffs, NJ: Prentice-Hall.

Kafai, Y., & Resnick, M. (Eds.). (1996). *Constructionism in Practice*. Mahwah, NJ: Lawrence Erlbaum Associates.

Newman, D., Griffin, P., & Cole, M. (1989). *The Construction Zone: Working for Cognitive Change in School*. Cambridge: Cambridge University Press.

Oldenburg, R. (1989). *The Great Good Place*. New York: Paragon House.

Papert, S. (1980). *Mindstorms: Children, Computers, and Powerful Ideas*. New York: Basic Books.

Papert, S. (1991). Situating Constructionism. In I. Harel & S. Papert (Eds.), *Constructionism* (p. 518). Norwood, NJ: Ablex Publishing.

Rogoff, B. (1994). Developing Understanding of the Idea of Communities of Learners. *Mind, Culture, and Activity, 1*(4), 209–229.

Spring, J. (1972). *Education and the Rise of the Corporate State*. Boston: Beacon Press.

10

From Ambitious Vision to Partially Satisfying Reality

An Evolving Socio-Technical Design Supporting
Community and Collaborative Learning
in Teacher Education

Sharon J. Derry, Jennifer Seymour, Constance
Steinkuehler, Julia Lee, and Marcelle A. Siegel

Our chapter relates to an ongoing and continuously evolving research and development project that has as its goal the design of a socio-technical system (a technical environment and related social structures and activities) that will constitute a good model for distributed teacher professional development programs conceptualized as knowledge-building communities. We focus primarily on a part of our work that is situated within the Secondary Teacher Education Program at the University of Wisconsin-Madison. We begin by describing the original ambitious vision for this program that we set out to implement, including its theoretical basis. Then we discuss how both our initial failures and the theoretical framework itself led us to more carefully consider how the historical and institutional contexts of such community-building efforts might influence the social processes of learning and teaching within the community. To illuminate this idea, we present a contextual analysis of the program as a prelude to an interaction analysis of a representative discourse from a group learning activity within the program. Throughout this chapter, we consider lessons learned from studies such as these and from our immersion in the experience of designing a socio-technical environment for supporting community-based teacher education. Drawing on these lessons, we describe our modified goal and the latest results of our efforts to develop an online system for structuring and supporting group learning, including the online mentoring of such learning, within teacher education programs.

ORIGINAL VISION

Previous work on building learning communities has produced fruitful results. Research demonstrates that collaboration, experimentation, and challenging discourse must be encouraged in order for teacher learning communities to succeed (Little, 1993; Norris, 1994). "Challenging discussions are not very common among teachers, who often equate criticism with personal inadequacies" (Loucks-Horsley, Hewson, Love, & Stiles, 1998). Yet a professional culture necessitates the analyzing, explaining of evidence, and communicating criticisms in order to learn. What we advocate for students, teachers need to learn as well (Loucks-Horsley et al., 1998). Reforms in education are often fundamentally flawed because they do not attempt to alter the structure of classroom discourse (Sarason, 1996). Studies find that using computer support for collaborative learning can drive changes in teacher practices from didactic to constructivist (Henze, Nejdl, & Wolpers, 1999; Resta, Christal, Ferneding, & Puthoff, 1999). A shared mission, continuous improvement, and results orientation are also important for professional learning communities to thrive (DuFour & Eaker, 1998).

Accordingly, our original vision for the Secondary Teacher Education Project (STEP) was to develop a technology-based distributed professional learning community as a model for teacher education. We wanted to design a learning environment that integrated academic coursework and practice in schools through collaborative instructional design projects carried out by teams composed of teacher education majors, university faculty, and classroom teachers from local area schools. Teams were to be student centered and include professional mentors from university faculty and area schools. Through participation on teams, members of the community would examine their beliefs about schooling in light of current science, educational theory, and authentic school contexts. This professional learning community would construct and reconstruct knowledge about teaching and learning in classrooms. Because teams would be geographically dispersed, online synchronous forums would be used to support collaborative work that could not feasibly take place without them. Also, collaborative projects would produce artifacts, such as model lessons, constituting an evolving base of instructional "cases." A case-based web technology would be developed to support maintenance of this communal knowledge base, as well as access and use of it for collaborative teaching and learning. That was the ambitious vision written in a proposal to the National Science Foundation (NSF) in 1998. Three years later we examine what STEP is now, where it is headed, and how and why the project's original vision changed.

The Knowledge-Building Community Framework

Both the original and evolving visions of STEP have been informed by the Knowledge-Building Community (KBC) Framework (see Figure 10.1), a perspective that focused us, as designers, on supporting group and community interactional processes, on considering how social and historical contexts might shape such interactions, and on the evolution of knowledge and beliefs at both the individual and community levels (Derry, Gance, Gance, & Schlager, 2000; Hewitt, this volume; Riel & Polin, this

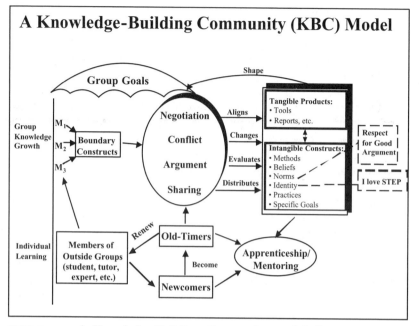

FIGURE 10.1. A Knowledge-Building Community model (from Derry, Gance, Gance, & Schlager, 2000)

volume). The KBC Framework represents a synthesis of four theoretical viewpoints regarding the nature of social knowledge construction: sociocultural/situative, sociocognitive, argumentative, and group information processing. The constructs we borrowed from these views and fused in our framework are briefly described below.

SOCIOCULTURAL/SITUATIVE PERSPECTIVE. A sociocultural/situative viewpoint (Greeno, 1998; Wertsch, 1991) dominates this framework. From this view, knowledge construction involves work activity, a process through which key "boundary constructs" (e.g., Wenger, 1999) evolve into mutually understood "new" ideas, behavioral norms, and other intangible constructs that shape and are shaped by teamwork. Boundary constructs are ideas brought to the work initially by members of diverse backgrounds, and are so named because they represent shared general ideas within overlapping boundaries of disciplinary knowledge. Documentation that boundary constructs emerge and evolve into shared concepts that drive and support group work is evidence that a knowledge-construction system is operating. Sociocultural/situative theory implies that processes of negotiation and apprenticeship drive such knowledge construction. Hence, presence, frequency, and quality of these processes within work groups dictate and indicate how well a group or community functions as a knowledge-construction system. This viewpoint led us, as designers, to consider such issues as attracting or selecting members for diversity and overlapping knowledge boundaries, and creating a system to support and facilitate collaboration, viewed as negotiation, apprenticeship, and mentoring.

SOCIOCOGNITIVE PERSPECTIVE. Figure 10.1 also represents a sociocognitive perspective, so named because it views knowledge construction as an individual cognitive activity driven by social interaction. Knowledge construction is seen as involving changes and realignments in individuals' mental representations of their work. Theoretically, as community members collaborate, their individual mental models of group tasks, community constructs, and the community itself become more aligned with one another. Some degree of mental-model alignment is considered a necessary precondition for productive work, although some misalignment is desirable (e.g., DuRussel & Derry, 1998; Orasanu & Salas, 1993; O'Donnell, DuRussel, & Derry, 1997). When people with different points of view work together, their interactions produce cognitive conflicts that individuals seek to resolve through argumentation, theoretically driving conceptual change. Hence, from the sociocognitive perspective, communities are operating as knowledge-construction systems if there is evidence of conceptual and belief change within individuals and a trend toward increasing compatibility among members' task-related viewpoints. Like the sociocultural/situative view, this perspective also focused us, as designers, on constituting groups with members having diverse but overlapping systems of knowledge and belief. In addition, this view encouraged design of activities that create some cognitive conflict but that embed within them mentoring processes that manage this conflict toward desired learning goals.

ARGUMENTATION PERSPECTIVE. The KBC model also incorporates a literature that views knowledge construction as both process and product of argumentation and informal scientific reasoning. This "critical thinking" (e.g., Halpern, 1996; Kuhn, 1991) viewpoint suggests that such processes as negotiation, apprenticeship/mentoring, and conflict resolution be judged against established standards for argument form and content, recognizing that argument in conversation is ill-structured and both temporally and socially distributed (Resnick et al., 1993). It suggests that the knowledge resulting from valid argument is superior to knowledge resulting from less logical processes. It suggests that "respect for good argument" should be a social norm that is promoted and supported within the community (Hewitt, this volume). The degree of adherence to critical thinking norms can theoretically be detected in transcripts of conversations and reports of individual beliefs. In addition, individual and group products can be assessed on whether judgments and decisions are based on evidence and valid argument (cf., Bell & Linn, 2000; Ranney, Adams, Siegel, & Brem, 1999; Siegel, 1999; Siegel & Lee, 2001; Watson, Swain, & McRobbie, 2001). Recognizing that valid argument in instructional conversation may be infrequent and difficult to promote (e.g., Derry, Gance, Gance, & Schlager, 2000), as designers we saw the need for system design that would scaffold good argumentation within the community's learning and working groups.

GROUP INFORMATION PROCESSING. Finally, Figure 10.1 incorporates group information processing theory (Hinsz, Tindale, & Vollrath, 1997; Smith, 1994). From this view, the potential for knowledge construction depends on such interacting factors as: (1) available knowledge within working groups; (2) extent to which shared knowledge overlaps among group members; (3) processes by which information is shared among members; and (4) stages by which information is transformed from one form (e.g., private, shared/unshared knowledge) to another (e.g., a tangible group product). As designers we were encouraged by this view to attend to the constructing of a system with affordances and constraints that shape these group information-processing factors. These include social factors, such as status of individual members and their group allegiances. For example, desirable group characteristics include moderate cultural/professional diversity (broad knowledge capacity with an overlapping base for starting communication) accompanied by high levels of information sharing among all social categories (broad knowledge distribution). Other factors shaping group information-processing include behaviors and contexts that impact important information-processing phases, such as the attentional phase. For example, environmental events (e.g., overlapping talk, distracting noise) that interfere with information sharing and inhibit group work must be minimized by socio-technical designs. Also, working groups must be supported in effective processes of transforming talk (planning, thinking, analysis) into the final required products that will be evaluated.

We have found the theories outlined above to be commensurate and overlapping in important ways. Briefly, the sociocultural/situative, sociocognitive, and group information processing viewpoints focused our design team on issues pertaining to membership, such as populating the community and constituting work groups with diverse but overlapping systems of knowledge and belief. All four views required us to consider how to support and manage the knowledge-construction processes whereby these systems interact. These processes are: negotiation, apprenticeship/mentoring, resolution of cognitive conflict, argument, and information sharing. Although these processes are named and conceptualized differently across theories, their boundaries and definitions overlap, and we adopt the view that knowledge construction can and should engage all these forms of interaction. Hence, one of our design goals has been to promote and manage these types of interaction. We have also been concerned with supporting stages of information processing, such as group attention, by creating environments that minimize overlapping talk and other distractions, such as technology difficulties. Finally, the information-processing aspect of the KBC model has prompted us to consider the importance of tools and procedures for helping work groups translate their discussions into tangible products, such as designs for classroom instruction.

However, perhaps the most critical aspect of the KBC model, for purposes of guiding program design, is its overall unified nature. The KBC model is a complex system requiring certain forms of communication, joint work, artifact use, and processes of membership renewal, all operating in synchrony. Thus a KBC cannot exist without "buy-in" from many constituents. And because the ability to achieve such buy-in is largely determined by the historical, institutional, and social contexts of the system-design project, these will be examined next.

The Secondary Teacher Education Program as a Context for Design

The context in which much of our design work is taking place is the secondary teacher education program at University of Wisconsin (UW)-Madison. It is a grade 6–12 certification program at the baccalaureate level involving five broad majors: mathematics, science, foreign languages, English, and social studies. Students usually enter the program in their junior or senior year or beyond, after completing coursework in their academic majors. The program is four semesters long and integrates eight methods and foundations courses with field experiences and student teaching. The program is relatively new and is still evolving. Program faculty from multiple departments try to meet monthly and strive for both vertical (between semester) and horizontal (within semester) integration across courses and field experiences. The program vision shared by faculty and promoted to students when they enter is one of an evolving knowledge-building community that includes university faculty and staff, the teacher education students, and teachers in cooperating schools.

In this chapter we examine the program from the perspective of third-semester instructional staff in charge of a foundations course in the learning sciences that is horizontally integrated with courses on literacy and diversity and a practicum field experience in local schools, and vertically integrated with methods courses and student teaching in the five certification areas. Our role within the program has involved viewing and influencing design of the program as a socio-technical learning community, with funded research obtained by the first author in support of this endeavor.

There are many positive forces operating within the program that support and encourage development and evolution of the socio-technical learning community vision. In the constraint category, legal credentialing requirements imposed by the state legislature and Department of Public Instruction have had the positive benefit of forcing busy faculty from different departments to come together to write standards for the new program and coordinate their courses and syllabi in working toward standards. Additional constraints include scarcity of staffing resources, practical limits on faculty and student time, as well as travel requirements associated with participation in and supervision of field experiences, including urban and foreign field experiences, which together encourage development and appreciation of online courses and meetings as alternatives to face-to-face interaction. In the category of positive affordances, the faculty and institution are collegial, supportive, and have proved willing to tolerate risks associated with innovative instructional programming.

Despite this necessary and positive context, we have also experienced numerous problems and resistances to developing the socio-technical learning community originally envisioned. In conceptualizing these resistances, we have found Wertsch's concept of "voice" (e.g., 1991) to be helpful in describing the program in terms of overlapping subdiscourses that do not easily interact in accordance with the KBC framework. These voices represent concerns and belief systems that are sometimes in conflict. They include various academic disciplines and epistemologies represented in the program; the cooperating school personnel, principally teachers, who interact with the program; the university administrators concerned with meeting accreditation and certification requirements; university faculty and instructional staff who teach and supervise program students; and the pre-service teachers who are students in the program.

An important and influential voice within the program is that of the university staff, including administrative program heads, administrative support personnel, teaching faculty, lecturers, field supervisors, and teaching assistants. Many of these staff members are graduate students. While these constituents do not always agree or speak with one voice, they meet regularly, tend to reach decisions cooperatively and collegially, and generally support one another as members of a team. However, there is substantial turnover in this group from semester to semester, and the group is scattered among offices in several buildings. While there are several long-term core members, the responsibilities of instructional staff often shift from semester to semester. Because time constraints are substantial, many participate extensively only during meetings and semesters that most directly relate to their specific areas of responsibility, and communication between meetings is relatively limited. One difficulty for the instructional staff is moving from newcomer status to old-timer status because of the shifting group structure; another is sufficient collaborative interaction. While this group has some degree of communal cohesiveness, it is loosely connected.

Another critical but currently even less cohesive part of the evolving community is the group of cooperating teachers who mentor students' field experiences. This group is geographically dispersed and never meets as a group, and its primary contacts with the program are through the individual student teachers who work in classrooms and the program's field supervisors for these students. Through indirect communication with field supervisors and students, program faculty who teach university courses strive to help coordinate their students' course-related field assignment with cooperating teachers' needs and constraints in mind.

By contrast, student cohorts seem more tightly connected. The program admits one or two cohorts per year that range in size from about 65 to 75 students. These students are assembled into three interdisciplinary learning communities (to promote the KBC goals of interaction among overlapping knowledge bases and systems of belief) that take courses and are assigned field placements together during the two-year program. In addition, the entire cohort meets on a regular basis. Students seem to quickly cohere and form relationships. They sometimes organize to make their wishes known and can function effectively as a political bloc.

Many instructional staff work intensely with cohorts for only one semester. This is the case for our psychological foundations instructional staff, which encounters a cohort only after it has been together for a year. And while there are only a few instructional staff during the third semester, there are a great many students. Thus the semester begins with allegiances reflecting an in-group/out-group structure, with instructional staff on the "outside." Such structural asymmetries in group composition tend to create comparable asymmetries in group interaction, such that in-group members dominate conversation and tend to share and impose common knowledge and belief systems (e.g., O'Donnell et al., 1998).

Goals of pre-service teachers are often in conflict with those of faculty and other instructional staff in schools of education. For example, our instructional staff expects students to acquire in-depth understanding of learning science concepts and learn to flexibly apply these concepts to the analysis and design of learning environments. Whereas an important goal for some students is to develop such knowledge and ability, many want other competing things from their teacher education program, such as rapid career entry, efficient credentialing, and specific instructional methods and materials. This tension between supporting immediate needs and facilitating more general professional development is described elsewhere as well (Barab, MaKinster, & Scheckler, this volume; Kling & Courtright, this volume). This ability of a socio-technical system to meet the immediate instructional needs of the users of the system may account, in part, for the success of the Math Forum (Renninger & Shumar, this volume).

The instructional staff asks students in the program to engage with a variety of unfamiliar theories and concepts and to use these in helping reformulate their practices and vision for education. Simon (1992) characterized this as a fear-provoking situation. He believes the sources of such fear are legitimate and include students' feelings of marginalization due to lack of facility with a new discourse they are being asked to acquire. They include realizations of the time commitment involved and resistance to examining and possibly abandoning currently held values and practices.

Hence the voices of the students sometimes reflect impatience, resistance, perhaps even fear, toward theoretical material they are expected to learn.

Further, research on collaborative learning has repeatedly documented the effects of status on individual student experiences within groups. For example, high-status group members tend to gain and maintain group attention; they talk more, and they derive greater learning benefits from group interaction. Lower-status group members are often marginalized and discouraged from participating (O'Donnell et al., 1997; O'Donnell & King, 2000). Of course individual personality matters greatly and students do not always conform to expectations based on group norms. Nevertheless, we believe that many group-membership characteristics that affect status are inherently present within the UW secondary teacher education program. For example, like Tannen (1990), we observe conversational styles associated with gender, whereby males seem more aloof and/or communicate for the purpose of providing information or gaining status, while females seem more concerned with affiliation and maintaining community relationships. Moreover, the program is multidisciplinary, with different academic disciplines holding different ranks associated with status in the university community. For example, physical scientists are generally regarded with higher status than are social scientists (O'Donnell et al., 1997). So, for example, if a group comprises several male scientists and one female social scientist, it is likely that the female social scientist will be marginalized in group interaction.

It was with these social contexts in mind that we began to examine social processes within the newly developing program, trying to gain a better understanding of what kinds of interactions our socio-technical design must mediate (e.g., Derry, Seymour, Feltovich, & Fassnacht, 2001; Siegel & Lee, 2001; Steinkuehler, 2001). So far our work has concentrated largely on trying to understand the interactions among the teacher education majors and the graduate student instructional staff in our learning sciences course, in which TAs (teaching assistants) supervise small-group learning activities, including extended projects. In the following we spotlight one analysis of a short segment of face-to-face classroom discourse that we believe is characteristic of such small-group instructional interactions. The analysis was conducted at a time when the program was just beginning to incorporate technology in various ways, but was not yet offering online instruction. A discussion of how such analyses influenced design of the online system, which we believe mediates and improves those interactions and promotes community, will follow.

A STUDY OF COLLABORATION WITHIN THE PROGRAM

The forces of resistance previously described are clearly present and influential within the collaborative interactions that take place in program classrooms. How these conflicts were manifest within the science education program during spring semester, 2000, is illustrated through analysis of a videotape of an instructional discussion that took place within the third-semester psychological foundations (learning sciences) course. This course is designed to help future teachers develop a scientific stance toward learning and development that can be used as a basis for analyzing classroom practice. A goal of this ongoing course is to help future educators develop a respectful, self-critical, scientific stance toward their own and others' classroom practice, as a basis for continuing professional development and improving instructional designs. A typical assignment in this course may require several weeks to complete. A representative assignment is one in which a small group of student teachers works with a teaching assistant to apply learning sciences concepts in critiquing a case of actual classroom teaching, and in justifying a redesign or adaptation of the example lesson given in the case.

This method of problem-based learning (PBL) was developed for medical education (e.g., Barrows, 1988) and has spread to many other types of classrooms, including K–12 classrooms. Elsewhere (Derry & the STEP Team, in press) we have described the purpose of PBL as helping students acquire domain knowledge, usually scientific knowledge, in the context of solving a real-world problem that is based on a real-world case. Our knowledge of this method is largely gleaned from wisdom of practice, from writings by its developer, Howard Barrows, and from the widespread PBL community that uses this method and has begun to conduct research on it. There are standard steps in PBL instruction, and many users of the method feel strongly that they work well and shouldn't be modified. PBL takes students through a facilitated small-group process in which students discuss and "solve" a problem case (e.g., a case of medical diagnosis) as they fill in labeled columns on a "whiteboard" (often a giant post-it note) that has been structured to guide discussion and thinking. In completing the whiteboard, students proceed through steps in which they notice facts about the case, formulate hypotheses, identify learning issues for further investigation, conduct research, and revisit and discuss hypotheses until a problem solution is reached. The main purpose of this activity is to learn about a conceptual domain as that conceptual domain is "shaped" and restructured in the context of realistic problem solving.

Here we examine a small segment of discussion that took place within a group of five science education majors who spent four weeks in a PBL activity, studying and redesigning a teacher's videotaped science lesson on static electricity. The case assigned to this group of science majors was "Students Get a Charge out of Static Electricity." The case materials were obtained from the STEP website, http://eSTEPWeb.org, which has been developed to provide access to instructional resources to support case-based and problem-based teacher education in the learning sciences. This case includes readings, videos, and inquiry materials, and tells the story of an actual science unit in a public school taught by a popular teacher and representing good traditional instruction. The group's instructional task was to advise Mr. Johnson (the teacher) on how to improve the unit and to justify the group's redesign in learning-sciences language. One solution that students could propose is to redesign the lesson as a more authentic, inquiry-based unit.

As is typical within this course, a relatively inexperienced teaching assistant served as facilitator for this discussion group. In PBL terms, such facilitators are typically called tutors. This teaching assistant had received two days of training in a PBL tutoring workshop, conducted by an expert PBL teacher. In accordance with this method, the tutor guided her group through a series of steps that included identifying learning issues – things students needed to learn more about in order to solve the redesign problem. Between classes, students researched assigned learning issues (a process facilitated by the STEP website), bringing varied findings to their group discussions.

Method

To examine classroom discourse, we employed an analytical approach known as *interaction analysis,* an interdisciplinary approach for investigating the interaction of people with each other and with their environment (Jordan & Henderson, 1995). This chapter reports an interdisciplinary interaction-analysis team's observations of a two-minute segment of video recorded on the first day of the students' four-week PBL exercise. This segment was chosen by the team as a case representing cognitive and social conflict within a PBL group. A detailed transcription of the segment was prepared using traditional Jeffersonian notation (Atkinson & Heritage, 1984).

Analysis Participants

This segment has been analyzed by two groups, the first one at the University of Wisconsin-Madison. Analysts in this group included two professors of cognitive science, one a specialist in medical education and the PBL method, the other the first author of this chapter and the developer of the subject course. Another participant was a specialist in medical education and PBL with advanced coursework in educational psychology. Seven graduate students in education and one education and research technology specialist with advanced training in conversation analysis (who faciliated the session) also participated in the analysis session. Five of these graduate students had been PBL tutors for the course, and one was the tutor being viewed in the videotape. The second interaction analysis session took place at Southern Illinois University-Carbondale. The same professors and medical education specialist took part. Four additional professors – a conversation analyst (who facilitated the group), a science educator, a cognitive scientist specializing in collaborative learning, and a history professor developing an undergraduate PBL curriculum – also took part. Nine graduate students in various social science fields and with no connection to the course participated as well.

DATA ANALYSIS. In the first analysis session, the video segment was viewed without any comments three times. During this time the analysts made notes on their transcripts. At the end of the third viewing, the analysts wrote for approximately 10 minutes about what they had observed. Then, each analyst in turn explained his or her analysis of the video segment without comment by others. This was followed by a general discussion of various analyses. The session was videotaped and audiotaped. Participating analysts' notes were also collected as a record of the analysis. In the second analysis session, the video segment was viewed repeatedly and discussed. The first author took detailed notes of the session. All recordings and notes were studied and synthesized by the first author of this chapter, with other authors contributing feedback and revisions. The following represents an attempt to synthesize and capture the analysts' collective viewpoint regarding the selected video segment.

Results

The two-minute segment that follows is a small portion of a discussion that occurred over several weeks of class in which five student teachers, Dean, Bo, Cindy, Paula, and Lou, led by their tutor, Janice, applied learning science concepts to the analysis and improvement of a high school static electricity lesson presented to them as a video case. The analysis of this segment is developed in four segments labeled: I. The Memory Incident; II. Lightning as a Vehicle for Teaching Static Electricity; III. Think in My Terms; and IV. The Conflict. The discourse in segment I is course-term banter pertaining to one student's effort to recall a concern she had about the lesson. In segment II, this student recalls that her concern is about connecting the lesson topic to things students might know and care about, which leads to a discussion of whether lightning would be a good vehicle for presenting the topic. In segment III, the tutor attempts to have the students translate the discussion into course terminology and reinforces one student for naming a correct term. In segment IV, the dominant student in the group challenges the use of this term, drawing support from another student and creating the stage for escalation of a conflict.

The group of analysts, including the tutor, unanimously agreed that this section was largely a story of conflict between the female tutor (Janice) and a dominant male student, Dean. All agreed the conflict negatively impacted the group and interfered with collaborative learning. During multiple sessions, analysts reflectively examined the discourse of the conflict in detail, developed informed hypotheses about its history and causes, and considered how a tutor might intervene (or how a system might be designed) to manage such conflict. The segmented transcript and a summary analysis of each segment are given next.

I. The Memory Incident

The PBL format is requiring students to generate and write on a whiteboard ideas for improving the instruction they are analyzing. The segment begins when Cindy has an idea for improvement but suddenly loses it from memory. This display provides Dean an opportunity to poke fun at course terminology. The tutor's response, line 7, appears to serve multiple functions. It corrects, builds relations among course terms, allows her to join in a joke with the cohort, and reprimands Dean for his resistance to terminology.

1. (15:53) CINDY: OKAY I HAVE A THING. Where did it go . . . to change.

2. (15:57) JANICE: Okay.

3. (15:57) CINDY: Um. [*hands to head*] Now I just lost it. Oh! Okay I'll – it'll all come back to me.

4. (16:02) DEAN: Ah did you lose it in your, working memory or your long-term or your SENSORY memory? [*layering his arms for emphasis*]

5. (16:05) CINDY: Yeah I JUST thought of it and then I lost it.

6. (16:08) CINDY: Shoot.

7. (16:09) JANICE: Let her try to recall it from the long-term memory back into the short-term or working memory.

8. (16:12) PAULA: Um hm. [*chuckling*]

9. (16:13) DEAN: Okay.

II. Lightning as a Vehicle for Teaching Static Electricity

II.1. INTRODUCING THE TOPIC AND PREPARING FOR DISCUSSION. The next segment of the transcript begins with Cindy's gaining the group's attention and presenting her issue – that the instruction is not connected to real-world experience. This reveals her belief that teaching should help students relate science to life experience. The tutor supports the direction of Cindy's thinking and the group's excitement (with an approving nod). That Dean agrees and values Cindy's comment is indicated by his eagerness to get it on the board. Dean's gestures, intonation, and volume suggest that he is taking a directive role of authority, while the tutor seems to follow his direction in preparing the board:

    10. (16:15) CINDY: OH. How does this apply to like what they're...
                          WHO cares? [*Laughs, Janice nodding*] I – Like if you're
                          sitting here who cares they're going to be like great.
                          I'm going to poke Paula and she's getting a shock
                          who cares. What, is this going to help them in the
                          real world kind of...
    11. (16:29) DEAN: Okay, let's – where is it?
    12. (16:30) CINDY: That would be my thing to change.
    13. (16:32) JANICE: Okay, [*inaudible*] for you. [*She changes a part of the whiteboard*]

II.2. DISCUSSION OF LIGHTNING. With the board prepared for writing, Dean indicates that he has an idea. However, the group does not attend to Dean. Rather, in talk that overlaps with Cindy's continued expression of belief that science instruction should be connected to real-world issues, Bo makes a suggestion that lightning would be a good basis for teaching static electricity. In line 19, Cindy responds positively to Bo, sharing her pleasure at having learned something interesting about lightning. Dean corrects Cindy (line 20) as though she has expressed a misconception. The tutor sees in this discussion an opportunity to make a connection to a course concept and attempts to encourage the group to conceptualize the idea as such by asking in line 21, "What would *I* call that?" The tutor's question is part of much overlapping talk and is not attended by the group. This segment ends with Cindy's resorting to gesture to overcome overlapping talk and communicate to Dean that she is not misinformed.

    14. (16:35) DEAN: Well I have an example of how does this help in the
                          real world.
    15. (16:38) BO: Sort of like how does, how does...
    16. (16:38) CINDY: Okay but they don't see how...THEY'RE not getting
                          that.
    17. (16:41) BO: How does how does like, something they see every-
                          day like lightning, how does how does that...
    18. (16:42):   [*Various students talk*]
    19. (16:44) CINDY: Okay which actually, comes from the ground.
                          [*laughing*] I was really pleased when I learned that.
    20. (16:46) DEAN: Well actually it comes from both.
    21. (16:48) JANICE: What would, what would *I* call that?
    22. (16:48) CINDY: Well I mean like people think... [*she motions with her hands*]

II.3. OWNING AND DEVELOPING THE LIGHTNING IDEA. Dean opens the next phase of talk by using intonation and gesture to "proclaim" that the lightning idea is an amazing one, appearing at once to both "own" the idea and grant Cindy (not Bo) credit for it. In line 24 Bo meekly indicates that Dean is reiterating his thinking. Dean continues to proffer the lightning idea and think out loud about it, using tone and gesture in ways that suggest he is stating new information, although he is largely reiterating and confirming what Cindy and Bo have attempted to express. His statements reveal something about his teaching philosophy, that instruction should begin with topics familiar to students. It is clear that Dean, Bo, and Cindy are in basic agreement about the use of lightning as a basis for redesigning the static electricity unit:

23. (16:49) DEAN: (gesturing toward Cindy) Now LIGHTNING, would be an AMAZING way for them to talk about static electricity.
24. (16:54) BO: That's what I was thinking.
25. (16:54) DEAN: Because, that's a great idea because they all know, about lightning. They've seen it, but I don't think . . .
26. (16:59) CINDY: But you know what?
27.   [*Cindy pointing with pen at table*]
28. (17:00) DEAN: I don't think they even realize it's static electricity.
29. (17:01) CINDY: EXACTLY, because they're talking about putting, electrons here, and there's no reference to what, they do in the world . . .

III. Think in My Terms

In the following segment, the tutor (line 30) begins by asking the group to conceptualize the discussion in learning sciences terms by asking, "What would I call that?" Although Cindy immediately responds with the desired term (authentic learning), this response is masked by Dean's overlapping response to the tutor in line 33 expressed in a very sarcastic tone, "I've no idea what YOU would call that . . ." Cindy then repeats her answer (authentic learning) audibly, which the tutor enthusiastically reinforces as "correct." Cindy responds to the tutor's reinforcement with obvious joy and delight. Dean's responses in lines 37 and 39 can be viewed as attempts to dismiss the topic as something irrelevant that they have already discussed. Paula's turn is likely a suggestion to put Cindy's term on the whiteboard. It seems significant also that in lines 32, 35, and 38, Cindy gradually changes the referent term so that "authentic learning" first becomes "authentic learning application," and finally "authentic instruction."

30. (17:06) JANICE: So what – so what would I call that?
31. (17:09) PAULA: [*inaudible*]
32. (17:09) CINDY: Authentic learning.
33. (17:09) DEAN: I have no idea what YOU would call it to be honest.
34. (17:11) PAULA: [*inaudible*] . . . better than I am.

35. (17:12) CINDY: Is it authentic learning application?
36. (17:13) JANICE: YES! [*throwing her head back to look at Cindy, who starts to laugh*]
37. (17:15) DEAN: Oh yeah we, we talked ALL about that last time. [*Cindy laughing and raising arms*]
38. (17:19) CINDY: Okay, it's authentic instruction.
39. (17:20) DEAN: We were all over that.
40. (17:21) PAULA: So put . . .

IV. The Conflict

IV.1. THE ASSIGNMENT. In the next segment, Dean questions whether using lightning to teach static electricity should be labeled as authentic instruction. Although he might be trying to recover from some lost status due to another student's being reinforced for naming the correct term when he did not, this was also a legitimate question. The tutor responded by suggesting that Dean make *authentic instruction* his learning issue (meaning investigate the term further). In line 45, Dean responds to this assignment with incredulity and an argument erupts in which the tutor repeatedly insists he conduct the research and Dean protests that he has already read and reread material on the Web. Paula supports Dean in lines 47 and 49, indicating that she feels the assignment is unreasonable.

43. (17:22) DEAN: But, talk about lightning (I think) that's authentic? [*pause*] See I wouldn't have thought about that as authentic instruction.
44. (17:28) JANICE: I think that that needs to be YOUR [*indicating Dean with her pen*] learning issue then.
45. (17:32) DEAN: WHAT? [*dropping pen on table*]
46. (17:33) JANICE: I need you, I think you need to investigate authentic learning?
47. (17:36) PAULA: Aw . . .
48. (17:36) DEAN: I've looked on the Web like NINE times.
49. (17:38) PAULA: Yeah.
50. (17:38) JANICE: Can you look somewhere else, can you try to think about why, ah?

IV.2. THE FACE-OFF. In lines 51–53 Paula and Dean offer a joint argument that authentic instruction is not teaching science using real-world examples but teaching through a process that involves real-world activity. Cindy begins to reconcile the two ideas, noting that authentic instruction refers to both. However, the tutor cuts her off in responding to Dean. Noting the tutor's emphasis, pausing, and tone, the analysts concluded that the tutor's response was a reprimand. Noting the nonverbal gestures between Dean and the tutor, one analyst described the scene as "dueling rams." Dean grudgingly concedes, capitulating to the tutor as a way of ending debate rather than agreeing. Following an awkward pause, Bo defuses the situation with a humorous comment.

51. (17:42) DEAN: Well because they're not, going to do . . .
52. (17:43) PAULA: That's not an authentic method that's just, something that happens that they've seen, is what he's saying.
53. (17:47) DEAN: Is that what makes it authentic instr – because my understanding of authentic instruction, it's doing things that REAL people, in the REAL world, would do.
54. (17:53) CINDY: Oh, I think it's both.
55. (17:55) JANICE: So, would REAL people, in the REAL world, LOOK at lightning, and NOT know, what it was!? And would they Wonder. And would it HELP them in any way, to understand, weather, or electricity?
56.   [*long silent pause*]
57. (18:10) DEAN: Yes.
58.   [*silent pause*]
59. (18:13) BO: It would help them to know that if they have a [*brushing head with hand*] whole bunch of electrodes in their head, they should go somewhere else.

Perhaps, all's well that ends well. Immediately after this PBL session the tutor requested a private meeting with Dean, the dominant student. Dean confessed that out of frustration with his previous tutor's lack of guidance during PBL sessions, he was used to taking control. Janice expressed her determination to help Dean see that PBL could be worthwhile, which she believed could be accomplished by providing more structure to the PBL process than Dean had previously encountered. Janice and Dean left the meeting agreeing to work together to include the voices of all other members of the PBL group and make the extensive time and effort necessary for PBL to be "worth it." Nonetheless, this session was challenging and provides an excellent illustration of pitfalls tutors may encounter.

Summary Analysis

This two-minute segment illustrates patterns in conversational styles that reflect the findings of another study (Siegel & Lee, 2001) of the roles played by the members of this PBL group. By analyzing the number of turns, coding the types of utterances, and noting interactions and body language, researchers characterized the participants as:

Dean   Science authority
Cindy   Synthesizer

Paula   Questioner
Lou   Collaborator and questioner
Bo   Peripheral member

Dean acted as and was reacted to as a leader and resource in the group. In another clip from this PBL group, Dean provided the most science answers or declarative statements and asked the least number of questions (Siegel & Lee, 2001). In addition to challenging the tutor, Dean's play on terminology, combined with his sarcasm, intonation, and gestures, suggest resistance to the course content and the instructional format. The resistance was also evident in interviews with Dean in which he described his frustration with PBL due to his experiences with his first PBL group led by a different tutor, and voiced suspicions of learning sciences concepts with regard to their usefulness for teaching. This resistance is important for the tutor to address because a dominant member voices it.

The talk in segment II.2, which follows Cindy's recall, is animated and lively. Members of the group are eager to develop Cindy's idea and begin to suggest specific ways to improve the instruction in accordance with it. Given what appears to be strong group motivation at this point, it is instructive to ask how the social interactions that follow undermined the group's work and what kinds of socio-technical solutions might be possible.

Segment II.2 exposes several patterns of group interaction that could be minimized by an experienced tutor. First, overlapping talk and animated voices illustrate how motivated excitement within a group can create confusion and lack of communication: Dean has an idea but will not get a chance to share it. Bo puts forth an idea that is well received, but he is cut off before having a chance to elaborate and own it. The tutor herself sees an opportunity to connect the conversational topic to an important course concept, but her words also are lost in the confusion.

An important issue, then, is how to recognize and take advantage of conversational confusion, produced by motivated excitement, and manage it toward productive work. For example, one strategy for disentangling conversational threads and insuring that less dominant students get turns is to temporarily establish a speaking order ("OK, let's hear what Bo has to say and get group reactions, then let's hear Dean's idea"). Or, each student might be given a number of tokens representing the number of turns to talk allowed. Students give up a token with each turn and only when all students' tokens are depleted are they redistributed.

Second, the segment highlights a contrast between collaborative versus authoritarian talk in group work: As Cindy shares her pleasure with having learned something about static electricity, Dean jumps in to let her know she is wrong. So another important question is how to encourage collaborative sharing and reduce inappropriate authoritative talk that may reduce motivation and status for some students. Such strategies become a part of an experienced tutor's repertoire, but a system can be designed to achieve these strategies even with inexperienced tutors.

Similarly, segment II.3 illustrates additional patterns of problematic interaction that an experienced tutor or a good system design might alleviate. One is the situation in which a dominant student is claiming or delegating ownership of a good idea that another student has contributed. Appropriate tutorial responses could include such moves as agreeing with the dominant student while giving credit to another ("Right, and we have Bo to thank for bringing that up"). A tutor can also watch for situations in which a dominant and resistant student's expressed beliefs can be used as a basis for building conceptual links and bolstering the validity of course content ("Dean has made a good point. Does anyone other than Dean have an idea about exactly how to connect this idea of atomic models to the lightning thing?")

The goal of the course is to help future teachers acquire learning science concepts and vocabulary as analytical lenses for discussing and thinking about teaching and learning. In segment III, the tutor appropriately notes an opportunity for mentoring students into the learning sciences vocabulary by asking them to focus on and name a course-relevant concept their discursive talk is reflecting. However, analysts agreed that the tutor made a mistake in framing the question, "What would *I* call that?" Analysts noticed as problematic consistent use of the pronouns "I," "we," and "you" to reinforce and exacerbate the in-group/out-group nature of the tutor-student relationship. To maintain camaraderie and avoid emphasizing group membership, the tutor might have asked instead, "What could we call that?" or "What would the cognitive community call that?"

Segment IV illustrates a growing tension between the tutor and Dean. The issue at hand is a valid one, whether the label *authentic instruction* is appropriate for a given application. However, instead of taking advantage of an opportunity to explore cognitive conflict and probe a student's understanding in depth, the tutor engages in the conflict, cutting off discussion and instructing Dean to conduct further research. The assignment is directed to one student in particular and was viewed by another student (line 47) as punitive.

In the process of an escalating social conflict between Dean and the tutor, other students have been left out and ignored. Using conciliatory talk, Cindy tries to reconcile the conflict in line 54. The tutor's response following 54 might have been, "What do you mean, Cindy?" Such a question would have brought another student into the discussion and taken advantage of cognitive conflict and its resolution as a learning opportunity. However, the tutor's actual response to Dean, although instructive, demanded concession.

In evaluating this PBL segment in terms of the KBC model, it is clear that the instructional interaction is less than ideal in several respects. The interaction appears to limit possibilities for developing *authentic instruction* as a community concept. Although the tutor does provide some scaffolding and mentoring in helping this construct develop, the process of negotiating the meaning of this concept among students was cut off at critical moments. An escalating social conflict over classroom control, which occurred between a dominant male science student and the female tutor, a social scientist, appeared to curtail students' efforts to legitimately argue through and resolve a legitimate cognitive conflict about the nature of authentic learning and instruction. Dominance and overlapping talk in conversation sometimes diverted group attention away from important ideas offered by less-dominant students and drastically limited information sharing among students. In fact, one student did not participate at all in this segment, and analyses of other segments of the longer tape verified that this student participated very little throughout the entire unit (Siegel & Lee, 2001).

The previous discussion illuminates an interesting conflict between the design goals of building a spontaneously interacting and self-sustaining community versus facilitating the construction of ideas. Other socio-technical designers have encountered this conflict in online asynchronous discussions (e.g., Cuthbert, Clark, & Linn, 2000). One project's solution was to increase the support for constructing ideas through several types of reflection prompts; however, they left the problem of how to sustain interaction as an open question (Cuthbert et al., 2000).

Designing and Institutional Context

Not all interactions within the course are problematic. Student ratings from this and subsequent semesters indicate that students believe this and similar activities are valuable and relevant to their teaching careers. However, the kinds of conflicts and resistances just illustrated are far from rare in teacher professional development (e.g., Simon, 1992) and in this case, as analysts noted, probably had multiple origins, many grounded in the following institutional contexts.

TAs with minimal training often serve as tutors as part of their own doctoral training. As noted by Steinkuehler, Derry, Hmelo-Silver, and DelMarcelle (2002), the high turnover rate endemic to such positions means that each semester, the course manager may have to start over with a new group of tutors. As is typical, the beginning TA in this case had little teaching experience. Although relative to the student teachers she was advanced in terms of her knowledge of the learning sciences content, she was not versed in the science that was the topic of the case discussion. This situation likely exacerbated a perceived status difference between the pre-service students, all senior-level science majors, and the tutor, a graduate student but still a social scientist. Second, although the students belonged to a cohesive cohort that had worked together for two years, the tutor was a newcomer, an outsider "imposed" upon them along with a third-semester required course. Further, a course in educational foundations that deals with learning theory may not seem useful to students who are concerned with developing practical methods and anxious to get on with the business of actually teaching. Also, these students had previously taken education courses with teacher education professors whose philosophies and approaches may be in conflict with premises of the learning sciences foundations course. This is the pervasive problem of ideational fragmentation in teacher education as discussed by Ball (2000) and others.

We are attempting to engineer a socio-technical solution to many of these problems, although these solutions may appear quite different from those we originally envisioned and proposed. Originally our plan was to bring pre-service teachers together online with instructional staff, disciplinary mentors (subject-matter specialists), and cooperating teachers, to work on instructional projects that would be implemented by student teachers in classrooms. Our vision was that such teams would work together online in a relatively unstructured synchronous discussion environment.

Our reality three years later is that we have created a more structured socio-technical design, including a communications technology, instructional materials, and social activities, to guide student teachers' thinking and help them acquire course content as they work collaboratively to design instruction they will perceive as having immediate and future usefulness. A central part of that design is the STEP pbl[1] System, currently in use by the educational foundations courses at Rutgers University and UW-Madison. This system provides scaffolding to guide individual students and groups through pbl problems, and both training and scaffolding to support the tutoring process and help TAs function as online facilitators. An earlier pilot version of STEP pbl was described in Steinkuehler et al. (2002). The following description of the substantially revised system that is currently in use at UW-Madison and Rutgers University is taken from Derry and the STEP Team (in press), a source that also provides a theory-based discussion of the design of the full STEP environment, including the case library and online hypertext book, which

---

[1] We use PBL to refer to the Problem-Based Learning technique originally designed by Barrows (1988); we use "pbl" (all lowercase letters) to refer to the modified version of problem-based learning used by STEP. We maintain this distinction throughout our work in order to acknowledge the fact that we have modified the procedure and employ online *asynchronous* discussions whereas Barrows specifies that such discussions should always occur synchronously.

together comprise the STEP Knowledge Web (KWeb) that is integrated with STEP pbl.

THE STEP pbl SYSTEM

The STEP pbl system scaffolds online instruction in which students deepen their understanding of learning sciences as they work collaboratively, or collaboratively share and discuss individual work, on various types of problems. Course managers can create new problems and customize the system in various ways to meet various instructional needs. The system is described here using an instructional design challenge that was created for mathematics majors in the fall 2002, learning sciences course at UW-Madison. This example is a prototype but it illustrates only one of many possible forms that STEP pbl instruction can take.

Several years ago, PBL was introduced into the STEP course as a face-to-face small-group method that was practiced once a week in the classroom. It was introduced simultaneously with the STEP KWeb (which did not at that time have a site supporting online problem-based learning). PBL presented cases of instruction to be improved, and the instructional design projects lasted several weeks. Between classes, students conducted research using the STEP website and other resources. The group that we described previously in this chapter consisted of five science education majors and their tutor, one of the earliest PBL groups in the course. Our studies of this group and our observations of the STEP course as a whole led us to conclude that PBL is a difficult instructional method, unlike any that most people have experienced. The facilitation of PBL is important to its success and the unseasoned TAs who served as facilitators for PBL groups struggle with it. Student teachers are often initially resistant to the unfamiliar method, and there are larger institutional and program contexts that make it likely that conflicts will arise. PBL is also resource intensive since one trained, preferably experienced, facilitator is required for every 7–10 students. In large courses, tutors must monitor multiple groups. This is a substantial burden for TAs, but we felt this was a problem that might be addressed through technology.

Hence we created and added to our website the STEP pbl system for online support of problem-based learning. The STEP pbl system is a collaborative environment that is integrated with other eSTEPWeb.org resources. The STEP pbl system supports either online small-group instruction or a hybrid model in which students meet face-to-face in small groups during class and then extend their work outside of class through online interaction. In both online and hybrid models, students are guided by a human facilitator, typically a teaching assistant, and are required to complete and submit individual and group artifacts, typically products related to and documenting various stages of instructional design, through the online system. The online system collects and displays data on student performance and affords detailed monitoring of work by individuals and small groups, permitting detailed (and powerful) formative assessment of individuals and groups throughout the course.

Although they can be set up in different ways by the course manager, most STEP pbl activities so far have included a phase of individual study and preparation, followed by a phase of facilitated small-group design work, followed by a final phase in which the individual analyzes, extends, and reflects upon the group's work and how much the individual gained from it. The online environment guides students through a series of steps. The number of steps and required activities for each step may vary from problem to problem, as desired by the course manager/designer. Here we describe one of the activities created for the fall 2002 course at UW-Madison, which took students through a four-week, nine-step design challenge. This example was the second online activity completed by the mathematics majors. Pbl problems customized to specific disciplines were also assigned to students in secondary science, English, social studies, and foreign language.

When students entered the STEP pbl system to start their design challenge, they saw a "sidewalk" with nine steps, each step associated with a particular due date for completion (Figure 10.2). Each student began the task by mouse clicking on step 1, which opened a page of instructions and a design problem appropriate to that student's academic teacher certification area. The design problem for mathematics majors, Bridging Instruction in Mathematics, is shown in the appendix at the end of this chapter, titled, Bridging Instruction in Mathematics – Problem Statement. Previously, each student had been assigned to a small discipline-based work group that was maintained in this problem activity and throughout the course.

Like design problems for other disciplines, the mathematics problem referenced and linked to a particular video case in the STEP video library, a classroom story that students were asked to analyze in preparation for their design work. Students were asked to draw lessons and ideas from the case under study and then apply those lessons and ideas by working with their group to design or redesign a similar type of instruction. All design problems for all disciplines required students to warrant their instructional designs through learning science research. This research was facilitated by availability of the STEP KWeb, the online hypertext book (Figure 10.3) of learning sciences concepts and library of classroom video cases (Figure 10.4), which is integrated with the STEP pbl system.

Pbl activities in the fall 2002, UW-Madison course required students to apply a process of "backward design" leading to the creation of a "group product," a plan for an instructional unit. The unit to be developed in the mathematics teachers' groups (see their problem) was to employ an approach based on bridging instruction (e.g., Nathan & Koedinger, 2000)

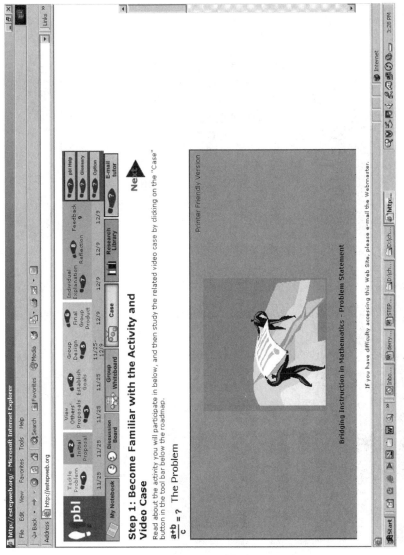

FIGURE 10.2. STEP pbl system interface

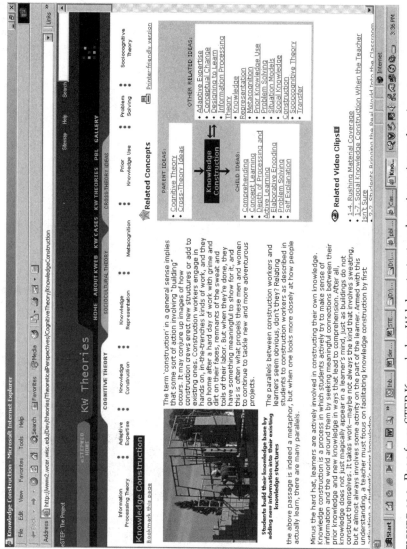

FIGURE 10.3. Page from STEP Knowledge Web hyptertext on learning science theories

280

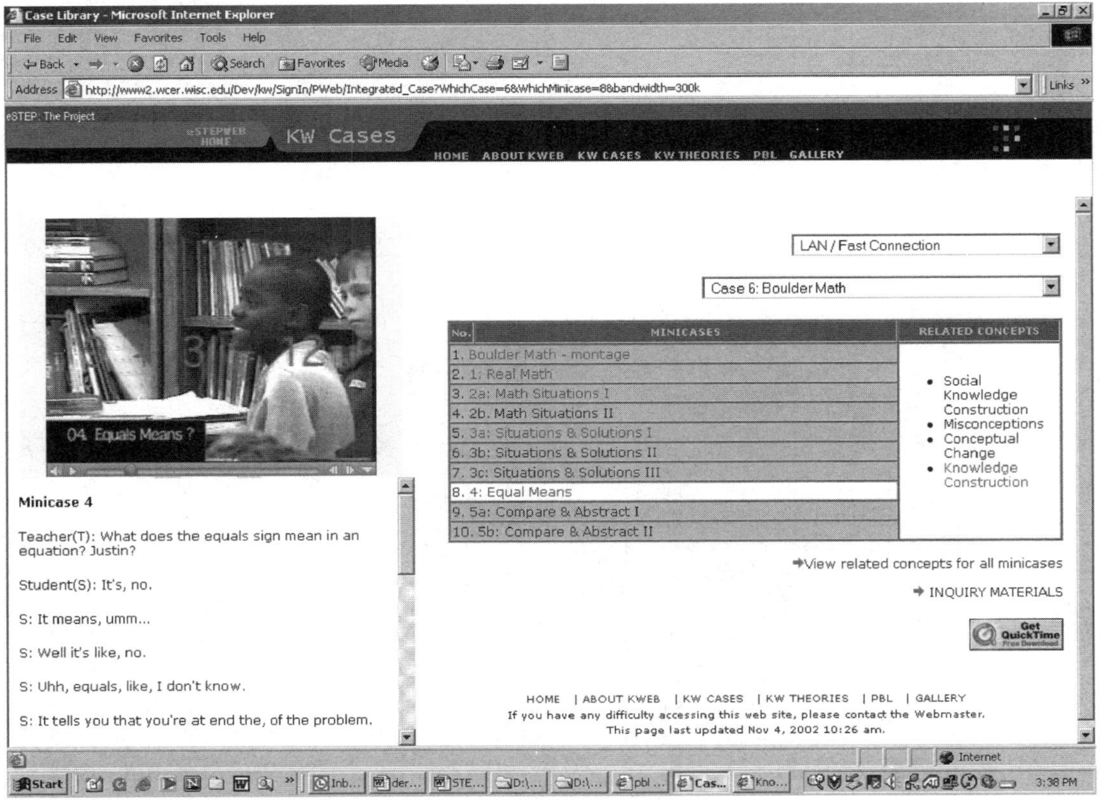

FIGURE 10.4. Page from STEP case library

in which teachers employ students' prior knowledge to help them create a mathematical situational model prior to developing a solution equation (the approach used in the video case the students were required to study). Students learned about backward design through readings in the KWeb and an assigned text. Adhering to the steps in their pbl "sidewalk," students first completed their reading assignments and studied their case, entering their thoughts and reflections about the case into an online notebook (see Figure 10.5). After completing initial assignments by the due date, students were at step 3, where they viewed each others' preliminary work and then joined their group of 4–5 other students online and began working together to plan an instructional unit. Groups were allowed to choose whether to work online at all times or to supplement online work with face-to-face meetings during class. Most groups continued to meet face-to-face, at least occasionally.

During the instructional design phase in steps 4–6, the pre-service teachers were scaffolded, by the system and by a tutor, through a group process in which they first decided upon what "enduring understandings" their unit would teach. Next, they developed ideas for how they would assess their students, to determine whether goals for understanding were being acquired. Finally, they worked together to design goal-related instructional activities. Each step in the process involved submission and discussion of the various teacher-learners' ideas for goals, assessments, and activities. Ideas were refined online through discussion and voting, with ideas receiving strongest group support becoming part of the final group product. Group activity was supported online by a group whiteboard (Figure 10.6 shows the whiteboard for a mathematics group viewed through the tutor's interface) and a supplementary discussion board. As shown in Figure 10.6, the whiteboard contained sections (marked by "tabs") for each stage of the group's work. For example, during the design-of-assessments stage, the group members worked within the assessment tab of the group whiteboard. During each major phase of the group activity, such as the assessment or activities design phases, students entered their "proposals" for what the group's design should include, plus a justification for their proposals, onto the group whiteboard. Students also used the group whiteboard to view and comment on others' proposals and justifications, read comments about their own proposals made by group members or the tutor, and modify their own proposals in response to feedback. Students controlled what the system put into their final product with a voting mechanism through which proposals receiving group support were automatically included in a group product that could be viewed by clicking on step 6. Upon finishing the group product – a justified plan for an instructional unit specifying goals, assessments, and activities – individual students completed steps 7–9 individually. In step 7 individual students wrote their own critique and analysis of the group product.

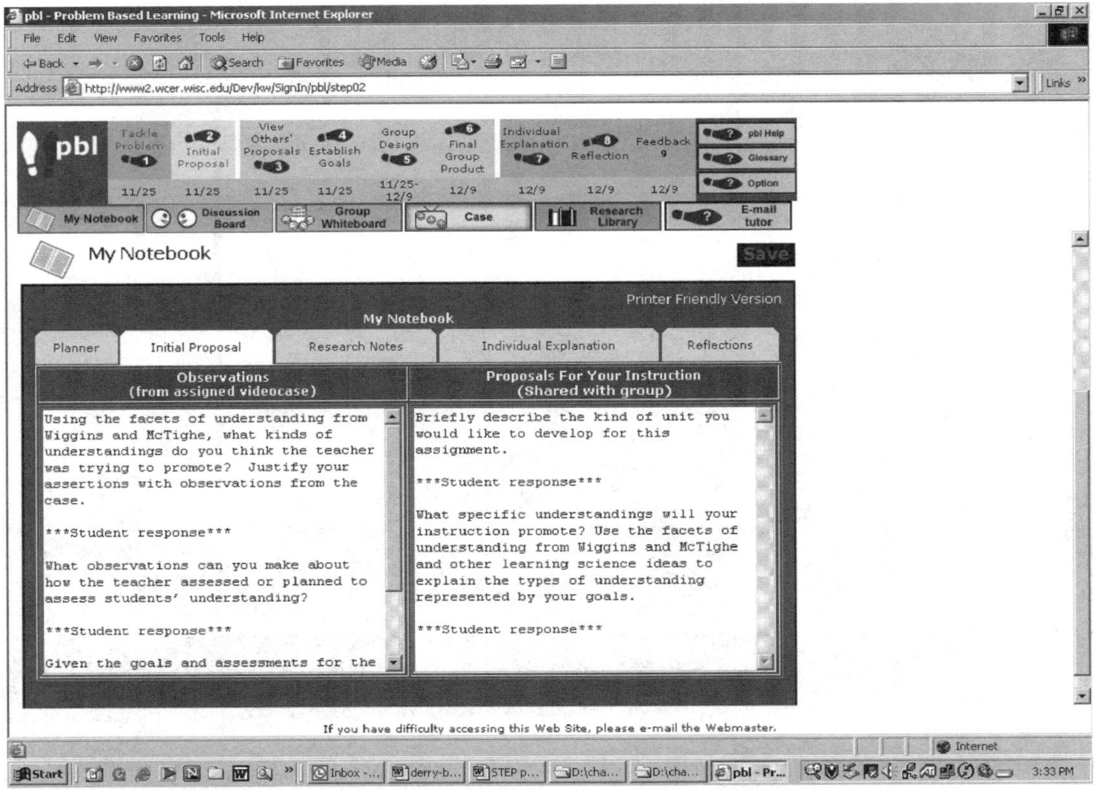

FIGURE 10.5. STEP pbl student online notebook

283

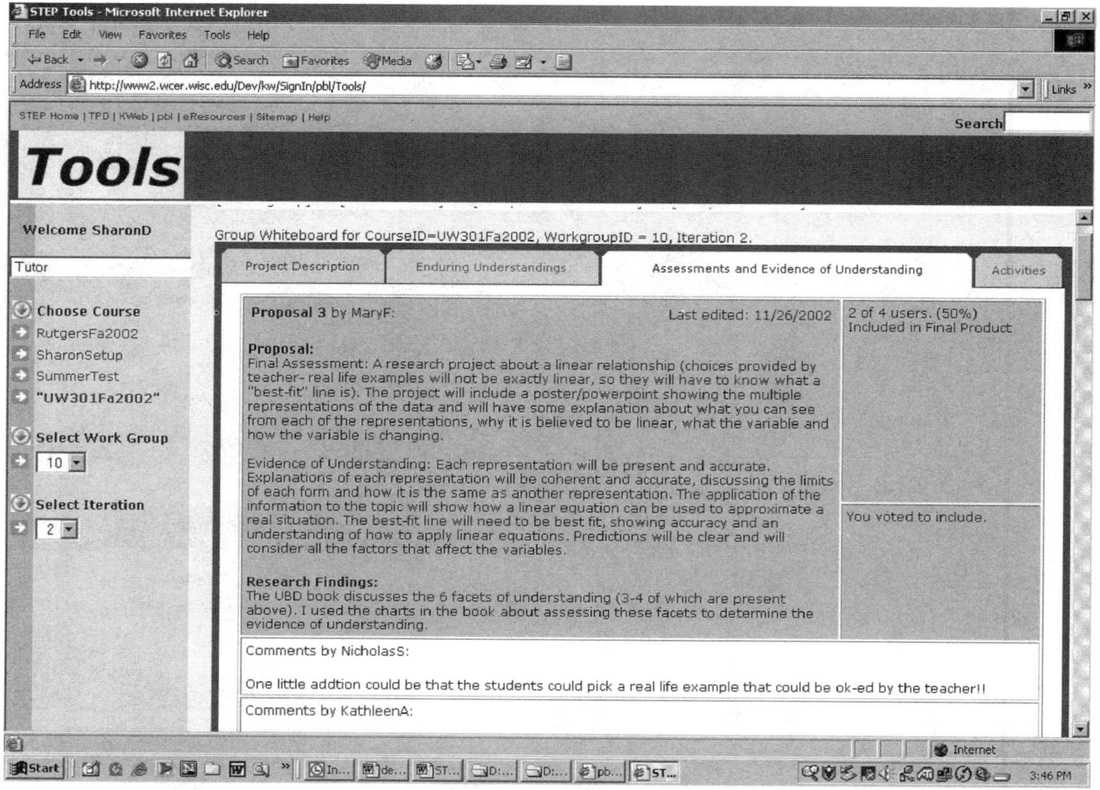

FIGURE 10.6. STEP pbl tutor interface showing group whiteboard with student work

In step 8 students reflected on their learning, and in step 9 provided anonymous feedback on the activity and site. The tutor monitored and provided technical and conceptual assistance during every step in the activity.

Thus, the group whiteboard, as set up for this activity, required students to design an instructional unit, thinking about assessments and activities in a certain order and in terms of how they would lead to the enduring understandings that the group had established as their instructional goals. The STEP pbl is a general tool that allows course managers to change these requirements by altering the number of tabs, tab headings, and instructions to learners within each tab.

A TA facilitated all steps online. Each TA in the fall course managed four small groups of about five or six students each. An online tutoring tool that permitted monitoring of each group and individual facilitated the TA's task. The tutoring tool provided instructions and assistance for tutors, including a history of advice from previous tutors. As previously noted, the screen shot in Figure 10.6 is taken from the tutor's tool and illustrates how a tutor accesses and participates in group work through the tool's interface.

Student Ratings of STEP pbl Activities and Site Tools

Students in the fall UW-Madison course participated in two instructional design pbl activities, similar to the one just described. Based on a class size of 60 and a response rate of about 97 percent, ratings of components of the two pbl activities and the system tools used during the pbl activities indicated that they were valued and generally well received. Several patterns in these responses were observed. First, from pbl-1 to pbl-2, there was a substantial increase in student satisfaction. This is likely due to a number of factors, including student and TA experience with the method and system, as well as the use of discipline-specific cases and problems in pbl-2 (rather than the generic instructional design scenario grounded in a case on design-based instruction in a science class, which was employed in pbl-1). Also, it is notable that the most rewarding activities for students were those involving collaboration rather than individual work. Also, a highly rated tool was the hypertext and case-based information resource, the STEP KWeb. A sample of student ratings of the instruction and system, aggregated by disciplinary group, is provided in Table 10.1. Although all ratings were generally positive, these ratings indicate that not all disciplinary groups were equally well served, an issue to be investigated further.

That students perceived the activity as useful is indicated by the following "anonymous" assessments that were made in response to the question, "How will you use what you have learned in your future teaching practice?" Two characteristic responses are supplied for each discipline.

TABLE 10.1. *Sample of Student Ratings of Two STEP pbl Experiences by Discipline*

	Time 1	Time 2
How much did you learn from pbl activity overall (1 = Nothing – 5 = A Lot)?		
English ($n = 8$)	3.75	4.5
Language ($n = 5.5$)	4.0	4.36
Math ($n = 12.5$)	3.8	3.9
Science ($n = 12.5$)	3.8	4.6
Social Studies ($n = 11$)	3.7	4.6
How much did you learn from the group design steps (1 = Nothing – 5 = A Lot)?		
English ($n = 11$)	3.9	4.5
Language ($n = 5.5$)	4.4	4.7
Math ($n = 14$)	3.57	4.4
Science ($n = 13.5$)	4.1	4.5
Social Studies ($n = 14$)	4.1	4.1
How well did the Knowledge Web work for you (1 = Very poorly – 5 = Very Well)?		
English ($n = 11$)	4.1	4.8
Language ($n = 5.5$)	4.6	4.3
Math ($n = 14$)	4.2	4.4
Science ($n = 13.5$)	4.4	4.6
Social Studies ($n = 12.5$)	4.3	4.2

English

I will make it a goal to utilize this method in designing curriculum for my classes.

I will definitely use aspects of backward design in my planning. I find myself now in designing courses for next semester thinking about enduring understandings and assessments before I jump into planning activities throughout the course . . . I will also take away conscious choices a teacher has to make when teaching controversial topics. Censorship and getting into trouble over a book seemed in far-away school districts until this activity.

Social Studies

I would use the unit itself. It was a good final product. I would also use this method of creating lesson plans.

I found this process an exciting way to design lessons. It held me, as a teacher, to a high standard to justify lesson plans and choose the most important understandings in a topic.

Foreign Language

I would definitely like to use this unit when I teach, as well as the different assessments and activities that my group came up with. It is really nice to see others' viewpoints on the same unit because you are able to see different perspectives that can give you some new and different ideas.

The plan that we made up as a group will be extremely useful for me as a teacher. I also learned the value of input from others and how it can help you design a unit. I also learned how time-consuming planning a unit can be.

Science

I will try to use this process of developing lessons. I will also consult other teachers when developing a lesson to try and incorporate multiple ideas.

I will be sure to cover these areas thoroughly with other teachers involved in designing a lesson as well as using my colleagues for feedback. There were several ideas I had that they said, "no, that won't work because . . ." and they were reasons I had never thought of.

Mathematics

Well, this lesson we have designed as a group is definitely something I could see myself using down the road when I have my own classroom. I feel it is a well thought out lesson that can be easily modified to meet the needs of whatever type of class "make-up" I may have.

I will attempt to use this method when creating lesson plans for next semester. I think it is a valid model that helps the teacher keep objectives clear and plan meaningful activities which cater to the objectives.

CONCLUDING COMMENTS

Many researchers (Ball, 2000; Wideen, Mayer-Smith, & Moon, 1998) have argued that divisions among departments, schools, and courses are creating a structural fragmentation (Wideen et al., 1998, p. 161) within teacher education programs. Ball (2000) suggested that the fragmentation appears in the prevailing curriculum of teacher education by imparting knowledge in different domains, such as educational psychology, sociology of education, foundations, methods of teaching, and the subject matter disciplinary knowledge. She suggested that this kind of fragmentation creates a difficult challenge for beginning teachers, who must integrate disparate or conflicting pieces of knowledge into the contexts of classroom practice. There are also conflicting messages (Borko & Putnam, 1996) that confuse novice teachers because their practicum and student teaching experiences may be very different from approaches advocated in the teacher education programs.

Also, pre-service teachers' learning experiences are affected by their beliefs that they bring with them from personal life experience, schooling, instructional experience, and formal knowledge experience (Richardson, 1996). Because these beliefs are a collection of influences in the life of teachers, beliefs act as filters (Borko & Putnam, 1996; Wideen et al., 1998, p. 145; Richardson, 1996). One common belief held by entering pre-service teachers is that experience is the best teacher (Richardson, 1996, p. 108). The receptivity of the student teachers to the knowledge that teacher educators wish to impart in the teacher education program depends very much on how these prior beliefs are addressed. Many studies on teaching interventions, such as the Second-Grade Mathematics project by Paul Cobb et al. and the Cognitively Guided Instruction project by Thomas Carpenter et al., have shown that the way teachers teach and learn depends on whether their beliefs are confronted in ways that allow for change to take place (Borko & Putnam, 1996). Beliefs should be surfaced and acknowledged during teacher education programs if programs are to make a difference in the deep structure of knowledge and beliefs held by the students (Richardson, 1996).

The challenge for teacher education thus goes beyond imparting a knowledge base that is, at best, uncertain, to fostering a discourse that incorporates the preconceptions and varied interests and messages that affect how student teachers view and learn from their teacher education programs. This is a difficult instructional design problem, particularly in the context of large university programs that may provide a supporting environment in some ways, but also must deal with problems of departmental fragmentation, limited resources, placing responsibility on relatively inexperienced teaching assistants, substantial turnover among instructional staff, overloaded senior faculty, and social conflicts created by personalities, status differences, and institutional contexts.

We have described our recent attempts to address some of these problems through design of a socio-technical environment for shaping group interactions so that they are in greater accord with a KBC model of learning, which encourages diverse viewpoints and mentored work activities that involve interaction among those viewpoints. We began with a more ambitious vision for a larger, more cohesive online community, but this vision could not be immediately realized, largely because the change required to achieve it would be too great and would involve overcoming many socially and historically rooted forces of resistance. We scaled back to a more modest goal, to create a model for that part of the curriculum in which learning sciences are infused into the teacher education program. Our approach engages small groups of students in mentored problem-based learning activities that involve analysis and design of learning environments.

Prior to the online version of STEP pbl, PBL activities took place in classrooms. We studied discourse in these classrooms in conjunction with considering the program's broader social contexts and their possible reflection in classroom discourse. We observed that many pedagogical demands are placed on relatively untrained and inexperienced TAs. Various contextual issues, such as conflicting voices and goals and discipline-based status differences within the program, exacerbate the difficulty of a TA's position. It is not surprising that conflict occurs and that a TA might have trouble managing it. Moreover, large-course implementation requires that TAs manage several pbl groups at once. We concluded that an online approach to the course might alleviate many of these problems. Our design provides a structured and supportive environment for facilitated, online problem-based learning. Because students investigate and discuss learning sciences in the context of design problems, they have the opportunity to socially construct knowledge about learning sciences and integrate it with other points of view as they work on authentic instructional tasks that are perceived as meaningful. The instructional design problem for us is how to scaffold and support social knowledge construction through system design. The evolving solution is the STEP pbl system reported here.

Did our original vision fail? Definitely not. Consistent with other accounts in this volume (Barab, MaKinster, & Scheckler, this volume; Schlager & Fusco, this volume), our greatest error was the naïve idea that we could pull one already-complex community into the shape of a newly envisioned complex community, in one fell swoop. Designing a knowledge-building community requires support and active participation from many people, and the altering of many ingrained habits, communication channels, and beliefs. Bringing these changes about is an evolutionary process. It takes time, and substantial grant money helps. Socio-technical communities evolve simultaneously as social systems and interwoven technologies. STEP is at an intermediate stage of its evolution. Cooperating teachers are not yet real members of the STEP community, but there are important roles for teachers in the structure we have designed and we will soon be ready to actively court their participation. The STEP pbl system currently serves only one type of foundations course, but we are organizing projects involving cross-course use of STEP resources in vertical and horizontal curriculum integration. For example, we are now developing cases for joint, coordinated use in methods, psychology, and diversity courses. So the original vision is not lost; in many ways we are slowly moving toward it. Through our work we will continually develop and integrate the STEP pbl system so that it becomes part of and facilitates the evolution of our existing community.

APPENDIX: BRIDGING INSTRUCTION IN MATHEMATICS – PROBLEM STATEMENT

Bridging instruction in mathematics means utilizing students' informal strategies and understandings to make sense of more formal mathematical

Basketball Problem: A Dad and his four daughters went to a sporting goods store to look for a basketball. The daughters wanted to purchase a basketball for $42. The Dad said he would pay $18, but that the daughters would need to pay for the remaining cost. If the daughters pay for the rest, how much does each daughter need to contribute for her share?	
Situation Equation	**Solution Equation**
(4 X D) + $18 == $42 D = Amount of money each daughter pays	($42 - $18)/4 = $6

FIGURE 10.7. STEP pbl problem for mathematics

strategies and representations. The classroom depicted in this video case (Case 6: Boulder Math) is an example of an effort to implement this concept of bridging to help sixth grade students make the transition from arithmetic to algebraic types of reasoning that will be critical to their success in pre-algebra and algebra classes in middle and high school. The case includes video taken from five class sessions, although the organization of the cases is largely thematic as opposed to sequential. The teacher in this case worked closely with Dr. Mitchell Nathan in the development, implementation, and recording of these lessons. The lessons revolve around the class's efforts over several class periods to solve word problems, many of which were authored by students in the class. An example problem is shown in Figure 10.7.

Students at this level of development are often able to arrive at "the answer" to this type of question through strategies such as unwinding (see Nathan/Koedinger articles in the case's Inquiry Materials for a more thorough explanation of student strategies). In the basketball problem students will often start with the total cost of the basketball, $42, and "unwind" or work backward until they reach a solution. They might say, "If the basketball costs $42 and Dad gives me $18, then we can subtract 18 from 42 and we only need to pay $24. Since there are four of us, we will divide 24 by 4 and each pay $6." These operations are then depicted in the solution equation column. What the teacher is trying to do with these problems is help students represent the situation using an algebraic model that doesn't yet answer the question. So she tries to help them create a mathematical description of the situation, shown in the situation column, and uses various methods to accomplish this, including having them develop and act out skits of the situation for the class. On several occasions she even films (only briefly depicted in this case) these skits, so that students are able to reflect on what occurred as it relates to the mathematical representations of the situation. Once they have developed these two representations of the problem, situation, and solution equations, she asks them to examine the structure of these two mathematical sentences to see how they are related. In this way they can "bridge" the relationship between their representation and strategies from the solution equation, and the target representation depicted by the situation equation.

From a learning sciences perspective this case has many interesting facets as well. Bridging curriculum begins with what the students already know how to do and attempts to build on their prior knowledge and representations. This case also demonstrates various methods and tools for involving students in their learning and building on their contributions, including using problems they authored as part of the instruction. The teacher uses these problems in interesting ways, revisiting previously solved problems on several occasions to draw out new relationships. Another point of interest is the fact that this teacher was working hand-in-hand with researchers who are experts in both the subject domains of algebra learning/teaching and the learning sciences, who were trying to apply what they had discovered about student and teacher strategies into an actual classroom.

This case revolves around the class's interaction with various word problems. Of particular interest are students' efforts to move from informal strategies depicted in the result-unknown solution equations to more symbolic beginning-unknown representations of the problem in the situation equations, and their understanding of the relationships between the two. In order to get the most from this case, it is highly recommended that you review the math problem index in the inquiry materials and become familiar with the problem statements and situation and solution equations so that you can better understand the students' activities.

Your Task

After studying the video case, your group's task is to design its own bridging instruction unit, where the objective is to identify and incorporate students' informal strategies into the target strategies and representations of your unit. You may choose to redesign the unit depicted in this case, or to use it as a model to design a unit on a topic of interest to you. As you watch the video try to answer the following questions:

> What do you think the teacher is trying to accomplish?
> Why is she doing what she is doing?
> How useful are the activities?
> How would you build on what seems to be working?
> What changes would you make and why?

What instructional activities would you include?

What types of assessments would you use to evaluate your own teaching and your students' progress?

To answer these questions and complete your design assignment you will need to become familiar with the problems described in the inquiry materials, read the articles by Nathan and Koedinger on teachers' and students' understandings of the development of algebraic reasoning, and investigate the learning science concepts listed within each minicase. Your group will then need to determine whether they want to redesign the unit depicted in this case, or apply the principles and methods from this case to a related unit of interest. Once this is decided, the group should evaluate the case together and identify their target enduring understandings (see Wiggins and McTighe textbook) they want from their unit. Following these decisions, your group will generate and develop proposals for assessments and instructional activities that will support the enduring understandings. These are the only real parameters of the activity. It is up to the group to make any other design decisions that aren't specified here. ***Good Luck!!***

References

Atkinson, J. M., & Heritage, J. (1984). *Structures of social action: Studies in conversation analysis.* Cambridge: Cambridge University Press.

Ball, D. (2000). Bridging practices: Intertwining content and pedagogy in teaching and learning to teach. *Journal of Teacher Education, 51,* 241–247.

Barab, S., Moore, J., Cunningham, D., and the ILF Design Team. (April, 2000). The Internet learning forum: A new model for online professional development. Paper presented at the 2000 Annual Meeting of the Americana Educational Research Association, New Orleans, LA.

Barrows, H. (1988). *The tutorial process.* Springfield: Southern Illinois University Press.

Bell, P., & Linn, M. C. (2000). Scientific arguments as learning artifacts: Designing for learning from the web with KIE. *International Journal of Science Education, 22*(8), 797–817.

Borko, H., & Putnam, R. (1996). Learning to teach. In R. Calfee & D. Berliner (Eds.), *Handbook of Educational Psychology* (pp. 673–725). New York: Macmillan.

Cuthbert, A. J., Clark, D. B., and Linn, M. C. (2002). WISE Learning communities: Design considerations. In K. A. Renninger & W. Shumar (Eds.), *Building virtual communities: learning and change in cyberspace* (pp. 215–248). Cambridge, U.K.: Cambridge University Press.

Derry, S. J., Gance, S., Gance, L. L., & Schlager, M. (2000). Toward assessment of knowledge building practices in technology-mediated work group interactions. In S. P. Lajoie. *Computers as cognitive tools volume two: No more walls* (pp. 3–29). Mahwah, NJ: Erlbaum.

Derry, S. J., Seymour, J., Feltovich, P., & Fassnacht, C. (2001 May). Tutoring and knowledge construction during problem-based learning: An interaction analysis.

Paper presented at the Annual Conference, National Association for Research in Science Teaching (NARST), St. Louis, MO.

Derry, S. J., & the STEP Team (in press). STEP as a case of theory-based web course design. To appear in A. O'Donnell & Cindy Hmelo-Silver (Eds). *Collaboration, reasoning and technology*. Mahwah, NJ: Erlbaum.

DuFour, R., & Eaker, R. (1998). *Professional learning communities at work: Best practices for enhancing student achievement*. Bloomington, IN: National Educational Service.

DuRussel, L., & Derry, S. J. (1998 May). Mental models in educational research teams. Poster presented at the 1998 American Educational Research Association Conference in San Diego, CA.

Feltovich, P., Spiro, R., Coulson, R., & Feltovich, J. (1996). Collaboration within and among minds: Mastering complexity, individually and in groups. In T. Koschmann (Ed.), *CSCL: Theory and practice of an emerging paradigm* (pp. 25–44). Hillsdale, NJ: Erlbaum.

Frederiksen, J. (1999, November). *Supporting professional development and improving practice using video case examples of classroom practices collected for that purpose*. Paper presented at the meeting of the Board on International Comparative Studies in Education, National Academy of Sciences invitational meeting, Washington, DC.

Glenn, P. J., Koschmann, T., & Conlee, M. (1999). Theory presentation and assessment in a problem-based learning group. *Discourse Processes*, 27(2), 119–133.

Greeno, J. G. (1998). The situativity of knowing, learning, and research. *American Psychologist*, 53(1), 5–26.

Halpern, D. F. (1996). *Thought and knowledge*. 3rd ed. Mahwah, NJ: Erlbaum.

Henze, N., Nejdl, W., & Wolpers, M. (1999). Modeling constructivist teaching functionality and structure in the KBS Hyperbook System. In D. Hoadley & J. Roschelle (Eds.), *Proceedings of the Computer Support for Collaborative Learning (CSCL) 1999 Conference*, (pp. 223–231). Mahwah, NJ: Erlbaum.

Hinsz, V. B., Tindale, R. S., & Vollrath, D. A. (1997). The emerging conceptualization of groups as information processors. *Psychological Bulletin, 121*, 43–64.

Jordan, B., & Henderson, A. (1995). Interaction analysis: Foundations and practice. *Journal of the Learning Sciences*, 4, 39–104.

Kuhn, D. (1991). *The skills of argument*. Cambridge: Cambridge University Press.

Lave, J., & Wenger, E. (1991). *Situated learning: Legitimate peripheral participation*. Cambridge: Cambridge University Press.

Lewis, C. C., & Tsuchida, I. (1998). A lesson is like a swiftly flowing river: How research lessons improve Japanese education. *American Educator*, Winter: 12, 23–32.

Little, J. W. (1993). Teachers' professional development in a climate of educational reform. *Educational Evaluation and Policy Analysis*, 15, 2, 129–151.

Loucks-Horsley, S., Hewson, P. W., Love, N., & Stiles, K. E. (1998). *Designing professional development for teachers of science and mathematics*. Thousand Oaks, CA: Corwin Press.

Nathan, M. J., & Koedinger, K. R. (2000). Moving beyond teachers' intuitive beliefs about algebra learning. *Mathematics Teacher*, v93 March, 218–223.

Norris, J. H. (1994). What leaders need to know about school culture. *Journal of Staff Development*, 15, 2, 2–5.

O'Donnell, A. M., DuRussel, L. A., & Derry, S. J. (1997). *Cognitive processes in interdisciplinary groups: Problems and possibilities* (Research Monograph No. 5). Madison: University of Wisconsin-Madison, National Institute for Science Education.

O'Donnell, A. M., & King, A. (Eds.). (2000). *Cognitive perspectives on peer learning.* Mahwah, NJ: Erlbaum.

Orasanu, J., & Salas, E. (1993). Team decision making in complex environments. In G. A. Klein, J. Orasanu, R. Calderwood, & C. E. Zsambok (Eds.), *Decision making in action: Models and methods* (112–136). Norwood, NJ: Ablex Publishing.

Ranney, M., Adams, S., Siegel, M., & Brem, S. (1999). Reasoning about the environment: Prototypical cases and their educational implications. *Fifth Conference on environmental education.* Zurich, Switzerland.

Resnick, L. B., Salmon, M., Zeitz, C. M., Wathen, S. H., & Holowchak, M. (1993). Reasoning in conversation. *Cognition and Instruction, 11*(3&4), 347–364.

Resta, P., Christal, M., Ferneding, K., & Puthoff, A. K. (1999). CSCL as a catalyst for changing teacher practice. In C. Hoadley & J. Roschelle (Eds.), *Proceedings of the Computer Support for Collaborative Learning (CSCL) 1999 conference* (pp. 488–494). Mahwah, NJ: Erlbaum.

Richardson, V. (1996). The roles of attitudes and beliefs in learning to teach. In J. Sikula (Ed.), *Handbook of research on teacher education* (pp. 102–119). New York: Macmillan.

Sarason, S. (1996). *Revisiting the culture of school and the problem of change.* New York: Teachers' College Press.

Siegel, M. A. (1999). Changes in student decisions with *Convince Me*: Using evidence and making tradeoffs. In *Proceedings of the twenty first annual conference of the Cognitive Science Society,* (671–676). Mahwah, NJ: Erlbaum.

Siegel, M. A., & Lee, J. A. C. (2001 May). "But electricity isn't static": Science discussion, identification of learning issues, and use of resources in a problem-based learning education course. Paper presented at the Annual meeting of the National Association for Research in Science Teaching, St. Louis, MO.

Simon, R. L. (1992). *Teaching against the grain. Texts for a pedagogy of possibility.* New York: Greenwood Publishing Group.

Smith, J. (1994). *Collective intelligence in computer-based collaborations.* Hillsdale, NJ: Erlbaum.

Steinkuehlker, C. A. (2001 May). The quality of preservice science teachers' social argumentative reasoning. Paper presented at annual conference of the 2001 National Association for Research in Science Teaching, St. Louis, MO.

Steinkuehler, C. A., Derry, S. J., Hmelo-Silver, C., & DelMarcelle, J. (2002). Cracking the resource nut with distributed problem based learning in secondary teacher education. *Distance Education, 23,* 23–39.

The STEP Project Group* (2000). Promoting teachers' flexible use of the learning sciences through case-based problem solving on the WWW: A theoretical design approach. In B. Fishman & S. O'Connor-Divelbiss (Eds.), *Proceedings of the Fourth International Conference of the Learning Sciences* (pp. 273–279). Mahwah, NJ: Erlbaum. (*Siegel, M., Derry, S., Kim, J., Steinkuehler, C., Street, J., Canty, N., Fassnacht, C., Hewson, K., Hmelo, C., & Spiro, R.)

Stigler, J. W., & Hiebert, J. (1999). *The teaching gap.* New York: Free Press.

Tannen, D. (1990). *You just don't understand.* New York: Ballantine Books.

Watson, J. R., Swain, J. R. L., & McRobbie, C. (2001). Students' discussions in practical scientific inquiries. In J. V. Wertsch. *Voices of the mind: A sociocultural approach to mediated action* (pp. 91–113). Cambridge, MA: Harvard University Press.

Wenger, E. (1999). *Communities of practice: Learning, meaning and identity.* Cambridge: Cambridge University Press.

Wertsch, J. V. (1991). *Voices of the mind: A sociocultural approach to mediated action.* Cambridge, MA: Harvard University Press.

Wideen, M., Mayer-Smith, J., & Moon, B. (1998). A critical analysis of the research on learning to teach: Making the case for an ecological perspective on inquiry. *Review of Educational Research, 68*(2), 130–178.

PART IV

RESEARCHING ONLINE COMMUNITY

11

Scholarly Networks as Learning Communities

The Case of TechNet

Emmanuel F. Koku and Barry Wellman

WIRING SCHOLARLY NETWORKS

Rapid developments in computer-mediated communication are associated with a paradigm shift in the ways in which institutions and people are connected. This is a shift from being bound up in small groups to surfing life through diffuse, variegated social networks. Although the transformation began in the pre–Internet 1960s, the proliferation of the Internet both reflects and facilitates the shift.

Much social organization no longer fits a group-centric model of society. Work, community, and domesticity have moved from hierarchically arranged, densely knit, bounded groups to social networks. In networked societies, boundaries are more permeable, interactions are with diverse others, linkages switch between multiple networks, and hierarchies are flatter and more recursive. People maneuver through multiple communities, no longer bounded by locality. They form complex networks of alliances and exchanges, often in transient virtual or networked organizations (Bar & Simard, 2001). Workers – especially professionals, technical workers, and managers – report to multiple peers and superiors. Work relations spill over their nominal work group's boundaries and may even connect them to outside organizations. In virtual and networked organizations, management

Our research has been supported by the Bell University Laboratories, the Social Science and Humanities Research Council of Canada, and Daniel Keating's grant from the Telelearning National Centre of Excellence. Ronald Baecker, Gale Moore, and Nancy Nazer gave much good advice. H. Russell Bernard, Kathleen Carley, Noshir Contractor, Laura Garton, Caroline Haythornthwaite, Charles Kadushin, Ronald Rice, Thomas Schott, and David Tindall gave useful pretest advice on our interview schedule. Kristine Klement and Nadia Bello coded much of the data. The Centre for Urban and Community Studies has been a supportive home for our research. Most of all, we deeply appreciate the time and interest that the members of TechNet gave to us. We dedicate this chapter to Ronald Baecker, a pioneering guide in computer-mediated communication.

by network has people reporting to shifting sets of supervisors, peers, and even nominal subordinates (Wellman, 2001).

How people learn is becoming part of this paradigm shift. There has been some movement away from traditional classroom-based, location-specific instruction to online, virtual classrooms. There has also been some movement away from teacher-centered models of learning to student-centered models and flatter hierarchical relations. Physically dispersed learning is part of this shift. It has moved beyond traditional many-to-teacher correspondence and educational television courses to computer-supported many-to-many learning. Even before the development of the Internet, text-based computerized communication supported communication and collaboration among physically dispersed scholars (Finholt, 2001; Finholt, Sproull, & Kiesler, 2002). This is now being joined by online audiovisual technologies supporting collaborative work (Ragusa & Bochenek, 2001; Barrett, 2000; Churchill, Snowdon & Munro, 2001). Distance education programs now offer a variety of courses, supplementing traditional means of instruction with computer-mediated activities and projects (Harasim, Hiltz, Teles, & Turoff, 1995). In some cases, computer-mediated communication has enabled the operation of entire university programs online (Acker, 1995; Noam, 1998). Instead of university faculties localized at their university departments, formalized "collaboratories" link far-flung scholars, institutions, and research centers (see Barab, Kling, & Gray, this volume; Finholt, 2001). Even more prevalent are informal collaborations between researchers and professors located in different universities spanning the globe (Koku, Nazer, & Wellman, 2001).

Computer-mediated communication is providing a technological basis for new forms of spatially dispersed, loosely bounded networks of scholars that are more connected than the fitful, amorphous relationships of the past and less physically proximate and bureaucratically structured than contemporary universities. The velocity of communication is more rapid, distant scholars stay in touch more, and email and its attachments fill gaps between face-to-face meetings.

The ability of all to communicate rapidly with all, no matter where located, has created hopes that peripheries would become as well-connected as centers. As distance matters little for computer-mediated communication, spatial isolation should not be a problem. As all are connected to all, formerly disconnected persons, groups, and branch plants should be as able as those at the center to communicate with others. This should affect the structure of scholarly networks: As email helps maintain direct ties, social density increases and the periphery – whether spatial, social, or scholarly – can become better connected with the core.

Preliminary research has shown that computer-mediated communication supports a range of instrumental, informational, social, and emotional exchanges in work and leisure contexts (e.g., Baym, 1995, 1997; Rice,

D'Ambra, & More, 1998; Wellman & Gulia, 1999). Building on this work, there is a need to understand the types of interpersonal interactions, multiple exchanges of material and emotional support, intimacy, trust, and self-disclosure that characterize learning communities online and offline (Granovetter, 1973; Marsden & Campbell, 1984; Wellman & Berkowitz, 1988; Wellman, 2001). By "opening up the black box of community and looking inside, [analysts] can examine what types of interactions and associations make for a community" (Haythornthwaite, 2002, p. 160). Social network analysis provides an approach that can facilitate understanding of communities. Viewing community as comprising social networks of relations enables analysts to examine the types of interactions – such as information, emotional support, material support, companionship – that affect online communities. It facilitates the assessment of the extent to which computer-mediated communication supports online learning communities with low levels of centralization and hierarchy (Ahuja & Carley, 1999).

In this chapter, we analyze social network ties and structures of *TechNet*, a scholarly network in a North American university. We address a series of questions:

- What is the size and heterogeneity of scholarly work, friendship, and communication networks?
- To what extent are such work, friendship, and communication relationships associated?
- How are the size and heterogeneity of scholarly networks related to communication patterns?
- What is the role structure of this scholarly network?
- Is the role structure of the email contact network more egalitarian than that of the face-to-face contact network?
- What are the implications of the network's role structure for communication patterns?

In the next section of this chapter, we describe social network analysis and discuss how it can aid understanding of scholarly networks, online and offline. The chapter continues with a description of TechNet as a community of practice (Wenger, 1998) engaged in peer-to-peer interaction and learning. In the last sections of the chapter, we use survey and qualitative data about TechNet's structure and relationships to address our research questions.

SOCIAL NETWORK ANALYSIS OF COMPUTER-SUPPORTED NETWORKS

Much research on computer-mediated communication has focused on how the characteristics of different communication media affect what each medium can convey (Garton, Haythornthwaite, & Wellman, 1998). Such characteristics include the richness of cues a medium can convey (for example, whether a medium is text-only such as email or also includes visual and auditory cues); the visibility or anonymity of the participants (video-mail versus voice mail); whether communication exchanges identify the sender by name, gender, and/or title; and the timing of exchanges (e.g., synchronous or asynchronous communication). Until recently, social scientific research into computer-mediated communication has concentrated on how individual users interface with computers, and how two persons and small groups interact and function online. Much less attention has been paid to how computer networks fit into the broader social networks and contexts in which these individuals, dyads, and groups are connected. Yet, the social relationships that people have with each other are embedded in social networks that affect their social resources, mobility, happiness, and work habits (Wellman, 1999, 2001).

Social network analysis stresses the importance and patterns of relationships among interacting units, such as people, organizations, states. The social network approach enables analysts to go beyond viewing relationships only in terms of groups and isolated duets. It incorporates into research a set of structural variables such as the density, clustering, heterogeneity, and multiplexity of networks (Wellman, 1988, 1999; Berkowitz, 1982; Scott, 1991; Wasserman & Faust, 1994; Wellman & Berkowitz, 1988; Ahuja & Carley, 1999; Tindall & Wellman, 2001). Social network analysts have developed procedures for seeing how different types of relationships interrelate, detecting structural patterns, and analyzing the implications that structural patterns have for the behavior of network members. For example, the fact that Person A and Person B interact online may be understood better if one takes into consideration their offline reporting relationships to Person C, the company vice president.

Thinking about relationships in terms of social networks rather than in groups can allow analysts to examine the social contexts of online relationships and focus on the potential of computer-mediated communication to support less-bounded, sparsely knit interactions (Rice, Grant, Schmitz, & Torobin, 1990; Fulk, Steinfeld, Schmitz, & Power, 1987; Fulk & DeSanctis, 1995; Wellman & Gulia, 1999; Wellman, Salaff et al., 1996). For example, analysts may enquire whether there are core and periphery clusters in a particular network structure and then examine how involvement in such structural locations help explain the behavior and attitudes of network members. For example, do peripheral people send more email and do they communicate only with members of their own clusters or with others?

Network analysts look at both *whole networks* and *personal networks*. Whole network analyses look at patterns of relationships in a social system with clearly defined boundaries, be it a set of scholars in a university lab, an office, or work group. Personal network analyses look at each person's own network, such as each scholar's associates from office, family, or tennis club, among others (Wellman & Berkowitz, 1988).

In the past four decades, the social network approach has evolved into a set of theories, models, and substantive applications in many domains that have traditionally interested social scientists. The growth of the social network approach is partly reflected in the longevity of the International Network for Social Network Analysis (INSNA), a multidisciplinary scholarly organization founded in 1977. It publishes two refereed journals, *Social Networks* and *Journal of Social Structures*, and an informal journal, *Connections*; holds annual conferences; maintains a lively listserv, *SocNet*; and hosts an information-rich website. Network analysts have demonstrated the role of social networks in understanding the following:

- Communities (Fischer, 1982; Wellman, 1999; Newman, 2001)
- Provision of interpersonal support (Lin & Dumin, 1986; Lin & Westcott, 1991; Wellman, 1992; Wellman & Wortley, 1989, 1990)
- Social capital (Lin & Gao, 2000; Lin et al., 2001)
- Diffusion of innovations (Rogers, 1979; Valente, 1995)
- Sociology of science (Carley & Wendt, 1991; Carley, Hummon, & Harty, 1993; Crane, 1972; Newman, 2000)
- Computer-mediated communication (Haythornthwaite, 2000; Haythornthwaite & Wellman, 1998; Rice, 1991, 1994, 1997; Rice & Gattiker, 2001; Teigland & Wasko, 2000; Wellman & Gulia, 1999; Wellman et al., 1996).

The social network approach has developed a battery of concepts and methods that can aid analysis of communities, online and offline. Using examples from online communities in general, and learning communities in particular, the next section of this chapter examines the usefulness of social network concepts such as range (size and heterogeneity), density and boundedness, centrality, tie strength, multiplexity (multiple roles), and structural equivalence (blocks or blockmodeling) for understanding online communities and social relationships.

Network Range (Size, Heterogeneity)

The concept of network range pertains to the size and diversity of the population within the network's boundaries (Burt, 1983; Haines & Hurlbert, 1992). Networks with high range (large, heterogeneous) are good for seeking and obtaining new resources (Wellman, 1999; Newman, 2001). On the other hand, networks with low range (small, homogeneous) are able to conserve resources and information within their boundaries.

Computerized conferences, newsgroups, and listservs facilitate and increase the range of social networks (Smith, 2000). The asynchronicity and relatively inexpensive cost of online communication transcends spatial and temporal limits, enabling system users to communicate over different time zones and maintain contact with their weak ties. Therefore, online communication links can increase the range of social networks. Given that email relationships have few social cues and social presence, the only personal details that communicators may initially know about each other are their email addresses and signatures. Such limited personal information allows development of relations based on shared interests rather than on shared social status (Hiltz & Turoff, 1993).

Centrality

Network centrality indicates the extent to which certain network members are prominent in a given network in terms of connectivity among network members. Centralization scores (measured as a percentage) indicate how variable or heterogeneous the individual network member centrality scores are. It records the extent to which a single network member has high centrality scores, and the others lower scores. A high centralization score means a network's activity centers on a particular member.

Two important types of centrality are pertinent to this study: degree centrality and betweenness centrality. Scholars with high degree centrality are those who have many connections with other network members. Such scholars are involved in relations with many others and could be recognized by other scholars as a major channel of scholarly information and activity. Well-connected network members usually play a key role in shaping the behavior and perceptions of others in the network, particularly in the diffusion of innovations (Rogers, 1983; Valente, 1995) and the use of available media. Central network members tend to use a variety of media (Haythornthwaite & Wellman, 1998), have the most positive experiences with media use, are early adopters of a new information system, and facilitate the development of critical mass of users for the system (Rice et al., 1990; Rice, 1997).

When directionality is taken into account, there are two kinds of degree centrality: *In-degree centrality* measures how many nominations or choices a person receives from other network members. For example, participants mention scholars with high in-degree centrality as people they approach for advice or discussions. Thus, in-degree centrality is one measure of the prestige of a network member. By contrast, *out-degree centrality* measures how many other network members a person contacts for a specific resource such as advice. Thus it is an indicator of the extent to which a scholar reports reaching out to others.

Betweenness centrality measures the extent to which a network member "straddles" or "lies between" the communication paths of non-adjacent network members. A scholar with a high betweenness centrality is positioned in the collaborative and communication networks paths of other scholars who are not directly connected to each other. Network members with high betweenness centralities facilitate communication and information flow. They broker information, linking otherwise disconnected scholars. They transmit information across disciplinary and organizational boundaries (Burt, 1992; Tushman & Scanlan, 1981; Ahuja & Carley, 1999; Orlikowski & Barley, 2001). Thus, scholars with high betweenness are in powerful collaborative and communication brokerage positions between otherwise disconnected scholars.

Earlier studies of scholarly networks have drawn attention to the importance of centrality in the control and diffusion of information (Crane, 1972). Central scholars are able to sustain a more central communication role than peripheral ones in part because of prestige, popularity, and grant funding. This has positive feedback effects, leading to increased conference attendance, speaking engagements, and interaction with disparate others (Perry & Rice, 1998). All of these interactions expose scholars to more ideas, make them better known within professional and policy circles, and popularize their research. This sustains the cycle of centrality and prestige because central scholars are better able to respond to promising ideas, influence the direction of policy, and retain funding.

Central scholars tend to have a sophisticated level of knowledge of the things worth knowing: the debates and lore that are crucial for leading-edge scholarship. They usually play essential roles in introducing peripheral ideas into the mainstream, which otherwise might lack the attention or awareness within the scientific community (Perry & Rice, 1998). As Erickson (1996) suggests, one of the useful consequences of being in the center is that central people know what they can afford not to know.

Density

The density of a social network is the extent to which its members are in direct contact with each other. Hence, the rate of information flow in networks partly depends on whether networks are densely or sparsely knit. Densely knit, bounded networks (i.e., groups) are characterized by frequent contact among members. In such networks, most relationships remain within the population, with the exception of a few boundary spanners and gatekeepers who maintain links outside. Frequent contact within these groups and the wide range of group activities often fostered by members create close relationships among them.

By contrast, members of sparsely knit networks have fewer ties with each other but maintain more ties with others outside their networks. Ties in sparsely knit networks tend to be more variable than those in densely knit networks (Danowski, 1986; Wellman, 1997) in terms of what network members do together, how supportive they are, and how frequently they interact.

Computer-mediated communication supports both densely knit and sparsely knit networks. Focused task and work groups, MUDs[1], and some

---

[1] MUDs refer to "Multi User Dimensions" or "Multi User Dungeons" or "Multi User Dialogues."

moderated newsgroups and listservs are densely knit communities, as they evolve rules and leadership structures and require attention and commitment from their members (Kollock & Smith, 1998). Message management features of email systems can increase network density and enable friends and colleagues to keep each other informed. Third parties spread the word about who has help, who needs help, who has been helpful in the past, and who has been a free-rider. Forwarding communications to third parties also provides indirect connections between previously unconnected people. Ease of direct reply can then transform a transitive, indirect tie to a direct tie.

Computer networks also support sparsely knit networks. Participants can send email to anyone whose address they know, and they can belong to multiple discussion lists and chat groups simultaneously. They can engage in different kinds of discussions about different subjects on different lists, varying their involvement and commitment in different work groups, maintaining connections with distant acquaintances, and forming new ties with strangers. Information may come unsolicited through distribution lists, chat groups, forwarded messages from friends, and direct email from strangers connected through mutual ties. Sparsely knit networks are usually connected through weak ties to a variety of social circles. Hence, they are more apt to be sources of new information and potential alliances (Granovetter, 1973, 1983).

Tie Strength

The strength of a tie is a multidimensional construct comprising social closeness, voluntariness, and multiplexity (Granovetter, 1973, 1983; Wellman & Wortley, 1990). Strong ties often provide more support and information and a sense of belonging. However, Granovetter shows that weak ties are useful for specific purposes. He argues that people live in a cluster of others with whom they have strong relations. Information circulates at high velocity within these clusters and each person tends to know what other cluster members know. The spread of new information, ideas, and opportunities must therefore come through the weak ties that connect people in separate clusters.

Some studies have focused on the effect of tie strength on resource and information flow among scholars. Friedkin's (1980, 1982) study of university faculty contrasts the importance of strong versus weak ties for information flow. He shows that in the aggregate, the large number of weak scholarly ties contributes significantly to information flows. Although strong ties provide much information about activities within an organization, weak ties provide useful information about activities outside of a work group or organization (Levin, Cross, & Abrams, 2002).

Marshall McLuhan (1962) claimed that the medium is the message. Does computer-mediated communication determine the content of messages and the pattern of their communication? In particular, does computer-mediated communication support only weak, narrow, and instrumental messages as analysts once feared (Fulk et al., 1987)?

Despite email's limited social presence and absence of social cues, its ease and ubiquity support strong, frequent, supportive, and companionable contact (Nie, 2001; Wellman & Gulia, 1999; Garton & Wellman, 1995; Kling, 1996; Rheingold, 2000; Sproull & Kiesler, 1991). So strong and supportive are some online relationships that some participants in an online group come to feel that fellow members are their closest friends (Hiltz & Turoff, 1993). Concerns about how computer-mediated communication supports strong ties ignore the many relationships that combine online and offline communication. Computer-mediated communication is often used to maintain contact between face-to-face meetings and phone calls. Indeed, computer-mediated communication often coincides with in-person meetings, fills in gaps between, and helps arrange future meetings. Conversations begin in one medium and drift to another. For example, most computer scientists working in the same physical space communicated by email as well as face-to-face (Haythornthwaite & Wellman, 1998). Learning communities are no different, with friendship and informal relationships – online and offline – being the fluid that lubricates the formality of collegial and academic collaborations (Carley & Wendt, 1991; Grimshaw, 1989; Gresham, 1994; Toren, 1994; Glanz, 1999).

Blockmodels

Traditional tests of social influence explain the similarity of attitudes among a set of individuals according to personal attributes such as age, occupation, or degree of innovation (Rice & Aydin, 1991). However, network analysts argue that people's attitudes are, in part, a function of their patterns of relations with others (Wellman, Carrington, & Hall, 1988; Erickson, 1988). The structural context of their relationships provide the mechanisms by which individuals are influenced by the information, influence, and behavior of others. Specifically, such structural contexts are important in explaining perceptions of communication media and media use. One indicator of such a structural context is *structural equivalence* and *blockmodeling*.

Unlike many network analytic techniques, blockmodel analysis does not examine the direct connectivity of members of a network. The notion of *equivalence* underlies blockmodeling, a quantitative technique that assigns members of a network to blocks. Two scholars are equivalent if they have similar relationships to and from the same scholars in the network (Wasserman & Faust, 1994). Blockmodel analysis starts by partitioning (subdividing) and permuting (reordering) the rows and columns of the socio-matrices of relationships under study to discover patterns of links among network members. Specifically, the goal of this reordering is to arrange network members into sets (termed blocks) so that those who are assigned to the same block occupy adjacent rows and columns in the permuted matrix.

Equivalent persons may share similar attitudes – not necessarily because they are directly related to each other but because they occupy similar positions and are exposed to similar sets of influences, obligations, and expectations (Rice & Aydin, 1991; Burt, 1980). For example, equivalent organizational members often perceive and use information systems in similar ways (Contractor & Eisenberg, 1990).

The previous discussion shows that network analysis concepts such as size, heterogeneity, centrality, density, tie strength, and blockmodeling can facilitate our understanding of the underlying structures of online and offline communities, and can also help us understand use of communication media in such communities. Network density, for example, shows the extent of direct connectivity among network members and how this affects communication patterns and access to resources; tie strength shows the extent to which communities are differentiated by different degrees of closeness and how this affects their choice of communication media and work relations. The next section describes TechNet as a scholarly community and analyzes the network structure and communication behavior of the scholars.

TECHNET: A SCHOLARLY COMMUNITY

TechNet is a network of scholars and professionals in a North American university interested in a coherent set of issues at the intersection of the social sciences, humanities, sciences, and engineering. It began informally in the early 1990s and formally became a university research institute in the mid-1990s. Its goals are to do the following:

- Facilitate an intellectual community of scholars, researchers, and students from a number of disciplines.
- Facilitate appropriate partnerships with other universities, the private sector, nonprofit organizations, and government.
- Afford the intersection of the relevant disciplines a more prominent place and role within the university.
- Create and support colloquia and lecture series.
- Facilitate visits of distinguished scholars to the university, support researchers working in these areas, and increase support for graduate students.
- Establish one or more appropriate funded chairs and professorships.
- Create additional relevant courses and increase awareness of existing courses that cross disciplinary boundaries.

- Create a new collaborative degree program.
- Develop and offer short professional development courses for industry and society.

TechNet's activities have been guided by a multidisciplinary steering committee that meets monthly. Membership in TechNet is voluntary and open to all faculties with an interest in TechNet's domain. At the time of our data gathering at an early stage of TechNet's development, administration was informal, with only one part-time paid administrative assistant. There were 24 members of TechNet from the social sciences, physical sciences, medical sciences, humanities, and engineering. Members of TechNet organize and meet in a variety of online and offline forums to exchange ideas, discuss emerging research, and to socialize. Some of these are weekly multidisciplinary seminars, annual conferences and symposia, retreats, and end-of-semester/year parties.

TechNet is a scholarly network or more broadly, a community of practice with a shared history and cosmology (Barab & Duffy, 2000). Many founding members and some other members were initially linked through participation in joint research, conference attendance, reading the same journals, membership in university committees, and advising on graduate student projects. TechNet is also linked with other communities interested in the intersection of the humanities, social sciences, and technology. As one member explains in an interview:

The ways that an entire citizenry can be much more actively and successfully involved in knowledge development and knowledge society is the core interest of mine and that of a number of TechNet members. I just think that this interest is grossly underrepresented in the kind of work that is done in the university and underrepresented in formal structures. There are lots of faculty who are doing exciting things, but there are no formal structures to network together.

Scholarly networks similar to TechNet have existed since at least the Middle Ages. Fragmented archival records attest to the correspondence among scholars showing that scholarly networks communicated actively during the Enlightenment. In England and elsewhere, some were recognized as royal societies (Marshall, 1970). Studies of scholarly networks have increased since the early 1960s when Price (1961) coined the term *invisible colleges* to describe the patterns and structure of scholarly networks (see also Crane, 1972).

Scholarly networks contain:

- A core group of elite scholars;
- A high degree of communication through formal (conferences, papers) and informal channels among members;
- Frequent communication between prominent core scholars and subsets of less prominent, noncore scholars;

- Interactions among core members and their adherents holding the invisible college together;
- Contacts between members of invisible colleges and outsiders enabling mutual exchange of information.

Within the last three decades, developments in transportation, telecommunications, and computer-mediated communication have transformed some invisible colleges into "visible colleges" (Nazer, 2000; Walsh & Bayama, 1996). With the advent of the Internet, there are fewer constraints of time and place on communication. Scholars can stay in their locale to connect, interact, and collaborate with each other over great distances (Finholt, 2001; Assimakopoulos & Macdonald, 2002; Koku et al., 2001; Matzat, 2001; Mutschke & Quan-Haase, 2001). To facilitate the design of communication tools to aid scholarly communication and online learning behavior, it is useful to understand the social structure of scholarly networks, the types of media used by these networks, and the conditions under which different media are used.

METHODS

We interviewed all 24 TechNet members in 1997–1998 about their work, friendship, and media use inside and outside of TechNet, asking members to describe their scholarly and social relations with other TechNet member. This elicited reports from about 405 pairs of scholars: their work relationship, social closeness, friendship, frequency of scholarly communication, and type of communication media used. Although much of these interviews are analyzed statistically in this chapter, we also rely on notes of conversations held during the interviews and our own active participation in TechNet since its inception.

Relationships

COLLABORATING RELATIONS. TechNet members report about the presence or absence of a collaborative tie with other members. As there are nonacademic members of TechNet (those holding administrative or quasi-research blocks) and there are academics who engage in collaborative work with the nonacademics, we define collaborative work as all professional work that has scholarly related outcomes. Hence, joint participation in grant applications, university review committees, research projects, and collaborative teaching are all considered as collaborative work.

DISCUSSING RESEARCH. TechNet members' reports about which other members they discuss research questions or seek advice about research issues. These relationships are important in their own right and are often corollaries to collaborative relationships.

READING WORK. Members' reports about whether they read the work of each other member.

SOCIAL CLOSENESS. Members' reports about the type of social relationship they have with each other member. Respondents were asked if they are a "friend," "colleague," "acquaintance," or just "aware of" each other member. This variable was recoded into four matrices indicating the presence or absence of a friendship, collegial, acquaintanceship, and awareness relationship between pairs of scholars.

FREQUENCY OF COMMUNICATION. Members' reports of their frequency of contact with each other member within the past month. This is recoded into yearly estimates by multiplying the monthly counts by 12.

PERCEIVED EFFECTIVENESS OF MEDIA FOR SCHOLARLY WORK. Members' rating of the effectiveness of email and face-to-face media for accomplishing scholarly activities. The ratings are: "not effective," "moderately effective," "effective," and "very effective."

Network Structure

(calculated with UCINet software; see Borgatti, Everett, & Freeman, 1999):

NETWORK DENSITY. Measures the proportion of relationships that are actually present in a network. Density ranges between 0 for a network with no relations among members, to 1 for a network with all members directly connected to each other.

NETWORK HETEROGENEITY. Standard deviations indicate the extent of variation in the composition of a scholar's collaborative, discussion, reading, interpersonal, and communication relationships.

NETWORK SIZE. The total number of other TechNet scholars with whom each scholar maintains relations of a specified tie (e.g., discussing work).

CENTRALITY OF NETWORK MEMBERS. Each scholar's prominence in scholarly relations. We use the following measures:

- *Out-Degree Centrality*: Scholars with high out-degree make many choices, reaching out to others.
- *In-Degree Centrality*: Scholars with high in-degree are the object of many choices and hence, the members of many others' networks.
- *Degree Centrality*: Degree centrality counts the number of specified relationships that a person has, without regard to directionality. The degree centrality measure is applicable to relationships where one cannot clearly distinguish choices made (out-degree) and choices received (in-degree).
- *Betweenness Centrality*: A scholar with high betweenness centrality straddles the communication or interaction paths between two nonadjacent scholars. Such a scholar mediates the communication or relationship between other scholars. Scholars with high betweenness centrality are

more likely to control interactions between pairs of other scholars in the network.

We computed these indices for each scholar's collaborative, discussion/advice seeking, and reading work networks. To enable comparisons across these different relational networks, we standardized the indices by dividing the individual degree values by the maximum possible degree expressed as a percentage (Borgatti et al., 1999).

RELATIONSHIPS AND NETWORKS IN TECHNET

Range

TechNet scholars report having an average of five friends within TechNet (22 percent of the total membership), ten colleagues (43 percent), nine acquaintances (39 percent), and are "just aware" of four others (17 percent; Table 11.1, see also Table 11.3; Koku et al., 2001). They are in email contact with nineteen (82 percent) other members and in face-to-face contact with fourteen (61 percent). Most use email where necessary for work relationships (such as discussion of research) and supplement this with face-to-face communication when they meet in person in workshops, seminars,

TABLE 11.1. *Selected Characteristics of Work, Interpersonal, and Media Use Personal Networks*

Variable	Mean Size of Personal Network	Heterogeneity (Standard Deviation)	Density
Work Relation			
Collaboration	5.0	0.34	0.21
Discuss	17.4	0.50	0.76
Read Work	5.2	0.32	0.12
Interpersonal Relationship			
Friend	3.1	0.34	0.19
Colleague	6.7	0.46	0.41
Acquaintance	5.1	0.42	0.29
Aware	2.0	0.28	0.11
Media Use			
Email	18.9	0.47	0.64
Face-to-Face	13.4	0.49	0.40

Note: If all 24 network members are in contact with each other, we would have a maximum of 552 asymmetric (one-way) ties (24 × 23). In practice, we have only 405 active ties. The summary characteristics are based only on these 405 ties.

and other collegial gatherings. Sheer statistics underestimate the significance of face-to-face contact, as it is usually of longer duration and provides more communication possibility than email contact. Those pairs of TechNet scholars who are in touch are in relatively frequent contact: a mean of twenty times per year and a median of ten times per year. As all TechNet members are comfortable with computers, they use email often: 56 percent of all TechNet pairs have some email contact.

Email supplements rather than supplants face-to-face contact, with members using it to arrange face-to-face meetings, disseminate news, and exchange documents. Those TechNet members using email send messages to each other at a mean rate of twenty-four times per year, an average of twice per month. To TechNet members, non–face-to-face communication means computer-mediated communication. Only a minority use telephones, faxes, and couriers, and those who do use these media use them infrequently. The most widely used of these are local telephone calls, used by only 25 percent of the members. Those who telephone do so on the average of once per month (mean = 11 calls per year). Most TechNet pairs use a combination of communication media to keep connected. Thirty-two percent use two media, while 23 percent use three or more.

Discussing and seeking research advice are not uniformly distributed in collegial communities (see, for example, Lazega and Duijin's study of law firms, 1997). The more intense the work relationship, the smaller the scholar's network. The average TechNet member discusses work with seventeen other TechNet members (74 percent), but reads the work of only five (22 percent) and also collaborates with five (22 percent; not necessarily the same five) in research and proposal writing. These may be overlapping networks, with some scholars discussing each other's work, reading these works, and collaborating in research.

Larger scholarly networks vary more in the intensity of their communications (e.g., email) and scholarly (e.g., discussion) networks. Thus, email contact networks are as large and heterogeneous as face-to-face contact networks. Similarly, research discussion networks are larger and more heterogeneous than reading or collaborative networks. The size and heterogeneity of email networks stem in part from the ease of making contact without regard to spatial and temporal separation and the ease of including several scholars in the same message. Moreover, forwarding email messages fosters the development of more extensive and intensive relationships among scholars. The development of such heterogeneous linkages is facilitated by TechNet's weekly face-to-face seminars, workshops, and other social events that provide an in-person focus (Feld, 1981) where scholars make and sustain collegial and sociable contact with colleagues from different disciplines (for a similar pattern in another scholarly network, see Koku et al., 2001; Nazer, 2001). Such networks are important avenues for the provision of social, instrumental, and emotional support, and the mobilization and coordination of collective activity.

Network Density

TechNet's email contact network is quite densely knit (0.64; Table 11.1). That nearly two-thirds of all possible TechNet pairs are connected by email reflects the ease with which people can communicate one-to-one or one-to-many. The lower density of face-to-face contact networks (0.40) reflects the greater effort needed to journey across a large campus in what often is below-freezing weather. Nevertheless, two-fifths of all TechNet pairs do have face-to-face contact, testifying to the success of this visible college in fostering ties across dispersed disciplines and buildings.

The high density of the discussing work network (0.76) also shows TechNet's success in fostering contact and awareness of the members' work. Within TechNet, small sets of members work together, reflected in the lower collaboration network density of 0.21 and reading work density of 0.12. There are no projects involving a majority of members.

In terms of informed relations, TechNet is composed of awareness and contact-based networks of colleagues (density = 0.41) and acquaintances (0.29). The low friendship network density of 0.19 shows that TechNet does not have a dominant friendship cluster, although as blockmodeling will show later, there are coherent sets of planners and researchers within it.

The Intertwining of Scholarly Relationships

There is a moderately strong correlation between scholars' interpersonal and work relationships. "Friends" and "colleagues" are likely to collaborate (Table 11.2).[2] Collaborators also communicate more frequently both by face-to-face and email contact. By contrast, acquaintances and colleagues are more likely to have the weaker relationship of discussing research. Reading each other's work is widely diffused through TechNet. It is not significantly associated with either TechNet members' frequency of contact or the intensity of their relationships (friendship, colleagueship, etc.).

There is a social aspect to scholarly relationships (Hert, 1997). Having a collegial tie is usually not enough for having collaborative ties: Friendship is usually involved. Strong scholarly and friendship relations develop in positive feedback loops. Friends collaborate and discuss each other's work,

---

[2] UCINet's QAP correlation function examines this by permuting the rows and columns (together) of one of the input matrices, and then correlating the permuted matrix with the other data matrix. This process is repeated hundreds of times to build up a distribution of correlations under the null hypothesis of no relationship between the matrices. A low p-value (<.05) suggests a strong relationship between the matrices that is unlikely to have occurred by chance.

TABLE 11.2. *QAP Correlation between Work, Interpersonal and Media Use Relations*

	Collaborative	Discuss Research	Read Work	Friend	Colleague	Acquaintance	Aware	Email Contact	Face-to-Face Contact
Work Relationships									
Collaborative	–								
Discuss Research	–0.30	–							
Read Work	0.03	–0.12	–						
Interpersonal Relationships									
Friend	0.45*	–0.00	0.04	–					
Colleague	0.15*	0.35*	–0.07	n/a	–				
Acquaintance	–0.18	0.48*	–0.06	n/a	n/a	–			
Aware	–0.12	–0.29	–0.01	n/a	n/a	n/a	–		
Media Use									
Email	0.32*	0.03	–0.02	0.25*	0.02	0.02	–0.08	–	
Face-to-Face	0.44*	0.04	–0.03	0.48*	0.03	–0.11	–0.11	0.49*	–

$*p < .05$: A low p-value ($< .05$) suggests a strong relationship between the matrices that is unlikely to have occurred by chance.
n/a = not applicable.

TABLE 11.3. *Pearson Correlation between Network and Tie Characteristics with Frequency and Perceived Effectiveness of Email and Face-To-Face Contact*

	Frequency of Face-to-Face Contact	Frequency of Email Contact	Multiple Media Use	Perceived Effectiveness of Face-to-Face Contact for Scholarly Communication	Perceived Effectiveness of Email Contact for Scholarly Communication
Size					
Collaboration	.13**	.24**	.19**	.25**	.05
Discussing Research	−.04	−.04	−.03	.06	−.03
Reading Work	.11*	.11*	.08*	.25**	.33**
Density					
Collaboration	.13**	.06	.14**	−.42**	−.01
Discussing Research	.04	−.11*	−.11*	−.24**	−.07
Reading Work	.12*	.03	.03	−.18**	.03
Degree Centrality					
Collaboration	.13**	.24**	.19**	.26**	.05
Discussion *(Out Degree)*	−.02	−.01	.13**	−.14**	.16**

Discussion (*In Degree*)	.00	.02	–.05	.28**	–.06
Reading Work (*Out Degree*)	.10*	.10*	.10*	.21**	.22**
Reading Work (*In Degree*)	.00	.03	–.04	.04	.24**
Betweenness Centrality					
Collaboration	.01	.19**	.12*	.37**	.01
Discussing Research	–.02	.06	.07	.15**	.05
Reading Work	–.08	–.06	–.22	.12	.12
Tie Strength					
Friend	.22**	.50**	.36**	.10*	.01
Colleague	.13*	.06	.21*	–.19**	.16**
Acquaintance	.05	–.28**	–.12*	.05	–.02
Aware	–.56**	–.31**	–.61**	.11*	–.23**

*$p < 0.05$
**$p < 0.01$

and collaborating scholars develop stronger friendship ties. As cosmologist James Hartle (University of California, Santa Barbara) says of his collaboration with Nobel Prize winner Stephen Hawking (Cambridge University): "Generally, it is the science that drives it, while friendship naturally follows" (Glanz, 1999, p. D2). Frequent email and face-to-face contact are significantly related to having both collaborative and friendship relations. All media are used in such collaborative/friendship relationships. These scholar-friends use whatever means are necessary and handy (Haythornthwaite & Wellman, 1998; Koku et al., 2001).

Each medium plays a different role in supporting scholarly activities. For instance, the positive and moderately strong correlation ($r = 0.24$) between collaborative work and the frequency of email contact suggests that the velocity and timelessness of email supports collaboration. Although the scholars perceive face-to-face contact as effective for accomplishing scholarly activities, computer-mediated communication means that TechNet collaborators can work effectively despite being dispersed throughout a large university (Kraut, Egido, & Galegher, 1990).

Centrality and Communication

TechNet's email contact network is less centralized (centralization score = 34) than its face-to-face network (score = 56). Most TechNet members send and receive emails, but face-to-face contact between them is more variable.

TechNet scholars with large personal networks of collaborators and high (degree) centrality communicate more face-to-face and by email (Table 11.3).[3] Scholars with high betweenness centrality have a similar pattern, except that they have appreciably more face-to-face contact with their collaborators. Scholars with large collaborative and reading networks use more media to communicate, and are more likely to perceive email and face-to-face contact as effective for scholarly communication (see also Ahuja & Carley, 1999).

The centrality of scholars in a network is significantly related to their communication behavior in four ways:

1. Scholars who reach out (have high out-degree) to other scholars for advice and to discuss research tend to use several media (QAP $r = 0.19$) in their communications and to value email as an effective means of fostering discussions ($r = 0.26$). Scholars who need advice and want to discuss their research increase their opportunities by using multiple

---

[3] We analyze associations between the size, density, heterogeneity, and centrality of the networks by importing personal network and centrality indices from UCINet into SPSS. Given that these indices are on an individual level, we treat them as personal attribute information and merge them with respondent-level data (Wellman, & Frank, et al., 1991; Wellman, 1992). This enables us to analyze the implications of individual attributes for communication behavior of scholars.

communication media. However, the frequency of email contact itself is not related to scholarly centrality because much TechNet email traffic is administrative or public service broadcasts, such as notices of forthcoming lectures.

2. High-prestige (high in-degree scholars), those who report being asked by many others for advice, perceive face-to-face contact as effective in scholarly work (0.28). Such central TechNet members tend to be frequent seminar goers, making them accessible for such spontaneous encounters. Face-to-face contact enhances the status of prestigious scholars by giving them more information and visibility in TechNet. When such face-to-face contact is scheduled, it indicates the seriousness with which the advice-seeker regards the knowledge given. When face-to-face contact results from spontaneous encounters (such as encounters at seminars), it is a less intrusive medium than email for acquiring advice.

3. The high betweenness centrality scores of frequently collaborating scholars are related to their frequency of email contact ($r = 0.19$), use of multiple communication media ($r = 0.12$), and especially, perception of the effectiveness of face-to-face communication for scholarly work ($r = 0.37$). High betweenness implies greater capacity for brokerage, with email and face-to-face communication combining to facilitate such brokerage. The forwarding features of email facilitate the development of collaborative relations between two scholars through the intervention of a third party. Thus, scholars perceive email contact to be just as effective in scholarly work as face-to-face meetings, conferences, and other offline contexts. Both settings can be used to initiate and solidify collaborative relations.

4. The strength of TechNet members' ties is related to the frequency of face-to-face and email contact as well as to the perceived effectiveness of email and face-to-face communication. Friends are much more likely than acquaintances to use email ($r = 0.50$) and face-to-face ($r = 0.22$) contact and to use multiple media for contact ($r = 0.36$). Colleagues are also more likely than acquaintances to be in face-to-face contact ($r = 0.13$), use multiple media ($r = 0.21$), and perceive email as an effective medium for scholarly activities ($r = 0.16$). Scholars who are only aware of each other have less face-to-face and email contact ($r = -0.56$ and -0.31). There are differences in the relative strengths of the association, with the frequency of email contact between a pair of scholars related to the strength of their tie. Friends communicate more frequently than those who are work colleagues only. Yet, colleagues communicate more than acquaintances, with those who are just aware of each other communicating the least.

The foregoing analysis has drawn attention to the salience of email and the use of multiple media for supporting scholarly relations. Connectivity is associated with communication: Those central within TechNet – whether through out-degree, in-degree, or betweenness – are the most active communicators. Tie strength is associated with communication: Those with stronger ties of collaborative work and friendship communicate more. The demands for maintenance of scholarly relationships across time and space, and the increasing importance of friendship and other social aspects of the scholarly life, call for flexibility and adaptability in choice of media. Email, supported by face-to-face communication, is instrumental in fulfilling these tasks.

ROLE STRUCTURE

Blockmodeling TechNet

What would the structure of TechNet look like if all the relationships of its scholars were aggregated to reveal patterns *across* the multiple networks they are involved in? An answer to this question lies in *blockmodel analysis* (White, Boorman, & Breiger, 1976), which examines similarities in relational patterns, such as collaborative, friendship, and email networks in TechNet.

Blockmodeling is important for our analysis for two reasons: First, TechNet is an interdisciplinary network, and the scholarly activities of its scholars span disciplines. Given that boundary-spanning and inter-network communication are possible characteristics of scholarly networks such as TechNet, blockmodeling can usefully describe which subsets of scholars are jointly engaged in working relationships with similar others. Second, focusing on the blocks of scholars can aid in understanding the informal and underlying structure of TechNet and the roles of individual scholars within it.

We use the CONCOR blockmodeling procedure of UCINet to analyze TechNet's collaborating, discussing, and reading networks (Breiger, Boorman, & Arabie, 1975). CONCOR works from the top down, starting by partitioning all network members into two nonoverlapping mutually exclusive subgroups. Partitioning is based on the similarity of choices made and choices received by all scholars across all relationships under study. In other words, two scholars are grouped in the same block if their overall patterns of choices made and received are similar and not necessarily because they are directly or indirectly connected to each other.

CONCOR produced a four-block partition of TechNet members. Our knowledge of scholars' attributes and involvement in TechNet helps us to interpret these blocks in terms of scholars' roles in the establishment, continuing operation, and visibility of TechNet. Given the interdisciplinary aspirations of TechNet, it is noteworthy that the blocks are based on varying roles in TechNet and not entirely on disciplinary affiliation.

Block 1 (six persons) contains many of the founding core planners of TechNet, who are also on its executive committee. The monthly face-to-face meeting of the executive committee, frequent meetings of other committees, and much emailing keeps this block in active and coordinated contact. Its members mostly come from one scientific and one social scientific discipline.

Block 2 (twelve persons) comprises members who are less managerially central but who often have scholarly visibility. They come from many disciplines.

The two members of the small Block 3 work within one well-defined area at the intersection of a scientific and a social scientific discipline. They are not frequent interactors with most other TechNet members.

Block 4 contains four faculty members who are less active in TechNet.

Relationship between Blocks

Each block comprises equivalent scholars. Analyzing scholarly relationships between blocks can aid understanding of how scholarly networks operate. Figures 11.1a–11.1c represent *block matrix* structures of the collaborative, discussion of research, and reading work relationships. To facilitate

```
                    1 1                   1 2 1 1 1 2 1     2         1     1 2 2 1
          1 2 3 7 8 9       4 7 8 0 3 2 3 4 1 6 6 4     5 1     9 2 0 5
         ------------------------------------------------------------------------
 1       |   1 1 1 1 1 | 1 1           1   1         |       |       1 |
 2       | 1       1 1 1 |                            | 1 1   |         |
 3       | 1           | 1         1   1       1     |       |         |
17       | 1 1     1 1 |     1               1       | 1 1   |         |
18       | 1 1   1   1 |       1         1           |       | 1       |
 9       | 1 1     1 1 |                            | 1 1   |         |
         ------------------------------------------------------------------------
 4       | 1   1       |       1   1               |       1 |         |
 7       | 1           |                           |         |         |
 8       |     1       |                   1 1     |         |       1 |
10       |       1     | 1         1 1 1       1   |       1 |         |
23       |             |             1             |         |   1 1   |
12       | 1   1       | 1                         |         |         |
13       |             |     1 1                   |         |       1 |
14       | 1   1   1   |     1               1     |         |     1 1 |
21       |             |     1           1   1     |         |       1 |
16       |             |             1             |         |         |
 6       |     1 1     | 1                         |         | 1   1 1 |
24       |             |     1 1         1 1       |         |       1 |
         ------------------------------------------------------------------------
 5       | 1   1 1     |                           |       1 |   1     |
11       | 1   1 1     | 1         1               | 1       |         |
         ------------------------------------------------------------------------
19       |             |                 1         |         |         |
22       |     1       |       1                   |         |     1   |
20       |             |       1   1 1       1     |   1     |   1     |
15       | 1           |       1         1 1   1 1 |         |         |
         ------------------------------------------------------------------------
```

Overall Network Density = .21
Standard Deviation within Blocks = .41

FIGURE 11.1a. Block matrix structures for collaborative work

```
             1 1               1 2 1 1 1 2 1   2       1   1 2 2 1
         1 2 3 7 8 9       4 7 8 0 3 2 3 4 1 6 6 4   5 1   9 2 0 5
        ----------------------------------------------------------------
 1      |     1 1 1 1 |   1 1 1 1 1 1 1 1 1 1 1 | 1 1 | 1 1 1 1 |
 2      |         1 1 |   1 1 1 1 1 1 1 1 1 1 1 1 | 1   | 1 1 1   |
 3      | 1       1 1 |   1 1 1   1 1 1 1   1 1 |     |   1 1   |
17      | 1 1 1   1   |   1 1 1 1 1 1 1 1   1 1 1 | 1   | 1 1 1   |
18      | 1 1 1 1     |   1 1 1 1 1 1 1 1 1 1 1 1 | 1 1 | 1 1     |
 9      | 1           |   1 1 1 1 1 1 1 1 1 1 1 | 1 1 |   1 1   |
        ----------------------------------------------------------------
 4      |   1 1 1 1 1 |   1 1 1 1 1 1 1 1 1 1 1 | 1 1 |   1 1 1 |
 7      | 1 1 1 1 1 1 |   1   1   1 1 1 1 1 1   1 |     | 1 1 1 1 |
 8      | 1 1 1 1 1 1 |   1 1   1 1   1 1 1 1 1 | 1   |   1 1 1 |
10      | 1 1   1 1 1 |   1   1   1   1 1 1 1 |     | 1 1 1 1 |
23      | 1 1 1 1 1 1 |   1 1 1 1   1   1 1 1 1 1 | 1 1 | 1 1 1 |
12      | 1 1 1 1 1 1 |   1 1     1     1 1 1 1 1 |     | 1       |
13      | 1 1 1 1 1 1 |   1 1 1 1     1 1 1 1 1 | 1   | 1 1   1 |
14      | 1 1 1 1 1 1 |   1 1 1   1 1 1   1 1 1 1 | 1 1 | 1 1 1 1 |
21      | 1 1 1   1 1 |   1 1 1 1 1 1 1 1 1   1 1 1 | 1   | 1 1 1 1 |
16      | 1 1   1 1 1 |   1 1 1 1 1 1 1 1 1 1   1 |     | 1 1 1   |
 6      | 1 1 1 1 1 1 |   1   1 1 1 1 1 1 1     1 | 1   | 1 1   1 |
24      | 1 1 1 1 1 1 |   1 1 1 1 1 1 1 1 1 1 1 1 |     |         |
        ----------------------------------------------------------------
 5      | 1 1   1 1 1 |   1       1   1 1   1   |     |   1     |
11      | 1         1 1 |   1   1   1     1 1   |     | 1 1 1 1 |
        ----------------------------------------------------------------
19      | 1 1   1 1   |     1   1 1   1 1 1 1 1 |   1 |         |
22      | 1 1 1 1 1 1 |   1 1 1 1 1 1 1 1 1 1 1 |   1 |         |
20      | 1 1 1 1   1 |   1 1 1 1 1     1 1 1 |   1 1 |         |
15      | 1           |   1 1 1 1     1 1 1   1 |   1 |         |
        ----------------------------------------------------------------
```

Overall Network Density = .76
Standard Deviation Within Blocks = .43

FIGURE 11.1b. Block matrix for discussing research

detection of relational patterns between the blocks, we suppress the "0s" in the matrices that signify the absence of relations. Concentrations of 1s in the matrices indicate the relative presence of relationships among the scholars in the various blocks. For example, the matrices in Figure 11.1a (collaborating) and 11.1c (reading work) are relatively sparse compared to Figure 11.1b (discussing research), implying denser connections among scholarly blocks when discussing research. The larger size of the research discussion networks (Table 11.1) clearly aids communication between blocks.

To aid detection of relationships between the blocks, we converted the block matrices in Figures 11.1a, 11.1b, and 11.1c to *reduced block matrices* and *reduced graphs*. We show links between the blocks in Figure 11.2, rows 2 and 3. The reduced block matrices and graphs enable us to describe the structural patterns of the blocks with respect to the scholarly relationships under study.

COLLABORATING. Members of Blocks 1 (the planners) and 3 (technology, science, and social science interests) collaborate within their own blocks and with the other block. There is a similar pattern for Blocks 2 (researchers) and 4 (periphery). This suggests a pattern of two alliances.

```
                1 1                   1 2 1 1 1 2 1     2       1     1 2 2 1
          1 2 3 7 8 9     4 7 8 0 3 2 3 4 1 6 6 4     5 1     9 2 0 5
         ----------------------------------------------------------------------
   1  |       1       |   1 1       1           |       |       |           |
   2  |       1       |   1                     |       | 1     |           |
   3  |           1   |                         |       |       |           |
  17  |               |                         |       |       |           |
  18  |           1   |       1     1       1   |       |       1 1         |
   9  |   1           |       1                 |       | 1 1   |         1 |
         ----------------------------------------------------------------------
   4  |               |                         |       |       |           |
   7  |               |                         |       |       |           |
   8  |         1     |       1     1           |       | 1     |           |
  10  |               |                         |       |       |           |
  23  |               |                   1     |       |       |           |
  12  |               |   1             1       |   1   | 1     |           |
  13  |               |                         |       |       |           |
  14  |               |                         |       | 1     |       1 1 |
  21  |             1 |       1                 |       |       |           |
  16  |   1           |   1                     |       |       |           |
   6  |               |                         |       |       |           |
  24  |         1     |                         |       |       |           |
         ----------------------------------------------------------------------
   5  |               |   1             1   1   |   1   |       1           |
  11  |               |   1       1           1 |       |       1           |
         ----------------------------------------------------------------------
  19  |       1       |   1             1       |       | 1     1           |
  22  |       1       |   1       1         1   |   1 1 |       1           |
  20  |   1           |                     1 1 |       |     1             |
  15  |   1           |                 1   1   |       |     1 1           |
         ----------------------------------------------------------------------
```

Overall Network Density = .12
Standard Deviation Within Blocks = .32

FIGURE 11.1C. Block matrix for reading work

The first is based on the planning and technological interests, as evidenced by the ties between Blocks 1 and 3. The second is based on the researchers in Block 2, with some links to the two scholars in Block 4. At the same time, the reduced graphs show that members of Blocks 1 and 2 discuss research with each other, but not with the members of the smaller Blocks 3 and 4.[4]

There is more to the structure than two separate alliances. The data provide some evidence of a cross-cutting core-periphery pattern, with the planners (Block 1) and the researchers (Block 2) collaborating only with each other and not with the members of the other two blocks. There are no links between the peripheral Blocks 3 and 4. Scholars in these blocks are peripheral either because they have not actively represented their interests in TechNet or because they are inactive participants in TechNet. One Block 3

[4] All block descriptors are oversimplifications, as the "planners" are also scholars, the "researchers" sometimes help plan TechNet activities, and "peripheral people" sometimes get involved in core projects. The difference is principally in the extent of involvement in planning.

	Collaboration	Discussing Research	Reading Work
Block Densities	$\begin{array}{ccccc} & 1 & 2 & 3 & 4 \\ 1 & .73 & .17 & .50 & .08 \\ 2 & .17 & .18 & .08 & .23 \\ 3 & .50 & .08 & 1.0 & .13 \\ 4 & .08 & .23 & .13 & .17 \end{array}$	$\begin{array}{ccccc} & 1 & 2 & 3 & 4 \\ 1 & .60 & .94 & .67 & .67 \\ 2 & .94 & .89 & .42 & .73 \\ 3 & .67 & .42 & .00 & .63 \\ 4 & .67 & .73 & .63 & .00 \end{array}$	$\begin{array}{ccccc} & 1 & 2 & 3 & 4 \\ 1 & .17 & .11 & .25 & .13 \\ 2 & .06 & .05 & .08 & .08 \\ 3 & .00 & .25 & .50 & .25 \\ 4 & .17 & .19 & .36 & .33 \end{array}$
Reduced Block Matrices	$\begin{array}{ccccc} & 1 & 2 & 3 & 4 \\ 1 & 1 & 0 & 1 & 0 \\ 2 & 0 & 0 & 0 & 1 \\ 3 & 1 & 0 & 1 & 0 \\ 4 & 0 & 1 & 0 & 0 \end{array}$ Rule: $y(i,j) = 1$ if $x(i,j) > 0.21$, and 0 otherwise.	$\begin{array}{ccccc} & 1 & 2 & 3 & 4 \\ 1 & 1 & 1 & 0 & 0 \\ 2 & 1 & 1 & 0 & 0 \\ 3 & 0 & 0 & 0 & 0 \\ 4 & 0 & 0 & 0 & 0 \end{array}$ Rule: $y(i,j) = 1$ if $x(i,j) > 0.76$, and 0 otherwise.	$\begin{array}{ccccc} & 1 & 2 & 3 & 4 \\ 1 & 1 & 0 & 1 & 1 \\ 2 & 0 & 0 & 0 & 0 \\ 3 & 0 & 1 & 1 & 1 \\ 4 & 1 & 1 & 1 & 1 \end{array}$ Rule: $y(i,j) = 1$ if $x(i,j) > 0.12$, and 0 otherwise.
Reduced Graphs	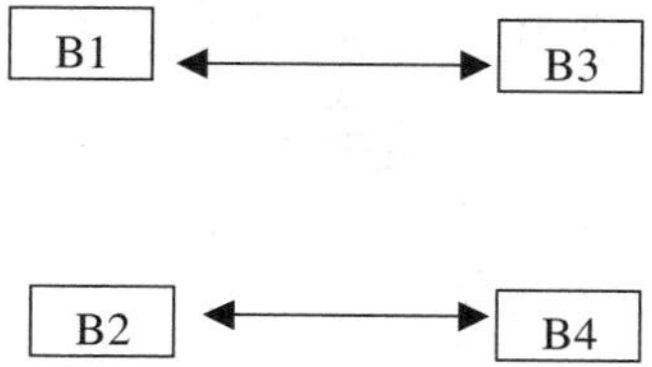 B1 — B3 ; B2 — B4	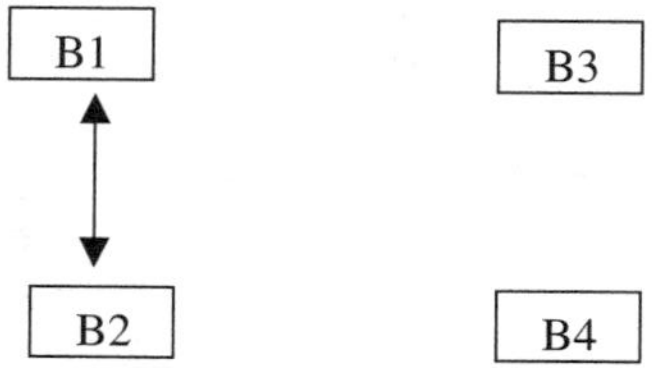 B1 — B2 ; B3 ; B4	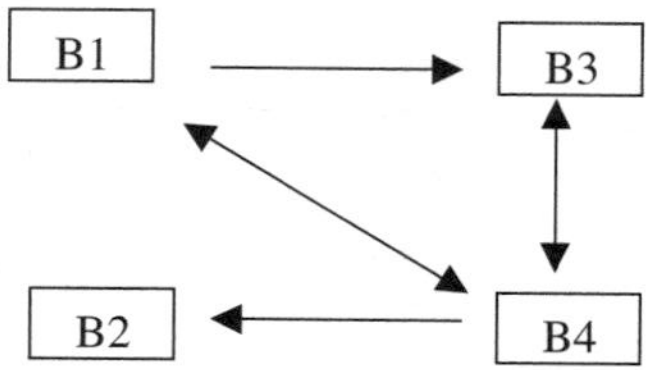 B1, B2, B3, B4 (B3 ↔ B4, B1 → B3, B4 → B2, B1 ↔ B4)

FIGURE 11.2. Representation of block densities, reduced block matrices, reduced graphs, and frequency of ties within and between positions

scholar says, "I don't recognize myself as an academic in terms of connections to other academics," while another reports, "I am a technical administrator. [Hence, I] concern [myself] only with technical details of or interests within TechNet."

READING EACH OTHER'S WORK. There is more interconnectivity between blocks in terms of reading each other's work than there is for collaboration. Members of the large planners Block 1 read the work of the members of Blocks 3 and 4. In other words, core and peripheral scholars want to learn about each other's work. Thus, some members of Block 1 read the work of the two Block 3 scholars whom they regard as eminent even though these Block 3 scholars keep to themselves and rarely reciprocate by reading Block 1's work. In addition, the two Block 4 members read the work of some leading researchers in Block 2. Members of the peripheral Blocks 3 and 4 also read each other's work, possibly to remain intellectually and socially connected with TechNet members. Note that some of the scholars peripheral to TechNet are important to their own disciplinary specializations, and core TechNet members can learn what is happening outside of their network through their relationships with the TechNet periphery.

The block models suggest that TechNet members read widely. In this way, the TechNet's ideal of interdisciplinary cross-fertilization is being realized. However, when it comes to the actual practice of research, TechNet scholars stay more narrowly within their own disciplines and blocks.

Blocks and Communication

How do scholars who occupy various positions or blocks differ in email and face-to-face contact, as well as in the perceived effectiveness of email and face-to-face communications for scholarly activities? In this section, we analyze the implications of occupying structurally equivalent positions or blocks for email and face-to-face contact, the use of multiple communication media, and varying perceptions about the effectiveness of face-to-face and email contact for accomplishing scholarly tasks.

FACE-TO-FACE CONTACT. Nearly three-quarters (73 percent) of TechNet pairs (405/552) have at least one type of relationship with each other: collaborating, discussing, or reading. The block location of scholars is associated with their face-to-face contact (Table 11.4). In general, 38 percent of TechNet members have face-to-face contact somewhat frequently (5–12 times/year), while 19 percent have frequent (more than 12 times/year) face-to-face contact with their scholarly ties. Almost a third (29 percent) have infrequent face-to-face contact (< 5 times/year), while only a few (12 percent) have no face-to-face contact. For example, one of the 405 pairs could be a frequent discussion tie and another could be an infrequent reading tie between the same two TechNet members. That slightly more than

TABLE 11.4. *Relationship between Scholarly Blocks and Overall Monthly Face-to-Face and Email Contact with Perception of Effectiveness of Media*

Block and Number of Ties	Block 1 (N = 105)	Block 2 (N = 219)	Block 3 (N = 23)	Block 4 (N = 58)	N	Total (%)	Contact (%)
Monthly Face-to-Face Contact		*Percent Within Blocks*					
None (0)	3	18	13	10	51	12	–
Infrequent (0.1–4.9)	26	30	44	31	121	29	34
Somewhat Frequently (5.0–12.9)	50	37	17	31	156	38	44
Frequent (13–441)	21	15	26	28	77	19	21
TOTAL	100	100	100	100	405	100	100
		$X^2 = 27.3\ DF = 9\ P < 0.01$					
Monthly Email Contact							
None (0)	55	47	35	36	189	46	–
Infrequent (0.1–4.9)	11	22	26	24	81	20	37
Somewhat Frequent (5.0–12.9)	9	14	22	16	53	13	24
Frequent (13–441)	25	17	17	24	82	20	38
TOTAL	100	100	100	100	405	100	100
		$X^2 = 14.9\ DF = 9\ P < 0.09$					

Multiple Media Use

No Media	2	17	13	7	47	11	–
One Media	46	28	22	26	129	31	36
Two Media	28	32	57	41	135	33	37
Three Media	25	24	9	24	94	23	26
TOTAL	100	100	100	100	405	100	100

$X^2 = 31.4\ DF = 9\ P < 0.001$

Perceived Effectiveness of Face-to-Face Contact

Not Effective	9	9	0	0	29	7.2	–
Slightly Effective	0	23	52	32	81	20	21
Effective	51	25	0	17	117	28.9	31
Very Effective	41	43	48	50	178	44.0	47
TOTAL	100	100	100	100	405	100	100

$X^2 = 74.2\ DF = 9\ P < 0.001$

Perceived Effectiveness of Email Contact

Not Effective	0	10	0	0	22	5.4	–
Slightly Effective	35	19	0	17	89	22	23
Effective	34	33	100	33	150	37	39
Very Effective	31	38	0	50	144	35	37
TOTAL	100	100	100	100	405	100	100

$X^2 = 72.3\ DF = 9\ P < 0.001$

half (57 percent) of TechNet pairs maintain frequent or somewhat frequent face-to-face contact, suggests that face-to-face contact is an important means of communication. It brings strong ties together for meetings and tête-à-têtes, and both strong and weak ties for larger scheduled events.

Different roles in TechNet affect variations in face-to-face contact within and between blocks. Block 1 planners stand out with 71 percent of their face-to-face relationships in TechNet being frequent or somewhat frequent. By contrast, only 43 percent of the two peripheral Block 3 members' face-to-face relationships are frequent or somewhat frequent. Block 1 planners and Block 2 researchers have frequent or somewhat frequent face-to-face relationships through informal chats and joint participation in TechNet's meetings, workshops, and seminars (Figure 11.2).

EMAIL CONTACT. Email contact relationships for collaborating, discussing, and reading research have different characteristics than face-to-face relationships. Nearly half (47 percent) of all TechNet pairs do not use email to communicate. In keeping with this, most pairs (60–69 percent) of each block never or infrequently communicate by email. However, those TechNet pairs who are in email contact tend to use it more frequently than face-to-face contact. For example, although only one-fifth (20 percent) of all TechNet pairs are in frequent email contact (82/405), 38 percent (82/216) of those pairs that use email use it frequently (more than 12 times/year). Thirteen percent of all TechNet pairs are in somewhat frequent email contact (5–12 times/year), while 20 percent are in less frequent contact.

In general, there are differences in email and face-to-face contact and in the perceived effectiveness of each medium in scholarly activities. These relate to the roles and research interests of various scholars in TechNet. Face-to-face contact brings together both active TechNet members and otherwise-disconnected TechNet members. Face-to-face contact is the predominant medium of contact for the planning Block 1 and the researchers in Block 2, because it suits the context of their reciprocal discussion of research and other interactions. By contrast, email connects active TechNet members in a focused, selective way and allows core planners to broadcast to and communicate with peripheral members. Different patterns of email use among blocks fit the scholarly roles of TechNet members. The planning Block 1 uses email to communicate with the peripheral, Internet-habituated members of Block 3. The planning Block 1 and research Block 2 communicate less by email because their TechNet activities bring them into frequent face-to-face contact at seminars, conferences, grant preparation, and administration. Email is the natural medium of choice for the peripheral members of Blocks 3 and 4 as it gives them remote access to the rest of TechNet while removing the burden of journeying to face-to-face meetings.

A SCHOLARLY NETWORK IN A COMPUTER-MEDIATED WORLD

Our analysis shows that TechNet is a learning community focused on peer-to-peer learning. Most TechNet members discuss and seek advice about their work with each other, but only read the work of a few and collaborate with few others in research and proposal writing. Social network analysis provided us with an approach to understand the structure of relations underlying this scholarly community. It reveals overlapping networks, with some scholars discussing each other's work, reading these works, and collaborating in research. Two kinds of networks affect the scholars' communication behavior: formal work relations and informal friendships. The centrality of TechNet members varies markedly, both in internal prominence (choices by others) and in how they are in brokerage positions that link different parts of the TechNet networks. TechNet members use both email and face-to-face contact to get advice from prominent members. Email is used extensively among friends and collaborators, as well as for communication within the core, and between the core and the periphery.

The nature of the tie predicts media use more than the nature of the communication task does. Friendship as well as collaboration drives frequent face-to-face and email communication. Strongly tied collaborators and friends use whatever communication means are necessary to interact, exchange information, and coordinate. The more types of relationships they have, the more frequently they communicate by email and face-to-face. Those scholars with larger (personal) networks have varied communication patterns, and mostly use email as a medium of communication. Even when working nearby, they often find email communication handier for spontaneous communication than walking a few hundred, often-cold meters to talk face-to-face. These ties are strong enough that they can be maintained extensively through the narrower bandwidth of email and refreshed through occasional face-to-face get-togethers.

Blockmodeling provides a view of internal differentiation within TechNet. This is not a densely knit network where all are connected to all. Neither is it a disconnected aggregate. There is much communication within and between the blocks, and TechNet members are scarcely aware that the blocks exist. This is not a set of mutually exclusive cliques. Indeed, all TechNet members are probably connected to all others by only one or two steps. TechNet has sizeable core blocks of planners and researchers plus two peripheral blocks. The block configurations are related to communication patterns of scholars. Face-to-face contact continues to play a strong role in inter- and intra-block communications. The core planning block of TechNet uses face-to-face contact both as a means of reaching out to peripheral members and because they are active in all of TechNet's public and private activities. TechNet members with higher administrative or research prestige are frequently sought out for advice when they are in public, face-to-face gatherings. Email is extensively used among friends and colleagues working together, for contacts to and from peripheral blocks, and for broadcasting announcements from the core planners.

Email and face-to-face contact play complementary roles and reinforce each other. The impact of email is not so much in what is communicated, but in who communicates with whom, how frequently, and over what distances. Despite TechNet's frequent public gatherings, face-to-face contact is more centralized than email contact. Core planners and researchers combine face-to-face, email, and occasional phone contacts. Peripheral members are more apt to use one of these media to keep in touch with TechNet activities. Some rely on scheduled face-to-face get-togethers to find out what is happening administratively and intellectually. Others, who do not want to go across campus to meetings, rely on email broadcasts and occasional focused exchanges. These blocks have fluid and permeable boundaries for the structure of relationships in TechNet that vary according to the activity being performed (for similar findings, see Ahuja & Carley, 1999). These networked scholars use email for a wide range of tasks: exchanging drafts among co-authors, setting up meetings, asking for information, or gossiping about colleagues. Although pundits worried a decade ago about whether merely textual email could sustain a wide range of interactions – from information seeking to emotional stroking – it is the social context, more than the nature of the medium, that affects whether email will be used. Expectations only a decade ago that email would only be used for purely instrumental communication appear to have been a product of early fascination with the novelty of email and an overemphasis on McLuhan's (1962) speculation that the medium is the message.

In short, TechNet has been a success in building a scholarly network and turning it into a semi-visible college. At the time of our data collection in 1997–1998, in TechNet's brief period of operation, it had already achieved the following:

1. Linked scholars across a variety of disciplines in the humanities, social sciences, and sciences.
2. Provided a milieu where most members are aware of each other's work.
3. Fostered a large amount of innovative collaborative work and discussions across disciplines.
4. Integrated the use of email and face-to-face contact into useful means of communication.

TechNet has continued to build from these early strengths. The scholarly network has become more visible and somewhat institutionalized. As of writing in 2002, collaborative research has become more extensive, and well-attended lecture series solidify internal communication and reach out to other scholars, policymakers, technology companies, and the public. A new graduate program offers a set of core interdisciplinary courses and an extensive list of affiliated courses with collaborating scholarly departments in the social sciences, physical sciences, and engineering. In addition, there is a full-time paid administrator and additional paid part-time staff.

Our findings suggest that scholarly communities of practice are not homogeneous entities, whether they are online, offline, or both. Online mutual-learning communities consist of scholars with varying roles, levels of involvement, positions, and varying levels of connectivity with other community members (Hiltz & Wellman, 1997). Further, the structure of these relationships is related to the types and variety of communication media used. Rather than seeing the Internet as a separate interaction system, they use it opportunistically to fit into their everyday lives. For designers of online educational communities, our study suggests the need to take a broad look at the social networks of community members and how their internal structure and media use facilitate and constrain mutual peer-to-peer learning.

References

Acker, S. R. (1995). Space, Collaboration, and the Credible City: Academic Work in the Virtual University. *Journal of Computer Mediated Communication, 1*(1). Available online at http://www.ascusc.org/jcmc/vol1/issue1/acker/acktext.htm.

Ahuja, M., & Carley, K. (1999). Network Structure in Virtual Organizations. *Organization Science, 10*(6), 741–757.

Assimakopoulos, D., & Macdonald, S. (2002). A Dual Approach to Understanding Information Networks. *International Journal of Networking and Virtual Organizations, 1*(1) 1–16.

Bar, F. with Simard, C. (2001). New Media Implementation and Industrial Organization. In L. Lievrouw & S. Livingstone (Eds.), *Handbook of New Media*. London: Sage.

Barab, S., & Duffy, T. (2000). From Practice Fields to Communities of Practice. In D. H. J. S. M. Land (Ed.), *Theoretical Foundations of Learning Environments*. Mahwah, NJ: Lawrence Erlbaum.

Barrett, R. (2000). Virtual Communities and the Internet. Working Paper: The Reginald H. Jones Center for Management Policy, Strategy, and Organization. Wharton Business School, University of Pennsylvania, Philadelphia.

Baym, N. (1995). The Performance of Humor in Computer-Mediated Communication. *Journal of Computer-Mediated Communication, 1*(2). Available online at http//www.usc.edu/dept/annenberg/vol1/issue2.

Baym, N. K. (1997). Interpreting Soap Operas and Creating Community: Inside an Electronic Fan Culture. In S. Kiesler (Ed.), *Culture of the Internet* (pp. 103–120). Mahwah, NJ: Lawrence Erlbaum.

Berkowitz, S. D. (1982). *An Introduction to Structural Analysis: The Network Approach to Social Research.* Toronto: Butterworth.

Borgatti, S., Everett, M., & Freeman, L. (1999). *UCINet 5 for Windows.* Natick, MA: Analytic Technologies.

Breiger, R., Boorman, S., & Arabie, P. (1975). An algorithm for Clustering Relational data with applications to social network Analysis and Comparison with Multidimensional Scaling. *Journal of Mathematical Psychology, 12,* 328–383.

Burt, R. (1980). Models of Network Structure. *Annual Review of Sociology, 6,* 79–141.

Burt, R. (1983). Range. In R. Burt & M. Minor (Eds.), *Applied Network Analysis* (pp. 176–194). Beverly Hills, CA: Sage.

Burt, R. (1992). *Structural Holes.* Chicago: University of Chicago Press.

Carley, K. M., Hummon, N., & Harty, M. (1993). Scientific Influence: An Analysis of the Main Path Structure in the Journal of Conflict Resolution. *Knowledge: Creation, Diffusion, Utilization, 14*(4, June), 417–447.

Carley, K., & Wendt, K. (1991). Electronic mail and Scientific communication. *Knowledge, 12*(4), 406–440.

Churchill, E. F., Snowdon, D. N., & Munro, A. J. (Eds.). (2001). *Collaborative Virtual Environments: Digital Places and Spaces for Interaction.* London: Springer-Verlag.

Contractor, N. S., & Eisenberg, E. M. (1990). Communication Networks and New Media in Organizations. In J. Fulk & C. Steinfeld (Eds.), *Organizations and Communication Technology* (pp. 143–172). Newbury Park, CA: Sage.

Crane, D. (1972). *Invisible Colleges: Diffusion of Knowledge in Scientific Communities.* Chicago: University of Chicago Press.

Danowski, J. A. (1986). Interpersonal Network Structure and Media Use: A Focus on Radiality and Non-Mass Media Use. In *Inter/Media: Interpersonal Communication in a Media World* (pp. 168–175). New York: Oxford University Press.

Erickson, B. (1988). The Relational Basis of Attitudes. In B. Wellman and S. Berkowitz (Eds.), *Social Structures: A Network Approach* (pp. 99–122). Cambridge: Cambridge University Press.

Erickson, B. H. (1996). The Structure of Ignorance. *Connections, 19*(1), 28–38.

Feld, S. (1981). The Focused Organization of Social Ties. *American Journal of Sociology, 86,* 1015–1035.

Finholt, T. (2001). Collaboratories. *Annual Review of Information Science and Technology, 36,* 73–107.

Finholt, T., & Sproull, L. S. (1990). Electronic Groups at Work. *Organization Science, 1*(1), 41–64.

Finholt, T., Sproull, L., & Kiesler, S. (2002). Outsiders on the Inside: Sharing Know-How Across Space and Time. In P. Hinds & S. Kiesler (Eds.), *Distributed Work: New Research on Working Across Distance Using Technology* (pp. 357–379). Cambridge, MA: MIT Press.

Fischer, C. (1982). *To Dwell Among Friends.* Berkeley: University of California Press.

Friedkin, N. (1978). University Social Structure and Social Networks Among Scientists. *American Journal of Sociology, 83*(6), 1444–1465.

Friedkin, N. (1980). A Test of Structural Features of Granovetter's Strength of Weak Ties Theory. *Social Networks, 2,* 411–422.

Friedkin, N. (1982). Information Flows Through Strong and Weak Ties in Intraorganizational Social Networks. *Social Networks, 3,* 273–285.

Fulk, J., & DeSanctis, G. (1995). Electronic Communication and Changing Organizational Forms. *Organization Science, 6*(4), 337–349.

Fulk, J., Steinfeld, C., Schmitz, J., & Power, J. G. (1987). A Social Information Processing Model of Media Use in Organizations. *Communication Research, 14*(5), 529–552.

Garton, L., Haythornthwaite, C., & Wellman, B. (1998). Studying On-Line Social Networks. In S. Jones (Ed.), *Doing Internet Research* (pp. 75–105). Thousand Oaks, CA: Sage.

Garton, L., & Wellman, B. (1995). The Social Uses of Electronic Mail in Organizations: A Review of the Research. *Communication Yearbook, 18*, 434–453.

Glanz, J. (1999). What Fuels Progress in Science? Sometimes, a Feud. *New York Times*: D1–2.

Gottlieb, B. (Ed.). (1981). *Social Networks and Social Support*. Beverly Hills, CA: Sage.

Granovetter, M. (1973). The Strength of Weak Ties. *American Journal of Sociology, 78*, 1360–1380.

Granovetter, M. (1983). The Strength of Weak Ties: A Network Theory Revisited. *Sociological Theory 1983*, 201–233.

Gresham, J. J. (1994). From Invisible College to Cyberspace College: Computer Conferencing and the Transformation of Informal Scholarly Communication Networks. *Interpersonal Computing and Technology, 2*(4), 37–52.

Grimshaw, A. (1989). *Collegial Discourse: Professional Conversation among Peers*. Norwood, NJ: Ablex.

Haines, V., & Hurlbert, J. (1992). Network Range and Health. *Journal of Health and Social Behavior, 33*, 254–266.

Harasim, L., Hiltz, S. R., Teles, L., & Turoff, M. (1995). *Learning Networks*. Cambridge, MA: MIT Press.

Haythornthwaite, C. (2000). Online personal networks. *New Media & Society, 2*(2), 195–226.

Haythornthwaite, C. (2002). Building Social Networks via Computer Networks: Creating and Sustaining Distributed Learning Communities. In K. A. Renninger & W. Shumar, *Building Virtual Communities: Learning and Change in Cyberspace* (pp. 159–190). Cambridge: Cambridge University Press.

Haythornthwaite, C., & Wellman, B. (1998). Work, Friendship and Media Use for Information Exchange in a Networked Organization. *Journal of the American Society for Information Science, 49*(12), 1101–1114.

Haythornthwaite, C., Wellman, B., & Mantei, M. (1995). Work Relationships and media Use: A Social Network Analysis. *Group Decision and Negotiation, 4*(3), 193–211.

Hert, P. (1997). Social Dynamics of an On-Line Scholarly Debate. *The Information Society, 13*, 329–360.

Hiltz, S. R., & Turoff, M. (1993). *The Network Nation* (2d ed.). Cambridge, MA: MIT Press.

Hiltz, S. R., & Wellman, B. (1997). Asynchronous Learning Networks as Virtual Communities. *Journal of the ACM, 40*(9), 44–49.

Kling, R. (1996). Social Relationships in Electronic Forums: Hangouts, Salons, Workplaces and Communities. In R. Kling (Ed.), *Computerization and Controversy: Value Conflicts and Social Choices* (2d ed., pp. 426–454). San Diego: Academic Press.

Koku, E., Nazer, N., & Wellman, B. (2001). Netting Scholars: Online and Offline. *American Behavioral Scientist, 44*(5), 1750–1772.

Kollock, P., & Smith, M. (Eds.). (1998). *Communities in Cyberspace.* London: Routledge.

Kraut, R., Egido, C., & Galegher, J. (1990). Patterns of Contact and Communication in Scientific Research Collaboration. In J. Galegher, R. Kraut, & C. Egido (Eds.), *Intellectual Teamwork: Social and Technological Foundations of Cooperative Work* (pp. 149–171). Hillsdale, NJ: Lawrence Erlbaum.

Levin, D., Cross, R., & Abrams, L. (August 2002). The strength of weak ties you can trust: The mediating role of trust in effective knowledge transfer. Paper presented at the Academy of Management conference, Denver, CO.

Lin, N. (2001). *Social Capital: A Theory of Social Structure and Action.* Cambridge: Cambridge University Press.

Lin, N., Cook, K., & Burt, R. S. (Eds.). (2001). *Social Capital: Theory and Research.* New York: Aldine de Gruyter.

Lin, N., & Dumin, M. (1986). Access to Occupations through Social Ties. *Social Networks, 8,* 365–383.

Lin, N., & Gao, B. (August, 2000). *Cybernetworks and a Social-Capital-Based Economy.* Paper presented at the American Sociological Association Meeting, Washington, DC.

Lin, N., & Westcott, J. (1991). Marital Engagement/Disengagement, Social Networks, and Mental Health. In J. Eckenrode (Ed.), *The Social Context of Coping* (pp. 213–237). New York: Plenum Press.

Marsden, P., & Campbell, K. E. (1984). Measuring Tie Strength. *Social Forces, 63,* 482–501.

Marshall, J. (1970). *The Castle's Keep: The Villa Serbelloni in History.* Bellagio, Italy: Bellagio Center for Study and Conferences.

Matzat, U. (2001). *Social Networks and Cooperation in Electronic Communities: A Theoretical–Empirical Analysis of Academic Communication and Internet Discussion Groups.* Unpublished doctoral thesis. Interuniversity Center for Sociological Theory and Methodology, University of Groningen, Netherlands.

McLuhan, M. (1962). *The Gutenberg Galaxy: The Making of Typographic Man.* Toronto: University of Toronto Press.

Mutschke, P., & Quan-Haase, A. (2001). Collaboration and Cognitive Structures in Social Science Research Fields. *Scientometrics, 52*(3) 487–502.

Nazer, N. (2000). *The Emergence of a Virtual Research Organization: How an Invisible College Becomes Visible.* Unpublished doctoral thesis. Department of Sociology, University of Toronto.

Nazer, N. (2001). *Operating Virtually within a Hierarchical Framework: How a Virtual Organization Really Works.* Unpublished doctoral dissertation, University of Toronto, Canada.

Newman, M.E.J. (2000). *The Structure of Scientific Collaboration Networks.* Working paper: Santa Fe Institute, Santa Fe, NM.

Newman, M.E.J. (2001). Ego-centered networks and the ripple effect: Why all your friends are weird. Working paper: Santa Fe Institute, Santa Fe, NM.

Nie, N. (2001). Sociability, Interpersonal Relations, and the Internet: Reconciling Conflicting Findings. *American Behavioral Scientist 45*(3), 420–435.

Noam, E. M. (1998). CMC and Higher Education. *Journal of Computer Mediated Communication, 4*(2). Available online at http: //jcmc.huji.ac.il/vol4/issue2/. pp7.

Orlikowski, W., & Barley, S. (2001). Technology and Institutions: What Can Research on Information Technology and Research on Organizations Learn from Each Other? *MIS Quarterly, 25*(June): 145–165.

Perry, C., & Rice, R. (1998). Scholarly Communication in Developmental Dyslexia: Influence of Network Structure on Change in a Hybrid Problem Area. *Journal of the American Society for Information Science, 49*(2), 151–168.

Price, D.d.S. (1961). *Science since Babylon.* New Haven: Yale University Press.

Ragusa, J., & Bochenek, G. (Eds.). (2001). *Collaborative Virtual Design Environments.* Special issue of *Communications of the ACM, 44,* 12(December): 40–90.

Rheingold, H. (2000). *The Virtual Community* (rev. ed.). Cambridge, MA: MIT Press.

Rice, R. E. (1991). Network Analysis and Computer-Mediated Communication Systems. In *Anthropology and Communication* (pp. 167–199).

Rice, R. (1994). Network Analysis and Computer-Mediated Communication Systems. In S. Wasserman & J. Galaskiewicz (Eds.), *Advances in Social Network Analysis* (pp. 167–203). Thousand Oaks, CA: Sage.

Rice, R. (1997). Relating Electronic Mail Use and Network Structure to R&D Work Networks. *Journal of Management Information Systems, 11*(1), 9–29.

Rice, R. E. (2001). Diffusion of Innovations and Communication. In J. Schement (Ed.), *Encyclopedia of Communication and information* (pp. 248–253). New York: Macmillan Reference.

Rice, R., & Aydin, C. (1991). Attitudes toward New Organizational Technology: Network Proximity as a Mechanism for Social Information Processing. *Administrative Science Quarterly, 36,* 219–244.

Rice, R., D'Ambra, J., & More, E. (1998). Cross-Cultural Comparison of Organizational Media Evaluation and Choice. *Journal of Communication, 48*(3) 3–26.

Rice, R. E., & Gattiker, U. E. (2001). New Media and Organizational Structuring. In F. Jablin & L. Putnam (Eds.), *The New Handbook of Organizational Communication: Advances in Theory, Research, and Methods* (pp. 544–). Thousand Oaks, CA: Sage.

Rice, R., Grant, A., Schmitz, J., & Torobin, J. (1990). Individual and Network Influences on the Adoption and Perceived Outcomes of Electronic Messaging. *Social Networks, 12,* 27–55.

Rogers, E. M. (1979). Network Analysis of the Diffusion of Innovations. In P. Holland & S. Leinhardt (Eds.), *Perspectives on Social Network Research* (pp. 137–165). New York: Academic Press.

Rogers, E. (1983). *Diffusion of Innovations.* New York: Free Press.

Scott, J. (1991). *Social Network Analysis.* London: Sage.

Smith, M. A. (2000). Some social implications of ubiquitous wireless networks. Working Paper: Microsoft Research, Redmond, WA.

Smith, M. A., & Kollock, P. (Eds.). (1999). *Communities in Cyberspace.* London: Routledge.

Sproull, L., & Kiesler, S. (1991). *Connections.* Cambridge, MA: MIT Press.

Teigland, R., and Wasko, M. M. (2000). *Creative Ties and Ties that Bind: Examining the Impact of Weak Ties on Individual Performance.* ICIS 2000 (International Conference on Information Systems), Brisbane, Australia.

Tindall, D., and Wellman, B., (2001). Canada as Social Structure: Social Network Analysis and Canadian Sociology. *Canadian Journal of Sociology, 26*: 265–308.

Toren, N. (1994). Professional-Support and Intellectual-Influence Networks of Russian Immigrant Scientists in Israel. *Social Studies of Science, 24*, 725–743.

Tushman, M. L., & Scanlan, T. J. (1981). Boundary Spanning Individuals: Their Role in Information Transfer and their Antecedents. *Academy of Management Journal, 24*(2), 289–305.

Valente, T. (1995). *Network Models of the Diffusion of Innovations.* Cresskill, NJ: Hampton Press.

Walsh, J. P., & Bayama, T. (1996). The Virtual College: Computer-Mediated Communication and Scientific Work. *Information Society, 12*, 343–363.

Wasserman, S., & Faust, K. (1994). *Social Network Analysis: Methods and Applications.* Cambridge: Cambridge University Press.

Wellman, B. (1988). Thinking Structurally. In B. Wellman & S. Berkowitz (Eds.), *Social Structures: A Network Approach* (pp. 15–19). Cambridge: Cambridge University Press.

Wellman, B. (1992). How to Use SAS to Study Egocentric Networks. *Cultural Anthropology Methods, 4*(2), 6–12.

Wellman, B. (1997). An Electronic Group Is Virtually a Social Network. In S. Kiesler (Ed.), *Culture of the Internet* (pp. 179–205). Mahwah, NJ: Lawrence Erlbaum.

Wellman, B. (1999). *Networks in the Global Village.* Boulder, CO: Westview Press.

Wellman, B. (2001). Physical Place and Cyber-Place: Changing Portals and the Rise of Networked Individualism. *International Journal for Urban and Regional Research, 25*(2), 227–252.

Wellman, B., & Berkowitz, S. D. (Eds.). (1988). *Social Structures: A Network Approach.* Cambridge: Cambridge University Press.

Wellman, B., Carrington, P., & Hall, A. (1988). Networks as Personal Communities. In B. Wellman & S. D. Berkowitz (Eds.), *Social Structures: A Network Approach* (pp. 130–184). Cambridge: Cambridge University Press.

Wellman, B., Frank, O., Espinoza, V., Lundquist, S., & Wilson, C. (1991). Integrating Individual, Relational and Structural Analysis. *Social Networks, 13*, 223–250.

Wellman, B., and Frank, K., et al. (2001). Network Capital in a Multi-Level World: Getting Support in Personal Communities. In N. Lin, K. Cook, & R. Burt (Eds.), *Social Capital: Theory and Research* (pp. 233–273). Hawthorne, NY: Aldine DeGruyter.

Wellman, B., & Gulia, M. (1999). Net Surfers Don't Ride Alone. In B. Wellman (Ed.), *Networks in the Global Village* (pp. 331–366). Boulder, CO: Westview Press.

Wellman, B., & Hampton, K. (1999). Living Networked On and Offline. *Contemporary Sociology, 28*(6),648–654.

Wellman, B., Salaff, J., Dimitrova, D., Garton, L., Gulia, M., & Haythornthwaite, C. (1996). Computer Networks as Social Networks: Virtual Community, Computer Supported Cooperative Work and Telework. *Annual Review of Sociology, 22*, 213–238.

Wellman, B. and Wortley, S., (1989). Brothers' Keepers: Situating Kinship Relations in Broader Networks of Social Support. *Sociological Perspectives, 32*, 273–306.

Wellman, B., & Wortley, S. (1990). Different Strokes from Different Folks: Community Ties and Social Support. *American Journal of Sociology, 96*, 558–588.

Wenger, E. (1998). *Communities of Practice: Learning, Meaning, and Identity.* Cambridge: Cambridge University Press.

White, H., Boorman, S., & Breiger, R. (1976). Social Structure from Multiple Networks: I Blockmodels of Roles and Positions. *American Journal of Sociology, 81,* 730–780.

Zack, M. H. (1994). Electronic Messaging and Communication Effectiveness in an Ongoing Work Group. *Information and Management, 26,* 231–241.

12

Computer-Mediated Discourse Analysis

An Approach to Researching Online Behavior

Susan C. Herring

Over the past fifteen years, the Internet has triggered a boom in research on human behavior. As growing numbers of people interact on a regular basis in chat rooms, web forums, listservs, email, instant messaging environments and the like, social scientists, marketers, and educators look to their behavior in an effort to understand the nature of computer-mediated communication and how it can be optimized in specific contexts of use. This effort is facilitated by the fact that people engage in socially meaningful activities online in a way that typically leaves a textual trace, making the interactions more accessible to scrutiny and reflection than is the case in ephemeral spoken communication, and enabling researchers to employ empirical, micro-level methods to shed light on macro-level phenomena. Despite this potential, much research on online behavior is anecdotal and speculative, rather than empirically grounded. Moreover, Internet research often suffers from a premature impulse to label online phenomena in broad terms, for example, all groups of people interacting online are "communities";[1] the language of the Internet is a single style or "genre."[2] Notions such as *community* and *genre* are familiar and

---

[1] See, e.g., Burnett (2000), who characterizes virtual communities broadly as "discussion forums focusing on a set of interests shared by a group of geographically dispersed participants." According to this characterization, almost any Internet discussion group is a virtual community.

[2] For examples of this usage, see Ferrara, Brunner, and Whittemore (1991), who employ the term "register" in this broad sense, and, more recently, Crystal (2001), who refers to the language of the Internet as "netspeak."

This chapter could not have been written without the feedback from the students in two graduate Computer-Mediated Discourse Analysis courses I taught at Indiana University in 2001–2002. I am grateful to those students for teaching me through their learning. Thanks are also due to Sasha Barab, Zilia Estrada, and John Paolillo for helpful comments on the writing and organization of the chapter, and to Anthony Aristar for up-to-date information about the Linguist List. Any remaining errors of fact or interpretation are my own.

evocative, yet notoriously slippery, and unhelpful (or worse) if applied indiscriminately. An important challenge facing Internet researchers is thus how to identify and describe online phenomena in culturally meaningful terms, while at the same time grounding their distinctions in empirically observable behavior.

Online interaction overwhelmingly takes place by means of discourse. That is, participants interact by means of verbal language, usually typed on a keyboard and read as text on a computer screen. It is possible to lose sight of this fundamental fact at times, given the complex behaviors people engage in on the Internet, from forming interpersonal relationships (Baker, 1998) to implementing systems of group governance (Dibbell, 1993; Kolko & Reid, 1998). Yet these behaviors are constituted through and by means of discourse: language is doing, in the truest performative sense, on the Internet, where physical bodies (and their actions) are technically lacking (Kolko, 1995). Of course, many online relationships also have an offline component, and as computer-mediated communication becomes increasingly multimodal, semiotic systems in addition to text are becoming available for conveying meaning and "doing things" online (cf. Austin, 1962). Nonetheless, textual communication remains an important online activity, one that seems destined to continue for the foreseeable future. It follows that scholars of computer-mediated behavior need methods for analyzing discourse, alongside traditional social science methods such as experiments, interviews, surveys, and ethnographic observation.

This chapter describes an approach to researching online interactive behavior known as Computer-Mediated Discourse Analysis (CMDA). CMDA applies methods adapted from language-focused disciplines such as linguistics, communication, and rhetoric to the analysis of computer-mediated communication (Herring, 2001). It may be supplemented by surveys, interviews, ethnographic observation, or other methods; it may involve qualitative or quantitative analysis; but what defines CMDA at its core is the analysis of logs of verbal interaction (characters, words, utterances, messages, exchanges, threads, archives, etc.). In the broadest sense, any analysis of online behavior that is grounded in empirical, textual observations is computer-mediated discourse analysis.[3]

The specific approach to computer-mediated discourse analysis described here is informed by a linguistic perspective. That is, it views online behavior through the lens of language, and its interpretations are grounded in observations about language and language use. This perspective is reflected in the application of methodological paradigms that originated in the study of spoken and written language, for example, conversation analysis, interactional sociolinguistics, pragmatics, text analysis, and critical

---

[3] "Textual" is intended here broadly, to include any form of language, spoken or written, that can be captured and studied in textual form.

discourse analysis. It also shapes the kinds of questions that are likely to get asked. Linguists are interested in language structure, meaning, and use, how these vary according to context, how they are learned, and how they change over time. CMDA can be used to study micro-level linguistic phenomena such as online word-formation processes (Cherny, 1999), lexical choice (Ko, 1996; Yates, 1996), sentence structure (Herring, 1998), and language switching among bilingual speakers (Georgakopoulou, in press; Paolillo, 1996). At the same time, a language-focused approach can be used to address macro-level phenomena such as coherence (Herring, 1999a; Panyametheekul, 2001), community (Cherny, 1999), gender equity (Herring, 1993, 1996a, 1999b), and identity (Burkhalter, 1999), as expressed through discourse. Indeed, the potential – and power – of CMDA is that it enables questions of broad social and psychological significance, including notions that would otherwise be intractable to empirical analysis, to be investigated with fine-grained empirical rigor. The present chapter is intended as a practical contribution toward helping researchers realize this potential.

Because of its practical focus, this chapter will be most useful to readers who already have some study of computer-mediated communication in mind and who have given some thought to how they might approach their investigation. Readers who have made preliminary observations about a behavior (or behaviors) of interest in a specific online environment, and who have collected (or have access to) a relevant corpus of data, will be even better positioned to appreciate the methodological concerns addressed here. At the same time, the chapter is not intended as a step-by-step "how to" guide, but rather as an overview of how a CMDA researcher might conceptualize, design, and interpret a research project involving identifying and counting discourse phenomena in a corpus of computer-mediated text.[4] For details regarding the implementation of specific analytic methods, readers are referred to the research studies cited in the references.

I begin by providing some historical background on CMDA and the kinds of research that have been carried out in the linguistic CMDA tradition, broadly construed. I then present a detailed overview of one version of the CMDA approach based on the "coding and counting" paradigm of classical content analysis, identifying a set of conceptual skills necessary for carrying out a successful analysis. These skills are illustrated with reference to the problem of analyzing virtual community in two professional development sites on the Internet. In concluding, the limits of the coding and counting paradigm, and the CMDA approach as a whole, are identified and future directions are charted.

---

[4] For a relatively current discussion of ethical issues associated with collecting and analyzing data from the Internet (although as of this writing, understandings of what is acceptable practice are still evolving), see Mann and Stewart (2000).

BACKGROUND

The term *computer-mediated discourse analysis* was first coined in 1995 (see Herring, 2001), although research meeting the definitional criteria for CMDA has been carried out since the mid-1980s (in the linguistic sense: e.g., Murray, 1985, 1988; Severinson Eklundh, 1986), and arguably, as early as the 1970s (in the general sense: Hiltz & Turoff, 1978). Starting in the mid-1990s, and corresponding to the upsurge in computer-mediated communication (CMC) research that followed closely on the heels of the popularization of the Internet (Herring, 2002), an increasing number of researchers began focusing on online discourse as a way to understand the effects of the new medium. However, different researchers approached computer-mediated discourse with different questions, methods, and understandings, often working in isolation from one another – and in the case of researchers outside the United States, unaware that other researchers shared their interests. The present chapter attempts to systematize some of the goals, understandings, and procedures implicitly shared by this emerging cadre of researchers.

As background to the remainder of the chapter, it is useful to think of CMDA as applying to four domains or levels of language, ranging prototypically from smallest to largest linguistic unit of analysis: (1) structure, (2) meaning, (3) interaction, and (4) social behavior. Structural phenomena include the use of special typography or orthography, novel word formations, and sentence structure. At the meaning level are included the meanings of words, utterances (e.g., speech acts), and larger functional units (e.g., "macrosegments," Herring, 1996b; cf. Longacre, 1992). The interactional level includes turn-taking, topic development, and other means of negotiating interactive exchanges. The social level includes linguistic expressions of play, conflict, power, and group membership over multiple exchanges. In addition, participation patterns (as measured by frequency and length of messages posted and responses received) in threads or other extended discourse samples constitute a fifth domain of CMDA analysis.

The kinds of understandings obtainable through a language-focused approach can be illustrated by summarizing briefly a few studies that focus on phenomena from each domain. Nonstandard spelling and typography have been analyzed structurally in Internet Relay Chat as an example of creative play (Danet, Ruedenberg-Wright, & Rosenbaum-Tamari, 1997), on the French Minitel system as an illustration of the tension between efficiency and expressivity (Livia, in press), and in a social MUD as evidence of participants' "insider" status (Cherny, 1999). Studies that consider what online participants mean by what they say – for example, by classifying their utterances as speech acts – have discovered differences between educational and recreational uses of IRC, as well as differences associated with teacher/leader versus other roles (Herring & Nix, 1997). Studies of interactional phenomena have identified system-imposed constraints on turn-taking (Herring, 1999a; Panyametheekul, 2001) and topic coherence (Herring & Nix, 1997; Lambiase, in press). One stream of socially focused CMDA, research on group identity, has identified discourse styles associated with participant age (Ravert, 2001), gender (Hall, 1996; Herring, 1993, 1996a, 1996b, 2003), ethnicity (Paolillo, in press), and race (Burkhalter, 1999; Jacobs-Huey, in press), even in supposedly anonymous text-only CMC. Finally, participation patterns have been observed to vary according to the synchronicity of the medium (Condon & Čech, 2001, in press), and to reveal social influence and dominance in online groups (Herring, in press a; Herring, Johnson, & DiBenedetto, 1992; Hert, 1997; Rafaeli & Sudweeks, 1997). This brief survey is intended to provide a sense of the range and diversity of topics that have been researched thus far using CMDA. More detailed surveys of the findings of previous CMDA research can be found in Herring (2001, 2002).

THE CMDA APPROACH

CMDA is best considered an approach, rather than a "theory" or a single "method." Although the linguistic variant described here is based on a loose set of theoretical premises (those of linguistic discourse analysis, plus a rejection of a priori technological determinism; see below), it is not a theory in that CMDA (as an abstract entity) makes no predictions about the nature of computer-mediated discourse. The findings of CMDA studies neither support nor falsify the premises of the approach, beyond confirming that it is useful or indicating that it is in need of further refinement. Rather, the CMDA approach allows diverse theories about discourse and computer-mediated communication to be entertained and tested. Moreover, although its overall methodological orientation can be characterized (see below), it is not a single method but rather a set of methods from which the researcher selects those best suited to her data and research questions. In short, CMDA as an approach to researching online behavior provides a methodological toolkit and a set of theoretical lenses through which to make observations and interpret the results of empirical analysis.

The theoretical assumptions underlying CMDA are those of linguistic discourse analysis, broadly construed. First, it is assumed that *discourse exhibits recurrent patterns*. Patterns in discourse may be produced consciously or unconsciously (Goffman, 1959); in the latter case, a speaker is not necessarily aware of what she is doing, and thus direct observation may produce more reliable generalizations than a self-report of her behavior. A basic goal of discourse analysis is to identify patterns in discourse that are demonstrably present, but that may not be immediately obvious to the casual observer or to the discourse participants themselves. Second, it is assumed that *discourse involves speaker choices*. These choices are not conditioned by purely linguistic considerations, but rather reflect cognitive

(Chafe, 1994) and social (Sacks, 1984) factors. It follows from this assumption that discourse analysis can provide insight into nonlinguistic, as well as linguistic, phenomena. To these two assumptions about discourse, CMDA adds a third assumption about online communication: *computer-mediated discourse may be, but is not inevitably, shaped by the technological features of computer-mediated communication systems.* It is a matter for empirical investigation in what ways, to what extent, and under what circumstances CMC technologies shape the communication that takes place through them (Herring, u.c.).

The basic methodological orientation of CMDA is language-focused content analysis. This may be purely qualitative – observations of discourse phenomena in a sample of text may be made, illustrated, and discussed – or quantitative – phenomena may be coded and counted, and summaries of their relative frequencies produced. (It should be noted that quantitative CMDA comprises a qualitative component, e.g., in deciding what counts as an instance of a phenomenon to be coded and counted, especially when the phenomena of interest are semantic rather than syntactic [structural] in nature; see Bauer, 2000, and the section titled "Analytical Methods.") An example of the quantitative approach is Simeon Yates' (1996) comparison of a corpus of asynchronous computer conferences with spoken and written English corpora with respect to range of vocabulary, modality, and personal pronoun use. An example of the qualitative approach is Lori Kendall's (2002) ethnographic, participant-observer study of gendered behavior in a social MUD. An earlier ethnography of a social MUD carried out by Lynn Cherny (1999) applies both approaches, but to different phenomena: qualitative description of novel word creations (chap. 3) and quantitative analysis of turn-taking patterns (chap. 4). Alternatively, Herring (1996b) combines the two approaches: the same patterns of email message structure are identified by both qualitative and quantitative means.[5]

As with other forms of content analysis, the CMDA researcher must meet certain basic requirements in order to conduct a successful (i.e., valid, coherent, convincing) analysis. She must pose a research question that is in principle answerable. She must select methods that address the research question, and apply them to a sufficient and appropriate corpus of data. If a "coding and counting" approach is taken, she must operationalize the phenomena to be coded, create coding categories, and establish their reliability, for example, by getting multiple raters to agree on how they should be applied to a sample of the data. If statistical methods of analysis are to be used, appropriate statistical tests must be identified and applied. Finally, the findings must be interpreted responsibly and in relation to the original research question. These requirements have been discussed

---

[5] Gathering and comparing evidence from multiple analytical approaches is known as *triangulation.*

extensively in the literature on the conduct of empirical research (see, e.g., Alford, 1998 for research in sociology; Bauer, 2000 for content analysis methods in communication); a basic familiarity with them is assumed here. Of interest in the present chapter is how to apply this general research schema to the particular constellation of issues and challenges associated with the study of computer-mediated behavior.

As an illustration of the CMDA approach, the following sections consider a currently popular research theme – that of *virtual community* – and how CMDA can be applied to determine empirically whether a group of people interacting online constitutes a community. In keeping with the focus of this volume on *learning*, the two online environments chosen for illustration have professional development as their reason for existence and both are associated with educational contexts: secondary science and mathematics education in the first case, and tertiary linguistics education and research in the second. To address the volume's focus on *system design*, the environments were selected to contrast in their technological affordances (one is a multimodal website, the other a text-based listserv); furthermore, one was intentionally designed with the goal of creating community, whereas the other was not. A comparison of these two environments can shed light on how the technological and social properties of CMC systems relate to the phenomenon of virtual community.

ANALYZING *VIRTUAL COMMUNITY*

Since it was first articulated in print (Rheingold, 1993), the concept of virtual community has become increasingly fashionable in Internet research (e.g., Baym, 1995a; Cherny, 1999; Werry & Mowbray, 2001), although it has also been criticized (Fernback & Thompson, 1995; Jones, 1995a; see also Kling & Courtright, this volume). The criticisms include a pragmatic concern that the term has been overextended to the point of becoming meaningless – for some writers, it seems that any online group automatically becomes a "community" – and a philosophical skepticism that virtual community can exist at all, given the fluid membership, reduced social accountability, and lack of shared geographical space that characterize most groups on the Internet (e.g., McLaughlin, Osborne, & Smith, 1995). For the purposes of the present discussion, we assume that virtual community is possible, but that not all online groups constitute virtual communities. The task of the researcher then becomes to determine the properties of virtual communities, and to assess the extent to which they are (or are not) realized by specific online groups.

Two Learning Environments

Two online professional development environments will serve as examples to ground our discussion of how CMDA can be applied to investigate virtual community. Professional development environments are online learning environments in which people participate voluntarily and intermittently – that is, for the purpose of acquiring information and skills to advance professionally – rather than in formal courses with students, instructors, and syllabi, as is the case for distance education. In successful cases, participation in such environments is continuous and self-sustaining, unlike course-based CMC, which is task-focused and temporally bounded. An example of a genre of professional development environment that dates back to the early days of computer networking is listserv discussion groups for professionals in academic disciplines (e.g., Hert, 1997; Korenman & Wyatt, 1996). A more recent example is the growing genre of professional development websites that combine discussion forums with access to documents and other online resources (e.g., Renninger & Shumar, this volume).

The environments selected as illustrations for this chapter represent these two types. The first, the Linguist List, was founded in November 1990 by a husband and wife team of academic linguists as a means for disseminating information and engaging in public discussion about issues of interest to professional (and aspiring professional) linguists; it has been in continuous existence since 1990. Originally a text-only, by-subscription list that made archived messages available only to subscribers, in 1994 it established a website and posted the discussion archives there, making them widely publicly accessible.[6] For further description and analysis of the Linguist List, see Herring (1992, 1996b). The second environment, the Inquiry Learning Forum (ILF), was opened to registered members in March 2000. It was designed with National Science Foundation support by a team of faculty and graduate students in the School of Education at Indiana University, with the explicit goal of fostering online community among secondary math and science in-service and pre-service teachers interested in the inquiry learning approach (National Research Council, 2000). Members must go to the ILF website to post messages and access the other resources there (which include videos of teachers using inquiry methods in their classrooms); past messages remain on the site alongside current messages. For further description and analysis of the ILF, see Barab, MaKinster, and Scheckler (this volume) and Herring, Martinson, and Scheckler (2002).

These environments are plausible candidates for virtual community status in several respects. First, both bring together people who arguably already constitute real-world professional communities: academic linguists and secondary math and science educators. Second, their online participation is centered around a shared professional focus, as in Wenger's (1998) "communities of practice." Third, the Linguist List is active and long-lived,

---

[6] The Linguist List has subsequently expanded its Web presence, coming to serve as an electronic clearinghouse for language- and linguistics-related resources.

which some might take as prima facie evidence that it has achieved online community status. In contrast, the ILF has struggled to establish and maintain an active level of participation, but might be considered to have a prima facie claim to community status on the grounds that it was explicitly designed to support community (Barab, MaKinster, Moore, Cunningham, & The ILF Design Team, 2001). For these reasons, it is germane to ask: to what extent does participation in these two environments in fact constitute "community" (as opposed to being simply "people interacting online")?

The following sections describe how a researcher making use of CMDA might go about addressing this question. Five conceptual skills involved in the research process are highlighted and discussed, first, with reference to CMDA in general, second, with reference to virtual communities, and last, with reference to the two professional development sites. The order of presentation of the five skills is roughly sequential (i.e., a researcher generally starts with the first, and progresses to the last), although the research process – in CMDA, no less than in other scientific disciplines – is frequently iterative, involving many feedback loops (Harwood, Reiff, & Phillipson, 2001). However, it is important to stress that what follows is not intended as an analysis in and of itself; to answer the question of what constitutes online community definitively would take us well beyond the scope of this chapter.

Research Questions

To carry out an investigation by means of CMDA, it is first necessary to have a research question, a problem to which the analyst desires to find a solution. Typically, the research question is based on prior observation – the researcher may have noticed some online behavior or behaviors and may have formed a preliminary hypothesis concerning them. Articulating a research question is a first step toward testing the hypothesis.

A good CMDA research question has four characteristics:

1. It is empirically answerable from the available data;
2. It is nontrivial;
3. It is motivated by a hypothesis; and
4. It is open-ended.

A CMDA research question should ideally ask about *empirically observable phenomena*, or phenomena that can be operationalized empirically, as opposed to purely subjective or evaluative ones. A question about the nature and frequency of joking in an online forum, for example, can be addressed empirically more readily than a question about whether the participants are having fun. Further, the question should be *answerable from the data selected for analysis*. For example, if only computer-mediated data are to be examined, the question should not ask whether CMC is better or worse than face-to-face communication along some dimension of comparison, since the CMC data can not tell us anything directly about face-to-face communication. Equally important in CMDA, the question should be *answerable on the basis of textual evidence*. Text is direct evidence of behavior, but it can only be indirect evidence of what people know, feel, or think. If it is important that the researcher try to understand participants' internal conscious or unconscious states, CMDA should be supplemented with other methods of analysis such as interviews or psychological experiments.

A good research question should be *nontrivial*; that is, the answer should be *of some ostensible interest* to at least a portion of the larger research community, and *not already known* in advance. Additionally, the research question should not be worded so as to presuppose an answer; that is, the answer should not appear to be a foregone conclusion.

At the same time, a research question *motivated by a hypothesis* – even if it is no more than an informal hunch – is more interesting and more interpretable than one that is not. Note that it is not necessary to posit a hypothesis that the researcher expects will be confirmed by the results of the analysis, although the hypothesis should be prima facie plausible. In some cases, a researcher may advance a popular hypothesis that she suspects is incorrect, in order to disprove it. For example, she might postulate that participant gender is invisible in CMC (a commonly held view in the early 1990s, based on the paucity of social status cues in text-only CMC), suspecting that such is not the case in her data.[7] The empirical results, if negative, are all the more illuminating for running counter to the prevailing wisdom.

Whether the researcher's hypothesis is supported or not, the results of the study should contribute new knowledge. Phrasing the question as an *open-ended* question (what, why, when, where, who, how) leaves the door open to unexpected findings to a greater extent than closed (yes/no) questions, generally speaking. One caveat is that unexpected answers to yes/no questions can be informative, as noted above, when the hypothesis underlying the question is favored by popular opinion or common sense, but receives no empirical support. Similarly, positive support for an unobvious hypothesis can also cause us to understand the world in new ways. However, support for obvious hypotheses does not advance knowledge, nor does lack of support for unobvious hypotheses. In contrast, a systematic study will always reveal something new in response to a well-crafted "what," "why," or "how" question.

What kinds of questions about virtual community can be researched from a CMDA perspective? Although all are legitimate foci of intellectual curiosity, the researcher is setting herself up for difficulty if she asks questions such as: (i) "Does virtual community exist?" (ii) "Is virtual community a good thing?" (iii) "Does membership in virtual communities

---

7 This strategy was adopted, for example, by Herring (1992, 1993).

satisfy needs previously satisfied only in face-to-face communities?" or
(iv) "Do people interact regularly in groups online?" Note, first of all, that
these are closed questions, to which the answer can only be "yes" or "no." In
addition, the first is effectively biased toward an affirmative answer, in that
exhaustive evidence would be required in order to answer it negatively.
The second question both presupposes the existence of virtual community
(a problem if virtual community hasn't already been empirically demonstrated) and asks a subjective, evaluative question about it; "goodness" is
difficult to measure empirically. The third question involves a comparison;
it can only be answered if empirical evidence (gathered by comparable
means) is available from both virtual communities (presupposed to exist)
and face-to-face communities. Finally, the fourth question, although neu-
trally worded and answerable, is trivial – the answer is obvious to anyone
who has spent any time on the Internet.

The following, in contrast, are examples of open-ended questions that
can usefully be addressed using CMDA: (a) "What are the discourse characteristics of a virtual community?" (b) "What causes an online group to
become a community?" (c) "What causes a virtual community to die?"
(d) "How do virtual communities differ from face-to-face communities?"[8]
(e) "What happens to face-to-face communities when they go online?"
and (f) "In what ways do communities constituted exclusively online differ from online communities that also meet face-to-face?" However, these
questions are not all equally easy to answer; their answerability depends
on the data available for investigation. Thus, (a)–(d) and (f) require an independent determination of virtual community, for example, in terms of
participants' perceptions; (b), (c), and (e) require longitudinal data; and
(d) and (e) require face-to-face data (see discussion of data in section on
Data Selection).

In addition, particular data samples will generally exhibit characteristics that invite more specific questions to be asked about them. The
question raised in the previous section – "[t]o what extent does participation in these two environments constitute 'community' (as opposed to
being simply 'people interacting online')?" – is a straightforward application of question (a) to the Linguist List and the ILF data samples. But
these samples, by their nature, also give rise to questions about virtual
community and professional development (e.g., "What is the nature of
virtual community in professional development environments, and how
does it differ from virtual community in structured learning environ-
ments/unstructured social environments/etc.?"). Furthermore, the two
environments contrast according to a number of technological and social

---

[8] This question assumes a common set of criteria for both domains, and the availability of
data for face-to-face communities.

TABLE 12.1. *Dimensions of Contrast between the Linguist List and the ILF*

Linguist List	ILF
Text-only	Multimodal (text + video + limited audio and graphics)
Messages come to subscriber ("push" technology)[a]	Member must go to site to post messages ("pull" technology)
Archives stored separately	Past messages appear alongside current ones
Public (by subscription)	Semi-public (by registration; password required; limited membership)
. . . .	. . . .
Pre-existing face-to-face "community" (meets at annual professional meeting)	Loosely defined pre-existing "community" (most members have never met face-to-face)
Relatively homogeneous population of users (academic linguists at universities) with similar access opportunities	Heterogeneous population of users (pre-service teachers; in-service teachers; ILF researchers) with differential access
Founders' goals were specific, limited in scope (i.e., information exchange and discussion)	Creators' goals were broad, ambitious (i.e., create intentional community; foster inquiry learning)
Moderators present themselves as peers, "facilitators" (but exercise behind-the-scene control over postings)	ILF development team members have higher status (but post messages themselves, and do not control postings)
Discussion is on topics selected by participants	Discussion is often focused around artifacts (video clips, instructional technology, lesson plans, etc.)

[a] In 1997, Linguist made available a new distribution option, Linguist Lite, which sends subscribers a single message containing the subject headers of the day's messages; subscribers must then go to the Linguist website to read the messages. This option, which exists alongside the traditional listserv distribution format, combines both "push" and "pull" elements.

dimensions, as summarized in Table 12.1.[9] Additional questions can be asked to focus on the contributing effects of a particular dimension to online behavior (e.g., "Is a multimodal environment more conducive to virtual community than a text-only environment?"; or "How does the self-presentation of the group 'owners' [e.g., as peers or as experts] affect the likelihood that a group will develop community characteristics?").

[9] Cells above the dotted line in Table 12.1 indicate medium (technological) variables; cells below the dotted line indicate situational (social) variables (see Herring, u.c. for a full description of this system of classification).

The comparison of the two groups in Table 12.1 suggests *too* many possible questions about the variables that condition virtual community, in fact. Ideally, two data samples that are compared should differ according to only one dimension, such that if differences in behavior are found between the samples, they can plausibly be attributed to that dimension of variation. If, however, it turns out that either the Linguist List or the ILF exhibits more "community" behaviors than the other, to what should the difference be attributed: (multi)modality? ease of posting messages? ease of access to the group's history? availability of face-to-face interaction? the intentions/behavior of the group's founders? Causal indeterminacy is a common problem in research that analyzes naturally occurring behavior.[10] The experimental research paradigm controls for this by holding all variables constant except for the variable that is hypothesized to condition the experimental result. For examples of experimental research that make use of CMDA methods, see Condon and Čech (1996a, 1996b, 2001).

Data Selection

In CMDA, as in other empirical social science approaches, a data sample must be selected that is appropriate to the study. By appropriate we mean that the sample should be of a nature and size to answer the research question(s); if the research question involves a comparison, more than one sample may be required. Each of these considerations is discussed separately. For the purposes of this discussion, it is assumed that the data of interest are produced naturally (i.e., by online discourse participants for their own purposes), and logged or culled from online archives by the researcher, rather than elicited experimentally.

It is often impossible to examine all the phenomena of relevance to a particular research question; this is especially true in CMDA, for which a vast amount of textual data is available in the form of online interactions. (Even in groups with relatively low participation, such as the ILF in its first year, the total amount of text quickly adds up to more than can easily be analyzed by a human coder using micro-linguistic methods.) For this reason, the researcher must usually select a sample from the totality of the available data. In CMDA, this is rarely done randomly, since *random* sampling sacrifices context, and context is important in interpreting discourse analysis results. Rather, data samples tend to be *motivated* (e.g., selected

---

[10] Causal indeterminacy in CMDA research can be minimized in two ways. First, data samples that are more similar than different can be selected, in an attempt to approximate the experimental approach of holding all but one feature constant. Second, dimensions of variation within the data sample(s) can be considered in interpreting the research findings (see Herring, u.c., and section on "Issues of Interpretation"). In some cases, although differences could result in principle from multiple contrasting dimensions, in practice, the evidence points more strongly to one than to the others.

TABLE 12.2. *CMDA Data Sampling Techniques*

	Advantages	Disadvantages
Random (e.g., each message selected or not by a coin toss)	Representativeness; generalizability	Loss of context and coherence; requires complete data set to draw from
By Theme (e.g., all messages in a particular thread)	Topical coherence; a data set free of extraneous messages	Excludes other activities that occur at the same time
By Time (e.g., all messages in a particular time interval	Rich in context; necessary for longitudinal analysis	May truncate interactions, and/or result in very large samples
By Phenomenon (e.g., only instances of joking; conflict negotiation)	Enables in-depth analysis of the phenomenon (useful when phenomenon is rare)	Loss of context; no conclusions possible re: distribution
By Individual or Group (all messages posted by an individual or members of a demographic group, e.g., women, students)	Enables focus on individual or group (useful for comparing across individuals or groups)	Loss of context (especially temporal sequence relations); no conclusions possible re: interaction
Convenience (whatever data are available)	Convenience	Unsystematic; sample may not be best suited to the purposes of the study

according to theme, time, phenomenon, individual, or group), or samples of *convenience* (i.e., what the researcher happens to have access to at the time). Some advantages and disadvantages of these various sampling techniques are summarized in Table 12.2.

Of the techniques in Table 12.2, sampling by time preserves the richest context. If a long enough continuous time period is captured, the sample will most likely include coherent threads, thereby incorporating the advantages of thematic sampling as well. Analogously, a thematic sample is typically organized by time, enabling some longitudinal observations to be made. Because of their multiple advantages, these two sample types are favored in CMDA research. In addition, it is possible to break down a sample of any type by individual or group, thereby achieving additional focus while avoiding the disadvantages of individual or group sampling. (For example, an extended thread was isolated for analysis from the Linguist List, then broken down by gender of participants, in Herring, 1992, 1996b.)

The richest possible context is required for the purposes of analyzing virtual community, as are data that can show change over time, if questions about the inception, evolution, and demise of virtual communities are to be addressed. The sample should include, as much as possible, the typical activities carried out on the site. These considerations suggest intermittent time-based sampling (e.g., several weeks at a time at intervals throughout a year) as particularly appropriate.[11] Ideally, in any analysis of virtual community, textual analysis would be supplemented by ongoing participant observation.[12]

The ILF environment imposes some limitations on sampling, as well as suggesting alternative sampling possibilities. Discussions take place in different parts of the ILF site, making it difficult to capture a representative overall time-based sample; rather, samples must be collected from individual "rooms" and collated, if a single sample is required. Moreover, discussions in the "classroom" portion of the ILF site are organized around videos of teachers using inquiry methods in their classrooms, with one discussion forum attached to each video (Herring et al., 2002). This configuration suggests new categories of data sampling: by room, and by artifact (in this case, video). A sampling technique based on units of interaction determined by the site design (and/or by participants' actual usage) has the advantage of allowing discourse patterns to emerge that are internally coherent to such units, whereas if data are combined across units, those patterns might be less apparent.

How much data is required to conduct a successful CMDA study? There is no simple answer to this question. The data should be sufficient to address the research question, such that tests of statistical significance could meaningfully be conducted on the key findings (regardless of whether or not the researcher actually conducts such tests). What counts as a sufficient amount of data will depend, therefore, on the frequency of occurrence of the analytical phenomenon in the data sample, the number of coding categories employed to describe the phenomenon, and the number of external factors that are allowed to vary (e.g., modality; topic of discussion; participant gender). Two general rules of thumb are (1) the more infrequent the phenomenon in the data, the larger the sample should be; and (2) the more variables considered in the analysis, the larger the sample should be. This is so that (1) enough instances of the phenomenon are available to analyze, and (2) when the sample is broken down into subsamples for purposes of comparison, there are still enough instances

---

[11] Even then, this method is likely to produce more data than can reasonably be analyzed using most linguistic methods, such that further winnowing of the sample may be required.

[12] Among the advantages of ongoing observation is that it allows the researcher to capture data opportunistically, should interesting interactions take place outside the formally established data collection periods.

in each category to allow for statistical testing.[13] Since it is often difficult to know all of this in advance, a recommended practice is to start with a pilot study based on a small amount of data, and expand the sample size as necessary in a larger study, according to the tendencies revealed in the pilot study.

A related issue concerns the number of samples required for purposes of comparative analysis. Earlier we noted that some CMDA research questions presuppose a comparison with face-to-face discourse. While it may be legitimate to draw a comparison with previous research on face-to-face communication in interpreting one's results (see "Issues of Interpretation"), no key results should be founded on such a comparison, unless the researcher can assure that the face-to-face study was carried out using comparable methods (e.g., because it was conducted by the researcher herself, or because the same methods that were applied in the face-to-face study were applied to the computer-mediated data). Otherwise, a comparable face-to-face sample is normally required. What the researcher hopes to find are cases in which the same people are communicating about the same topics, for the same purposes, both face-to-face and via CMC. Unfortunately, this situation rarely occurs naturally. Left to their own devices, people tend to use different modalities for different communicative purposes; moreover, CMC enables certain behaviors that would be difficult or impossible offline,[14] and vice versa. Data collected in experimental settings are superior to naturally occurring data for the purposes of comparing CMC with face-to-face (and traditional written) communication (see, e.g., Condon & Čech, 1996a, 1996b, 2001). However, since evidence of community is highly unlikely to surface in laboratory settings, given that experimental subjects typically have no past (or anticipated future) interaction (Walther, 1996), empirical comparison of face-to-face and online community is difficult. This may be one question for which interpretive, rather than strictly empirical, answers will have to suffice for the present time (cf. Etzioni, 1999).

Multiple CMC samples (or subsamples) may also be required in order to carry out a single study, depending on the research question. These are usually easier to collect, but care should be taken to hold constant as many dimensions of variation as possible, to maximize the interpretability of the results. Our two professional development samples in fact vary according to too many dimensions to enable straightforward comparison, as previously noted. A better example of contrasting samples is Paolillo's (in press)

---

[13] For example, chi-squared tests, which compare actual with expected distributions of results, typically require a minimum of five instances in each sub-category.

[14] For example, people can engage in large group conversations online, whereas a conversation involving one hundred or more people would be impossible face-to-face (Herring, 1999a).

comparison of an asynchronous Usenet newsgroup and a (synchronous) IRC channel frequented by the same participant demographic group (and to some extent, the same individuals): expatriate South Asians. When differences are found in language choice in the two samples, they can plausibly be attributed to differences in synchronicity between the two CMC modes.

Dividing a larger sample into subsamples by demographic group, topic, or other category is another means to insure that the subsamples share all but one feature. Applying this principle to research on virtual community, we might, for example, compare the behaviors of individuals within a single group who are known to interact face-to-face with other group members, with those individuals who do not, to test the hypothesis that face-to-face contact enhances involvement in online community (cf. Diani, 2000). Or we might consider participant behavior by role or status in relation to hypothesized community behaviors. In the case of the Linguist List, the behavior of professors might be compared with that of students, or U.S. linguists with non-U.S. linguists; in the ILF, pre-service teachers might be compared with in-service teachers, and teachers with researchers, to determine if higher status groups are more invested in the "community" than lower status groups.[15]

Operationalization of Key Concepts

The coding and counting approach to CMDA research described in this chapter requires that key concepts be operationalizable (and operationalized) in empirically measurable terms. This entails defining the concepts unambiguously, such that another researcher, examining the same data, could in principle reproduce the identification of a given token as an exemplar of the concept.[16] Equally or more important, it is necessary to define a concept in concrete, textual terms in order to be able to code it consistently. In the case of highly abstract concepts, this necessarily entails a reduction (and a risk of distortion) of the concept; content analysis is sometimes criticized on these grounds (cf. Bauer, 2000). At the same time, it is the requirement of operationalization, more than any other single requirement, that lends CMDA its rigor and makes it a useful tool for getting an empirical grasp on otherwise slippery or intractable concepts.

Concepts vary in the degree to which they are inherently operationalizable. This can be represented as a continuum, as in Figure 12.1. In a

---

[15] In their study of participation in the video-centered "classroom" discussions on the ILF, Herring et al. (2002) found that male in-service teachers featured in the videos, and female ILF development team members, were the most active participants, suggesting that both status and gender are associated with level of engagement in the site.

[16] The criterion of research reproducibility has traditionally been a guiding force in scientific methodology (cf. Swales, 1990).

More operationalizable   Less operationalizable

<--->

External, directly observable behavior   Internal, subjective states

Concrete, bounded, measurable   Abstract, ambiguous, generalized

Directly related to coding categories   Not obviously related to coding categories

FIGURE 12.1. Continuum of operationalizability

previous section, it was suggested that a researcher should avoid asking questions about concepts that are too far toward the subjective, abstract end of the continuum. In fact, such questions are often the most interesting to ask, but in order to address them quantitatively using CMDA, they must be defined in terms of textual phenomena that can be directly observed, coded, and counted. Thus, for example, concepts of widespread interest in CMC research such as affect, democracy, depth of discussion, empowerment learning, and trust, can be operationalized by identifying discourse behaviors (plausibly) characteristic of each phenomenon and then articulating interpretive links between those behaviors and the larger concepts. Alternatively, it might be necessary to supplement CMDA with other methods in order to make a meaningful demonstration that the evidence addresses the concept. For example, it is unlikely that CMC evidence alone could make a definitive case for changes in offline states of affairs; such a demonstration would normally require offline evidence, observational or self-reported.

Community is an inherently abstract concept. It also has a subjective component, especially when it is applied to online contexts, where it is always, in some sense, a metaphorical extension of the literal meaning of community as "grounded in a shared physical space" (cf. Jones, 1995a). Accordingly, definitions of community (and virtual community) abound, although Wellman's (2001) tripartite characterization of community as providing "sociability, support, and identity" constitutes a useful point of departure. More specifically, six sets of criteria can be identified from the literature on virtual community (e.g., Haythornthwaite, Kazmer, Robins, & Shoemaker, 2000; Jones, 1995a, 1995b; Reid, 1991, 1994, 1998; Riel & Polin, this volume):

1. active, self-sustaining participation; a core of regular participants
2. shared history, purpose, culture, norms, and values
3. solidarity, support, reciprocity
4. criticism, conflict, means of conflict resolution
5. self-awareness of group as an entity distinct from other groups
6. emergence of roles, hierarchy, governance, rituals

Criteria (1) and (4) relate to "sociability"; criteria (3) and (6) (loosely) to "support"; and criteria (2) and (5) to "identity."[17]

These six criteria suggest concrete ways in which the notion of *virtual community* might be broken down into component behaviors that can be objectively assessed.

1. *Participation* can be measured over time, and *core participants* identified on the basis of frequency of posting and rate of response received to messages posted (Herring, in press a), or via text-based social network analysis (Paolillo, 2001; cf. Koku & Wellman, this volume).

2. Shared *history* can be assessed through the availability and use of archives (Millen, 2000). *Culture* is indexed through the use of group-specific abbreviations, jargon, and language routines (Baym, 1995a; Cherny, 1999; Jacobs-Huey, in press; Kendall, 1996), as well as through choice of language, register, and dialect (Georgakopoulou, in press; Paolillo, 1996). *Norms and values* are revealed through an examination of netiquette statements (Herring, 1996a), FAQs (Voth, 1999), and verbal reactions to violations of appropriate conduct (McLaughlin et al., 1995; Weber, in press).

3. *Solidarity* can be measured through the use of verbal humor (Baym, 1995b); *support* through speech act analysis focusing, for example, on acts of positive politeness (Herring, 1994); and *reciprocity* through analysis of turn initiation and response (Rafaeli & Sudweeks, 1997).

4. *Criticism* and *conflict* can be analyzed through speech acts violating positive politeness (Herring, 1994). *Conflict resolution* might usefully be considered as an interactive sequence of acts (cf. Condon & Čech, 1996b, on decision-making sequences); it also lends itself to ethnographic analysis (e.g., Cherny, 1999).

5. A group's *self-awareness* can be manifested in its members' references to the group as a group, and in "us versus them" language, particularly in statements such as, "We do things this way here" (implying an awareness that they might be done differently elsewhere; Weber, in press). (See also "norms" in point 2.)

6. Evidence of *roles* and *hierarchy* can be adduced through participation patterns (see "participation" in point 1) and speech act analysis (e.g., Herring & Nix, 1997, which considers the different acts performed by group leaders and nonleaders). The study of *governance* and *ritual* would appear to require an ethnographic approach in which a group's practices are observed over time and described in terms of

[17] For an alternative set of criteria, and an attempt to operationalize them empirically, see Liu (1999), who bases his analysis of community in Internet Relay Chat (IRC) on Jones's (1997) four criteria for a "virtual settlement": (1) a virtual common-public-space; (2) a variety of communicators; (3) a minimum level of sustained stable membership; and (4) a minimum level of interactivity.

their meanings to participants (Cherny, 1999; Jacobson, 1996; Kolko & Reid, 1998). Note, however, that the reification of cultural practices in the form of governance and ritual appears to represent a relatively advanced stage of community (see, e.g., Dibbell's 1993 account of how this happened in LambdaMOO); thus it probably should not be taken as part of the basic definition of virtual community.

Some of these features are more useful than others as potential indicators of virtual community on the Linguist List and the ILF. Certain features occur rarely or not at all in either group: language routines, code switching, humor, and governance and ritual. Their relative absence is due to a variety of circumstances, for example the professional (serious) focus of the groups, and the fact that their members are proficient in written English.[18] Other features occur only or nearly exclusively on the Linguist List, e.g., criticism, conflict, and netiquette statements.[19] Conversely, such features as participation patterns, reciprocity, indicators of group self-awareness, and evidence of roles and hierarchy are evident in both and might usefully be assessed as community indicators for these environments.

Analytical Methods

Analytical methods in CMDA are drawn from discourse analysis and other language-related paradigms, adapted to address the properties of computer-mediated communication. In principle, nearly any language-related method could be so adapted; in practice, this chapter focuses on methods of linguistic discourse analysis, these being the methods with which the author is most familiar. These include approaches traditionally used to analyze written text and spoken conversation, approaches to discourse as social interaction, and critical (socio-political) approaches.

Given that we have already identified content analysis as the basic methodological apparatus of CMDA, the question might arise as to what the more specific linguistic approaches add to the research endeavor. In fact, it is possible to conduct a perfectly responsible CMDA analysis without drawing on any more specific paradigm than language-focused content

---

[18] The Linguist List has many international subscribers, but most messages are posted in English, the international language of scholarship.

[19] There are several possible reasons why the Linguist List is more conflict-prone than the ILF, despite the fact that the former is moderated and the latter is not. The Linguist List is larger and more impersonal than the ILF, which has restricted membership and makes available individual user profiles. Linguist messages are archived out of sight, while ILF messages remain on the site. The off-line professional discourse of academic linguists is also probably more antagonistic than that of secondary school teachers. Social accountability, message persistence, and generally supportive professional norms of communication could inhibit criticism and conflict in postings to the ILF. Alternatively, it could be that ILF participants are not as engaged in their interactions as are Linguist List participants.

analysis. For example, one could let the phenomenon of interest emerge out of a sample of computer-mediated data and devise coding categories on the basis of the observed phenomenon, as in the grounded theory approach (Glaser & Strauss, 1967). This approach is especially well suited to analyzing new and as yet relatively undescribed forms of CMC, in that it allows the researcher to remain open to the possibility of discovering novel phenomena, rather than making the assumption in advance that certain categories of phenomena will be found.

However, grounded theory is less useful for evaluating specific research hypotheses, or for making systematic comparisons across data samples. For these purposes, the CMDA researcher can profit from the structure, experience, and understandings available through specific discourse analysis paradigms. Such paradigms define issues of theoretical interest, a set of discourse phenomena about which much may already be known in other modalities and contexts, and discovery procedures for revealing the patterns and constraints that characterize the phenomena. Table 12.3 summarizes this information for five discourse analysis paradigms commonly invoked in CMDA research.

However, even though it is useful to be cognizant of these research paradigms as part of the CMDA toolkit, and to draw on them as appropriate, most CMDA research does not take as its point of departure a paradigm, but rather observations about online behavior as manifested through discourse. That is, rather than starting off with the intention of using conversation analysis (for example) to investigate some aspect of CMC and then selecting a behavior to focus on, a researcher is more likely to become interested in studying patterns of message exchange (for example), and then select conversation analysis as a useful methodological tool. In this sense, the approach is inductive – the phenomena of interest are primary – rather than deductive, or theory-driven. This orientation is reflected in Table 12.4, in which essentially the same CMDA issues and methods are re-organized around the four domains of language (plus participation) identified at the beginning of this chapter. Each domain includes subsets of linguistic phenomena, listed in the second column of Table 12.4.

Participation, while not a level of linguistic analysis per se, constitutes a fifth domain, in which the phenomena of interest are number of messages and responses and message and thread length. Such numbers can be interpreted to address social issues such as power, influence, engagement, roles, and hierarchy. Participation is not associated with a particular set of discourse analysis methods, but rather with descriptive statistics (i.e., the phenomena are simply counted).

Bauer (2000) draws a useful distinction in content analysis between *syntactic* (structural) and *semantic* phenomena. The former are invariant in form, or their members comprise a limited set of variants that can be formally identified. Examples of structural CMC phenomena include

TABLE 12.3. *Five Discourse Analysis Paradigms*

	Issues	Phenomena	Procedures
Text Analysis (cf. Longacre, 1996)	Classification, description, "texture" of texts	Genres, schematic organization, reference, salience, cohesion, etc.	Identification of structural regularities within and across texts
Conversation Analysis (cf. Psathas, 1995)	Interaction as a jointly negotiated accomplishment	Turn-taking, sequences, topic development, etc.	Close analysis of the mechanics of interaction; unit is the turn
Pragmatics (cf. Levinson, 1983)	Language as an activity – "doing things" with words	Speech acts, relevance, politeness, etc.	Interpretation of speakers' intentions from discourse evidence
Interactional Sociolinguistics (cf. Gumperz, 1982; Tannen, 1993)	Role of culture in shaping and interpreting interaction	Verbal genres, discourse styles, (mis)communication, framing, etc.	Analysis of the socio-cultural meanings indexed through interaction
Critical Discourse Analysis (cf. Fairclough, 1992)	Discourse as a site in which power and meaning are contested and negotiated	Transitivity, presupposition, intertextuality, conversational control, etc.	Interpretation of meaning and structure in relation to ideology; power dynamics

TABLE 12.4. *Four Domains of Language*

	Phenomena	Issues	Methods
Structure	Typography, orthography, morphology, syntax, discourse schemata	Genre characteristics, orality, efficiency, expressivity, complexity	Structural/ Descriptive Linguistics, Text Analysis
Meaning	Meaning of words, utterances (speech acts), macrosegments	What the speaker intends, what is accomplished through language	Semantics, Pragmatics
Interaction	Turns, sequences, exchanges, threads	Interactivity, timing, coherence, interaction as co-constructed, topic development	Conversation Analysis, Ethnomethodology
Social Behavior	Linguistic expressions of status, conflict, negotiation, face-management, play; discourse styles, etc.	Social dynamics, power, influence, identity	Interactional Sociolinguistics, Critical Discourse Analysis

emoticons, abbreviations, lexical items (such as personal pronouns), word formatives (such as *cyber-*), syntactic patterns (such as passive voice), and quoting (when marked by a formal signal, such as quotation marks or an angle bracket > at the beginning of a line of text). Such phenomena are objectively identifiable; they can be coded and counted more or less automatically, on the basis of a predefined set of structural features. Obviously, these are advantages if the researcher wishes to conduct computer-assisted data analysis.

Semantic coding categories, in contrast, hold the meaning or function constant, but vary (sometimes endlessly) in form. Examples of semantic CMC phenomena include speech acts and most social phenomena such as conflict and politeness.[20] Coding such phenomena necessarily involves an interpretive, subjective component; in most cases it can only be carried out by human coders. Despite the greater challenges they pose for empirical investigation, semantic phenomena are often the most interesting to study. Empirical rigor can be maintained if the researcher operationalizes and

---

[20] While some of these phenomena are conventionally associated with particular linguistic means of expressions (e.g., "Thanks" and "I'm sorry" as expressions of politeness), they can also be expressed indirectly or unconventionally (e.g., "That's sweet of you" and "What a klutz I am"). Given the creativity of language users, it is nearly impossible to predict in advance what all the variants might be.

TABLE 12.5. *Discourse Behaviors Hypothesized to Indicate Virtual Community*

Structure	Jargon, references to group, in-group/out-group language
Meaning	Exchange of knowledge, negotiation of meaning (speech acts)
Interaction	Reciprocity, extended (in-depth) threads, core participants
Social behavior	Solidarity, conflict management, norms of appropriateness
Participation	Frequent, regular, self-sustaining activity over time

defines each coding category in explicit terms and applies the codes consistently to the data. To insure consistency of coding, inter-rater reliability measurements can be made in CMDA, as in other forms of content analysis. This is especially advisable when the coding incorporates a subjective component.

The structural language phenomena in Table 12.4 are generally structural (or syntactic) in Bauer's sense. Interactional phenomena such as threading (based on subject line) can also be identified on structural grounds. To the extent that key words identify social phenomena, the frequency of those words can be counted, making structural methods appropriate to some social questions as well. Word and message counts are purely structural. In contrast, meaning, most social phenomena, and any interactional phenomena that require interpretation are semantic in Bauer's sense. One practical consequence of the greater ease with which structural phenomena can be automated is that analyses of such phenomena can be carried out on large samples of data. Conversely, semantic analyses, because they must be done "by hand," effectively limit the amount of data that can be analyzed.[21]

In the previous discussion of "operationalization," various discourse behaviors were identified as possible indicators of virtual community. These represent both structural and semantic phenomena, and span all five domains of CMDA. Table 12.5 summarizes these behaviors.

In an actual CMDA analysis of the evidence for virtual community in the Linguist List and the ILF, one or more behaviors would be selected from Table 12.5 and explicit coding categories devised for each. For example, in-group/out-group language might be operationalized structurally as the uses of first-person plural pronouns ("we," "us," etc.) in contrast to third-person plural pronouns ("they," "them," etc.); reciprocity might be operationalized interactionally as "response to previous message" or "response to previous message exchange" (cf. Rafaeli & Sudweeks, 1997);

---

[21] This need not be a problem, provided enough data are analyzed to meet the criterion of sufficient data to run tests of statistical significance, as noted in the section on "Data Selection." If structural and semantic analyses are conducted of the same data sample, it is possible to code all of the data for the relevant structural phenomena, and a selected subset of the data for the semantic phenomena.

and solidarity might be operationalized in social terms as the occurrence of humorous utterances (which would, in turn, need to be explicitly defined). An investigation that attempted to address *all* of the behaviors in Table 12.5 would probably not be feasible, since each behavior would need to be coded whenever it applies in a sufficiently large enough sample to achieve meaningful results for each demographic, temporal, topical, or other subdivision of the data that is being considered, for each of the two groups. Unless many of the features were coded automatically, the coding involved would be excessively time-consuming, and the results too numerous to present and discuss in an article-length work (although such a project might be appropriate in scope for a doctoral dissertation). In light of these constraints – and since in any event few CMDA studies are able to analyze *all* the possible evidence pertinent to a given research question – a researcher will normally select those features to code that she believes will produce the most valid and convincing results in relation to the research question, which in this case concerns the presence or absence of virtual community.

Although space and scope considerations prevent us from undertaking a full-fledged analysis of the hypothesized community behaviors in the Linguist List and the ILF in this chapter, a superficial consideration of the behaviors in Table 12.5 nonetheless reveals some differences between the two groups. The Linguist List has an explicit set of norms and guidelines for appropriate posting behaviors that are periodically posted to the list; such norms, if they exist on the ILF at all, are implicit. The Linguist List is characterized by regular conflict episodes, some of which are resolved behind the scenes by the moderators (see, e.g., Herring, Johnson, & DiBenedetto, 1995). Indeed, conflict was a feature of the Linguist List from the outset (Herring, 1992). In contrast, the ILF has virtually no conflict episodes. Perhaps most significantly, the Linguist List is active and self-sustaining; it grew rapidly from about 500 to 4,000 subscribers in the first year, doubling to 8,000 after a few years; today, at over 12,000 subscribers, message volume is so great as to overwhelm some subscribers, even when messages are consolidated and distributed as daily digests. In contrast, the ILF has had to work hard to recruit members – as of January 2002, the number was around 1,000, most of them pre-service teachers who were required to subscribe as part of their course work at Indiana University – and most members do not post. If they do, they do not return to the site subsequently, and few exchanges turn into extended threads. There are also similarities. Both sites make use of professional jargon; both reference themselves as an in-group in relation to an out-group (nonlinguists, students); both exchange knowledge[22] (although more of this takes place on the Linguist List

---

[22] Knowledge tends to be expressed as opinions on the Linguist List (Herring, 1996b), and as advice and personal experience on ILF (Herring et al., 2002).

than on the ILF); and both make limited use of expressions of solidarity. In a quantitative study, these observations would be supported with numerical evidence of frequency distributions for each behavior, compared across the two sites. How might we interpret such evidence in relation to the question of whether the two environments are virtual communities?

Issues of Interpretation

Responsible interpretation of research findings is necessary to insure the validity of any study. Skillful interpretation, moreover, makes the difference between a competent investigation and an insightful one. Interpretation is thus both a craft and an art. Interpretation of the results of CMDA should ideally take into account medium and situational variables, and take place on three levels: close to the data, close to the research question, and (optionally) beyond the research question.

Medium and situational variables are dimensions according to which computer-mediated data can vary and which potentially condition significant variation in online behavior. An example of a medium variable is synchronicity; an example of a situational variable is participant demographics (for a longer list of variables of each type, see Herring, u.c.). Such variables often enter into decisions about data selection early in the research process and can function as explicit dimensions of contrast within a study – for example, a synchronous sample may be compared with an asynchronous sample; native English speakers may be compared with non-native English speakers, males with females, teachers with students, and so forth. These same dimensions are also relevant in interpreting analytical results, even in studies with relatively homogeneous data sets. The issue is one of generalizability of the research findings: for what kinds of CMC – beyond the specific sample(s) analyzed – might the findings hold true? Strictly speaking, every sample is unique, and thus all generalization should be undertaken with caution. At the same time, results that do not generalize beyond the sample in the study are less valuable and interesting than those that do, a consideration that argues against excessive conservatism in interpretation. Advancing explanations that take into account medium and situational variables is one way to balance these competing requirements.

Another strategy for balancing caution with generalization is to interpret the research findings at multiple levels. *Interpretation close to the data* involves summarizing and synthesizing the results obtained by applying the analytical methods to the data. At this most conservative level of interpretation, patterns of results should be identified. *Interpretation close to the research question* requires the researcher to revisit the research questions raised at the outset of the study and indicate explicitly how the results answer the questions. Some creative reasoning may be required here; for example, the steps necessary to reason from the larger concepts in the research question to the specific, operationalizable features of the text may need to be reversed. At this level of interpretation, the researcher should also point out which results are expected and which are unexpected, and propose explanations for the unexpected results. The third and *broadest level of interpretation* calls upon the researcher to extrapolate from the findings of the study to their theoretical, methodological, and/or practical (e.g., design) implications. This level is necessarily the most speculative, and is not strictly speaking required to complete a study. However, broader interpretation helps others to appreciate the significance of the analysis, and can suggest productive avenues for further research.

Because interpretation is a creative intellectual act and because there can be more than one possible (broad) interpretation for any given analytical result, care should be taken that plausibility is always preserved (i.e., that the interpretations do not run counter to the evidence, writ large). The limitations of textual evidence should also be borne in mind: text can *only* tell us what people do (and not what they really think or feel). Any interpretations of the latter based on the former necessarily contain an element of speculation and risk being incorrect. At the same time, the researcher should try to construct the strongest possible evidential case for those interpretations she believes to be true.

What can be concluded about virtual community on the basis of the discourse evidence identified in the preceding sections? Specifically, what does CMDA reveal about the status of the two professional development sites as virtual communities? Our necessarily superficial analysis suggests some tentative interpretations. A close-to-the-data interpretation would summarize the results given in the last paragraph of the preceding section: statements about the relative presence or absence of each of the community features analyzed in each of the two professional development environments. At this level, we might conclude that both environments manifest at least some of the hypothesized community behaviors. At the same time, differences exist in the degree to which each environment manifests the behaviors, and in which behaviors are manifested.

Our overall research question was: to what extent are these environments virtual communities? If *community* is operationalized according to the discourse behaviors in Table 12.5, and assuming for the sake of simplicity that all of the behaviors are equally indicative of community (a proposition open to debate), the Linguist List appears to be more community-like than the ILF, in that it manifests more community behaviors: presence of conflict and norms, and active, self-sustaining participation (in addition to the behaviors that the two environments share). Depending on our initial hypotheses, this result might be considered surprising: some theorists would predict that the ILF, as a multimodal environment, would create a richer social experience for users than a text-only environment (e.g., Media Richness Theory, Daft & Lengel, 1986). Moreover, the ILF was designed around a system of values (inquiry teaching), which its participants presumably share. How can we explain the greater evidence of community in the Linguist List?

The dimensions of variation summarized in Table 12.1 provide clues to interpretation. Listservs may be more effective than websites at promoting professional development communities, in that the former are "push" technologies and the latter "pull" technologies. Time being a resource in short supply for most teaching professionals, the convenience of receiving messages automatically (a medium variable) might make group members more likely to read and respond to them. The Linguist List also has a pre-existing offline community – professional linguists who meet face-to-face at conferences and read one another's work in professional journals, and so forth – which provides and sustains a basis for online interaction. Regular offline contact (a situational variable) may facilitate virtual community, raising levels of participant trust and emotional investment in the group. Two other situational factors that conceivably facilitate the formation of virtual community are the fact that the Linguist List "owners" are peers in relation to the other participants (all are academic linguists), and that participants are free to select topics of discussion within the broad theme of academic linguistics. On the ILF the "owners" and participants are in a hierarchical relationship (university professors and doctoral students versus secondary school teachers and undergraduate teachers-in-training), and topics of discussion in the different areas of the site are more narrowly prescribed. A sense of shared ownership and empowerment to raise topics of discussion in an online environment may facilitate virtual community.[23] Additional analysis would be required to determine which of these factors is most explanatory.[24]

The question of whether the extent of community-like behavior is sufficient to justify labeling either environment a virtual community poses further interpretive challenges. How community-like must a group be in order to be a community? A researcher could establish objective criteria

---

[23] Cf. Bruckman & Resnick's (1995) suggestion that "letting the users [of a professional development MOO] build a virtual world rather than merely interact with a pre-designed world gives them an opportunity for self expression, encourages diversity, and leads to a meaningful engagement of participants and enhanced sense of community."

[24] One direction such analysis might take would be to hypothesize that a given difference is especially significant, and analyze new data samples that vary only (or predominantly) according to that dimension. For example, two web-based forums targeting similar audiences for similar purposes, one created and maintained on a volunteer basis by peers, and the other created and controlled by "experts," could be compared for evidence of community behaviors to test the hypothesis that a sense of "shared ownership" facilitates virtual community. Another possibility would be to conduct multivariate analyses on a large number of samples that vary according to multiple dimensions.

(e.g., certain key behaviors must be evident, or a certain combined frequency of a set of behaviors must be found), but this would necessarily be somewhat arbitrary. Ideally, such an assessment would take into account the perceptions of the participants themselves: it would hardly be satisfying to pronounce a group a community on the basis of empirical discourse evidence, only to find that the participants themselves did not feel any sense of community-hood.[25]

At the broadest level, we might make theoretical interpretations about how the technological and social properties of CMC systems relate to the phenomenon of virtual community, extrapolating from the preceding observations. For example, we might use the comparison of the Linguist List and the ILF to argue against the Media Richness Theory (Daft & Lengel, 1986), since a lean, text-only environment was found to be more "community-like" than a rich, multimodal environment (cf. Walther, 1999). The properties of CMC systems also have practical implications for designers interested in creating environments to optimize community-like behavior. Designers need to be especially aware of the ways in which the features of such sites – for example, push versus pull message access, co-present versus archived past messages, use of visual modalities such as video – encourage or discourage participation, arguably the *sine qua non* of community (Herring et al., 2002; but cf. Nonnecke & Preece, 2000). Finally, our analysis of virtual community necessitated the invention of new methods (e.g., coding categories) for identifying and quantifying communicative behaviors associated with virtual community. This is itself an original research contribution that could be refined and extended to other computer-mediated contexts in future studies.

The steps in the CMDA research process and their application to the problem of assessing the virtual community status of the two professional development groups are summarized in Table 12.6.

CONCLUSIONS

This chapter has presented a methodological overview of computer-mediated discourse analysis (CMDA), highlighting one empirical, linguistic approach.[26] This approach enables a level of empirical rigor, and reflects

---

[25] Conversely, participants might experience a sense of belonging and identity even in groups where discourse behaviors associated with community are lacking. For example, Nonnecke and Preece (2000) interviewed "lurkers" in online discussion groups and found that some expressed a sense of belonging, even though they never posted messages to the group.

[26] Interpretive approaches to CMDA, drawing on methods from, e.g., anthropology and rhetoric, also exist. See, for example, Cherny (1999) and Kendall (2002) for anthropological (ethnographic) approaches; Gurak (1996) and Herring (1999b) for rhetorical approaches.

TABLE 12.6. *Summary of the CMDA Research Process Applied to a Hypothetical Question about Virtual Community*

CMDA Research Process	Application to Virtual Community
Articulate research question(s)	E.g., "To what extent do two online professional development environments, listserv X and website Y, constitute 'community'?"
Select computer-mediated data sample	E.g., intermittent time-based sampling (several weeks at a time at intervals throughout a year) of public messages from each group
Operationalize key concept(s) in terms of discourse features	Community → core participants + in-group language + support + conflict + group self-awareness + roles, etc.
Select and apply method(s) of analysis	Frequency counts of, e.g., messages and message length, rate of response ("core participants") Structural analysis of, e.g., abbreviations, word choice, language routines ("in-group language") Pragmatic analysis of, e.g., speech acts of positive politeness ("support"), etc.
Interpret results	
1. summarize/synthesize results of data analysis	1. Listserv X has community features a, b, c, . . . ; website Y has community features c, f, . . .
2. answer research question(s); explain unexpected results	2. Both have some community features; X is more community-like than Y. This is due to . . .
3. consider broader implications	3. Results have implications for: CMC theory (e.g., Media Richness); system design (e.g., push vs. pull access); research methodology (e.g., coding categories for community features)

a heightened linguistic awareness, that sets it apart from other approaches to the study of Internet behavior. Five conceptual skills necessary for carrying out a CMDA using the code and count method were discussed and applied to the concept of virtual community, specifically the question of whether it exists in two asynchronous professional development environments. The existence of virtual community is a fundamental question that needs to be addressed if the term is to be used meaningfully, rather than purely metaphorically or (in Kling & Courtright's term) aspirationally, reflecting the user's desire that the positive aspects of community-hood be attributed to an online group.

Our hypothetical analysis suggested ways in which CMDA can shed empirical light on the notoriously slippery concept of virtual community. Crucially, CMDA requires that virtual community be operationalized according to behavioral criteria; on the Internet, such behavior takes place primarily through discourse. Although there is room for disagreement as to the best definition of virtual community, an operationalization need only be plausible and concrete in order to be applied and interpreted. Discourse measures are especially useful for comparing hypothesized community characteristics in different online environments or samples of data from the same environment. Further, once virtual community has been identified by discourse-independent means in some contexts, the discourse behaviors associated with it can be analyzed and extended as heuristics to identify virtual community in other contexts.

In other respects, virtual community remains a challenging concept to demonstrate. Operationalizations are inevitably somewhat arbitrary; their value resides in being empirically testable, not in being true in an ultimate, philosophical sense. But what is virtual community, really? The concept is derivative of face-to-face community; thus a comparison between the two would seem to be logically required. However, CMC, by its very nature, arguably favors different kinds of group interactions than are possible face-to-face, causing other circumstances to vary in addition to the modality of the communication. Face-to-face community and online "community" may not be strictly comparable (Jones, 1995a); to what, then, can the latter be referenced to establish its existence? Moreover, the concept of community itself is inherently abstract, especially when stripped of its geographical basis, as is the case in virtual community. Whereas certain behaviors, such as articulating norms and supporting others, might plausibly be associated with virtual community status, the same behaviors could also be interpreted in other ways, for example, as power negotiation, or strategies to promote personal gain. That is, concluding on the basis of specific discourse features that a group is a virtual community might ultimately require too great an interpretive leap, given the abstractness of the target concept.

To a certain extent, these problems reflect the limitations of CMDA as an empirical, text-based approach. We can only directly analyze discourse behavior, and must infer larger social and cognitive formations (such as perceived group identity) indirectly. In fact, CMDA is most useful for comparing discourse features with independently established technical, social, or psychological phenomena. Thus there are limits on what kinds of phenomena can be investigated via online discourse behaviors. However, this is also the case for self-report studies, ethnographic observation, social network analysis, and indeed for any other methodological approach to analyzing human behavior.

The coding and counting approach to CMDA illustrated in this chapter also has its strengths and limitations. The approach has the advantage of being based on a familiar social science paradigm, classical content analysis (Bauer, 2000), the usefulness of which has been repeatedly demonstrated for the analysis of communication media (Riffe, Lacy, & Fico, 1998; see also Bell & Garrett, 1998). It is particularly well-suited to analyzing and comparing discrete online phenomena, and for revealing systematic regularities in discourse use. However, quantitative content analysis may not be the best approach for analyzing complex, interacting, ambiguous, or scalar phenomena, which risk distortion by being forced into artificially discrete categories for purposes of counting. Such phenomena may be more richly revealed by qualitative, interpretive approaches, which illuminate through exemplification, argumentation, and narration.[27]

The question then arises whether virtual community might more appropriately be analyzed by qualitative than by quantitative means. Its complexities and ambiguities have been illuminatingly discussed in ethnographic studies of recreational CMC environments by Baym (1999), Cherny (1999), Kendall (2002), and Reid (1991, 1994), among others. The ethnographic approach has been especially revealing in describing insider language use, rituals, norms, and sanctions, and in narrating the histories of these practices. However, as Liu (1999) notes, most such studies assume a priori that the environments in question are communities (or in the case of Cherny, "speech communities"), rather than assessing empirically the extent to which they meet a consistent set of criteria for community-hood. As a result, although ethnographic research can provide valuable insights into online environments in which participants may experience a strong sense of subjective belonging, the studies do not prove or disprove the existence of virtual community, nor can they be compared in any systematic way. It seems likely that both qualitative and quantitative approaches are needed in order to arrive at a full understanding of the nature of the online social groupings that currently proliferate in cyberspace.

At the same time, computer-mediated groups, including those that meet the subjective criterion of "feeling" like community to their members, are increasingly interacting via multimodal interfaces, including web logs, online videoconferencing, and navigable virtual reality environments

---

[27] Qualitative approaches fall within the purvue of CMDA, provided they are based on analysis of actual records of online interaction. Examples of qualitative CMDA research, in addition to those mentioned in note 26, include Baym (1995b); Danet et al. (1997); Herring, Job-Sluder, Scheckler, & Barab (2002); Livia (in press); and Weber (in press). Moreover, even rigorously quantitative CMDA analysis can benefit from a theoretically informed interpretive framework, "thick" description of users, systems, and contexts, and discourse examples to lend analytical nuance.

(Bowers, 2000; Kibby & Costello, 2001; Naper, 2001). The CMDA "toolkit" as articulated here is lacking in methods for analyzing meanings communicated through semiotic systems other than text. An important future direction for CMDA is to identify and adapt appropriate methods of graphical, video, and audio analysis to computer-mediated communication, on the assumption that these modalities communicate discourse meanings (Naper, 2001; Soukup, 2000; cf. Kress & van Leeuwen, 1996). With regard to online learning environments, Herring et al. (2002) have begun to do this in analyzing video clips on the ILF site; much more work remains to be done in this direction.

References

Alford, R. A. (1998). *The Craft of Inquiry: Theories, Methods, Evidence.* New York: Oxford University Press.

Atkinson, J. M., & Heritage, J. (Eds.) (1984). *Structures of Social Action: Studies in Conversation Analysis.* Cambridge: Cambridge University Press.

Austin, J. L. (1962). *How to Do Things With Words.* Cambridge, MA: Harvard University Press.

Baker, A. (1998). Cyberspace couples finding romance online then meeting for the first time in real life. *CMC Magazine*, July 1998. Retrieved July 21, 2002 from the World Wide Web: http://www.december.com/cmc/mag/1998/jul/baker.html.

Barab, S., MaKinster, J., Moore, J., Cunningham, D., & The ILF Design Team. (2001). Designing and building an online community: The struggle to support sociability in the Inquiry Learning Forum. *Educational Technology Research & Development*, 49(4), 71–96.

Bauer, M. (2000). Classical content analysis: A review. In M. Bauer & G. Gaskell (Eds.), *Qualitative Researching with Text, Image and Sound* (pp. 131–151). Thousand Oaks, CA: Sage.

Baym, N. (1995a). The emergence of community in computer-mediated communication. In S. Jones (Ed.), 138–163.

Baym, N. (1995b). The performance of humor in computer-mediated communication. *Journal of Computer-Mediated Communication*, 1(2). Retrieved July 21, 2002 from the World Wide Web: http://www.usc.edu/dept/annenberg/vol1/issue2/baym.html.

Baym, N. (1999). *Tune In, Log on: Soaps, Fandom, and Online Community.* Thousand Oaks, CA: Sage.

Bell, A., & Garrett, P. (Eds.) (1998). *Approaches to Media Discourse.* Oxford: Blackwell.

Bowers, J. (2000). *Weblog communities.* Posted February 28, 2000. Retrieved December 31, 2002, from the World Wide Web: http://irights.editthispage.com/stories/storyReader$115.

Bruckman, A. S., & Resnick, M. (1995). The MediaMOO project: Constructionism and professional community. *Convergence*, 1(1), 94–109.

Burkhalter, B. (1999). Reading race online. In M. Smith & P. Kollock (Eds.), 60–75.

Burnett, G. (2000). Information exchange in virtual communities: A typology. *Information Research*, 5(4). Retrieved June 15, 2001 from the World Wide Web: http://www.shef.ac.uk/~is/publications/infres/paper82a.html.

Chafe, W. (1994). *Discourse, Consciousness and Time*. Chicago: University of Chicago Press.

Cherny, L. (1999). *Conversation and Community: Chat in a Virtual World*. Stanford, CA: Center for the Study of Language and Information.

Cherny, L., & Weise, E. R. (Eds.) (1996). *Wired_Women: Gender and New Realities in Cyberspace*. Seattle: Seal Press.

Condon, S. C., & Čech, C. (1996a). Discourse management strategies in face-to-face and computer-mediated decision making interactions. *Electronic Journal of Communication*, 6(3). Retrieved June 15, 2001 from the World Wide Web: http://www.cios.org/www/ejc/v6n396.htm.

Condon, S. C., & Čech, C. (1996b). Functional comparisons of face-to-face and computer-mediated decision making interactions. In S. Herring (Ed.), 65–80.

Condon, S. C., & Čech, C. (2001). Profiling turns in interaction: Discourse structure and function. *Proceedings of the 34th Hawaii International Conference on System Sciences*. Los Alamitos: IEEE Computer Society.

Condon, S. C., & Čech, C. (in press). Discourse management in three modalities. In S. Herring (Ed.).

Crystal, D. (2001). *Language and the Internet*. Cambridge: Cambridge University Press.

Daft, R. L., & Lengel, R. H. (1986). Organizational informational requirements, media richness and structural design. *Management Science*, 32, 554–571.

Danet, B., Ruedenberg-Wright, L., & Rosenbaum-Tamari, Y. (1997). Hmmm . . . where's that smoke coming from? Writing, play and performance on Internet Relay Chat. In S. Rafaeli, F. Sudweeks, & M. McLaughlin (Eds.), *Network and Netplay: Virtual Groups on the Internet* (pp. 41–76). Cambridge, MA: AAAI/MIT Press.

Diani, M. (2000). Social movement networks virtual and real. *Information, Communication & Society*, 3, 386–401.

Dibbell, J. (1993). A rape in cyberspace, or how an evil clown, a Haitian trickster spirit, two wizards, and a cast of dozens turned a database into a society. *Village Voice*, December 21, 1993, 36–42.

Etzioni, A. (1999). Face-to-face and computer-mediated communities, a comparative analysis. *The Information Society*, 15, 241–248.

Fairclough, N. (1992). *Discourse and Social Change*. London: Polity Press.

Fernback, J., & Thompson, B. (1995). Virtual communities: Abort, retry, failure? Retrieved December 31, 2002 from the World Wide Web: http://www.well.com/user/hlr/texts/VCcivil.html.

Ferrara, K., Brunner, H., & Whittemore, G. (1991). Interactive written discourse as an emergent register. *Written Communication*, 8(1), 8–34.

Georgakopoulou, A. (in press). 'On for drinkies?': E-mail cues of participant alignments. In S. Herring (Ed.).

Glaser, B., & Strauss, A. L. (1967). *The Discovery of Grounded Theory: Strategies for Qualitative Research*. Aldine Press.

Goffman, E. (1959). *Presentation of Self in Everyday Life*. Garden City, NY: Anchor.

Gumperz, J. J. (1982). *Discourse Strategies*. Cambridge: Cambridge University Press.

Gurak, L. (1996). The rhetorical dynamics of a community protest in cyberspace: What happened with Lotus Marketplace. In S. Herring (Ed.), 265–277.

Hall, K. (1996). Cyberfeminism. In S. Herring (Ed.), 147–170.

Harwood, W. S., Reiff, R., & Phillipson, T. (2001). *Conceptions of scientific inquiry: Voices from the front*. Unpublished ms, Indiana University, Bloomington.

Haythornthwaite, C., Kazmer, M. M., Robins, J., & Shoemaker, S. (2000). Community development among distance learners: Temporal and technological dimensions. *Journal of Computer-Mediated Communication*, 6(1). Retrieved October 2, 2000, from the World Wide Web: http://www.ascusc.org/jcmc/vol6/issue1/haythornthwaite.html.

Herring, S. C. (1992). Gender and participation in computer-mediated linguistic discourse. Washington, D. C.: ERIC Clearinghouse on Languages and Linguistics. Document no. ED345552.

Herring, S. C. (1993). Gender and democracy in computer-mediated communication. *Electronic Journal of Communication*, 3(2). Retrieved June 15, 2001, from the World Wide Web: http://www.cios.org/www/ejc/v3n293.htm.

Herring, S. C. (1994). Politeness in computer culture: Why women thank and men flame. In M. Bucholtz, A. Liang, L. Sutton, & C. Hines (Eds.), *Cultural performances: Proceedings of the Third Berkeley Women and Language Conference* (pp. 278–294). Berkeley, CA: Berkeley Women and Language Group.

Herring, S. C. (1996a). Posting in a different voice: Gender and ethics in computer-mediated communication. In C. Ess (Ed.), *Philosophical Perspectives on Computer-Mediated Communication* (pp. 115–145). Albany: SUNY Press.

Herring, S. C. (1996b). Two variants of an electronic message schema. In S. Herring (Ed.), 81–106.

Herring, S. C. (Ed.) (1996c). *Computer-Mediated Communication: Linguistic, Social and Cross-Cultural Perspectives* (pp. 81–106). Amsterdam: John Benjamins.

Herring, S. C. (1998). Le style du courrier électronique: variabilité et changement [Variation and change in e-mail style]. *Terminogramme, 84–85*, 9–16.

Herring, S. C. (1999a). Interactional coherence in CMC. *Journal of Computer-Mediated Communication*, 4(4). Retrieved June 15, 2001, from the World Wide Web: http://www.ascusc.org/jcmc/vol4/issue4/.

Herring, S. C. (1999b). The rhetorical dynamics of gender harassment on-line. *The Information Society*, 15(3), 151–167.

Herring, S. C. (2001). Computer-mediated discourse. In D. Tannen, D. Schiffrin, & H. Hamilton (Eds.), *Handbook of Discourse Analysis* (pp. 612–634). Oxford: Blackwell.

Herring, S. C. (2002). Computer-mediated communication on the Internet. In B. Cronin (Ed.), *The Annual Review of Information Science and Technology* (pp. 109–168). Medford, NJ: Information Today Inc./American Society for Information Science and Technology.

Herring, S. C. (2003). Gender and power in online communication. In J. Holmes & M. Meyerhoff (Eds.), *Handbook of Language and Gender* (pp. 202–228). Oxford: Blackwell.

Herring, S. C. (in press a). Who's got the floor in computer-mediated conversation? Edelsky's gender patterns revisited. In S. Herring (Ed.).

Herring, S. C. (Ed.) (in press b). *Computer-Mediated Conversation*. Cresskill, NJ: Hampton Press.

Herring, S. C. (Under consideration). A classification scheme for computer-mediated discourse.

Herring, S. C., Job-Sluder, K., Scheckler, R., & Barab, S. (2002). Searching for safety online: Managing "trolling" in a feminist forum. *The Information Society, 18*(5), 371–383.

Herring, S. C., Johnson, D. A., & DiBenedetto, T. (1992). Participation in electronic discourse in a "feminist" field. In K. Hall, M. Bucholtz, & B. Moonwomon (Eds.), *Locating Power: The Proceedings of the Second Berkeley Women and Language Conference* (pp. 250–262). Berkeley, CA: Berkeley Women and Language Group.

Herring, S. C., Johnson, D. A., & DiBenedetto, T. (1995). "This discussion is going too far!" Male resistance to female participation on the Internet. In M. Bucholtz & K. Hall (Eds.), *Gender Articulated: Language and the Socially Constructed Self* (pp. 67–96). London: Routledge.

Herring, S. C., Martinson, A., & Scheckler, R. (2002). Designing for community: The effects of gender representation in videos on a Web site. *Proceedings of the 35th Hawaii International Conference on System Sciences*. Los Alamitos: IEEE Press.

Herring, S. C., & Nix, C. G. (1997, March). *Is "serious chat" an oxymoron? Academic vs. social uses of Internet Relay Chat*. Paper presented at the annual meeting of the American Association of Applied Linguistics, Orlando, FL.

Hert, P. (1997). Social dynamics of an on-line scholarly debate. *The Information Society, 13*, 329–360.

Hiltz, R. S., & Turoff, M. (1978). *The Network Nation: Human Communication Via Computer*. New York: Addison-Wesley.

Jacobs-Huey, L. (in press). . . . BTW, how do YOU wear your hair? Identity, knowledge and authority in an electronic speech community. In S. Herring (Ed.).

Jacobson, D. (1996). Contexts and cues in cyberspace: The pragmatics of naming in text-based virtual realities. *Journal of Anthropological Research, 52*, 461–481.

Jones, Q. (1997). Virtual communities, virtual settlements & cyber-archaeology: A theoretical outline. *Journal of Computer-Mediated Communication, 3*(3). Retrieved July 25, 2002 from the World Wide Web: http://www.ascusc.org/jcmc/vol3/issue3/jones.html.

Jones, S. (1995a). Understanding community in the information age. In S. Jones (Ed.), 10–35.

Jones, S. (Ed.) (1995b). *Cybersociety: Computer-Mediated Communication and Community*. Thousand Oaks, CA: Sage.

Jones, S. (Ed.) (1998). *Cybersociety 2.0: Revisiting Computer Mediated Communication and Community*. Thousand Oaks, CA: Sage.

Kendall, L. (1996). MUDder? I hardly know 'er! Adventures of a feminist MUDder. In L. Cherny & E. R. Weise (Eds.), 207–223.

Kendall, L. (2002). *Hanging Out in the Virtual Pub*. Berkeley: University of California Press.

Kibby, M., & Costello, B. (2001). Between the image and the act: Interactive sex entertainment on the Internet. *Sexualities: Studies in Culture and Society, 4*(3), 353–269.

Ko, K-K. (1996). Structural characteristics of computer-mediated language: A comparative analysis of InterChange discourse. *Electronic Journal of Communication*, 6(3). Retrieved June 15, 2001, from the World Wide Web: http://www.cios.org/www/ejc/v6n396.htm.

Kolko, B. (1995). Building a world with words: The narrative reality of virtual communities. *Works and Days*, 13(1/2), 105–126. Retrieved June 15, 2001, from the World Wide Web: http://acorn.grove.iup.edu/en/workdays/toc.html.

Kolko, B., & Reid, E. (1998). Dissolution and fragmentation: Problems in online communities. In S. Jones (Ed.), 212–229.

Korenman, J., & Wyatt, N. (1996). Group dynamics in an e-mail forum. In S. Herring (Ed.), 225–242.

Kress, G., & van Leeuwen, T. (1996). *Reading Images: The Grammar of Visual Design*. London: Routledge.

Lambiase, J. (in press). Hanging by a thread: Topic development and death in an electronic discussion of the Oklahoma City bombing. In S. Herring (Ed.).

Levinson, S. (1983). *Pragmatics*. Cambridge: Cambridge University Press.

Liu, G. Z. (1999). Virtual community presence in Internet Relay Chatting. *Journal of Computer-Mediated Communication*, 5(1). Retrieved June 15, 2001, from the World Wide Web: http://www.ascusc.org/jcmc/vol5/issue1/liu.html.

Livia, A. (in press). BSR ES TU F? Brevity and expressivity on the French Minitel. In S. Herring (Ed.).

Longacre, R. E. (1992). The discourse strategy of an appeals letter. In W. Mann & S. A. Thompson (Eds.), *Discourse Description: Diverse Linguistic Analyses of a Fund-Raising Text* (pp. 109–130). Amsterdam: John Benjamins.

Longacre, R. E. (1996). *The Grammar of Discourse*, 2d ed. New York: Plenum.

Mann, C., & Stewart, F. (2000). *Internet Communication and Qualitative Research: A Handbook for Researching Online*. Thousand Oaks, CA: Sage.

McLaughlin, M. L., Osborne, K. K., & Smith, C. B. (1995). Standards of conduct on Usenet. In S. Jones (Ed.), 90–111.

Millen, D. (2000). Community portals and collective goods: Conversation archives as an information resource. *Proceedings of the 33rd Hawaii International Conference on System Sciences*. Retrieved June 15, 2001 from the World Wide Web: http://dlib.computer.org/conferen/hicss/0493/pdf/04933030.pdf.

Murray, D. E. (1985). Composition as conversation: The computer terminal as medium of communication. In L. Odell & D. Goswami (Eds.), *Writing in Nonacademic Settings* (pp. 203–227). New York: Guilford.

Murray, D. E. (1988). The context of oral and written language: A framework for mode and medium switching. *Language in Society*, 17, 351–373.

Naper, I. (2001). System features of an inhabited 3D virtual environment supporting multimodality in communication. *Proceedings of the 34th Hawaii International Conference on System Sciences*. Retrieved June 15, 2001 from the World Wide Web: http://www.hic.ss.hawaii.edu/HICSS_34/PDFs/DDPTC10.pdf.

National Research Council. (2000). *Inquiry and the National Science Education Standards: A Guide for Teaching and Learning*. Washington, DC: National Academy Press.

Nonnecke, B., & Preece, J. (2000). Persistence and lurkers in discussion lists: A pilot study. *Proceedings of the 33rd Hawaii International Conference on System*

Sciences. Retrieved June 15, 2001 from the World Wide Web: http://dlib.computer. org/conferen/hicss/0493/pdf/04933031.pdf.

Panyametheekul, S. (2001). Disrupted adjacency and cohesion in Thai chat. Unpublished manuscript, Indiana University, Bloomington.

Paolillo, J. (1996). Language choice on soc.culture.punjab. *Electronic Journal of Communication*, 6(3). Retrieved June 15, 2001, from the World Wide Web: http://www.cios.org/www/ejc/v6n396.htm.

Paolillo, J. (2001). Language variation on Internet Relay Chat: A social network approach. *Journal of Sociolinguistics*, 5(2), 180–213.

Paolillo, J. (in press). Conversational codeswitching on Usenet and Internet Relay Chat. In S. Herring (Ed.).

Psathas, G. (1995). *Conversation Analysis: The Study of Talk-in-Interaction*. Thousand Oaks, CA: Sage.

Rafaeli, S., & Sudweeks, F. (1997). Networked interactivity. *Journal of Computer-Mediated Communication*, 2(4). Retrieved June 15, 2001, from the World Wide Web: http://www.ascusc.org/jcmc/vol2/issue4/.

Ravert, R. (2001). Adolescent chat style. Unpublished manuscript, Indiana University, Bloomington.

Reid, E. M. (1991). *Electropolis: Communication and Community on Internet Relay Chat*. Senior Honors thesis, University of Melbourne, Australia. Retrieved December 31, 2002, from the World Wide Web: http://www.aluluei.com/.

Reid, E. M. (1994). *Cultural Formations in Text-Based Virtual Realities*. Unpublished master's thesis, University of Melbourne, Australia. Retrieved June 15, 2001, from the World Wide Web: http://home.earthlink.net/~aluluei/cult-form.htm.

Reid, E. M. (1998). Hierarchy and power: Social control in cyberspace. In M. Smith & P. Kollock (Eds.), 107–133.

Rheingold, H. (1993). *The virtual community: Homesteading on the electronic frontier*. Reading, MA: Addison-Wesley. Retrieved June 15, 2001, from the World Wide Web: http://www.rheingold.com/vc/book/.

Riffe, D., Lacy, S., & Fico, F. (1998). *Analyzing Media Messages: Using Quantitative Content Analysis in Research*. Hillsdale, NJ: Erlbaum.

Sacks, H. (1984). On doing "being ordinary." In J. M. Atkinson & J. Heritage (Eds.), 413–429.

Severinson Eklundh, K. (1986). *Dialogue Processes in Computer-Mediated Communication: A Study of Letters in the COM system*. Linköping Studies in Arts and Sciences 6. University of Linköping.

Smith, M., & Kollock, P. (Eds.) (1999). *Communities in Cyberspace*. London: Routledge.

Soukup, C. (2000). Building a theory of multi-media CMC. *New Media & Society*, 2, 407–425.

Swales, J. (1990). *Genre Analysis*. Cambridge: Cambridge University Press.

Tannen, D. (Ed.) (1993). *Framing in Discourse*. New York: Oxford University Press.

Voth, C. (1999). *The Facts on FAQs: Frequently Asked Questions Documents on the Internet and Usenet*. Unpublished master's thesis, University of Texas at Arlington.

Walther, J. (1996). Computer-mediated communication: Impersonal, interpersonal and hyperpersonal interaction. *Communication Research*, 23(1), 3–43.

Walther, J. (1999). Visual cues and computer-mediated communication: Don't look before you leap. Retrieved December 31, 2002, from the World Wide Web: http://www.rensselaer.edu/~walthj/ica99.html.

Weber, H. L. (in press). Missed cues: How disputes can socialize virtual newcomers. In S. Herring (Ed.).

Wellman, B. (2001). Message posted to AIR-L@aoir.org, December 25, 2001.

Wenger, E. (1998). *Communities of Practice: Learning, Meaning, and Identity.* Cambridge: Cambridge University Press.

Werry, C., & Mowbray, M. (Eds.) (2001). *Online Communities: Commerce, Community Action, and the Virtual University.* Upper Saddle River, NJ: Prentice Hall.

Yates, S. J. (1996). Oral and written linguistic aspects of computer conferencing. In S. Herring (Ed.), 29–46.

13

Shared "We" and Shared "They" Indicators of Group Identity in Online Teacher Professional Development

Kirk Job-Sluder and Sasha A. Barab

Currently, many educators are adopting community of practice theory (CoP) as a framework for designing environments to support learning (Lave & Wenger, 1991; Wenger, 1998). An assumption underlying community of practice theory is that learning occurs not only as a cognitive change in the learner but also as a social trajectory within a group. The social identities of learners change as the learners become recognized as experts within a social group that shares a set of practices. Wenger uses the example of insurance claims processors to illustrate how communities of practice work. The actual practice of claims processors is as much a product of the informal social networks and war stories of experienced members as it is a product of the formal procedures mandated by the company.

Not surprisingly, CoP as a descriptive theory has been applied as a design framework for online learning in addition to an analysis framework for examining workplaces bounded by a common location (Johnson, 2001; Schwen & Hara, this volume). The hope is to combine the information sharing and shared enterprises that characterize physical CoPs, along with characteristics of longstanding communities that have emerged on the Internet. Although the definitions of Internet community differ, most of the work on online communities makes a distinction between groups of people forming cohesive social structures in an online space and groups

The authors would like to thank the following people who helped with the development of this study: Dr. Susan Herring provided guidance and advice at critical points, Jamie Kirkley and Laura Job Sluder assisted in inter-rater reliability coding, many teachers and visiting researchers traveled to Indiana University, Bloomington to help build the ILF, and the National Science Foundation provided the means to build it. In addition, this chapter would not be possible without the help of the students, faculty, and staff on the ILF design and development teams who provided a rich community for this research to develop.

of people who just happen to use an online space (Barab, 2003). Internet communities are not defined by space or time, but by patterns of social networks built and sustained over time. The goal for designers in attempting to build online CoPs is to create the infrastructure and tools for participants to share information and engage in social dialogue (Grossman, Wineberg, & Woolworth, 2000). Hopefully, from this structure participants will develop the social networks and behaviors that form a CoP, and from an education standpoint, make learning meaningful. So far most of the literature regarding CoPs can be divided into two categories. The first category consists of case studies of an existing social network in physical or virtual spaces that already have well-defined histories, norms, identities, and shared practices (Cherny, 1999). The second category consists of case studies of attempts to design infrastructures for online communities within a given educational setting and studying the results of that design (Johnson, 2001). Both approaches have advantages and disadvantages. Studying an existing online or in-place community can yield a rich description of interactions. However, in many cases the studies are biased toward examples of successful communities. Many online spaces are underpopulated in both participants and messages. At the other end of the spectrum are spaces that are overloaded with the same arguments repeated by the same antagonists drowning out other forms of social interaction. Describing the handful of Internet success stories obscures the many attempts of community-building that do not get off the ground. On the other hand, studying a designed social network can describe the evolution of the social group from the start. However, most case studies involving planned educational collaboration usually take place over the course of an academic semester for a few years at most. Also, the case studies of designed online social groups usually include some external motivation such as working for a grade.

The case studies also are limited in their ability to provide a generalized design theory for online communities of practice: the observations are limited to a particular group within a particular domain. While the design literature provides us with plenty of "war stories" for attempting to design infrastructures for online communities, there are still many questions left to be answered. What distinguishes an online community from a gathering of people? How can we identify the difference through the evidence available from Internet spaces such as text transcripts? Are there developmental stages for community building? Are there aspects of community that can be quantified and measured? Is it possible to create a measurement methodology for looking at online community that can translate across different computer media (e-mail, Usenet, Web boards)? Most relevant to this study are useful methodological approaches to evaluating shared group identity, thereby characterizing the degree to which a group is an online community.

RELEVANT RESEARCH

There are a handful of studies that break significant ground toward developing a methodology that identifies online communities. Bucholtz (1999) used a linguistic study of "nerd girls" in a southern California high school to identify them as a separate community of practice from their peers. She observed that nerd girls used language differently from their peers at all levels, from their pronunciation of words, use of more advanced vocabulary words, and use of language to establish expertise in a subject.

Gunawardena (Gunawardena, Lowe, & Anderson, 1997) developed a model for how knowledge is socially constructed in computer-mediated debates. She proposed that groups actively engaged in constructing knowledge through a cyclic process of stating apparently contradictory viewpoints, creating a synthesis, and then challenging that synthesis as it becomes applied to new situations. Communities actively involved in creating knowledge progress through this cycle, while individuals that just inhabit a specific online space tend to remain stuck at the stage of stating contradictory viewpoints.

Another approach to the study of community is social network analysis (Koku & Wellman, this volume). Social network analysis examines the ways in which participants communicate with each other and by what medium. This method involves questioning participants to identify who they communicate with, the depth of those collaborations, and the frequency of communication between participants. Social network analysis serves to identify "a set of structural variables such as the density, clustering, heterogeneity, and multiplexity of networks" (Koku & Wellman, this volume). An advantage to social network analysis is that it incorporates all of the methods through which the group interacts rather than just computer-mediated communication.

Most of the descriptions of online communities and face-to-face communities in practice tend to agree that community is complex and multifaceted (Schweir, in press; Wellman & Gulia, 1999; Wenger, 1998; Winograd & Milton, 1999). Herring (this volume) advances six criteria for community:

1. active, self-sustaining participation; a core of regular participants;
2. shared history, purpose, culture, norms, and values;
3. solidarity, support reciprocity;
4. criticism, conflict, means of conflict resolution;
5. self-awareness of a group as an entity distinct from other groups; and
6. emergence of roles, hierarchy, governance, rituals (Herring, in press)

Herring (this volume) also claims, "A group's *self-awareness* is plausibly manifested in its members' references to the group as a group, and in 'us vs. them' language." In earlier pilot work, we attempted to juggle many of the different dimensions of community in order to develop a viable coding scheme. Rather than trying to work on all the different dimensions simultaneously, we have chosen to focus on expressions of a shared group identity. We hope by developing reliable coding schemes and methods for the individual dimensions, later we can merge our analysis into a holistic view of online communities.

Most of the literature seems to agree that a group identity is one of the central parts of a CoP. The group identity is usually defined according to implicit or explicit limits or boundaries around a group. In contrast, we suggest that a group identity is defined not only by boundaries but also by a sense of communal agency. The group "we" is not only something that is not "they," but an abstract entity capable of action and ownership in regard to "they." Teachers define themselves by what they do to or with students. Technical support consultants talk about users and clients and vegetarians on the Internet contrast their diet with "omni's."

In this chapter, rather than examining the big question of community, we have chosen to focus instead on evaluating sociability (Preece, 2001), the degree to which a socio-technical system enables participants to interact with each other. While community is considered to be an emergent property of participant behavior, sociability is a designed property of technical systems, which has parallels to the traditional definition of usability (Preece, 2001). Preece writes, "Whereas usability is primarily concerned with how users interact with technology, sociability is concerned with how members of community interact with each other via the supporting technology" (p. 83).

Because sociability focuses on design affordances rather than emergent patterns of behavior, we believe that sociability is applicable to more problems in designing learning environments. One-semester classes may not have enough time to develop the shared language, culture, and history that are generally considered to be requirements for community. Also, sociability is a necessary prerequisite but not sufficient in itself to create online communities.

CONTEXT OF THIS STUDY

The data analyzed for this study are derived from an examination of participation in the Inquiry Learning Forum (ILF) project (see *http://ilf. crlt.indiana.edu*). The ILF is a National Science Foundation–funded project that endeavors to build a CoP for math and science pre-service and in-service teachers (Barab, MaKinster, & Scheckler, this volume; Barab, MaKinster et al., 2001). Under this grant the ILF had two goals. First, we intended to build a professional development environment focused on inquiry-based teaching methods in math and science. Second, the ILF was a design experiment for advancing the methods for building online CoPs. We designed the ILF around a "visit to the classroom" metaphor. The ILF design team videotaped teachers using inquiry-based methods in the classroom. This is loosely defined as teaching methods that encourage students to develop their own answers to complex questions rather than methods that focus on effective transfer of information from teacher to students. The videotaped lesson was digitized for distribution over the World Wide Web. Along with the videotaped lesson we included commentary from the teacher regarding the lesson, links to state standards, resources, the lesson plan, and examples of student work. Attached to each lesson was a discussion forum for discussion of each lesson. In addition to the classrooms, the ILF included two different types of discussion spaces. The "Lounge" was designed as a discussion space open to all members of the ILF. Later we added "Inquiry Circles" to support small-group discussions around a specific topic.

Initially our audience consisted of in-service and pre-service math[1] and science teachers for grades 6 through 12. In the third year of the project, membership in the ILF was expanded to include elementary teachers and teachers outside of Indiana (although we chose to gear the content toward Indiana standards). As part of our goals to protect students and provide a safe space for teachers to interact, we require registration before participation and attempt to verify employment as a teacher or pre-service status at a college or university.

We designed the framework of the ILF around a metaphor of the school. Major areas include the "library," "lounge," "classrooms," "office," "my desk," and "collaboratory" (see Figure 13.1). A button bar at the top provides navigation links to major areas of the site. A secondary menu provides links within a given topic area. Informational content appears in the bottom frame. When visiting a classroom, the participants see a small video window embedded in the upper left corner of the screen, and a list of video clips from the lesson to the right of the video window.

During the first two years of the project, discussions primarily occurred in the classrooms and lounge. The classrooms consist of a collection of inquiry-based lessons that had been videotaped by ILF staff, digitized, and put on the Web with supporting materials. The videos were usually cut into six to eight segments. Discussion threads were started for each video segment with questions from the featured teacher. The lounge is a general discussion space with topics suggested by ILF participants or ILF staff.

In the second year of the project, we re-evaluated our goals to focus on sociability as well as usability (see Barab, MaKinster et al., 2001 for a

---

[1] In-service describes teachers currently working in K–12 schools, while pre-service describes students in college teacher education programs seeking teaching certification.

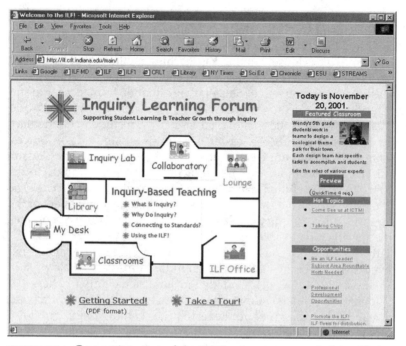

FIGURE 13.1. Current iteration of the ILF home screen, consisting of links to the *Visit Classrooms, ILF Office, Collaboratory, Lounge, Library,* and *My Desk*

discussion of the design trajectory of the project). Sociability was envisioned as the ability of our Web interface to support knowledge-sharing and interaction between groups of users rather than just the ability of the single user to get information. An important question raised by this commitment is how we evaluate sociability as a design goal. Evaluation of sociability requires developing frameworks that look beyond individual users and on to how groups use the tools to interact.

RESEARCH QUESTIONS

1. To what extent and in what manner do participants in the Inquiry Learning Forum express a shared group identity as part of their discussions?
2. To what extent and in what manner do the shared group identities differ from location to location within the ILF? (For example, are the group identities expressed in math-focused discussions different from the group identities expressed in science-focused discussions? Are discussions focused on personal biographies different from discussions on practice?)

Methods

Sample and Selection

Three discussion areas of the ILF were selected for this chapter. All three samples were chosen because they had comparatively high activity over an extended period of time. Two samples were selected to contrast a discussion of primarily in-service science teachers with a discussion of primarily in-service math teachers. "Science Misconceptions" was a discussion focused on misconceptions in science education. "Useless Math" started with a question of what could safely be eliminated from the math curriculum toward the goal of deeper exploration of critical topics. The third sample served as a contrast sample. "Introduce Yourself" was a discussion in which participants were requested to introduce themselves to the ILF community. The initial hypothesis was that the discussion in Introduce Yourself would incorporate a higher quantity of self-focused language and a lower quantity of group-focused language compared to the other two groups. In addition, we expected Introduce Yourself to include a much lower quantity of references to external groups. The contrast sample served to provide an obvious nonexample of group interaction that helped to focus on the similarities between the science and the math groups. The contrast sample also revealed ways that some members of the ILF staff interacted with teachers and pre-service education students in that ILF staff were very active in this discussion forum.

Analysis

Computer-mediated communications discourse analysis (CMDA or CMC-DA) examines how people use electronic tools to communicate. It was primarily developed for studying text-based human-computer-human modes of interactions such as chats, e-mail, Usenet, and bulletin boards. It treats computer-mediated communications (CMC) as an emerging genre of human language with styles and characteristics that are distinct from traditional modes of speech and writing (Herring, 1996). The hope of CMDA researchers is to develop an overall theory of how the technical features of CMC affect the way we use computers to communicate. In this case, CMDA involved three stages: contextual analysis, case characterization, and content analysis (see Table 13.1).

The first stage of CMDA involves some form of contextual analysis. For this study, participant demographics were presented and then Herring's (this volume) classification scheme was used for describing the data in terms of medium and context variables. Her chapter includes a discussion of these variables for the ILF classrooms but does not focus specifically on the discussion spaces. This classification scheme permits easy comparisons among multiple different types of CMC. Medium variables include synchronous versus asynchronous communication, the theoretical and

TABLE 13.1. *Stages of the Computer-Mediated Discourse Analysis*

Stage	Description
I. Contextual Analysis	
a. Participant demographics	This involves identifying important characteristics of the participants. For this study, we classified the participants by the subjects they taught and their current job status.
b. Medium variables	This involves characterizing the medium of communication used in the sample. Critical variables include synchronicity, buffer size, and message persistence. The goal here is to describe the technical features of the medium that may influence how the participants structured their discourse.
c. Context variables	This involves describing the context of the discussion using key variables such as discussion purpose, language, participation structure, and anonymity. The goal here is to describe contextual features as a basis for comparison to other contexts.
II. Case Characterization	This involves cycling through the raw data, examining the meaning of posts, reviewing the analysis of the first two stages of the CMDA, and offering a summary characterization of each discussion forum being examined. The spirit of the characterization should be ethnographic in that the goal is to provide the reader with an "insider" feel.
III. Content Analysis	
a. Structural analysis	This involved calculating frequency counts of first-person plural pronouns, first-person singular pronouns, and second-person pronouns. In addition, we collected statistics on words per post.
b. Semantic analysis	This involved coding statements made by the participants as statements about members of other groups or statements made indicating membership in a group.

practical size of the message buffer, the length of time messages are available to users, who can access the messages, and the capabilities of the interface for handling text formatting and/or multimedia. Context variables include the purpose of the discussion space, whether the participants are relatively homogenous or diverse, and obvious power differences between the participants.

Participant demographics were collected using two different methods. As part of registration, participants filled out a survey form including gender, their current position (classroom teacher, university student, university instructor, ILF staff, or other), and the subject areas they teach. The list of subject areas was collapsed into four categories: science, math, both, and none reported. In addition to the registration survey, we use data compiled from usage logs in order to obtain information about frequency of use and total number of posts for each member throughout the entire ILF – not simply in the discussion groups analyzed for this study. These data were cumulative as of June 1, 2002 and include data about participation before and after the discussions were active.

Following content analysis, the next stage of our process involves building a descriptive case characterization. While qualitative characterizations necessarily involve some research interpretation, at this stage in the analysis the goal is to be more descriptive than interpretive. A case characterization can be thought of as an abbreviated case study or a "thin" description (see Geertz, 1983, for a discussion of a "thick" description, which is a much more detailed account than being suggested here). This involves cycling through the raw data, examining the meaning of posts, reviewing the analysis of the first two stages of the CMDA, and offering a summary characterization of each discussion forum being examined. While not ethnographic in scale, the spirit of the case characterization should be ethnographic in that the goal is to provide the reader with an "insider" feel of the forum, but to do so in a manner that can have "outside" significance (Barab, Thomas, & Merrill, 2001; Geertz, 1983).

The final stage of our approach involves some form of content analysis. The literature usually differentiates between two different types of content analysis: structural analysis and semantic analysis (Bauer, 2000). Structural analysis examines features such as word counts, word frequencies, sentence or utterance length, message length, and vocabulary size. These are features that can usually be counted using automated tools such as concordance software. Semantic analysis classifies text features into categories according to various types of meaning. This requires that the researcher interpret what the writer of the text meant to say. Language is usually multilayered in meaning. For example, the phrase "How is it going?" can serve simultaneously as an inquiry, a greeting, and an expression of positive politeness. In looking at expressions of group identity, we used both structural and semantic analysis. In terms of the former, we first examined participation in terms of frequency counts regarding the amount of participation of each ILF member. Second, transcripts of the forums were converted to plain text format and analyzed using Simple Concordance Program (SCP) (Reed, 2002). We selected only the posts from the Introduce Yourself forum that were created during the same time period as the other two forums. Once in SCP, the word count was obtained by eliminating header labels, however, signature files were included in the total word count. Then SCP was used to count first-person singular pronouns, first-person plural pronouns, and second-person pronouns. These values and the total word count were imported into Microsoft Excel for further analysis. The counts for the different types of pronouns were aggregated and converted into frequency per 1,000 words. To correct for differences in pronoun use among the three groups, the final index calculates the percentage of a pronoun type out of all the pronouns counted. In terms of semantic analysis, we examined group references in posts and the relationships among posts, and content analysis was used to interpret the nature of the discussions. The coding scheme for categorizing "In-group" and "Out-group" references was developed through multiple rounds of open coding (Strauss & Corbin, 1998). Eventually, two primary themes emerged from the open coding. Personal identity statements identified the person as a member of the specific group working within a specific context. External references described a relationship between the self and a different group. The coding scheme is not meant to be exhaustive of all types of references, but to reflect the most frequent references.

The coding scheme for external references included three codes. The first is to incorporate the concept of transitivity: who is doing what to whom. "Out-group as object" incorporates those phrases in which members of the Out-group are the object or recipient of In-group actions. Members of the Out-group are placed into a passive role. "Out-group as subject" is used for those phrases in which members of the Out-group are engaged in independent action. This typically involves a description of Out-group behavior. The third Out-group code is the "parallel statement." This consists of a statement regarding the actions of the In-group coupled with a statement regarding the actions of the Out-group. These are usually used to explicitly contrast In-group behavior and Out-group behavior.

We used two identity statement codes. The basic "identity statement" describes an individual's role, or context. This usually consisted of personal narrative including details such as where the participant worked, years of experience, and subject areas taught. "Transformation identity statements" describe changing group membership over time. For example, participants described working summer jobs in construction or transitioning from pre-service student teaching to full-time professional teaching.

Units of text coded usually included one or more complete noun-verb phrases. Adjacent units coded with the same label were collapsed into one unit. The codes were counted and entered into a Microsoft Excel spreadsheet. To normalize the data for different word counts, we calculated the frequency of each code per 100 words. These frequencies were used in two different ways. First, frequencies of identity statements were contrasted with frequencies of external references for major subgroups. Second, the frequencies were used to construct a map of the identities expressed in the sample.

In addition, the types of external references used offer tentative conclusions about the nature of the relationship between the "in-groups" and the "out-groups." For example, direct object phrases imply that the participant is directly trying to change members of the external group, while parallel statements ("we do this . . . they do that") highlight differences in perspective or practice between the two groups. Two coders also went through each of the posts in the different discussion groups to qualitatively characterize the overall nature of the discussions. This involved each coder reading all the posts and writing a one-page summary, comparing these summaries, and then re-writing the summaries until we had a version of each discussion group that both coders felt represented the nature of the discussion.

Inter-rater Reliability

Two coders independently coded the three discussion samples. After coding the samples, the two coders then reviewed each other's coding selections. Pre-discussion agreement averaged 59 percent among the three samples. As part of the review we negotiated on each code to reach 100 percent agreement. The discussions revealed systematic issues that needed to be resolved with the original coding scheme. As a result of inter-rater reliability, we collapsed two codes, "Out-group as independent object" and "Out-group as dependent object" into one code, "Out-group as object." Distinguishing between these two codes added some error without a clear theoretical distinction. Another major source of error came from possessive statements that overlapped with other codes. In retrospect, the use of possessive pronouns is better incorporated as a structural analysis feature. A third major source of error consisted of confusion over when to combine two adjacent codes. The data in the results section of this chapter reflect the revised coding scheme and not the original.

The two coders also went through each of the posts in the different discussion groups to qualitatively characterize the overall nature of the discussions. This involved each coder reading all the posts and writing a one-page summary, comparing these summaries, and then re-writing the summaries until we had a version of each discussion group that both coders felt represented the nature of the discussion.

RESULTS

Contextual Analysis

Participant Demographics

Some basic statistics about the participants in the three forums are summarized in Table 13.2. The three forums were dramatically different in terms of participant gender, the current position of the participants, and the subject area taught by participants. With regard to participant gender, Introduce Yourself had more than three times as many female participants

TABLE 13.2. *Participant Demographics*

	Useless Math	Introduce Yourself	Science Misconceptions
Total Participants	15	32	18
Gender			
Female	6	25	9
Male	9	7	9
Current Position			
Classroom teacher	9 (60%)	20 (63%)	6 (33%)
University student	3 (20%)	5 (16%)	7 (39%)
University instructor	1 (7%)	3 (9%)	1 (6%)
ILF staff	2 (13%)	3 (9%)	3 (17%)
Other	0 (0%)	1 (3%)	1 (6%)
Subject Area			
Science	6 (40%)	6 (19%)	3 (17%)
Math	4 (26%)	10 (31%)	0 (0%)
Both	3 (20%)	12 (38%)	4 (22%)
None reported	2 (13%)	3 (9%)	11 (61%)
Participation Statistics			
Mean number of posts in ILF	35.20	20.19	58.22
Median number of posts in ILF	27	4	14
Mean days since registration	578.34	504.14	419.61
Median days since registration	652.47	504.14	322.64

as male participants. Science Misconceptions had equal numbers of male and female participants, and Useless Math had nine male participants to six female participants. In terms of current position, Useless Math and Introduce Yourself included similar percentages of classroom teachers (60% and 63%) and similar percentages of university students (20% and 16%). "Science Misconceptions" was very different for its larger percentage of university students participating. Thirty-nine percent of participants in Science Misconceptions identified themselves as university students and 33 percent identified themselves as classroom teachers. Another interesting feature of the participant demographics is that participants in Useless Math and Science Misconceptions on average posted more frequently than participants in Introduce Yourself. This seems to suggest that issue-focused discussion forums tend to attract participation from participants who post more frequently.

Medium and Context Variables
Classification of the data samples by medium and context variables helps to permit generalizations between CMC studies. Different electronic media offer different affordances for communication. In particular, the features of

synchronicity and message size tend to have a large impact on how people use CMC. Synchronicity is defined by the assumption that the participants are using the system at the same time, while asynchronous communication does not make this assumption. Buffer size is defined by the size of the message a person can enter into the system. With most asynchronous media the actual physical buffer size is far larger than is needed by the user.

Both synchronicity and buffer size influence how a message is structured. Asynchronous communication encourages participants to expand their thoughts in detail. Large text buffers permit the use of text structures characteristic of written text, such as paragraph breaks, introductory and summary sentences, and identifying signature files. Table 13.3 includes a breakdown of the medium variables.

The ILF as a messaging medium both is asynchronous and has a large message buffer. As a result, it is more analogous to similar forms of asynchronous CMC such as e-mail, Usenet, and Web-based bulletin boards than to synchronous environments such as chat utilities or MUDs (such as Tapped In: Schlager & Fusco, this volume). Participants used an average of

TABLE 13.3. *Medium Variables for ILF Discussions*

Variable	Description
Synchronicity	Asynchronous: potential extensive time delay between when messages are posted and when they are read.
Directionality	One-way message transmission: posts appear on the forum in their entirety. In addition, no mechanism exists for users to edit their posts after they appear.
Persistence	Highly persistent: messages remain on the ILF for months at a time.
Buffer size	Large message buffer: technical constraints limit message size to 1 MB. Practical message size is approximately one screen of text.
Mode	Primarily text communication: although users can attach additional files, this ability was not used in the sample.
Anonymity	Anonymous messaging is not an option: participation in the site requires registration and verification of identity.
Private messaging	Private messaging is an option: users can send private messages through the system.
Filter capabilities	Messaging filtering is not an option: users do not have the ability to block messages.
Quoting capabilities	Minimal quoting options: individuals can quote using cut and paste.

Source: Some text adapted from Herring (this volume).

105 words per post. Most posts were divided into multiple paragraphs, and some contained an e-mail–like signature file identifying the participant.

Table 13.4 summarizes the context variables. The context variables describe the context of the interactions that take place on the site. The participation structure variable describes how the participants communicate with each other. The ILF forums are a "many-to-many" venue in which multiple voices are present and anyone can respond to a particular post. The same technical system can be used as a "many-to-one" (a dropbox for assignments), a "one-to-many" (a space for posting announcements), or a "one-to-one" (two people talking in a private forum). The ILF registration system strongly encourages the use of real-life identities by asking for names, addresses, and a verification reference that can confirm an applicant's identity. In many other online forums, some degree of identity deception is assumed to occur or is actively encouraged (for example, role-playing MUDs). Other forums place a high value on identity concealment to protect individuals from unwanted commercial e-mail. The ILF encourages participants to interact with their real-life identities and restricts membership to educators in order to provide a semi-private space for interaction.

The participant characteristic variables describe overall aspects of the participants as a group. The ILF is a professional development environment for math and science teachers originally in the state of Indiana and expanded to a national audience. Other participants include professional ILF developers and research staff, university faculty associated with schools of education, and pre-service education students participating as part of a class requirement. The participants share a common language (American English), a common interest (inquiry practices in education), but different goals, levels of experience, and levels of familiarity with the ILF.

The purpose of the discussion is related to the topic or theme. The activity variable describes what the participants are doing in the forum. The tone variable describes the overall atmosphere of the discussion. The participants were relatively informal, addressing each other by first name, using personal greetings, and joking around with each other.

Case Characterization

Introduce Yourself

The Introduce Yourself forum was originally intended to be the location for new members to introduce themselves and for established members to greet newcomers, and this is generally how the forum was used by participants. New members describe who they are, where they work, and in which aspects of education they are most interested. Most of the responses to messages from newcomers came from ILF staff, suggesting resources posted on the ILF or resources hosted elsewhere. In a few cases, established

TABLE 13.4. *Context Variables for the ILF Sample*

Variable	Description
1. Participation structure	Many-to-many. Semi-private: membership restricted to math and science educators, university students, and faculty. Participants interact with real-life identities (Herring, in press). Population from 20 members to 1,600 over three years. Infrequent, slow participation (Herring, in press).
2. Participant characteristics	Primarily Indiana math and science teachers. Native English speakers. Little face-to-face contact. "Role hierarchy: ILF researchers > in-service teachers > pre-service teachers." Teachers featured in classroom video enjoy special status (Herring, in press). Share socio-cultural knowledge as Americans and schoolteachers; share subject-matter knowledge of math and science (Herring, in press).
3. Purpose	Of group: to facilitate implementation of inquiry-based teaching in the classroom. Goals of interaction: to share experiences with other teachers.
4. Topic or theme	Of group: inquiry-based teaching in the classroom. Useless Math: unnecessary topics in secondary math curriculum. Science Misconceptions: misconceptions adopted by students, teachers, and others. Introduce Yourself: personal introduction.
5. Tone	Relatively informal, friendly.
6. Activity	Sharing stories, debating proposals.
7. Norms	Of organization: the ILF was designed as a research project (Herring, in press). Of social appropriateness: "polite and supportive"(Herring, in press), emphasis on providing useful information. Of language: some jargon associated with both teaching philosophy and subject-matter.
8. Code	"Standard written English." "Roman alphabet in ASCII characters"(Herring, in press).

Source: Some text adapted from Herring (this volume).

members responded to new members who shared a common location, a common interest, or a "friend of a friend" connection.

Overall, posts in the Introduce Yourself forum tended to be short and chatty. Most of the posts started with an explicit welcome such as "hello" or "howdy." The ILF staff members tended to push features of the ILF in the responses to new members. Pre-service or in-service teachers often congratulated new members for joining the ILF. Overall, participants tended to use a larger proportion of first-person singular pronouns than other pronoun types. Participants also tended to use personal identity statements rather than talking about external groups.

Science Misconceptions

The Science Misconceptions topic started with a recommendation for resources about misconceptions and science. From this start, participants discussed the most frequent misconceptions that they deal with when working with students and misconceptions held by other adults and teachers. Misconception topics ranged from chemistry (the definition of "freezing"), biology (the belief that plants do not require oxygen), and environmental science (the belief in a link between the ozone layer and the greenhouse effect). In contrast to the Introduce Yourself discussion, the focus was more on students and their misconceptions than about the poster.

Overall, posts in the science misconceptions forum tended to include multiple paragraphs of narration about a specific misconception and ended with an invitation for further discussion. A few other posts provided links to research about science misconceptions. Participants were about equally split among in-service teachers, university students, and a third group consisting of university instructors and ILF staff. Discussion tended to be very "other" focused with most of the examples about misconceptions held by students. A lot of the discussion focused on how to transform misconceptions into proper conceptions.

Useless Math

The Useless Math forum started with a provocative statement by a high school geometry teacher claiming that he did not see a reason to teach a specific topic. He suggested cutting some "useless" topics out of the curriculum in the hopes of making more space for in-depth study into more "useful" topics. This statement set off a running debate about how to create a curriculum that was not "a mile wide and an inch deep." In the process, science teachers started participating in the discussion talking about the links between math and science curricula. Overall, posts in this forum tended to be at least three paragraphs in length. The first paragraph usually included an acknowledgment of what other people had said in the forum. The second paragraph usually developed an argument about how to redesign the math curriculum. Last, there was frequently a very short

TABLE 13.5. *Summary of Participation Across the Three Forums*

	Useless Math	Introduce Yourself	Science Misconceptions
Total Posts	48	51	50
Count	14	32	18
Average posts per person	3.43	1.59	2.78
Total Words	6782	3419	5642
Average words per post	141.29	67.04	112.84
Average words per person	484.43	106.84	313.44

paragraph with an invitation for further comment. As with the Science Misconceptions forum, Useless Math involved quite a bit of discussion about students. This was reflected by a very high frequency of references to students as an Out-group.

Content Analysis

Structural Analysis

PARTICIPATION COUNTS. Table 13.5 summarizes participation statistics for all three discussions. The Introduce Yourself forum had the fewest number of words contributing to the lowest words per post. It also included the most number of participants resulting in a very low number of words per person and a low average number of posts (1.6 per person compared to 3.4 posts per person for Useless Math and 2.8 for Science Misconceptions). Participants posted slightly more frequently in the math and science forums, and included more words per post. For the most part, conversation in Introduce Yourself consisted of either single posts or two-post answer-response couplets. The science and math forums had longer conversations in which earlier contributions were actively referenced.

USE OF PRONOUNS. The structural analysis revealed differences in pronoun use among the three discussions. The total pronoun frequency was highest in the Introduce Yourself sample with a frequency of 10.1 pronouns counted per 100 words. Science Misconceptions had the lowest pronoun frequency at 3.0 pronouns per 100 words. Because of the differences in pronoun use among the three groups, comparisons were made on the basis of each group of pronouns as a percentage of all pronouns counted. Table 13.6 summarizes the structural analysis results.

There were significant differences in the types of pronouns used among all three groups. The frequency of first-person singular ("I") pronouns was greatest in the Introduce Yourself sample ($X^2 = 102.7$, $p < .01$). The frequency of second-person ("you") pronouns was also highest in the Introduce Yourself sample ($X^2 = 54.1$, $p < .01$). The Introduce Yourself forum

TABLE 13.6. *Structural Analysis Summary Statistics*

	Useless Math	Science Misconceptions	Introduce Yourself	Chi-Square
Total Words	**6,299**	**5,168**	**2,933**	
First-Person Singular (count)	244	102	190	102.7*
Frequency (per 100 words)	3.87	1.97	6.48	
Second Person (count)	69	39	77	54.1*
Frequency (per 100 words)	1.10	0.75	2.53	
First-Person Plural (count)	94	30	19	28.2*
Frequency (per 100 words)	1.49	0.58	0.65	
Third-Person Plural	83	59	10	18.7*
Frequency (per 100 words)	1.32	1.14	.341	
Total Pronouns	490	230	296	
Pronoun Frequency	7.78	4.45	10.1	
% first-person singular	49.8%	44.4%	64.2%	
% second person	14.1%	17.0%	26.0%	
% first-person plural	19.2%	13.4%	6.42%	
% third-person plural	19.6%	25.7%	3.38%	

$^*p < .01$

had fewer first-person plural ("we") pronouns ($X^2 = 28.2, p < .01$) and third-person plural ("they") pronouns ($X^2 = 18.7, p < .01$). These differences are shown graphically in Figure 13.2.

Semantic Analysis

IN-GROUP/OUT-GROUP REFERENCES. The semantic coding also revealed dramatic differences among the three groups. As expected, the two discussion forums had dramatically lower frequencies of personal identity statements ($X^2 = 132.3, p < .01$) and transformation identity statements ($X^2 = 10.3, p < .01$). Participants in Science Misconceptions and Useless Math had higher frequencies of Out-group references to students ($X^2 = 17.2, p < .01$). The semantic coding revealed that the Useless Math and Science Misconceptions discussions were more similar to each other than to Introduce Yourself. Participants in Useless Math and Science Misconceptions referred to students more than five times as frequently as participants in Introduce Yourself. These results are summarized in Table 13.7. All numbers are expressed as frequency per 100 words. Out-group statements are subtotaled as statements about students, statements about nonstudents, and all Out-group statements.

A summary of the Out-group statement totals is displayed graphically in Figure 13.3. Out-group statements about students are compared to other Out-group statements for each discussion sample. This suggests that participants use different ways of expressing identity in Science

TABLE 13.7. *Summary of Semantic Coding for In-Group and Out-group References (Frequency per 1,000 words)*

	Useless Math	Science Misconceptions	Introduce Yourself	Chi-Square
All Out-group Codes	1.56	1.19	0.35	13.4*
All Student Codes	1.33	0.94	0.22	17.2*
All Nonstudent Codes	0.24	0.25	0.13	.50
Identity Statement	0.12	0.03	0.72	132.3*
Transformation Identity Statement	0.01	0.00	0.06	10.3*

*$p < .01$

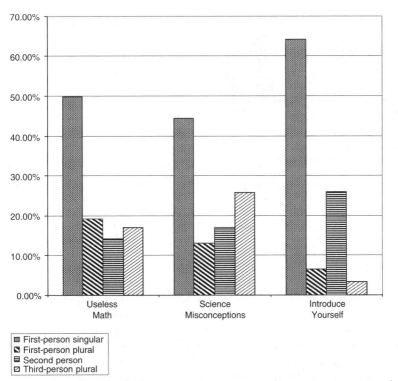

- First-person singular
- First-person plural
- Second person
- Third-person plural

FIGURE 13.2. Singular first-person pronouns, second-person pronouns, and plural first-person pronouns as a percentage of all pronouns counted

Misconceptions and Useless Math compared with Introduce Yourself. In Introduce Yourself the primary mode of identity expression is personal. Participants identify who they are and attempt to make links with other participants based on similar contexts or goals. In contrast, participants in Science

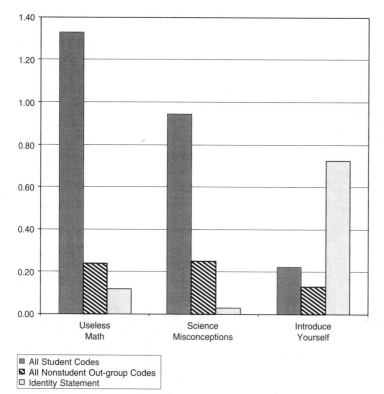

FIGURE 13.3. Out-group codes referring to students and Out-group codes referring to other groups as frequency per 100 words

Misconceptions and Useless Math rarely explicitly describe themselves as teachers in isolation, but as teachers in contrast with students.

In addition we separated the results by type of participant. One interesting pattern emerged in Introduce Yourself where 71 percent of the Out-group references made by ILF staff members referred to teachers rather than students. Most of these Out-group references were embedded in offers of assistance or references to teachers in videotaped classrooms. The semantic coding also revealed the type of relationship expressed. Direct object clauses and indirect object clauses imply a relationship in which the speaker is attempting to change members of the Out-group through action. Parallel sentence statements imply a difference of action or worldview between the groups. Other statements include observations of what the Out-group is doing without explicitly connecting the observation to In-group actions. The subtotals of Out-group references by type of code are given in Table 13.8.

TABLE 13.8. *Frequencies for Contrasting Identity Statements*

	Useless Math	Science Misconceptions	Introduce Yourself
Out-group as Object	**0.47**	**0.32**	**0.15**
Student subtotal	0.43	0.29	0.07
Out-group as Subject	**0.69**	**0.62**	**0.07**
Student subtotal	0.55	0.40	0.06
Parallel Statement	**0.29**	**0.16**	**0.00**
Student subtotal	0.25	0.16	0.00
Possessive Statement	**0.10**	**0.09**	**0.13**
Student subtotal	0.10	0.09	0.09

Participants in the Useless Math and Science Misconceptions discussions used references to students to define their own identity in terms of the teacher-student relationship. Participants in these discussions rarely directly identify themselves as a teacher at a specific school, or in a specific topic area; instead they usually identify themselves by describing their relationship to students. Parallel statements were used to contrast the way teachers see their subject area with the way that students see their subject area. For example:

EXAMPLE 1: Useless Math: Jan. 18, 2001: Tracy:
If technology continues, and of course if our computers don't crash (like in *Dark Angel*), then those basic skills will be obsolete. Even if the computers crash, we will still have calculators . . . which my students declare. My simple answer to them is: sometimes it's not the actual problem that we learn from, sometimes we learn from HOW we try to solve them. (C: Parallel statement) Also, many of the things we (educators) see as "useless" the students see as "short cuts." (C: Parallel statement)

EXAMPLE 2: Science Misconceptions: June 27, 2001: Tom
When a student walks into my cool room and says "It's freezing in here," I usually tap on something solid and say, "Yes, it is for some things." (C: Parallel Statement) Of course they don't get it. (B: Out-group as subject)

Object clauses defined students as the indirect or direct object of teacher action. In indirect clauses the teacher is providing students with something, in direct clauses the teacher is actively changing the student. These clauses define the teacher-student around a set of verbs such as expect, improve, get ("get the kids to . . ."), prepare, serve, and of course teach:

EXAMPLE 3: Useless Math: Dec. 2, 2000: abmckirk:
Obviously this is a generalization, but if we want to improve the standing of our students in comparison with other students throughout the world then we need to have higher expectations of them. (A: Out-group as object)

EXAMPLE 4: Useless Math: Nov. 28, 2000: David
I agree that part of our job is to prepare the students for their educational future. . . .
[A: Out-group as object] I would like to get my students to understand what is
essential before they move on instead of trying to "cover" everything. [A: Out-
group as object]

CONCLUSIONS AND DISCUSSION

Structural Coding Alone Is Not Enough

The first hypothesis for this study was that a rough indicator of group
identity can be found by looking for a higher frequency of "we" pronouns
and "they" pronouns versus "I" pronouns and "you" pronouns. This relationship would make it easier to quickly look for discussions in which
there is a possibility of group identity because frequency counts can be
obtained through automated computer tools. The results of looking for a
relationship in terms of frequency counts were complicated by differences
in how the three groups used personal pronouns. The science forum had
a lower frequency of personal pronouns per 1,000 words of total text than
the other two forums.

One way around this is to examine the frequencies as a percentage of the
personal pronouns actually used. Using this ratio, the Useless Math group
and the Science Misconceptions group demonstrated a higher percentage
of "we" pronouns and "they" pronouns compared to "I" pronouns and
"you" pronouns. This matched the prediction of our earlier hypothesis that
the two forums will be more alike than different in their comparative use of
pronouns. But this ignores the differences in total pronoun use among the
three groups. As a result, we have a low level of confidence in this ratio.

Linking Identity and Contrasting Identity

In looking at how the groups expressed a shared identity, our developing
coding scheme suggests that there are two different types of discourse used
to establish identity. Contrasting identity relies on defining distinctions between the group and one or more other external groups. In all three forums,
the primary object of the contrasting identity is the student. Students are
described as having different goals, different understandings of both the
topic and post-instructional applications, and different behaviors. Teachers
use parallel statements to describe how they are different from students.
Teachers also use subject/object statements to define students as either the
object acted on or as a recipient of an object provided by the teacher.

Contrasting identity was the primary form of identity expression in both
the science forum and the math forum. Participants rarely explicitly identified themselves as teachers or university students; instead they described

the ways in which they are different from their students. In talking about teaching practice the students occupied a central role.

Linking identity consists of statements that attempt to find points of commonality or identification within a larger community. This was the dominant form of expression in the introduction forum. Participants identified themselves by talking about locations, roles, levels of experience, and common social ties. While contrasting identity defines the boundaries of the community and provides a useful foil for describing group behavior, linking identity establishes personal context and invites others to link to that personal context.

The choice between contrasting identity and linking identity appears to depend on the purpose and the topic of the online space. The Introduce Yourself discussion forum focused on personal disclosure and had more expressions of linking identity in the form of describing similar personal contexts. The discussion spaces focused on in-classroom practice focused on contrasts between teachers and students.

Shared "Us" and Shared "Them" as Contrasting Identity

Contrasting identity serves to define identity by highlighting what the members are not. What are teachers? Teachers are not students. What do teachers do? Teachers are employed in the education of students. How do they do it? They do it differently from students. Contrasting identity was central to discussion in Useless Math and Science Misconceptions. Almost every description of teacher practice involved some form of relationship or contrast with students. The teacher-student relationship is not only an aspect of teacher practice; it is the central definition of teacher practice.

This is an apparently trivial result, but it has some key implications for using CMDA as a method to distinguish between a group of loosely associated individuals who just happen to communicate using the same computer-mediated channel, and online community. Much of the research on online communities has focused on interconnectedness and interdependence. Identifying the shared "them" of the online space might be an important indicator as to whether there is a shared "we." The "them" may extend to defining moral, social, and political values within a community.

However, one of the issues is that contrasting identity appears to be strongly determined by the context of the discussion. The Introduce Yourself forum had a much smaller frequency of contrasting identity statements than the other two forms. It makes sense that topics focused on individual disclosure may encourage participants to talk about themselves more and talk less about the "other." One of the interesting results is that Useless Math included such a high frequency of contrasting identity statements even though students were not the primary focus of the initial topic.

IMPLICATIONS

The most critical limitation of the study is the small number of discussion forums used. The study only includes three discussion forums, two of which were deliberately selected to be similar to each other and a third forum deliberately selected to provide contrast. All three forms came from the same teacher professional development environment. This method would need to be applied to several additional CMC samples in order to determine its usefulness. Another limitation is a factor of the choice of a teacher professional development environment. Compared to other CMC samples, the ILF sample is very civil and polite. As a result, this coding scheme might not be adequate to cover environments where two mutually antagonistic groups inhabit the same space. As a result, the coding scheme needs to be applied to many different types of discussion in order to expand it to a full group of generalizable codes. In spite of these limitations, this study and the methods used did provide useful insights into what extent and in what manner each discussion forum had some sense of shared identity. Further, examining how members of a group talk about and contrast themselves with other groups can provide a way to map the boundaries and identity of the group. The identities expressed by teacher members of the ILF were based on contrasting relationships to students more than references to schools or personal history. Drafting discussion leaders and moderators who share the same sense of identification should become a future goal for the ILF.

The next step in this research is to triangulate the CMDA data with other ways of looking at online social groups such as social network analysis, questionnaires, and interviews with members. This technique also needs to be applied to other forms of computer-mediated communication to check generalizability. A possible application of this method might be to track the development of group identity in a distance education cohort over the course of a semester or school year. While development of a shared group identity is probably not sufficient to say whether a group is a "community" or not, it may be one critical piece of the picture.

In summary, we believe that examining how participants in online discussions talk about themselves as members of a group, and talk about other groups, is critical to understanding if or how those participants express a shared group identity. Communities are defined as much by their boundaries as by their internal networks, shared language, or shared practices. Communities not only share common networks, language, and practice, but they also share relationships to external groups. In service professions such as teaching, the shared "they" is central not only to the shared "we" but impacts other aspects of community such as history, norms, participation, and roles. In this manuscript, we were able to develop and apply a framework that will allow others to more readily identify group identity in their particular contexts so that we can better understand and improve sociability in online spaces.

APPENDIX 1: SEMANTIC CODING USED TO ANALYZE IN-GROUP AND OUT-GROUP STATEMENTS

Code	Description	Examples
A: Out-group as object	Explicit reference to singular or multiple members of the Out-group as the direct or indirect object of In-group action.	"I tell them . . ." "I do something for them . . ." "I show them . . ."
B: Out-group as subject	Explicit reference to singular or multiple members of the Out-group as the subject of an action.	"They like to . . ." "They do . . ." "They say . . ."
C: Parallel in-group; Out-group statement	A compound statement describing the actions of members of an In-group with actions of members of an Out-group.	"They tell me . . . I reply . . ." "They do this . . . We do that."
E: Identity statement	An explicit statement of identity, usually starting with "I" or "We."	"I am a . . ." "I work at . . ." "We as teachers . . ."
F: Transforming identity statement	A statement of changing identity.	"I used to . . ." "During the summer I . . ."

IMPLIED REFERENCES: Avoid coding examples where the subject or object of the statement is implied. Code only explicit references. For example, code "I teach algebra to 7th graders." (Explicit reference to Out-group "7th graders.") Do not code "I teach algebra." (Students are implied but not referenced.)

COMBINING CODES: Combine identical codes when they are adjacent to each other. For example, "I am a pre-service Elementary teacher. I am currently placed in a first grade classroom once a week for field experience" can be counted as a single "E: Identity Statement."

References

Barab, S. A. (2003). An introduction to the special issue: Designing for virtual communities in the service of learning. *Information Society*, 19(3), 197–202.

Barab, S., MaKinster, J. G., Moore, J., Cunningham, D., & the ILF Design Team. (2001). Designing and building an online community: The struggle to support sociability in the Inquiry Learning Forum. *Educational Technology Research and Development, 49*(4), 71–96.

Barab, S. A., MaKinster, J., & Scheckler, R. (this volume). Designing system dualities: Characterizing an online professional development community.

Barab, S. A., Thomas, M. K., & Merrill, H. (2001). Online learning: From information dissemination to fostering collaboration. *Journal of Interactive Learning Environments, 12*(1), 105–143.

Bauer, M. (2000). Classical content analysis: A review. In G. Gaskell (Ed.), *Qualitative researching with Text, Image and Sound* (pp. 131–151). Thousand Oaks, CA: Sage.

Bucholtz, M. (1999). "Why Be Normal?": Language and identity practices in a community of nerd girls. *Language and Society, 28*(2), 203–223.

Cherny, L. (1999). *Conversation and Community: Chat in a Virtual World.* Stanford, CA: Center for the Study of Language and Information.

Geertz, C. (1983). Thick description: Toward an interpretive theory of culture. In R. M. Emerson (Ed.), *Contemporary Field Research: A Collection of Readings* (pp. 37–59). Prospect Heights, IL: Waveland Press.

Grossman, P., Wineberg, S., & Woolworth, S. (2000). *What Makes Teacher Community Different from a Gathering of Teachers?* (occasional paper): Center for the Study of Teaching and Policy.

Gunawardena, C. N., Lowe, C. A., & Anderson, T. (1997). Analysis of a global online debate and the development of an interaction analysis model for examining social construction of knowledge in computer conferencing. *Journal of Educational Computing Research, 17*(4), 397–431.

Herring, S. C. (1996). Two variants of an electronic message schema. In S. C. Herring (Ed.), *Computer-Mediated Communication* (vol. 39, pp. 81–107). Philadelphia: John Benjamins.

Herring, S. C. (this volume). Computer-mediated discourse analysis: An approach to researching online behavior.

Johnson, C. M. (2001). A survey of current research on online community of practice. *Internet and Higher Education, 2001*(4), 45–60.

Koku, E., & Wellman, B. (this volume). Scholarly networks as learning communities: the case of TechNet.

Lave, J., & Wenger, E. (1991). *Situated Learning: Legitimate Peripheral Participation.* Cambridge: Cambridge University Press.

Preece., J. (2001). Sociability and usability and online communities: determining and measuring success. *Behavior & Information Technology, 20*(5), 347–356.

Reed, A. (2002, Feb. 20, 2002). *Simple Concordance Program* [Software]. Textworld. com. Retrieved Feb. 26, 2002, 2002, from the World Wide Web: http://web.bham.ac.uk/a.reed/textworld/scp/.

Schwier, R. A. (in press). Catalysts, emphases, and elements of virtual learning communities: Implications for research and practice. *The Quarterly Review of Distance Education.*

Schlager, M., & Fusco, J. (this volume). Teacher professional development, technology, and communities of practice: Are we putting the cart before the horse?

Strauss, A., & Corbin, J. (1998). *Basics of Qualitative Research, Techniques and Procedures for Developing Grounded Theory* (2d ed.). Thousand Oaks, CA: Sage.

Wellman, B., & Gulia, M. (1999). Virtual communities as communities: Net surfers don't ride alone. In P. Kollock (Ed.), *Communities in Cyberspace* (pp. 331–366). New York: Routledge.

Wenger, E. (1998). *Communities of Practice: Learning, Meaning and Identity.* Cambridge, MA: Cambridge University Press.

Winograd, D., & Milton, K. (1999). Asynchronous Online Listserve Exchange as a Conduit to Conflict. Unpublished study received by author.

14

Sociocultural Analysis of Online Professional Development

A Case Study of Personal, Interpersonal, Community, and Technical Aspects

James H. Gray and Deborah Tatar

Robert[1] is from Iowa, now living in a small town near the Rhone river valley in central France with his French wife and two children. He teaches English as a foreign language in the local high school, where he has only a handful of colleagues who share his educational interests. He turned to the Internet five or six years ago to find "intelligent contact with English-speaking people." More recently, he joined an email list about an online pedagogical approach called InternetInquiry.[2] Then, while planning to lead local workshops on "teacher training in educational technology," Robert joined Tapped In (http://www.tappedin.org) – a multi-user virtual environment (MUVE) designed to promote teacher professional development – and soon "fell in love" with the environment. By the time we interviewed him seven months later, he had designed his online office, attended more than forty seminars – including monthly sessions on the topic of InternetInquiry – and launched his own weekly seminar about language learning.

In this chapter, we describe and analyze Robert's experience in Tapped In and related changes in his professional practice. While his experience is not necessarily typical of participants in Tapped In or other online communities, the particular details of his activities illustrate issues common to many educators who seek to develop their professional practice through participation with colleagues in online communities. By presenting a detailed view of Robert's experience in light of appropriate theory and literature, we provide the reader with a salient example with which to compare similar instances of online professional development efforts.

---

[1] All names are pseudonyms and identifying information has been changed.

[2] "InternetInquiry" is a structured approach to web-based student research. It began in 1995, and has evolved into a very popular tool for teachers across grades and subject areas.

This research was supported in part by the Center for Innovative Learning Technologies (CILT), an NSF-funded center (grant # 9720384).

A primary aim of this chapter is to illustrate a particular analytic approach to understanding processes of learning and development in relation to multiple contexts. Our approach draws on sociocultural theory and uses ethnographically oriented case study methods to highlight the interconnections between online and offline contexts in the professional trajectory of one Tapped In participant.

Through Robert, we ask how individuals enter and participate in particular professionally oriented online environments. What do they do there? Why do they remain or leave? What do they gain from the experience? How does their online activity relate to other aspects of their professional practice? In posing these questions, we begin to identify the complex set of personal, social, institutional, cultural, and technological issues that underlie efforts to design and facilitate online teacher professional development. Answers to these questions are necessarily complex, and they are at the heart of why one online environment may be vibrant and fulfilling for certain types of participants, situated in a particular sociocultural context, while another becomes stagnant and disappointing.

We begin the chapter by describing our particular sociocultural approach to analyzing learning and development in online community settings. We then outline the methods used in the larger study of Tapped In of which this case study is a part. Next, we present an overview of the Tapped In environment to set the stage for the in-depth case study of Robert that follows. Finally, drawing on insights from this case study, we extend it by discussing implications for the design and study of online learning communities and their participants. At the end of the chapter, Appendixes provide a guide to the interview questions and an excerpt of an after-school online seminar.

A SOCIOCULTURAL APPROACH TO ONLINE LEARNING AND DEVELOPMENT

As researchers, our dilemma is how to grasp the complexity of online teacher professional development, while retaining analytic focus. Toward this end, we draw on sociocultural theory to help make sense of Robert's experience and extend its implications to other settings. The hallmark of sociocultural theory is in the analytic connection it affords between the thoughts, feelings, and actions of individuals and their social-historical contexts by way of mechanisms variously called cultural tools (Vygotsky, 1978), artifacts (Cole, 1996), or mediational means (Wertsch, 1998). In this view, the appropriate unit of analysis is never an individual in isolation or in interaction with a separate environment (Rogoff, Baker-Sennett, Lacasa, & Goldsmith, 1995); rather it is "activity," an "activity system" (Engestrom, Miettinen, & Punamaki, 1999), or "practice" (Bourdieu, 1977; Holland & Lave, 2001, Lave, 1988; Wenger, 1998) that encompasses individuals, their social partners, and cultural, institutional, and historical traditions.

From this perspective, development involves changes in patterns of participation in sociocultural activity and a reciprocal relationship between person and context in which "individuals' changing roles are mutually defined with those of other people and with dynamic cultural processes" (Rogoff et al., 1995, p. 45). The research reported in this chapter contributes to our understanding of how learning and development occur in computer-mediated environments and how these processes may compare and contrast with similar processes in traditional offline cultural settings (Rogoff, 1990). More broadly, we ask whether the sociocultural contexts of online learning are more flexible and adaptive than traditional settings; or, do they simply replicate traditional forms of enculturation, socialization, learning, and development – in what ways, and under what conditions? In either case, online communities provide a valuable source of data about these kinds of sociocultural processes, especially when the majority of communication among members occurs within the community and is easily documented. As new socio-technical innovations continue to emerge in the design of online learning communities, it will be increasingly important to study how these communities and the individual members learn and develop.

In the following pages, we organize our analysis of Robert's experiences in terms of personal, interpersonal, and community "planes"[3] (Rogoff et al., 1995). These three aspects of analysis provide sufficient structure to be a useful heuristic within the umbrella of sociocultural theory, while being broad enough to accommodate constructs from related perspectives – such as activity theory (Engestrom, Miettinen, & Punamaki, 1999), communities of practice (Wenger, 1998), cultural models (D'Andrade, 1987, 1995; Holland & Quinn, 1987; Shore, 1996; Strauss, 1992), figured worlds (Holland, Lachicotte, Skinner, & Cain, 1998), the dramatic pentad (Burke, 1945/1969; Wertsch, 1998) – or derived as grounded theory (Glaser and Strauss, 1967) particular to Robert and his experiences. Additionally, to address the issues particular to online communication and community, we integrate technology as a fourth aspect of our analytic framework.

While we make an analytic distinction among personal, interpersonal, community, and technological aspects of socio-technical systems, in practice, they are deeply intertwined. Therefore, while examining one plane of analysis, it is important to note connections to the others. It is useful to

---

[3] In recent writings Rogoff (in press; Rogoff, Topping, Baker-Sennett, & Lacasa, 2002) has changed terminology from "planes of analysis" to "foci of analysis" to avoid the suggestion of separate, self-contained levels of reality, and to emphasize the interrelatedness of individual, interpersonal, and community processes. In this chapter, we will retain the term "planes" but emphasize this interrelatedness in our descriptions of the data.

TABLE 14.1. *Overview of the Four "Planes" or Foci of Analysis Used to Understand Interrelated Aspects of Robert's Professional Activity*

Plane	Analytic Focus	Case Study Example
Personal	How individuals change through involvement in sociocultural activity	Learning French and teaching English as a second language shapes and is shaped by Robert's life trajectory and self-understanding
Interpersonal	How people communicate and coordinate their activities	Robert's interactions with close colleagues and students are organized around his expertise with language and learning technologies
Community	Patterns of participation in culturally organized activity	Robert attends and leads online sessions structured like face-to-face academic seminars
Technology	Use of information and communication technologies by individuals and groups to construct meaning	Projecting a common web page to seminar participants fosters coordination of attention and content of discourse

Source: Adapted from Rogoff (1995)

think of this relationship between the analytic parts and whole as a kind of photograph in which the subject (one plane) is "in focus" while the others are visible but blurred, their general shape being recognizable but not their details (Rogoff, 1998). In our writing, this is achieved by occasionally juxtaposing discussion of different planes of analysis rather than keeping them entirely confined to separate sections.

In this way, we remind ourselves that each plane emphasizes a different aspect of the broader socio-technical system. As Table 14.1 summarizes, the personal plane of analysis focuses on how individuals change through involvement in sociocultural activity; the interpersonal plane examines how people communicate and coordinate their activities; and the community plane of analysis focuses on people participating with others in culturally organized activity. For our purposes, the technology plane of analysis examines information and communication technologies as cultural artifacts used by individuals and groups to manipulate symbolic material (e.g., to record, transmit, store, organize, and display information) in the process of constructing meaning.

Through this additional analytic lens we see how the technology of Tapped In mediates activities at each of the other levels of organization.

As we discuss in detail later in the chapter, the underlying MOO technology on which Tapped In is built (Curtis, 1997; Schank, Fenton, Schlager, & Fusco, 1999) affords the exchange of text to simulate multiple modalities of communication, including verbal (e.g., talk, whisper), gestural (emote), and written (projections of signs, whiteboard). These forms of communication mediate all interpersonal interaction on Tapped In in a very direct way, and more indirectly shape personal and community aspects of the activity system. Projection is a feature that allows participants to show a web page to one or more people in the same virtual room. As such, it can help coordinate the attention and discourse of a group in ways that foster community processes, such as the construction of shared values. Aspects of Tapped In features that are particularly aligned with the personal plane of analysis include self-descriptions (visible when one "looks" at another participant), customizable private offices, and personal recorders that allow participants to review and reflect on their previous social interactions. Finally, textual descriptions, graphic elements, movement-oriented commands, and computational objects support the spatial metaphor of an academic campus with buildings, offices, hallways, elevators, and functioning physical objects. These features organize personal, interpersonal, and community aspects of online activity in Tapped In by, for example, allowing groups to conduct private conversations in their own offices.

Whereas we discuss Robert's life trajectory and professional roles under the rubric of personal and interpersonal planes of analysis, we might also examine them in terms of *activity theory* (Engestrom et al., 1999) to emphasize a systemic view of meaning-making and the mediating role of artifacts. Alternatively, we could analyze these issues in relation to social processes of learning in *communities of practice* (Wenger, 1998). Likewise, our discussion of the community norms and structures of Tapped In and the After School Online seminar series could be re-cast in terms of *cultural models* (D'Andrade, 1987, 1995; Holland & Quinn, 1987; Shore, 1996; Strauss, 1992), *figured worlds* (Holland et al., 1998), or the *dramatic pentad* (Burke, 1945/1969; Wertsch, 1998) to emphasize the construction of identity and agency in particular cultural worlds. While we will mention these kinds of related perspectives where they seem to illuminate the issues being discussed, it is beyond the scope of the chapter to fully develop and apply multiple theoretical perspectives.

Nonetheless, we highlight two essential aspects of sociocultural theory in our work. First, our unit of analysis is not Robert as an individual, it is the systems of activities or practices in which he operates and which include him. Through the multiple "planes" metaphor, we examine different aspects of this system, but try to not lose sight of its totality. While we talk about Robert's personal life trajectory and professional roles, we also examine them in relation to the communities in which he acts.

Second, we keep the notion of mediational means (Wertsch, 1991) relatively prominent in our analysis. That is, when we talk about what Robert does with colleagues, we note the cultural tools he uses. Foremost among these tools are the technological features of Tapped In (TI) and the symbolic systems that it carries as a mediator of interaction and understanding among people. Hence, for example, we examine how the "whisper" command and personal office space feature of TI make possible and more likely private interactions and close interpersonal relationships with colleagues. While the technological design of TI affords these kinds of interactions, it does not guarantee them. Rather, interactions are determined by factors in all four planes – for example, the personal goals of the individuals involved, their interpersonal history and relationships, the prevailing cultural models of communication shared by participants, and the communicative affordances of the TI technology.

It is important to note that each plane is both an analytic lens – a way of looking at the whole socio-technical system – and an ontological reality – a set of potentially observable events. As researchers, it is useful to examine and label our analytic tools, to acknowledge our own processes of interpretation and biases. In this sense, each plane represents a type of analysis. Concomitantly, each plane has an ontological correlate. Individual people, interpersonal interactions, patterns of community, and technological features are each manifest in the observable world. Hence, we use the four planes of analysis to organize our descriptive, analytic, and reflexive writing.

Finally, in this view we do not make a sharp distinction between learning and development, since a single change in an individual – such as learning how to facilitate an online inquiry – can have a wide range of meanings in the various social settings in which the individual interacts, and across multiple timeframes ranging from collegial discourse to career trajectory. Likewise interpersonal, community, and technological change can have multiple levels of impact. When we consider learning and development in the socio-technical system, we consider changes over time from all four perspectives.

RESEARCH METHODS

The case study of Robert presented here is part of a larger study of Tapped In designed to examine issues of professional development in terms of online discourse, values related to learning and technology, professional identity, and social networking (cf., Tatar, Gray, & Fusco, 2002). To examine the relationship among these factors, we chose a single focal event in which to locate key examples of discourse and from which to trace evidence related to the other topics. This was achieved by recording a logfile of all conversations, public and private, during a one-hour seminar on the topic of InternetInquiry.[4] Within a few days we conducted one- to two-hour telephone interviews with 12 of the 15 participants, those who granted permission. The interviews were designed to gather data on the four topics previously mentioned and included questions about specific parts of the conversation in order to reveal how participants interpreted particular online events [see Appendix A for sample interview questions].

Decisions about what data to collect were based on a variety of criteria. For the focal event, we chose an After School Online (ASO) seminar because these meetings are a core institution within Tapped In. Hence, the analysis would be likely to inform our understanding of other ASO seminars and their role in Tapped In. We chose to examine an ASO session on InternetInquiry because it is a popular monthly seminar conducted by the originator of this approach to online pedagogy. The popularity of the session together with its focus on a specific academic topic meant that it was likely to produce data useful for understanding teacher professional development from each of the perspectives we had defined, including values for learning.

Of the 12 participants we interviewed, we chose Robert for this case study for several reasons. First, he was an active participant in the focal event, other InternetInquiry seminars, ASOs on other topics, and Tapped In more generally. Second, he seemed to have used these experiences for his own professional development. Finally, he was willing to talk at length about his online experience and professional practice during the interview. In short, Robert seemed to be a model Tapped In community member, and we reasoned that if we could understand his particular experiences – what drew him to Tapped In, how he participated in the focal event, what he got out of the experience – we would understand something important about how this and other online communities do or do not support educators' efforts toward their professional development.

TAPPED IN

Tapped In is a multi-user virtual environment (MUVE) dedicated to teacher professional development. It is organized around the metaphor of a conference site, with multiple buildings, public meeting rooms, private offices, and outdoor areas. Launched in 1997, it grew steadily to 1,000 members by early 1998, to 5,000 in mid-1999, and 11,000 by mid-2001 (Fusco, 2002; Schlager, Fusco, & Schank, 2002). Approximately 10% of members log on

---

[4] We were not able to acquire permission in advance because the sessions are open to the entire Tapped In community and anyone else who logs in as a "guest." Participants who attended this session were notified of the recording at the beginning of the seminar, and permission to use their comments in our research was obtained afterward.

TABLE 14.2. *Duration of Memberships in Tapped In from Launch (1997) to Mid-2001*

Months	Members	
	Number	Percent
1–3	835	10.2
4–7	1,322	16.2
8–14	2,165	26.5
15–24	1,855	22.7
25–30	1,247	15.2
31–40	562	6.9
40–55	195	2.4

Note: "Duration of Memberships" does not differentiate between different start times, or reasons for ending time, such as member request, automatic termination, or end of sampling period.
Source: Fusco, 2002

each month with logon times averaging roughly 4 hours per month (Fusco, 2002; Schlager, Fusco, & Schank, 2002).

While there is a core of regular activity, participation patterns vary significantly across Tapped In members. Some individuals log on regularly, every week or month for the length of a particular online course or project, or across multiple events for the duration of their entire membership. As Table 14.2 illustrates (Fusco, 2002), length of membership – time from first logon to termination[5] – ranges from one to fifty-five months, with half of all memberships remaining open for approximately one academic or calendar year (8–14 months). It is not uncommon, while remaining members, for individuals to be very active for a period of time and then go dormant for many weeks or months before coming back when their professional circumstances change (Schlager et al., 2002).

During their memberships, individuals vary in their level of activity. On average, approximately 80 percent of individuals log on (at least once) during fewer than 20 percent of their membership months (e.g., during 1 or 2 months over the course of a 1-year membership); 10 percent of members log on during 20 percent to 50 percent of membership months (e.g., between 3 and 6 months per year); and another 10 percent of members log on between 50 percent and 100 percent of available months (e.g., between 6 and 12 months per year).

[5] Tapped In memberships are terminated in two ways: (1) by member request, or (2) by system administrators if a member does not log on for a period of approximately six months, and does not respond to email notification of termination. This procedure is designed to assist individuals who no longer wish to be members but do not know how to unsubscribe (Fusco, 2002).

TABLE 14.3. *Number of Logins per Member in Tapped In from Launch (1997) to Mid-2001*

Logins	Members	
	Number	Percent
1–5	5,066	62
6–20	2,031	25
21–200	1,018	12
201	66	1

Note: "Number of Logins" does not control for length of membership – e.g., 30 logins may occur over one week or two years.
Source: Fusco, 2002

The wide range of membership duration and login frequencies means that members also vary significantly in the total number of visits to Tapped In. As Table 14.3 illustrates (Fusco, 2002), the majority (62%) of members log on only 1 to 5 times, suggesting a process of initial exploration and evaluation that does not move into sustained activity. Another 25 percent of members logged on between 6 and 20 times, indicating long-term occasional activity, or perhaps a short burst of moderately active use. The 12 percent or approximately 1,000 members who logged on between 21 and 200 times appear to be regular or very active members, perhaps those who consistently attend organized classes or community activities. A much smaller group of 66 members, constituting less than 1 percent of Tapped In members, logged on more than 200 times. These members are likely to represent the core group of highly active and long-term Tapped In members, volunteer leaders, and staff. The case study of Robert presented in this chapter focuses on one of these highly active members – specifically, he logged on for 100 percent of the months of his membership, with nearly 700 logins during the first 12 months of membership (Fusco, 2002).

About half of Tapped In members are K–12 teachers, with the remainder including K–12 support staff, university faculty, researchers, staff developers, technology support providers, and pre-service teachers (Schlager et al., 2002). Members join Tapped In either through their affiliation with one of its "tenant" organizations (e.g., Pepperdine University, Lawrence Hall of Science), or as individuals interested in attending organized events or interacting informally with colleagues. Interactions among members are facilitated by a small group of paid and volunteer staff who greet newcomers, guide participants to scheduled meetings, and provide helpdesk services such as advice on how to record conversations or set up an office for private meetings. Typically, at least one such facilitator is available in the reception area during daytime and evening hours in the United States.

Interactions on Tapped In are predominantly text-based real-time discussions with additional capabilities like "facial expressions"(e.g., "Jenny smiles with understanding") and "gestures" (e.g., "Audrey waves at Marty") also supported by the MUVE. As Figure 14.1 illustrates, there is also a graphical interface, "Tapestry," that provides maps of the environment, point-and-click access to various functions (e.g., acquiring a personal tape recorder, or transcripts of past meetings), and display of optional photos or icons of each person who is logged on and present in the same room. TI also supports *projection* of web pages in which one person can cause a window with a web page in it to open on other people's screens. Participants use projection so that they can view and discuss a common web object.

Participation occurs in various structures. Informal interactions are common in the Reception Area where newcomers first arrive and are met by TI staff or volunteer HelpDesk personnel. Individuals can acquire and customize personal offices, which are then available for private meetings, informal conversations, or other activities. Groups come to TI and set up meeting rooms or even entire buildings to host their various activities. Large groups like Pepperdine University are paying "tenants" and receive customized services from the TI staff, such as the construction of their own virtual building. Many existing educationally oriented groups (e.g., Museum of Tolerance, Lawrence Hall of Science, PBS Teacherline) use TI to meet, discuss common interests, plan projects, and the like. Finally, the Tapped In staff sponsors professional development activities, such as the After School Online seminar series. The staff provides planning and logistical support for these seminars by sending out email newsletters to all TI members alerting them to upcoming activities, posting a web calendar of events, facilitating meetings, and providing transcripts of meetings to both attendees and others not present for the real-time discussion.

The participation structure most widely accessible to all members of the Tapped In community is the After School Online seminar series. A typical monthly Event Calendar at Tapped In includes 30–50 ASO seminars on topics such as social studies, language learning, science, math, school administration, technology coordinators, and "Tapped In Tours and Tips." Seminars are offered on a weekly and monthly basis, as well as special one-time events. While existing organizations contract for customized services, and individuals can interact informally in private offices and public spaces of TI, it is the ASO seminar format that most readily affords small groups discussion around a focal topic.

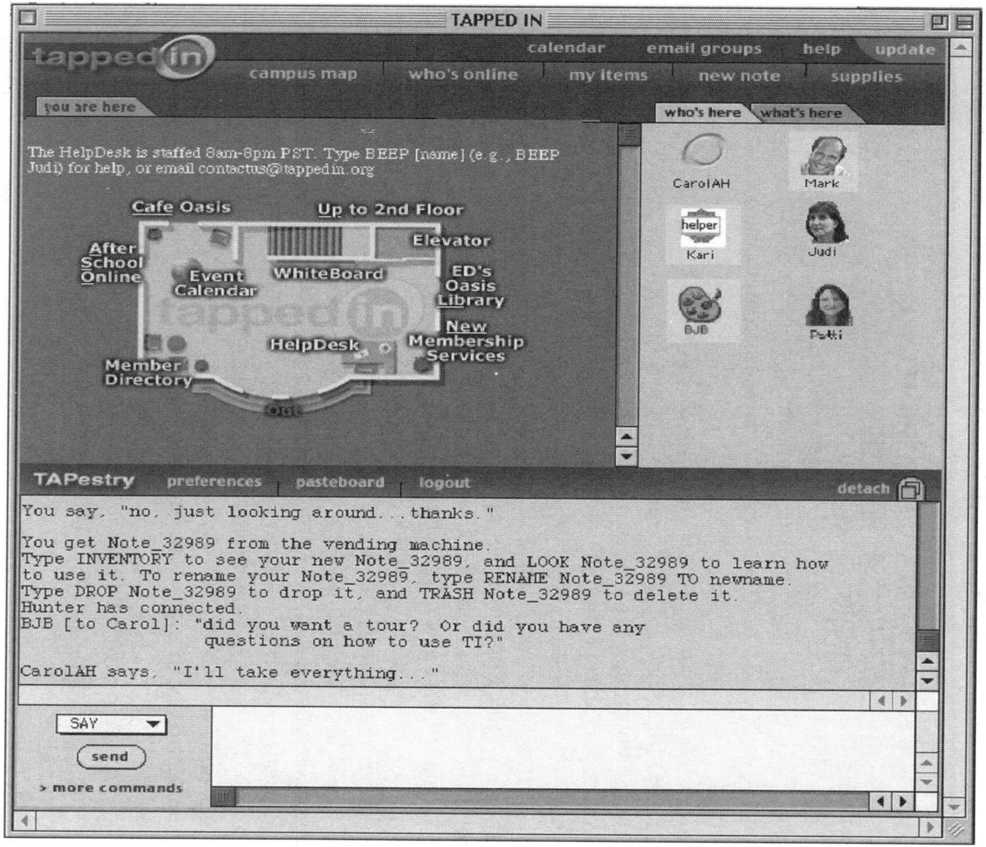

FIGURE 14.1. The "Tapestry" graphical interface, including maps of the environment, point-and-click access to various functions, and optional images of individuals present in the same room

The Tapped In ASO format is notable for its adaptability to diverse topics and participants, opportunities for sharing web-based resources, knowledge construction through real-time discourse, and potential for fostering professional development. While a few ASO sessions are sponsored by TI staff, most are designed and run by volunteers from the community. The TI staff encourages people to organize ASO seminars and provides help in planning and leading them. Hence, the institutionalized participation structure of the ASOs and the available scaffolding provide a significant professional development opportunity for educators. Individuals can join TI, participate in existing ASOs, and then launch their own seminars to expand their professional circle of like-minded colleagues, enhance their content knowledge, and expand their leadership abilities. The case study presented in this chapter traces one such developmental process, and illustrates how the four-planes-of-analysis framework helps to identify the presence or absence of factors that shape development.

ROBERT: A CASE STUDY OF PROFESSIONAL DEVELOPMENT IN TAPPED IN

In this section, we examine processes of development from personal, interpersonal, community, and technological perspectives. We ask how Robert, his interactions with colleagues, and the Tapped In environment change over time and in relation to each other. The aim is to illuminate why Robert comes to Tapped In, what makes it inviting and meaningful to him, what he gets out of it, and how his activities in turn shape the environment.

In our analysis, we have identified three main themes that link Robert's personal and professional trajectories to his experience in Tapped In and give it meaning: *literacy* (French, English, and learning technologies), *expertise/leadership* (vis-à-vis colleagues and students), and *interpersonal connection*. The third theme of connecting to others is what Robert himself articulates most clearly. He describes his own changes online as lessening his "bad habit" of being "too enthusiastic," talking "over other people," and hence "not leaving them time to talk." He also reports using what he learns online with his young students and in his teacher-training workshops. In the coming pages, we examine these themes across multiple planes of analysis.

A Personal View of Professional Development: French-English Literacies and Identities

Robert is a high school (lycée) English language teacher in France. He comes from Iowa and now lives with his French wife and two children in a small town of 12,000 near the Rhone river valley. He counts among his local colleagues three other English teachers in his lycée, two more

English teachers in this local town, four or five other technology teacher-trainers, and the many teachers who have participated in his educational technology sessions – "five workshops so far this year," as of mid-March.

At the time of our data collection, Robert had been a member of Tapped In for seven months, and had been "involved with using the Internet with teaching" for three years. During this time, he has established many valuable professional relationships. As he put it, "I've gotten far more out of contact with people that I've never seen with my own eyes than with colleagues that I can actually speak to and listen to." He finds several aspects of the Tapped In environment especially valuable, a topic we will address later in more detail.

The French and English languages – learning them, teaching them, speaking them – play a key role in the trajectory of Robert's professional development and identity. More recently, computer literacy has taken on a similar role. As a college student, he moved from the United States to Québec to study French literature and ultimately to get a bachelor's degree in English as a second language. From there he went on to study comparative literature at the University of Iowa before moving to France, getting a French teaching certificate, and starting his current career teaching English as a foreign language.

Robert's facility with language allowed him to study in Québec and learn how to teach English to French speakers. Language literacy became a key component in shaping his personal and professional path. As Robert put it, "teaching English was my ticket out of Iowa." With an ability to speak and teach both English and French, Robert was able to use "the educational system for my own agenda" and live and work in [Francophone country] and then [a Northern region of France] before settling in Central France.

Robert used the literacies that he had developed to shape his professional path, and those experiences have shaped his sense of self. "Learning French for me was building a new identity" he told us, "basically, because I had changed almost every aspect of my life from working for Pizza Hut." As Robert tells it, "when I moved out to Québec and studied French literature, that was a complete switch for me, and I completely changed my life and became a whole other person in many different ways."

Speaking in retrospect, Robert is quite consciously aware of how he has used his education to build a life for himself and how this process has made him feel like a new person; and yet, while living in France he remains, in many respects, an American:

I've kind of exiled myself in the middle of all these French-speaking people . . . and I love French, and I love French culture and food (too much) and I love everything here; but, my first reason for getting on the Internet about 5, 6 years ago, was to have contact with, intelligent contact, with English-speaking people who had intelligent things to say and not just my family giving me a guilt trip about not visiting them often enough.

Despite having French citizenship, Robert identifies himself as an American; indeed, when asked about his "ethnicity or race" he replied "White, Iowan." Like many immigrants he has a dual sense of allegiance and identity (Deaux, 2000). For Robert, information and communication technologies afford the kind of social interactions that keep his intellectual identity and his more geographically distant, American sense of self alive.

Interpersonal Interactions and Relationships: Intellectual Connections and the Construction of Expertise

As previously mentioned, Robert has a range of both local and online colleagues with whom he discusses educational issues. The professional identity he constructs in these conversations appears to be focused in large part on expertise. Robert presents himself and is known as a competent professional who shares his knowledge and takes on leadership roles. We discuss his relationship to local French colleagues and students, to a variety of online peers and novices, and to other experts.

Local Colleagues and Students
In his local town, Robert aligns himself most strongly with other English teachers who are "at least somewhat interested in the same issues" and identifies himself in contrast to all of the other teachers. There are four English teachers in his lycée, only one of whom Robert has "a lot of exchange with." The other three, like the other lycée teachers, are not very interested in learning technologies. Although Robert attempts to share his interests and expertise, "often my exchanges with them are trying to show them other educational technologies and ways they can use the Internet." Their school has only been connected to the Internet for "a very short period of time" and Robert is "one of the very few teachers who uses, maybe the only one, who makes intense use of the Internet." Apparently only two or three others have "taken students to the Internet at all" and according to Robert, they "have no real idea of what they're doing." From Robert's perspective, the other teachers are quite different from him in many respects:

Basically all the other teachers in my school are very reluctant and consider themselves far too busy to bother listening to what I have to say. . . . They're a very unreceptive bunch and spend most of their time smoking cigarettes when it's illegal to smoke cigarettes in a French school. That's another issue.

In contrast to his school environment, Robert has cultivated a small group of colleagues in the local area who do share his interests in technology and pedagogy. As he describes it, "we're a group of four English teachers in my town," including one from his school, and "two other colleagues who are at least somewhat interested in the same issues." They have been getting together once a month and "talking about lesson plans, mostly oriented around cinema, and showing each other things [they've] been doing and sharing resources."

These collegial activities do, in fact, affect how Robert interacts with his lycée students. As he notes, "trying to motivate them is the number one issue and of course using the Internet or using film clips and so on, all those things, anything that gets them out of their textbook is a big motivating factor." As an English teacher, Robert "can use pretty much whatever source material" he wants to, and he is "successful using things like the FBI site or NASA and exploring Mars and all these things . . ." These types of Internet activities appeal to his students because many of them are technologically oriented, it's new for them, and it is not what they expect in an English class. It works well for both students and teacher, as Robert sums up, "It's motivating for them and they like it. So that's good. That's valorizing for me. It makes me feel better about my job and so on."

While Robert values teaching his students, he is especially enthusiastic about working with educators who want to explore new ways to use technology. He notes that "the really interesting exchanges" have been in the teacher-training sessions and with other teacher trainers. He appreciates the people in his seminars for their openness to his ideas, "my agenda with all those people has been a lot more fulfilling and interesting because they're closer to actually accepting using technology . . . but don't know most of the stuff that I've been doing." Likewise, Robert finds mutual exchanges with other teacher trainers especially rewarding:

Some of them have been doing really interesting things on their end, in different areas that I'm not that familiar with. So we've had really interesting exchanges. And all those have been really fulfilling, valuable exchanges, which is a real contrast with my typical exchanges with other teachers in my school. Well, since we're all doing teacher training basically on the same topic, which is educational technology and language learning, but since we all have different ideas of what that is and what things can be done.

Robert's professional development represents change for both himself and his students. He emphasizes both. When asked if he is happy in his current job, he replied:

Yeah, everything's been great and I've been able to reduce, I mean I like my students a lot, but I've been able to reduce the number of hours I spend in the classroom with students, which is good, and spend more time doing creative things and teacher training on Internet and pedagogical strategies of using the Internet and film and things like that, which is great. And it's like I'm working and not working because they're interesting subjects.

Online Colleagues

While the Internet provides a source of information and resources that Robert can use in his high school classes and teacher workshops (e.g., educational websites), it also offers access to a wide range of like-minded colleagues. His first reason for getting on the Internet about five or six years ago was to have contact with English-speaking people who had intelligent things to say. More recently, during the last three years that Robert has been "using the Internet with teaching," he has explored a range of online venues, including educationally oriented email lists (e.g., FLT, NetTeach L) and chat environments (e.g., IRC and ICQ). For example, about a year and a half ago, Robert's students introduced him to IRC chat, where he then participated for a while in different subject-oriented rooms "trying to find other writers and people interested in some of the subjects [he's] interested in."

Then, in August of 2000, Robert began two new activities. He started doing "teacher training in educational technology" for local educators and he joined Tapped In. His initial reason for coming to Tapped In was to support his new workshop activities, as he put it, "I do teacher training in educational technology. Thus, my interest in Tapped In." However, for Robert, Tapped In is more than a source of new lesson ideas for teachers. As he tells the story, "I fell in love with [Tapped In] right away. I think I designed my office within 10 days of joining, and created a bunch of ritual objects, and so on, and then just started attending sessions, and I really liked them." Over the next six months he reports that he attended a total of 40–50 Tapped In seminars on topics ranging from social studies to science. "I can't say I really spend a lot of time socializing, just talking about the weather . . ." he adds; rather, most of his time is spent engaging with colleagues in the context of online educational seminars or informal conversations about educational matters.

When asked about who he interacts with on Tapped In, Robert first mentions Pat and Jenny, two staff members who are most often in the Reception area where new members arrive and where many informal discussions occur. Next are two nonstaff people: Yuki, who teaches Japanese in the United States, and Hiro, who teaches English in Japan and "often comes" to the seminars led by Robert. As in his local setting, Robert seeks out other language teachers online.

Robert values both the organized and informal social atmosphere of Tapped In. He notes that "the most important thing with Tapped In . . . is the ability to be able to come in at almost any time and find people doing things, so it's always open. You don't have to just come for scheduled events." However, he also acknowledges the importance of structure. "Plus, there's the scheduled reception people like Jenny and Pat and Audrey who facilitate things, keep it rolling, help enroll new people, and so on." Similarly, Robert emphasizes his reliance on the events calendar "which warns about important sessions like Marty's regular InternetInquiry sessions, [and] social studies sessions." Thus, the efforts of a few staff people, a regular schedule of activities, and the communicative affordances of Tapped In offer Robert opportunities for both structured and informal interactions with a wide array of colleagues who share his interests.

It is important to note that Robert's collegial interactions and professional development span both online and local settings. Processes of professional change in one setting seem readily applicable in the other, akin to the issue of "transfer" in cognitive psychology (cf., Bransford, Brown, & Cocking, 2000). From a sociocultural perspective, this transfer can be seen as an interpretive process in which the two settings are understood as being analogous in relevant respects (Pea, 1987).

In Robert's case, we might ask to what extent he perceives his roles and the settings of Tapped In and his local teacher-training seminars to be similar. He explicitly acknowledges the connection between these settings when he commented that his interest in Tapped In is because he does training in educational technology. Based on this and other descriptions of his online activities, it appears that Robert sought out a role in Tapped In that would facilitate his local professional development. Because Robert moved between online and local experiences on a nearly daily basis, it appears that he engaged in a dual process of negotiating new leadership roles in both settings concurrently. This pattern of professional development is distinct from traditional weekend or summer in-service sessions in which newly learned skills and their application in other settings are separated in time. By contrast, Robert engaged in a very incremental process of changes in himself and his interpersonal relationships in two settings simultaneously. What could be seen as transferring a series of newly learned skills between settings can also be seen as a process of negotiating two sets of similar roles and settings in which to enact them.

Robert as Expert

We now turn to a recent InternetInquiry seminar to illustrate in more detail the various roles that Robert plays on Tapped In. This is one of the monthly sessions led by Marty, the originator and expert on the InternetInquiry approach to web-based pedagogy. Approximately 15 people attended the seminar, which lasted one hour. It was preceded by a 15-minute period when we introduced the research project and gathered contact information for follow-up phone interviews and informed consent. Regular attendees of this meeting noted that this initial period was unusual and disrupted normal conversation, but that the seminar itself was typical. These reactions to change in normal functioning are an important source of data regarding the established norms, expectations, and cohesiveness of this group.

One of the roles that Robert assumed in this group was to orient newcomers to the normal patterns of activity and to make sense of the unusual events. For example, at the end of the research introduction, Hugh, a first-time participant, complained, "If this is how difficult it is to get to a session, then it doesn't seem worthwhile." In response, Audrey, a Tapped In designer and researcher, quickly replied (15 seconds) directly to Hugh, "this is a very unusual session." Similarly, Robert replied (27 seconds) to offer his reassurance and explanation, "Hugh, this is quite rare. Usually, we just walk in and start talking." A few minutes later when Hugh was having trouble with the interface ("How do you make the text screen larger. things are flying by"), Robert repeated Audrey's earlier public instructions for expanding the text window by whispering his advice, "hugh click on the 'detach' button just above your text window." Also while the researchers were talking to individual participants, Robert suggested that the group start with its usual routine, "Shall we do intros while we're waiting?" It was not until minutes later, when Audrey declared that the researchers were done and the seminar could start, that Marty repeated this suggestion, stating, "OK . . . shall we start with the usual (Very Quick) self-introductions?"

During the substantive discussion, Robert expresses empathy with novices trying to understand the pedagogical approach of Internet-Inquiries. For instance, when the group is talking about some poorly designed InternetInquiries, he notes that some people "have scavenger hunts mixed up with InternetInquiries." Marty agrees, "yup," and Robert explains, "The specificity of the InternetInquiry model is not always easy to grasp. I heard the label 'InternetInquiry' more than a year before I read the training material on The InternetInquiry Page and found out what they were really about."

While these activities are normally the duty of the designated seminar leaders and facilitators, Robert, as a participant, took the initiative to conduct them on his own. This sort of understanding of multiple roles within a community, awareness of group needs, and ability to respond is a sign that an individual has developed to be a relatively central member of a community (Rogoff et al., 1995). Robert started as a newcomer in August, and by March he interacts with novices like Hugh as an experienced member who is responsible for the group as a whole.

How does Robert interact with other experienced participants? Of the twenty-four (24) comments that he made during this seminar, eight (8) were oriented toward group process (e.g., "shall we do intros . . .") or social goals (e.g., "Thanks! See you soon."), while sixteen (16) were on the topic of InternetInquiry. One-quarter of these were general comments about this approach or the day's seminar, while three-quarters were specific, substantive expressions of Robert's opinions on a particular website or issue.

When Marty showed a site that promoted a pedagogy of "retelling" information gathered from the Internet rather than engaging in true inquiry, several participants noted the limitations of this and offered alternatives [see Appendix B for logfile]. Robert defends the pedagogical value of "retelling" as "an important first step" to which Marty agreed, but "wonders if that's a good use of $2,000 per desk." Later, Robert reported that he "wanted to come back on that, but it wasn't really germane to the way the discussion was going." The issues that Robert would have wanted to discuss were "more like InternetInquiry philosophy issues and that would be more e-mail type discussion than real time." Robert might have pushed his point and "talked over" others to pursue the debate during the seminar (as he said he used to do); instead, to help maintain the leader's direction, he "restrained" himself on this particular issue.

In this section we have seen in some detail how Robert constructs a professional identity of expertise and leadership in relation to local and online colleagues. Through interactions with local French educators, he has established himself as an authority on educational technology and language learning. While it appears that this knowledge is unappreciated by most local colleagues, it is valued by a small group of fellow English language teachers who share his interest in learning technologies. Through exploration and interactions on the Internet, Robert develops the skills and knowledge that then structure his interactions with students in his classroom and less knowledgeable peers in his teacher-training workshops. Similarly, Robert takes on an expert role among online colleagues. During the InternetInquiry seminar he engaged in sophisticated debates about the details of a particular pedagogical approach with its creator and other colleagues, and guided newcomers into this professional discourse. In the next section, we examine the socio-technical context in which this development has been possible.

Community Development: A New Seminar Emerges

Researching development in the community plane involves the examination of changes in institutional structures in relation to the generations of people who participate in the community (Rogoff et al., 1995). Here we discuss the institutionalized structures of Tapped In that appear to be most influential in shaping Robert's online activity and professional development, the Help Desk, and After School Online seminar series.

As already mentioned, when Robert talks about with whom he interacts on Tapped In he first mentions the HelpDesk staff, " . . . Pat and Jenny, usually in Reception." These are the people who help the guests and members of Tapped In learn how to perform various online actions, find resources and colleagues, and feel welcomed. "Reception" is the room where all guests first arrive and it is "home" for members unless they reset it to be their office or other room. The tradition of the HelpDesk is an essential component of giving participants like Robert the feeling that Tapped In is "always open." The staff comprise a significant social presence themselves, and they facilitate the online activities of others. As a result, participants have the "ability to be able to come in at almost any time and find people doing things."

In the socio-technical system of Tapped In, actions of HelpDesk staff shape the roles of other participants. When Jenny greets new guests in Reception, she asks how she can help and offers to show them around if she has the time. She thereby makes a bid for a particular kind of inter-personal interaction and relationship – assistance from a relative expert and for a novice. Guests may accept her offer, ask a question that brought them to Tapped In, state their preference to explore on their own, ignore the statement altogether, or respond in any number of other ways. In this way Jenny and the guest negotiate their roles with respect to one another. In some cases this interaction will have little relationship to later online activity, because the guest does not return to TI or establishes a pattern of activity that avoids the reception area. Other times, this first interaction may initiate a relationship of expanding interdependence between the guest and the established TI community. Like Robert, the guest may soon become a member of Tapped In, attend ASO sessions, assist newer members informally or as a volunteer HelpDesk staffer, and create new online events. In this way, the norms and structures of Tapped In established over a relatively long time and across many individuals are present in the enacted roles of greeter and guest.

Along with the HelpDesk, After School Online seminars are a central activity structure in Tapped In. ASO meetings are modeled after academic seminars, in which a leader facilitates discussion among a relatively small number of students or colleagues. Typically there are eight to twelve participants, and occasionally up to twenty or more. ASO seminars have a clearly defined topic that is listed in the Tapped In calendar and "On the Tapis" email newsletter. The topic is defined by the session leader, who is usually a subject-area expert or interested practitioner. The seminars often take advantage of the project feature to examine and discuss particular websites pre-selected by the leader or offered spontaneously by participants.

While ASO leaders are typically experienced members of Tapped In, they need not be experts on the technical features of TI or running an on-line seminar. Instead, members of the HelpDesk staff are available to help plan and run the seminars. Audrey, Pat, Jenny, and sometimes other experienced TI participants help greet participants as they arrive to a seminar. They often whisper special instructions, praise, or empathic comments to novices who seem unsure of how to interact in this context. They typically explain the less intuitive aspects of the TI interface, such as how to "detach" the text window so that participants can keep up with the scrolling dialogue. Also, they prepare novices to expect their web browser to automatically display a second window with another website when the "project" command is given – usually by the leader but sometimes by a facilitator or knowledgeable participant.

Facilitators help maintain a professional tone through their own interactions and by monitoring the discussion. For example, if someone starts chatting about an especially private matter before the meeting starts, they might whisper a reminder that the seminar is a public forum that is often recorded by participants. Likewise, if another group arrives in the meeting room unaware of the seminar in progress, the facilitators would explain the current discussion and help the new group join the seminar or find an alternative meeting place. On the rare occasion of a person logging on to disrupt the discussion purposefully, the facilitators can disconnect the individual from Tapped In.

For a participant like Robert, attending ASO sessions and participating over time at increasingly sophisticated levels is an apprenticeship model of learning how to lead one's own seminar. Indeed, after three months of participation in ASO seminars, Robert launched his own seminar designed around issues of language learning. This seminar has continued to meet weekly.

Technology: Affordances and Constraints

In this section we examine some of the technological features of Tapped In that support the kinds of interactions and meaning-making evident in the previous sections. While the underlying technological infrastructure profoundly shapes how participants use the system, the specific technical details of how the system works (data types, programming languages, etc.) is beyond the scope of this chapter. Rather, here we focus on how the availability and use of particular symbolic systems mediate interpersonal interactions, reference to shared cultural models, and individual learning/development.

For Robert, part of the appeal of Tapped In is feeling like he is in a physical place. Specifically, he says that "it feels like I'm back at university talking to other grad students and researchers and things like that about subjects that I'm interested in. So, it works out well that way." How does this happen? According to Robert, "you really have a sense of being somewhere because you see the room. You see the little heads for the people . . . you have a feeling that you're actually somewhere and that you're really talking to people." Apparently, the perceived experience of being on a college campus evokes related cultural models of academic discourse, which supports ASO activities.

Other features that shape Robert's online experience are the whisper and page functions that allow for private dialogue with other colleagues. For example, Robert whispered to Marty to negotiate a time when he could visit Robert's language seminar. He also whispered to a novice to explain how to "detach" the text window, and sent a "page" to someone in another room to announce the start of the seminar. These uses of whisper and page are consistent with the way HelpDesk staff members use these functions to facilitate the meeting without disrupting the substantive discussion and to help novices without embarrassing them by publicly drawing attention to their lack of knowledge. Since these communications are private, they may be especially well-suited to interpersonal relationship-building.

Web projections are especially important to many ASO seminars; in the InternetInquiry seminar they are essential. The discussion is structured around the set of InternetInquiry websites that Marty locates and prepares to show during a particular seminar. By allowing the participants to all easily view and explore the same website at the same time, it functions to coordinate participants' attention and the content of the conversation. When asked what it's like using Tapped In technology, Robert replied:

Yeah, the sharing websites basically is the main thing. That's really good, I mean, it's something that you can't do on other sites that I've seen. I think it's really important because you can talk about the same thing instead of just talking and look at things together and say "click on that, see what that does?" "Oh, yeah, I like this because," and you're looking at the same thing so it gives you more of the feeling of being in the same place with other people who are sitting at their computers across the other side of the planet.

For Robert, web projection evokes a sense of cohesion with others. This is the experience of social connection that first motivated Robert to seek out computer-mediated communication on the Internet, and it is part of what he finds satisfying about being a regular participant on Tapped In.

Robert's virtual office is the final feature of Tapped In that was prominent in his interview. As mentioned, customizing his office was the first thing he did after joining Tapped In. During the interview, he joked about the interviewers joining him in his online office for a "virtual glass of rum." (One of the other experienced TI users whom we interviewed invited us into her TI office to continue our conversation where she felt comfortable and could talk with us.) On a similar note, when the interviewers asked if they could visit his home page, he suggested they should "go into [his] office and click on the overhead projector, and get into [his] site directly that way." Like whisper and page, the capacity of having one's own personal space and customizing it with virtual objects seems to foster a sense of belonging and affords interpersonal interactions and relationship-building.

Summary: A Sociocultural System Develops

Examining learning and development as the transformation of participation in sociocultural contexts has involved highlighting, in turn, the personal, interpersonal, community, and technological aspects of Robert's activities on Tapped In. These multiple foci offer complementary views of Robert's professional development. In the personal plane of analysis, we see how Robert's life trajectory from Iowa to central France is intertwined with his present-day professional interactions on Tapped In. He connects to distant colleagues in part to avert certain kinds of isolation and to re-create his identity as an American and as an intellectual interested in serious educational issues more than idle socializing that he finds in some online chat rooms and local teachers' cliques. We also see how he has transformed his participation among colleagues, both in Tapped In and his local community. Online he became a leader of a new ASO session while concomitantly in France, he became a teacher trainer.

Both of these new roles are extensions of Robert's professional identity, not simply as an expression of private psychological change, but as new ways of being constructed in interpersonal interactions – both online and locally. Robert transformed from a Tapped In novice to an expert in relation to the HelpDesk staff, colleagues like Marty who led other seminars, and a host of new guests and members who accepted and benefited from his growing expertise (in the norms of ASO seminars and educational topics like InternetInquiry). During this same time, he also launched his career as a teacher trainer. Interacting with local French teachers interested in his technological expertise was a new role, an expansion of Robert's identity in his small town that draws directly on his online interactions and explorations.

From the community perspective, Robert's development extends beyond himself and his immediate interpersonal interactions to include changes in the sociocultural activity structures available in Tapped In and in the educational institutions in his region of central France. The most obvious development includes the addition of a new ASO seminar that, following Robert's professional interests, makes new kinds of knowledge available to the Tapped In community. There are also likely to be myriad other more subtle changes that result from Robert's expanding online participation. Teachers who interact informally with him may be influenced by his knowledge of InternetInquiry to try this pedagogical approach with their students. Teacher educators who attend his ASO sessions may be inspired to start their own seminars, on Tapped In or elsewhere.

Similarly, we can only speculate about the new opportunities made available through the institutionalization of Robert's technology expertise in teacher-training workshops. Whereas his efforts to inspire his local school colleagues often seemed to fall on deaf ears, perhaps those who choose to attend his workshops will take up new approaches to teaching their students or log on to Tapped In and try their hand at sharing their local knowledge more widely. Colleagues who had seemed uninterested in

Robert's ideas may turn out to be willing to listen if he establishes greater status as a leader in his local community.

The technological plane of analysis highlights how the Tapped In infrastructure constrains and affords development in each of the other planes, and how the TI technology itself can develop. At the level of community, TI combines a set of technological features that tend to evoke particular cultural worlds in the imagination of participants, such as a U.S. university campus. Graphic images of a campus, textual floor plans, written descriptions of the TI mission, and many other features lead participants to imagine themselves in an academically oriented setting.

From the interpersonal plane, we see how commands like *talk, whisper,* and *look* combine with public and private "rooms" to allow interpersonal interactions inside group boundaries. Within this set of constraints, focused discourse is possible. Whether or not it occurs, of course, depends on the particular participants at a given meeting, the leader, choice of topic, web projections, facilitators, and so forth. The emergent discourse is then the source of individual learning and development.

The same features that support the community processes of a regularly meeting seminar group, when viewed from the perspective of the personal plane of analysis, can be seen to support processes of learning and development for individuals. Through interactions with more able colleagues, educators new to a topic like InternetInquiry gain a particular pedagogical lexicon of "rubrics," "journalistic tasks," and so forth. As we saw with Robert's leadership in the ASO seminar (e.g., explaining the difference between scavenger hunts and InternetInquiries), they may master this way of speaking and thinking, and take the role of leader in the group.

From the perspective of sociocultural theory (Rogoff et al., 1995), being a leader in this online community also prepares participants to play parallel roles in other similar sociocultural settings. An essential question – both theoretical and practical – is what makes another setting similar and how an individual re-negotiates a similar role in a new context, whether online or off. For Robert, this process may occur because he came to Tapped In specifically to enhance his local professional practice and therefore interprets his Tapped In experiences as essentially linked to his local professional development. Teaching less knowledgeable colleagues about learning technology, for example, involves enacting essentially the same role in both settings. In contrast to more isolated or generic professional development activities, Robert's personal choice of using Tapped In for his professional goals and the sort of collegial interactions he found there allowed him to engage in essentially the same developmental process across ostensibly different settings.

We have seen how this process of reciprocal change unfolded with Robert. The academic campus metaphor in TI was very engaging for him, and he soon imagined his online interactions to be occurring in a cultural world of intellectual pursuit akin to his college days in Iowa and Québec. His desire for intelligent discourse on the topic of education was satisfied in many of the ASO seminars he found on TI. Among them was the monthly InternetInquiry seminars where he developed a personal relationship with Marty, the originator of InternetInquiry, and several other English language teachers, like Hiro and Yuki. While we have not studied the discourse of Robert's new language seminars, we can imagine him leading this group in much the same way that he helped orient newcomers in the InternetInquiry session described earlier.

Regardless, it is clear that Robert built on his previous TI experiences to create a new seminar series, which was then available to the wider TI community. In this way we see development in the systems of activity of Tapped In from community, interpersonal, and personal perspectives. Likewise, the TI technology continues to develop. At the time of this writing, the TI infrastructure is undergoing a re-design, based in part on the research of Robert and the InternetInquiry seminars (cf., Tatar et al., 2002). Hence, changes in Robert – which might be defined as the acquisition of new knowledge and skills – are intertwined with interpersonal, community, and technological changes around him. Understanding how change is co-constituted across planes of analysis may be useful in the design and facilitation of online communities like Tapped In.

LESSONS LEARNED

In this final section, we examine how the particular details of Robert's experiences, considered through four analytic foci, may inform design, facilitation, and research in relation to learning, development, and online community. We use specific aspects of the present analysis to think about related issues in other settings. Our hope is that readers will further extend this process to examples they know.

Implications for Community Design and Facilitation

How might the sort of description and analysis presented here illuminate processes of design and facilitation in other online environments? Comparisons between Robert's case and others would likely take different forms depending on one's goals. As with established strategies like participatory design (Schuler & Namioka, 1993) and value-sensitive design (http://www.ischool.washington.edu/vsd/), the process of launching a new community would start with an analysis of the target membership. From our sociocultural perspective, we might begin by looking for common patterns in personal identities and life trajectories, interpersonal interactions, and community affiliations as they relate to the themes of the planned community. From that perspective, specific features could be designed to build on the existing repertoire of social roles. Alternatively, a designer or facilitator working in an existing online environment might start with a comparison of the technological features of Tapped In and his or her environment, and from that perspective consider the other planes of analysis.

Let us take the *whisper* feature as an example. In Tapped In it affords private interaction in the midst of public activities. In the case study of Robert, we saw how he used it to arrange for Marty to visit his language seminar. This simple act is meaningful in relation to Robert's professional development along each of the planes of analysis. It is an interpersonal interaction that helps build a collegial relationship between Robert and Marty. As a whispered conversation, it was able to proceed in private, between the two individuals, without the possibility of interference by others. Nonetheless, the interpersonal interaction has a community dimension. Robert's role in this relationship has meaning in the wider community, namely being an educational leader with the status to interact as peers with a well-established, senior member of the community. More personally, it may shape Robert's sense of himself as an educator and will likely prepare him to speak with authority when he leads teacher workshops on technology and learning.

Other community designers can consider details of this socio-technical system and compare them to similar features and activities in their settings. For instance, how might teachers investigating the use of classroom inquiry use similar private communication venues such as Instant Messaging or private discussion threads? In light of Robert's motivation to discuss issues related to his professional development, the designer might ask what in their larger sociocultural setting would motivate the particular teachers involved? Are they early adopters who, like Robert, might want to use their online experiences to prepare for leadership roles in their schools? Alternatively, are they being required to learn new pedagogical practices, and want a private space to commiserate and discuss fragile new ideas with just one or two trusted peers?[6]

Whereas Robert and Marty had sufficient common ground to carry out a private interpersonal negotiation of a future meeting, the designers might want to consider the interpersonal dynamics that would support the sort of goal they have for their community. Should the community

---

[6] Barab, MaKinster, and Scheckler (this volume) hypothesize from their data that teachers inexperienced in sharing constructive criticism with colleagues do not post online critiques in order to avoid the appearance of attacking their colleagues' personal teaching style and online identity. In contrast, they suggest, receiving an invitation to offer specific feedback may shift the meaning of online critiques toward a more mutually supportive activity. This sort of (potential) transformation could be analyzed as the relationship between a new pattern of interpersonal discourse (initiated by a request) and subsequent development of interpersonal relationships, personal identity and agency, and shared (cultural) models for collegiality.

infrastructure group teachers in particular ways? Should it encourage particular kinds of diversity? How should issues of affiliation and inclusion be approached? Participant information could be made public and searchable. Recommender engines could be used to suggest particular connections with others that might be productive for joint project work. Alternatively, community designers could structure the environment according to pre-arranged groups, according to criteria such as: local affiliation (i.e., school building or district), shared background (e.g., grade level, subject), or nonacademic interests.

Finally, designers might ask how these teachers see themselves in relation to the online community. Do the goals of the community designers align with the teachers' understanding of themselves in their current roles (vis-à-vis colleagues, administrators, students) and imagined career trajectories? What sort of changes does aligning with the community's goals require of teachers? Can the new roles draw directly on existing roles in some way? For example, if leading inquiry with students is the aim of the community, one might ask where in teachers' professional and personal lives they enact similar roles. Perhaps the personal, interpersonal, and social aspects of games like "twenty questions" or comparison shopping can be used as preparation for data gathering and analysis for the sake of scientific inquiry.

Implications for Research

Another approach to learning from Robert's case study is to distill research guidelines for the sociocultural study of learning and development in online communities. We organized our analysis around an extension of Rogoff's *three planes of analysis* approach (Rogoff et al., 1995; Rogoff, 1990) and suggested options from other related theoretical perspectives such as *activity theory* (Engestrom et al., 1999), the *dramatic pentad* (Burke, 1945; Wertsch, 1998), *figured worlds* (Holland et al., 1998), and *cultural models* (D'Andrade, 1987, 1995; Holland & Quinn, 1987; Shore, 1996; Strauss, 1992). However, at its core, the kind of analysis we are presenting involves three questions: How do members participate online? How do they make sense of the online activity? and, How are online and offline activities related? These three essential questions provide a useful starting point for researchers who want to take a holistic view of learning and development in online community – that is, to understand online activity in the wider contexts of participants' lives. How do members participate online? What do they actually do, together and alone? These questions examining participation can draw on various methodologies such as computer-mediated discourse analysis (see Herring, this volume; Tatar et al., 2002) to emphasize linguistic and communicative patterns, or grounded theory (Glaser & Strauss, 1967) to describe and explain online activities in the terms used by participants themselves. Discovering how participants make sense of online activity – their own and others' – is likely to require the supplement of online texts (e.g., logfiles) with observational and interview data. While collecting multiple forms of data may provide a richer picture of online learning and development, it may still miss much of the larger significance of these processes in the personal and professional trajectories of participants. In this sense, it is essential to gather data that illuminate how specific online and offline activities are related. Understanding how a group of teachers form a vibrant online community is not enough, if their goal is to enhance their professional practice in the classroom.

APPENDIX A: INTERVIEW GUIDE: INTRODUCTION AND SAMPLE QUESTIONS

In each of the interviews we began by reviewing the research topic, confirming participant consent, and soliciting questions about the project. After answering participant questions and establishing rapport, we gathered some personal background information (e.g., age, city of residence, profession, education, etc.). Throughout the interview, we attempted to maintain an informal, conversational tone in which we could follow each interviewee's train of thought while still covering all the relevant topics. Hence, we occasionally varied the order of questions to facilitate the discussion, but addressed each of the questions in our interview guide. Here are sample questions in each of the major categories.

Tapped In Experience

> *What* brought you to TI the *first time*? (A class, a listserv? What was your purpose in being there?) *When* was that?
> What do you *usually* do in TI? *Who* do you talk to? *Where* do you go? (<first timers>: Did you do *anything else* on TI besides the Internet-Inquiry session?)
> If you had to label yourself, would you call yourself a *regular*, an *occasional*, or an *infrequent* user of TI?
> When you think about TI, what's *important* to you? What do you *value* about the environment?
> People think of TI in different ways, to you, *what is TI*? (What is TI most like in the "real world"?)

Specific InternetInquiry Seminar

> *How many times* would you say you have attended a TI seminar like the InternetInquiry?
> *Tell me about* the InternetInquiry seminar. What was it like from your perspective? (What were the important *events*? What else happened?)

Who ran the meeting? Anyone *else*? How would you describe their *roles*?

Did it feel like a *big* meeting or a *small* meeting? If you had to give me a guess, could you tell me *how many* people were there?

Do you *remember the other* participants? Know any from before the meeting? (For each: How *long* know? In TI? *Outside* TI? Meet *f2f*? *Name*?)

[*Note list of names for later use*]

[*Prompt for Marty, Pat, and any other facilitators*]

Were there people there who seemed to know each other? (*Groups*? Interpersonal?)

How much did you *feel a part* of the group? Did you feel *excluded* at times? (Want to be a part of some conversation, but not able to?)

Did you have specific *goals* for attending this seminar? What were you hoping to get out of it?

Did you *learn* anything in the session? Did you *share* anything that you thought was of value to others?

. . .

Do you remember the Titanic InternetInquiry that Helen had made? What did you think of it? What did other people think of it? Did you feel able to express criticism?

Earlier when she expressed some doubt about sharing it, Marty said:

(16:59:29) MARTYG: Awww . . . you're among friends here.

Do you think that's true? Would you ever share something like that?

Participation

<if TI REGULAR/NON-FIRSTTIME> What's your *style* of participation in TI? Do you *usually* lead sessions, facilitate, join in the conversation, just listen? How would you describe your role?

Have you always done this? How has your role *changed* since you first started logging on TI?

<FIRSTTIMERS> We'd like to ask about your *style* of participation in TI. As you saw in the InternetInquiry session, some people lead, others facilitate, join in the conversation, or just listen. How would you describe your role?

<if NON-LEADER> Have you ever *thought* of *leading* a session? Would you *want* to ever lead a session?

Are you in a leadership role in other areas of your *professional life*?

(Do you mentor others? Organize workshops? Do others come to you with questions or for assistance?)

Teaching

How did you come to be a teacher <or other occupation> ?

When you think about *your teaching practice*, what *values* come to mind? (What's really *important* to you about teaching?)

Could you describe your *goals* for your *teaching practice* (your *approach* to teaching and learning) ?
What *helps* you meet your goals or make changes?
Does *TI* help you with that? How? What *else* do you get from TI?

Technology

In general, how do you *feel* about computer technology? Do you tend to *seek* it out, or *avoid* it, or somewhere in *between*?
How do you feel about computer technology in *educational* practice? What does it *add* or *detract*?

APPENDIX B: LOGFILE EXCERPT OF ASO SEMINAR

(16:40:06) BENNET: Right off the bat . . . a news report.
(16:40:17) MARTY: Ah . . . a journalistic task.
(16:40:35) BENNET: Have the students write from the perspective of victim/volunteer and so on.
(16:40:39) BARBARA: How about a mystery where we see the results of a disaster and have to figure out what happened?
(16:40:50) MARTY: Cool, Barbara.
(16:40:50) ROBERT: Retelling tasks can be an important first step to InternetInquiry elements that will be completed later in the classroom with more student involvement.
(16:41:00) DOUG: Being in role in many of these tasks is what makes them meaningful.
(16:41:16) ROBERT: *agrees with Doug*
(16:41:21) MARTY: *agrees with Robert but wonders if that's a good use of $2,000 per desk*
(16:42:06) MARTY: Other task types that might lend themselves to disasterology?
(16:42:19) BARBARA: Here's another one. You are part of the National Committee on something to prevent disasters and you need to make plans about earthquakes in Washington state?
(16:42:36) BENNET: Maybe have the learners design possible plausible escape routes.
(16:42:36) MARTY: Hmmmm . . . a design task perhaps.
(16:43:03) MARTY: This is a well-informed crowd, I see.

References

Barab, S., McKinster, J., Scheckler, R. (this volume). Designing system dualities: Characterizing online community.

Bourdieu, P. (1977). *Outline of a Theory of Practice*. New York: Cambridge University Press.

Bransford, J. D., Brown, A. L., & Cocking, R. R. (2000). *How People Learn: Brain, Mind, Experience, and School*. Washington, DC: National Academy Press.

Burke, K. (1945/1969). *A Grammar of Motives*. Berkeley: University of California Press.

Cole, M. (1996). *Cultural Psychology: A Once and Future Discipline*. Cambridge, MA: Harvard University Press.

Curtis, P. (1997). Mudding: Social phenomena in text-based virtual realities. In Kiesler, S. (Ed.). *Culture of the Internet* (pp. 121–142). Mahwah, NJ: Lawrence Erlbaum Associates.

D'Andrade, R. G. (1987). A folk model of the mind. In Dorothy C. Holland & Naomi Quinn (Eds.). *Cultural Models in Language and Thought* (pp. 112–148). New York: Cambridge University Press.

D'Andrade, R. G. (1995). *The Development of Cognitive Anthropology*. Cambridge: Cambridge University Press.

Deaux, K. (2000). Surveying the Landscape of Immigration: Social Psychological Perspectives. *Journal of Community & Applied Social Psychology*, 10 (5), pp. 421–431.

Engestrom, Y, Miettinen, R., & Punamaki, R. (1999). *Perspectives on Activity Theory*. New York: Cambridge University Press.

Fusco, J. (2002). Personal communication.

Glaser, B. G., & Strauss, A. L. (1967). *Discovery of Grounded Theory: Strategies for Qualitative Research*. Chicago: Aldine.

Holland, D., Lachicotte, W., Skinner, D., & Cain, C. (1998). *Identity and Agency in Cultural Worlds*. Cambridge, MA: Harvard University Press.

Holland, D. & Lave, J. (2001). *History in Person: Enduring Struggles, Contentious Practice, Intimate Identities*. Santa Fe, NM: School of American Research Press.

Holland, D. C., & Quinn, N. (Eds.). (1987). *Cultural Models in Language and Thought*. New York: Cambridge University Press.

Lave, J. (1988). *Cognition in Practice: Mind, Mathematics and Culture in Everyday Life*. Cambridge MA: Cambridge University Press.

Pea, R. D. (1987). Socializing the knowledge transfer problem. *International Journal of Educational Research*, 11 (6), pp. 639–663.

Rogoff, B. (1990). *Apprenticeship in Thinking: Cognitive Development in Social Context*. New York: Oxford University Press.

Rogoff, B. (1995). Observing sociocultural activity on three planes: Participatory appropriation, guided participation, and apprenticeship. In J. V. Wertsch, P. del Rio, & A. Alvarez (Eds.). *Sociocultural Studies of Mind* (pp. 139–163). Cambridge: Cambridge University Press.

Rogoff, B. (1998). Cognition as a collaborative process. In W. Damon (series ed.) & D. Kuhn & R. S. Seigler (vol. eds.), *Handbook of Child Psychology: Vol. 2. Cognition, Perception and Language* (pp. 679–744). New York: Wiley.

Rogoff, B. (2003). *The Cultural Nature of Human Development*. New York: Oxford University Press.

Rogoff, B., Baker-Sennett, Lacasa, P., & Goldsmith, D. (1995). Development through participation in sociocultual activity. In J. J. Goodnow, P. J. Miller, & F. Kessel. *Cultural Practices as Contexts for Development*. No. 67. Spring. San Francisco: Jossey-Bass Publishers.

Rogoff, B., Topping, K., Baker-Sennett, J., Lacasa, P. (2002). Mutual contributions of individuals, partners, and institutions: Planning to remember in Girl Scouts cookie sales. *Social Development*, 11(2) pp. 266 – 289.

Schank, P., Fenton, J., Schlager, M., & Fusco, J. (1999). From MOO to MEOW: Domesticating Technology for Online Communities. In C. Hoadley (Ed.), *Proceedings of Computer Support for Collaborative Learning 1999* (pp. 518–526). Hillsdale, NJ: Erlbaum.

Schlager, M., Fusco, J., & Schank, P. (2002). Evolution of an On-line Education Community of Practice. In K. A. Renninger and W. Shumar (Eds.). *Building Virtual Communities: Learning and Change in Cyberspace.* (pp. 129–158). Cambridge University Press.

Schuler, D., & Namioka, A. E. (1993). *Participatory Design: Principles and Practices.* Mahwah, NJ: Lawrence Erlbaum.

Shore, B. (1996). *Culture in Mind: Cognition, Culture and the Problem of Meaning.* New York: Oxford University Press.

Strauss, C. (1992). Models and motives. In Roy D'Andrade & Claudia Strauss (Eds.), *Human Motives and Cultural Models* (pp. 1–20). New York: Cambridge University Press.

Tatar, D., Gray, J., & Fusco, J. (2002). *Rich Social Interaction in a Synchronous Online Community for Learning.* Paper presented at the Computer Support for Collaborative Learning Conference, Boulder, CO.

Vygotsky, L. S. (1978). Mind in Society: The Development of Higher Psychological Processes. In M. Cole, V. John-Steiner, S. Scribner, & E. Souberman (Eds.), Cambridge, MA: Harvard University Press.

Wenger, E. (1998). *Communities of Practice: Learning, Meaning, and Identity.* New York: Cambridge University Press.

Wertsch, J. V. (1991). *Voices of the Mind: A Sociocultural Approach to Mediated Action.* Cambridge, MA: Harvard University Press.

Wertsch, J. V. (1998). *Mind as Action.* New York: Oxford University Press.

Index

(*continued from page iii*)

Philip E. Agre   *Computation and Human Experience*

William J. Clancey   *Situated Cognition: On Human Knowledge and Computer Representation*

Etienne Wenger   *Communities of Practice: Learning, Meaning, and Identity*

John Singleton   *Learning in Likely Places: Varieties of Apprenticeship in Japan*

Magdalene Lampert and Merrie L. Blunk   *Talking Mathematics in School: Studies of Teaching and Learning*

Yrjö Engeström, Reijo Miettinen, and Raija-Leena Punamäki   *Perspectives on Activity Theory*

Gordon Wells   *Dialogic Inquiry: Towards a Sociocultural Practice and Theory of Education*

Carol D. Lee and Peter Smagorinsky   *Vygotskian Perspectives on Literacy Research: Constructing Meaning Through Collaborative Inquiry*

Christian Health and Paul Luff   *Technology in Action*

Martin Packer   *Changing Classes: School Reform and the New Economy*

K. Ann Renninger and Wesley Shumar   *Building Virtual Communities: Learning and Change in Cyberspace*

Peter Sawchuk   *Adult Learning and Technology in Working-Class Life*

Alex Kozulin, Boris Gindis, Vladimir S. Ageyev, and Suzanne M. Miller   *Vygotsky's Educational Theory in Cultural Context*

The Learning in Doing series was founded in 1987 by Roy Pea and John Seely Brown